EXAMPLES&EXPLANATIONS

Environmental Law

Environmental Law

Sixth Edition

Steven Ferrey
Professor of Law
Suffolk University Law School

Wolters Kluwer
Law & Business

Published by Wolters Kluwer Law & Business in New York.

Wolters Kluwer Law & Business serves customers worldwide with CCH, Aspen Publishers, and Kluwer Law International products. (www.wolterskluwerlb.com)

To contact Customer Service, e-mail customer.service@wolterskluwer.com, call 1-800-234-1660, fax 1-800-901-9075, or mail correspondence to:

Wolters Kluwer Law & Business
Attn: Order Department
PO Box 990
Frederick, MD 21705

Printed in the United States of America.

2 3 4 5 6 7 8 9 0

ISBN 978-1-4548-0938-8

Library of Congress Cataloging-in-Publication Data

Ferrey, Steven.
    Environmental law / Steven Ferrey, Professor of Law, Suffolk University Law School. — Sixth Edition.
        pages cm. — (Examples & explanations)
    Includes bibliographical references and index.
    ISBN 978-1-4548-0938-8 (alk. paper)
    1. Environmental law — United States. I. Title.

KF3775.Z9F45 2012
344.7304′6 — dc23

                                                    2012042142

About Wolters Kluwer Law & Business

Wolters Kluwer Law & Business is a leading global provider of intelligent information and digital solutions for legal and business professionals in key specialty areas, and respected educational resources for professors and law students. Wolters Kluwer Law & Business connects legal and business professionals as well as those in the education market with timely, specialized authoritative content and information-enabled solutions to support success through productivity, accuracy and mobility.

Serving customers worldwide, Wolters Kluwer Law & Business products include those under the Aspen Publishers, CCH, Kluwer Law International, Loislaw, Best Case, ftwilliam.com and MediRegs family of products.

CCH products have been a trusted resource since 1913, and are highly regarded resources for legal, securities, antitrust and trade regulation, government contracting, banking, pension, payroll, employment and labor, and healthcare reimbursement and compliance professionals.

Aspen Publishers products provide essential information to attorneys, business professionals and law students. Written by preeminent authorities, the product line offers analytical and practical information in a range of specialty practice areas from securities law and intellectual property to mergers and acquisitions and pension/benefits. Aspen's trusted legal education resources provide professors and students with high-quality, up-to-date and effective resources for successful instruction and study in all areas of the law.

Kluwer Law International products provide the global business community with reliable international legal information in English. Legal practitioners, corporate counsel and business executives around the world rely on Kluwer Law journals, looseleafs, books, and electronic products for comprehensive information in many areas of international legal practice.

Loislaw is a comprehensive online legal research product providing legal content to law firm practitioners of various specializations. Loislaw provides attorneys with the ability to quickly and efficiently find the necessary legal information they need, when and where they need it, by facilitating access to primary law as well as state-specific law, records, forms and treatises.

Best Case Solutions is the leading bankruptcy software product to the bankruptcy industry. It provides software and workflow tools to flawlessly streamline petition preparation and the electronic filing process, while timely incorporating ever-changing court requirements.

ftwilliam.com offers employee benefits professionals the highest quality plan documents (retirement, welfare and nonqualified) and government forms (5500/PBGC, 1099 and IRS) software at highly competitive prices.

MediRegs products provide integrated health care compliance content and software solutions for professionals in healthcare, higher education and life sciences, including professionals in accounting, law and consulting.

Wolters Kluwer Law & Business, a division of Wolters Kluwer, is headquartered in New York. Wolters Kluwer is a market-leading global information services company focused on professionals.

For Curran and Cameron, and the many wondrous days
ahead on this mystical planet:

"To see a World in a Grain of Sand
And a Heaven in a Wild Flower,
Hold Infinity in the palm of your hand
And Eternity in an hour."

— *William Blake*
Auguries of Innocence

"A small group of thoughtful people could change the world.
Indeed, it's the only thing that ever has."

— *Margaret Meade*

Summary of Contents

Contents

Chapter 3   **The National Environmental Policy Act   83**

Contents

Chapter 4   Constitutional Issues: The Commerce Clause and Environmental Preemption   147

Chapter 5   Air Quality Regulation   179

Contents

Contents

Chapter 10   Local Environmental Controls   485

Contents

Chapter 11 Preservation of Natural Areas: Wetlands and Open Space 527

Contents

Chapter 14   TSCA and FIFRA: Regulating Chemical Manufacture and Distribution   629

Chapter 15   International Environmental Law   649

Contents

Preface and Acknowledgments

"What's past is prologue."

William Shakespeare, The Tempest

Environmental law is everywhere and influences every type of law. This book will help you decipher and understand the complex multitude of issues, statutes, agency regulations, and court decisions that make up environmental law. It breaks down the primary topics of environmental and energy law into key concepts and rules, and then it reassembles them in a format that makes them easier to work with.

There is an emphasis herein on providing you with the scientific background to understand each area of environmental and energy law. Each chapter is intended to ground you in the technical, legal, scientific, and policy aspects of real-world environmental law practice. In addition, each chapter provides questions with answers, or Examples and Explanations, that place you in the position of counsel to corporations, environmental groups, the government, or lenders, and in the position of prosecutor or environmental policymaker, to help you see how the law applies in real situations. This information is detailed enough to provide a complete foundation even for advanced-level environmental and energy law courses.

The sequence of chapters follows the order of topics as they appear in many environmental law casebooks. Specific topics may be located easily either in the table of contents or in the index. There also is a detailed glossary of key terms and a list of abbreviations at the back of the book.

Environmental and energy law are new, exciting, and growing areas of the law. And there is no end in sight to their growth. There is no Restatement of Environmental Law. We are still just beginning the "statement"—the Restatement is something *you* may author during your career.

In preparing this book and the Sixth Edition, I gratefully acknowledge the generous support of the Dean at Suffolk University Law School. I also express a special thanks to my friend and colleague, Professor Joseph Glannon, whose vision and creativity paved the way for the *Examples and Explanations* series. I also acknowledge the valuable contributions of my environmental law students and research assistants over the years who helped with the creation of the original book and later editions: Abigail Albee, Neil Alexander, Caroline Cho, Joseph Cipriano, William D'Alissandro, Jennifer

Preface and Acknowledgments

Davis, Donna Drewes, Mark Evangelista, Deborah Gilburg, Andrew Grimes, Douglas Martland, Maureen Medeiros, Susan Mulholland, Carla Munroe, Joe Perillo, James Sullivan, Charmaine Surette, Olga Titova, Maureen Vallatini, Edy Warren, and Gemma Ypparila. Grateful thanks are also due to the professional staff at Wolters Kluwer, including Eric Holt, John Lyman, Melody Davies, Betsy Kenny, Carol McGeehan, and Peter Skagestad. Most of all, I acknowledge with love the support of my wife and partner, Kathleen, who has made me rich in sons.

Steven Ferrey

November 2012

Environmental Law

CHAPTER 1

Environmental Ethics, Standards, Markets, and the Common Law

"The more I examine the universe and study the details of its architecture, the more evidence I find that the universe in some sense must have known we were coming."

Freeman Dyson

"The Whole of nature is a metaphor of the human mind."

E. E. Cummings

"Every thing is connected to everything else."

John Muir

"Universe to each must be all that is, including me. Environment in turn must be all that is, excepting me."

R. Buckminster Fuller, Shelter, 1979

"The future is purchased by the present."

Samuel Johnson

"Study the past, if you would divine the future."

Confucius

THE CONCEPT OF ENVIRONMENTAL REGULATION

Ecosystems and Cycles

The earth is comprised of interrelated ecosystems. The rationale for environmental law is to restore, preserve, and protect natural systems working throughout the atmosphere, the hydrosphere, and the lithosphere. There are related cycles involving solar radiation, water, carbon, oxygen, nitrogen, phosphorus, and sulfur. Disturbances in any of these systems can disturb other parts of the cycle or other systems.

The earth is powered by a basic energy cycle that derives elementally from the sun. Solar radiation penetrates the earth's atmosphere and is absorbed as heat. The absorption of heat in the world's oceans drives ocean currents and latent heat produces water vapor. As heat rises through the atmosphere, winds are created, and ultimately determine climatic conditions. The oceans also work as massive heat sinks storing heat in the summer, and releasing heat in winter months, with that heat ultimately radiated back into space.

Aside from the solar heat, the light spectrum in sunlight is captured by plants for photosynthesis. Only about one-tenth of 1 percent of the sun's light in the atmosphere is involved in photosynthesis. However, this is enough to produce approximately 2 billion tons of additional organic matter each year, which is essential to the ecosystem.

The plants that utilize the sunlight are an essential element of "producer" organisms in the environment. "Producer" organisms, such as plants and bacteria, convert inorganic compounds to organic materials (even humans can do this). "Consumer organisms," typical of animals and humans, consume the plants directly (or indirectly by consuming other species that consume the plants). In addition, there are "decomposer" organisms that degrade organic compounds into simpler forms that can be reabsorbed by green plants. Typical "decomposer" organisms are fungi and bacteria.

Water moves in the hydrologic cycle. Water is essential for plant and animal life and is essential in the creation of terrestrial weather patterns. Water is the most abundant substance in the biosphere. Hydrogen, which is a primary element in water, is the most abundant element on earth, and plays an essential role in current fossil fuel utilization and prospects for future innovative energy resources.

The amount of water on the earth is constant, and is constantly recycled. Most of the water arrived through a billion years of collisions with meteorites and comets, which brought enough water to fill the oceans. The oceans were of their current size 3.8 billion years ago. The earth now has all the water molecules it will have over time.

More than 90 percent of all of the water on earth is in the oceans, with another 2 percent in glaciers and polar ice caps, with 90 percent of that in Antarctica. Four percent of water is in the lithosphere including groundwater, and less than one-tenth of 1 percent of water is in freshwater bodies such as lakes, rivers, and streams. Therefore, freshwater constitutes less than 6 percent of all the water on earth. Yet this freshwater is essential to survival. While humans can go for months without food, they can only last for a few days without water. Seventy-five percent of the world's freshwater supply is frozen in glaciers and ice formations.

Through the hydrologic cycle, water moves through the biosphere. Precipitation of water to earth and evaporation of water from earth are balanced on a global basis. The majority of water in a rainstorm returns to the atmosphere within a day or two. Water that precipitates to earth recharges groundwater supplies, is absorbed by soil and plants, and eventually is either returned to the atmosphere through transpiration, or runs off into the oceans. The soil acts as a natural buffer regarding precipitation. It soaks up and restores any deficit in soil moisture before surplus water moves down to the groundwater table beneath the soil. Permanent streams are sustained by groundwater. More detail on the hydrologic cycle is contained in the beginning of Chapter 6.

Pure water is found only in water vapor, ice, and distilled water. Water in the liquid state will dissolve almost any substance to some degree into solution, and this can result in water pollution. Human discharge of wastes into water bodies changes the contents of the water by adding dissolved or suspended pollutants or contaminants. Dissolved and suspended materials, including many pollutants, exist in much of the water in the world.

Carbon molecules also move through a distinct cycle in the biosphere. Carbon is critical to earth's life forms (as anyone who watches old reruns of *Star Trek* can testify). Carbon moves from carbon dioxide (CO_2) in the atmosphere to living organisms. Carbon and decayed organic matter also are the basis of fossil fuels — coal, oil, natural gas — upon which modern Industrial society is built. The burning of these fossil fuels releases CO_2 back to the atmosphere. The combustion by modern society of these fuels at a much greater rate than the redeposition of the released CO_2 into carbon sinks in oceans and forests, changes the carbon balance in the biosphere.

Plant photosynthesis on land and in marine plants is the mechanism by which carbon is reabsorbed. Utilizing sunlight, carbon dioxide combines with water and enzymes of chlorophyll to produce sugar and release oxygen. This oxygen is essential for many animal species and humans. Plants also release some carbon dioxide through respiration at night when photosynthesis is not occurring because of the absence of sunlight.

Carbon is only the fifteenth most common element on earth and comprises less than 10 percent of the human body; nevertheless, it is essential. Humans are about 60 percent water. Oxygen is the most abundant element on earth, with silicon (used for solar photovoltaic panels) in second place. Both are essential to the future of life on earth.

The oxygen in the atmosphere also works in its own cycle. Oxygen exists primarily because of photosynthesis by green plants. About 20 percent of all oxygen molecules is in the atmosphere. It is believed that it took billions of years on earth until oxygen began to accumulate in the atmosphere about 1.8 billion years ago. The oxygen formed ozone (O_3) in the upper atmosphere as a protective layer to absorb ultraviolet radiation and further protect living species. As the supply of carbon dioxide increases, the supply of free oxygen consequently decreases.

Approximately 80 percent of the atmosphere is composed of nitrogen, as an inert gas. Bacterial action in soil fixes nitrogen. Plants use nitrogen in the form of ammonia soluble nitrates to produce protoplasm. Nitrogen then is incorporated into amino acids and proteins in the plant. When the plant or animal protein eventually decays, bacteria in the soils then denitrify the nitrogen so that it may be returned to the atmosphere. There are a dozen or so essential bacteria involved in the nitrogen cycle, without which life would not be possible on earth.

Modern fertilizers produce artificially fixed nitrogen, increasing the nitrogen in soil and in water runoff. When this runoff reaches lakes or streams, it enriches algae respiration, which then depletes the oxygen content of the water to sustain the algae growth. The deprivation of oxygen content of the water then kills fish and other oxygen-dependent water species. Eutrophication takes place as the water body dies, and can no longer function as a host to more complex animal species. Significant amounts of nitrogen also can make water unsafe for human consumption.

Phosphorus is much less prevalent in the biosphere than nitrogen. Phosphorus is an element of plant and animal protoplasm and, when broken down into dissolved phosphates, is essential for protein synthesis as well as becoming ferric and calcium phosphates in rocks. As phosphorus is lost from modern agricultural practices in the temperate zones, by topsoil loss and runoff, the soil becomes less able to sustain plant growth. When phosphates enter lakes or streams, they also cause eutrophication.

Sulfur also is critical for protein synthesis. It is not a limited element as is phosphorus, and can be recycled independently from green plant growth. The amount of sulfur is estimated to have increased by 50 percent from power plant emissions. All of these cycles are highly interdependent, and the imbalance of one can have significant implications for the operation of others. These cycles form our global ecosystem.

Modern agriculture in the United States and other industrialized countries has become dependent upon fossil fuels. Feed-lot agricultural practices for the raising of cattle and other animals constitute an energy-intensive environmentally polluting activity. Feed-lot cattle are fed low-cost corn to fatten the animals over a period of slightly more than a year to the point of slaughter, whereas range-fed and grazed animals might take up to five years to achieve a similar size and be ready for slaughter. The use of corn to fatten cows in feed-lot agriculture consumes more chemical herbicide and fertilizer than any other crop. The nitrogen runoff from that crop fertilizer runs off into water bodies and groundwater in the farming communities, and then into major rivers traversing multiple states.

The fertilizer necessary to grow that corn is derived from oil fields (principally in the Persian Gulf and other foreign nations). Thus, modern animal agriculture is driven by, and dependent on, fossil fuels. A cow that eats 25 lbs. of corn per day so as to reach a weight of 1,250 lbs. at the point of slaughter has indirectly "consumed" approximately 284 gallons of oil in the form of the petrochemical fertilizers necessary to grow that corn. Thus, our modern agricultural system is dependent upon fossil fuels across the food cycle. In essence, this fossil fuel agricultural "machine" has replaced a natural solar-powered renewable system in which animals previously grazed on an open range, eating grasses that were naturally produced by photosynthesis driven by solar power and the natural nitrogen and phosphorus cycles.

The natural environmental balance is maintained by the natural ecology and the physics of the universe. The presence of the moon and its gravitational attraction actually steadies the orbit of the earth and keeps it from wobbling. This is critical in maintaining the natural solar, hydrologic, and other cycles. More eccentric orbits or wobble would affect the length and intensity of sunlight reaching the earth.

Natural, and inevitable, events and forces are responsible for many significant environmental phenomena. One thunderstorm can contain the equivalent of the electricity used in the United States in a day. About 200 million tons of carbon are released into the atmosphere annually from decaying plants and volcanic activity. This is 30 times what humans expel from machines and cars. A volcanic eruption in Tuba, Sumatra, Indonesia, 74,000 years ago caused emission of six years of ash, blanketing the earth and blocking the infiltration of sunlight, dramatically reducing the human population. More recently, in 1815, a volcanic eruption in Sumbawa, Indonesia, the most significant in 10,000 years, with the explosive force of 60,000 Hiroshima-sized atomic bombs, instantly killed 100,000 people and led to cooling climate change of 1.5°F and the famine and associated typhoid epidemic in Ireland that killed 65,000 more. Yellowstone National Park is the center of major volcanic activity in the United States and appears due for a major blast now, about 630,000 years since its last major eruption.

Significant environmental destruction resulting from major long-term volcanic activity as well as asteroid collisions is expected to continue.

Asteroid collisions with earth over the past several billion years are responsible for major physical changes and possibly for the extinction of dinosaurs and many other formerly living species. The entire Chesapeake Bay is the result of an impact crater from a single asteroid collision with earth. About 4.5 billion years ago, an asteroid the approximate size of Mars crashed into the earth, exploding material from the earth's crust, which formed the moon.

It would be almost impossible for the few earth telescopes surveying the sky for such events to pick up a large asteroid hurtling to earth until it has virtually arrived. When a string of 21 asteroids struck Jupiter in July 1994, the force of just one, known as Nucleus G, had the explosive impact of 6 million megatons, or 75 times the impact of all the nuclear weapons in existence. Such force once unleashed, whether from nuclear weapons or space collision with asteroids orbiting the sun's planets, would wipe out most life on earth. Nucleus G made an impact crater in Jupiter the size of the earth. Entering the earth's atmosphere, an asteroid would rapidly compress and heat the air below to $60,000°K$, or ten times the surface temperature of the sun. On impact, the blast would level everything from 150 to 1,000 miles, killing every living thing in that radius and setting this area ablaze, affecting the earth's climate for thousands of years.

The natural environment can be viewed as infinite space or as finite. While the earth is often viewed as crowded, there is incredible space at the atomic level. The neutrons and protons inside the nucleus of a single atom occupy only one-millionth of a billionth of the volume of the atom, yet contain virtually all of the atom's mass. If the atom were the size of a large cathedral, the nucleus would be the size of a fly inside that cathedral. Negatively charged electrons without any significant mass are everywhere else in the vast empty space of that cathedral. Given these dimensions and scale, what is the purpose of environmental regulation?

Ethics and Efficiency: The Moral Basis of Pollution Control

Environmental protection laws have been enacted to further two primary goals: preventing irreparable environmental damage and forcing the consideration of environmental values into all realms of private and commercial activities. Beginning in the 1960s, much of the American public recognized that protection of the environment was imperative to preserving its social and cultural values, as well as the nation's natural resources.

The underlying vision of environmentalism shared by most Americans, that of bringing industrial society into balance with environmental ethics, forms the basis of pollution control laws. This vision embraces two generally accepted themes molding all aspects of environmental legislation: ethical and cultural considerations, and economic efficiencies. Proponents of these two views often differ with each other.

Those who see pollution as an ethical issue treat it as inherently negative, a manifestation of humankind's greed and disregard of social consequences. They advocate legislative action to police corporate and personal behavior to improve environmental quality and ensure public health and safety.

Adherents of the efficiency theme invoke economic pragmatism: If polluters were required to pass on the costs of pollution to society as a whole by charging prices that reflected the environmental costs of production, there would be a market incentive to reduce levels of pollutants in order to stay competitive. The free market system would thus ensure the conservation of the world's valuable limited resources.

Environmental protection laws reflect a sense of community, wherein the health and safety of individuals are as important as the economic well-being of the nation as a whole. The National Environmental Policy Act of 1969 (NEPA) (see Chapter 3) established a national policy to "assure for all Americans safe, healthful, productive, and aesthetically and culturally pleasing surroundings." This expression of a national environmental policy was carried into substantive legislation, including the Clean Air Act (see Chapter 5) and the Clean Water Act (see Chapter 6) to protect the public health.

The EPA and Its Authority to Permit and Enforce

Created in 1970 during the administration of President Nixon, the Environmental Protection Agency (EPA) was the product of a wellspring of social activism coalescing into a political consensus yielding a series of environmental legislation. The EPA is neither a cabinet-level department, such as the Department of Energy (DOE), nor an independent government agency, such as the Federal Energy Regulatory Commission (FERC) or the Securities and Exchange Commission (SEC). The EPA administers nine major environmental statutes passed by Congress between 1969 and 1980:

- Clean Air Act
- Federal Water Pollution Control Act (the Clean Water Act)
- Comprehensive Environmental Response, Compensation and Liability Act (the "Superfund")
- Marine Protection, Research and Sanctuaries Act (MPRSA)
- Solid Waste Act, more commonly known as the Resource Conservation and Recovery Act (RCRA)
- Federal Insecticide, Fungicide and Rodenticide Act (FIFRA)
- Toxic Substances Control Act (TSCA)

- Noise Control Act
- Safe Drinking Water Act

In addition, the EPA exercises some responsibility over four other environmental statutes. It operates under the restraints of the Administrative Procedure Act, the National Environmental Policy Act (NEPA), and constitutional principles.

The Departments of Interior, Commerce, Transportation, Labor, and the Council on Environmental Quality and others have primary responsibility for administering numerous other environmental laws, including:

- Coastal Barrier Resources Act
- Coastal Zone Management Act
- Deepwater Port Act
- Endangered Species Act
- Environmental Programs Assistance Act
- Environmental Quality Improvement Act
- Federal Land Policy and Management Act
- Fish and Wildlife Coordination Act
- Fishery Conservation and Management Act
- Marine Mammal Protection Act
- Marine Protection, Research, and Sanctuaries Act
- National Environmental Education Act
- National Environmental Policy Act
- National Forest Management Act
- National Park System Mining Regulation Act
- National Wildlife Refuge System Act
- Occupational Safety and Health Act
- Oil Pollution Act of 1990
- Outer Continental Shelf Lands Act Amendments of 1978
- Pollution Prevention Act
- Pollution Prosecution Act
- Radon Gas and Indoor Air Quality Research Act
- Shore Protection Act
- Soil and Water Resources Conservation Act
- Surface Mining Control and Reclamation Act
- Water Resources Conservation Act
- Wild and Scenic Rivers Act
- Wilderness Act

None of these statutes, however, provides the agency with a general charter. The executive action creating the EPA merely transferred existing executive branch functions from other agencies without regard to a specific mandate or policy statement. To a large extent, the EPA establishes and administers pollution control regulations in the absence of an enumerated, comprehensive environmental strategy. It must identify those agents that cause or contribute to environmental hazards and ensure that, once identified, these pollutants (with few exceptions) are reduced to levels that have minimal effect on the environment.

Each of these substantive statutes expresses specific goals of environmental quality, and the EPA is required to work toward these objectives within the narrow scope of the purpose specified in each act. One of the purposes of the Clean Water Act, for example, is to provide for the protection and proliferation of fish, shellfish, and wildlife and to provide for public recreation in and on the water. The Clean Air Act seeks to provide an ambient level of air quality sufficient to protect the public health.

Agriculture enjoys broad exemption from the environmental laws applicable to most other pursuits in the United States. Farming pollutes groundwater, surface water, air, and soils. It also contributes to open space loss and destruction of wildlife habitat, as well as soil erosion, sedimentation of lakes and rivers, and depletion of freshwater resources. Farms cover almost 1 billion acres in the United States; farms utilize 36 percent of global land surface. Farms are extremely energy intensive, owning an estimated $110 billion in machinery and equipment, and spending $6 billion annually on gasoline and fuels, $18 billion annually on chemical fertilizers, and almost $3 billion on electricity. The impacts of traditional farming practices in the United States are:

- Degradation and loss of habitat, including the drainage of wetlands, and diminishment of wildlife species.
- Farming is the leading cause of soil erosion, with more than 25 percent of all acreage considered highly erodible. Between 25 and 40 percent of soil that erodes from a farming field will eventually reach a water body, resulting in sedimentation in reservoirs and lakes, at the rate of over 1 billion tons of sediments and approximately half that amount of dissolved solids lost annually to water bodies by U.S. farms.
- Vast depletion of water reserves by irrigating approximately 50 million acres of agricultural land annually. In many areas, the withdrawal of water reduces the water table, causes land subsidence and desertification. Worldwide, agriculture accounts for 66 percent of freshwater withdrawal and 85 percent of water consumption.
- Agricultural water use results in salinization of soils and water, from leachate of salt and minerals from the soil. More than 500 million acres in the United States have a moderate to severe potential for soil and water salinity problems, which can reduce crop yields.
- Herbicides, insecticides, and fungicides find their way through air, soil, and water to become an environmental pollutant. Annually,

more than 750 million pounds of pesticides are applied to agricultural crops, constituting by far the vast majority of all pesticides used in the United States. Many of these pesticides persist in the environment for long periods of time after their application. Nitrogen, phosphorus, and potassium used to promote crop growth become pollutants to the environment when they run off into streams.

- The production of animal wastes constitutes a major source of non-point water pollution from runoff from large commercial farms. About 70 percent of American farms congregate animals on dense feedlots, rather than allowing livestock to graze. American livestock produce approximately 1.8 billion tons of wet manure annually, much of which reaches surface water supplies along with nitrogen and phosphorus runoff from farming operations. See Chapter 7. In many places this accounts for the majority of pollution in waterways; in more than 40 states, nonpoint sources are the predominant source of water pollution in lakes. Nearly 60 percent of pollution in U.S. rivers and streams and 45 percent of pollution in U.S. lakes stem from agricultural sources.

- Fertilizers in agricultural use also are a source of greenhouse gases, including CO_2 and NO_x. It is estimated that farming operations account for up to 25 percent of the emissions from global fossil fuel combustion. Deposition of NO_x leads to acidification, eutrophication, and changes in ecological balance. In addition, many pesticides are dispersed in the air. See Chapter 13.

Notwithstanding all of these significant environmental impacts from agricultural operations, farming operations are exempted from almost all of the significant national environmental statutes. For example, farming waste discharge can be exempted from requirements to obtain NPDES permits under the Clean Water Act. Similarly, the Clean Water Act stormwater discharge permit program is not applied to farm discharges, nor do farms require a Section 404 Clean Water Act permit for normal farming practices that alter, dredge, or fill protected wetlands areas. Only in those selected states that enact stricter state statutes is there authority over farm nonpoint discharges. See Chapter 6.

Similarly, under the Clean Air Act, most farm discharges do not constitute "major sources" subject to permitting, nor do most states have state statutes that cover such discharges. Excluded are such farming practices as seasonal burning of biomass and agricultural waste.

FIFRA regulates the application of pesticides by requiring labeling. Even though FIFRA pesticides are registered, labeled, and records are required to be maintained, there is no regulatory "hammer" to enforce the appropriate use and volume of pesticides in the agricultural environment. Neither does TSCA impose any use or application restrictions on pesticides and herbicides other than their initial registration at the manufacturing stage.

CERCLA excludes "the normal application of fertilizer" from covered "releases" for cleanup liability. EPCRA, which includes emergency planning and storage notification requirements, exempts "routine agricultural operations," and incorporates the Superfund exemption for pesticides. Farms are not covered by the TRI toxic reduction program. Farming operations with pesticides and fertilizers also are not required to comply with the complex RCRA regulations on handling of hazardous wastes. Farm irrigation return flows are not considered solid waste or subject to RCRA regulation, notwithstanding that they are conduits for chemicals, pesticides, animal waste, and other contaminants to the environment.

That said, the environmental statutes that the EPA administers are not self-executing, however. The EPA must use its discretion to identify the specific pollutants causing the most serious problems and then establish a framework by which the goals of the statutes are translated into concrete standards of permissible geographic concentrations of designated pollutants. The EPA designs the programs to facilitate achievement of the established standards; the states, in large part, must administer them. In many cases, the EPA has established numerical standards of environmental quality that objectively quantify the threshold triggering a response action. If a designated pollutant exceeds its established threshold, cleanup is mandated without any further evaluation until the levels of the specified pollutant fall below the threshold level for initial response.

Five of the environmental statutes administered by the EPA have specific provisions authorizing the EPA to delegate administration to those states that have created permit systems meeting the federal statutory criteria. By delegating responsibility for enforcing compliance to the states, the EPA can restrict its role to issuing comprehensive legislative rules and to issuing and enforcing permits only in those states that have not yet adopted environmental protection programs that meet federal standards. (The EPA exercises sole authority over ocean dumping and registering pesticides, as well as reviewing and regulating the manufacture of toxic substances and motor vehicles.) This delegation system is a cooperative federalism. Although the EPA delegates enforcement authority to federally approved state programs, the agency retains concurrent authority to enforce permit requirements in sanctioned programs and veto power over individual state permits. In addition, the EPA requires that emission limitations under the Clean Air Act, usually included in state operating permits, be submitted for EPA approval. Consequently, state actions seemingly independent of the EPA's scope of authority are in fact subject to federal supervision.

Common procedural requirements for permits can be complex. They include public notice with a request for comment to the agency issuing the permit, receipt of public comments during a stated period of time, and possibly a public hearing on the matter. These procedures are covered in more detail in Chapter 2. Actions not within the scope of these common procedures are ocean dumping permits, emergency permits, RCRA permits-by-rule, federally issued Section 404 dredge-and-fill permits, and state new-source air pollution permits issued under nonattainment area rules, as well as nonpermit actions under TSCA and FIFRA, RCRA interim status, and Safe Drinking Water Act authorization by rule.

In the 30-year period between 1969 and 1999, 240 environmental and natural resource law cases were decided on the merits by the U.S. Supreme Court. Justice White wrote three dozen of these opinions, the most of any Justice, with Justice O'Connor writing 22 of the opinions. Justice Kennedy was most often in the majority in these environmental cases, but only wrote two of the opinions. The Court has shown little affirmative interest or philosophy in a substantive position on environmental and land use issues. The decisions have often been made on procedural or narrow grounds. In the 2008-2009 Supreme Court term, four of five environmental cases heard by the Supreme Court were appeals from the 9th Circuit, and in four of these five it upheld the government position. In the four from the 9th Circuit, the Circuit was reversed in all.

Setting the Standard for Emissions to the Environment

Historically, governmental response to environmental hazards has depended on recognition of a problem as being a sufficiently serious threat to public health and safety as to warrant intervention. The EPA is empowered to designate the *specific* pollutants to be controlled and to establish numerical standards for ambient levels of these pollutants and thus the threshold levels that require a response to these contaminants.

Given the difficulties in ascertaining "safe" levels of certain pollutants, the EPA has struggled at times to establish numerical thresholds of pollution compatible with public health. Scientists cannot always determine which levels of a contaminant are safe, which chemical substances are carcinogenic, or the statistical increase in the incidence of a particular disease caused by exposure to a given toxic substance. In the absence of scientific certainties, and in light of the personal and economic costs associated with protecting the environment, individuals, businesses, and communities may question the benefits of controlling specific contaminants.

The general threshold for implementing environmental protection regulations is the "imminent and substantial hazard" standard; this is the government's general emergency response authority. Each of the environmental statutes that the EPA administers gives it the authority to respond to imminent and substantial hazards, be they discharges requiring a local response or more widespread problems threatening broader public health damage. This standard triggering mechanism is common to all the EPA statutes, with the exception of the Noise Control Act. The EPA must weigh the nature of the risk and the damage posed against the burden of regulation. In effect, the EPA must analyze the probability that a harm is likely to occur and the nature of its consequences in light of the burden to society of taking measures to prevent or mitigate the damage.

Conventional Pollutants

The various types of pollutants regulated by the EPA include both conventional and toxic substances. There is no common definition distinguishing toxic from conventional pollutants under the various environmental protection statutes. As early as 1900, conventional pollutants such as sewage, smoke, and dust were limited by quality control standards set by local communities. Conventional pollutants today, as long as they are in low concentrations, are treated as though they had no ill effect on the environment or on public health. Government response to such emissions is mandated only if their levels exceed an established threshold level of safety.

Toxic Pollutants

Toxic pollutants, on the other hand, are subject to far more rigorous standards, approaching total prohibition. The divergence of treatment of these two types of pollution is a result of the perception that for toxic pollutants, there is no safe threshold of risk. Stringent control standards are necessary to drastically reduce levels of toxic contaminants to ensure the public an ample margin of safety.

To be designated a toxic pollutant, a substance must pose a significant or unreasonable risk of hazard to the public health or welfare. This determination is made using modern risk analysis. Significant risks to public health are weighed against the social burden of controlling such substances. Once a substance is categorized as toxic, it is subject to the strictest of controls, including the federal authority to completely ban the manufacture or use of designated chemicals. The EPA has made compromises with the industrial sector. The general understanding is that the goal of total elimination of toxic pollution will be achieved only as quickly as the best available technologies allow.

Tools and Techniques of Environmental Protection

In the early phases of environmental regulation, states were permitted great discretion in determining local environmental quality standards and setting the mechanisms to reduce pollutants. Discontent with the states' slow pace of improving air quality standards, and the disparity between environmental standards and ambient air conditions, caused Congress to gradually institute uniform levels of nationwide control.

Technology Forcing Standards

The passage of the Clean Air and Clean Water Acts by Congress in the early 1970s represented a shift in thinking on environmental issues. Both statutes require the states to improve air and water quality levels to a minimum acceptable standard — regardless of currently available technologies. Congress's intent was to force industries to use technologies believed to be readily available but not widely in use, as well as to force them to develop new technologies. This policy is called "technology forcing." An example: Section 202(b) of the 1970 Clean Air Act required a 90 percent reduction in emissions from new cars by 1975 (see Chapter 5).

These "technology forcing" emission limits generally are instituted on an industry-by-industry basis, and the discharge limits are periodically tightened. A more accurate description of these statutes, however, might be "compliance-forcing." The time schedules for compliance often do not permit sufficient time for the development of advanced technologies to meet the stringent environmental requirements. They are, in effect, mandates to clean up or shut down production without primary regard to cost.

In addition, all proposed new sources of pollution are compelled to adhere to state-of-the-art pollution control technologies. Congress intends that each technological advance should become an industry-wide norm that, with gradually tighter standards, will eventually eliminate all significant pollution.

The means by which these action-forcing and technology-forcing schemes are implemented typically require the discharger to meet performance standards, such as individual facility permits that require a cap or limit on emissions. These limits determine the amount or concentration of a given contaminant that the site may discharge into the environment. They do not generally prescribe the use of any specific pollution control devices. The limits are not based primarily on cost considerations or availability of technology. An example of such a limit is the technology standard of lowest achievable emission rate (LAER) in the Clean Air Act (see Chapter 5).

A second kind of "technology-forcing" performance standard is based on an industrial benchmark, such as the performance of the industry's best plant. This category of performance standards is often applied differentially. For existing sources of conventional pollutants, this kind of standard demands only that the facilities perform as well as the best models within their industries. The standard for new sources of conventional and toxic pollutants, as well as hazardous waste facilities, is tied more stringently to the best technology currently available, whether or not widely deployed.

Compliance with performance standards can be achieved by any means the operator of a site chooses. In practice, however, some kinds of pollution effectively decide the types of control devices that can be used, such as scrubbers to eliminate sulfur dioxide emissions from coal burning facilities.

Regulation of Existing Versus New Emitters

Pollution control regulation represents a relatively new field of law, developed only in the latter half of the twentieth century. Accordingly, a distinction exists between the laws affecting *existing* sources of pollution and laws affecting *new* facilities. While environmental protection law is focused on improving public health, regulators understand that existing industrial sources of pollutants, which represent employment and large-scale investments, are limited in their ability to adapt to more stringent environmental regulations. As a result, existing sources of pollution are the beneficiaries of "grandfather" clauses whereby they are either exempted or granted a transition period before they must comply with the more exacting standards applied to new facilities. "Existing" facilities include those already in operation at the time the more stringent standards are enacted as well as those for which substantial commitments have been made. Existing sources are eligible for variances and waivers under circumstances where compliance cannot be attained.

Taxes and Subsidies

Some economists believe that regulatory action alone will never achieve the goals of the environmental statutes administered by the EPA. According to their theory, the best way to ensure the reduction of pollutants is to treat the environment as a commodity and allow the free market to allocate resources efficiently. This system can only be effective, however, if the added costs and benefits of controlling pollution are internalized by industry and reflected in the prices paid by customers and by society as a whole.

One of the primary difficulties encountered by the free market system is that the costs of the consequences of pollution to society are often unquantifiable. How can one accurately put a price on a reduction in respiratory illnesses as a result of improved air quality in a community? And how is such a price then internalized by the emitters of pollutants? There is no inherent economic mechanism providing industries with incentives to reduce emissions in order to remain competitive.

When private decisionmakers internalize environmental costs such that their decisions are based on their own profit rather than on rules imposed on them by government, then they are obviously subject to market forces. There are several ways to achieve this kind of internalization. One proposal for reap-portioning environmental externalities (external impacts) involves a pollution tax system. Under such a system, the government would set a tax rate for each type of pollution at levels that encourage self-imposed pollution reduction. The tax rates could be structured so that a unit of one type of pollutant would be more heavily taxed than another type, depending on the risk to human health or to the general environment. With a fixed tax per ton of pollution discharged, each emitter would be forced by market forces to reduce the levels of pollution to the point where the marginal cost of reducing further emissions was at least equal to the marginal tax imposed. The higher the tax rate for each type of contaminant, the less of that pollutant would be produced. The price of products whose production results in taxed pollution would be higher than that of products generated with less pollution. Consumers rationally choose to purchase lower-priced substitute goods.

The direct regulatory approach does not give polluters any economic incentive to reduce pollution levels below the statutory requirements. A range of economic incentives or taxes, on the other hand, could be adjusted periodically to reflect changes in environmental conditions or to provide a greater financial incentive for controlling pollution and promoting environmental quality. Issues of global environmental concern, such as acid rain, ozone depletion, and global warming are good candidates for testing such a system.

Pollution taxes, despite their seeming advantages over the standard regulatory system, have several drawbacks. First, there are administrative costs. Some form of constant monitoring of individual polluters is necessary to ensure that each emission subject to taxes is measured. Second, pollution taxes may seem appropriate mechanisms for controlling pollution across national or regional levels, but unforeseen pollution results may occur on a local level where an individual polluter(s) determines that discharging pollutants is worth the high cost of such taxes. This structure encourages those who can reduce effluents at the lowest cost to do so, not those who actually cause the greatest environmental damage. (Note that the same effect of a pollution tax could be achieved by the inverse policy of subsidizing environmentally benign nonpolluting products.) Another drawback of a pollution tax system is that it would be ineffective in the control of toxic pollutants because there is no adequate margin of safety for such substances. Absolute prohibitions are the only means of adequately assuring that discharges of these pollutants will be minimalized. Moreover, in a competitive market economy, selective taxes cause a less than optimal amount of production of the taxed items. For all these reasons, some environmentalists contend that the best way to control pollution emissions is to combine the regulatory approach with the market incentives provided by pollution taxes and subsidies.

Flexible Market Incentives

Several mechanisms currently used to regulate air quality (see Chapter 5) utilize flexible market trading in pollution rights/credits. "Offset" requirements mandate that a polluter offset proposed pollution with reductions of that same or similar pollutants in the same geographic region. Major new sources of emissions must be offset by the elimination of existing sources or the reduction of emissions from those sources.

The goal is therefore to reduce the emission levels for each pollutant in a geographic area despite the addition of a new source, such that the overall reduction in emissions represents further improvement of ambient air quality. The effect is intended to be ratchet-like — in theory, emissions can never go up significantly from existing levels but must always spiral downward. The government-imposed regulations set a ceiling on the total levels of pollution allowed in a given region, and the private sector bargains for the distribution of these pollution rights amongst themselves.

Thus, in practice, the operator of a proposed new facility need not be the party reducing emissions; reductions may be made by any existing source within the region. This market-based system allows polluters who can reduce their levels of emissions at low cost to do so, while permitting those who cannot do so cheaply (or simply refuse to do so) to pay others for the right to pollute. Consequently, a private market in emission rights has emerged. As long as the total levels of pollutants are reduced, the system cares little which parties make that achievement possible.

The principal advantage claimed by proponents of this type of emissions trading system is that polluters are given an economic incentive to reduce effluents at the least total collective cost possible. There are critics. They argue that companies are given credit or cash for emission reductions that they would have made anyway purely for business reasons, completely removed from any environmental considerations. To other critics, the microlevel income transfers are troubling. For example, if a manufacturer shuts down a production line because it is too expensive to operate, the EPA will be forced to grant the company tradable credits for reductions in emissions because it does not consider the manufacturer's motivations. Also, the EPA can financially favor older industries that pollute by giving them credits for reducing pollutant emissions, whereas new entrants to the market cannot do that.

A market-based pollution control methodology related to offsets is the "bubble" concept. Emissions are measured as if a hypothetical dome covered the entire plant. As long as there is no significant net increase in total emissions from any given bubbled facility, a proprietor may offset increases and decreases in emissions within the facility without triggering the imposition of additional environmental regulation. An industrial complex with multiple smokestacks, for example, may shut down a furnace or render a production process more efficient with less resulting waste, thereby offsetting new emissions with a reduction of older ones. The bubble concept allows private decision-making as to how emission standards are to be met on a plant-by-plant basis, as long as the net effect is to maintain or decrease total emissions in the region.

One of the major criticisms of this bubble approach is that it supports the present levels of acceptable pollution; there is no downward pressure of tighter air quality standards, and polluters have no continuing incentive to reduce overall emission levels. The bubble approach, like the offset system, also favors existing polluters who can take advantage of their "bubble," at the expense of new entrants to the market. These flexible market approaches may allow the region as a whole to achieve pollution reductions at the lowest cost, as long as one is not too concerned about the micro-level allocation among "winners" and "losers." This also underscores the complementary nature of regional or area-wide standards as opposed to individual emitter standards. Regional standards regulate media quality — air or water quality for an entire geographical region. Individual regulations control the amount that an individual or corporation can discharge into the environment. Permitting or controlling individual actions can meet the goals of area-wide improvement. The two approaches are intimately related, as we will see in the air (Chapter 5) and water (Chapter 6) sections.

Risk Assessment

When dealing with hazardous or toxic substances, it is important to assess the likely human impact of long-term exposure, even to relatively small amounts of these substances. Increasingly, an objective scientific method is used to assess the risk. Risk assessment is the objective weighing of scientific data to estimate the risk to a human population from exposure to a given substance. This process is distinctly different from risk management, which is the process of deciding how to remediate or deal with a risk that has been previously identified.

There are two primary applications of risk assessment. EPA employs risk assessment to determine at what level of stringency, if any, it should regulate a particular pollutant. Second, EPA or the states use risk assessment to determine the level of remediation required at a particular site where pollution poses a long-term risk to the local population.

The process of risk assessment involves four steps: (1) The hazard is identified by determining the pollutant at issue and its likely concentration; (2) the human carcinogenic, mutagenic, or pathogenic response to a particular dose or level of the pollutant is identified; (3) an assessment is made of the likely exposure of human populations through the various environmental media — air, water, soil, or food chain; and (4) the likely incidence of disease or damage is calculated. This last value is typically expressed as a probability of illness or death over a lifetime of exposure to the chemical or pollutant; the risk characterization may include a sensitivity analysis of the range of variables and outcomes that affect the analysis. Risk is a function of the toxicity of the chemical times its intake by humans at the site times the concentration of the pollutant.

The great advantage of risk assessment is that it quantifies risk. Quantification allows comparison of the risk of various pollutants on a consistent basis. It permits comparison of the risk against the cost of pollutant containment, reduction, or remediation. For policymakers, risk assessment can be the first step in meaningful cost-benefit analysis of regulating pollutants or cleaning up contaminants.

Even though it yields a quantitative value from a rigorous process, risk assessment still involves great uncertainty. First, extrapolation is often made from laboratory animal tests to likely human responses. Exactly when does the proclivity of laboratory mice to contract disease from exposure to chemicals indicate reliably the dose-response risk to humans from the same exposure? Human exposure levels often are much lower than those to which laboratory animals are exposed. Extrapolation of results to lower levels of exposure, as well as across species, creates significant degrees of scientific uncertainty.

Despite these problems, the process is important. Many scientists believe that the majority of cancers in humans are a result of environmental exposure, defined to include diet, drinking water, and tobacco, as well as ambient environment. Risk assessment becomes important to determine the degree to which we should regulate each potentially dangerous chemical or pollutant.

The objective of risk assessment is not to eliminate risk but to determine the level of risk that is acceptable. The risks that are assessed are principally public risks from general exposure to the environmental media (air, water, soil), the food chain, drinking water, or to workplace exposure to certain chemicals. The population at large tends often to discount latent or long-term risk and to concentrate instead on catastrophic risk with irreversible or large-scale injury, such as that posed by a serious malfunction at a nuclear power plant located in a populous region. Congressional action often reflects these public perceptions more than the application of a rigorous risk assessment.

In many cases, courts have directly considered the issue of risk in the level of chemical exposure. In *Reserve Mining Co. v. EPA*, 514 F.2d 492 (8th Cir. 1975), regarding water pollution, the court considered the risk from ingesting, rather than inhaling, asbestos by-products dumped in Lake Superior. The scientific evidence was disputed, with uncertain and conflicting testimony from experts for both sides. Ultimately, the court could only conclude that "the probability of harm is more likely than not . . . of some health risk." Because of this indefinite conclusion and Reserve Mining's willingness to undertake alternative methods of disposal in the future, the court balanced the equities and refused to enjoin the operation of the plant.

Regarding air pollution and risk assessment, the court in *Ethyl Corp. v. EPA*, 541 F.2d 1 (D.C. Cir. 1976), deferred to EPA's evaluation of the risk in lead as a gasoline additive pursuant to Section 211(c) of the Clean Air Act. There was a high degree of scientific uncertainty in the scientific data as to exactly how dangerous was lead in the ambient air. The court held that where the Clean Air Act sought prophylactically to preserve public health by an "adequate margin of safety," absolute scientific certainty is not required before regulations may issue.

Regarding workplace environmental exposure (rather than ambient exposure) to toxic chemicals, the Supreme Court, in *Indust. Union Dep't, AFL-CIO v. Am. Petroleum Inst.*, 448 U.S. 607 (1980), evaluated more stringent government regulation of permissible workplace levels of benzene, a known carcinogen, and overturned the regulation on a risk assessment basis by a divided Court. Benzene had no known safe level of human exposure, thus qualifying as a substance posing "significant risk of harm." However, the agency (the Occupational Safety and Health Administration) had made no finding that benzene present at the traditional level of regulation posed a significant risk of harm. The plurality opinion was based on an interpretation of the statute by which the justices believed the agency's risk assessment had to validate the "significant risk of harm" finding. Since the agency had not made a finding on whether the risk posed by the prior level of allowed workplace benzene was significant, the agency's attempt to lower the allowable workplace level was statutorily deficient. A stinging dissent by Justice Thurgood Marshall accused the plurality of bending over backwards to lessen the environmental burden on regulated industry.

In *Am. Textile Mfrs. Inst., Inc. v. Donovan*, 452 U.S. 490 (1981), the issue was OSHA workplace regulation of cotton dust that caused brown lung disease, byssinosis. OSHA had determined on the record that cotton dust presented a significant health hazard to employees, 25 percent of whom were affected by byssinosis. The Court held that no cost-benefit risk assessment was required prior to the government's setting a level of regulation for cotton dust. All that was required was an analysis that demonstrated that the regulation was feasible.

Under the Toxic Substances Control Act (TSCA), EPA regulates the manufacture and distribution of chemicals to prevent an unreasonable risk of injury to health or the environment. The court in *Corrosion Proof Fittings v. EPA*, 947 F.2d 1201 (5th Cir. 1991), applying a substantial evidence standard on review, reversed EPA's regulation of asbestos because the regulation failed to consider the costs and benefits of alternatives to a complete ban on asbestos. In essence, the EPA risk assessment was inadequate to conclude that alternative asbestos regulation posed an unreasonable risk to the public.

Environmental Equity

Despite consideration of average risk or area-wide environmental standards, certain micro-areas or communities can experience disparate environmental impact. Various research studies have found a correlation between race of local inhabitants and poverty on the one hand, and the location of hazardous waste facilities and other polluting industrial activities on the other hand. See U.S. General Accounting Office, *Siting of Hazardous Waste Landfill and Their Correlation with Racial and Economic Status of Surrounding Communities*, GAO/RCED-83-168 (1983); Robert D. Bullard, *Dumping in Dixie: Race, Class, and Environmental Quality* (2d ed. 1994). But for a contrasting view, see Vicki Been, "What's Fairness Got to Do with It? Environmental Justice and the Siting of Locally Undesirable Land Uses," 78 Cornell L. Rev. 1001 (1993).

There is a "chicken and egg" conundrum: Do hazardous facilities locate in industrial zones, which happen to be bordered by low-income or racially minority communities, or is there intent to locate near racial minorities as a matter of intentional discrimination? Litigation was prosecuted asserting violations of equal protection of the laws in the disproportionate environmental impact imposed on some communities from facility siting decisions. The litigation has been unsuccessful. See *Washington v. Davis*, 426 U.S. 229 (1976) (racially disparate impact alone does not violate the Constitution); *Vill. of Arlington Heights v. Metro. Hous. Dev. Corp.*, 429 U.S. 252 (1977) (developing five factors for equal protection claims generally); *R.I.S.E. v. Kay*, 768 F. Supp. 1144 (S.D. Va. 1991) (no discriminatory intent when economic factors motivate decision); *East-Bibb Twiggs Neighborhood Ass'n v. Macon-Bibb Planning and Zoning Comm'n*, 896 F.2d 1264 (11th Cir. 1989) (no discriminatory intent demonstrated).

Environmental equity litigation was dealt a severe blow by the Supreme Court in *Alexander v. Sandoval*, 532 U.S. 275 (2001), holding that there is no private right of action available to enforce disparate impact regulations promulgated under Title VI of the Civil Rights Act. *Sandoval* involved a challenge to the Alabama policy of administering driver's license examinations only in English, and the court held that the statute prevents only intentional discrimination. Relying on *Sandoval*, the Third Circuit reversed the lower court determination that the New Jersey Department of Environmental Protection discriminated against racial minorities by issuing an air permit for a cement facility that could have an adverse disparate racial impact under Title VI of the Civil Rights Act of 1964. *S. Camden Citizens In Action v. N.J. Dep't of Envtl. Prot.*, 274 F.3d 771 (3d Cir. 2001). The court held that plaintiffs cannot maintain an action under Section 1983 for disparate impact discrimination in violation of Title VI because no such interest is implicit in the statute and Title VI proscribes only intentional discrimination.

In 1994, President Clinton issued Executive Order 12,898, requiring all federal agencies to make achieving environmental justice part of their missions. It requires each federal agency to have an environmental justice strategy that identifies the distributional impacts of existing programs and to collect data on demographic outcomes of agency decisions.

COMMON LAW ENVIRONMENTAL REMEDIES

Key Distinctions

In the modern era, environmental statutes provide one-stop shopping for environmental claims. They typically provide both the procedural basis and the substantive remedy for redressing environmental problems. But statutes leave some gaps. The principal advantage of the common law is that it is decentralized and remedies can be tailored to individual circumstances, providing monetary damages to those directly injured or injunctive relief. Tort actions by individual plaintiffs can attack a problem with a specificity that generic regulations may overlook.

However, this advantage also suggests the limitations of tort common law remedies. Individual plaintiffs must have the resources to sustain lengthy litigation. The injury to health or the environment may occur long after the release or discharge of pollution, making detection, causation, and linkage difficult to prove. Moreover, environmental damages often affect aesthetic or recreational interests, or they create fear of future illness, torts which may be more difficult to evaluate than direct economic loss. See *Metro. Edison Co. v. P.A.N.E.*, 460 U.S. 766 (1983); *Ayers v. Jackson Township*, 106 N.J. 557, 525 A.2d 287 (N.J. 1987).

Despite the numerous environmental statutes and regulations, common law remedies still play a vital role in environmental protection. Common law actions can provide remedies where federal or state statutes do not. In some instances, environmental pollution does not meet the threshold for violating a federal statute; however, it may have caused either personal or property damage cognizable at common law. Common law can provide those harmed by pollution an easier threshold for bringing the defendant to court. Plaintiffs can recover common law damages, including those for pain and suffering, and even punitive awards, and they may be able to demand a jury trial — all of which are seldom available statutorily. Recovery for economic loss may not be available statutorily, nor may typical damage remedies.

Some common law actions have found damages for emotional distress where contamination migrates onto the property of another. *Curran v. Mass. Tpk. Auth.*, 2 Mass. L. Rep. 260 (Mass. Super. 1994). This action does not compensate for damages caused by the actual migration of the pollutants themselves, but for ailments caused by emotional distress from knowing that the pollutants are migrating. *Payton v. Abbott Labs*, 386 Mass. 540, 556, 437 N.E.2d 171 (Mass. 1982); *Parr v. Goodyear Tire & Rubber Co.*, 641 So. 2d 769, 770 (Ala. 1994); *Rodrigues v. State*, 472 P.2d 509 (Haw. 1970). This is distinct from recovery for the fear of injury, but rather compensates for the actual emotional injury related to the migration of chemicals.

An important role common law plays in environmental protection is as a *supplement* to federal regulation. For example, under the Comprehensive Environmental Response, Compensation and Liability Act (CERCLA), a private person may sue only for equitable restitution of response costs. By asserting a common law claim in addition to the CERCLA claim, the plaintiff may have a jury trial and recover damages. Further, the plaintiff may gain attorney fees.

Private litigants, seeking remedies for harms caused by environmental pollution, file cases based on common law theories of nuisance, trespass, negligence, strict liability, and the public trust doctrine. Which doctrine fits where? Plaintiffs will use negligence and strict tort liability to gain damages for *personal* injury from environmental pollution. For invasions of *property* interests, plaintiffs rely on trespass and nuisance actions to address environmental harm. The public trust doctrine stems from Roman law, which held that resources such as air, running water, the seas, and the shores of the sea are common to all; this doctrine typically is used to protect waterways and their associated lands.

Common law contract claims also find their way into environmental claims. The Uniform Commercial Code provides an implied warranty of merchantability on sales by merchants. This includes adequate labeling. U.C.C. 2-314(2)(e). An implied warranty of fitness for a particular purpose also can be created, whether or not the vendor is a merchant. Claims for breach of warranty where a product causes environmental injury can invoke these provisions. Express warranties also can be breached.

In every common law action, the plaintiff must bring the case within the statute of limitations and establish the causation between the harm and the defendant's conduct. Let's take a closer look at each of these common law actions and key case law.

Nuisance

Nuisance is the most frequently pled common law tort action in environmental litigation. Nuisance law traditionally protected the right of a landowner to use and enjoy property. This is a broad interest that can be violated without direct physical invasion. Nuisance actions come in two forms: public and private.

Under both private and public nuisance law, the plaintiff must prove that the defendant's activity unreasonably interfered with the use or enjoyment of a protected interest and caused the plaintiff *substantial* harm. An activity that affects the physical environmental conditions of land usually will meet the substantial harm requirement. Additionally, substantial harm may be shown if the activity caused a single, significant injury, or if the activity was a sequence of minor but steadily increasing-in-harm activities.

Potential harm may be considered substantial in some nuisance actions if the plaintiff can show that the harm is significant and probable. The connection between the interference and the polluter's acts, however, often is difficult to establish because of the long time period and attenuated nexus in which some pollution manifests harm.

Most states have explicitly barred same-property private nuisance claims by a current landowner seeking damages or equitable relief for contamination originating on his property. A public nuisance is one which affects at the same time an entire community, neighborhood, or any considerable number of persons, although the extent of the annoyance or damage inflicted on individuals is unequal. Only private individuals who suffer special damage distinct from damages of the general public may pursue an action for public nuisance. *Newhall v. Superior Court*, 19 Cal. App. 4th 334, 340 (Ca. 1993)(cause of action for a continuing trespass, using public nuisance to satisfy the "tortuous" element of a continuing trespass).

Section 821D of the Restatement Second of Torts defines private nuisance as a nontrespass invasion of another's interest in the private use and enjoyment of land. The majority of states restrict private nuisance claims to disputes between neighboring landowners, which precludes the use of private nuisance to recover for same-property contamination. *Philadelphia Elec. Co. v. Hercules, Inc.*, 762 F.2d 303 (3rd Cir. 1985). Oklahoma courts held that a successor landowner may be entitled to pursue a claim for public nuisance against a predecessor who is responsible for groundwater contamination. *Moore v. Texaco, Inc.*, 244 F.3d 1229, 1231 (2001).

The trier of fact determines whether an activity is unreasonable by balancing the social utility of the activities against the harm they create. The court or jury considers the benefits and damages that each party will gain if the polluting activity is terminated. Other factors the trier of fact will consider are the local conditions, the right of the plaintiff to use the protected interest, and whether the defendant could have prevented the activity that caused the harm. Section 822 of the Restatement Second of Torts specifies that:

> one is subject to liability for a private nuisance if, but only if: his conduct is a legal cause of an invasion of another's interest in the private use and enjoyment of land, and the invasion is either (a) intentional or unreasonable, or (b) unintentional and otherwise actionable under the rules controlling liability for negligent or reckless conduct or for abnormally dangerous conditions or activities.

Complainants have used *private* nuisance actions to gain individual compensation and force polluters to discontinue interference with their physical private *property* as well as with their comfort and enjoyment of their property. In *Boomer v. Atlantic Cement Co.*, 257 N.E.2d 870 (N.Y. 1970), the prior-in-time plaintiffs claimed that the dirt, smoke, and vibrations coming from the defendant's 1,544 acre, $45 million cement plant caused injury to their property. The property owners sought damages and an injunction to close the plant. The plant already employed the best pollution control technology. The *Boomer* court addressed the economic consequence of the injunction and the effect of the nuisance. The court weighed the economic effect of closing the plant, which paid half the town's property taxes, against the harm to the individual plaintiff's land, and concluded that the cement company could pay permanent damages in lieu of an injunction or closing.

The court's order gave Atlantic Cement a choice: It could pay permanent damages to plaintiffs to compensate for all present and future economic loss to their properties attributable to Atlantic's operations, or an injunction against the nuisance would issue. This was novel in two regards. First, it offered defendant Atlantic control — and a choice — of remedy. Usually the choice of remedy belongs to the aggrieved plaintiff. Second, the damages award was for future damages, even when those had not occurred, and it was not clear that they would continue to occur. Moreover, the court concluded that the state statutory scheme regulating air pollution was a better means to address air pollution than common law negligence. Note, however, that the former mechanism largely eviscerates effective direct citizen use of the common law in favor of government regulation.

Justice Jasen dissented, stating that the long-standing New York rule which held that a nuisance must be enjoined when it results in continuing damages should not be disregarded, thereby licensing the continuation of a nuisance and escalating the serious problem of air pollution. Essentially, Atlantic was able to continue its nuisance as long as it paid for property condemned or damaged thereby.

This case illustrates the limitations of private nuisance law to remedy pollution. Courts typically balance the equities and hardships. Private nuisances do not always outweigh the economic contribution of the polluting entity. In *Weinberger v. Romero Barcello*, 456 U.S. 305 (1982), the Court reversed the circuit court's order of injunctive relief. For widespread pollution, public nuisance law might be more appropriate than private nuisance law. However, there are standing problems for individuals who want to assert public nuisance.

Public nuisance law protects from interference a "right common to the general public." Plaintiffs may bring a public nuisance action if there are damages, interference, or inconvenience to the health or safety of the public. A state may assert a public nuisance action as an exercise of its police powers — the typical situation. A private citizen may bring a public nuisance action only if he or she can show that he or she has suffered from a harm that can be distinguished from that suffered by the members of the general public.

This so-called "special injury" rule has been interpreted to require that the individual injury must be distinct from the environmental injury to all persons in the area, in order for the individual to be granted standing to bring a public nuisance action. The individual private injury must be qualitatively different, not just quantitatively different, from the public injury. Some courts have held that this standard can be satisfied by personal injury to one's health, as opposed to property damage. In the well-known W. R. Grace case in Woburn, Massachusetts (popularized in J. Harr, *A Civil Action*), plaintiffs alleged that contamination of their groundwater caused specific fatal illnesses. The court in *Anderson v. W. R. Grace & Co.*, 628 F. Supp. 1219 (D. Mass. 1986), held that this constituted a special injury to public water supply to ground a public nuisance claim. If proven, compensation could include value for physical injury, emotional distress related to the physical injury, and diminution in property values.

It also can be difficult for private plaintiffs to demonstrate the individual personalized material harm necessary to be successful in a nuisance action. Where pollution emanates from several sources, no one of which alone causes the harm, but cumulative harm is caused, the material harm may be difficult to prove. Moreover, nuisance actions are a case-by-case one-shot attempt to cure a particular problem. Nuisance law does not provide an ongoing construct to supervise discharges to the ambient air or water supply.

In *Spur Indus., Inc. v. Del Webb Dev. Co.*, 494 P.2d 700 (Ariz. 1972), the plaintiff, a developer who was building homes near a 15-year preexisting well-kept, rural animal feed lot owned by Spur, complained that the feeding operation was a *public* nuisance because of the associated flies and odors that would drift or blow over the development. The developer sought a permanent injunction. The court imposed a permanent injunction as a public and private nuisance holding that the damages to the people who bought homes in the new development required such a decision. Yet the new homeowners had moved to the nuisance and thus assumed some risk. The court ordered the developer to pay Spur a reasonable amount for the cost of moving or shutting down.

The *Spur* court held that if the developer alone had been injured, the doctrine of "coming to the nuisance" would have barred Webb's recovery. However, Webb had induced residents to move to its development and to incur foreseeable harm from the feedlot nuisance. Only because Webb brought residents to the nuisance was he given the opportunity to pay Spur to cease operation or relocate, rather than lose his (Webb's) investment in the new development. Here again is a balancing of the equities — the pollution was abated, but at the direct expense of the developer.

Some states allow demonstration of a plaintiff having "come to the nuisance" as a complete defense to the nuisance action. In essence, this establishes a priority of use in favor of the defendant. Cf. *Pendoley v. Ferreira*, 187 N.E.2d 142, 345 Mass. 309 (1963) (defendant provided a reasonable amount of time to relocate piggery); *Terhune v. Methodist Episcopal Church*,

87 N.J. Eq. 195, 100 A. 342 (N.J. 1917) (plaintiff moving to an area where one could hear church bells prevented him from enjoining their ringing).

Other states consider "coming to a nuisance" as a factor in fashioning equitable relief, but not a dispositive one. This is to prevent the first-in-time settlors from controlling use of nearby land, especially when uses and development evolve. In states that consider multiple factors, these include relocation of a nuisance, knowledge of the nuisance, any financial discount in acquisition of the burdened property, and whether requested relief is temporary or permanent. *Williams v. Oeder*, 659 N.E.2d 379, 103 Ohio App. 3d 333 (Ohio 1995); *Boomer v. Atlantic Cement Co.* 257 N.E.2d 870, 872, 26 N.Y.2d 219 (N.Y. 1970); *Rassier v. Houim*, 488 N.W.2d 635, 638 (1992) (considering many factors to enjoin preexisting wind generator that created noise in residential neighborhood).

Urban sprawl threatens many traditional agricultural areas because residential developments may characterize the odors, noise, and other problems from these agricultural areas as nuisances. So-called "right-to-farm" statutes protect farmers and ranchers from nuisance lawsuits filed by residential newcomers who "come to the nuisance." They essentially codify the "coming to the nuisance" defense to defeat nuisance actions against the preexisting practices.

Although these statutes differ in the various states, if an agricultural or ranching activity has been established for a specified minimum length of time (typically one year) before the land use change that creates the nuisance situation, then the owner or operator of the nuisance is protected from suit. *Buchanan v. Simplot Feeders Ltd. P'ship*, 952 P.2d 610, 614, 134 Wash. 2d 673 (Wash. 1998); *Jerry Harmon Motors, Inc. v. Farmers Union Grain Terminal Ass'n*, 431 N.W.2d 427 (1983). At least one court has ruled such statutes unconstitutional and a taking. *Bormann v. Bd. of Supervisors In And For Kossuth County*, 584 N.W.2d 309 (Iowa 1998).

In *Vill. of Wilsonville v. SCA Servs., Inc.*, 426 N.E.2d 824 (Ill. 1981), the plaintiffs, a village and other governmental bodies, alleged that the defendant's hazardous chemical landfill was a *public* nuisance. The plaintiffs successfully sought to enjoin the operations of the landfill and require removal of toxic waste and contaminated soil. Although the damages were *prospective*, the nuisance already was present. Where damages are not adequate, a wide variety of activities have been enjoined by state governments employing the doctrine of public nuisance. Public nuisance can enjoin or remedy hazardous waste, *Town of Mt. Pleasant v. Van Tassell*, 7 Misc. 2d 643, 166 N.Y.S.2d 458 (N.Y. Sup. Ct. 1957), water pollution, noise pollution, *Bd. of Health v. Copcutt*, 140 N.Y. 12, 35 N.E. 443 (1893), and noxious odors, *N.Y. Trap Rock Corp. v. Clarkstown*, 299 N.Y. 77, 85 N.E.2d 873 (1949).These three cases illustrate the flexibility of nuisance remedies. All invoke *state* common law. Of note, all were initiated before CERCLA (see Chapter 9).

Nuisance law and other common law remedies are subject to the claim by defendants that such remedies are preempted by the elaborate federal and state pollution control regulations. The resolution of this issue is not fully matured.

In *Milwaukee v. Illinois*, 451 U.S. 304 (1981) (*Milwaukee II*), the Court held that the federal Clean Water Act preempted any federal common law. Illinois and Michigan sued Milwaukee for creating a public nuisance by dumping untreated sewage into Lake Michigan. The EPA had already cited Milwaukee for violating the Clean Water Act and had imposed a timetable for the city to come into compliance. The nuisance suit sought to impose a more stringent timetable. The Supreme Court held that, while a federal common law of nuisance does exist, it is preempted by federal regulation of the area in question. In this case, although there was ongoing harm to the plaintiff states caused by Milwaukee, the suit was preempted by the Clean Water Act. This decision is criticized by some because the Clean Water Act contains an explicit savings clause (see Chapter 4 regarding savings clauses and Chapter 6 regarding the Clean Water Act) that protects all more stringent state law. Some argue that this clause protects state common law claims.

In *Int'l Paper Co. v. Ouellette*, 479 U.S. 481 (1987), the Court allowed a state nuisance and trespass claim to be lodged against a discharger of water pollutants that otherwise complied with regulatory discharge requirements. The U.S. Supreme Court held that while a Vermont citizen could sue a New York-based polluter in Vermont state court for harm to his land in Vermont, the court had to apply New York water-quality standards and common law in determining whether a nuisance existed. International Paper's wastewater pipe ended at the bottom of the lake just short of the Vermont border, so the court ruled that it was subject only to New York standards, not those of Vermont. The federal precedent construing *Ouellette* (involving the Clean Water Act) applies also to the Clean Air Act, requiring source-state rather than recipient-state nuisance law to apply to pollution source emissions. *N.C. ex rel. Cooper v. TVA*, 615 F.3d 291 (4th Cir. 2010). In the area of toxic waste cleanup and liability, private citizens often bring suit pleading federal statute (CERCLA) (see Chapter 9), state statute (the state equivalent of CERCLA), and common law actions for nuisance, trespass, or strict liability. These common law actions typically survive and are prosecuted simultaneously with the statutory claims. *New York v. Shore Realty Corp.*, 759 F.2d 1032 (2d Cir. 1985).

Trespass

Trespass is closely related to nuisance and sometimes easily confused with it. Trespass is a *direct* physical invasion or intrusion of the plaintiff's land — by the defendant, the defendant's agent, or an object that the defendant has caused to be deposited on the land. Nuisance interferes with the plaintiff's use and enjoyment of the land and can thus be considered indirect injury. The interest protected in a nuisance claim is the property owner's use and enjoyment of the land, as opposed to trespass where the owner's interest is the exclusive possession of the land. *Martin v. Reynolds Metals Co.*, 342 P.2d 790, 795 (1959). A major issue is whether a former owner, selling contaminated property, commits a trespass to the land owned by the buyer by leaving pollution behind after the sale. California allows such novel claims. Nuisance and trespass often are both pled.

Need an environmental trespass be directly visible? In *Martin v. Reynolds Metal Co.*, 342 P.2d 790 (Or. 1959), plaintiff landowners argued that fluoride particles which emitted from the defendant's plant and settled on the plaintiff's land constituted trespass. The defendants contended that because the fluoride particles were invisible, there could be no direct invasion. The court stated that although one cannot see an atom with the naked eye, "even the uneducated know the great and awful force contained in the atom and what it can do to property if released." The court held that the intrusion of the invisible fluoride particles constituted trespass.

In the modern environmental context, courts may require minimum levels of injury before affording a remedy for the trespass. Therefore, actions in nuisance have been used more by plaintiffs for environmental injury than claims in trespass. Some courts allow actions for trespass or nuisance against prior property owners, *Mangini v. Aerojet-Gen. Corp.*, 281 Cal. Rptr. 827 (1991), although the majority of courts deny such actions, *Philadelphia Elec. Co. v. Hercules, Inc.*, 762 F.2d 303 (3d Cir. 1984) (caveat emptor); *Wellesley Hills Realty Trust v. Mobil Oil Corp.*, 747 F. Supp. 93 (D. Mass. 1990).

Negligence

The common law doctrine of negligence is used most frequently to govern relief for *personal* injuries due to environmental pollution. In a negligence-based cause of action, the plaintiff must show (1) a legal duty requiring the actor to conform to a certain standard of conduct for the protection of others against an unreasonable risk, (2) a breach of that duty, (3) a reasonably close causal connection between the conduct and the resulting injury, and (4) an actual injury. The third item — linking release of pollution to an actual injury — has proven most difficult to plaintiffs raising environmental torts.

Some common law tort actions may employ the doctrine of *res ipsa loquitor*. This doctrine permits the inference of negligence in the absence of findings of a specific cause of occurrence, when the accident is of a kind that does not ordinarily happen unless the defendant was negligent in some respect and other responsible causes, including the conduct of plaintiff-injured party, are sufficiently eliminated. To invoke *res ipsa loquitor* the plaintiff bears the burden of proving that the accident would not have happened except for the negligence of the defendant. *Trefney v. Nat'l Super Mkts.*, 803 S.W.2d, 119 121 (Mo. Ct. App. 1990).

The standard of proof for the admissibility of expert scientific evidence requires that in federal court the Federal Rules of Evidence require that the expert's testimony rest on a reliable foundation and is relevant to the issues at hand based on scientific knowledge. *Daubert v. Merrill Dow Pharms., Inc.,* 509 U.S. at 579 (1993). The trial judge makes "a preliminary assessment of whether the testimony's underlying reasoning or methodology is scientifically valid and properly can be applied to the facts at hand." *Id.* at 580.

With negligence claims in many jurisdictions, contributory negligence can bar recovery for the plaintiff. For example, if the plaintiff's injury was due to exposure to asbestos but also to smoking and other voluntary actions, recovery may be barred. See *Borel v. Fibreboard Paper Prods. Corp.,* 493 F.2d 1076 (5th Cir. 1973), *cert. denied, Fibreboard Paper Prods. Corp. v. Borel,* 419 U.S. 869 (1974).

Negligence per se can be claimed where the defendant violated a statutory (or in some cases regulatory) standard of conduct or obligation. The plaintiff must be a member of the class of persons whom the statute or regulation was designed to protect.

Strict Liability

Plaintiffs may prefer a strict liability standard to that of negligence. Certain actions or conduct impose liability so that the defendant does not have to prove the elements of negligence. The concept emanates from the case of *Rylands v. Fletcher*, 3 H.C. 774, 159 Eng. Rep. 737 (1865), in which the owner or occupier of land was strictly liable for injury from a thing that is "likely to do mischief if it escapes." Reasonable care by the landowner is not a defense to a strict liability claim for ultrahazardous activities.

The doctrine of strict liability, liability without intent or negligence, may be used in cases where the defendant has carried on an *abnormally dangerous* activity and has subjected a plaintiff to a foreseeable harm resulting from that activity. Section 520 of the Restatement Second of Torts states factors used in determining whether an activity is abnormally dangerous: "(a) whether the activity involves a high degree of risk of some harm to the person, land, or chattels of others; (b) whether the gravity of harm which may result from it is likely to be great; (c) whether the risk cannot be eliminated by the exercise of reasonable care; (d) whether the activity is not a matter of common usage; (e) whether the activity is inappropriate to the place where it is carried on; and (f) the value of the activity to the community." Additionally, to recover under strict liability, the plaintiff must show actual damages.

Courts have imposed strict liability in hazardous waste cases where plaintiffs have alleged damages caused by improper disposal and subsequent leaking of hazardous waste. For example, in *State Dep't of Envtl. Prot. v. Ventron Corp.*, 468 A.2d 150 (N.J. 1993), the New Jersey Supreme Court considered whether a company that owned a mercury processing plant which had polluted a tidal creek and neighboring land would be strictly liable for damage caused. The court applied the six Restatement factors (above) and found that disposal of waste was an abnormally dangerous activity for which the company could be held strictly liable. See also *Sterling v. Velsicol Chem. Corp.*, 647 F. Supp. 303 (W.D. Tenn. 1986), *aff'd in part and rev'd in part*, 855 F.2d 1188 (6th Cir. 1988). Other courts have declined to hold that the handling or storage of hazardous chemicals constitutes an ultrahazardous activity. Cf. *Avemco Ins. Co. v. Rooto Corp.*, 967 F.2d 1105 (6th Cir. 1992).

Courts have applied strict liability to cases involving contamination from oil wells, leaking fuel tanks that leach into groundwater and contaminate drinking water wells, and radioactive emissions, among others. The use of strict liability, however, is on a case-by-case basis. The court will consider evidence regarding the activity and the defendant's management of that activity.

Strict liability also has application in environmental law in product liability claims. Plaintiffs claim that they are injured by exposure to toxic elements contained in consumer products. Section 402A of the Restatement Second of Torts permits a claim against someone in a trade or business who sells a defective product that is unreasonably dangerous to the user or consumer or to his or her property.

The basis of a plaintiff's claim can be that there is a design defect, a manufacturing defect, a failure to warn of foreseeable toxic hazards, or other risks in or associated with a product. The manufacturer is held to the standard of an expert in the field in terms of assessing the foreseeable risks of a product; there is an affirmative obligation to keep up with the science in a relevant area. See *Davis v. Wyeth Labs., Inc.*, 399 F.2d 121 (9th Cir. 1968) (polio vaccine manufacturer had duty to warn of one in a million risk of contracting the disease from the administration of the vaccine).

A variety of defenses may be raised against environmental product liability claims. These include the state-of-the-art defense against failure-to-warn claims, in which the defendant claims not to have known and to have had no reasonable ability to know of the hazard or risk at the time of plaintiff's exposure or injury. See *Anderson v. Owens-Corning Fiberglas Corp.*, 281 Cal. Rptr. 528, 810 P.2d 549 (Cal. 1991). Most states allow this defense to be made to environmental claims.

In addition, there is a recognized defense for unavoidably unsafe products that are of great value to society and cannot be made safe. Much of the case law in this area has developed around drug-related injuries. There is also a sophisticated user defense, in which the consumer is in a superior or sophisticated position vis-à-vis the seller of the product to know of its inherent toxic risk. The seller must have given any appropriate warning to the purchaser. See *Adams v. Union Carbide Corp.*, 737 F.2d 1453 (6th Cir. 1984), *cert. denied*, 469 U.S. 1062 (1984) (where Union Carbide sold toxic chemicals to General Motors to be used in the workplace, provided information about the toxic chemicals, and conducted safety discussions with General Motors, Union Carbide was not liable for injury to General Motors' employees).

Public Trust Doctrine

The public trust doctrine is based on the principle that certain resources are too unique and valuable to be privately owned; they must be available for public use. The roots of the doctrine lie in Roman law, described by Justinian:

> Things common to mankind by the law of nature, are the air, running water, the sea, and consequently the shores of the sea. . . . The use of the seashore . . . is also [governed] by the law of nations . . . and all persons are at equal liberty to land their vessels, unload them, and to fasten ropes to the trees upon the banks as to navigate upon the river itself . . . for the shores are not understood to be property in any man, but are compared to the sea itself, and to the sand or ground which is under the sea.[1]

England adopted a similar rule, describing all riparian land as being held by the crown in the name of the people. After the American revolution, the rights of the sovereign passed to the governments of the individual colonies, not the central federal government. The state's role as sovereign over trust lands gives it certain trustee environmental duties that it owes to the public and that are thus enforceable by the public.

There is judicial recognition that certain rights of the public are paramount to individual common law rights. For example, most states recognize the public right or trust in certain waterways and coastal zones. This right or trust is interpreted to include tidelands — those lands that sometimes are underwater and other times are not. *Phillips Petroleum Co. v. Mississippi*, 484 U.S. 469 (1988). States and state court interpretations can expand public trust authority to nonnavigable waterways. The public trust doctrine establishes a set of public rights in water that are subject to the public trust.

---

1. J. Inst. bk. 2, tit. 1, pts. 1-5, at 67-68 (T. Cooper trans. 1852).

The basis for this doctrine is that title to certain beds beneath navigable waters was vested in the states at the time of their statehood. Though originally derived from the federal government's control over navigable waters, at statehood these powers were vested in the states. Therefore, the public trust doctrine arises under and is interpreted pursuant to state common law, rather than federal law. *New York v. DeLyser*, 759 F. Supp. 982 (W.D.N.Y. 1991). This doctrine works to restrict the states from passing title to these submerged lands or the waters above them to a private interest in such manner that it impairs the obligation to hold use of these lands and waters for the public at large.

In *Ill. Cent. R.R. v. Illinois*, 146 U.S. 387 (1892), the state of Illinois granted 1,000 acres of submerged lands on the shores of Lake Michigan to Illinois Central Railroad in fee simple. Five years later, the legislature changed its mind and repealed the grant. The state sued to quit title. The United States Supreme Court noted that conveyances of trust property to private citizens were possible; however, this grant was invalid because the state had "abdicated its trust." If the public is deprived of access to trust resources, the state has the burden of justifying the purpose of the conveyance.

In *Nat'l Audubon Soc'y v. Superior Court*, 658 P.2d 709 (Cal. 1983), the plaintiffs alleged that water diversions from Mono Lake in northern California to the city of Los Angeles resulted in a significant drop in the lake's water level, causing damages to the environment, and violated the public trust doctrine. Los Angeles defended by emphasizing that the state had issued permits allowing the diversions. The California Supreme Court held that the state had continuing supervisory responsibility over its navigable waters under the public trust doctrine; the doctrine prevented any party from appropriating water in a manner that harmed public trust interests. But as is so common in common law remedies, expediency mitigated the rule of law. The court acknowledged that Los Angeles depended on water diversions and held that the state could permit water transfers even though some damage to the sources would occur. The court concluded it would allow only minimal harm; the state had an affirmative duty to protect the public trust whenever feasible.

Although the public trust doctrine does not prevent conveyance of affected property to private interests, it does impose a condition subsequent on the future use of the land to further the public purpose. The legislature and courts of a given state enjoy substantial discretion in defining exactly what that public purpose is. As technology has changed, our rivers and waterfronts are used less for waterborne commerce and transportation and more for recreational purposes. The public trust doctrine has been employed to preserve a public interest in recreation, swimming, access, and recreational fishing. *Marks v. Whitney*, 98 Cal. Rptr. 790, 491 P.2d 374 (Cal. 1971).

The Availability of Criminal Sanctions

Civil penalties are assessed by federal environmental agencies, as set forth in Exhibit 1.1. Despite practical problems, criminal prosecution has assumed center stage in environmental enforcement. For a business executive, the prospect of incarceration with violent felons focuses the attention like few other sanctions. In return for no jail time, defendants often are willing to plead guilty to violations carrying very large fines. Defendants' costs usually are paid by the corporation, not by the accused executive. These legal costs are tax-deductible business expenses. Corporations often also pay the fines on behalf of their executives. Nevertheless, criminal prosecution remains a potent weapon in the expanding arsenal of environmental enforcement. Recent federal prosecutions are illustrated in Exhibits 1.2 and 1.3.

1.1 EPA Civil Enforcement and Compliance Activities, 2008

Referrals of civil judicial enforcement cases to Department of Justice (DOJ)	280
Supplemental referrals of civil judicial enforcement cases to DOJ	35
Civil judicial complaints filed with court	164
Civil judicial enforcement case conclusions	192
Administrative penalty order complaints	2,056
Final administrative penalty orders	2,084
Administrative compliance orders	1,390
Cases with SEPs	188

1.2 Criminal Enforcement Program, 2008

Years of incarceration	57
Fines and restitution	$63,500,000
Value of court-ordered environmental projects	$12,000,000
Environmental crime cases initiated	319
Defendants charged	176
Estimated pollution reduced, treated, or eliminated commitments (pounds)	1,600,000

1.3 Criminal Enforcement Program Major Activities

Fiscal Year	Number of Cases Initiated	Number of Defendants Charged	Sentences (years)	Fines and Restitution (in $M inflation-adjusted to FY '08 dollars)
'04	425	293	77	$54
'05	372	320	186	$111
'06	305	278	154	$46
'07	340	248	64	$66
'08	319	176	57	$63.5

In aggravated situations, some environmental polluters may be held criminally liable for the human deaths their pollution caused. Here's one example: Film Recovery Inc., a company near Chicago, extracted trace amounts of silver from hospitals' discarded X-ray film by using sodium cyanide.[2] In its heyday, the company employed 80 workers and earned about $18 million annually.

But in its unventilated workroom, employees hunched over 140 bubbling, foaming cauldrons of sodium cyanide. They were issued no protective gear and were not instructed in safety measures. While the workers manually stirred these vats, sodium cyanide slopped over the sides, soaking the workers' clothing and skin. The air was choked with the fumes of hydrogen cyanide gas.

Film Recovery employed undocumented immigrant laborers almost exclusively in its silver-recovery process. The common antidote for cyanide poisoning, amyl nitrite, was not available at the facility. Even the "skull-and-crossbones" warning labels on the drums of cyanide were covered over or obscured by management. One day in February 1983, Stefan Golab, a Polish immigrant, stumbled into the lunchroom, fell to the floor with nausea, and died from acute cyanide poisoning. He was 59 years old.

The tragedy of Stefan Golab's death was compounded by the fact that the government agency responsible for regulating Film Recovery had given the firm a clean bill of health only months before. In the fall of 1982, inspectors from the federal Occupational Safety and Health Administration (OSHA) visited the plant but never went beyond the front office, where they saw nothing out of the ordinary in the company's paperwork. They did not walk the additional 25 feet beyond the office doors to observe Golab and others

---

2. This example is adapted from S. Ferrey, *Toxic Shell Game*, Amicus, Summer 1987, at 70.

hunched over vats of cyanide. After Golab's death, OSHA inspectors descended on the plant, fining management the amount of $4,855. Film Recovery refused to pay, so OSHA reduced the fine by half.

These on-site activities were just the tip of the criminal iceberg. Investigators later discovered almost 15 million pounds of cyanide waste from Film Recovery that had been dumped illegally in rented truck trailers parked in other parts of Illinois. The EPA used $4.5 million of taxpayers' funds to clean up this toxic debris.

The county prosecutor filled the prosecutorial void. He prosecuted Film Recovery president Steven O'Neil, the plant manager, and the foreman, for murder. Although they had never wielded a gun or voiced a threat, the three were convicted and sentenced to 25 years in jail.

Federal and state laws covering hazardous waste, clean air, clean water, and workplace safety impose stiff civil and criminal penalties for knowing violations or repeated offenses (see Chapter 9). Like expanding reflections in a carnival mirror, one transgression magnifies into multiple dimensions. A single polluting action can violate several laws simultaneously, and each day of violation is counted by the courts as if it were a new violation. A single act of pollution becomes a serious and compounded felony.

Common law is an important adjunct to statutory remedies, as you will see in the following Examples and Explanations. In later chapters, we'll look at specific environmental statutory requirements.

Examples

1. Because he has a difficult time withstanding the elements, and to prevent rusting, Tin Man frequently squirts key joints with oil from a large supply he keeps in 55-gallon drums on his property. He also supplies oil to several farmers with large combines. Unfortunately, Tin Man has not properly stored the drums, and they have begun to rust and leak. Lubricating oil has seeped into the ground, and it has even contaminated Scarecrow's drinking water well and is flowing into the nearby stream. Remember that Tin Man has no heart. Scarecrow is concerned and angry that Tin Man's problem has now become his headache. Remember that Scarecrow has no brain. What can Scarecrow do?

2. Could Scarecrow bring a public nuisance action?

3. If Tin Man's oil has not yet actually contaminated Scarecrow's drinking water, can Scarecrow bring a common law action? If so, what kind?

4. If Tin Man were an important element of the local economy who employed many people, how would the court come to its conclusion

and what might be the likely outcome if it found Tin Man's operations to be a nuisance?

5. What would be the defense of Tin Man if his practices were visible, obvious, and well known in this location before Scarecrow moved to the neighborhood?

6. If Tin Man defends by claiming that his operations satisfy all applicable federal, state, and local environmental statutes and regulations, is this a valid defense to Scarecrow's common law action?

7. If Tin Man's environmental injury were an unavoidable result of the manufacturing of a product with great societal benefit, and Tin Man otherwise attempted to minimize the amount of such environmental damage, what defense might he invoke to a common law action for strict liability?

Explanations

1. In Chapter 9, we will see that the federal CERCLA statute does not cover oil and provides no private right of action for damages. So it's time for the common law. Scarecrow can pick his legal weapon. Scarecrow first can seek an injunction to stop Tin Man from improperly storing the oil drums on his property and force him to clean up the contamination. Additionally, Scarecrow can bring common law actions in nuisance or trespass for the physical incursion on his property. Scarecrow can seek damages from Tin Man. This is an important factor in all common law actions, because any remedies under federal statutes, even where allowed, usually include only clean-up costs and not additional damages. Under a private nuisance action, Scarecrow could obtain damages for the contamination to his drinking water well and an order for Tin Man to clean up the site and provide an alternative water supply.

2. An individual seeking to bring a public nuisance action must demonstrate a "special injury." Unless the individual injury is distinct from the environmental injury to all persons in the area, the court will not grant individual standing to bring a public nuisance action. Some courts have held that this standard can be satisfied by personal injury to one's health, as opposed to property damage. This argument was sufficient in a case where plaintiffs alleged that contamination of their groundwater caused specific fatal illnesses in *Anderson v. W. R. Grace & Co.*, 628 F. Supp. 1219 (D. Mass. 1986) (groundwater contamination is a special injury on which to base a public nuisance claim). Scarecrow's groundwater is impacted. If proven, compensation

could include value for Scarecrow's physical injury, for his emotional distress related to any physical injury, and for diminution in his property values.

3. Actions could lie in private nuisance or trespass. It is unlikely that strict liability rules would apply to the use of oil, as it is not considered ultra-hazardous.

4. The court will balance the equities, as in *Spur* and *Boomer*. The tort remedies are quite flexible. If Tin Man employs many people and is a vital part of the local economy, remedies might be limited to money damages and not an injunction that would require cessation of activities.

5. The *Spur* case holds that if one comes to the nuisance, it can be a defense to the environmental source of the nuisance. In *Spur*, it could not be used as an absolute defense because the developer, Webb, had induced the residents to move to his community notwithstanding the nuisance. When only the primary plaintiff party is involved, this defense can be invoked.

6. Although not entirely clear, meeting statutory requirements is probably not a defense in this environmental context. In *Int'l Paper Co. v. Ouellette*, 402 U.S. 558 (1987), the Court allowed a state nuisance and trespass claim to be lodged against a discharger of water pollutants that otherwise complied with regulatory discharge requirements. Common law actions for nuisance, trespass, or strict liability can be prosecuted simultaneously with statutory claims. *New York v. Shore Realty Corp.*, 759 F.2d 1032 (2d Cir. 1985).

7. There is a recognized defense to strict liability claims for unavoidably unsafe products that are of great value to society and cannot be made safe. Much of the case law in this area has developed around drug-related injuries.

Administrative Procedure for Environmental Regulation

"We were not born to sue, but to command."

William Shakespeare, King Richard II

"Nothing changes more constantly than the past; for the past that influences our lives does not consist of what actually happened, but of what men believe happened."

Gerald White Johnson, American Heroes and Hero-Worship, 1943

"As rapidly as—indeed, sometimes more rapidly than—causes could be isolated and problems defined, administrative agencies were created to wrestle with them."

James Landis, The Administrative Process

Pythagorean Theorem:	24 words
Lord's Prayer:	66 words
Archimedes' Principle:	67 words
Ten Commandments:	179 words
Gettysburg Address:	286 words
Declaration of Independence:	1,300 words
Federal Environmental Regulations:	31 book volumes

WHERE THE ACTION IS

Agencies of the executive branch of government make law in the form of regulations. We rely on agencies to implement and enforce congressionally enacted statutes. Agency actions to make law are governed by administrative law and procedure.

Let's take a short walk through history to the modern environmental agency. Although the primary environmental statutes did not appear in the United States until after the first Earth Day in 1970, environmental legislation existed long before. For instance, ordinances in England in the fourteenth century prohibited the disposal of refuse or garbage into city waterways, in order to improve sanitation in urban areas. In the nineteenth century, England passed urban protection legislation that restricted emission of smoke and noxious fumes and the discharge of sewage.

At that time the Unites States left public health and safety regulation to state and local governments. The U.S. federal government in the nineteenth century focused its environmental agenda on *development*, not protection, of natural resources. The Homestead Act of 1862 and the Mining Act of 1872 encouraged such development by allowing private parties to claim public land and the mineral resources in it. Even the passage of the Refuse Act of 1899, prohibiting the discharge of refuse into navigable waters without a permit, was triggered by *commercial*, not environmental, concerns: Congress's desire to keep the waterways of commerce free of debris. The Act's impact on the environment was not widely recognized until the 1960s, when environmentalists discovered that the Act could underwrite citizen suits to prevent surface-water pollution.

Most initial pre-1970 attempts by Congress at environmental regulation simply regulated government agencies or provided research and funding grants to assist states with environmental planning. Private industry was virtually ignored.

But things changed dramatically around 1970. The concept of the "environment" broadened to encompass not just natural resources but all living creatures — plants, animals, and humans. The environmental movement, which began in earnest in the 1960s, highlighted the ineffectiveness of the common law to prevent harm to the environment. Thus protection of the environment shifted from the often inadequate common law to a statutory formulation.

In 1970 Congress passed the first two environmental statutes to regulate and impact both private *and* public entities. Quite logically, the holistic concept came first: The National Environmental Policy Act (NEPA), 42 U.S.C. §§4321-4370a (analyzed in Chapter 3), established environmental policy goals and required all federal agencies to complete an environmental impact statement whenever "major federal actions significantly impact human environment." Next, came air: The Clean Air Act, 42 U.S.C. §§7401-7671q (reviewed in detail in Chapter 5), went beyond NEPA's procedural context. It attacked the emissions of factories, power plants, and cars. It established deadlines for air quality standards to be implemented by the states, national emission standards for hazardous air pollutants, and auto emission standards.

In rapid-fire over the next 15 years, Congress passed an array of substantive environmental statutes (see Exhibit 2.1).

2.1 Major Historic Environmental Statutes

Name of Statute	Known as	Year Passed	Chapter in This Book
National Environmental Policy Act	NEPA	1970	3
Clean Air Act	CAA	1970	5
Clean Water Act	CWA	1972	6 and 11
Federal Insecticide, Fungicide, and Rodenticide Act	FIFRA	1972	14
Ocean Dumping Act		1972	6
Endangered Species Act	ESA	1973	13
Safe Drinking Water Act	SDWA	1974	6
Toxic Substances Control Act	TSCA	1976	14
Resource Conservation and Recovery Act	RCRA	1976	8
Comprehensive Environmental Response, Compensation, and Liability Act	Superfund or CERCLA	1980	9
Emergency Planning and Community Right-to-Know Act	EPCRA	1986	9

In 1970 an executive order created the Environmental Protection Agency (EPA) to exercise the administrative powers first described in the Clean Air Act and then the powers in each of the subsequent acts listed in Exhibit 2.1. The formation of the EPA consolidated most of the environmental protection responsibilities into one agency. However, several other federal agencies also exercise authority to protect the public health and the environment, including:

- Department of Agriculture (pesticides)
- Department of the Interior (parks and federal lands)
- Department of Health and Human Services (food and drugs)
- Department of Energy (energy resources)

- Nuclear Regulatory Commission (nuclear plant safety)
- Department of Commerce (marine and coastal resources).

In the environmental arena, the "action" is at the agency level. Agencies are part of the executive branch, but they are created by statutes or by executive order. Congress creates agencies by passing statutes like the Clean Air Act, which empower, restrict, and give direction to an agency's permissible behavior. That is, congressional legislation identifies an environmental area and vests an agency with administrative powers to implement and enforce the substantive law.

But agencies are more than just "agents" of the legislative branch. Typically, Congress legislates at the *macro* or "big picture" level, delegating or leaving to the agency the detailed *micro*-level substantive regulation. An agency can make laws, govern private conduct, issue rules and regulations that have the force of law (unless successfully challenged in court), adjudicate, and provide extensive benefits, subsidies, and government services. Thus agencies do more than administer — they make the law at the micro level and enforce the law. The reason for this is twofold. First, 535 members of Congress would have great difficulty agreeing on the details of something as complex as most environmental statutes. Second, a specialized agency can develop expertise in an environmental area more than can Congress.

The interaction of all three branches of government — the legislative, executive, and judicial — as well as the public, gives rise to what we call administrative law. Each branch has power that *may* be exercised over the agencies. *Congress* can change the agencies' powers by amending a statute, control their budgets through the annual appropriations process, hold oversight hearings at a moment's notice to publicly scrutinize agency action. It can also place a "sunset" provision in the enabling statute that ends an agency or its authority at a specified time, unless reauthorized. The *President* has power of appointment and removal over top agency personnel, the ability to implement his or her own agenda through executive orders and policy or enforcement memoranda; ultimately the President is responsible for agency actions. The *judiciary* has power to interpret rules and statutes.

Drawing the Line: The Nondelegation Doctrine

Where is the line between legislative and agency power? Whenever Congress by statute authorizes an agency to carry out or execute certain environmental duties, it delegates its micro-level legislative authority to the executive branch. In 1892 *Field v. Clark*, 143 U.S. 649, 692 (1892), held "[t]hat

Congress cannot delegate legislative power" to the President. The principle, known as the nondelegation doctrine, is based on Article I of the Constitution, which itself states that "[all] legislative power herein granted shall be vested in a congress."

Yet through the years the Supreme Court has increasingly allowed congressional delegation, provided that Congress specifies an "intelligible principle" to guide the agency's discretion. *Yakus v. United States*, 321 U.S. 414 (1944). As long as Congress creates sufficient limitations on an agency's (micro-level) rulemaking authority that allow a court to determine whether the agency acted within its granted authority, the delegation will be upheld. In determining whether an intelligible principle exists, courts consider rule-making delegation or limitations included in an agency's enabling act, the statute as a whole, and the legislative history of the act. Since the 1930s, very little legislation has violated the nondelegation doctrine. The EPA NO_x and fine particulate standard ultimately was upheld against challenge under the long-moribund "nondelegation" doctrine. *Whitman v. Am. Trucking Ass'n*, 531 U.S. 457 (2001) (see Chapter 5).

Staying Within the Tent: The Ultra Vires Doctrine

Whereas the nondelegation doctrine requires a specific *procedural* pass-down of authority from the legislative to the executive branch, the ultra vires (without authority) doctrine requires an agency to operate within the *substantive* statutory "tent" created by that hand-off. An agency receives only the authority that is legislatively delegated. It must not venture outside the substantive "tent" erected by Congress.

When a court is faced with a potential delegation problem, it simply looks at the face of the enabling act to find authority and does not normally inquire into any subsequent agency actions. Challenges to an agency's authority under the ultra vires doctrine go a step further to determine compliance with the nondelegation doctrine. While it is presumed that the agency is functioning within its statutory authority, one may dispute this presumption by showing that the agency action is not authorized under the enabling act. The Supreme Court described the ultra vires doctrine in *Stark v. Wickard*, 321 U.S. 288, 309 (1944), as "[w]hen Congress passes an Act empowering agencies to carry on governmental activities, the power of those agencies is circumscribed by the authority granted." The judiciary is responsible for enforcing the limits of statutory authority when an agency oversteps its legal bounds.

Examples

1. Assume that in the name of truth, justice, and the American way, Congress passes the Environmental Harms Act, granting the EPA authority "to pass any rules relating to environment harm and to take any action necessary to identify, root out, and eliminate environmental harm, wherever it may lurk." How would you decide if this statutory delegation from Congress is legal?

2. Assume the same facts as in Example 1. What if the act passes muster as a proper delegation and the EPA, acting pursuant to the Environmental Harms Act, proposes a rule (i.e., an enforceable legal provision) limiting the number of children that parents on welfare can have and still receive federal assistance. The agency's rationale is that population growth is the fundamental environmental issue linked ultimately to resource consumption. Is the EPA acting within its statutory authority?

Explanations

1. This example implicates the *nondelegation doctrine*. All-American motives are not enough to uphold a statute. First, answer two related questions about standards: Is there a standard set forth in the statute? And, if so, what is that standard? After confirming that the text of the statute and its legislative history shed no more light on what Congress intended to delegate, the closest express standard is the phrase "environmental harm." This vague phrase is not a justiciable standard. Second, answer the question, To whom is the decision-making power delegated? The answer here is obvious — the EPA. However, given the broad and imprecise nature of the statute's delegation, it is void because it fails to state an intelligible principle to guide the agency's actions.

2. This one is easy. After reviewing the statute and any legislative history, one would conclude "no." Even though the statute is broad in its delegation, it never gave the EPA authority to regulate federal welfare assistance programs. The generality of the statute is resolved against an agency assertion of power.

THE ADMINISTRATIVE PROCEDURE ACT

Types of Agency Actions

The bulk of environmental law is made by agencies, not by Congress. The details — the micro level — are the province of the agency. The Clean Air

Act, a very elaborate environmental statute, for example, is set out in a few hundred pages. The EPA regulations under the Act occupy several volumes. And the EPA makes changes to them constantly — every month.

Professor Jerry Anderson has made an interesting quantitative comparison about the amount of executive branch regulations in modern America: In 1970, the CFR took up 76 horizontal inches of shelf space; by 2009, it consumed 276 horizontal inches of shelf space — approaching a fourfold increase in the text of applicable regulations. The increase in environmental regulations has been particularly dramatic: Between 1972 and 2010, Title 40 of the CFR, pertaining to protection of the environment, went from a single CFR volume to 31 volumes.

Are there additional constraints on agency discretion beyond the two doctrines just discussed? Yes. The Administrative Procedure Act (APA), 5 U.S.C. §551 et seq., passed by Congress in 1946, long before any modern environmental statutes, acts as a control. The APA prescribes basic procedural rules that agencies must obey to ensure the public's access to information and public participation in the rulemaking process. All federal agencies, including the EPA, must follow the procedures of the APA except where it contradicts the enabling statute of the agency or any congressional mandate. The President is not an "agency" within the meaning of the APA. Dalton v. Specter, 511 U.S. 462, 476 (1994); Franklin v. Massachusetts, 505 U.S. 788, 800-801 (1992).

A rulemaking is the way that an agency makes law. Through required procedures and judicial control of the administrative process, the APA determines the exercise of agency preemptory power. The primary powers exercised by an agency are:

1. Rulemaking — issuance of rules or regulations with wide applicability
2. Formal adjudication — issuance of orders in particular cases
3. Permitting and approval of specific projects
4. Enforcement against violators of the statute or rule (discretionary)

The APA only directly addresses the first two of these powers. Permitting under the federal statutes regulating the primary media — air (Chapter 5), water (Chapter 6), and the lithosphere (Chapter 8) — is delegated to the states to administer. Therefore, these delegated permits have no final federal agency action and are not subject to the federal APA. They are subject to state due process as determined by state courts. In rare instances of significant legal issues, the EPA Environmental Appeals Board will grant a petition to hear an appeal of such a delegated state permit decision, which would then create a final federal agency action. Therefore, it is critical to identify which one of these four categories of action is under consideration in order to determine whether the APA covers the action. The majority of EPA decisions fall into the last two categories.

Let's focus on the rulemaking process. The APA provides for two types of rulemaking procedure, *formal* and *informal*. An agency promulgates a rule through either formal or informal rulemaking in order to carry out the authority delegated to it by Congress. Many times, Congress will provide specific deadlines by which an agency, like the EPA, must propose a rule and then actually promulgate it in effective final form.

There is general judicial deference to the substance of administrative rules if it turns on disputed issues of technical fact or policy, or if the statute does not precisely answer the question the rule addresses, as in *Chevron v. NRDC*, 468 U.S. 1227 (1984). On the other hand, where the disputed issue is characterized by a court as a question of law, courts tend not to defer to agency determinations and to decide questions independently. Interpretive rules that are not rulemakings do not enjoy the strong deference accorded legislative rulemaking by an agency, but still enjoy an initial presumption of (*Skidmore*) deference. *Skidmore v. Swift & Co.*, 323 U.S. 134 (1944); *Christiensen v. Harris*, 522 U.S. 576 (2000) (stronger deference to agency interpretive rule interpreting a regulation than interpreting a statute); *United States v. Mead Corp.*, 533 U.S. 218 (2001). In some cases, courts will strike interpretive rules made by an agency on the ground that the rules were in fact legislative rules that require a full notice and comment, under formal or informal rulemaking. While distinguishing between legislative and interpretive rules thus is critical, there is little agreement among the courts on this distinction. Where mathematical or technical standards are imposed, or a new duty is imposed on a party by the rule, this typically requires the formal requisites of APA notice and comment.

Proposed and final rules are published for public notification daily in the Federal Register. The Federal Register was created by statute in 1935 to ensure that the public received notice of executive and agency orders and rules having the effect of law. The Federal Register is an official federal government publication in which federal rules, regulations, orders, and other documents of "general applicability and legal effect" must be published.

In addition, there is a Code of Federal Regulations (C.F.R.), which is revised regularly. The Code is divided into 50 topic areas and arranged on an agency-by-agency basis. The title numbering of the C.F.R. roughly corresponds to that used for statutes under the U.S. Code. For instance, by looking at Title 40 of the U.S. Code §7401, one can find the provisions of the Clean Air Act; by looking at Title 42 of the C.F.R., one can then find the air pollution regulations of the EPA.

Informal Rulemaking

Informal rulemaking is governed by §553 of the APA. Its main requirements include public notice in the Federal Register of the proposed rule and of the authority under which the agency is operating, a comment period during which interested persons have the opportunity to comment on the proposed rule, agency consideration of public comment, and production of a reasoned rationale and purpose when the final rule is printed in the Federal Register.

What does this mean in practice for an environmental regulation? A typical regulatory life cycle might be as follows.

1. Either at its own behest or at the suggestion of an interested party, the EPA conceives of a regulatory concept or amendment.
2. The agency compiles factual support for the key elements of the new rule.
3. The EPA issues a notice of *proposed* rulemaking (NOPR) — its concept of the regulatory direction it proposes to go — in written form in the Federal Register. This notice will contain a narrative explanation, reference the key factual and legal information on which the agency relies, explain its reasoning, and typically propose the exact language for the regulation. At this point, the regulation has no legal effect. The exception is where an emergency regulation is effective immediately on proposal.
4. The public has a stated period (usually at least 30 days) to comment in writing.
5. At the close of the designated comment period, which can be extended by the EPA, the EPA must read and *consider* each comment. It need not follow or adopt the substance of any comments.
6. The EPA then revises the proposed regulation — if it chooses — and promulgates it in the Federal Register a second time. It may or may not change the regulation based on comments or on the evolution of its own thinking. The second publication in the Federal Register *promulgates* the regulation, making it effective as of the date specified. As part of this promulgation, the EPA must provide a statement summarizing the comments and other information, responding to key comments, and explaining why it chose the final rule that it did. This final step is important both for the process and for judicial review.

Approval by the Office of Management and Budget (OMB) is also required as to compliance with executive orders and benefits/costs, before promulgation. OMB administers the Paperwork Reduction Act and Executive Order 12866 during both the proposed and final stages of the rulemaking process. If a rule would have an annual economic effect of $100 million or more, the OMB can require the agency to prepare a regulatory impact analysis.

The Congressional Review Act allows Congress to amend or disapprove proposed agency actions by passing a joint resolution within 90 days of the action becoming final. 5 U.S.C. §§801-808. It has almost never been used, as it would require disapproval by both houses of Congress and either the signature of the President or an override of a veto by two-thirds of both houses. One view is that the unitary executive theory exclusively vests agency power in the President pursuant to the Vesting Clause in Article II of the Constitution. Elena Kagan, before she became a Supreme Court Justice, wrote that Congress has the power to abrogate that authority via statute.

After a major rule is published in the Federal Register, it takes effect 60 days later, while non-major rules take effect 30 days later. 5 U.S.C. 801(a)(3)(A). Congress can disapprove a rule through a joint resolution under the Congressional Review Act, retroactive to the date the rule became effective. 5 U.S.C. 801(f). If a rule has been challenged in court, the executive branch can postpone the effective date of a rule under §705 of the Administrative Procedure Act. An indefinite postponement by the executive branch is similar to a rule revoking the regulation, which, if not done in compliance with the Administrative Procedure Act, is not allowed. If a rule proposed by one political administration is rescinded by the subsequently elected political administration, there must be a justification why such rescission is not arbitrary or capricious or an abuse of discretion. *Motor Vehicle Mfrs. Ass'n v. State Farm Mut. Auto Ins. Co.*, 463 U.S. 29 (1983).

Formal Rulemaking

Formal rulemaking utilizes the procedures found in §553 and adds the hearing-type procedures found in §§556-557. These include a full trial-type process, representation by counsel, discovery, motions, production of evidence, a written transcript, and cross-examination. In essence, a mini-trial is held before the agency, with a designated agency person sitting as the administrative judge or hearing examiner. At the conclusion, a decision is made on the record.

Formal rulemakings thus are more complex and time consuming for all parties. But intervenors have a more robust process within which to press their position. The record created and the decision itself are subject to judicial review. Formal rulemaking is rare because it is usually discretionary with the agency; it is ordered only when statute requires that the proposed rules be made *on the record* after an agency hearing.

Adjudications

In a formal adjudication, an agency must follow the requirements in §554 of the APA. An adjudication determines specific rights. Its main requirements include (a) notice to the parties of the time, place, and nature of the hearing and of the matters of fact and law asserted, (b) public opportunity to submit arguments, (c) a formal hearing under §§556-557 (if settlement efforts fail), and (d) an independent decision-maker bound to decide in a reasoned manner based on the compiled record.

Hybrid Procedures

Hybrid procedures for rulemakings and adjudications are not prescribed by the APA, but represent a combination of both formal and informal processes. They are undertaken at the initiative of the agency itself, by order of a court, or when required by some other particular substantive statute. For economy of process, most rulemakings and adjudications proceed informally. Exhibit 2.2 enumerates the appropriate statutory sections of the APA that govern rulemakings and adjudications.

An agency must comply with the APA whenever it promulgates, amends, or cancels a regulation. The APA requirements are purely *procedural* — they regulate the process of agency decision making, but not the substance.

Staying Current

So how do you determine current environmental regulations? First, you consult the C.F.R. Second, you scan the finding guide index of the Federal Register to determine if there have been any relevant changes proposed or promulgated in the Federal Register since the publication of your edition of the Code. Finally, care must be taken to ensure that the judiciary has not overruled or interpreted the regulation.

In addition, the EPA and other agencies can issue guidance documents and informal interpretative policy statements without utilizing the APA procedures. If not issued pursuant to the APA, these do not have the force of law. Yet these documents indicate how the EPA will react under certain situations.

Reg-Neg

The rulemaking process has been criticized because of its slow pace and adversarial nature. Many insist that the use of hybrid procedures has not solved the problems inherent in the rulemaking process. One increasingly popular alternative is rulemaking by negotiation, known as "reg-neg."

2.2 APA Rulemaking and Adjudication Sections

	Rulemaking	Adjudication
Formal	§§553, 556-557	§§554, 556-557
Hybrid	§553, parts of §§556-557	No prescribed process
Informal	§553	No prescribed process

2. Administrative Procedure for Environmental Regulation

Rather than imposing rules on resistant interest groups, agencies gather representatives of interested parties to bargain collectively toward a consensus rule. Agencies have been encouraged to use the "reg-neg" process during informal rulemaking when such use is in the public interest.

An agency seeking to use "reg-neg" must consider a variety of factors including whether there are a limited number of identifiable interests that will be significantly affected by the rule, whether the use of negotiation will unreasonably delay the promulgation of the rule, and whether the agency is willing to honor the consensus reached by the negotiating group. Although agency action regarding the existence and function of a "reg-neg" committee is not subject to judicial review, the final rule itself is subject to review just like any other final rule issued by an agency.

Examples

1. Your client, Perry White, editor of the *Daily Planet*, a great metropolitan newspaper, comes into your office seeking advice as to compliance with environmental requirements and standards. The *Daily Planet* generates waste ink from its printing process and emits a wastewater discharge into a local water body. Where would you obtain necessary information about the legality of these activities?

2. Another client, Lex Luther, the evil archenemy of Superman, contacts you for information regarding the proper procedure for obtaining a permit from the EPA to store kryptonite. He may be evil, but he has a green conscience. Where would you obtain the necessary information?

Explanations

1. The very first place you should consult is any applicable federal, state, or local statutes. Second, you should refer to any underlying regulations implementing those statutes. Consult the C.F.R. and the Federal Register to obtain the most recent versions. Third, you may discuss the type of business and its waste streams with federal and state environmental agency personnel. Fourth, you should check to see if any guidance documents are available that interpret applicable statutes and regulations or show the extent of agency enforcement discretion. Finally, you should research the interpretation and status of the statutes and regulations found in any court decisions. Sources of regulatory information overlap to a considerable degree. All levels of government — federal, state, and local — produce statutes, regulations, and policy statements, and all must adhere to APA requirements.

2. Since the APA does not mandate a required *process* to be followed for the issuance of permits, you would not want to look there. The APA does not cover permit decisions. Substantive agency regulations will tell you about any required permits. It is probable that the agency has established a set of permit procedures through guidance memoranda or policy statements. You should obtain copies of any such documents that are applicable. Also, talk informally — with federal and state environmental regulators. Anonymity can be maintained. Regulators have great discretion with their permit decisions.

The Process and Judicial Review

Section 7 of the APA provides judicial review of most agency actions, including *final* rules and orders. A federal court has authority under the APA to "compel agency action unlawfully withheld or unreasonably delayed." 5 U.S.C. §706(1). Unless a statute expressly precludes judicial review, or the agency action is subject to agency discretion by law, any administrative action is reviewable by a court of law. The aggrieved party must assert proper jurisdiction, as well as satisfy the threshold requirements of standing, ripeness, and exhaustion of administrative remedies.

Standing to Sue

The standing requirement emanates from Article III of the U.S. Constitution, which requires that courts hear only cases or controversies. Standing limits the docket to justiciable issues, so as to prevent court forums from airing generalized grievances. *Flast v. Cohen*, 392 U.S. 83, 106 (1968). Citizen suit provisions satisfy prudential requirements of standing.

An environmental group may sue on behalf of either its members or itself, assuming that it can satisfy standing requirements for the individuals. *Dubois v. U.S. Dep't of Agric.*, 102 F.3d 1273, 1277 (1st Cir. 1996) (the suit must be germane to the objectives of the organization and not otherwise require individual participation). To summarize, these requirements are that the organization show that the interests it is seeking to protect are germane to organizational purposes, demonstrating that neither the claim nor relief require the participation of individual members of the group, and demonstrating that members of the group otherwise could sue in their own rights. *Hunt v. Wash. State Apple Adver. Comm'n*, 432 U.S. 333 (1977). The party seeking review must be injured or the harm must be imminent.

Who may obtain review of agency action? Who is a proper plaintiff? This *standing* gets one into court. Whether or not a challenger has standing turns on three different tests: (1) Is there personal injury-in-fact, which is necessary to establish Article III "case or controversy" standing? (2) Is the claimed injury within the "zone of interests," drawn from the APA's §702 requirement that claimants be within a class that Congress intended to benefit when it passed the underlying law? (3) Should judge-made "prudential principles" be used by the court to deny standing because the judicial remedy would not redress the claimed injury or it is not ripe? Let's look at these three tests sequentially.

Under the injury-in-fact test, the Supreme Court held in *Sierra Club v. Morton*, 405 U.S. 727 (1972), that the plaintiffs' mere allegation of a sincere interest in an area affected by environmental degradation did not constitute injury-in-fact. The organization could not claim standing as a guardian of the environment without showing specific injury to the organization or its members. However, the Court also showed potential plaintiffs how easily this standing requirement can be met for environmental organizations: The Court eventually allowed the Sierra Club to amend its complaint by merely alleging that injury would in fact occur to at least one of its members that used the affected recreation area. The court held in *Sierra Club* that even if the interest is shared only by an environmentally aware few, rather than the masses, it is still worthy of protection if the injury is distinct and palpable. A justiciable injury cannot be comprised of simply emotional harm. *Humane Soc'y of the United States v. Babbitt*, 46 F.3d 93 (D.C. Cir. 1995) (sleeplessness, depression, and anger were not deemed an injury).

Later, the Court expanded citizens' rights to seek redress against government abuses when it found that the plaintiffs in *United States v. SCRAP*, 412 U.S. 669 (1973), had alleged sufficient individual harm to demonstrate standing. The plaintiffs were able to challenge an Interstate Commerce Commission decision that encouraged use of raw materials over recycled materials by assigning higher transport tariffs to the latter. Through an attenuated line of causation, plaintiffs demonstrated to the court that the alleged injury of increased use of nonrecyclable commodities would eventually occur, and that injury of greater litter ultimately could affect them. A mere allegation of a remote and attenuated injury was sufficient to establish standing. In ruling on a motion to dismiss a complaint, the district court must draw all reasonable inferences in favor of the plaintiff ". . . and must not dismiss the complaint unless it appears beyond doubt that the plaintiff can prove no set of facts in support of its claim that would entitle it to relief. *Conley v. Gibson*, 355 U.S. 41, 45-46 (1957)." *Mountain States Legal Foundation v. Bush*, 306 F.3d 1132 (D.C. Cir. 2002), *cert. denied*, 540 U.S. 812 (2003). Cognizable injuries can be somewhat attenuated as well as aesthetic, recreational, or conservational. *Animal Welfare Inst. v. Kreps*, 561 F.2d 1002 (1997) (unable to enjoy or photograph fur seals subject to slaughter, was a sufficient injury to satisfy standing); *Japan Whaling Ass'n v. Am. Cetacean Society*, 478 U.S. 221 (1986) (whale watching interests can be sufficient for standing regarding whale slaughter).

2. Administrative Procedure for Environmental Regulation

Using reasoning similar to that in *SCRAP*, the Court held that there was a sufficient basis for plaintiffs' standing in *Duke Power Co. v. Carolina Envtl. Study Group, Inc.*, 438 U.S. 59 (1978). The environmental group had challenged the constitutionality of the Price-Anderson Act. The Act limits the liability of the nuclear industry for damages resulting from a nuclear accident. The plaintiffs claimed that without this liability limitation, reactors would not be built, and that absence of a reactor would in turn prevent immediate environmental injuries like injury to fishing and water quality.

Yet, their ultimate claim on the merits did not involve these immediate environmental fishing injuries; rather, it involved an argument of unconstitutional "taking" of property without just compensation. Plaintiffs asserted that a taking (environmental injuries) would occur in the future because of the potential liability limitation *if and when* a reactor in their area had a nuclear accident *and* they were injured *and* their damages exceeded the amount allowed by the statute. Thus, due to the possibility that the potentially unconstitutional Price-Anderson statute might be used to the plaintiffs' detriment in the future, the plaintiffs alleged that they were suffering an immediate environmental injury. Despite the obviously attenuated chain of causation, the Court found for the plaintiffs on standing. The Court also held that only a "fairly traceable" nexus between the plaintiffs' alleged injury and the claim on the merits is needed.

But the stretched string of standing snapped back. The Court now takes a more restrictive stance on citizen standing. In *Lujan v. Nat'l Wildlife Fed'n*, 497 U.S. 871 (1990), an environmental group challenged the Department of the Interior's "land withdrawal review program," which reclassified public lands to allow them to be used for mining. The plaintiffs attempted to support their claim for standing by submitting affidavits of members who stated that their recreational and aesthetic enjoyment of public lands was injured by the department's reclassification. The Court held insufficient to establish standing the Federation members' declarations that they used "unspecified portions of an immense tract of land," some areas of which were affected by allegedly illegal governmental action. In addition, the majority of the Court called into question the continuing validity of the rationale in *SCRAP*, asserting that its expansive expression of standing has never since been followed by the Court.

In applying context to the *Lujan I* opinion, the court has noted that "the limitation to discreet agency action precludes the kind of broad programmatic attacks we rejected in *Lujan*." *Norton v. Southern Utah Wilderness Alliance*, 542 U.S. 55 (2004). This court also noted that ". . . when an agency is compelled by law to act within a certain time period, but the manner of its action is left to the agency's discretion, a court can compel the agency to act, but has no power to specify what the action must be." *Id.*

The requirement of redressability was weakened by the decision in *Massachusetts v. EPA*, 549 U.S. 497 (2007) (regulation of CO_2 for global warming mitigation, finding that redress can be even an incremental improvement in emission of generalized environmental pollutants, without addressing whether that small incremental improvement would give the plaintiffs relief). The four dissenting justices noted that

> domestic motor vehicles contribute only about 6% of global carbon dioxide emissions, and 4% of global greenhouse gas emissions. . . . [The Clean Air Act] covers only new motor vehicles and new motor vehicle engines, so petitioners' desired emission standards might reduce only a fraction of 4% of global emissions. . . . Redressibility is even more problematic. To the tenuous link between petitioner's alleged injury and indeterminant fractional domestic emissions at issue here, add the fact that petitioners cannot meaningfully predict what will come of the 80% of global greenhouse gas emissions that originate outside the United States . . . and any decreases produced by petitioners' desired standards are likely to be overwhelmed many times over by emission increases elsewhere in the world.

States are held to a lesser standing requirement: "[A] litigant to whom Congress has 'accorded a procedural right to protect his concrete interests' . . . 'can assert that right without meeting all the normal standards for redressability and immediacy'" (quoting Judge Scalia's majority opinion in *Lujan*). States enjoy "special solicitude" in demonstrating standing, greenhouse gases are air pollutants under the Clean Air Act's "capacious definition of air pollutant," and it was arbitrary and capricious for the EPA to refuse to decide whether these emissions "endanger public health and welfare."

The dissent of Chief Justice Roberts notes that such lack of causative scientific connection makes the injury "speculative" and returns the Court to the era of diluted standing requirements in *Scrap*. Note the difference between causation and redressability: The causative scientific link may be proven to link CO_2 emissions with global warming, yet the regulation of only a tiny part of CO_2 emissions may not redress the plaintiff's alleged injury.

Moreover, in *Lujan v. Defenders of Wildlife*, 504 U.S. 555 (1992), the Court stated that when a plaintiff brings an action, and that plaintiff is not the person whose injury is being asserted in the action, "standing is not impossible, but substantially more difficult." Justice Scalia, writing for the Court, stated that "the plaintiff must have suffered an 'injury in fact' — an invasion of a *legally protected interest*." The Court's concerns stem from the difficulty in establishing causation and redressability of an injury to a third party that is not a party in the action before the court. In *Defenders of Wildlife*, the Court found that the plaintiffs failed to establish either injury or redressability (the latter requirement joined by only four Justices), and they thus lacked standing to pursue their claims. Even if plaintiffs prevailed, it would not necessarily stop the construction activities that the United States was funding in part. Independent actions are not redressable. Past recreational use does not establish a concrete future injury. Provided that environmental plaintiffs can adequately resolve these concerns, the Court will grant them standing.

The standing requirement originates in Article III as part of the minimum constitutional requirements to prosecute an injury that meets the following requirements described by the Supreme Court in *Bennett v. Spear*, 520 U.S. 154 (1997): "(1) that the plaintiffs have suffered an 'injury in fact' — an invasion of a judicially cognizable interest which is (a) concrete and particularized and (b) actual or imminent, not conjectural or hypothetical; (2) that there be a causal connection between the injury and the conduct complained of — the injury must be fairly traceable to the challenged action of the defendant, and not the result of independent action of some third party not before the court; and (3) that it be likely, as opposed to merely speculative, that the injury will be redressed by a favorable decision" (referring to *Defenders of Wildlife*). This "fairly traceable" requirement leads to some form of "causation in fact." The exact contours of this causation nexus is not clear from the precedent, although the court did extend standing under §1533 of the Endangered Species Act to any person, including those arguing against species protection.

A general emotional harm is insufficient to satisfy the Article III injury-in-fact requirement. *Asarco v. Kadish*, 490 U.S. 605, 616 (1989). The injury-in-fact requirement requires a showing of injury to oneself or one's organization, but does not require a showing of injury to the environment, although for an aesthetic or recreational interest, there logically would be environmental degradation as a foundation for the personal injury. *Friends of the Earth, Inc. v. Laidlaw Envtl. Servs., Inc.*, 528 U.S. 167, 181 (2000). The injury can be shown by affidavits that go beyond the mere "general averments," "conclusory allegations," or "someday intentions" to visit impacted areas that were found insufficient in *Defenders of Wildlife*. Standing is not defeated by the fact that the government has settled its complaints with an industry in the form of civil payments, where a citizen group wants an injunction of the actual threatened injury, and not monetary damages to the government. *Id.*

Moreover, a citizen group claim for civil damages is not immediately mooted once a company reachieves compliance with a permit limitation that it has violated. "A case might become moot if subsequent events make it absolutely clear that the allegedly wrongful behavior could not reasonably be expected to recur." *Id.* The burden of demonstrating this lies with the party asserting mootness. Mootness is more than simply "standing set in a time frame." The prospect of future harmful conduct may be too speculative to support standing, but not too speculative to overcome mootness. There is an exception to the mootness doctrine for acts that are "capable of repetition, yet evading review." There is no similar exception for the standing requirement. Where a plaintiff lacks standing at the time an action commences, despite the fact that a dispute is capable of repetition yet evading review, there still will not be the ability to maintain the action.

While recreational and aesthetic interests are cognizable for environmental claims and can establish standing, by their very nature they are not personal to the parties alleging a grievance, but are associated with often-broad tracts of often-remote land. It is the connection between individual injury and these often-broad and often-remote geographic areas that the Supreme Court has found not proximate enough to ground a complaint.

The causal link between the alleged injury and the remedy/remediation cannot be purely speculative. *Japan Whaling Ass'n, supra.* However, while a link is required, the link can be to a third party rather than directly to the plaintiff. *Defenders of Wildlife, supra* (1992). Where the environmental claim is principally procedural, most courts have interpreted the precedent as not requiring plaintiff to show that he/she would benefit directly from the requested court action. *Lujan v. Nat'l Wildlife Fed'n*, 497 U.S. at 572 n.7 (1990); *Cantrell v. City of Long Beach*, 241 F.3d 674, 682 (9th Cir. 2001) (interpreting the APA and granting standing even though plaintiffs could not establish that a different ultimate substantive result would occur because of the success of their suit). Linking environmental impacts to specific tax credit policies regarding the use of agriculture-based fuel additives in motor fuels was deemed too speculative and remote to satisfy the new nexus requirement for standing. See *Fla. Audubon Soc'y v. Bentsen*, 94 F.3d 658 (D.C. Cir. 1996). Inherently, economic or behavioral linkages, rather than direct physical linkages, to the environment run the risk of being more speculative and more remote.

In its decision in *Summers et al. v. Earth Island Institute et al.*, 129 S. Ct. 1142 (2009), the Supreme Court held that the environmental organization plaintiff lacked standing to challenge regulations regarding timber sales from fire-damaged land, absent a live dispute over a concrete application of those regulations. Relying on *Lujan v. Defenders of Wildlife*, 504 U.S. 555, 559-560, the Court limited the judicial power to cases and controversies under Article III to redress or prevent actual or imminent threatened injury to persons caused by violations of law. The majority opinion noted that the organization had already settled that part of the case pertaining to its only member who suffered any injury that was "concrete and particularized" because he had visited the exact site and planned to return. For other organizational members with general plans to visit national forests, the majority found no standing because the

> vague desire to return is insufficient to satisfy the requirement of imminent injury: Such someday intentions — without any description of concrete plans, or indeed any specification of when the some day will be — do not support a finding of the actual or imminent injury that our cases require.

In dissent, Justice Breyer found that this focus on imminent harm was appropriate to determine ripeness or injunctive relief, but inappropriate as part of the standing test, without negating the recent holding in *Massachusetts v. EPA*, 549 U.S. 497 (2007):

> To know, virtually for certain, that snow will fall in New England this winter is not to know the name of each particular town where it is bound to arrive. . . . [T]hreat of future harm may be realistic even where the plaintiff can not specify precise times, dates and GPS coordinates.

The government had unsuccessfully pressed for an even more restrictive holding that the matter was not ripe until regulatory programs were implemented by the government causing a demonstrable concrete, often economic, injury. The Supreme Court did not reach the ripeness issue because it resolved the case on the standing issue alone. Relying on *Sierra Club v. Morton*, 405 U.S. 727, 734-736, the *Summers* Court majority held that while recreational or esthetic interests of members of an environmental group are cognizable for standing, general harm to the environment is not sufficient. The Supreme Court also held that "the threat must be actual and imminent, not conjectural or hypothetical; it must be fairly traceable to the challenged action of the defendant; and it must be likely that a favorable judicial decision will prevent or redress the injury" (citing *Friends of the Earth, Inc. v. Laidlaw Envt. Serv., Inc.*, 528 U.S. 167, 180-181 (2000)).

A number of lower courts have not applied the rigor of the Supreme Court in the *Lujan* holdings to deny standing to environmental plaintiffs. In fact, a number of lower federal courts have generously construed the facts, affidavits, and pleadings of environmental plaintiffs to create standing where the Supreme Court might deny standing. As the arbiters of factual issues, the lower courts' readings of pleadings and key facts can be determinative in the standing contest. See *Comm. to Save the Rio Honcho v. Lucero*, 102 F.3d 445 (10th Cir. 1996) (causation and redressability requirements relaxed so NEPA challenge to Forest Service decision to allow summer use of a national forest could proceed even though area of plaintiffs' concern was at least 12-15 miles downstream); *Pub. Interest Research Group of N.J., Inc. v. New Jersey Expressway Auth.*, 822 F. Supp. 174 (D.N.J. 1992) (quoting *SCRAP* to the effect that plaintiff's injury "may be quite indirect" and finding that plaintiffs did not have to allege that they used the exact water tributary that might be affected by defendants' discharges); *Resources Ltd., Inc. v. Robertson*, 35 F.3d 1300 (9th Cir. 1994) (rejecting that the *Lujan* opinions establish a new stricter burden on plaintiffs to establish specifically an injury in fact caused by a challenged government action); *Fla. Audubon Society v. Bentsen*, 54 F.3d 873 (D.C. Cir. 1995) (IRS to prepare an EIS regarding tax credit for fuel additive could be challenged as causing additional corn and sugar cultivation without pointing to any precise location where such increase might occur or a close nexus); *Friends of the Earth, Inc. v. Chevron Chemical Co.*, 900 F. Supp. 67 (E.D. Tex. 1995) (four mile distance between Chevron plant and potentially affected lake was not so great as to deny standing); *Humane Soc'y of the United States v. Brown*, 920 F. Supp. 178 (Ct. Int'l Trade 1996) (where plaintiffs were unable to pinpoint planned return to affected area from unauthorized fishing practices and trade sanctions, other than a desire to in the future visit "Southern France, Spain or Italy," standing still allowed); *Southwest Center for Biological Diversity v. FERC*, 967 F. Supp. 1166 (D. Ariz. 1997) (alleged violation of Endangered Species Act challenge granted standing despite plaintiff's expert's inability to distinguish the particular species from other similar nonthreatened species absent killing the species and dissecting it in a laboratory, where standing predicated on the "spiritual" enjoyment from viewing the indistinguishable species). However, agency action that somewhat arbitrarily relieves other smaller entities from regulatory requirements while imposing them on larger entities was held not to cause any "injury in fact" or redressable injury that the affected covered entities could assert for standing to contest the regulations. *Coalition for Responsible Regulation, Inc. v. EPA*, 684 F.3d 10 (D.C. Cir. 2012) (no standing to challenge CO_2 "tailoring rule" regulating only much larger emitters than specified in the statute, therefore not reaching the merits of the claim).

Congress established direct standing in various environmental statutes. These allow citizens to step in to enforce statutes when government agencies such as the EPA fail to act. For instance, in §505 of the Clean Water Act, Congress provided that, unless the EPA has previously commenced a civil action:

> [A]ny citizen may commence a civil action on his own behalf . . . (1) against any person . . . who is alleged to be in violation of (A) an effluent standard or limitation under this chapter or (B) an order issued by the Administrator or State with respect to such a standard or limitation, or (2) against the Administrator where there is alleged a failure of the Administrator to perform any act or duty under this chapter which is not discretionary with the Administrator. . . .
>
> No action may be commenced . . . (A) prior to sixty days after the plaintiff has given notice of the alleged violation (i) to the Administrator, (ii) to the State in which the alleged violation occurs, and (iii) to any alleged violator of the standard, limitation, or order, or (B) if the Administrator or State has commenced and is diligently prosecuting a civil or criminal action in a court of the United States or a State to require compliance with the standard, limitation, or order, but in any such action in a court of the United States any citizen may intervene as a matter of right. . . .

More than a dozen environmental statutes include similar standing provisions. These legislative creations are called "citizen suit provisions."

Ripeness of the Action

Plaintiffs must also present a case *ripe* for judicial review of an agency action. Section 704 of the APA provides that only "final" agency actions are subject to judicial review. The basic rationale of the ripeness doctrine is to restrain courts from deciding hypothetical cases and to shield them from involvement in disagreements over legislative or administrative policies. The ripeness doctrine also serves to protect agencies from judicial interference until an administrative decision is final. In addition, the agency action must have an immediate and direct adverse impact on the petitioning party. The courts will not anticipate a question of administrative law in advance of the necessity of deciding it.

In *Port of Boston Marine Terminal v. Rederiaktiebolaget*, 400 U.S. 862 (1970), the Court stated that the "relevant considerations for determining finality are whether the process of administrative decision making has reached the stage where judicial review will not disrupt the orderly process of agency adjudication and whether rights or obligations have been determined or legal consequences will flow from the agency action." Agency orders denying relief requested by an individual, such as denying a license or permit, are usually ripe for review upon issuance since the agency orders have direct impact upon the individual's rights and duties. However, it is more difficult to judge the ripeness of general administrative regulations that are not directed at certain individuals. Agencies have tried to argue that such regulations are not ripe for review by petitioners until a specific enforcement action has been undertaken against the petitioners.

The Supreme Court rejected this argument in *Abbott Labs. v. Gardner*, 387 U.S. 136 (1967). The commissioner of Food and Drugs had promulgated a regulation requiring labels, advertisements, and other printed material relating to prescriptive drugs to designate the established name of the drug. The question was whether the commissioner had authority to issue the rule. The parties agreed that the question turned entirely on congressional intent — a purely legal issue.

Withholding review would have been extremely burdensome to the petitioning companies because they were threatened with numerous penalties if they did not change their labeling immediately. The *Abbott Labs* two-part test evaluates (1) the fitness of the issues for judicial decision and (2) the hardship to the parties of withholding court consideration. It is not always necessary to await implementation of an action to satisfy a ripeness requirement, as interpreted by the lower courts. In *Salmon River Concerned Citizens v. Robertson*, 32 F.3d 1346, 1355 (9th Cir. 1994), the plaintiffs were allowed to challenge an EIS regarding herbicides use during reforestation, despite an argument that absent a specific decision to apply such herbicides to a particular tract, the issue would not be ripe.

However, the Court's decision in *Lujan v. Nat'l Wildlife Fed'n*, 497 U.S. 871 (1990), suggests that it may make significant changes in ripeness doctrine to reduce the court's role in government policy making. Following the facts as stated prior, the Court concluded that the "program" was not reviewable because there was no legally cognizable "program." The only potentially reviewable agency action was each of the Department of the Interior's reclassification decisions — of which there had been hundreds.

The majority then suggested that even those separate decisions were not ripe for review since reclassification of land does not by itself lead inevitably to mining. For a DOI action to be ripe for review in this case, the agency would have had to grant a *permit* to authorize mining on the land. Obviously, it is easier for plaintiffs to challenge a generic program than each individual permit.

A challenge to the credible evidence rule was held by the D.C. Circuit to not be ripe for review until the rule is applied in an actual enforcement action. *Clean Air Implementation Project v. EPA*, 150 F.3d 1200 (D.C. Cir. 1998); *cert. denied sub nom. Appalachian Power Co. v. EPA*, 527 U.S. 1021 (1999).

Exhaustion of Administrative Remedies and Estoppel

Plaintiffs must demonstrate, prior to securing judicial review, that they have exhausted all possible administrative remedies. According to the D.C. Circuit, exhaustion serves four main purposes: (1) It carries out the legislative purpose in granting authority to an agency by discouraging frequent and deliberate flouting of administrative procedures. (2) It protects agency autonomy by allowing the agency the opportunity in the first instance to apply its expertise and correct its own errors. (3) It aids judicial review by allowing the parties and the agency to develop the facts of the case in the agency proceedings. (4) It promotes judicial economy by avoiding needless repetition of administrative and judicial fact-finding, perhaps avoiding the necessity for any judicial involvement. *Andrade v. Lauer*, 729 F.2d 1475, 1484 (D.C. Cir. 1984).

The exhaustion of administrative remedies doctrine states that "no one is entitled to judicial relief for a supposed or threatened injury until the prescribed administrative remedy has been exhausted." *McKart v. U.S.*, 395 U.S. 185, 193 (1969). This doctrine determines whether judicial review is appropriate for an agency action that is not the last agency word on that matter. The decision in *McKart* described four main factors that must be considered to determine whether a petitioner should be granted judicial review:

- The degree of plaintiff's injury
- The need to protect the integrity of agency functions

- The likelihood that judicial review would be enhanced by application of agency experience or the accumulation of a record
- The improvement of judicial efficiency by avoiding intervention and first giving the agency a chance to correct the matter

In environmental cases, courts strive to apply the *McKart* exhaustion factors to determine judicial reviewability. The exhaustion defense has been rejected — judicial review granted — in a number of cases: *State v. United States Steel Corp.*, 240 N.W.2d 316 (Minn. 1976) and *State v. Dairyland Power Coop.*, 187 N.W.2d 878 (Wisc. 1971) (water and air pollution cases where no administrative proceedings were pending and none were contemplated); *NRDC v. Tennessee Valley Auth.*, 367 F. Supp. 128 (E.D. Tenn. 1973) (NEPA case where claims of failure to comment on draft impact statements were raised as a complete bar to an attack on statement adequacy). At the same time, the exhaustion defense has been raised successfully — judicial review denied — in cases where allowing the administrative process to proceed to the end would be of great assistance to any subsequent judicial review.

In theory, at common law, any party may be estopped if it makes an intentional or negligent misrepresentation of a fact, and the other party relies on that fact to its detriment. This estoppel precludes the party from asserting a claim or defense that otherwise is available. See Restatement (Second) of Torts §894(1). All American jurisdictions, including federal and state courts, recognize the common law theory of estoppel.

Where an environmental agency misrepresents a fact and another party relies on it, can that other party use equitable estoppel where it relies on the government's action or inaction? Especially where an environmental statute or regulation is vague, can a party rely on the government's position to raise estoppel against government enforcement of that statute in a particular situation? While the doctrine of equitable estoppel should apply equally to the government as to a private party, there are few cases estopping the government from enforcing an environmental law where the affected party relied on the mistaken advice of a government employee regarding the interpretation or enforcement of that law. Despite efforts of lower federal courts to find an appropriate case of estoppel against the government, the U.S. Supreme Court has reversed every estoppel case against the government that has reached it.

Reasonable reliance by a private party on a state environmental agency's interpretation of RCRA did not estop the federal government from enforcing an RCRA violation, even where the state's advice was in written form to the private party and the private party complied with that advice. See *United States v. Marine Shale Processors*, 81 F.3d 1329 (5th Cir. 1996) ("When a court refuses to enforce the law on the basis of a previous representation from a government official, it renders the current executive unable to enforce the law and thus discharge its responsibilities under the Take Care Clause"). The court also relied on the fact that the misinterpretation of RCRA did not amount to affirmative misconduct, but rather a negligent interpretation. The court in *Marine Shale* also asserted that a private party is charged with knowledge of the law, notwithstanding the agency's official interpretation of that law. While not rising to the level of estoppel, reliance on a negligent interpretation of a statute can be a mitigating factor in determining the penalty against the private party who detrimentally relies on that interpretation.

In *United States v. Toledo*, 867 F. Supp. 603 (N.D. Ohio 1994), regarding enforcement of an NPDES permit for effluent discharge from the city, the lack of affirmative misconduct, as opposed to passive, indifferent, or negligent misconduct by the enforcing government agency, eliminated an estoppel defense, although remaining relevant for determining the amount of penalty the private party must pay in an enforcement action. In *United States v. Smithfield Foods, Inc.*, 969 F. Supp. 769 (E.D. Va. 1997), a matter involving violation of the Clean Water Act, the EPA was not estopped from enforcing violations of the Act even where it knew that the Commonwealth of Virginia had changed the permit. The public interest in enforcement of environmental laws is likely to outweigh a private party's interest in equitable estoppel of a government enforcement action.

See also *United States v. Boccanfuso*, 882 F.2d 666 (2d Cir. 1989) (estoppel denied against enforcement of Clean Water Act where landowner built a seawall without necessary permits from Army Corps of Engineers, based on failure of Corps to follow its own deadlines and oral misstatements of Corps personnel regarding lack of need for permit). The court in this case stated that "oral statements by Government employees are not accorded the same weight as written ones." Parties are still charged with knowledge of, and their own correct interpretation of, the law. This is true even where an agency misinterprets or violates its own regulations; it is not estopped to later enforce those regulations in a contrary manner against the same party that relied on the misrepresentation. *Conn. Fund for the Env't v. Upjohn Co.*, 660 F. Supp. 1397 (1987).

In *United States v. Martell*, 844 F. Supp. 454 (N.D. Ind. 1994), equitable estoppel was denied as a defense in a §107 CERCLA matter. The related topics of "grandfathered" rights and takings are discussed in Chapter 10.

Standards of Judicial Review

After waiving all the hurdles to permit judicial review, the court must determine the scope of its inquiry into the merits of the challenged agency action. The question of which standard of review a court will use is very important: It controls the balance of power. If the scope of review is too broad, agencies essentially relinquish all decision making to the judiciary, dismissing the advantage of agency expertise in complex areas like environmental law. If the scope of review is too limited, agencies would receive a rubber stamp of approval from the judiciary, making the right to review meaningless.

Courts have found that while the APA does not include its own statute of limitations, the general six-year statute of limitations of 28 U.S.C. §2401 applies to claims against the government brought thereunder, as well as claims under NEPA (see Chapter 3).

What Can Be Appealed to the Courts

What is appealable? One can successfully appeal an agency decision that

1. exceeds the statutory grant of agency authority,
2. misapplies the law,
3. violates correct administrative process,
4. construes the factual record in a manner that is not justifiable.

In interpreting the law, an agency must take into account constitutional and statutory commands, weigh them appropriately, and avoid relying on factors the law sought to exclude from consideration. The interpretation of a statute whose text clearly states a set of factors to be considered presents a question of *law* that courts will usually examine independently. One situation: If the text of the statute is clear and the agency's interpretation of the statute is at odds with it, the court will freely disregard what it considers to be an erroneous agency view. However, not all statutes are clear. A second situation: Congress may not have foreseen the circumstances that give rise to a particular application of the statute and, in those unforeseen circumstances, the statute may be capable of more than one reasonable interpretation. A third situation: Congress may not have considered certain circumstances at all, and the statute is entirely silent on those issues.

The Supreme Court faced such a case in *Chevron v. NRDC*, 467 U.S. 837 (1984). It remains today the key opinion on interpreting EPA discretion. The Court opinion in *Chevron* established a deferential judicial approach to agency interpretations of law embodied in legislative rules, when Congress has been wholly silent in the statute on such interpretation.

The Court disagreed with the lower court's willingness to substitute its legal interpretation for that of the EPA when the statute in question was ambiguous. The Supreme Court established a two-step approach to the review of questions of law:

> If Congress has not directly addressed *the precise question at issue*, the court does not simply impose its own construction on the statute as would be necessary in the absence of an administrative interpretation. Rather, if the statute is silent or

ambiguous with respect to the specific issue, the question for the court is whether the agency's answer is based on a *permissible construction of the statute.*

The *Chevron* case remains the most cited case in modern American law. Step one of *Chevron* requires the court to determine whether an agency interpretation of statute is contrary to clear congressional intent and must reject any contrary regulatory decisions. *Motor Vehicle Mfrs. Ass'n v. State Farm Mut. Auto Ins. Co.,* 463 U.S. 29 (1983). Step one allows the court to impose independent judicial judgment rather than merely oversee agency decision making. If congressional intent is ambiguous, under Step 2, the *Chevron* Court defers to any reasonable or permissible agency interpretations of the statute. Where *Chevron* does not apply, courts apply the arbitrary and capricious standard of review. If *Chevron* does not apply to a particular agency action, then under *Skidmore v. Swift & Co.,* 323 U.S. 134 (1944), while not controlling upon the courts, the body of agency experience and informed judgment guide the court. See *United States v. Mead, supra.*

An agency is not afforded any deference to its position where it makes a determination that is not embodied in a regulation. *United States v. Mead Corp.,* 533 U.S. 218 (2001). Deference is only afforded to an agency interpretation where "it appears that congress delegated authority to the agency to make rules carrying the force of law, and that the agency interpretation claiming deference was promulgated in the exercise of that authority." *Id.* The EPA's interpretation of its own regulatory scheme was entitled to "a measure of deference" because the interpretation was not "plainly erroneous or inconsistent" with properly enacted agency regulations. *Coeur Alaska, Inc. v. Southeast Alaska Conservation Council,* 557 U.S. 261 (2009); *Alaska Department of Environmental Conservation v. EPA,* 540 U.S. 461, 487 (2004)(*Chevron* deference did not apply; *Mead* analysis and deference). The Seventh Circuit held regarding the EPA administrative process that ". . . the EPA has changed its view so often that it is no longer entitled to the deference normally accorded an agency's interpretation of the statute it administers." *Chicago v. EDF,* 985 F.2d 303 at 304.

Where Congress, through a statute, makes a determination, and thus leaves no room for an agency to make a determination by order or regulation, an agency's contrary position is accorded no deference whatsoever by the court. *Id.,* quoting *E.E.O.C. v. Arabian Am. Oil Co.,* 499 U.S. 244, 257 (1991); *Gen. Electric Co. v. Gilbert,* 429 U.S. 125, 141 (1976). Where a statute, such as the APA, is administered by more than one agency, the interpretation of that statute by any particular agency "is not entitled to *Chevron* deference." *Proffit v. F.D.I.C.,* 200 F.3d 855, 860 (D.C. Cir. 2000).

In *Environmental Defense v. Duke Energy Corp.,* 549 U.S. 561 (2007), in a narrow opinion, the Supreme Court held that the EPA did not have to define or conform key regulatory definitions ("modification") consistently throughout different provisions of the Air Act, specifically NSPS and PSD, even if the terms share a common statutory definition. Ambiguities in identical statutory terms need not be construed identically, regardless of surrounding context. Judicial deference is accorded to the agency's interpretation provided it falls within the outer limits of statutory allowance. That is consistent with the *Chevron* decision.

There is general judicial deference to the substance of administrative rules if it turns on disputed issues of technical fact or policy, or if the statute does not precisely answer the question the rule addresses, as in *Chevron*. On the other hand, where the disputed issue is characterized by a court as a question of law, courts tend not to defer to agency determinations and to decide questions independently. Interpretive rules that are not rulemakings do not enjoy the strong deference accorded legislative rulemaking by an agency, but still enjoy an initial presumption of (*Skidmore*) deference. *Skidmore v. Swift & Co.*, 323 U.S. 134 (1944); *Christiensen v. Harris*, 522 U.S. 576 (2000) (stronger deference to agency interpretive rule interpreting a regulation than interpreting a statute); *United States v. Mead*, 533 U.S. 218 (2001).

"[A] preliminary injunction is an extraordinary remedy never awarded as of right." *Winter v. Natural Resources Defense Council, Inc.*, 555 U.S. 7 (2008) — remanded by NRDC v. Winter. 560 F.3d 1027 (9th Cir. 2009). The Court emphasized that a mere "possibility" of irreparable harm was insufficient to warrant an injunction, if it is not "likely." In *Winter v. NRDC*, for seeking preliminary injunction, the 9th Circuit "possibility of irreparable harm" test was overturned in favor of the traditional four-part test of likelihood of success on the merits, the likelihood of plaintiff suffering irreparable harm, the balance of equities, and whether the public interest is served by an injunction. For the balance of the equities, national security was deemed superior to environmental requirements and allowed the Court to make ad hoc assessments of relative hardships to plaintiffs and defendants.

In some cases, courts will strike interpretive rules made by an agency on the ground that the rules were in fact legislative rules that require a full notice and comment, under formal or informal rulemaking. While distinguishing between legislative and interpretive rules thus is critical, there is little agreement among the courts on this distinction. Where mathematical or technical standards are imposed, or a new duty is imposed on a party by the rule, this typically requires the formal requisites of APA notice and comment. *Columbia Falls Aluminum Co. v. EPA*, 139 F.3d 914 (D.C. Cir. 1998) (finding EPA rulemaking under Section 3004 of RCRA arbitrary and capricious where the agency relied on an analytical model that they knew was flawed and not an accurate predictor).

Under the APA, any agency guidance document, which is not a rule, must be available to the public before it can be relied upon as precedent. The EPA violates the APA by relying on interpretive guidance, rather than a regulation. *NRDC v. EPA*, 643 F.3d 11 (D.C. Cir. 2011)("Given that the Guidance document changed the law, the first merits question — whether the Guidance is a legislative rule that required notice and comment — is easy. [The Guidance cannot] be considered a mere statement of policy; it is a rule" for ozone non-attainment areas); *Nat'l Mining Ass'n v. Jackson*, 816 F. Supp. 2d 37 (D.D.C. 2011) and 2012 WL 3090245 (D.D.C. July 31, 2012)(EPA exceeded its statutory authority and violated the APA by relying on interpretive guidance, rather than a regulation, and infringes on state authority as "Final Guidance constitutes final agency action . . . even if facially nonbinding [once] applied by the regional field offices . . ."). If an agency adopts a new position inconsistent with an existing regulation, or effects a substantive change in the regulation, notice and comment are required pursuant to the Act. If the EPA rejects a petition for action, that rejection is the final agency action.

Only legally binding final agency action is governed by the APA rule-making requirements and carries the force of law. 5 USC §553(b); *Cement Kiln Recycling Coalition*, 493 F.3d 207, 228 (D.C. Cir. 2007) ("an agency's pronouncement that a document is non-binding" does not actually render the document interlocutory "where there is evidence or practice to the contrary"); *Appalachian Power Co.* 208 F.3d 1015, 1024 (D.C. Cir. 2000)(it is "well-established that an agency may not escape APA notice and comment requirements by labeling a major substantive legal addition to a rule a mere interpretation").

A regulation is final if it operates in ". . . a binding manner and has been implemented in its current version." A court considers to determine finality, the agency characterization of the action, whether the agency action was published in the Federal Register or the Code of Federal Regulations and whether the agency action "has binding effects on private parties or the agency." To determine if agency action is final, the court determines whether an action is "merely tentative or interlocutory" or whether the action creates legal rights, obligations, or consequences. *Bennett v. Spear*, 520 U.S. 154, 178 (1997). While facts need to be judicially noticed under the Federal Rules of Evidence, a guidance document is not a fact. As such, guidance documents are entitled to *Skidmore* deference ("respectful consideration") as opposed to *Chevron* deference ("if the statute is silent or ambiguous ask if the agency construction is permissible").

The Choice of Standard

Exactly how closely will a court examine agency decisions? The APA defines three different standards of judicial review applicable to agency findings of fact. In a few cases, §706(2)(F) allows a court to review the facts de novo, as if the court, rather than the EPA, were the trier of fact in the first instance.

In regard to formal rulemakings and to on-the-record adjudicatory proceedings, §706(2)(E) of the APA provides for a "substantial evidence" standard of review of agency fact-finding. What this means in practice is that if the record includes substantial evidence supporting the agency's order

2.3   Judicial Review of Rulemaking

Rulemaking	Standard of Judicial Review
Formal	Substantial evidence
Informal	Arbitrary, capricious, abuse of discretion

or rule, a court will affirm an agency's findings, even if it would not have made those same findings if it had been the initial fact finder.

In *informal* rulemaking proceedings, as well as other informal agency actions subject to judicial review but falling outside the specific provisions of the APA, §706(2)(A) of the APA states that the "arbitrary and capricious" standard of review applies. This standard allows the most deference to an agency action. As long as the agency decision is not clearly erroneous and has *some* rationality, even if not supported by substantial evidence or a majority of the evidence, it will be upheld by the reviewing court. Thus different types of rulemakings are subject to different levels of judicial review (see Exhibit 2.3).

In *Citizens to Preserve Overton Park, Inc. v. Volpe*, 401 U.S. 402 (1971), the Court made it clear that judicial review of agency actions affecting environmental concerns must be conducted with attentive oversight — sometimes called strict scrutiny or the "hard look" doctrine. A quick review of this seminal case is in order. The Department of Transportation Act of 1966 stated that the secretary of transportation shall not approve any highway project that requires the use of publicly owned land from parks unless (1) there is no feasible and prudent alternative, and (2) the project includes all possible planning to minimize harm.

Former secretary of transportation Volpe approved a highway through Overton Park and rejected two alternatives that were more expensive and displaced schools and houses. A citizen group sued to enjoin the release of federal money to fund the project because Volpe failed to make an independent determination and the plan did not include all possible methods for reducing the harm to the park as required by statute.

The Court held that judicial review was proper here since Congress did not prohibit such review *and* the agency action was not one "committed to agency discretion." Moreover, the Court remanded the case to the district court to review the administrative record under an *arbitrary and capricious* standard of review. The Court found the "substantial evidence" standard applicable only to formal rulemaking; and the "de novo review" standard suitable only when an adjudication's fact-finding procedures are inadequate or when issues not before the agency are raised in a proceeding to enforce a nonadjudicatory action.

2. Administrative Procedure for Environmental Regulation

The Supreme Court required that the arbitrary and capricious standard be applied in a three-step analysis. First, the court must ask whether the secretary of transportation acted within the scope of his authority in *Citizens to Preserve Overton Park*. Second, it must consider whether the secretary's decision was based on relevant factors or whether there was a clear error of judgment — recognizing that a court cannot substitute its own opinion for that of an agency. Third, the court should inquire whether the secretary followed proper APA procedural requirements. One significant result of *Massachusetts v. EPA*, 549 U.S. 497 (2007), is that it makes agency inaction and decisions not to make findings reviewable under the similar "hard look" standard that the court applies in reviewing affirmative agency actions.

The Supreme Court also held that although the secretary was not required to make formal findings under the Department of Transportation Act, the reviewing court needed to base its decision on the *materials that the agency used to make its decision* — "post hoc" rationalizations are not sufficient. Thus only the original of administrative record must be placed before the reviewing court to assist its review of whether the agency acted in an arbitrary or capricious manner. A fundamental principle of judicial review was established in *S.E.C. v. Chenery Corp.*, 332 U.S. 194 (1947) (*Chenery I*), that administrative agency actions and decisions must be judged on the basis of the justifications offered by the agency at the time the agency took the actions in question, not on some post-hoc rationalizations or new grounds not raised in the prior proceedings. See also *United States v. Mead*, 533 U.S. 218, 230-231 (2001).

To justify an administrative action, agencies should not be able to place on the litigation record documents that were not available at the time of the proposed rulemaking. This denies effective comment by the public in the administrative process. Where Arizona provided documents justifying its plan for particulate emission control in the ambient air after the rulemaking had expired, these additional documents could not be considered as part of the record against which the agency decision would be adjudicated. See *Ober v. EPA*, 84 F.3d 304 (9th Cir. 1996). Similarly, where argument by counsel before the trial court is the basis for excusing an agency from making a full investigation of all alternatives more properly weighed in that investigation, "such *post hoc* rationalizations are inherently suspect, and in any event are no substitute for the agency's following statutorily mandated procedures. . . . [E]ven if the agency's actual decision was a reasoned one, the EIS is insufficient if it does not properly discuss the required issues." *DuBois v. U.S. Dep't of Agric.*, 102 F.3d 1273, 1289 (1st Cir. 1996).

Courts have not allowed federal agencies to revise, or even reconsider, their regulations without going through proper rulemaking procedures. Where the agency explains its reasoning in retaining an old rule as-is or substantively responds to comments about any aspect of the old rule, the agency has implicitly reopened the rule to new challenges. See *Ohio v. EPA*, 838 F.2d 1325, 1328 (D.C. Cir. 1988). When a court determines that a federal agency has "reopened" one of its regulations, "challenges to the rule are in order," and "a new comment period is triggered." *Columbia Falls Aluminum Co. v. EPA,* 139 F.3d 914, 921 (D.C. Cir. 1998).

In *Vt. Yankee Nuclear Power Corp. v. NRDC,* 435 U.S. 519 (1978), the Supreme Court rejected the idea that courts may impose procedural requirements on agencies beyond those contained in the APA. The Atomic Energy Commission, predecessor to the Nuclear Regulatory Commission (NRC), evaluated the environmental effects of radioactive waste. The NRC was authorized to use informal rulemaking in issuing this type of rule, but it voluntarily held a more formal oral hearing at which witnesses were questioned by agency representatives. On review, the District of Columbia Circuit held that the NRC had not allowed sufficient cross-examination of the witnesses regarding the disposal plans for nuclear waste.

The Supreme Court unanimously reversed the appellate court's decision. It held that judges lack the authority to impose any *additional* procedures on agencies beyond those required by statute, the Constitution, or the agency's own rules, except in undefined "extremely rare" cases.

In general, courts have adhered to *Vermont Yankee* and have not imposed additional procedures on agencies. However, such adherence does not mean that judicial supervision of the rulemaking process is meaningless. Not only did the Court leave open the possibility that in extremely compelling circumstances some additional procedures might be imposed, but under the "hard look" doctrine the APA requirements themselves can be enforced aggressively. Courts give an expansive reading to statutes relating to agency procedures; some environmental statutes contain detailed provisions regarding agency procedures that go far beyond the APA's minimum requirements.

Is an agency's revocation of an order reviewable, and if so, what standard of review is applicable? In *Motor Vehicle Mfrs. Ass'n v. State Farm Mut. Auto Ins. Co.,* 463 U.S. 29 (1983), the National Traffic and Motor Vehicle Safety Act of 1966 authorized the secretary of transportation to issue vehicle standards. The secretary revoked standard 208 requiring that passive restraints be in all vehicles by 1982. The Court of Appeals held that the revocation was arbitrary and capricious. The Supreme Court agreed and required the agency to make further findings. Essentially, the Court held that the revocation is subject to the same standard of review as informal rulemaking because the purpose of the Act is to promulgate safety standards under APA §553. The Court outlined the manner by which one determines whether an agency action is arbitrary or capricious:

1. Has the agency relied on factors that Congress had not intended it to?
2. Has the agency entirely failed to consider an important aspect of the problem?

3. Does the agency's explanation of the decision run counter to the evidence?
4. Is the decision so implausible that it could not be explained as a difference in opinion or the product of agency expertise?

The Court concluded that when an agency changes its course, it must supply a reasoned analysis. Again, the Court stated that post-hoc rationalizations are not sufficient. Based on the four factors above, one can see why many critics have stated that there is no longer much practical difference between the "substantial evidence" standard and the "arbitrary, capricious" standard coupled with a "hard look."

In summary, how does a court decide whether a plaintiff is entitled to judicial review of an agency action, and if so entitled, which standard of review to use? Recall that all final agency actions are entitled to review unless Congress explicitly prohibited review or the agency action is "committed to agency discretion" by law. Two important factors to consider are congressional intent and the purpose of the statute. Moreover, plaintiffs must always meet the tests for standing, ripeness, and exhaustion of administrative remedies. To determine the standard of review, the court starts by looking at the enabling statute, and if a reviewing standard is not specified therein, it looks to the APA for the "default" position as to the correct standard for review.

Examples

1. Recall that Lex Luther wants to store kryptonite. You have looked at the federal and state requirements and determined that a permit from the EPA is necessary. Specifically, the EPA has a set of engineering regulations promulgated pursuant to RCRA for the treatment, storage, and disposal of kryptonite. Lex Luther has supplied the necessary information in a permit application and has submitted it to the EPA for approval. The EPA has denied the permit to Lex. He wants to appeal the agency's decision.
   a. Given these facts, is Lex entitled to judicial review of the agency's permit denial? Why or why not?
   b. Assuming Lex Luther is entitled to judicial review, what standard of review should the court use? How is this determined?
   c. If the EPA denies Lex Luther's application because he is disliked by Superman fans within the agency, is this procedure proper?

2. Let's revisit Perry White, editor of the *Daily Planet*, which is generating waste ink from its printing processes. The EPA promulgated a set of regulations that mandate a new disposal method for waste ink — jettisoning it into outer space. The EPA did not publish a proposed rule nor did it allow for public comment. Compliance with the new regulations will cost the *Daily Planet* over $1 million. Perry White decides he cannot

afford to comply with the new rules and continues to dispose of the waste ink by the old method — sending it to a landfill. The EPA initiates an enforcement action against the newspaper. Perry comes into your office and asks what options he has at his disposal (no pun intended). Advise him.

Explanations

1a. To determine if Lex Luther is entitled to judicial review, we must first determine whether Congress has explicitly prohibited review or whether the agency action is exclusively "committed to agency discretion" by law. The important factors to consider are congressional intent and the purpose of the statute. Let us assume that our review of RCRA reveals no intent to prohibit such review. There is no express delegation of unlimited discretion to the EPA in the statute. Thus review of agency rules is permissible.

The next consideration is whether Lex Luther has *standing* to request judicial review of the agency decision. Here it is easily established that, through the denial of a permit that affects his commercial interests, Lex meets the "injury-in-fact" test necessary to establish an Article III case or controversy. He is within the protected zone of interests and is directly and personally affected.

The third consideration is whether Lex's case is *ripe* for judicial review. Only final agency actions are subject to judicial review. The relevant factor for reaching a ripeness determination is whether the process of administrative decision making has reached the stage where judicial review will not interfere with the agency's adjudicatory process. In this case, the denial of the permit is the final action and is ripe for review immediately when the decision is issued. There is a real case or controversy. The agency order has a direct impact upon the rights of Lex Luther.

The final consideration is whether Lex Luther has exhausted all possible administrative remedies. If Lex has already pursued all administrative appeals, then there is no reason for judicial review not to be granted. If Lex has not proceeded to use all administrative remedies, then the court could refer to the *McKart* factors (i.e., degree of Lex's injury; likelihood that judicial review would be enhanced by application of agency experience or accumulation of a record) and consider whether to grant judicial review anyway.

1b. The court starts by looking at the enabling statute — here, RCRA. If a reviewing standard is not specified therein, it looks to the APA for direction as to the correct one. Under the APA, permit proceedings are not specifically mentioned, but courts have stated that actions falling outside APA provisions will be reviewed under the "arbitrary and capricious" standard. The appropriate standard of review of a permit denial is the arbitrary and capricious standard.

1c. An agency must act on the basis of the factual record before it. The agency has discretion on how it assembles this record, pursuant to the public comment provisions of the Administrative Procedure Act. Any decision not supported by the record—in some manner—is considered arbitrary and capricious. Therefore, a decision based on a personal perspective by some decision-maker at the agency is not warranted. It is arbitrary, capricious, and an abuse of agency discretion. It is not consistent with legal requirements.

2. Perry White can defend against the EPA's enforcement action by claiming that the outer-space disposal regulations were not promulgated properly. Recall that under the APA rulemaking procedures, rules must be proposed and published in the Federal Register. In addition, the public must be given an opportunity to comment, and the EPA must review and address such comments, rationalizing its decision, when it publishes its final rule. The set of regulations mandating a new disposal method for waste ink did not follow these mandatory procedures. Therefore, the agency's enforcement action is ultra vires, without authority, and Perry White should not be forced to comply with the new regulations. To avoid being subject to an EPA enforcement action, Perry should initiate a declaratory judgment action to have the regulations declared void. During the interim until new rulemakings occur, his old disposal practices are permissible.

REMEDIES AND FEES

What should one do if the agencies "get it wrong"? Persons harmed by administrative actions often seek a declaratory judgment to invalidate the administrative decision and/or request an injunction of the agency's enforcement action. However, injured persons often also seek to recover damages from the government to compensate them for their injuries.

Unless such efforts have a statutory basis, they will probably fail on the basis of the sovereign immunity doctrine—the principle that the government may not be sued without its consent. Congress can assign non-Article III courts, such as administrative agencies, the power to adjudicate claims of "public rights." Moreover, Congress can create new statutory rights between private individuals and assign adjudicatory power over these rights to agencies—commonly referred to as private rights of action.

Federal Tort Claims Act

For tort claims, the proper avenue for redress is the Federal Tort Claims Act (FTCA). The FTCA generally renders the government liable in tort for any "negligent or wrongful act or omission . . . in the same manner and to the same extent as a private individual under like circumstances." 28 U.S.C. §1346(b). Yet, the Act also lists a number of exceptions that effectively preserve much of the sovereign immunity doctrine. The exceptions deny tort liability for many intentional torts like defamation, misrepresentation, deceit, and interference with contract rights.

The broadest of the FTCA exceptions prohibits the suit if the responsible administrators were exercising a "discretionary function," regardless of whether they abused their discretion. In *United States v. S.A. Empresa de Viacao Aerea Rio Grandense (VARIG)*, 467 U.S. 797 (1984), concerning a fire in an airplane lavatory that killed most of the passengers and damaged the plane, the Court ruled in favor of the government agency — the F.A.A. The Court explained that Congress had intended the discretionary exemption "to prevent judicial second-guessing of legislative and administrative decisions grounded in . . . policy through the medium of an action of tort."

However, four years later the Court limited *Varig*. In *Berkovitz v. United States*, 486 U.S. 531 (1988), the Court sustained the injured party's FTCA complaint against a government motion to dismiss. The petitioner had contracted polio after ingesting a vaccine disseminated under federal administration. The Court announced a test to determine whether the discretionary function exemption is applicable to governmental conduct — "the permissible exercise of policy judgment" test. Under this standard, the discretionary function exemption does not apply to governmental conduct that violates a statute, regulation, or policy that specifically prescribes a course of action for an employee to follow. In addition, the exception now protects only judgments based on public policy considerations, not every exercise of judgment by a government employee. This new standard exposes the federal government to tort liability for certain environmental indiscretions.

Equal Access to Justice Act

Prevailing parties, including intervenors, may claim the right to attorney fees under the Equal Access to Judgment Act (EAJA), 28 U.S.C. §2412, but only if the government's position was not "substantially justified." The EAJA works in two ways.

First, the EAJA waives the government's sovereign immunity as to claims for attorney fees. This only gets one part way to receive fees. Because of the "American Rule," whereby winning and losing parties each pay their own attorney fees, removing sovereign immunity does not guarantee fee

Examples

1. Suppose Senator Jackson had been unsuccessful in getting §102(2)(C), the EIS requirement, included as an amendment in the final draft of NEPA. Could a citizen subsequently have challenged an agency for not considering environmental concerns in a particular project plan?

2. The Department of Transportation (DOT) decides to fund a project to build additional entrance and exit ramps onto a major interstate highway. A local citizen's group, the Neighborhood Knights, is concerned because the nearby location of a proposed ramp will dramatically increase the traffic flow in and around its neighborhood. The community is located in a small valley, and many children live in the area. The Knights are afraid that the increase in traffic will cause a higher concentration of NO_x and ozone, combining to produce smog, which will have a detrimental effect on the air quality of the valley. Also, the increase in traffic during both the construction period and later may be dangerous for the children, who frequently play outdoors in the neighborhood.

   The group submitted its concerns to the DOT, but in its final environmental impact statement, the DOT states that after consideration of these possible consequences it has decided that the advantages of the project outweigh the potential adverse environmental impacts. The Knights file suit, claiming that the DOT violated NEPA, and present convincing evidence at trial that the adverse effects with which they are concerned will most likely occur.

   a. Is this a procedural or substantive claim? Why? Do the Knights win or lose?
   b. Can a judge overrule the DOT's decision? Why or why not?
   c. How would you answer (b) differently if this fact pattern was set in 1978?

Explanations

1. Section 102(2)(C) is the core of the NEPA process. It provides the concrete steps and stages to structure the consideration of environmental values. It provides the procedural standards. A citizen would have no effective ability to challenge an agency in the absence of §102(2)(C), because courts give great deference to agency decision making. If an agency claims it has considered environmental impacts and made its decision accordingly, there would be no procedural means for a citizen to prove otherwise in the absence of the defined §102(2)(C) process. Without §102(2)(C), nothing is *mandatory* about NEPA. Note that

§102(E) requires all agencies to "study, develop, and describe appropriate alternatives to recommended courses of action in any proposal which involves unresolved conflicts concerning alternative uses of available resources," whether or not an EIS is prepared.

2a. If the DOT formally complied with all NEPA requirements and made the decision on the administrative record to go ahead with the project, the Knights essentially are challenging the *substantive* decision of the agency. Because it is the result of the agency's substantive decision that the Knights are challenging, not the decision-making process, their claim will be deemed substantive. However, after *Strycker's Bay*, NEPA prescribes only procedural requirements. The Knights lose. If the Knights were challenging the process by which the DOT made its decision, then it would be a procedural claim. If the Knights could stress procedural failures to evaluate relevant facts, they might be able to cloak their substantive claim in an effective procedural mantle.

2b. If the DOT fully complied with the NEPA process, under *Strycker's Bay* the judge is obligated to defer to the agency's decision. The courts' role is to make sure the agencies adhere to informed decision-making processes under the NEPA mandate. The substantive result of an agency decision, however, is beyond judicial reach unless the decision is "arbitrary or capricious" on the facts on record (as you will recall from the prior chapter). If the Knights had challenged the process by which the DOT made its final decision and the judge determined that the DOT did in fact violate a NEPA step or failed to engage in a "hard look," the agency would be forced to reevaluate the environmental impacts on record in accordance with the statute. The trial judge does, then, have some limited discretion to characterize an agency misstep as either "procedural" or "substantive." This can shape whether the judge has authority to strike the agency decision.

2c. Some courts believed that they did have the power to enforce substantive duties under NEPA, as was suggested in the *Calvert Cliffs'* opinion. If this fact pattern were set in 1978, before the *Strycker's Bay* decision, the Knights could argue that the DOT's final decision violated a substantive requirement under NEPA, mandating the agency to make decisions that minimized adverse environmental impacts. However, very few courts actually overruled agency determinations under such an argument, and the question was not firmly settled until 1980.

Imagine if *Strycker's Bay* had been decided differently, following the *Calvert Cliffs'* decision. Substantive challenges under NEPA could then be heard by the courts. This would effectively have given the judiciary power to override agency decisions. Would this kind of precedent have been consistent with the Administrative Procedure Act, discussed in Chapter 2? The answer is no, for under the APA, courts must give agencies considerable discretion in making a final decision on the record.

THE EIS PROCESS

The EIS process is "where the action is" in NEPA. It is mandated by a single sentence in §102(2)(C), yet every word in that sentence is of great legal significance. Before dissecting the statutory sentence, let's walk through the NEPA process. NEPA imposes an administrative process on federal agencies that may require the preparation of an environmental impact statement (EIS) before a final decision. The threshold determination of whether or not to prepare an EIS when an agency begins to plan an action is governed by NEPA, CEQ regulations, and the internal procedures and regulations of the individual agency. For an agency, there are *procedural* decision points at various "forks" in the EIS path. The following review outlines the administrative process from start to finish and then looks closely at the considerations necessary to determine whether or not an agency must prepare an EIS.

The Administrative Process

Once an agency begins the early planning process for a project, it must address whether or not to prepare an EIS. To make this determination, the agency first considers which of three categories the project falls into, as shown in Exhibit 3.1. The agency action is different in each situation. The first category includes projects that have been predetermined to have no significant impact on the environment, either individually or cumulatively. If the proposed project falls into this categorical exclusion, then the agency may proceed with the plan without preparing an EIS.

Various presidential administrations have moved aggressively to define as categorically excluded from NEPA a variety of practices by agencies, including federal land management, timber harvesting, temporary road construction, and certain oil and gas lease areas that are smaller than a

3.1 Agency Projects

Categorically Excluded	Project EIS in Dispute	Categorically Included
No EIS	EA	EIS

designated size. Decisions under the Clean Air Act and many decisions under the Clean Water Act and by the Department of Homeland Security "to attain border security" are exempt from NEPA. In these excluded situations, the activities can occur without the preparation of either an environmental assessment or an EIS because of the categorical exclusion.

The second category of projects includes those that, because of size or impact, always require an EIS. The agency should include the preparation of the EIS as part of the planning process from the onset. The third category involves projects for which the agency is unsure whether an impact statement is needed. In these circumstances, the agency will prepare an environmental assessment (EA) to determine whether or not the project will have a significant effect on the environment and thus require an EIS.

The EA is like a mini-EIS; it is designed to include enough evidence to help an agency decide whether it must go ahead and prepare an EIS or whether it can announce a finding of no significant (environmental) impact (FONSI). A FONSI shall "briefly present the reasons why an action, not otherwise [categorically excluded], will not have a significant effect on the human environment and for which an EIS therefore will not be prepared. It shall include the EA or a summary of it. . . ." 40 C.F.R. §1508.13. The EA should include a brief discussion regarding the need for the proposed action, optional alternatives to the action, and the possible environmental impacts of both the proposed action and its alternatives. The EA must also list the agencies and individuals consulted during its preparation.

The EA, if properly prepared, demonstrates to the court that the NEPA process was followed. If the agency decides there would be no significant environmental impact, then it prepares a FONSI and goes ahead with the plan for the proposed action. If the agency determines that there would be a significant impact, then it must prepare an EIS before deciding whether to proceed with the plan. If a judicial review shows that the environmental assessment omitted key facts that would tend to show a significant impact on the environment, the burden of proof can shift back to the agency to show that its negative determination was reasonable under the circumstances. *Lakes Region Legal Def. Fund v. Slater*, 986 F. Supp. 1169, 1191 (N.D. Iowa 1997).

The number of EISs prepared by federal agencies has fallen dramatically from approximately 2,000 annually in 1973 when NEPA was first enacted to approximately 500 annually from 1984 to the present. This does not count the large number of EISs filed by private parties.

If an agency prepares an EIS, the statement must first be prepared in draft form and shared with all relevant federal, state, and local agencies, those who apply to the agency for permits, and citizens. The responses by commenting agencies and other interested parties must be as specific as possible, and those agencies that are critical must include ways they think the problems should be addressed. Usually a 45-day comment period is provided, but this can be reduced or extended by the agency. Comments are made in writing to the clerk of the rulemaking agency. The agency must read and consider these comments before proceeding. The agency can alter the project, or proceed to a final version of the EIS.

In its final EIS (FEIS), the agency must respond to each comment, modifying its analyses where necessary and citing authority or a basis for its final determination. The FEIS then is circulated to interested parties, and the agency has approximately 30 days to make its final decision on the merits. Exhibit 3.2 offers a simple outline of the basic steps in the NEPA process.

3.2 Basic Steps in the NEPA Process

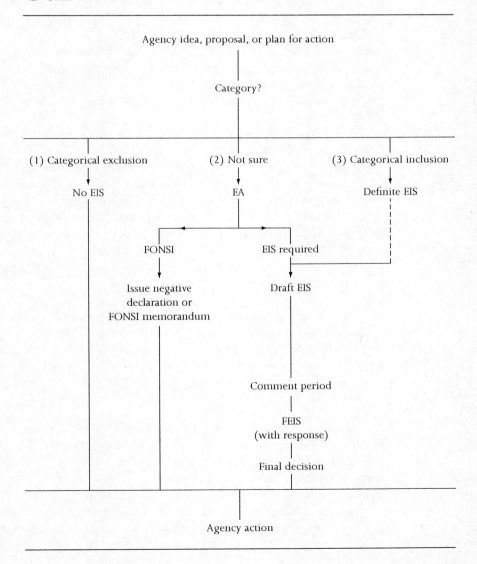

Agency idea, proposal, or plan for action

Category?

(1) Categorical exclusion   (2) Not sure   (3) Categorical inclusion

No EIS   EA   Definite EIS

FONSI   EIS required

Issue negative declaration or FONSI memorandum   Draft EIS

Comment period

FEIS (with response)

Final decision

Agency action

The CEQ regulations require agencies to balance environmental considerations in their decision-making process and to use all means to avoid and minimize environmental harm. 40 C.F.R. §1505.2(b)-(c). CEQ regulations also require agencies to state whether all practical means to avoid and minimize environmental harm from the alternatives selected have been adopted and if not, why not. 40 C.F.R. §1505.2(c).

The Threshold Decision

The administrative process is fairly straightforward. But it is the "forks" in the EIS road that are difficult to navigate: When must a federal agency prepare an EIS? This is known as the "threshold" question.

The most significant sentence in §102(2)(C) of NEPA states that an agency must prepare an EIS whenever "proposals for legislation or other major federal actions significantly [affect] the quality of the human environment." Each word has come to represent a battleground for NEPA litigation. A federal action must fall within the scope of all of these operative words to trigger an EIS.

To avoid preparing an EIS, an agency need only show that a proposed project does *not* fall under any *one* element of §102(2)(C). In other words, is a proposal (1) major, (2) federal, (3) an action, (4) significantly affecting the (5) human (6) environment? Those who wish to win an argument that an EIS is required bear the burden of squeezing a proposed project into the scope of each of those words. The agency makes its own threshold determinations; consequently, less than 10 percent of all federal proposals are accompanied by an EIS.

The CEQ regulation emergency provision at 40 C.F.R. §1506.11 provides:

> Where emergency circumstances make it necessary to take an action with significant environmental impact without observing the provisions of these regulations, the federal agency taking the action should consult with the Council about alternative arrangements. Agencies and the Council will limit such arrangements to actions necessary to control the immediate impacts of the emergency. Other actions remain subject to NEPA review.

The term "emergency" as it relates to 40 C.F.R. §1506.11 is not defined within the regulation. The lack of a definition has consistently given the CEQ wide latitude in determining whether or not it is appropriate to allow for alternative arrangements. To this end, in *Winter v. N.R.D.C.*, 555 U.S. 7 (2008) — remanded by *NRDC v. Winter*, 560 F.3d 1027 (9th Cir. 2009), the Court stated that since the Navy had been conducting SONAR training for over 40 years, it is not likely that the environmental harms are unknown.

What exactly constitutes *major federal action*? What kinds of acts *significantly affect* the human environment? And finally, what factors and concepts encompass the *human environment*? These issues were initially addressed by the courts, and later codified in regulations promulgated by the CEQ. These CEQ regulations provide guidelines to help agencies make the initial threshold determinations. Let's review the relevant threshold case law and the CEQ regulations, concept by concept — trigger by trigger.

Major Federal Action

Federal "Major federal action" contains two adjectives modifying the noun. An EIS is required only when the action proposed is *federal* action. When a federal agency itself embarks upon a project, its actions are clearly federal.

What if a nonfederal entity, like a state government or a private organization, undertakes a project that enjoys federal funding? Nonfederal projects that are eligible for federal assistance and/or require federal permits or approvals are considered *federal* actions because the federal agency enables the nonfederal entity to act. Many private projects require permits pursuant to federal law. Any federal nexus, as evidenced in the CEQ regulations quoted below, makes an action "federal." But watch your step: Federal funds delegated to state and local governments to assist with planning programs do not require an EIS unless federal approval of the plan is required.

Some courts have allowed nonfederal action to be considered "federal" when the federal agency possesses authority to exercise some discretion over the outcome of the project. *Sugarloaf Citizens Assoc. v. FERC*, 959 F.2d 508 (4th Cir. 1992) (FERC approval of an incinerator that qualified as a "small power production facility" under the Public Utility Regulatory Policies Act); *Save Barton Creek Assoc. v. Fed'l Highway Admin.*, 950 F.2d 1129 (5th Cir. 1992) (where federal agency can control outcome of a project in material respects or has discretion to exercise judgment regarding the outcome, this is "touchstone" of major federal action).

Action Whether a proposal involves an *action* within the scope of NEPA is determined by whether the federal activity is *major* and whether it *significantly* affects the human environment. Nondiscretionary actions, however, those actions in which an agency has no choice, are generally outside the scope of NEPA and do not require an EIS. For example, in *South Dakota v. Andrus*, 614 F.2d 1190 (8th Cir. 1980), the court held that the Department of the Interior's issuance of a mineral patent for mining claims in a national forest was a ministerial act that did not come within the scope of NEPA. Because the department is mandated to issue such patents and has no discretion in the matter, these acts are exempt from the EIS requirement. Informal advice by an administrative agency to a company subject to its regulations, or the failure of an agency to object to actions where it lacks clear authority, are not considered agency actions subject to NEPA. See *Marbled Murrelet v. Babbitt*, 83 F.3d 1068 (9th Cir. 1996); *Sierra Club v. Babbitt*, 65 F.3d 1502 (9th Cir. 1995).

What if an agency chooses *not* to act? Agency *inaction* is considered by courts to be outside the scope of NEPA because the language of the statute addresses "action" and not "a failure to act." The leading case on this issue is *Defenders of Wildlife v. Andrus*, 627 F.2d 1238 (D.C. Cir. 1980). There, the state of Alaska planned a wolf kill to protect caribou herds, and the Department of the Interior did not use its authority to prohibit the wolf kill. The court did not require the agency to prepare an EIS for its decision not to act. According to the court, the principles of NEPA would be trivialized if agencies were forced to prepare EISs when they failed to take action, as well as when they did act. The CEQ regulations take a contrary view. Failure to act by a responsible official, which is reviewable as agency action by courts or under the Administrative Procedure Act (APA) (see Chapter 2), may be considered "action" under NEPA, according to CEQ regulations.

Major   Once a court determines that an agency has taken an *action* and that it is *federal*, the next question is whether or not the act is *major*. One of the early cases addressing the meaning of "major" is *Hanly v. Mitchell (Hanly I)*, 460 F.2d 640 (2d Cir. 1972), in which the court reviewed a proposal by the General Services Administration to build a nine-story jailhouse in Manhattan. The court held that the term "major federal action" could refer to such variables as the cost of a project, the amount of planning that has gone into the project, and the time needed to complete it. The court believed that just because an action is "major," it does not necessarily mean that the impacts are "significant." This "dual standard" set out by *Hanly I* requires actions that call for an EIS to be both "major" *and* "significant." A number of courts adopted the dual standard, while some jurisdictions found a "unitary standard," whereby any significant action was automatically deemed to be major. The federal circuits remain split.

The following regulatory definition of "major federal action," promulgated by the CEQ, codifies most of the case law on the meaning and scope of the words in §102(2)(C). Note that the CEQ adopted the "unitary standard" for understanding the relationship between "major" and "significantly," stating "major reinforces but does not have a meaning independent of significantly."

Major Federal Action (40 C.F.R. §1508.18)
In CEQ regulations, "major Federal action" includes actions with effects that may be major and that are potentially subject to federal control and

responsibility. "Major" reinforces but does not have a meaning independent of "significantly":

> (a) Actions include new and continuing activities, including projects and programs entirely or partly financed, assisted, conducted, regulated, or approved by federal agencies; new or revised agency rules, regulations, plans, policies, or procedures; and legislative proposals. Actions do not include funding assistance solely in the form of general revenue sharing funds, distributed under the State and Local Fiscal Assistance Act of 1972 . . . with no Federal control over subsequent use of such funds. Actions do not include bringing judicial or administrative civil or criminal enforcement actions.
>
> (b) Federal actions tend to fall within one of the following categories:
>
> (1) Adoption of official policy, such as rules, regulations, and interpretations adopted pursuant to the Administrative Procedure Act . . . ; treaties and international conventions or agreements; formal documents establishing an agency's policies which will result in or substantially alter agency programs.
>
> (2) Adoption of formal plans, such as official documents prepared or approved by federal agencies which guide or prescribe alternative uses of federal resources, upon which future agency actions will be based.
>
> (3) Adoption of programs, such as a group of concerted actions to implement a specific policy or plan; systematic and connected agency decisions allocating agency resources to implement a specific statutory program or executive directive.
>
> (4) Approval of specific projects, such as construction or management activities located in a defined geographic area. Projects include actions approved by permit or other regulatory decisions as well as federal and federally assisted activities.

The Supreme Court relied on the CEQ regulations in *Andrus v. Sierra Club*, 442 U.S. 347 (1979), when it was asked to determine whether or not requests for appropriations from Congress were proposals for legislation or "major federal actions." The Court concluded that such requests were neither, for they did not fall into the CEQ definitions of "major federal action." Since this case, the CEQ regulations have been elevated to being an important source for interpreting the scope of NEPA threshold questions.

Significantly Affecting the Quality of the Human Environment

Significantly and Adverse   We have now examined half of the six key trigger concepts of NEPA §102(2)(C). There are three more to dissect. The question of whether or not a major federal action *significantly* affects the quality of the human environment receives the most consideration in

NEPA cases where a threshold determination is at issue. If the defined level of "significance" triggering an EIS were too high, then many agency actions would be able to escape NEPA altogether. The leading case on this issue is *Hanly v. Kleindienst (Hanly II)*, 471 F.2d 823 (2d Cir. 1972), where the court reexamined the General Services Administration's assessment of environmental impacts resulting from the construction of the nine-story jailhouse in Manhattan. The court considered two factors to be relevant in defining "significantly": the extent to which an action would cause a greater degree of *adverse* environmental effects in a particular area, and the quantitative effects of the action on the environment, including the *cumulative* harm of the proposed action added to existing adverse conditions.

To determine whether a greater degree of adverse effects would result from the proposed action, the court adopted a test that looked at the "baseline factor" of an area as the point of comparison, assessing the character of the area to be affected by the proposed action. For example, the adverse effects of a proposed highway in a wilderness area (pristine baseline) would exhibit a greater degree of significance than a highway built in an area traversed with roads (automania baseline). At the same time, the court noted that adverse impacts can be the last straw in an area that is already burdened by pollution and environmental degradation, and this too would affect the degree of "significance" of an action. The dissenting opinion, written by Judge Friendly, suggested a more lenient standard. He believed that an EIS should be required if an action exhibited only "arguably" adverse impacts.

Although the *Hanly II* court outlined important aspects in defining "significantly," few courts since have explicitly identified a "baseline" for determining significance. More commonly, courts look at the significance of environmental impacts from a proposed action on a case-by-case basis. The case law is split on whether only *adverse* impacts can be "significant." There is nothing in the statute to support the idea that beneficial impacts are not just as "significant." Reasonably foreseeable environmental effects and impacts of a proposed project that are sufficiently likely to occur and not too speculative or lacking sufficient detail to be useful must be considered. *Dubois v. U.S. Dep't of Agric.*, 102 F.3d 1273, 1288 (1st Cir. 1996).

The CEQ regulations incorporate some of the *Hanly II* considerations but divide the inquiry into areas of *context* and *intensity*. "Context" refers to the unique circumstances and settings of a proposed action that should be considered when determining whether the impacts are "significant." "Intensity" involves the severity of an environmental impact, including cumulative effects, precedent set for future actions, and any violations of federal, state, or local environmental protection laws.

The CEQ regulations diverge from the *Hanly II* focus on there being only adverse "significant" impacts. Beneficial as well as adverse impacts on the environment are considered "significant" by the CEQ. In reading through the CEQ regulations, keep in mind the likelihood of judicial deference so long as the agency thoroughly evaluates the effects of the proposed action in terms of both context and intensity.

Significantly (40 C.F.R. §1508.27)

"Significantly" as used in NEPA requires consideration of both context and intensity:

> (a) *Context*. This means that the significance of an action must be analyzed in several contexts such as society as a whole (human, national), the affected region, the affected interests, and the locality. Significance varies with the setting of the proposed action. For instance, in the case of a specific action, significance would usually depend upon the effects in the locale rather than in the world as a whole. Both short and long term effects are relevant.
>
> (b) *Intensity*. This refers to the severity of impact. Responsible officials must bear in mind that more than one agency may make decisions about partial aspects of a major action. The following should be considered in evaluating intensity:
>
> > (1) Impacts that may be both beneficial and adverse. A significant effect may exist even if the Federal agency believes that on balance the effect will be beneficial.
> >
> > (2) The degree to which the proposed action affects public health safety.
> >
> > (3) Unique characteristics of the geographic area such as proximity to historic or cultural resources, park lands, prime farmlands, wetlands, wild and scenic rivers, or ecologically critical areas.
> >
> > (4) The degree to which the effects on the quality of the human environment are likely to be highly controversial.
> >
> > (5) The degree to which the possible effects of the human environment are highly uncertain or involve unique or unknown risks.
> >
> > (6) The degree to which the action may establish a precedent for future actions with significant effects or represents a decision in principle about a future consideration.
> >
> > (7) Whether the action is related to other actions with individually insignificant but cumulatively significant impacts. Significance exists if it is reasonable to anticipate a cumulatively significant impact on the environment. Significance cannot be avoided by terming an action temporary or by breaking it down into small component parts.
> >
> > (8) The degree to which the action may adversely affect districts, sites, highways, structures, or objects listed in or eligible for listing in the National Register of Historic Places or may cause loss or destruction to significant scientific, cultural, or historical resources.
> >
> > (9) The degree to which the action may adversely affect an endangered or threatened species or its habitat that has been determined to be critical under the Endangered Species Act of 1973.

(10) Whether the action threatens a violation of Federal, State or local law or requirements imposed for the protection of the environment.

Effects   The types of effects that are caused by a major federal action must also be examined to determine whether an action is significant. The CEQ regulations define "effects" to include aesthetic, cultural, ecological, economic, health, historic, and social effects. This broadens the notion of environmental effects. In _Hanly II_, the General Services Administration failed to assess the possibility of increased crime in the neighborhood (as was ordered in _Hanly I_), and the court found this failure to be a violation of NEPA requirements.

Not all possible major federal effects, however, qualify as NEPA EIS triggers. According to the CEQ regulations, indirect or secondary effects, depending on the foreseeability of these effects and the time when they are likely to occur, may qualify. For example, if a new bank is approved by a federal agency and there is a chance the bank will finance a project that will significantly affect the environment, that project would be an indirect effect of federal action. In this case, such an effect is too speculative for courts to impose an EIS requirement on the action.

In the following CEQ regulation, indirect effects include effects that may change land use patterns, population growth, or ecosystem development.

Effects (40 C.F.R. §1508.8)
"Effects" include:

(a) Direct effects, which are caused by the action and occur at the same time and place.

(b) Indirect effects, which are caused by the action and are later in time or farther removed in distance, but are still reasonably foreseeable. Indirect effects may include growth inducing effects and other effects related to induced changes in the pattern of land use, population density or growth rate, and related effects on air and water and other natural systems, including ecosystems.

"Effects" and "impacts" as used in these regulations are synonymous. Effects include ecological (such as the effects on natural resources and on the components, structures, and functioning of affected ecosystems), aesthetic, historic, cultural, economic, social, or health, whether direct, indirect, or cumulative. Effects may also include those resulting from actions which may have both beneficial and detrimental effects, even if on balance the agency believes that the effect will be beneficial.

The Human Environment

Even with significant effects to study, an EIS is not required unless there is a triggering relationship with the human environment. What encompasses the *human environment* under NEPA? Impacts on urban environments as well as natural environments are within NEPA's consideration. Early on, the controversy lay in whether or not to consider socioeconomic effects as they relate to the human environment.

In *Hanly I*, the court found that NEPA included socioeconomic impacts, holding that quality of life (noise, traffic, transportation, crime, congestion, drugs) for city residents was a significant effect to be included in an impact statement. Most courts hold that NEPA's primary concern is humankind's impact on the physical or natural environment. Socioeconomic effects may be considered in the EIS, but *alone* they are not enough to trigger the EIS. This approach was taken by the court in *Image of Greater San Antonio v. Brown*, 570 F.2d 517 (5th Cir. 1978), where a managerial decision to eliminate a number of positions at an Air Force base was held alone not to trigger an EIS, despite the socioeconomic effects the decision would have on the discharged employees and their families. The action brought by the AFL-CIO questioned the reduction in force at Kelly Air Force Base. Socioeconomic impacts are not a trigger but must be included in effects evaluated if an EIS is otherwise triggered. The current CEQ regulations state that economic and social impacts by themselves do not require the preparation of an EIS but should be considered if they are interrelated with other significant impacts.

Human Environment (40 C.F.R. §1508.14)

"Human environment" shall be interpreted comprehensively to include the natural and physical environment and the relationship of people with that environment. This means that economic or social effects are not intended by themselves to require preparation of an environmental impact statement. When an environmental impact statement is prepared and economic or social and natural or physical environmental effects are interrelated, then the environmental impact statement will discuss all these effects on the human environment.

How about psychological effects? In *Metropolitan Edison v. People Against Nuclear Energy* (*PANE*), 460 U.S. 766 (1983), the Nuclear Regulatory Commission (NRC) granted permission to restart an infamous nuclear reactor located on Three Mile Island in Pennsylvania. A reactor on this site had failed, causing the worst U.S. nuclear accident to date. PANE was a group of nearby residents and neighbors who adamantly protested the NRC decision. Among other things, PANE argued that NEPA required the NRC to study and take into account the psychological distress that would accompany the restart of the reactor.

The Supreme Court held that psychological effects *alone* do not trigger an EIS. While human health is cognizable under NEPA, and human health includes psychological health, NEPA is limited to the physical environment as its fundamental EIS trigger. While other courts have required agencies to consider the environmental risks of their proposed actions, the Supreme

Court distinguished *Metropolitan Edison* because the environmental effect (fear) was a result of the risk of radiation poisoning, not of the radiation itself. In *Metropolitan Edison*, Justice Rehnquist qualifies that ". . . the context of the statute shows that Congress was talking about the physical environment — the world around us, so to speak." Moreover, ". . . anxiety, tension, fear [and] a sense of helplessness" do not give rise to NEPA litigation. Note, however, that if the physical environment trigger is pulled, causing an EIS, then nonphysical impacts, including direct psychological impacts, must be discussed in the EIS.

Metropolitan Edison injects the nexus requirement: A clear, causal relationship must be shown between a federal action and its environmental effect. The Court thus adopted a causation test to determine NEPA's applicability to psychological impacts. Under this test, the causal chain linking the environmental impact to the federal action cannot be too attenuated. While indirect, speculative environmental effects are beyond the scope of NEPA, there is no requirement that there be certainty of a potential impact. Since *Metropolitan Edison*, many courts have held that if the risk of a federal action causing an environmental harm is reasonably foreseeable, an EIS must be prepared. In some cases, even if the risk of an environmental effect has a low probability of occurrence, an EIS must still be prepared if the consequences of the occurrence are potentially severe.

Judicial Review Under NEPA

In 2004, there were only about 1,000 federal court cases filed that involved environmental issues, from more than 280,000 civil cases filed in federal court that year. Also in 2004, approximately 600 EISs were prepared by the federal government and 156 NEPA court cases were filed, with 11 of those resulting in the issuance of injunctions.

The agency informally makes NEPA threshold determinations. The standard for reviewing informal agency decisions is spelled out by §706(2)(A) of the Administrative Procedure Act, which authorizes the court to determine whether agency decisions are "arbitrary, an abuse of discretion, or otherwise not in accordance with law." The "arbitrary and capricious" standard has applied to all informal agency decisions since *Citizens to Preserve Overton Park, Inc. v. Volpe*, 401 U.S. 402 (1971).

A majority of the federal circuits apply a "reasonableness" standard, in which the court weighs evidence presented by the plaintiff and by the federal agency and determines whether the agency's decision not to prepare an EIS was reasonable under the circumstances. The *Hanly II* court, however, looked at the threshold determination of the GSA not to prepare an impact statement as both a question of law (the meaning of the word "significantly" under NEPA) and a question of fact (whether or not the jailhouse would have "significant" adverse environmental impacts on the surrounding community).

The Supreme Court, in *Marsh v. Oregon Natural Res. Council*, 490 U.S. 360 (1989), addressed the duty of the Army Corps of Engineers to prepare a supplemental EIS (SEIS) in light of new information on the impact of the construction of the Elk Creek Dam on the fish population of the stream. The Court rejected the *Hanly* "reasonableness" standard of review for NEPA threshold determinations and held that the proper standard to employ was the "arbitrary and capricious" test. To make this determination, the reviewing court must look to see whether the agency had applied all the relevant factors and then whether it has made a clear error of judgment under the circumstances. Some courts interpret *Marsh* to apply only to questions of fact, under the significance determination. For instance, an Eighth Circuit case has decided to continue to apply a "reasonableness" standard to threshold decisions based on questions of law. See *Goos v. Interstate Commerce Comm'n*, 911 F.2d 1283 (8th Cir. 1990).

The "hard look doctrine" increases the rigor with which a court reviews an agency decision, as discussed in the prior chapter. The Supreme Court in *Marsh* used language that affirmed the application of the "hard look" doctrine to NEPA threshold determinations. Cf. *City of Auburn v. United States Government*, 154 F.3d 1025 (9th Cir. 1998) (60-page environmental assessment including many mitigation measures supported deference to the agency under the substantial evidence test); *Nat'l Audubon Soc'y v. Hoffman*, 132 F.3d 7 (2d Cir. 1997).

Look again at our procedural flow chart, now expanded in Exhibit 3.3 to show the terms of contention and the considerations that each agency must examine when deciding whether or not to prepare an EIS. As we can see, every noun, verb, adverb, and adjective of NEPA §102(2)(C) is grounds for suit. Every federal agency must follow NEPA's procedural requirements whenever it creates a proposal for action. In the next section we will look at the EIS process itself to understand at what point in the planning process an agency should prepare an impact statement, and the scope of what the EIS should cover. First, however, try some Examples and Explanations to make sure the concepts are clear.

Examples

1. According to the CEQ regulations, which of the following agency proposals are "federal actions" as contemplated in the term "major federal actions"?
   a. Federal funding for any state project approved by the federal government designed to advance the restoration and protection of coastal wetlands in the qualifying state's jurisdiction.

3.3   Expanded Steps in the NEPA Process

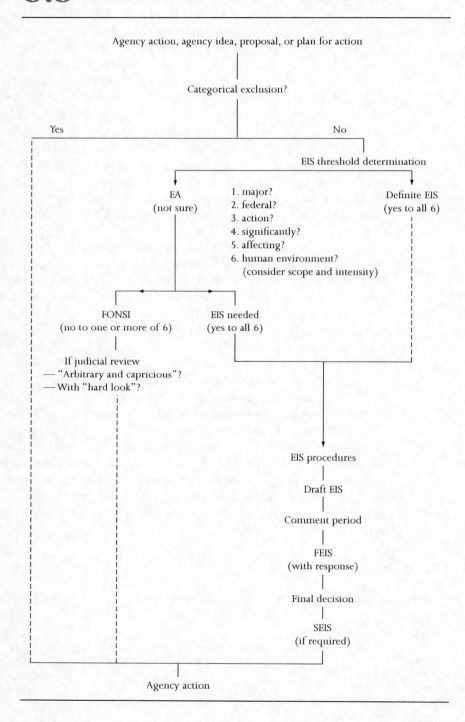

Agency action, agency idea, proposal, or plan for action

Categorical exclusion?

Yes   No

EIS threshold determination

EA
(not sure)

1. major?
2. federal?
3. action?
4. significantly?
5. affecting?
6. human environment?
   (consider scope and intensity)

Definite EIS
(yes to all 6)

FONSI
(no to one or more of 6)

EIS needed
(yes to all 6)

If judicial review
— "Arbitrary and capricious"?
— With "hard look"?

EIS procedures

Draft EIS

Comment period

FEIS
(with response)

Final decision

SEIS
(if required)

Agency action

    b. General federal funding for each state, to be used without qualification by local governments for their self-determined programs.

    c. A proposal for internal procedures to be used by the Department of the Interior for evaluating applications and issuing permits to prospective mining operations.

    d. An administrative enforcement action brought by the Internal Revenue Service against an environmental consulting firm for taking unlawful tax deductions related to environmental services.

2. The city of Dover, located on the Atlantic Ocean, has a major harbor that attracts cargo and passenger ships from all over the world. To better accommodate international liners, the Dover Port Authority (Authority) is planning to deepen the navigational channels, as well as a number of ship berths within the harbor. To accomplish this project, the Authority must enlist the help of the Army Corps of Engineers (Corps) to facilitate the dredging and disposal of the ocean sediment. The Environmental Protection Agency is concerned about this project because recent tests have found the harbor sediment to be contaminated with a number of toxins.

    The Corps and the Authority must decide where to dispose of the contaminated sediment. They have three options. Upland disposal is the first and most expensive option, in which the dredged materials would be transferred to a land-based disposal site where they could be properly treated and buried. The second two options involve dumping the sediment in designated areas in the open ocean. Area 1 is near a location frequently visited and fished by local fishermen, and Area 2 is located further out to sea, a quarter mile north of the Dover National Marine Sanctuary.

    The National Marine Fishery Service (NMFS) expressed its concern about Area 1, claiming the contaminated sediment would kill fish stocks in the nearby fishing location. The National Oceanic and Atmospheric Administration (NOAA), which is charged with the management and protection of endangered sea animals within the marine sanctuary, is concerned about Area 2 because there is a slight chance that the sediment could migrate into the sanctuary region. A local citizens' group, Sailors for Sealife, is opposed to any open ocean disposal because of the possible harmful effects on the marine ecosystem; it insists that upland disposal (option 1) offers the least adverse environmental consequences.

    a. What are the specific threshold determinations that must be considered by the Corps in deciding whether or not to prepare an EIS?

    b. Do the ocean sites fall into the category of "human environment" under NEPA, or are they marine environments?

c. NMFS, NOAA, and Sailors for Sealife each have complaints about the proposed open ocean sites. How "significant" and what kind of environmental effects under NEPA would there be from dumping at each site?

d. Assuming that NOAA has the authority to expand the ocean area around the sanctuary by a half mile, it could claim the extra space is needed for the protection of the sanctuary and its inhabitants. This action would effectively eliminate Area 2 from consideration by the Army Corps, as Area 2 would then fall within the sanctuary's boundaries and under NOAA's jurisdiction. NOAA declines to take action, however, and does not expand the sanctuary's boundaries to include the Area 2 dump site. Can Sailors for Sealife bring an action against NOAA for failing to prepare an EIS prior to its decision and thereby violating NEPA?

e. Suppose a local fishermen's organization, Fishing in Fear, opposes the dumping in Area 1 and brings an action against the Corps for not considering in its FEIS the socioeconomic and psychological effects that a severe drop in fish stocks would have on the fishing community. What would be the result?

3. The National Forest Service (NFS) undertakes a Land and Resource Management Plan (LRMP) for the Boise National Forest, located in Idaho. A forest development road runs through portions of the forest, along the South Fork of the Salmon River. The terrain is steep and mountainous, and the soil is full of fine sediments and highly erosive. The road currently is constructed of dirt and gravel, and a high volume of rain and snow causes a large amount of sediment to wash into the river, which is a critical spawning habitat for the Chinook salmon. The sediment is determined to be harmful to the salmon habitat because it covers the fish nests and suffocates salmon eggs. Consequently, the NFS would like to address the sediment problem and is considering what to do with the road in its LRMP.

   The first option is to close down the road and leave it as a hiking trail. Residents of Yellow Pine, a nearby logging town, contest this option because it would cut off access to their timber holdings in the forest. Even though the NFS issued a moratorium on logging in the area, the citizens of Yellow Pine claim they still have a right to access their holdings. The second option is to pave the road, which would substantially decrease the amount of washed-out sediment but increase vehicle use of the road and cause oil and other toxic runoff to enter the river. The National Marine Fishery Service declared the Chinook salmon to be a "sensitive species," and the NFS is required by law to make a decision that will benefit the salmon in the long run.

a. If the NFS determines in an environmental assessment (EA) that paving the road ultimately will benefit the salmon habitat and therefore no adverse environmental impacts will result, must it thereafter undertake the time-consuming task of preparing an EIS?

b. Suppose the NFS decides to close the road altogether to preserve the Chinook salmon's spawning habitat. It prepares an EA and thereafter files a FONSI. The citizens of Yellow Pine bring suit against NFS for violating NEPA, claiming that an EIS should have been prepared. What must the plaintiffs prove to win the suit? How will a judge review the evidence?

Explanations

1. To answer this question, you need to look again at the CEQ regulations and case law.

1a. This funding plan is major federal action because it is a federally funded and approved program, as specifically listed in the CEQ regulations at 40 C.F.R. §1508.18(a). Most federal funding qualifies as federal action because federal control is involved.

1b. Here is the exception. General state funding that does not require federal approval is exempt from the "major federal action" definition because it does not involve any federal control. This exemption is denominated as such in the above-cited CEQ regulation (40 C.F.R. §1508.18).

1c. Internal agency procedures and regulations are expressly listed as major federal action in the CEQ regulations, both in 40 C.F.R. §1508.18(a) and (b). Inclusion of internal agency policies and interpretations can be quite far-reaching in application of the EIS trigger. This extends into the internal mechanics of the agency.

1d. Administrative enforcement actions are specifically excluded from "major federal action" in 40 C.F.R. §1508.18(a). This exclusion applies to all agencies, including the EPA. Therefore, this enforcement action is not an EIS-triggering "action." It may also not qualify as "major."

2a. The first question that must be answered is whether the action of dredging the Dover harbor is a "major federal action." The Corps is a federal agency, and because it will be performing the work, this project is definitely "federal action." Under 40 C.F.R. §1508.18(b)(2), this covered federal action is an "adoption of formal plans." Recall that all six triggers must be pulled to require an EIS. One needs to analyze the remaining triggers.

Whether or not it is "major" action depends on the likely effects of the action and whether it will "significantly affect the human environment." These two concepts are intertwined. Because the sediment is contaminated, it will affect the environment wherever it is dumped. All of the possible dumping sites have their environmental drawbacks. If the Corps first does an environmental assessment (EA) to determine whether an EIS is necessary, a finding of potential "significant environmental impact" would probably be made. Therefore, depending on Explanation 2b below, the Corps would have to prepare an EIS as it develops its plans and chooses a dump site. In its EIS, the Corps would have to include all the attributes of each of the three options, both beneficial and adverse. A decision not to prepare an EIS is examined only if it is challenged by someone with standing to sue.

2b. To determine whether the ocean is part of the "human environment," it is helpful to look at the CEQ regulations: "Human environment shall . . . include the natural and physical environment and the relationship of people with that environment" (40 C.F.R. §1508.14). Humans do not live in the ocean and are not a part of the marine ecosystem. However, they rely on the resources of the ocean and use its waters for transportation and recreation. Human activities affect the marine ecosystem. Therefore, the ocean is part of the human environment, and any activities within U.S. waters that significantly affect this environment are subject to NEPA provisions.

2c. "Significant" effects are required to trigger an EIS. If an EIS is prepared, by definition some impacts are deemed to be "significant." In the EIS, the Corps would have to address the specific concerns of the government agencies and the citizen group, as well as any other important issues. In analyzing the "significance" of each effect, the Corps could follow the CEQ regulations and look at the context and the intensity of each effect.

NMFS claims that if the contaminated sediment is dumped into Area 1, the toxins would poison the fish and lower fish stocks in the area. Because fishermen frequently fish in this area, their catch would be lower and many would no longer be able to fish there. Locally, this could be a significant problem because the fishing communities rely on this trade to survive. It would be a socioeconomic impact or effect, which alone does not trigger NEPA. Nationally, the drop in fish stocks in Area 1 might not be significant, unless loss of fish is a nationwide problem. The effect of a drop in fish stocks may be more problematic if the same kind of thing is occurring in other areas; then the compounding cumulative effects could cause many fishermen to go out of business. There would also be adverse effects on the marine environment, which is covered by NEPA's physical "human environment." This cumulative concern is certainly "significant" and would have to be thoroughly considered in the EIS.

If the contaminated sediment is dumped in Area 2, NOAA is concerned about the possibility of the sediment migrating one-quarter mile south and entering the region of the Dover National Marine Sanctuary. Because the sanctuary provides protection to endangered marine species, it is certainly a critical ecological area (see 40 C.F.R. §1508.27(b)(3)). This is the physical human environment. However, the chances that the sediment will migrate into this area may not be very high. The Corps would have to gather scientific data on the water current patterns to determine if the possibility of migration is within the scope of NEPA. While the risk of occurrence may be small, however, the consequences could be great. Even a low probability of a major impact can be significant and trigger NEPA. Moreover, because the effects would be on the *physical* environment of the sanctuary, the *Metropolitan Edison* case is not a bar and such a risk is within the scope of NEPA.

Finally, the concern of Sailors for Sealife is that ocean dumping in general causes significant adverse effects on the marine ecosystem. Because little is known about the vulnerability of the marine ecosystem, the Corps may determine these claims to be too tenuous, indirect, and speculative to require an EIS. Can dumping in one area destroy the ecosystem of a massive body of water? There is some evidence that local sea life will suffer, but this may be localized and not "significant" in the NEPA context. However, the sediment is toxic, and the environmental effects it will have on the marine ecosystem must be considered by the Corps in an EIS, even though concerns of Sailors for Sealife are not as "significant" as those of the agencies.

2d. NOAA's decision not to expand the sanctuary boundaries, and thereby eliminate Area 2 from consideration for a dump site, is not a "major federal action" and therefore does not trigger the EIS requirement under NEPA. Courts have found that an agency's *inaction* does not require an EIS, even if the effects of the inaction significantly affect the environment. See *District of Columbia v. Schramm*, 631 F.2d 854 (D.C. Cir. 1980) (no EIS required regarding EPA's refusal to veto a state water pollution discharge permit on grounds that it had delegated authority to the state even though the EPA had authority to veto the permit); see also *Defenders of Wildlife v. Andrus*, 627 F.2d 1238 (D.C. Cir. 1980), *supra* (the Department of the Interior's refusal to prohibit a wolf kill instigated by the state of Alaska to protect caribou herds did not require the preparation of an EIS for its decision not to act). NOAA has chosen not to act by declining to expand the sanctuary's borders. Under CEQ regulations, agencies are required to prepare an EIS for "failure to act" when such a decision is reviewable under the Administrative Procedure Act (APA). See 40 C.F.R. §1508.18. The standard for reviewable agency decisions under the APA is "arbitrary and capricious" action. In this case, NOAA's failure to act will not be judicially reviewable because the agency's decision is afforded great discretion.

2e. If the Corps finds that there are no significant impacts on the human environment from dumping in Area 1, prepares a FONSI rather than an EIS, and ultimately does not consider the socioeconomic or psychological effects on the fishing community by dumping in this area, then Fishing in Fear would have to reckon with the precedent of *Metropolitan Edison*. There the court held that risk of psychological harm was not enough *alone* to trigger NEPA's preparation of an EIS. However, if the Corps prepares an EIS for any reason, these nonphysical impacts must be evaluated either as secondary, indirect effects from dumping sediment in Area 1 or as socioeconomic effects interrelated with the direct physical effects on the fishing area. Note that if these effects are proven to be "reasonably foreseeable," Fishing in Fear may prevail, and the Corps would have to include these effects in its FEIS (see 40 C.F.R. §1508.8(b)). However, if the causal connection between the dumping and the adverse socioeconomic and psychological effects suffered by the fishing community is too attenuated, Fishing in Fear will not be able to require consideration of these nonproximate impacts.

3a. NEPA requires an EIS even if the final effects of the federal action ultimately benefit the environment. More simply stated, either adverse or beneficial impacts — if significant on the human environment — trigger an EIS. Moreover, both the adverse and beneficial impacts of a proposal must be analyzed in an EIS (see 40 C.F.R. §1508.8(b) and §1508.14). In this case, even if paving the road is beneficial overall, the risk of toxic run-off may still affect the salmon habitat, and there is still the option of closing the road altogether. The NFS must explore all aspects of these possibilities in an EIS. If it does not, it violates the requirements of NEPA. Consequences that ultimately benefit the environment must be examined under NEPA especially if the long-term benefits are accompanied by some adverse trade-offs.

3b. NFS rendered a threshold determination of no significant impact for its decision to close the access road. The citizens of Yellow Pine must prove that this is a major federal action that will have a significant effect on the human environment. They must demonstrate that closing the road satisfies each of these criteria. Using the CEQ regulations as a guide, the citizens can argue that closing the road is major federal action because it is a project sponsored by NFS and because it will fundamentally change the character of the local environment; some case law on agency inaction is to the contrary. Beneficial effects, such as preserving the spawning ground for a sensitive species, are considered significant by the CEQ (40 C.F.R. §1508.27(b)(1)); therefore, the citizens could argue that the act of closing the road will affect the environment of the river by eliminating the sediment problem and protecting the Chinook salmon.

In court, the judge will use the "arbitrary and capricious" standard of review, taking a "hard look" to determine if the agency's decision, in light of the circumstances, was supportable. Doing this as part of the court's procedural review allows the judge to evaluate the significance of the impacts. If the court determines that the decision not to prepare an EIS was unwarranted under the circumstances, it will require the NFS to prepare an EIS before coming to a final decision on its major federal action. Preparing an EIS would obviously delay all action pending NEPA compliance.

TIMING AND SCOPE OF THE EIS

Once an agency makes the threshold decision that an EIS is necessary, the next step is to determine *when* in the planning process the impact statement should be prepared, and the *scope* of what it should consider. These questions, often intertwined, are critical to NEPA's implementation. The usefulness of an EIS depends upon when it is prepared and what it includes.

Agencies are faced with the following considerations: (1) Should an EIS be prepared in the early stages of a plan in order to highlight environmental considerations and consequences associated with fundamental policy decisions? (2) If a national program is implemented, should an agency prepare an EIS for each region? (3) Should a separate EIS be prepared for every action taken in a particular area, or will one comprehensive EIS suffice? (4) If more information about environmental impacts is collected after an EIS has been prepared, must an agency prepare a supplemental EIS (SEIS)? Each of these questions has an answer in the who, what, where, and when of NEPA.

When: Timing of the EIS

Federal agencies constantly undertake, fund, and approve projects, and deciding when in the planning process to prepare an impact statement frequently presents a major dilemma. If an EIS is prepared too early in the planning process, the agency may not have enough information available to make a worthwhile environmental analysis. On the other hand, if an agency waits too long to prepare a statement, it may delay the progress of underlying actions or commit itself to a particular decision such that an impact statement becomes merely a rationalization for what the agency already intends to do.

Some federal courts use the "ripeness" doctrine, which allows them to decline review of an agency decision unless it is final, to avoid requiring agencies to prepare an EIS (see Chapter 2). Agencies engaged in preliminary planning and decision making are protected by the "ripeness" doctrine from challengers claiming that an impact statement should be prepared at a particular stage. Because the ripeness doctrine is court made, courts retain ample flexibility to determine when to review an agency decision. While this approach resolves timing questions in some cases, by nature it avoids addressing the substantive issue of when NEPA requires an impact statement to be prepared.

In the first case to directly address the timing question under NEPA, *Scientists Inst. for Pub. Info., Inc. (SIPI) v. Atomic Energy Comm'n (AEC)*, 481 F.2d 1079 (D.C. Cir. 1973), the AEC issued a program plan to further the development of the liquid-metal fast breeder reactor. The agency neglected to prepare an EIS for the research and development program as a whole. The court held that an impact statement was required for the entire program because it was an "action" under NEPA. The *SIPI* court applied a policy-oriented and flexible balancing test, requiring a case-by-case application of the timing requirement. This approach, however, was short lived.

Two years later, the Supreme Court considered the timing question for the first time in *Aberdeen & Rockfish R.R. v. Students Challenging Regulatory Agency Procedures (SCRAP II)*, 422 U.S. 289 (1975). The timing question was considered for a formal agency ratemaking proceeding. The Interstate Commerce Commission (ICC) issued a report on a proposed general increase in railroad rates, after an informal hearing. SCRAP claimed the ICC should have prepared an impact statement on the proposed rate increase before issuing its report. The Supreme Court held that the ICC was not required to prepare an impact statement until after it had issued its report, stating "the time at which the agency must prepare the final 'statement' is the time at which it makes a recommendation or report on a *proposal* for federal action." By adopting this formal, mechanical approach to solve the timing question, the Court impliedly rejected the policy-based balancing test used by the *SIPI* court. While some would argue that the holding in *SCRAP II* is limited to formal agency hearings, subsequent cases apply its precedent widely.

The Supreme Court again addressed the timing issue and reinforced its *SCRAP II* decision in *Kleppe v. Sierra Club*, 427 U.S. 390 (1976). The Department of the Interior (DOI), in an effort to review its domestic coal leasing program, prepared a comprehensive EIS for coal development throughout the nation. The Northern Great Plains, a region composed of portions of four states (eastern Montana, northeastern Wyoming, and western areas of North and South Dakota), was the subject of three different studies over ten years, the third of which was devoted entirely to assessing potential environmental, social, and economic impacts of resource development in this area. While the DOI conceded that impact statements would be needed for coal leasing activities at specific sites, it did not prepare a regional EIS because there was no recommendation on a proposal for major federal action with respect to the Northern Great Plains. The court agreed with the DOI, and held that the express language of NEPA §102(2)(C) required an EIS to be prepared only upon a proposal for major federal action. The regional studies alone were not enough to trigger the statute. The Supreme Court clarified that courts are required to take a "hard look" at the environmental effects of proposed actions.

Exactly what constitutes the key concept of a "proposal" is not expressly defined in this decision. The Supreme Court held that even if the DOI was considering federal action in this region, contemplation of a project accompanied by a study does not necessarily result in "a proposal for major federal action." The court indicated that regardless of the statutory language of NEPA, a regional EIS could not be prepared "for practical reasons." Lower federal courts mirror the Supreme Court's restrictive holdings on the timing requirement, and they likewise reflect the ambiguities that run through the Kleppe decision. Some circuits concentrate on a precise definition of "proposal" and ultimately defer to the agency's determination that a proposal has not occurred. Other circuits stress the practical ineffectiveness of preparing an EIS too early in the decision-making process, in order to hold that an impact statement is not required, or that preliminary agency actions or proceedings are not final decisions or proposals under NEPA and therefore do not require an impact statement.

The CEQ regulations explicitly address the timing question, attempting to codify and elaborate on the relevant case law. Consider whether the interpretive problems found in Kleppe are reconciled by the CEQ's definition of "proposal" and its attempt to outline the timing of an impact statement.

"Proposal" exists at that stage in the development of an action when an agency subject to the Act has a goal and is actively preparing to make a decision on one or more alternative means of accomplishing that goal and the effects can be meaningfully evaluated. Preparation of an environmental impact statement on a proposal should be timed (§1502.5) so that a final statement may be completed in time for the statement to be included in any recommendation or report on the proposal. A proposal may exist in fact as well as by agency declaration that one exists. 40 C.F.R. §1508.23. An agency shall commence preparation of an environmental impact statement as close as possible to the time the agency is developing or is presented with a proposal (§1508.23) so that preparation can be completed in time for the final statement to be included in any recommendation or report on the proposal. The statement shall be prepared early enough so that it can serve practically as an important contribution to the decision making process and will not be used to rationalize or justify decisions already made. 40 C.F.R. §1502.5.

Finally, the following CEQ section reinforces §1502.5, outlining policy considerations for integrating NEPA with agency planning at early stages.

Agencies shall integrate the NEPA process with other planning at the earliest possible time to insure that planning and decisions reflect environmental values, to avoid delays later in the process, and to head off potential conflicts. 40 C.F.R. §1501.2 [in part].

Upon a full reading of CEQ directives, it is apparent that agencies are given considerable discretion for determining *when* in the planning process an impact statement should be prepared. This is consistent with both the Supreme Court's statutory interpretation of "proposal" in *Kleppe* and the "ripeness" doctrine, which precludes judicial intervention until agency actions are sufficiently final.

Who, What, and Where: Scope of the EIS

Before a federal agency prepares an EIS, it must determine the *scope* of the impact statement. The purpose of "scoping" is to identify issues related to the proposed action and to decide whether an action should be evaluated individually or together with other actions. The agency also must evaluate alternative measures to the proposed action and analyze these alternatives in its EIS.

The CEQ regulations offer general guidance to agencies in 40 C.F.R. §1508.25, which requires consideration of three types of *actions*, three types of *alternatives*, and three types of *impacts* in determining the scope of an EIS. Exhibit 3.4 is a 3 × 3 matrix of these scoping categories. Let's examine how the CEQ and the courts attempt to resolve these issues.

3.4 EIS Scoping Categories

Actions	Alternatives	Impacts
Connected actions	Primary	Direct
Cumulative actions	Secondary	Indirect
Similar actions	No action	Cumulative

Actions: Program Impact Statements, Segmentation, and the Small Handle Problem

Here we present the first trio — this time describing types of *actions*. The first question a federal agency must address is whether or not the EIS should consider a single action or a number of related actions. In addition, an agency must decide if its action is part of a larger project such that it must consider the larger project in its review of the action. Here are the three types of actions to consider in an EIS, outlined by the CEQ regulations.

(1) *Connected actions*, which means that they are closely related and therefore should be discussed in the same impact statement. Actions are connected if they:
  (i) Automatically trigger other actions which may require environmental impact statements.
  (ii) Cannot or will not proceed unless other actions are taken previously or simultaneously.
  (iii) Are interdependent parts of a larger action and depend on the larger action for their justification.
(2) *Cumulative actions*, which when viewed with other proposed actions have cumulatively significant impacts and should therefore be discussed in the same project impact statement.
(3) *Similar actions*, which when viewed with other reasonably foreseeable or proposed agency actions, have similarities that provide a basis for evaluating their environmental consequences together, such as common timing or geography. 40 C.F.R. §1508.25(a) [in part].

In sum, *connected actions* are those actions that somehow trigger, precede, or are interdependent on other actions, all of which significantly affect the environment. *Cumulative actions* are related to each other when their impacts, considered together, significantly affect the environment. "NEPA and implementing statutes require that 'when several proposals for action will have cumulative or synergistic environmental impact, their environmental consequences must be considered together.'" *Sierra Club v. Penfold*, 664 F. Supp. 1299, 1303 (D. Alaska 1987) (quoting *Kleppe v. Sierra Club*, 427 U.S. 390 (1976)). *Similar actions* are related geographically or are proposed at the same time. A federal proposal for a plan may involve one or a combination of these types of actions.

Program Impact Statements When an agency includes a number of related actions together in one impact statement, it is known as a program environmental impact statement (PEIS). If a PEIS is prepared at the outset of a federal project, the agency will decide later whether or not additional "site-specific" impact statements will be needed for each individual action. Where "an agency has prepared an EIS for a large action, the regulations encourage it to incorporate EIS conclusions into EAs prepared for smaller, subsequent actions." *Newton County Wildlife Ass'n v. Arkansas Forestry Ass'n*, 141 F.3d 803 (8th Cir. 1998); *Sierra Club v. Penfold*, 664 F. Supp. 1299 (D. Alaska 1987).

The CEQ regulations use the term "broad federal actions" to refer to programs that would require a PEIS. Guidance is given in 40 C.F.R. §1502.4(c) to evaluate broad federal actions (1) *geographically*, which includes actions planned for the same general location; (2) *generically*, which includes actions with relevant similarities such as timing, impacts, or alternatives; and (3) *technologically*, which refers to the stages of development for new technologies that could significantly impact the environment. So here is another trio within a triplet.

As discussed earlier, an impact statement is required only when an agency makes a *proposal*. A court may have no difficulty in finding a single, well-defined action to be a proposal; however, it becomes more problematic to view a group of interrelated actions as one comprehensive, well-defined program. The Supreme Court considered this question, prior to any CEQ regulations, in *Kleppe*, where the DOI's national coal development program was challenged by the Sierra Club because no PEIS had been prepared to assess the cumulative impacts of individual coal leases in the Northern Great Plains Region. The Court found no final proposal regarding this region, and therefore no impact statement was required. It did concede, however, that if a number of related actions are proposed at the same time, NEPA may require a PEIS if these proposed actions have a *cumulative* environmental impact on a particular region.

The CEQ regulations embody and make some attempt to clarify the standard set under the *Kleppe* decision. Lower courts have recognized the limits of judicial review under the arbitrary and capricious standard, and they generally confirm agency discretion when agencies claim a PEIS is not required.

If an agency prepares a PEIS, it may still be required to prepare a subsequent impact statement on site-specific actions. This process is called "tiering." Pursuant to 40 C.F.R. §1502.20, after a PEIS has been prepared, an agency need only incorporate by reference any of the broader issues discussed in the PEIS in subsequent statements or environmental assessments concerning each subsequent individual action.

Segmentation Problems   On the opposite side of the coin is the segmentation problem. In situations where federal agencies plan a number of related actions but decide to prepare individual impact statements for each action, a "segmentation" problem may develop. A good illustration of this type of problem is found in highway development planning. The highway agency may divide a highway plan into two segments of roadway and prepare impact statements for each segment. The first segment has no environmental impacts, and the agency proceeds to build it.

The second segment, however, runs through a wilderness area and therefore has significant environmental impacts. Because the two highway projects were not considered together, the agency essentially committed itself by constructing the first segment. If a comprehensive EIS had been prepared, the agency could have considered rerouting the road or reviewed its plan in light of the overall environmental consequences.

Similarly, segmentation can affect whether or not an action is deemed "major." By segmenting a project into many smaller slices, an agency can avoid proposing a "major federal action significantly affecting the quality of the human environment." This type of segmentation allows some agencies to circumvent NEPA's purposes.

Where federal funding was isolated to preliminary studies and feasibility analyses that were preliminary to permitting or construction, notwithstanding that the eventual project construction would have significant environmental impacts, courts have found that these segmented actions "lacked the degree of decision making power, authority, or control . . . needed to render it a major federal action." *Ka Makini O'Kohala Ohana, Inc. v. Hawaii*, 295 F.3d 955, 960 (9th Cir. 2002). Moreover, if the situation is reversed, and the federal government funds an earlier stage of a project but does not fund an unrelated extension or a later not interrelated stage of that project, absent any other EIS triggers, the former funding of a discrete element of a project does not forever link it to "major federal action" requiring perpetual EISs at every stage. *City of Boston v. Volpe*, 464 F.2d 254 (1st Cir. 1972).

However, where segmentation creates two projects, and neither can stand alone, this can result in the part with major federal action causing the entire aspect of the two projects to be federalized. See *Hawthorne Environmental Association v. Coleman*, 417 F. Supp. 1091 (N.D. Ga. 1976) (where no independent utility to the two segments, an EIS is required for entire highway project); cf. *Citizens for Balanced Environment and Transportation, Inc. v. Volpe*, 376 F. Supp. 806 (D. Conn. 1974). Any successful segmentation must occur *ab initio*: Stopping taking future federal funds after already accepting some, in an effort to avoid preparation of an EIS, has not been successful. *Ely v. Velde*, 497 F.2d 252 (4th Cir. 1974); *Thomasine Ross v. Federal Highway Administration*, 162 F.3d 1046 (10th Cir. 1998) (withdrawing federal funds for the last segment of a highway project funded up until then by federal funds could not successfully de-federalize the action so as to avoid an EIS, where the last highway segment had no independent utility).

The *Kleppe* decision, some argue, affects segmentation cases because it implies that actions that do not require a PEIS can be properly segmented for environmental review. In *Envt'l Defense Fund v. Marsh*, 651 F.2d 983 (5th Cir. 1981), the court took a different view of *Kleppe* in allowing the segmentation of a waterway project. The EDF court held that *Kleppe* did leave room for the prohibition of segmentation, and if an agency has used segmentation to arbitrarily violate the NEPA mandate, courts could require a PEIS for two or more projects, even if one is not yet proposed. See *Preserve Endangered Areas v. U.S. Army Corps*, 87 F.3d 1242 (11th Cir. 1996).

The Small Handle Problem   Federal permits, leases, or approvals for non-federal action may be too small or insignificant to trigger NEPA. This has given rise to the "small handle problem." Often a nonfederal project of which federal approval is a small part will result in significant environmental consequences if it is implemented. A number of projects receive some federal funding as a small incentive or to finance part of development efforts. Technically, the CEQ regulations specify that any direct financial aid to a project is "major federal action." While courts have not spoken with uniformity, there is significant sentiment for not triggering preparation of an Environmental Impact Statement for incidental federal funding. Under NEPA, unless the action is "major federal action," no EIS is required.

Courts have split as to whether to apply a dual standard or a unitary standard in analyzing small federal handles. Under the dual standard, there must be federal action that is truly major, *and* there must be significant environmental impact from the project. Under the unitary standard, there is no inquiry as to the substantive size of federal action, and the only question is whether there is significant impact on the environment from the project that has some federal involvement. See, for example, *City of Davis v. Coleman*, 521 F.2d 661 (9th Cir. 1975).

The trend is for courts to adopt the dual standard. See *National Association for the Advancement of Colored People v. The Medical Center, Inc.*, 584 F.2d 619 (3d Cir. 1978) (court must determine both whether the agency action is "major" and whether it has significant effects on the environment, pursuant to the express language of NEPA). Where the federal financial involvement is relatively small, the dual analysis can conclude that even where there is a significant environmental impact, there is no "major federal action" to require an EIS, absent other factors. *Landmark West! v. United States Postal Service*, 840 F. Supp. 994 (S.D.N.Y. 1993) (Postal Service contribution of $9.8 million toward a $250 million project was not major federal action).

An irony is that as projects and their environmental impacts get larger, it makes partial federal funding of that project a smaller percentage. Therefore, for very large projects that have significant environmental impacts, a set amount of federal financing may be a small percentage of total funding and qualify the project under the small handle doctrine to not require preparation of an EIS. Thus, smaller projects may be more subject to requirements to prepare an EIS, because federal funding constitutes a larger percentage of the total project financing.

Other courts, however, require the federal agency to examine the consequences of its action in the context of the entire project's impacts. In *Colo. River Indian Tribes v. Marsh*, 605 F. Supp. 1425 (D.C. Cal. 1985), the district

3.5 Three Kinds of Agency Paradigms

Paradigm	Program EIS	Segmentation	Small Federal Handle
Result	One EIS	No EIS	No EIS

court held that a permit from the Army Corps of Engineers to reinforce a riverbank, as part of a 150-acre private development project, required an EIS that included the potential environmental consequences of the entire development project. According to this court, NEPA implicitly requires reasonable forecasting of environmental effects of *any* project with federal involvement. Exhibit 3.5 reviews these issues.

Alternatives to the Proposed Action

Recall that NEPA mandates a process to consider environmental actions and impacts. Under the NEPA statute, federal agencies must also consider and discuss alternatives to their proposed actions. The CEQ describes the alternative requirement as the heart of NEPA. The statute requires agencies to consider alternatives both in a formal impact statement and *during* agency planning even when no EIS is required.

Alternatives are other methods, besides the proposed action, that an agency might employ to meet its objective. Agencies must determine whether they can accomplish their actions in less environmentally damaging ways or whether implementing an alternative makes the proposed action unnecessary. What alternatives an agency must discuss, and how many alternatives must be included in an analysis, are important questions that sculpt the scope of an impact statement.

There are two types of alternatives: primary and secondary. *Primary* alternatives are substitutes for the proposed action that will achieve similar results. For example, electric power production can be accomplished through burning coal as an alternative to building a nuclear power facility. *Secondary* alternatives are different ways in which an agency can go about its proposed action: Changing the location of a proposed housing project, or the materials used in a construction project, are examples. Agencies are more willing to examine secondary alternatives, as they are considerations that normally would be addressed in any planning phase. There also is a "no action" alternative, representing the status quo.

The more difficult challenge is how agencies deal with primary alternatives to their proposed actions, and this is the issue most frequently litigated in court. One of the leading cases addressing alternatives is *Natural Res.*

Def. Council, Inc. (NRDC) *v. Morton*, 458 F.2d 827 (D.C. Cir. 1972). In *Morton*, the DOI prepared an impact statement on a proposal for a lease sale for offshore gas and oil drilling rights, fostered in response to the nation's perceived energy shortage. No alternatives to addressing the energy crisis besides off-shore lease sales were discussed in the EIS. The DOI argued that the alternatives which must be discussed in an EIS are only those which the proposing agency is empowered to adopt.

The court in *Morton* held to the contrary. It read NEPA's alternative requirement to be very broad. Under this interpretation, federal agencies must discuss *all* relevant primary alternatives, even if they are beyond the scope of the agency's statutory authority. If the alternative requires legislative or administrative action, it still must be discussed by the agency. The court emphasized that an agency's discussion of alternatives must be subject to a "rule of reason."

Six years later, the Supreme Court addressed the issue of an agency's consideration of primary alternatives by significantly narrowing the *Morton* decision. *Vt. Yankee Nuclear Power Corp.* (*Vermont Yankee*) *v. Natural Res. Def. Council* (NRDC), 435 U.S. 519 (1978), gave the Court the opportunity to place important qualifications on the alternatives that federal agencies must consider. The Nuclear Regulatory Commission's (NRC) licensing board had declined to consider energy conservation issues during proceedings for a nuclear reactor license application. The NRC claimed that evidence was insufficient to warrant consideration of energy conservation; the proponents, on the other hand, indicated that energy conservation measures would eliminate the need to build more nuclear power plants.

The Supreme Court affirmed the "rule of reason" standard adopted in *Morton* but ruled that remote and speculative alternatives need not be considered. An EIS did not have to include "every alternative device and thought conceivable by the mind of man." The Court held that considering energy conservation, a broad and evolving concept, as an alternative to licensing a nuclear reactor, did not withstand the rule of reason and was beyond the scope of NEPA.

Vermont Yankee cut back the *Morton* decision by eliminating the requirement to consider alternatives that had not yet been fully studied. This decision undercut some of NEPA's basic policies, for it is the agency that has the knowledge, expertise, and resources to study an alternative and determine its merits. By placing the burden of presenting evidence of alternatives on the ordinary citizen or community group, the Court effectively narrowed the scope of agency review and the impact of NEPA on agency decision making.

The regulations later promulgated by the CEQ codify the rule of reason standard adopted in *Morton* and later affirmed in *Vermont Yankee*. In sum, here is the third and final trio of elements — the three required alternatives. Under 40 C.F.R. §1508.25, the scope of an impact statement includes three types of alternatives: (1) the no-action alternative, (2) other reasonable courses of action, and (3) mitigation measures not in the proposed action. The regulations also require agencies to consider alternatives outside their jurisdiction. Regarding license and permit situations, like the one in *Vermont Yankee*, the CEQ published a guidance memorandum stating that feasible alternatives must be considered, while remote and speculative alternatives may be ignored.

When Again: The Supplemental EIS

The world is an ever-changing arena. After preparing a final impact statement, new information or new circumstances can arise which may require an agency to prepare a supplemental EIS (SEIS). Nowhere does the statutory language of NEPA expressly make such a requirement, but the CEQ included guidelines for preparing an SEIS in specific circumstances:

> Agencies . . .
>
> (1) Shall prepare supplements to either draft or final environmental impact statements if:
>
> (i) The agency makes substantial changes in the proposed action that are relevant to environmental concerns; or
>
> (ii) There are significant new circumstances or information relevant to environmental concerns and bearing on the proposed action or its impacts. 40 C.F.R. §1502.9(c).

Is this regulating standard for determining when an SEIS is necessary entirely clear? Hardly. When new information is "significant," and whether or not a change is "substantial," are matters of opinion. An SEIS may be required where there is "reliance on stale scientific evidence," rendered stale by either the passage of time or new intervening events. See *City of Carmel v. Dep't of Transp.*, 95 F.3d 892 (9th Cir. 1996) (the intervening Loma Prieta earthquake could have altered wetlands and other environmental characteristics since the original studies undergirding the EIS). In *Marsh v. Oregon Natural Resources Council*, 490 U.S. 360 (1989), the Court construed an agency's duty to prepare an SEIS. The court found that, as in agency decisions made for the preparation of the initial impact statement, agency determinations regarding whether to prepare an SEIS must follow the "rule of reason":

> If there remains "major federal action" to occur, and if the new information is sufficient to show that the remaining action will "affect the quality of the human environment" in a significant manner or to a significant extent not already considered, a supplemental . . . [impact statement] must be prepared.

The *Marsh* court adopted the set of factors in the checklist below to determine whether an SEIS is necessary:

1. Environmental significance of the new information.
2. Accuracy of the new information.
3. Significance to which the agency considers and evaluates new information for its environmental impact.
4. Degree to which the agency's decision not to prepare SEIS is supported by explanation or additional data.

If new information is not environmentally significant, then it is not necessary for an agency to prepare a supplemental impact statement. At the time an SEIS is considered there must remain "major federal action" to be taken, such as federal permitting. An agency's decision not to prepare an SEIS is judged by the courts under an "arbitrary and capricious" standard. Therefore, agencies retain great discretion to decide whether new issues necessitate a supplemental impact statement.

Examples

1. The Department of Housing and Urban Development (HUD) is planning to construct a series of Native American housing projects for the Oglala Sioux, who live on the Pine Ridge Reservation in South Dakota. The agency is contemplating building two separate projects, each containing 25 home units, to be located in two different areas of the reservation. HUD commissioned a study of the reservation to better determine where to build the units. One of the areas studied is known to the Sioux as sacred ground where they often perform religious ceremonies. Another level area is a short distance from the reservation dump site. Finally, HUD evaluated a third area, not far from the main highway running through the reservation. Although the new homes are much needed, some Native American activists oppose building on sacred ground and are concerned about developing homes near the dump site. They want HUD to undertake an EIS on the proposed building sites, but HUD refuses.

    a. Under the *Kleppe* doctrine, at what point is HUD expected to prepare an EA or an EIS for this project? Enumerate some of the considerations for determining when an impact statement should be prepared.

    b. Can you make an argument, using case law and CEQ regulations, supporting the Native American activists' contention that HUD should prepare an impact statement for each possible location before finalizing the plan?

    c. How would your answer to (a) change if you applied the balancing test used in *SIPI v. AEC*?

2. The Federal Highway Administration (FHA) has agreed to fund the reconstruction of a major road artery that runs north-south through the city of Wilton. The State Highway Department (Department) must develop plans for construction and submit them to the FHA for approval prior to receiving the funding. The artery presently runs from the north along the coast, passes through the center of the city, and then terminates where it intersects the interstate highway seven miles south of Wilton. It is always congested because of the large amount of commuter traffic into Wilton.

   The Department divided its plan into three segments. The first involves rerouting the northern section of the highway further inland so that it connects to the northern interstate, which will provide out-of-state commuters with better access to Wilton. Doing this will also improve the aesthetic value of the coastal area and allow restoration of the coastal wetlands. The second segment involves expanding the portion of the artery that runs through the city from four lanes to eight, and submerging this highway segment underground to reduce auto emissions into the air and improve the central city. Finally, the Department would like to extend the southern section of the artery another five miles so that it will be more accessible to growing communities along the southern shore.

   The FHA has prepared an impact statement on the project, as required before approving the state plan and providing funds. A local environmental group, the Watchdogs, would like to file a suit against the FHA for violating NEPA. It claims that the EIS prepared by the FHA does not consider primary alternatives to reconstructing the artery, such as building a mass-transit system to transport commuters, which also would reduce air pollution from auto emissions as well as traffic congestion.

   a. If you worked for the FHA, how would you evaluate the highway proposal from the state when determining the scope of the impact statement? Refer to the CEQ regulations. What type of action is this? What kind of impact statement might you prepare? What alternatives and impacts should you consider?

   b. If you were to draft the brief for the Watchdogs, what arguments would you raise in support of their claims?

   c. If the FHA approves the state plan and refuses to prepare an EIS because it does not believe its actions constitute "major federal action," what problem does this present? Are there any arguments to support a claim that the reconstruction is "major federal action"?

   d. In anticipation of the challenge by the Watchdogs, the Department decides to submit each segment of the plan as a separate project to the FHA. Accordingly, the FHA analyzes the environmental impacts of each plan separately. What problem may result from this decision? How do you think the court would resolve a challenge to it?

e. Assume that the FHA makes a final decision to approve the state plan and prepares an EIS regarding the action. After construction begins, the federal and state departments become aware of a ventilation problem in the underground section of the new highway. To remedy this problem, special vents must be constructed that will release concentrated auto exhaust fumes from the dense underground artery traffic. The initial EIS did not include discussion of these vents, and the project is already under way. What is the proper NEPA response?

Explanations

1a. Under the *Kleppe* doctrine, HUD would be expected to prepare an EA or an EIS at the time it presented a proposal for federal action. "Proposal" itself is not expressly defined, but mere *contemplation* of a project by an agency, even when accompanied by a study, is not enough to trigger NEPA. *Kleppe* also suggests that certain "practical" considerations may affect the timing of an EIS.

In our problem, HUD still is contemplating its building scheme and has not officially made a *proposal* about building two housing projects. The study it has undertaken of three separate areas is not enough action in itself to require an EIS under the *Kleppe* doctrine. The concern that HUD may have about preparing an EIS prematurely, before completing the study, is that it may not have enough information to prepare an EIS. Because the timing obligation is judged under an "arbitrary and capricious" standard, HUD has discretion as to when it officially makes a "proposal." The activists must wait until HUD makes a recommendation or a proposal before the matter is ripe to press in court.

1b. According to 40 C.F.R. §1508.23 of the CEQ regulations, a "proposal" exists when an agency "has a goal and is actively preparing to make a decision on one or more alternative means of accomplishing that goal. . . ." Even so, this is hardly an example of regulatory clarity. The activists could argue that HUD has a goal: It wishes to build 50 housing units on the Pine Ridge Reservation. Deciding whether or not to build in one or two project blocks is deciding between alternatives, and as a prerequisite to any decision an EIS is necessary. If HUD were to decide on the basis of the studies, before an EIS, to build two projects, then a subsequent EIS would only serve as a tool for determining locations upon which to build.

By preparing an EIS for each site while it is studied and before any decision, HUD's decisions will be aided and informed by the impact statement. Under *Kleppe*, the "practical considerations" that the activists can invoke include the argument that the preparation of an EIS early in the project planning will be more effective in helping HUD plan its construction strategy. However, if HUD is not moved by these arguments, most courts will side with the agency's decision to wait, because the "arbitrary and capricious" standard under which a court can overturn an agency's decision is so limiting.

1c. The *SIPI* court adopted a policy-oriented and flexible balancing test to reconcile the competing concerns arising in a timing determination. The court in this case would look at whatever information is available this early in the decision-making process to determine if an EIS would be practical and effective. Finally, if the court interpreted the entire construction program as one action under NEPA, it could mandate an impact statement at the initial decision stages. This balancing test was rejected by the Supreme Court in *SCRAP II* and in *Kleppe*; however, some argue that the CEQ regulations suggest that balancing concerns may be appropriate.

2a. The CEQ regulations, 40 C.F.R. §1508.25, direct agencies to consider three types of actions, three types of alternatives, and three types of impacts. This is our rule of three set out in Exhibit 3.4 *supra*. Let's start with "actions." The first issue to be considered is, What type of action is this project? Actions can be of three types: (1) connected, (2) cumulative, or (3) similar, as well as independent and unconnected. The reconstruction of the artery is presented in three work segments that appear to be connected because they are closely related and interdependent parts of a larger action. Each segment is part of the whole highway project. The rule is that where segments proceed dependently, all should be connected in the same impact statement.

Second, the EIS must consider three types of alternatives: (1) the no-action alternative, (2) other reasonable primary and secondary courses of action, and (3) mitigation measures not in the proposed action. Building or expanding a mass transit system might be considered an alternative to reconstructing the highway. A combination of reconstruction and enhanced mass transit improvements may be an alternative, as well as a mitigation measure to the highway reconstruction. In addition to a "no-build" alternative, therefore, designs for mass transit or other mitigation must be included in the EIS.

The scope of the EIS must include the three types of impacts — (1) direct, (2) indirect, and (3) cumulative — that would accompany the building of a larger highway. The impacts might include air pollution, traffic congestion, the possibility of more commuters, coastal erosion, the effect of construction on the city, and so on. *Cumulative* impacts could be particularly nettlesome. Any infrastructure improvements that lessen travel times are likely to encourage additional commuter trips over time, thus adversely affecting the environment in the long run. Mitigation must focus on both the construction and permanent phases of the project.

Finally, the FHA may wish to prepare a PEIS on the entire highway project, especially if it is funding other such projects around the nation. This way, the entire project could be examined as a whole. Later, additional impact statements could be prepared on each segment. The decision on what type of impact statement to prepare rests within the FHA's discretion, and any judicial review would apply an "arbitrary and capricious" standard.

2b. The Watchdogs want to challenge the FHA impact statement because it fails to discuss *primary* alternatives to the highway reconstruction project. Primary alternatives are possible actions that can substitute for the proposed action. Implementing a mass transit system to address the traffic congestion and pollution problem is a primary alternative. Even if the FHA chooses to fund the highway reconstruction project anyway, it still must first consider in good faith primary alternatives in its impact statement. Under *Morton* and *Vermont Yankee*, federal agencies are required to consider alternatives that are reasonable. Mass transit is the quintessential alternative utilized by other cities to reduce traffic congestion and transport commuters. To ignore the possibility altogether would violate NEPA and its policies. Finally, the CEQ regulations require in 40 C.F.R. §1508.25(b) that an agency consider the no-action alternative.

2c. The FHA may believe that simple approval of a project is not enough to constitute "major federal action." This situation illustrates the "small handle" problem, where a minor federal action initiates other action that may cause a significant effect on the environment. Courts take different positions on the small handle problem, some requiring the approving agency to review the entire action, others upholding the federal agency decision that the approval is not major federal action. Federal funds given to state agencies to aid in implementing a state plan generally are not considered major federal action unless the state plan requires federal approval.

In this case, the FHA is in a weak position because, in addition to approval, it is also allotting funds to the state-level department for the highway project. If it is the federal government that is enabling a nonfederal entity to act, then courts deem the action to be federal. See *SIPI v. AEC*, 481 F.2d 1079 (D.C. Cir. 1973) (federal research and development program would lead to the development of private facilities); see also *Davis v. Coleman*, 521 F.2d 661 (9th Cir. 1975) (federally funded highway interchange would attract new industrial growth). In this situation the FHA is both approving and funding the state project; hence the project is considered major federal action.

2d. If the FHA looks at each highway reconstruction segment as a separate project and prepares individual impact statements on each, it will not be able to assess the cumulative environmental impacts of the entire project. This is the classic segmentation problem, in which the agency myopically focuses on the trees and misses the forest. For instance, the first segment involves rerouting the northern leg of the highway further inland, connecting it to an interstate highway. The environmental impacts of this project segment may be beneficial, especially if the coastal area is improved by the action and the restoration of coastal wetlands becomes possible. If the FHA approved this plan, construction would begin, committing the department and the FHA to further action. Constructing the other two segments, however, might create a larger number of adverse environmental impacts.

Some argue that the _Kleppe_ precedent allows segmentation when a PEIS is not required. However, other courts hold that a PEIS could be required if the agency uses segmentation to avoid analyzing the cumulative impacts of a project and thus arbitrarily violates the NEPA mandate. In the present case, the department is purposeful in segmenting its project, wishing to avoid litigation with the Watchdogs. For purposes of the EIS, the department may be considered arbitrary in its approval of such a segmented plan.

2e. The ventilation problem and its "solution" through a new vent is a project change that in itself has significant environmental impacts and requires preparation of an SEIS. According to §1502.9 of the CEQ regulations, supplemental impact statements shall be prepared if the agency makes "substantial" changes in its proposed action that are relevant to environmental concerns, or if "significant" new circumstances or information develop that bear on the environmental impacts of the project. Whether or not the ventilation problem is significant is left the discretion of the agency; however, the court in _Marsh_ requires agencies to take a "hard look" at their actions after a final decision is made. A court will look at the degree to which the new information was considered by the FHA. If no SEIS is prepared, the court will look to see if the agency's decision was supported by explanation and data. If constructing vents for the submerged artery would have significant environmental impacts, then the FHA has a duty to analyze these impacts in an SEIS. Again, the agency decision, if challenged, will be examined by the court under an "arbitrary and capricious" standard.

ADEQUACY OF THE EIS: ANALYSIS AND ALTERNATIVES

From here forward, let's accept that an EIS is required and prepared. When is it good enough? Once a federal agency prepares an impact statement, it can be challenged by a plaintiff on grounds that its discussion of environmental impacts and alternatives is inadequate. The NEPA statute defines basic adequacy of an impact statement, which is further classified by CEQ regulations and federal case law.

Generally, adequacy refers to the *analysis* applied to the environmental effects of an action, as well as the various *alternatives* to the action explored by the agency in its impact statement (see Exhibit 3.6). NEPA may also require a discussion of *mitigation* measures to offset possible adverse impacts. The degree to which these considerations must be discussed in an EIS is often circuit-driven. Nonetheless, judicial review of a challenge is limited to NEPA procedural considerations. A court cannot *substantively* reverse an agency's final decision; it can only order the agency to go back and prepare the EIS in a manner consistent with the *procedural* standards of the statute.

Analysis of Sufficient Environmental Impacts

How thorough and quantitative must the EIS be? Rigorous analysis of environmental impacts is an important part of the preparation of an impact statement. The CEQ regulations offer detailed guidelines for the environmental review process, as well as prescribing a "full and fair discussion of environmental impacts." The regulations set out nonbinding time limits for each part of the NEPA process.

According to CEQ regulations, *direct*, *indirect*, and *cumulative* environmental consequences of the proposed action, and those of any *alternatives* to the action, must be identified and discussed. In *Grand Canyon Trust v. Federal Aviation Admin.*, 290 F.3d 399 (D.C. Cir. 2002), the D.C. Circuit required the agency

3.6 The Adequate EIS

Analysis	Alternatives	Mitigation
No delay	No action	Of actions and alternatives
No worst-case analysis?	Primary action	
Cost-benefit analysis?	Secondary action	

to consider five factors in order to conduct meaningful cumulative impact analysis, involving area and expected impacts. Uncertainty and delay, worst-case risk analysis, and use of a cost-benefit analysis are specific issues addressed both by CEQ regulations and NEPA case law. We'll look at each briefly.

To Analyze or Not to Analyze? EIS Uncertainty and Possible Delay

If an agency is uncertain of relevant environmental information, or if such information is unavailable, its ability to prepare an adequate impact statement may be jeopardized. *SIPI v. AEC* addressed how to deal with uncertainty: "Reasonable forecasting" is an implicit agency duty under NEPA. According to the court, federal agencies are responsible for predicting possible environmental effects of proposed actions, even if those effects are not fully known. An agency cannot avoid this responsibility by labeling such a discussion as unrequired "crystal ball inquiry."

The alternative to early EIS preparation is delay of federal action until more information is acquired. In *Alaska v. Andrus*, 580 F.2d 465 (D.C. Cir. 1978), the Department of the Interior (DOI) prepared an impact statement regarding off-shore lease sales for gas and oil drilling; the statement included areas off the coast of Alaska. The EPA and the CEQ argued that the EIS was inadequate because the environmental effects of drilling in Alaskan waters were unknown. They claimed that more information must be sought before the EIS was prepared or final action taken. The court upheld the DOI's decision to proceed. While NEPA places an "affirmative obligation" on agencies to research information regarding possible environmental effects, the cost of uncertainty is a risk that must be weighed. The court may not "substitute its judgment" and require that the action be delayed until more information is acquired.

Worst-Case Risk Analysis

To what degree must the agency assume the worst? High-risk impacts with a low probability of occurrence are considered *worst-case risks*. The meltdown of the radioactive core of an atomic power plant is one well-litigated example. At one point, the CEQ required all agencies to perform a worst-case analysis to evaluate environmental risk.

In 1986, however, the CEQ revoked the worst-case analysis regulatory requirement. According to the new rule, an agency must make "reasonable efforts" to obtain information important to environmental impact evaluation and final decision making. Worst-case analysis as previously applied was thought to be unproductive and ineffective, lending itself to unending hypothesis and speculation. When catastrophic impacts that have a low probability of occurrence could result from a proposed action, an analysis still is required under the new rule.

The amended regulation was upheld by the Supreme Court decision in *Robertson v. Methow Valley Citizens Council*, 490 U.S. 332 (1989). In this case, the plaintiffs challenged the Forest Service for issuing a special use permit to a ski resort on national forest land. The impact statement considered possible effects of the resort on local wildlife, and it proposed mitigation measures that had not been fully developed or tested. In endorsing reasonably foreseeable impacts, the court did not discuss the worst-case analysis requirement in detail, nor did it elaborate on the kinds of analysis required by the amended regulation. See also *Baltimore Gas & Electric v. Natural Resource Defense Council, Inc.*, 462 U.S. 87 (1983) (concluding commission's zero-release assumption to be reasoned rulemaking as required by the APA, complying with NEPA; not arbitrary or capricious).

Cost-Benefit Analysis

Does an agency have to do the math? Section 102(B) of the NEPA statute requires federal agencies to develop methods to ensure that "presently unquantified environmental amenities and values be given appropriate consideration in decision-making along with economic and technical considerations." Must agencies quantify environmental values through cost-benefit analysis?

Because this method generates an equation or value, the substantive assumptions, values, and math greatly tempt judicial review. Assigning monetary values to various benefits and costs is always subjective, making general agreement difficult. Similarly, judgments are involved when selecting a rate for discounting the monetary value of future costs and future benefits. How these variables are quantified often results in a legal battle between an agency and a challenging plaintiff.

While the statutory language of NEPA requires agencies to take into account "unquantified environmental amenities and values," does NEPA *require* a cost-benefit analysis for proposed projects? In the early case of *Calvert Cliffs' v. AEC*, 449 F.2d 1109 (D.C. Cir. 1971), some judicial support can be found to require agencies to perform a cost-benefit analysis as part of an EIS for a proposed project. The court stated that NEPA mandates a "finely tuned and 'systematic' balancing analysis" to determine whether or not environmental costs outweigh the economic and technical benefits of a project. Later interpretations of *Calvert Cliffs'* and §102(B), however, adhere to the belief that there is no cost-benefit analysis *requirement* as part of an EIS.

Where a cost-benefit analysis is prepared voluntarily, its substantive use is not judicially reviewable. However, the cost-benefit analysis may be reviewed to determine whether or not the environmental costs of a proposed project have been adequately presented in the impact statement. Similarly, the failure to consider or quantify all environmental costs associated with a project, or faulty selection of critical components in a cost-benefit analysis, such as the discount rate or the project life, is unacceptable. In sum, a cost-benefit analysis cannot be required, but once voluntarily prepared by an agency, its quantitative values and assumptions provide grist for the "hard-look" mill of judicial review.

The scrutiny of the "hard look" can cause an EIS to fail to pass muster because of inaccurate cost-benefit calculations or distorted economic assumptions. Where distorted or inaccurate economic assumptions regarding environmental costs and economic/recreational benefits are discovered by the court, this can be grounds for overturning the EIS or requiring an SEIS. See *Hughes River Watershed Conservancy v. Glickman*, 81 F.3d 437 (4th Cir. 1996).

CEQ regulations follow the case law and do not require agencies to conduct cost-benefit analyses. However, agencies must list these considerations in their EIS when they are relevant to a decision. Failing to include *quantifiable* environmental costs in an analysis violates NEPA, but what about *unquantifiable* costs? While agencies must consider such costs, their final decisions will be as their discretion dictates, regardless of the substantive outcome of any cost-benefit analysis.

Treatment of Alternatives

Agencies must include an adequate discussion of alternatives to the proposed action in their impact statements. The range of alternatives that must be considered is specified in the CEQ regulations. What are some basic rules? Courts hold that agencies must discuss alternatives related to the statutory purposes of the action, even though it is not within the jurisdiction of the deciding agency. Speculative and remote alternatives are not required to be considered. The alternatives that must be considered, at a minimum, are:

1. *No-Action Alternative:* What if the agency did nothing?
2. *Primary Alternatives:* What else can be done, or on what scale besides the proposed action can an agency accomplish its goals? Can another action altogether serve to meet the same ends?
3. *Secondary Alternatives:* What other ways can an agency go about the proposed action? Are there other locations? Other scientific methods?

Section 1502.14 of the CEQ regulations requires federal agencies to present environmental impacts of proposed and alternative actions in a format that permits objective and comparative evaluation. If an agency rejects a particular alternative, it must discuss its reasons for doing so. If an alternative considered is "environmentally preferable," it must be identified as such and analyzed on the basis of economic, technical, and statutory factors. If a large number of alternatives are available for consideration, an agency may limit itself to consideration of a "reasonable number," but it must make selections from the full spectrum of possibilities. Some courts hold that the number of alternatives an agency must consider decreases as the environmental impacts of the proposed action become less significant.

All *reasonable* alternatives must be explored by an agency as part of the scope of an EIS. Where a particular mitigation measure or alternative has been used in practice at a similar development, it must be included and evaluated in an EIS. See *DuBois v. United States Dep't of Agric.*, 102 F.3d 1273 (1st Cir. 1996). Not every alternative must be considered in an EIS. The EIS must include enough information to allow the agency to "rigorously explore and objectively evaluate" each alternative. 40 C.F.R. §1502.14(a); *Dubois, supra* at 1287 (an alternative that has a reasonable probability to avoid "serious adverse consequences" must be explored). Adequacy of the EIS is a question of law subject to de novo review. *Id.*

Courts can find an agency's consideration of alternatives to be inadequate. In *California v. Block*, 690 F.2d 753 (9th Cir. 1982), the court held that the National Forest Service (NFS) had not considered an adequate number of alternatives in an EIS concerning the allocation of 62 million acres of land between wilderness and nonwilderness. No alternative considered in the EIS designated more than 33 percent of the land for wilderness areas, or less than 37 percent of the land for nonwilderness areas. Choosing a variety of alternatives is important to withstanding the "rule of reason" review, particularly if data support the possibility of such alternatives. The following subsections explore in more detail the three types of alternatives that agencies must consider in their impact statements.

No-Action Alternative

True to its name, the no-action alternative considers the environmental consequences of not pursuing the project or action at all. The CEQ regulations state that the no-action alternative is always appropriate, even if the federal agency is under a legislative mandate or a court order to act. Any predictable actions that may be taken by others if the no-action alternative is adopted also must be discussed in the EIS. Recently, courts are paying more attention to the adequacy of a no-action alternative, and they may find the EIS to be inadequate if this alternative is not properly addressed.

Primary Alternatives

Primary alternatives are substitutes for agency actions that accomplish the desired goals of the proposed plans, but in another manner. In *Vermont Yankee*, the decision not to consider energy conservation measures as a primary alternative to the building of a nuclear power plant was upheld by the

Supreme Court. In the few cases where an agency's discussion of primary alternatives was deemed inadequate, the court found the presentation of the primary alternatives to be conclusory. Most courts find an agency's discussion of a primary alternative to be adequate, and its rejection justifiable, for reasons like lack of feasibility, unsatisfactory accomplishment of the main objective, and equally damaging environmental effects.

Secondary Alternatives

Secondary alternatives are different ways in which an agency can carry out its proposed primary action: Modification of a project or an alternative building site are examples. Courts rarely find an agency's discussion of secondary alternatives to be inadequate, or its subsequent rejection of these alternatives to be unjustifiable. Generally, courts reason that secondary alternatives are appropriately rejected by lead agencies when the alternatives are environmentally disruptive, environmentally inferior, inadequate for meeting project goals, or just too costly. In the cases where an agency's discussion of secondary alternatives was held inadequate, the court found either that obvious problems were not addressed by the agency or that the discussion was too conclusory. Typically, deference to agency decision making limits a court's ability to substantively analyze an agency's discussion and subsequent rejection of alternatives.

Mitigation Measures

Section 102(2)(C) of NEPA implicitly requires federal agencies to discuss mitigation measures in their impact statements. The statute actually requires discussion of "any adverse environmental effects which cannot be avoided." The CEQ regulations interpret this language as requiring the discussion of (1) mitigation measures, which include avoiding or minimizing adverse environmental impacts, (2) rectifying adverse effects by restoring, rehabilitating, or repairing the damaged environment, (3) using preservation or maintenance plans to reduce or eliminate the impacts over time, and (4) providing substitute resources as compensation for adverse effects. Note that for mitigation purposes, as compared to the basic trigger to prepare an EIS, only *adverse* impacts must be mitigated.

The duty to mitigate was considered by the Supreme Court in *Robertson v. Methow Valley Citizens Council*. The plaintiffs challenged the National Forest Service (NFS) for issuing a permit to build a ski resort in a national forest, which construction could threaten a deer herd. The Court held that NEPA implicitly demanded a "reasonably complete discussion" of mitigation measures in the EIS in order for the NFS to properly evaluate the severity of the environmental effects associated with building the resort. However, the

Court pointedly distinguished the duty to *discuss* mitigation measures in an EIS from any duty to formally *adopt* or *implement* a mitigation plan. The latter requirement is substantive and not required under NEPA. The Court held that the Forest Service, if it complied with the procedural requirements of NEPA, could be left to wipe out 100 percent of the mule deer herd if it so chose. For example, if an agency plans to build a road through a national forest, it must discuss mitigation measures for water quality and fish habitat. See *Northwest Indian Cemetery Protective Ass'n v. Peterson*, 565 F. Supp. 586 (N.D. Cal. 1983). In sum, while federal agencies are required to discuss mitigation measures in their impact statements, NEPA does not impose any formal duty to mitigate.

Judicial Review of Adequacy: Substance Versus Procedure

Since there is no citizen suit provision in NEPA, plaintiffs must allege violations of §10 of the Administrative Procedures Act to gain standing for a NEPA challenge. *Lujan v. Nat'l Wildlife Fed'n*, 497 U.S. 871, 882-883 (1990).

The existence of a NEPA violation does not create a presumption that injunctive relief is available. See, e.g., *Weinberger v. Romero-Barcelo*, 456 U.S. 305, 312, (1982); cf. *Marsh v. Oregon Natural Resources Council*, 490 U.S. 360, 371 (1989). Under NEPA, "[a] preliminary injunction is an extraordinary remedy never awarded as of right" and plaintiffs must demonstrate that irreparable harm is likely if the injunction does not issue and that the balance of the harms favors plaintiffs. *Winter v. Natural Resources Defense Council, Inc.*, 555 U.S. 7, 22, 24 (2008). A court must determine that an injunction should issue under the traditional four-part standard for injunctive relief (irreparable injury, remedies available at law are inadequate, balance of hardships, and the public interest would not be disserved by a permanent injunction). *Monsanto Co, et al., v. Geertson Seed Farm, et al.*, 130 S. Ct. 2743 (2010).

Court review considers whether an agency took a "hard look" at the environmental consequences of its decision to go forward with the project. *Wilderness Society v. Salazar*, 603 F. Supp.2d 52 (D.C. Cir. 2009). "Agency action will be set aside upon judicial review pursuant to the Administrative Procedure Act if the agency identifies no rational connection between the facts found and the choice made, or if its explanation for its decision runs counter to the evidence before the agency or is so implausible that it cannot be ascribed to a difference in view of the product of agency expertise." *Envtl. Def. v. US Army Corps of Engineers*, 515 F. Supp. 2d 69 (D.D.C. 2007).

While there is no requirement under NEPA that an EIS include *all* of the underlying data on which it is based, *Sierra Club*, 595 F. Supp.2d at 1021, an EIS does violate NEPA when it fails to disclose and discuss responsible opposing views or data. *Pac. Coast Fed'n of Fisherman's Ass'ns v. Nat'l Marine Fisheries Serv.*, 482 F. Supp.2d, 1248, 1250 (W.D. Wash. 2007); see also *Silva v. Lynn*, 482 F.2d 1282 (1st Cir. 1973)("detailed statement" . . . required so that . . . information is provided which Congress thought the public should have concerning the particular environmental costs involved in the project"). NEPA does not allow an agency to rely on the conclusions and opinions of its staff without providing both supporting analysis and data which "reflected a cross-section of the related disciplines." *Id.*; *Sierra Nev. Forest Prot. Campaign v. Rey*, 573 F. Supp. 2d 1316, 1317 (E.D. Cal. 2008).

NEPA does not expressly provide the standard for judicial review regarding compliance with its terms. The Supreme Court first considered substantive judicial review of agency actions in *Kleppe*, where the Court held that a program impact statement was unnecessary for coal development in the Northern Great Plains region. The Court did not review the merits of the case but indicated in an influential footnote that "[t]he only role for a court is to insure that the agency has taken a 'hard look' at environmental consequences." The Court cannot substitute its discretion for that of the agency in choosing what action to take.

The Supreme Court reinforced this position in *Vermont Yankee v. NRDC*, where the Nuclear Regulatory Commission was not required to consider energy conservation as an alternative to nuclear power when deciding to grant a license for a nuclear power plant. In supporting its decision, the court stated that administrative decisions should be set aside only under the procedural context of NEPA, "not simply because the court is unhappy with the result reached."

The definitive case regarding substantive judicial review under NEPA is *Strycker's Bay v. Karlen*, 444 U.S. 223 (1980), holding a court cannot set aside an agency's decision on its merits unless it can be proven that the agency acted in an arbitrary or capricious manner. Although courts apply this standard to threshold determinations, the standard frequently applied to an adequacy review of an EIS is often called the "rule of reason." The Court stated clearly that these two standards are similar and that judicial review under the two should not differ significantly.

In adequacy reviews, lower courts elaborate on the rule of reason standard by reviewing three factors. First, has the agency made a "good faith effort" to consider environmental values; does an EIS fully explain its inquiry, analysis, and reasoning? Second, did the EIS provide full "environmental disclosure" to the public, containing a reasonable balance of scientific and nontechnical information? Finally, does the impact statement protect the integrity of the agency decision-making process by preventing problems and criticisms from being overlooked?

Note that if a court finds an agency's analysis to be procedurally inadequate, it may also be implying that the action's environmental effects make it unacceptable. This is particularly true if the court undertakes a detailed review of the factual basis underlying an impact statement and finds it inadequate. The Supreme Court has never sustained an environmental group on a substantive challenge under NEPA.

Exemptions from NEPA

CEQ regulation allows an emergency exemption after consulting with CEQ. 40 C.F.R. 1506.11. The NEPA statute itself does not exempt any federal agency from its reach, requiring all to comply with its terms "to the fullest extent possible." Regardless, like most rules, there are exceptions. Congress has the power to exempt agency programs and actions from NEPA through express and explicit statutory language. Generally such exemptions are created if statutorily mandated procedures or agency regulations provide the functional equivalent to NEPA's requirements. In a few instances, courts find statutory conflicts to exist between an agency's proposed action and NEPA procedures. While these kinds of exemptions are rare, they are nonetheless exceptions to the NEPA rule. The following is a brief review of several exemptions from the NEPA statute.

Statutory Exemptions

Through express language, Congress has written a number of statutory exemptions from the EIS requirement for federal programs. Some of the most important exemptions are those created for the Environmental Protection Agency (EPA), whose purpose is to establish regulatory programs designed to protect the environment. Because of the nature of this agency, Congress has exempted from NEPA requirements all EPA actions under the Clean Air Act and many actions under the Clean Water Act. These are the only exemptions for EPA programs expressly legislated by Congress. For other EPA environmental protection programs to be exempted from NEPA, the courts must find EPA's environmental decision-making procedures to be functionally equivalent to NEPA's requirements.

Some statutes other than the Clean Air Act (see Chapter 5) and the Clean Water Act (see Chapter 6) provide full or partial exemption from NEPA procedures for the administering agencies. The following is a selection of these federal statutes:

1. Deep Seabed Hard Mineral Resources Act: 30 U.S.C. §1419(d)
2. Defense Production Act: 50 U.S.C. §§2095(h), 2096(I) (synthetic fuels)
3. Disaster Relief Act: 42 U.S.C. §5159
4. Endangered Species Act: 16 U.S.C. §1636(k)
5. National Forest Management Act: 16 U.S.C. §5440(f)

6. Power Plant and Industrial Fuel Use Act: 42 U.S.C. §8473
7. Strategic Petroleum Reserve: 42 U.S.C. §6239(h)(3)(A)
8. Surface Mining Control and Reclamation Act: 30 U.S.C. §§1251(a), 1292(d)

Statutory Conflicts: The *Flint Ridge* Case

If an agency's action is not statutorily exempted from NEPA, a court may find that the agency's statutory obligations conflict with NEPA compliance. In *Flint Ridge Dev. Co. v. Scenic Rivers Ass'n of Okla.*, 426 U.S. 776 (1976), the Court considered the responsibilities of the Department of Housing and Urban Development (HUD) under the Interstate Land Disclosures Act. Under this Act, a developer is prohibited from marketing a subdivision in interstate commerce unless it files with HUD a statement disclosing specific information about the subdivision. The statement is effective after 30 days unless HUD determines that the developer's reporting is inaccurate or incomplete, in which case the developer has to remedy the defects. In *Flint Ridge*, the plaintiffs argued that HUD must prepare an EIS before it approves the report. The Court held that the statutorily mandated filing time of 30 days implicitly precluded the preparation of an EIS, which would take much longer. The Court did find, however, that HUD has the authority to require the developers to incorporate a wide range of environmental information into their statements.

Some courts hold that certain statutory decision-making duties do not meet the requisite of "major federal action," in which case environmental factors are irrelevant and need not be considered by the administering agency. See *Milo Cmty. Hosp. v. Weinberger*, 525 F.2d 144 (1st Cir. 1975) (a federal agency's decision to terminate its assistance to a community hospital did not require an EIS because environmental factors were not relevant to the termination criteria). Lower federal courts are mixed on this issue, as are federal circuits.

National Security

The federal government claims that actions relating to national defense and security are, by implication, exempt from NEPA's EIS requirement. The government has invoked the "secrecy exception" within the Freedom of Information Act (FOIA) to preclude judicial review for NEPA compliance.

The FOIA exemption was upheld by the Supreme Court in *Weinberger v. Catholic Action of Hawaii*, 454 U.S. 139 (1981). The Navy was planning to construct ammunition and weapons facilities for the storage of nuclear weapons. The plaintiffs claimed that an impact statement was required before a final decision could be made. The Court held that public disclosure under NEPA is expressly governed by FOIA, which exempts disclosure of any matters authorized "to be kept secret in the interest of national defense" by a Presidential Executive Order. Information relating to nuclear weapons storage was properly classified as "secret" under an Executive Order, so the Court concluded that the Navy did not need to prepare an EIS in this case. The agency could neither admit nor deny the existence of the facility for national security reasons, therefore compliance with NEPA was beyond judicial review. FOIA's exemption for classified materials was applicable because almost all information relating to the storage of nuclear weapons is classified. The Court cited its holding in *Kleppe v. Sierra Club*, which requires an EIS be prepared only when a project is proposed, not when a project has only been contemplated, noting that the Navy complied with NEPA "to the fullest extent possible." The Supreme Court's decision in *Weinberger* did not create a military exemption from NEPA; it applies only to maintaining the confidentiality of information dealing with the deployment and storage of nuclear weapons, and only precludes any judicial review of cases that involve classified information concerning nuclear weapons.

The Court narrowed this exemption to shield national defense activities that are not physically obvious and that if publicly disclosed would be in violation of FOIA's secrecy provision. Later courts elaborated on the restrictions in *Weinberger* by stating that NEPA does not have a national defense exemption. The defense project must fall under the protection of the secrecy provision in FOIA in order to escape disclosure and still comport with NEPA. In *McQueary v. Laird*, 449 F.2d 608 (10th Cir. 1971), the Tenth Circuit concluded that under the doctrine of sovereign immunity, the decision where to store chemical and biological weapons was within the discretion of the government, but stated that there was no NEPA exemption for federal agencies involved with national security.

Subsequent cases have arisen in the context of nuclear weapons or war. In *Hudson River Sloop Clearwater, Inc. v. United States*, 659 F. Supp. 674 (E.D.N.Y. 1987), the court concluded that the Navy did not have to release classified information in the context of NEPA that would admit a proposal to deploy nuclear weapons in Staten Island, New York. Neither the draft EIS nor the final EIS addressed nuclear weapons or the environmental risks associated with deploying them in New York's harbor. The court held that whether the Navy complied "to the fullest extent possible" with NEPA was not subject to judicial scrutiny.

In other contexts, courts have held that the Department of Defense can comply with reasonable alternatives to NEPA and thereby accomplish a similar purpose. In *Valley Citizens for a Safe Envt. v. Aldridge*, 695 F. Supp. 605 (D. Ma. 1988), an Air Force proposal to locate C-5A aircraft with noise and safety concerns was evaluated in an Environmental Impact Statement, which found that it included adequate considerations of alternatives (even though they weren't detailed) to satisfy NEPA. A challenge to the EIS of the Federal Aviation Administration regarding Air National Guard activities was found not to be inadequate in its limited consideration of noise impacts of flight activities. See *Custer County Action Ass'n v. Garvey*, 256 F.3d 1024 (10th Cir. 2001).

In *Ground Zero Center for Non-Violent Action v. United States Department of the Navy*, 383 F.3d 1082 (2004), the Navy homeport base for the Trident submarine fleet in Bangor, Washington, resulted in an EIS and four supplements. The Court of Appeals for the Ninth Circuit found that NEPA's requirements do not apply to presidential action because the President acts outside of NEPA's definition of a "federal agency." The court reasoned that based upon the Navy's study, an accidental explosion was such a remote possibility that the Navy was not required to examine the possible environmental impacts.

NEPA serves as no constraint on executive military action: The Supreme Court ignored the applicability of NEPA in situations involving military readiness and military operations and preparedness of the fleet. *Winter v. NRDC Inc.*, 129 S. Ct. 365 (2008). The majority opinion deems military interests, even in routine training, "not . . . a close question" to outweigh environmental public interests under NEPA regarding observation of marine mammals. The Court noted that a permanent injunction would be inappropriate on these facts of the possible interference of Navy sonar testing with whale habitats in the oceans, even if plaintiff NRDC were to prevail on the merits. This goes further than the earlier decision in *Romero-Barcelo* in that even NEPA review is negated. Even if the Navy had prepared a full EIS, it could still have decided to conduct sonar operations as long as it considered the EIS, but would not have to protect species or follow the balance of harms shown there.

In the post-*Weinberger* era, courts have generally found that there is no national security exemption for NEPA compliance. Recently, the courts' foci have shifted to consider whether the likely environmental consequences of a potential terrorist attack must be considered as part of the NEPA process. See, *Mothers for Peace v. Nuclear Regulatory Comm'n*, 449 F.3d 1016 (2006); *Ground Zero Center for Non-Violent Actions v. United States Department of Navy*, 383 F.3d 1082 (2004) (Navy did not have to include impacts of possible terrorist attacks on a Navy base as part of the EIS).

International Environmental Effects

NEPA contains a paragraph, found in §102(F), which states that all federal agencies shall "recognize the worldwide and long-range character of environmental problems and, where consistent with the foreign policy of the United States, lend appropriate support to initiatives, resolutions, and programs designed to maximize international cooperation in anticipating and preventing a decline in the quality of mankind's world environment." Some argue that NEPA requires federal agencies to evaluate the extraterritorial environmental consequences of their activities, when appropriate.

On January 4, 1979, President Jimmy Carter issued Executive Order 12,114 in an effort to clarify the questions surrounding NEPA's international application. 44 C.F.R. §1957. Covered are major federal actions outside the United States, its territories, and possessions that "significantly affect natural or ecological resources of global importance" by declaration of the President or international agreement binding on the United States. The compliance acceptable under this procedure includes EISs, bilateral or multilateral studies by the United States and one or more foreign nations, studies by an international organization or body of which the United States is a member, and "concise reviews of environmental issues" including environmental impact assessments, summary analyses, and other appropriate documents.

When read in conjunction with the decision in NRDC v. Morton, 458 F.2d 827 (D.C. Cir. 1972), this seems to imply that an individual agency's particular provisions, so long as they pass the foreign policy/national security consistency test, will be triggered when actions have reasonable alternatives within the jurisdiction of any federal agency. Of significance is the order's exemption of Presidential actions, intelligence activities and arms transfers, nuclear activities, actions arising from membership in international organizations, and emergency relief actions. Also exempted are actions which, in the view of the agency, do not have a significant effect on the environment. Noteworthy, the definition of "environment" is restricted to the "natural and physical environment" and expressly excludes "social, economic and other environments."

The courts are divided on the issue. With regard to U.S. Trust Territories, a district court held that NEPA did apply, by construing the term "United States" to include Trust Territories and by determining that the application of NEPA to activities affecting these areas would not raise foreign policy or world power issues. See *People of Enewatak v. Laird*, 353 F. Supp. 811 (D. Haw. 1973). This finding, however, did not directly involve environmental impacts *outside* the territorial jurisdiction of the United States. The courts generally skirt the issue by applying exceptions from other statutes involved or by relying on current foreign policy initiatives as a trump card, thereby supporting or precluding NEPA compliance.

In NRDC v. NRC, 647 F.2d 1345 (D.C. Cir. 1981), an environmental group sought judicial review of the Nuclear Regulatory Commission's (NRC) approval of nuclear expert applications to the Philippines. The Court of Appeals ruled that the NRC had acted properly by declining to consider the foreign impacts, and that its deference to the executive's analysis and foreign policy judgment was "fully consistent" with congressional objectives. More specifically, the court was not able to find that NEPA imposed a requirement for an EIS where the impacts fell exclusively within foreign jurisdictions. In analyzing the language of the statute, the court held that the deference to the presidential authority in foreign relations "dictate[d] that NEPA's putative extraterritorial reach be curbed" with respect to nuclear exports. The court concluded that NEPA's legislative history revealed nothing about extraterritorial application.

In *Greenpeace v. Stone*, 748 F. Supp. 749 (D.C. Haw. 1990), the court ruled that the portion of the project concerning the transportation of the weapons within the Federal Republic of Germany did not fall within NEPA's scope because the action was pursuant to a presidential agreement. In *Lujan v. Defenders of Wildlife*, 504 U.S. 555 (1992), groups unsuccessfully challenged a Department of Interior regulation providing that the Endangered Species Act did not create a duty for federal agencies funding projects in foreign countries to consult with the secretary of interior about the project's likely impacts on endangered species. One of the plaintiffs had visited parts of Sri Lanka that were also the site of a development project funded by USAID. Another plaintiff went to Egypt and observed the Nile crocodile's habitat, which coincided with the Aswan High Dam construction project. Both plaintiffs noted their intent to return to those areas, but the court found their complaints lacked standing. (See also Chapter 2.)

In *Envt'l Def. Fund, Inc. v. Massey*, 772 F. Supp. 1296 (D.C. Cir. 1991), the plaintiff environmental group sought to enjoin the National Science Foundation's program of food-related and domestic waste incineration in the Antarctic, because it had failed to prepare a proper environmental analysis in violation of NEPA, the CEQ Regulations, and Executive Order 12,114. The U.S. district court held that it could not "ferret out a clear expression of Congress' intention that NEPA should apply beyond the territorial jurisdiction of the United States." The court relied substantially on a 1991 Supreme Court decision that congressional legislation is meant to apply only within the territorial jurisdiction of the United States, unless a clear contrary intent is shown. In applying Executive Order 12,114 the court noted that based on case law, executive orders without specific foundation in congressional action are not judicially enforceable in private civil suits.

The Alien Tort Claims Act, 28 U.S.C. §1350, has been pled regarding environmental impacts overseas. See *Amlon Metals, Inc. v. FMC Corp.*, 775 F. Supp. 668 (S.D.N.Y. 1991) (alleging a shipment constituting an imminent danger violating norms of international law); *Beanal v. Freeport-McMoran*, 969 F. Supp. 362 (E.D. La. 1997), aff'd, 197 F.3d 161 (5th Cir. 1999) (alleging environmental torts and human rights violations in Irian Jaya, Indonesia, related to mineral mining operations); *Jota/Aguinda v. Texaco*, 157 F.3d 153 (2d Cir. 1998), on remand, *Aguinda v. Texaco, Inc.*, 142 F. Supp. 534 (S.D.N.Y. 2001) (environmental damage by Texaco and personal injuries alleged by indigenous tribes in South America, including dumping of toxic waste into rivers).

The United States is involved in many activities in other countries by nature of its membership in various international organizations. NEPA §4332(2)(f) expressly refers to international activities in calling on agencies to "recognize the worldwide and long-range character" of environmental problems and to "support [appropriate] initiatives, resolutions, and programs designed to maximize international cooperation in anticipating and preventing a decline in the quality of world environment." Regarding bilateral activities, NEPA procedures are only fully implemented if the action affects the environment of the United States, the global commons, or areas outside the jurisdiction of any nation.

USAID projects overseas are governed by Regulation 16, which differs from NEPA in three main respects: First, the Initial Environmental Examination (IEE), in contrast to NEPA's Environmental Assessment procedure, only requires a brief discussion of foreseeable environmental effects of the action; discussion of alternatives, including the no-action alternative, is not required, nor is any participation by the public in the IEE preparation process. Second, the scope and content of the IEE, which is to include "the direct and indirect effects of the project on the environment," is much less detailed than the guidance provided by the CEQ Regulations. Third, the IEE is not circulated for public comment; only the draft EIS receives public input.

The World Bank initiated an environmental policy in May 1984 mandating an EIA for all projects that may have significant environmental impacts. But the EIA requirement does not apply to projects that can be characterized as "environmentally beneficial," leaving this determination to Bank officials. In part to address this, in 1989 Congress passed the International Development and Finance Act, which prohibits American representatives of any international bank from voting for any development project unless an EIA has been performed. This would be a statement pursuant to the guidelines set by the United Nations Environment Programme (UNEP), and not NEPA.

Examples

1. The Department of Energy (DOE) is asked to respond to a perceived power supply shortage that recently gripped the nation. After much contemplation, the DOE decides to prepare an EIS and thereafter, if appropriate, to issue a permit authorizing the building of a new nuclear power plant. Due to recent technological advancements, a private company, "Newnuc," is confident it can build the plant for much less money than it would cost to build a conventional power plant. In fact, the greatest expense will arise in 50 years, when the on-site nuclear storage facility becomes full and the spent fuel rods are moved to a permanent

site. The DOE dutifully prepares an EIS to analyze environmental impacts, discuss alternatives to the proposed project, and suggest various mitigation measures.

Newnuc intends to build its plant on a river in Oklahoma, located 15 miles north of a small farming community and 20 miles south of the Kiowa Indian Reservation.

a. You work for the DOE and must oversee preparation of the EIS for the nuclear power plant permit. Others in your work group think a cost-benefit analysis of the project would add weight to the proposal, in light of the inexpensive building costs. Do you think the DOE should include a cost-benefit analysis in its EIS? Must it do so? How do you think a court would review a cost-benefit analysis, should the EIS be challenged?

b. In the EIS, primary and secondary alternatives are considered. However, the agency does not include the possibility of *no action*. The Kiowa tribe decides to challenge the adequacy of the EIS, claiming that the nation is not experiencing a power shortage and that more efficient use of existing power plants would eliminate any risk of such a problem. The Kiowa claim that the DOE violated NEPA by refusing to consider no action, or more efficient utilization of existing power plants, as alternatives. You are the judge. Is the DOE's treatment of alternatives adequate?

c. Representatives of the farming community bring an action in district court against the DOE for violating NEPA. The farmers claim that the EIS is inadequate because it does not perform a worst-case risk analysis on the proposed nuclear power plant. The farmers fear the possibility of a radioactive core meltdown and, at the very least, radioactive leakage into the river that they will share with Newnuc. The farmers rely on the river to irrigate their crops and support their livestock and community. You are an attorney for the Department of Justice, and you have been assigned to this case. What arguments would you offer in support of the agency? What do you think the court will say?

2. Reread Example 3.2 on page 103 about deepening the Dover harbor. Assume that the Army Corps of Engineers has decided to dump the dredged, contaminated sediment in Area 1, an ocean site located near a local fishing ground. To reduce the threat of a contaminated migration of sediment, the Corps proposes to "cap" the dirty sludge with clean sediment, a process that has succeeded only experimentally. The theory is that the cap will form a clean cover of sediment over the mound of contaminated sludge, burying it "forever." Only a six-inch cap is considered. Fishing in Fear, a local community group, challenges the adequacy of the Corps's EIS. The plaintiffs claim that the Corps did not include mitigation measures to ensure the integrity of the cap and

did not adequately consider alternatives to the capping procedure. Fishing in Fear argues that the Corps relied on incomplete data and did not consider the possibility of local organisms burrowing into the contaminated mound. The plaintiffs introduce evidence that these "bioturbators" do exist and are known to burrow as much as two meters into the ocean floor.

a. Assume that the existence of the bioturbators is well known; however, there is no scientific agreement on how deep they can burrow. At trial, the Corps introduces a study supporting a conclusion that the bioturbators known to inhabit Area 1 only burrow a few inches, and the cap of clean sediment will be at least six inches deep. Fishing in Fear's evidence is based on a study of bioturbators not local to Area 1. In its EIS, the Corps did not consider thickening the cap or testing the area first to gain more data on the local creatures. You are the judge. How would you analyze this issue? Is the Corps's discussion of alternatives adequate under NEPA? Why or why not?

b. Because capping is so experimental, there is a real possibility that the contaminated sediment will migrate into the surrounding area. The Corps has assumed that the cap will adequately contain the sludge and has proposed no mitigation measures should this assumption prove false. As the judge, how would you rule? Can the court compel the Corps to implement mitigation measures?

3. The Endangered Species Act (ESA) is administered by the Fish and Wildlife Service (FWS). The FWS must determine which species are endangered and, having listed them, must provide for the protection of their lives and habitat. The ESA requires the FWS to base its decision on whether a species should be listed as endangered on five statutory factors, none of which references NEPA.

The agency recently decided to list a small bird whose population had become so low that the species warranted protection. In an effort to protect the bird's habitat, the FWS restricted further development in a region in Texas where a number of these birds had recently been spotted. No EIS had been prepared prior to listing the endangered bird. A local development company, Concrete Paradise, looking for an opportunity to develop the restricted area, filed a complaint in district court against the FWS for violating NEPA.

a. Is the FWS in violation of NEPA's EIS requirement? You are an attorney representing the agency. What arguments might you make on its behalf?

b. Suppose a colony of the endangered birds is discovered on a small Mexican island, and the FWS proposes a plan to aid the Mexican government in developing a preservation park to manage the birds. Coincidentally, Concrete Paradise has spent the last year trying to negotiate a contract with the Mexican government to build a vacation resort on this same island. Now the contract negotiations have been terminated in light of the feathered discovery. Assume that the resources committed to the project by the FWS qualify it as "major federal action." Can Concrete Paradise bring a successful claim against the FWS for not preparing an EIS? What argument might it make? How will the court most likely rule?

Explanations

1a. First, assess the efficacy of the cost-benefit analysis. When an agency decides to perform a cost-benefit analysis on the environmental effects of a project, it is assigning monetary values to environmental consequences, as well as to the actual cost of the proposed project. If the DOE prepares a cost-benefit analysis on the building of a nuclear power plant, it will have to weigh the cost of the environmental consequences against the value of the energy benefits. Just because building a nuclear power plant costs less than alternative power sources, it does not follow that the *environmental impacts* of the project will be less costly. Nuclear waste is extremely hazardous and difficult to dispose of. Plutonium 239 has a half-life — a measure of the rate of decay of radioactive substances to half potency — of 24,100 years. Nuclear plants are expected to generate 800 tons of plutonium. The environmental costs of creating such waste inevitably will be high, regardless of when permanent disposal of the fuel rods takes place. Similarly, the environmental costs of a possible operating mishap are large, if assigned a monetary value. Because of the difficulty in quantifying environmental impacts, a cost-benefit analysis frequently invites litigation. Performing a cost-benefit analysis may not be in the best interests of furthering the project. Quantification actually makes it easier for a court to remand the EIS because of imprecise or erroneous quantification.

The next question is whether the DOE *must* prepare a cost-benefit analysis. The NEPA statute requires agencies to take into account "unquantifiable environmental amenities and values." This provision was interpreted by the court in *Calvert Cliffs'* to require a "systematic balancing test" that included weighing environmental costs against the project's benefits. Today, however, it is well established that no cost-benefit analysis *per se* is required by NEPA. Should an agency perform such an analysis, it had better be prepared to defend its assumptions and subjective determinations in court, for judges will take a "hard look" at the process.

1b. According to the CEQ regulations, agencies must discuss the no-action alternative as well as primary and secondary alternatives. The no-action alternative for the DOE in this example is the refusal to issue a permit to any power company. Even if the DOE is under a congressional or court order to permit a new facility, it will still be required to *consider* the no-action alternative in its EIS. Because the agency has not done so, its EIS is inadequate. The DOE will be required to reconsider the project in light of the no-action alternative. If the alternative is considered and subsequently rejected, typically the impact statement will be deemed adequate.

The DOE also neglected to consider more efficient utilization of existing power plants as an alternative. This is a primary alternative to issuing a permit for a new facility. While agencies are not required to consider every alternative, the court in *California v. Block* held that choosing a variety of alternatives is important for withstanding the "rule of reason" review. As long as other reasonable primary alternatives were considered by the DOE, it will not be required to consider this particular alternative. Furthermore, after the Supreme Court's decision in *Vermont Yankee*, courts generally uphold agency decisions not to consider energy conservation as a primary alternative. The Kiowa are unlikely to succeed on this issue.

1c. At one point, the CEQ regulations required all agencies to perform a worst-case risk analysis of a proposed project in their EIS. However, in 1986, this regulation was revoked and replaced with a softer requirement to make "reasonable efforts" to obtain information regarding all possible environmental impacts. The DOE would argue that the possibility of a core meltdown is so remote that no worst-case analysis is required. On the other hand, when catastrophic impacts could result, even if the probability is low, a worst-case risk analysis may still be appropriate. Thus the DOE will have to defend why it did not consider the possibility of a core meltdown, because of resulting catastrophic impacts.

There is also the possibility of radioactive contamination in the river from operations. This impact is not as remote as meltdown, and the farmers rely on the river for their water. This impact should be addressed. The DOE can still decide to issue the permit; however, it must consider all reasonably possible environmental impacts in its EIS. This procedural duty is enforced by the courts. Substantive decisions, however, will be left to the agency's discretion, subject to the "arbitrary and capricious" standard of review.

2a. This question involves secondary alternatives. The Corps presents evidence that supports its plan to cover the contaminated sediment with a six-inch layer of clean sediment. However, the agency did not discuss the possibility of the bioturbators in its EIS, nor did it consider forming a thicker mound of clean sediment. The data regarding the burrowing depth of local bioturbators are disputed in the scientific community and therefore uncertain. This is an environmental impact that should be discussed in the Corps's EIS, along with alternative cap thicknesses.

Generally, courts uphold the adequacy of an agency's discussion of secondary alternatives unless obvious problems are not addressed. If the Corps had considered the possibility of the burrowing creatures and concluded that a six-inch cap was adequate, then NEPA's procedural requirements would have been met. This is not the case, however; the discussion of alternatives and impacts is inadequate, and the Corps will have to readdress the problem and potential alternatives in a new EIS. See *Friends of the Earth v. U.S. Navy*, 841 F.2d 927 (9th Cir. 1988) (Corps's EIS held inadequate because it relied on incomplete data in considering alternatives).

2b. This question involves mitigation requirements. Section 102(2)(C) of NEPA requires federal agencies to discuss mitigation measures in their impact statements. The CEQ regulations specifically state that mitigation measures that restore, rehabilitate, repair, maintain, preserve, or eliminate environmental impacts must be included in an EIS. The migration of contaminated sediment into the surrounding area could jeopardize the integrity of the clean cap. The capping process is still experimental, and migrating sediment is a very real possibility. The Corps must discuss mitigation measures that address this environmental consequence, even if they only consider monitoring the cap and repairing any damage that may occur. However, once the agency has *discussed* these measures, they have effectively complied with NEPA. According to the court in *Robertson*, there is no duty to adopt or implement a mitigation plan. The discussion alone satisfies the procedural nature of NEPA. The Corps will have to reconsider the migration problem and discuss possible mitigation measures in order to comply. Once it has done so, the courts cannot force the agency to go forward with the mitigation plans.

3a. Concrete Paradise is claiming that the FWS has violated NEPA because no impact statement was prepared. The FWS is not required to prepare an EIS because it has complied with the ESA, whose procedures are mandatory and whose purpose is functionally equivalent to NEPA's. See *Pacific Legal Found. v. Andrus*, 657 F.2d 829 (6th Cir. 1981) (Court found the FWS was required to list species based on the five factors contained in the Endangered Species Act, and was therefore not required to prepare an EIS when listing species). In *Flint Ridge*, the Supreme Court suggested that statutory conflicts may exempt a planning agency from complying with NEPA. In this case, the ESA expressly lists the factors that the FWS is to consider, and there is no mention of NEPA compliance. The factors are meant to encourage environmental considerations; the ultimate result is the protection of the listed species and its habitat. It can be argued that the environmental decision-making criteria under the ESA are functionally equivalent to NEPA's procedures.

3b. Concrete Paradise may bring a suit against the FWS for violating §102(2)(F) of NEPA, requiring federal agencies to "recognize" environmental factors on a worldwide scale. The company will argue that no impact statement was prepared and that the agency is not acting under the protective mandates of the ESA. This is major federal action; therefore, the FWS must comply with NEPA and prepare an impact statement.

Unfortunately, courts have not interpreted NEPA to require an impact statement for agency actions abroad. The duty to "recognize" environmental effects is not equated with the duty to prepare an EIS. The *Laird* case states that impact statements are required when agencies plan actions in U.S. Trust Territories. However, Mexico is not a trust territory. Courts generally uphold agency positions, looking for exceptions in relevant statutes or in the nature of the project and its relationship to current foreign policy initiatives.

In this case, if the court finds that the U.S. government is engaged in improving relations with Mexico or assisting with its environmental management, then the action may be beyond judicial interference. Similarly, the court may believe that an ESA exception applies in this case, overriding NEPA. In either instance, it is unlikely that Concrete Paradise will succeed on a NEPA claim.

Constitutional Issues: The Commerce Clause and Environmental Preemption

"Think globally; act locally."

Anonymous

"Man is a singular creature. He has a set of gifts which make him unique among the animals: So that, unlike them, he is not a figure in the landscape — he is a shaper of the landscape. In body and in mind he is the explorer of nature, the ubiquitous animal, who did not find but has made his home in every continent."

J. Bronowski, The Ascent of Man, 1973

"Why may not that be the skull of a lawyer? Where be his quiddities now, his quillets, his cases, his tenures, and his tricks?"

William Shakespeare, Hamlet

"But I know it when I see it . . . "

Justice Potter Sewart, *Jacobellis v. Ohio*, 378 U.S. 184 (1964)

Do the states or the federal government regulate the air, the water, and the land? Does the answer change if pollution migrates across states' boundaries? Where are the lines?

Environmental pollution heeds no boundaries, a fact that gives rise to multiple levels of regulation and legal headaches. Tensions exist between the federal, state, and local authorities that attempt environmental protection. The prevailing question is, who has the authority to regulate, and who has the right to enforce regulations or impose standards on polluters? This chapter will discuss two constitutional issues: the ability of Congress to regulate through the commerce clause and dormant restrictions on states, and its ability to supersede state and local regulation through the supremacy clause.

THE COMMERCE CLAUSE AND ENVIRONMENTAL REGULATION

Article I, §8[3] of the U.S. Constitution provides that "the Congress shall have power . . . to regulate Commerce with foreign Nations, and among the several States, and with the Indian Tribes." This specific grant of power provides Congress with constitutional authority to govern activities that affect interstate commerce. Congress is not required to act, however; the commerce clause is a permission slip written specifically for Congress.

The Tenth Amendment of the Constitution provides, "[T]he powers not delegated to the United States by the Constitution, nor prohibited by it to the States, are reserved to the States respectively, or to the people." The Tenth Amendment does not *give* power to the states, but it explicitly allows states to keep and exercise their *inherent* powers. There is nothing more fundamentally local than police power, which has always included regulation of health, safety, and the environment.

States and localities impose their own environmental regulations to solve local problems. Subsequently, conflicts often arise between a state's interest in its environment and another state's interest in its economics, or between state, local, and federal interests. The issue in play is, who gets to regulate the environment? Federal courts serve as neutral forums for resolution of these interstate and state-federal disputes.

Issue One: The Plenary Power of Congress to Regulate Interstate Commerce

Direct Federal Regulation

The power of the federal government to regulate natural resource and environmental issues through commerce clause legislation is best demonstrated by a case involving the Surface Mining Control and Reclamation Act of 1977, 30 U.S.C. §1201 *et seq.* ("Surface Mining Act"). In *Hodel v. Indiana*, 452 U.S. 314 (1981), the Court considered whether certain provisions of the Surface Mining Act exceeded congressional constitutional powers. The challenged provisions had established special requirements for surface mining operations conducted on land that is "prime farmland" and has historically been used as cropland. These provisions included environmental protection standards, such as (1) restoration of the land to conditions capable of supporting uses that it supported before the mining, and (2) using the "best technology available" to minimize adverse impacts of the operation on fish, wildlife, and related environmental values. These land-use controls are traditionally police powers and are therefore considered state prerogatives (see Chapter 10 for a discussion of land use).

The *Hodel* court reasoned that federal legislative acts "adjusting the burdens and benefits of economic life come to the Court with a presumption of constitutionality." The Court applied the "rational basis" test, holding that a court may invalidate legislation enacted under the commerce clause if the court concludes that "there is no rational basis for a congressional finding that the regulated activity affects interstate commerce, or there is no reasonable connection between the regulatory means selected and the asserted ends." The Court examined the legislative history of the Surface Mining Act, found that the Senate considered evidence and testimony regarding acreage and agricultural productivity losses due to surface mining on prime farmland, and concluded that "Congress had a rational basis for finding that surface coal mining on prime farmland affects interstate commerce in agricultural products." That's an indirect linkage.

In the more than half century between 1937 and 1995, the Supreme Court did not strike a single regulation under the Commerce Clause, until decisions in *United States v. Lopez*, 514 U.S. 549, 549 (1995); *United States v. Morrison*, 529 U.S. 598, 598 (2000); and *Solid Waste Agency of Northern Cook County v. U.S. Army Corps of Engineers*, 531 U.S. 159, 159 (2001). However, the federal commerce power is still very broad. In *Lopez* and *Morrison*, the Supreme Court established the outer limits of the commerce power, setting out three broad categories of activity that Congress may regulate under its commerce power: (1) use of the channels of interstate commerce, (2) instrumentalities, persons, or things in interstate commerce (even if the threat comes only from intrastate activities), and (3) those activities that substantially affect interstate commerce. Where a federal statute is not sufficiently related to interstate commerce, it will be overruled. This situation naturally leads to the first question in every inquiry: Has Congress acted regarding the environment?

The Tenth Amendment Limitation on Federal Power to Regulate

The Supreme Court's interpretation of the commerce clause and the supremacy clause has confirmed the federal government's sweeping power to promulgate and enforce pollution control and other environmental regulations. In the 1980s, private parties constrained to comply with environmental regulations, as well as states responsible for implementing and enforcing the regulations (and in some instances also required to comply with the federal regulations themselves), began challenging the extent to which the federal government could control the states through the commerce clause powers. The Tenth Amendment was the weapon of choice: "The powers not delegated to the United States by the Constitution, nor prohibited by it to the States, are reserved to the States respectively, or to the people."

Two pivotal cases involving Tenth Amendment challenges to federal environmental regulations were decided in the 1980s. The plaintiffs in both cases sought Supreme Court intervention to balance the interests of the federal government as articulated in the commerce clause with what they saw as the inherent powers reserved in the Tenth Amendment to the states and the people. These cases did not challenge the fundamental rights of the federal government to promulgate and enforce environmental regulations, but rather attempted to redefine or limit specific federal powers.

The federal regulation at issue in *Hodel v. Virginia Surface Mining and Reclamation Ass'n, Inc.*, 452 U.S. 264 (1981), was the Surface Mining Control and Reclamation Act. The Act sought to minimize the damage inflicted on topsoil and the environment from surface mining. The case was a pre-enforcement challenge to the constitutionality of the Act. Plaintiffs alleged that the Act violated the commerce, equal protection, and substantive due process clauses and the Tenth Amendment, and that various provisions of the Act violated the just compensation clause of the Fifth Amendment. The lower federal court held that the federal performance standard provision of the Act was in contravention of the Tenth Amendment because it "operates to displace the state's freedom to structure integral operations" in those areas traditionally reserved for the police power of the states. The lower court also ruled that certain provisions of the Act were, in fact, a taking of private property in violation of the Fifth Amendment.

The Supreme Court in a unanimous decision reversed, holding the Act constitutional regarding the Tenth and Fifth Amendments. In deciding the Tenth Amendment question, the court corrected the district court's interpretation of its decision in *National League of Cities v. Usery*, 426 U.S. 833 (1976). It stated the "sharp distinction" between federal regulation impacting private persons and businesses versus federal regulation of the "States as States." Private persons and businesses are by necessity subject to the sovereign power of both the state and the nation. Therefore the Tenth Amendment is not violated when Congress exercises control over them.

The Court went on to examine federal regulation of "the States as States" by a three-part test to determine whether the federal government's authority under the commerce clause should be scrutinized under the Tenth Amendment. First, there must be proof that the statute in question regulates the state as a state and not the citizens of the state. Second, the regulation must regulate an area that is indisputably within the state's sovereign powers.

Third, the state's compliance with the federal law must directly impair its ability to promulgate operations or regulations in areas that were traditionally its own realm. The Court points out in a footnote that the presence of these requirements does not guarantee a Tenth Amendment challenge will be upheld, because in some situations the federal interest is so compelling that it justifies subjugation of state powers.

The Court found that the provisions of the Act that plaintiffs had challenged on Tenth Amendment grounds did not regulate the state as a state but rather the "activities of coal mine operators who are private individuals and businesses." In addition, the Court held that since the states were not compelled to take action, spend money, enforce the regulation, or even set up a permanent state program, no sound argument could be made that the Act subjugated or interfered in any way with the states' legislative processes. The Court cited a great body of precedent that allowed Congress to preempt state laws regulating private citizens and businesses, once it is established that the regulated activity affects interstate commerce. The federal government could have wholly preempted state regulation regarding surface mine reclamation and still be operating well within its constitutional authority. Point, set, match — federal government. In Chapter 12, we discuss a subsequent case applying this principle, *FERC v. Mississippi*.

In 1992 the state of New York brought suit against the United States government for violation of the Tenth Amendment in its promulgation of the Low-Level Radioactive Waste Policy Amendments Act of 1985. *New York v. United States*, 505 U.S. 144 (1992). The purpose of the Act was to require states that did not have low-level radioactive waste sites to begin disposing of their own wastes by 1992. The Act contained an incentive: States with sites would agree to accept waste from unsited states through 1992. The Act also contained three sticks, all of which were the issues challenged by New York.

First, the sited states were given permission to gradually increase their fees for accepting waste from unsited states. Second, states that missed certain deadlines would be charged higher surcharges and could be denied access to disposal facilities in sited states. Third, any state that had not developed its own disposal site would be required to take title of all low-level radioactive waste generated in that state after 1992. The third, "take title," provision (stick) was unique in requiring the states to accept and implement legislation enacted by Congress, with no other option for the states.

The Court recognized the federal government's right to encourage states to pursue policies consistent with federal goals by attaching conditions to federal funding. It also recognized the right of Congress to regulate private authorities under the commerce clause and to offer to allow the state (a) to regulate the activity by promulgation of state plans (approved by the federal government) or (b) to have the state law preempted by the federal regulation. Both of these latter methods preserved the right of the citizens of the individual states to decide the avenue of compliance. For instance, a state's citizens may refuse a federal grant or elect to have the federal government and not their state bear the cost of enforcing a regulation. The Court found that the "take title" provision in the 1985 radioactive waste act did not provide state citizens a choice since it invaded areas normally reserved for the states and thus violated the Tenth Amendment.

It is difficult to find a logical string to link *New York* with *Hodel.* Until the *New York* case, the federal government was given broad discretion as to how it enforced regulations promulgated under the commerce clause. The three criteria outlined in the *Hodel v. Virginia Surface Mining* case would be used to analyze whether Congress had exceeded the power granted by the commerce clause. In *New York,* the court changes direction: Here the Court analysis lets the people themselves, through the political process, strike the balance between federal and state power. Under this reasoning, federal action that worked to negate the reserved power of the citizens of a state could be found inconsistent with the Tenth Amendment.

Issue Two: Restriction of State Power — The Dormant Commerce Clause

The commerce clause is extremely permissive. It has long been interpreted to restrict state regulation where courts have invalidated state laws that unduly burden interstate commerce. They have done so even when Congress has not regulated a particular matter and has allowed its regulatory authority under the commerce clause to lie dormant. This "dormant commerce clause" interpretation protects federal jurisdiction. Congress, however, still maintains the direct power to either (1) permit a state action invalidated by a court, or (2) preempt state action because it directly interferes with interstate commerce, even if the state action was deemed constitutional by the court.

Under present commerce clause theory, state or local environmental legislation is unconstitutional if it interferes materially, directly or indirectly, with interstate commerce. But the analysis is complex. In the universe of environmental regulation, different judicial decision rules apply to different circumstances. If state environmental legislation is challenged, three critical issues emerge: (1) whether the legislation is discriminatory, (2) whether the state has a proprietary interest in the regulated activity, and (3) the impact of the statute, directly or indirectly, on interstate commerce weighed against the state's justification for the statute and the legitimate local interest in the regulation. There are three general categories where laws may fail such scrutiny: where (1) the state is discriminating in order to isolate itself from a problem common to many states, (2) a state is discriminating for purposes of economic protectionism, or (3) a state is discriminating to generate revenue. Let's look at each.

Geographically Discriminatory Legislation

The rubric for analysis of geographic discrimination in the guise of protection of health and safety emanates from *Dean Milk Co. v. Madison*, 340 U.S. 349 (1951) (ordinance prohibiting the sale of any milk or milk products in the city unless the product was pasteurized and bottled within five miles from the central square in Madison). The Supreme Court there noted, "A city cannot discriminate against interstate commerce, even in the exercise of its unquestioned power to protect the health and safety of its people, if reasonable nondiscriminatory alternatives, adequate to conserve legitimate local interests, are available." If the ordinance exists for a legitimate purpose, the court determines if this legitimate purpose can be served by a reasonable alternative.

The classic commerce clause challenge to state environmental legislation that *facially* discriminates against out-of-state articles of commerce is *City of Philadelphia v. New Jersey*, 437 U.S. 617 (1978). New Jersey had enacted a statute prohibiting the importation and disposal of most solid waste originating outside New Jersey, until the state determined that it would not endanger the public health, safety, and welfare of its citizens. The petitioners were operators of private landfills in New Jersey and cities from other states that had waste disposal agreements with the private operators. They argued that this statute violated the Constitution because it interfered with the free flow of interstate commerce. The petitioners claimed that the statute's purpose was primarily economic; by increasing the longevity of in-state landfills, by excluding out-of-state waste, it would delay the day when New Jersey cities would have to export their own waste at greater expense. New Jersey argued that the purpose of the statute was to protect the environment and the public health, safety, and welfare — all traditionally local obligations.

The Court applied *strict* scrutiny. It stated that it need not determine the legislative purpose of the statute because "the evil of protectionism can reside in legislative means as well as legislative ends." The Court reasoned that whatever its purpose, New Jersey cannot discriminate against articles of commerce originating in other states unless there is a "reason, apart from their *origin*, to treat them differently." In fact, out-of-state waste was no more harmful than waste generated in New Jersey.

Wastes *are* articles of commerce, subject to the clause: "All objects of interstate trade merit Commerce Clause protection, and none is excluded by definition at the outset. . . . Congress has power to regulate the interstate movement of these wastes, [and] States are not free from constitutional scrutiny when they restrict that movement." There was no balancing or weighing of interests. The statute was both facially and effectively discriminatory. A geographically based environmental restriction is unconstitutional. In a critical footnote, the Court reserved judgment on states claiming the same purpose, but as a market participant. We will discuss this below.

There are some exceptions to the rule that a geographically based restriction is unconstitutional. In *Philadelphia*, the court stated that some quarantine laws have not been considered a violation of the commerce clause, although directed at out-of-state commerce. The court distinguished the quarantine laws because they prohibit the entry and movement of articles that risked "contagion and other evils." The quarantine laws prohibit the traffic of noxious articles, whatever their origin. The New Jersey prohibition treated identical out-of-state waste differently from in-state waste, for no reason related to health or safety.

Maine v. Taylor, 477 U.S. 131 (1986), was a quarantine case where Maine banned the importation of an article of commerce, live baitfish, to prevent contamination of Maine's native fish with parasites present on the non-native baitfish. The Court stated that the ban on the baitfish was constitutional only if the "statute served a legitimate local purpose, and the purpose cannot be served well by available nondiscriminatory means." The Court then examined whether prevention of parasitic invasion and commingling of species could be accomplished in a nondiscriminatory manner. Relying on expert testimony, the court found that there was no "satisfactory way to inspect shipments of live baitfish for parasites or commingling of species." The Court held that the prevention of the threat of parasites and the commingling of native and non-native fish species was a legitimate local reason for banning the importation of live baitfish.

The *Philadelphia* decision was the impetus for more creative statute drafting. Clever attorneys drafted legislation that allowed the states and their subdivisions to allocate precious waste disposal land for in-state waste, yet created distinctions from the *Philadelphia* case. If the statute could be written to avoid a finding of facial or geographic-origin discrimination, then it might be reviewed by the courts under the less strict balancing test (discussed in detail in the next section). During a seven-year period spanning into the mid-1990s, the Supreme Court granted certiorari six times to decide the constitutionality of state and local restrictions on the interstate transportation of garbage. Garbage has become the quintessential commodity for commerce clause analysis, as well as the leading environmental issue before the Supreme Court.

In *Fort Gratiot Sanitary Landfill v. Michigan Dept. of Resources*, 504 U.S. 353 (1992), the state of Michigan enacted the Waste Import Restrictions to the Solid Waste Management Act. The state itself did not ban importation of waste from other states, but it allowed importation of waste into a county only if that county had authorized such receipt in its waste plan. If waste was generated in-state and sent to another county, a petition was required. The plaintiff owned and operated a landfill in a county with no provision in its plan for importing waste. When plaintiff's request for authority to accept out-of-state waste was denied, he sued the state, claiming that the Waste Import Restrictions Act was a violation of the commerce clause. The state argued that the law was not facially discriminatory. First, it treated waste from within the state the same as interstate waste; second, the state did not forbid counties to accept outside waste.

The Court rejected both arguments and instead found that the facts of this case were indistinguishable from those in *Philadelphia*. The Court found that equally burdening state residents does not negate the interstate discrimination. The fact that it was Michigan counties that, through inaction, might prevent the importation of waste would not exempt the state statute from strict scrutiny. Further, the fact that Michigan allowed some counties to accept the waste "reduced the scope" of the burden but did not alleviate it. The Court cited *Dean Milk*, comparing the intrastate nature of the challenged laws in the two cases to show that despite being mainly intrastate, the Michigan statute is still facially discriminatory against interstate commerce. The Court held that "a State (or one of its political subdivisions) may not avoid the strictures of the Commerce Clause by curtailing the movement of articles of commerce through subdivisions of the State, rather than through the State itself." Based on these findings, the Court applied the strict scrutiny test as it did in *Philadelphia* and held the statute facially discriminatory: "There is no valid health and safety reason for limiting the amount of waste that a landfill operator may accept from outside the State, but not the amount that the operator may accept from inside the State."

Alabama did not attempt to disguise the geographic-origin discrimination of the statute; it was in fact blatantly discriminatory against waste. The statute imposed a fee on all hazardous waste disposed of at in-state facilities and then added an additional fee for hazardous waste generated outside the state. The state argued that although the statute was facially discriminatory, it warranted the balancing test and not the strict scrutiny test, because the intent was to quarantine the hazardous waste as noxious articles. The state asserted that consistent with the Court's finding in *Philadelphia*, the additional fee fulfilled a legitimate local purpose and would therefore be held constitutional under a balancing test.

The Court in *Chemical Waste Management v. Hunt*, 504 U.S. 334 (1992), struck the Alabama statute that required a "base fee" of $25.60 per ton of hazardous waste disposed at commercial facilities to be paid by the operator of the facility and an additional fee of $72.00 per ton to be paid for hazardous waste that was generated outside Alabama. It found the statute facially discriminatory. While it did not dispute the fact that hazardous waste could be construed as noxious articles, it found that the state did not meet its burden of proving the unavailability of nondiscriminatory means of achieving its legitimate local purpose. In fact, the Court outlined three possible less discriminatory alternatives that would advance the legitimate local concerns of Alabama without violating the commerce clause. They included "a per-ton additional fee on all hazardous waste disposed of in Alabama," a per-ton tax on all vehicles transporting hazardous waste across Alabama roads, and an all-inclusive cap on "the total tonnage land filled," regardless of where the waste was disposed of.

In a 1989 regulation, similar to the Alabama statute in *Chemical Waste*, Oregon imposed a $2.25/ton surcharge on waste that was generated out of state and a surcharge for waste generated in the state of $0.85/ton. The U.S. Supreme Court reiterated that "the purpose of the law has no bearing on whether it is facially discriminatory. In making geographic distinction, the surcharge patently discriminates against interstate commerce. . . . [T]he virtually per se rule of invalidity provides the proper legal standard here." *Oregon Waste Sys. v. Department of Envtl. Quality*, 511 U.S. 93 (1994).

In 1997, the United States Supreme Court refused to hear a case determining whether portions of South Carolina's hazardous waste management program, which limited the amount of out-of-state hazardous waste that could be disposed within the state, violated the commerce clause. See *South Carolina v. Environmental Technology Council*, 521 U.S. 1103 (1997). The Court of Appeals for the Fourth Circuit ruled that the South Carolina plan violated the commerce clause strict scrutiny test, finding facial regulatory discrimination based on point of origin. *Environmental Technology Council v. South Carolina*, 98 F.3d 774, 780 (4th Cir. 1996). South Carolina, for any waste treatment facility in the state, prohibited accepting hazardous waste from a jurisdiction that did not have an interstate or regional agreement for disposing of hazardous waste pursuant to CERCLA, required reservation of space for waste generated in the state, and limited the amount of waste accepted from any one state. These measures were approved by EPA pursuant to RCRA. South Carolina argued that RCRA and CERCLA overrode the dormant commerce clause. South Carolina was unsuccessful in arguing reversible error to the Supreme Court regarding the application of the strict scrutiny test, alleging that the less strict "reasonableness" test should have applied.

In *C. & A. Carbone, Inc. v. Town of Clarkstown*, 511 U.S. 383 (1994), the Court held that regulation cannot be justified by desire to protect or regulate the environment outside the political jurisdiction of the regulatory agency: The town cannot "justify the flow-control ordinance as a way to steer solid waste away from out-of-town disposal sites that it might deem harmful to the environment. To do so would extend the town's police power beyond its jurisdictional bounds." Though the Clarkstown ordinance did not seek to burden interstate commerce, it based its ordinance on geographic origin and discriminated by practical effect.

The town of Clarkstown adopted an ordinance requiring all solid waste within the town to utilize a newly built transfer station where the town had guaranteed a minimum waste flow at an above-market tipping fee in order to finance the station. Carbone's waste-hauling truck struck an overpass on a parkway in New York, which caused the discovery that he was sending waste out of state rather than to the designated facilities. Thereafter, local police monitored Carbone's plant and seized more tractor trailers of waste headed for the Midwest and elsewhere. The town of Clarkstown sued Carbone to try to enjoin him from sending waste to other than the designated transfer stations. The Court held: "The flow control ordinance . . . hoards solid waste, and the demand to get rid of it, for the benefit of the preferred processing facility. Discrimination against interstate commerce in favor of local business . . . is per se invalid, save in a narrow class of cases in which the municipality can demonstrate, under rigorous scrutiny, that it has no other means to advance a legitimate local interest. . . . By itself . . . revenue generation is not a local interest that can justify discrimination against interstate commerce." In this case, the court found that Clarkstown had a number of other nondiscriminatory alternatives for addressing the health and environmental problems that justified the ordinance. The court found unconvincing the rationale that the town needed to raise revenue through the flow control ordinance.

A flow control statute requiring all garbage that was not sent out of state to be taken to a particular transfer station for disposal, at which fees were higher than market, violated the dormant Commerce Clause. *U & I Sanitation v. Columbus*, 205 F.3d 1063 (8th Cir. 2000). The court distinguished the case from *Carbone* because the city required solid waste to utilize the transfer station only if it was disposed of in the state, whereas the ordinance in *Carbone* required all solid waste to utilize the station. The court held that "[t]he purely intrastate designation of the Columbus ordinance, which does not explicitly favor local interest over out-of-state interests does not violate the Commerce Clause . . . however the ordinance may still violate [it] if the local interests that it serves do not justify the burden that it imposes on interstate commerce." While the court found that since there was an exemption for waste leaving the state, it did not overtly discriminate against interstate commerce, it nonetheless found the regulation unconstitutional because it imposed an excessive burden in relation to the local benefit (raising revenue).

A regulatory limitation on the amount of solid waste that can be delivered to a large regional landfill in a state, and prohibiting barge transportation of solid waste on a temporary basis, was found discriminatory against out-of-state commerce. *Waste Management Holdings v. Gilmore*, 87 F. Supp. 2d 536 (E.D. Va. 2000). The state of Michigan's requirement that only solid waste from a state or county that had enacted beverage container deposit laws, to encourage the return and recycling of bottles, could be accepted at Michigan landfills was found to be a violation of the Commerce Clause in *National Solid Waste Management Ass'n v. Charter County of Wayne*, 303 F. Supp. 2d 835 (D. Mich. 2004).

California's low carbon fuel program was enjoined as facially discriminatory under the dormant commerce clause against out-of-state fuel substitutes because it assigned a higher carbon index score to Midwest biofuels than it did to California-produced fuels due to the distances involved in delivery and use of coal in Midwest electricity production. *Rocky Mt. Farmers Union v. Goldstene*, 2011 U.S. Dist. LEXIS 149592 (E.D. Cal. Dec. 29, 2011). While these weights were factually and environmentally accurate, no facially discriminatory regulation based on geography of the commerce can survive unless it embodies the least restrictive means of achieving a legitimate environmental objective. *Id.*

Facial as well as applied discrimination based on *point of origin* is highly suspect and almost always fatal when embodied in environmental laws. Courts employ strict scrutiny, with no balancing of interests, to reach this conclusion. Exceptions are few.

The Balancing Test for State Legislation That Is Not Facially Discriminatory but May Burden Interstate Commerce

There is more than one way to accomplish a legislative goal. In many cases, environmental statutes are not based on point of origin and therefore not facially discriminatory. However, state legislation may still interfere with or adversely impact interstate commerce. To determine whether a statute *as applied* justifiably burdens interstate commerce, a court will balance the impact of the statute on interstate commerce against the state's reasons and legitimate purpose for the statute. By definition, this balancing test is *not* strict scrutiny. But there is much environmental precedent employing this balancing test to determine whether incidental discrimination *as applied* is impermissible.

The *Dean Milk* decision is an early precursor of what became the *Pike* balancing test. See *Pike v. Bruce Church, Inc.*, 397 U.S. 137 (1970) (a non-environmental case). *Dean Milk* was decided at the exact midpoint of the twentieth century. The local ordinance made it illegal to sell milk that was processed and bottled more than five miles outside the boundary of the city, or to import, store, receive, or sell milk in the city of Madison unless it was from a source inspected and permitted by Madison. However, the inspectors from Madison would not inspect sources more than 25 miles outside the center of the city. The court explained that the city could not discriminate against interstate commerce even though it had the power to protect health and safety of its citizens. Most importantly, the court held that an ordinance which burdens interstate commerce cannot be enacted if non-discriminatory alternative means adequate to protect legitimate state or local interests were available. The statute violated the commerce clause.

Essentially, *Dean Milk* requires regulators to implement the least burdensome alternatives to mitigate the burden on interstate commerce. While the marquee expression of the balancing doctrine awaited the decision in *Pike*, the *Dean Milk* decision became the foundation of the 1960 Supreme Court decision in *Huron Portland Cement*, 362 U.S. 440 (1960), and echoes through the decision in *Pike*.

In *Procter & Gamble v. Chicago*, 509 F.2d 69 (7th Cir. 1975), *cert. denied*, 421 U.S. 978 (1975), the city of Chicago had enacted an ordinance that banned the use of detergents containing phosphates. The plaintiff, Procter & Gamble, was a company that manufactured and sold phosphate detergents throughout the country — a good, clean business. The plaintiff argued that the statute affected sales of phosphate detergents because its warehouses, supplying stores in northern Illinois, northern Indiana, southern Wisconsin, and Michigan, refused to carry both phosphate and nonphosphate detergent.

As with many environmental laws, interstate commerce was involved. The court concluded first that the Chicago ordinance did affect sales of phosphate detergent in other states, thereby burdening interstate commerce. The court next examined the interest sought to be served by the ordinance, to determine whether it was a legitimate local concern. The court balanced: It found that Chicago's objective in enacting this ordinance was to prevent and eliminate algae in the Illinois River and Lake Michigan (see the discussion of water pollution in Chapter 6).

The court concluded that the burden placed on interstate commerce was slight and that it was outweighed by the legitimate environmental goal of decreasing algae. The ordinance was not impermissible under the commerce clause. This case also illustrates that local as well as state legislation can trigger commerce clause scrutiny.

Minnesota v. Clover Leaf Creamery, 449 U.S. 456 (1981), involved a statute that banned the retail sale of milk in plastic, nonreturnable, nonrefillable containers, but it permitted the sale of milk in nonreturnable, nonrefillable *paperboard* milk cartons. By a wild coincidence, Minnesota produces lots of trees milled to produce paperboard in its forest products industry; surprisingly, it produces little plastic. The petitioners contended that the statute violated the commerce clause because it imposed an unreasonable burden on interstate commerce.

The court balanced. First, the court found that the statute did not discriminate between interstate and intrastate goods, because the statute prohibits *all* Minnesota milk retailers from selling milk in plastic, nonreturnable, nonrefillable containers, regardless of the container's place of origin. Then (the balancing test) it examined whether the statute placed any burden on interstate commerce and whether local benefits as a result of this statute outweigh the burden. Dairies bore the cost of complying with this statute, and it disadvantaged out-of-state plastic manufacturers. The Court found that the state interest — promoting conservation of energy, protection of natural resources, and decreasing solid waste — outweighed the slight burden placed on interstate commerce.

The court found the classification to be reasonably supported, not a violation of equal protection, and found no Commerce Clause violation because the state regulated "even handedly" and did not prohibit or distinguish between in-state and out-of-state sellers of milk cartons.

One more illustration. The Third Circuit Court of Appeals used the balancing test in *Norfolk Southern Corp. v. Oberly*, 822 F.2d 388 (3d Cir. 1987). This case involved a Delaware environmental statute that imposed strict regulation on all *new* bulk fuel transfer facilities in the coastal zone and prohibited all "offshore gas, liquid, or solid bulk transfer facilities" that were not in operation as of 1971. The petitioners, seeking to start a coal lightering service in Delaware Bay, claimed that the statute violated the commerce clause. The petitioner's coal lightering service involved topping off "supercolliers," deep-draft cargo vessels, while they were anchored offshore in deep water. The petitioners claimed that Delaware Bay was the only safe harbor suitable from Maine to Mexico for anchorage deep enough for fully loaded vessels.

The court found that the Delaware statute was facially neutral and did not have a discriminatory effect because the prohibition included Delaware coal exporters. The court then balanced. It asked whether the statute burdened interstate commerce and if so, whether the burden was outweighed by the local benefits created by the statute. In this case, the court found that the local benefits were the protection of the coastal environment from potential transfer facility pollution and spills, and that there was "no legally relevant burden on interstate commerce." That is, the local benefits outweighed the burden (if any) placed on interstate commerce, and the statute was upheld. In sum, one can discriminate against *new* or *particular* industries, but *not* on the basis of point of origin.

In some cases the court engages in the balancing test but still finds that the local benefit does not outweigh the burden. *West Lynn Creamery v. Healy*, 512 U.S. 186 (1994), involved yet another attempt at drafting of a statute so as to circumvent a finding of facial discrimination and avoid the strict scrutiny test. At issue was a law created by the Massachusetts Department of Food and Agriculture that imposed an assessment (a tax) on all fluid milk sold by milk dealers to Massachusetts retailers. All the funds collected through the assessment were then distributed to Massachusetts dairy farmers.

Petitioners were licensed dealers who bought milk produced by out-of-state farmers and then sold it to Massachusetts retailers. The dealers refused to pay the assessment; the Commonwealth of Massachusetts revoked their licenses. The dealers then brought suit alleging that the provisions, as enforced, violated the commerce clause. One of the Commonwealth's arguments for upholding the provisions was that the local benefits outweighed any incidental burden on interstate commerce, because the Massachusetts dairy farmers needed the assistance and the dealers did not. The other argument asserted by the Commonwealth was that the provisions did not discriminate for two reasons: The assessment is paid by in-state residents and also is levied against milk produced within the state, and the dairy farmers who receive the funds were not competitors of the retail dealers who pay the tax. These arguments were successfully asserted in the *Minnesota* case. The last and unique argument made by Massachusetts was that the Commonwealth had a right to levy an assessment to subsidize an in-state industry.

The Court did not recognize balancing in this case and distinguished it from *Minnesota* because the subsidy to the Massachusetts dairy farmers came entirely from the assessment. Nor would the court sanction the ultimate goal of preserving the failing Commonwealth dairy industry as a legitimate local benefit. The goal of aiding a failing industry was not of such a compelling interest as to outweigh the burden it placed on the dealers with out-of-state sources. The Court comments, "Preservation of local industry by protecting it from the rigors of interstate competition is the hallmark of the economic protectionism that the commerce clause prohibits."

The New York Supreme Court struck down a tax that supported the state Superfund program as unconstitutional. *CWM Chem. Servs., L.L.C. v. Roth*, 6 N.Y. 3d 410 (N.Y. 2006). The tax was imposed on out-of-state hazardous waste shipments into the state, while in-state shipments were exempt from the tax. The tax was found to discriminate facially against interstate commerce, against out-of-state companies, and to violate the dormant commerce clause. The court suggested that if the tax were severed from the use of the proceeds to finance in-state-only Superfund cleanups, it might survive challenge.

In a few cases, the court does not get as far as a balancing test analysis because it finds that the state legislation does not discriminate even incidentally against interstate commerce. Instead, the court resolves the case based on whether the statute places an undue burden on interstate commerce, a burden being less serious than discrimination. In the 1960 case of *Huron Portland Cement v. City of Detroit*, 362 U.S. 440 (1960), the Court considered whether a Detroit ordinance that set a maximum limit for smoke emissions and created criminal liability for violations imposed an undue burden on interstate commerce. The petitioner was a corporation that owned five cement transport vessels that docked in Detroit. While docked, the vessels' hand-fired boilers periodically emitted smoke that exceeded the maximum standards set by the Detroit ordinance.

The owners and agents of the vessel were charged with criminal violations of the ordinance. They argued that the ordinance imposed an impermissible burden on interstate commerce. The Court held that the ordinance did not discriminate against interstate commerce, as its provisions were applicable to any person or corporation in Detroit, regardless of their origins. It also held that "no impermissible burden on commerce" was shown. No undue burden, no balancing.

Market Participant Analysis: When a State Does Not Regulate

The United States Supreme Court recognizes a relaxation of commerce clause restraints in cases where discriminatory action is taken by a government entity in the role of a *market participant* rather than as a *regulator*. When a state participates directly in the market as a purchaser, seller, or producer of articles of commerce, its activities will not be subject to the usual commerce clause restrictions, even if discriminatory effects flow from the state's actions. Recall that this possibility was not resolved in *Philadelphia v. New Jersey*. This concept can best be demonstrated by an environmental statute involving a state incentive to decrease the number of abandoned cars clogging urban areas.

In *Hughes v. Alexandria Scrap*, 426 U.S. 794 (1976), a Maryland statute provided that anyone who had an inoperable motor vehicle ("hulk") could transfer it to a licensed scrap processor who in turn could claim a financial bounty (payment) from the state of Maryland without any proof of title. In 1974 Maryland introduced geographic discrimination in dealing with these articles of commerce, the hulks. More stringent requirements were placed on out-of-state processors. A Maryland processor, under the new ordinance, needed to have only an "indemnity agreement" whereby any unlicensed hulk provider certified his or her right to the hulk and indemnified the licensed processor for any potential claims that might arise from the destruction of the vehicle. This made the hulk provider, not the processor, responsible for obtaining clear title. By comparison, non-Maryland processors had to submit a certificate of title, a police certificate that vested title in the processor, or a bill of sale from a police auction.

The plaintiff, a Virginia processor, claimed that the 1974 provision violated the commerce clause. He complained that the statute's more elaborate requirements caused a decrease in the number of bounty-producing hulks that he could redeem in Maryland. The court distinguished the *Hughes* case from other cases where states interfered *by regulation* with private parties engaged in interstate commerce. The Court emphasized the fact that Maryland did not seek to prohibit or regulate the flow of interstate hulks. The burden was on out-of-state *businesses*, not on out-of-state articles of commerce. Instead, Maryland was a participant in the market. The Court stated, "[N]othing in the purposes animating the commerce clause prohibits a State, in the absence of congressional action, from participating in the market and exercising the right to favor its own citizens over others." The Maryland statute did not violate the commerce clause.

Therefore, a state can choose to place in or withhold from interstate commerce an article it controls. In *Hughes*, that article was the bounty — state property. This choice by the state, acting in a market participant or proprietary mode, rather than a regulatory mode, is permissible. This concept also applies to environmental resources, such as landfill space or energy resources, for which the state acts in a proprietary capacity.

4. Constitutional Issues: The Commerce Clause and Environmental Preemption

By dominating waste markets, rather than regulating them, municipalities may find mechanisms to escape the limitations of *C. & A. Carbone*. Two federal circuits have held that as long as out-of-state facilities can apply to do the trash hauling work, requiring designated trash haulers, by contract, to take waste to a designated facility does not violate the dormant commerce clause. *Harvey & Harvey v. County of Chester*, 68 F.3d 788 (3d Cir. 1995); *SSC Corp. v. Town of Smithtown*, 66 F.3d 502 (2d Cir. 1995); *USA Recycling v. Town of Babylon*, 66 F.3d 1272 (2d Cir. 1995). In these jurisdictions, the town's acting in a proprietary capacity, via contracts with other parties who haul waste, can be sustained.

The Second Circuit allowed a municipality to establish a garbage collection district and give a private garbage hauler the exclusive right to collect garbage within that district (which eventually was burned in a municipal cogeneration plant). The court held that such a *contract* constituted municipal *market participation*, rather than municipal *regulation*. *SSC Corp. v. Town of Smithtown*. This court allowed the private contracting mechanism to insulate the town from the stricter constitutional scrutiny imposed on acts of a regulator. See *U.S.A. Recycling, Inc. v. Town of Babylon*, 66 F.3d 1272 (2d Cir. 1995).

In 2007, in a perplexing decision, the Supreme Court seemed to contradict *Carbone* by following its dissenting opinions, while claiming that *Carbone* involved a privately owned transfer station, holding that municipalities could undertake flow control by benefiting public-owned rather than private facilities. *United Haulers Ass'n, Inc. et al. v. Oneida-Herkimer Solid Waste Management Authority, et al.*, 550 U.S. 330 (2007). The affected counties had the state create a special-purpose solid waste management authority which was granted a local monopoly to process, recycle, or dispose of (but not collect) all solid waste emanating from the affected counties. The affected counties then implemented flow control ordinances, requiring trash collectors to obtain permits that obligated them to dispose of all trash at above-market prices exclusively through the authority. The tipping fee at the Herkimer fill was about 120 percent of the cost of the tipping fee at the private landfills in the two neighboring counties to which the waste otherwise could have been transported.

In *Oneida-Herkimer*, the plurality opinion written by Chief Justice Roberts applied the *Pike* balancing test and thereafter interpreted the ordinance not to violate the dormant commerce clause because it created at least "minimal" local benefits that outweighed whatever "insubstantial" differential burden was placed on interstate commerce. The plurality opinion found that there is "constitutional significance" to the public/private distinction for ownership under the market participant exception. The Court noted that in-state and out-of-state interests were equally disadvantaged. The Court stated that discriminatory regulation must benefit the former and burden the latter.

However, *Carbone* could be argued to have prohibited Commerce Clause violations where the in-state flow control ordinance burdened in-district

power. The protection of citizens' health, safety, and welfare has historically come under the states' police powers and includes the protection of the environment. There is no automatic preemption merely because Congress previously has acted. Oz can limit new facilities if the statute is carefully crafted.

Air Quality Regulation

"There is something in the wind."

William Shakespeare, A Comedy of Errors

"Air, wonderful Air, wonderful Air!"

The Muppets

"It is in our lungs that we connect to our earth's great aerial bloodstream, and in this way the atmosphere inspires us from our first breath to our last."

Tim Flannery, The Weathermakers

"The overwhelming importance of the atmosphere means that there are no longer any frontiers to defend against pollution."

Margaret Mead, Culture and Commitment, 1970

"We are thankful to the powers we know as the Four Winds. We hear their voices in the moving air as they refresh us and purify the air we breathe. They help to bring the change of seasons. From the four directions they come, bringing us messages and giving us strength."

Iroquois Nation, Thanksgiving Address

THE BASICS OF AIR POLLUTION REGULATION

Sources of Air Pollution

Take a deep breath. Now exhale. It is so common that we take it for granted. We each breathe 50 to 60 pounds, or approximately 20,000 liters, of air a day, making our lungs our primary point of contact with the environment. Air is an absolute necessity to sustain animal life. Earth's air, in its purest form, consists of nitrogen and oxygen in an approximate ratio of three to one. The supply of air is not centralized or fixed. It drifts and mixes. Its natural waste by-product from humans, CO_2, sustains plant life. Since 1950, the net growth of trees has exceeded the net harvest of trees every year in the United States. Forested areas cover 30 percent of the total land areas. Air is polluted when undesirable particles and gases are added to the basic combination of nitrogen and oxygen.

How does air pollution come about? The Clean Air Act simplifies the analysis by dividing all sources of air pollution into two categories: "mobile" and "stationary" sources. *Mobile* sources include automobiles, buses, trucks, trains, and airplanes. *Stationary* sources include factories, power plants, or any structure or facility that emits a significant amount of pollutant into the air. Stationary sources are easy targets for regulation — they cannot move or flee. Mobile sources are more problematic — cars are driven, owned, and adored by the voting public. Moreover, these sources of pollution move about freely. Societal dependence on the automobile and a continual increase in the number of vehicle miles traveled each year underscore the growing importance of controlling mobile sources.

An indirect source is any "facility, building, structure, installation, real property, road, or highway which attracts, or may attract, mobile sources of pollution." 42 U.S.C. §7410(a)(5)(C). Indirect sources are not stationary sources. Parking structures that otherwise do not emit pollutants are often regarded as indirect sources. States have the option of regulating indirect sources if they choose, or omitting any regulation of them. In major construction projects where a roadway is to be underground, there are lingering questions whether ventilation structures for an underground roadway are a mobile source or a stationary source. To avoid the stricter regulation of stationary sources, Massachusetts amended its SIP to declare that any tunnel ventilation systems were to be regarded as indirect sources. Litigation by environmental groups was unsuccessful in reversing this designation as an indirect source. *Sierra Club v. Larson*, 769 F. Supp. 420 (D. Mass. 1991).

Let's begin by identifying the key components of air regulation in the United States. We start with some ancient history (before 1970) in order to gain a sense of the evolution of air regulation. The important things to understand here are (1) the role of the states versus that of the federal government, (2) the distinction between regulating regional air quality and permitting individuals to emit air pollutants, (3) the ways in which technology-based pollution standards are translated into legal requirements and eventually into technological solutions to pollution problems, and (4) your role as environmental counsel. As we proceed through this material, we will note the ten key concepts that are most important to understand.

Air Pollution Regulation Prior to 1970

Until enactment of the Air Pollution Control Act of 1955, the problem of mitigating air pollution was reserved almost exclusively for local and state authorities. You'll notice similarities on this point when we subsequently discuss water pollution in Chapter 6. The initial Clean Air Act was adopted in 1963, expanding the federal role by authorizing the Department of Health, Education, and Welfare (HEW) to establish air quality criteria through conferences involving polluters and representatives from state and federal government. The 1965 Motor Vehicle Pollution Control Act extended the federal effort by authorizing the HEW secretary to prescribe national standards to regulate emissions from new motor vehicles. The initial standards for automobiles were applied to 1968 new model vehicles.

In November 1967, Congress enacted the first comprehensive federal scheme of air pollution control with passage of the Air Quality Act. And from this Act came the first key concept that it is important for us to understand: AQCRs. The Act required the HEW secretary to designate *air quality control regions (AQCRs)* within a state or within an interstate region. AQCRs are regions or airsheds in which air quality is monitored and controlled. It remains a key regulatory concept.

In designated AQCRs, the *states* were required to set standards to limit the levels of a pollutant described in *federal* air quality control technology documents. However, in the absence of enforceable national air quality standards, the Air Quality Act failed to clearly define its goals for these pollutants. Problems with implementation ensued. A state could set varying standards for different regions within its boundaries.

As before, the task of designing and implementing programs to remedy air pollution problems was shouldered by the individual states. The Air Quality Act also left enforcement of the air quality standards to the states and did not provide for effective federal enforcement. Enforcement of the Act's mandates was conducted through administrative action or a court proceeding against an individual polluter, a process that proved ineffective in redressing ambient air problems. The significant contribution of the 1967 Act was its role in starting to identify which air regions were particularly problematic and which sources of pollution were contributing to the problem.

What is interesting to note in this ancient history is that automobiles were regulated before stationary sources. It is also worth noting that this early approach to air quality monitoring and compliance was a disaggregated regional one, with a dual state/federal role. Let's move on now and track the evolution of this regulation to the individual polluting sources.

The Clean Air Act Amendments of 1970

The 1970 Clean Air Act passed the Senate unanimously and was adopted by the House by voice vote. The Clean Air Act Amendments of 1970 provide the basic structure and bedrock of the current Clean Air Act. Under the Clean Air Act Amendments of 1970, Congress envisioned a federal/state partnership. The *federal* role was to create (1) nationally uniform quality standards for ambient air, and (2) *technology-based* standards for individual polluters' emissions. In this federal vein, here is the second key concept: National Ambient Air Quality Standards (NAAQS). The states' role was to enforce these standards through a third key concept: SIPs, State Implementation Plans, to achieve the NAAQS.

Let's review each of these key concepts.

Ambient Air Quality: Area Regulation

National Ambient Air Quality Standards (NAAQS) and Criteria Pollutants What are NAAQS? Under the 1970 amendments, Congress abandoned the region-by-region approach it had favored under the Air Quality Act of 1967, instead mandating nationally uniform standards. The 1970 Act instructed the EPA to promulgate NAAQS for six "criteria pollutants" for which the EPA had issued scientific air quality criteria prior to 1970: (1) particulate matter, (2) sulfur dioxide, (3) ozone, (4) nitrogen oxides, (5) carbon monoxide, and (6) hydrocarbons. The EPA must review the adequacy of NAAQS at least once every five years.

The concept of *criteria pollutants* is the fourth key concept that we should keep in mind. These compounds are called "criteria pollutants" because, while undesirable, they are not toxic in typical concentrations in ambient air. *Toxic* air pollutants, as well as carbon dioxide, a "greenhouse" gas associated with global warming, were not included. In *Massachusetts v. EPA*, 549 U.S. 497 (2007), the Court held, 5-4, that states have standing to sue the EPA alleging injuries from climate change, the EPA has the authority to regulate greenhouse gases as "pollutants" under the Clean Air Act, and the EPA did not adequately justify its decision not to regulate greenhouse gas emissions from motor vehicles under the Act. See Chapter 12.

The National Research Council looked at human mortality from environmental impacts resulting from pollution, such as SO_2, NO_x, O_3, and particulate matter, and concluded that in 2005 about 19,000 people died prematurely from the harmful emissions from transportation and power generation-related emissions of criteria pollutants. Among the criteria pollutants, particulate matter may have the clearest and largest effects on mortality and morbidity. Ozone has been shown to have only a fraction of the mortality impact that is associated with particulate matter, although it is being linked to lung function development in children. The impact of carbon monoxide is generally localized around certain transportation corridors.

The human lung has an enormous surface area — as large as a tennis court. The alveolar walls of the lung, where gas exchange between the lung and the circulatory system occurs, is much thinner tissue than either the stomach or the skin, so as to allow fast diffusion of oxygen across this barrier. This makes the lung tissue susceptible to environmental pollutants. Once an airway or alveolar wall tissue is damaged or destroyed, it does not regenerate. Because of differences in surface-to-lung volume, metabolic rate, and activity, a child's lungs get a much larger dose of disseminated particulate pollution than do adult lungs.

As people age, they naturally lose about one percent of lung function each year (about 50 percent more than this for cigarette smokers). Thus, an average 70-year-old adult has lost approximately 50 percent of his or her lung function from natural aging, even in the absence of elevated pollution levels. Where particulate pollution decreases lung function even more, the reserve lung function capacity is significantly impacted.

As a lawyer, where do you find the NAAQS for these criteria pollutants? They are required by the statute and in the EPA air regulations. The federal air regulations are at 40 C.F.R. The NAAQS are expressed as "parts per million" of a pollutant in a sample of ambient air.[1] Ambient air quality standards are expressed as both a maximum concentration of criteria pollutants in air over a sampling period of 1 to 24 hours depending on the pollutant, as well as an annual arithmetic mean concentration. The limitation for a criteria pollutant typically is that the standard cannot be exceeded more than once per year. The standards are expressed as a threshold concentration of pollutant gas in the air. NAAQS are established, without regard to cost, to protect sensitive subpopulations. *Amer. Lung Ass'n v. EPA*, 134 F.3d 388 (D.C. Cir. 1998). NAAQS protect normal populations with an adequate margin of safety. They must be reviewed every five years and revised if necessary.

The NAAQS include both "primary" standards, designed to protect the *public health* while allowing for an adequate margin of safety, and "secondary"

---

1. Measurement units and conversions:

- 1 part per million (ppm) = 1 milligram/liter (mg/L)
  = 1 microgram/gram (μg/g)
  = 1 milligram/kilogram (mg/kg)
- 1 part per billion (ppb) = 1 microgram/liter (μg/L)
  = 1 microgram/kilogram (μg/kg)

standards. Secondary standards are intended to protect the *public welfare* from any known or anticipated effects of the criteria pollutants. "Public welfare" includes soils, water, crops, visibility, comfort, and human-made materials. The NAAQS must be achieved "as expeditiously as practicable." Would it surprise you to learn that the deadlines imposed for states to achieve these standards, originally set at three years from 1970 for the primary standards, and within "a reasonable time" for the secondary standards, were largely unattained at the prescribed times? Many areas still have not attained them.

In *Natural Resources Defense Council v. Train*, 411 F. Supp. 864 (S.D.N.Y. 1976), *aff'd*, 545 F.2d 320 (2d Cir. 1976), the NRDC brought an action against the Environmental Protection Agency for its failure to list *lead* as a criteria pollutant. The NRDC alleged that once the EPA administrator determines that a pollutant "has an adverse effect on public health and welfare," the administrator must regulate that criteria pollutant. The EPA argued that

5.1   Criteria Pollutants

Symbol	Precursor	Name	Environmental Impact	Major Source
SO_2		Sulfur dioxide	Acid rain	Fossil fuel
NO_x		Nitrogen oxides	Smog, global warming	Fossil fuel power plants, vehicle exhaust
PM-10 PM-2.5		Particulate matter (measured as less than 10 or 2.5 microns)	Respiratory irritant	Coal, various processes
CO		Carbon monoxide	Smog	Auto exhaust, combustion
Pb		Lead	Impairs brain function	Chemical processes, product additive
HC*		Hydrocarbons	Smog	Auto exhaust, chemical facilities
O_3	VOCs, NMOGs, HC	Ozone (precursors)	Smog	Auto exhaust, chemical facilities

*Hydrocarbons (HC) were originally listed separately from ozone. Now they are viewed as an ozone precursor.

its administrator has sole discretion in the initial decision regarding the listing of a pollutant. The court held that the EPA is obligated to list a pollutant once such pollutant has been determined by the agency *potentially* to have an adverse effect on public health and welfare. So now lead is on the list, but there are still only six criteria pollutants. Hydrocarbons (HC) have now been redefined as a precursor of ozone. A precursor chemical is a compound that reacts in the atmosphere with other chemicals to become or create the regulated compound. The six original criteria pollutants are listed in Exhibit 5.1. On the last line of Exhibit 5.1, the three precursors of ozone (other than NO_x) are also shown: volatile organic compounds (VOCs), nonmethane organic gases (NMOGs), and hydrocarbons (HC). In 2009 the EPA decided also to regulate CO_2. See Chapter 15 regarding carbon regulation.

But the battle about lead was not over. In *Lead Industries Ass'n v. EPA*, 647 F.2d 1330 (D.C. Cir. 1980), several organizations challenged the ambient air quality standards for lead that the EPA had promulgated. The court affirmed the standards set by the EPA, holding that the administrator's construction of the act will be upheld if it is reasonable. The EPA was not to consider economic or technological feasibility in setting the standards. The court noted that in fulfilling congressional orders to ensure "an absence of adverse effects . . . Congress directed the Administrator to err on the side of caution in making the necessary decision."

Exhibit 5.2 sets forth existing NAAQS for the six criteria pollutants.

State Implementation Plans (SIPs)   Now let's focus on the third key concept: SIPs. The SIP bridges the gap between *federally* established air quality standards and *state* enforcement of these standards. The new "partnership" in the fight to control air pollution is embodied by the state's development and submission to the EPA of SIPs designed to achieve the NAAQS. The state is undoubtedly the junior partner in this relationship, even though it is charged with doing much of the work.

The SIP process requires each state to submit a detailed plan for the implementation, maintenance, and enforcement of the national ambient air standards for each of the criteria pollutants. Once the EPA issues a primary NAAQS, states must propose a plan (a SIP) for its attainment. The states, through the use of emission inventories and computer models, must predict for each AQCR whether the national standards are in danger of being violated and what reductions in regional emission are necessary to meet the national standards.

After a SIP is submitted, the EPA has four months to make a finding that accepts, accepts in part, or rejects the plan in whole or in part. If the plan is adequate, the EPA must approve it. Once approved by the EPA, the state and local regulations in the SIP become enforceable as federal law. Any state changes are not effective until approved by the EPA. In the absence of an adequate SIP, the EPA is empowered to create a Federal Implementation Plan

5.2 NAAQS

Pollutant		Primary/ Secondary	Averaging Time	Level	Form
Carbon Monoxide		Primary	8-hour	9 ppm	Not to be exceeded more than once per year
			1-hour	35 ppm	
Lead		Both	Rolling 3-month average	0.15 $\mu g/m^3$	Not to be exceeded
Nitrogen Dioxide		Primary	1-hour	100 ppb	98th percentile, averaged over 3 years
		Both	Annual	53 ppb	Annual mean
Ozone		Both	8-hour	0.075 ppm	Annual fourth-highest daily maximum 8-hr concentration, averaged over 3 years
Particle Pollution	$PM_{2.5}$	Both	Annual	15 $\mu g/m^3$	Annual mean, averaged over 3 years
			24-hour	35 $\mu g/m^3$	98th percentile, averaged over 3 years
	PM_{10}	Both	24-hour	150 $\mu g/m^3$	Not exceeded more than 1x/year over 3 years
Sulfur Dioxide		Primary	1-hour	75 ppb	99th percentile of 1-hour daily maximum concentrations, averaged over 3 years
		Secondary	3-hour	0.5 ppm	Not to be exceeded more than once per year

(FIP) for a particular region and take over administration of a state's air program. Federal highway funds can be cut off.

The federal government creates the general "envelope" of uniform NAAQS. The states are free to optimize approaches and programs within the envelope to achieve NAAQS compliance within the AQCR. The state can restrict specific pollution sources by any means, and it can address ambient or fugitive sources. Controls can include technology or techniques, such as the use of tall emission stacks, to disperse pollutants to other regions.

The EPA's "preferred approach" for the drafting of SIPs called for states to enact immediately effective categorical emission limitations. These could include a "variance" procedure that allowed individual sources of pollutants to obtain relief from specified requirements. The EPA sought to treat these variances as SIP "revisions" in some circumstances, whereas environmental groups insisted that they amounted to "postponements of federal requirements." "Postponements" were subject to strict procedural and substantive standards, and the EPA was required to conduct hearings to determine whether a "postponement" should issue.

This distinction between "revisions" and "postponements" was important, as SIP revisions could be granted by the state alone, provided they did not interfere with attainment of NAAQS by specified SIP dates. In Train v. NRDC, 421 U.S. 60 (1975), the Court held that the EPA's treatment of variances as revisions was acceptable, provided that ultimate attainment dates were not adversely affected. This decision vested authority in the states to grant variances, unless they would delay attainment, in which case they would necessitate federal review.

In Union Electric Co. v. EPA, 427 U.S. 246 (1976), Missouri adopted a SIP for the metropolitan St. Louis region that required pollution emission reductions from three of Union Electric's coal-fired electric power plants. The company did not challenge the generic SIP within the guidelines enumerated under the federal act. Rather, it obtained variances to permit continued operation for a specified extension period. Upon expiration of the variances, Union sought a review of the EPA's prior approval of the SIP. Union Electric claimed that "the reductions required of Union were not technologically or economically feasible; if enforced, Union would be required to shut down its plants and curtail electric service." The Court held, "We agree that Congress intended claims of economic and technological infeasibility to be wholly foreign to the Administrator's consideration of a state implementation plan." Union Electric did not prevail. Compliance is always possible by shutting down the polluting source entirely.

In Abramowitz v. EPA, 832 F.2d 1071 (9th Cir. 1987), petitioner Abramowitz sought judicial review of an EPA decision to approve certain air pollution control measures in the South Coast Air Basin (including Los Angeles) portion of California's SIP without first requiring attainment of statutory air quality standards in compliance with prescribed deadlines. The EPA had taken final action by approving the portions of the California SIP pertaining to carbon monoxide (CO) and ozone control measures without requiring a demonstration that these measures would enable California to attain the primary standards by the statutory deadline. The Court of Appeals for the Ninth Circuit held that the EPA had erred in segregating attainment demonstration from the approval process for the proposed control measures.

Once a SIP is adopted at the federal level by the EPA, only an agreement with or variance granted by the EPA will allow noncompliance with the provisions of the SIP. A state court injunction pending a variance does not toll a federal SIP violation, *Getty Oil Co., Inc. v. Ruckelshaus*, 467 F.2d 349 (3d Cir. 1972), nor does a state court decree to which the EPA is not a party prevent EPA enforcement for noncompliance, *United States v. Ford Motor Co.*, 814 F.2d 1099 (7th Cir. 1987). Even federal courts have no discretion to vary the statutory deadlines for individual emitter compliance with a SIP. *United States v. Wheeling-Pittsburgh Steel Corp.*, 818 F.2d 1077 (3d Cir. 1987). Continuous emission controls, rather than intermittent or temporary controls, are required for SIP compliance. *Kennecott Copper Corp. v. Train*, 526 F.2d 1149 (9th Cir. 1975).

The timetable presented under the 1970 amendments mandated attainment of the NAAQS for all criteria pollutants by 1975, and in the case of extensions, by no later than 1977. Yet many areas of the nation still are not in compliance, more than three decades later. The specific requirements for SIPs are found at §110 of the Clean Air Act.

Air Quality Control Regions (AQCR)   The Clean Air Act of 1970 did not abandon the 1967 Act's AQCR structure, but it announced two significant changes. First, rural areas that had been ignored under the 1967 Act were included to emphasize the national scope of the new amendments. Second, the amendments directed the EPA to designate areas as part of an AQCR when necessary for attainment of the NAAQS, thus, "giving the federal government its first authority directly to define AQCRs." This change in the statute reduced state autonomy with the EPA ultimately controlling final designation of AQCRs.

Examples

1. You are the legal counsel to the newly elected governor Ross Parrot. Governor Parrot claims that he heard a "large sucking sound" of jobs being lost across the border to Mexico after ratification of the NAFTA treaty. He wants to attract more industry to the state. The state is divided into several Air Quality Control Regions (AQCRs). Governor Parrot wants to alter the parameters of pollution control monitoring so as to attract more industry. Please advise him as to whether he may do the following, and if so, how.
   a. Can he change the geographic lines of the different AQCRs so as to attract more industry? How?

b. List the criteria pollutants for Governor Parrot. Is he correctly concerned that carbon dioxide is a criteria pollutant, the regulation of which could restrict new industry?

c. Do the NAAQS vary for different AQCRs?

d. Is Governor Parrot correct that it is *improper* to establish NAAQS so as to protect that subset of persons suffering from emphysema and other bronchial ailments? Explain.

2. In his campaign for governor, Mr. Parrot was aided by large campaign donations from the beer industry in the state. The state is under requirements to revise the state implementation plan (SIP); in particular it is required to regulate VOCs more stringently. VOCs are designated as ozone precursors. Rather than tighten up on all industries that emit VOCs (volatile organic compounds), Governor Parrot decides to decrease restrictions on the alcoholic beverage industry while tightening up much more on all other industries. Can he do that? Why?

3. If the bakery industry is not satisfied that it has been treated fairly with tougher standards on VOC emissions, list the options that its counsel could recommend at both the state and federal levels to resist these tougher standards imposed on a particular bakery or on the industry.

4. If the plan devised by Governor Parrot, on paper, legitimately seems to provide a reasonable means to achieve NAAQS by the applicable deadline, can the EPA disapprove the SIP or otherwise alter the particular regulatory tack elected by the governor because the plan favors the brewery industry or is otherwise discriminatory?

5. Suppose Governor Parrot signs a variance for the brewery industry that contributed to his campaign, pending reduction of regulation of this industry in the upcoming SIP revisions. As counsel for the brewery industry, can you rely on the governor's variance? Why?

Explanations

1a. The states designate the AQCRs, but subject to federal EPA approval. As legal counsel for Governor Parrot, you can petition the EPA to change or otherwise redraw the lines of the AQCRs. However, you may not unilaterally do so at the state level without federal approval of the resultant revision to the SIP. The AQCRs are promulgated as a matter of federal regulation and therefore are federal law.

1b. The criteria pollutants are (1) particulate matter, (2) sulfur dioxide, (3) ozone, (4) nitrogen oxides, (5) carbon monoxide, and (6) lead. Hydrocarbons are now recognized as ozone precursors. Carbon *dioxide,* while a compound of concern, is not regulated as a criteria pollutant. Carbon monoxide is the criteria pollutant. Recall also that toxic air pollutants are not regulated as criteria pollutants.

1c. The NAAQS are federally uniform. They do not vary in different AQCRs. A governor, therefore, has no control over the NAAQS. They are set as a matter of federal law and do not vary.

1d. The governor could be right about the loud sucking sound but not about the establishment of the NAAQS. This is a tough question. Remember that the standards must protect the general population by an adequate margin of safety. The NAAQS are established to protect the public health of people who are sensitive receptors, including people who suffer from bronchial asthma. Setting the NAAQS for sensitive receptors ensures an adequate margin of safety in the setting of these standards for the general population, as required by the statute.

2. Although it may not seem evenhanded, the answer is a qualified "yes." The federal government establishes the NAAQS, and the states elect in their SIPs how to achieve the NAAQS in each AQCR. These micro decisions inside the federal NAAQS envelope are up to the state. Assuming that the governor and not the legislature ultimately determines on specific state regulations and plans to satisfy the NAAQS, the governor can reward friends and disadvantage others with environmental regulation. The micro decisions are discretionary. Obviously, procedural due process requirements overarch these decisions.

3. The bakery industry has options primarily at the state level. The industry can attempt to influence micro-level decisions in the executive or legislative branches as to which industries should bear the greatest burden for VOC reduction. If the industry believes that it has been treated unfairly or that procedural due process has not been observed, it can launch an administrative appeal or court challenge in state court, contesting the decision as a matter of state law. (See Chapter 2 for a discussion of administrative procedure.) At the federal level, there is little recourse for the bakery industry, other than lobbying the EPA to disapprove the SIP as "infeasible."

4. No. If on paper there is a reasonable approach that could conceivably achieve the goal by the deadline, the EPA has no choice but to approve the SIP. The EPA makes the macro choices, but it cannot influence or disapprove a state's decision as to the micro components for achievement. The EPA can only substitute a federal plan when the state plan will not, on an objective scientific basis, reasonably lead to achievement of the results by the deadline.

5. You cannot rely on this change. As developed in court precedent, no SIP changes, variances, or consent decrees are valid until approved at the

federal level. The industry still is subject to federal orders for emission noncompliance during the interim, until the SIP revisions are properly promulgated at the state level and accepted by the EPA. This EPA approval can take several months.

Source Controls: Regulation of Individual Emitters of Pollutants

Ambient standards require the states to achieve acceptable air quality. Standards for individual pollutant discharges to the air are the means by which the government translates this responsibility to individual sources causing the pollution. The 1970 Clean Air Act Amendments, besides requiring compliance by the states, also addressed individual air pollution sources. The statute forces technology to be developed and deployed by individual stationary sources. In *Friends of the Earth v. Potomac*, 419 F. Supp. 528, 535 (D.D.C. 1976), the court concluded that the 1970 amendment's legislative history contemplated that the requirements be "technology-forcing." For a case discussing the concept of "technology forcing" as it pertains to *mobile* source motor vehicle emission reductions, see *NRDC v. Thomas*, 805 F.2d 410 (D.C. Cir. 1986). By regulating specific industries through new-source performance standards (NSPS), by regulating the release of hazardous air pollutants not covered by NAAQS or SIPs, and by regulating mobile source vehicle emissions, the 1970 amendments force all new-source emitters to adopt additional control.

If a release does not occur to the ambient environment, there is no EPA jurisdiction pursuant to the Clean Air Act. There may be OSHA jurisdiction if an indoor release occurs in a workplace. However, if exposure occurs in space that is not a work space, such as a hotel room, residence, or certain commercial spaces, OSHA does not exercise jurisdiction. Therefore, only common law tort actions (see Chapter 1) or other statutory remedies could apply to redress any impacts of an indoor release of air toxics.

New-Source Performance Standards (NSPS) The 1970 amendments provided the federal government with the authority to regulate emissions from individual emission sources through application of *new-source performance standards* (NSPS). NSPS applies to either major new or modified stationary sources, but only to those sources in certain high-emission industries. The Clean Air Act defines "modification" to mean any change to a stationary source that "increases the amount of any air pollutant emitted by such source" or leads to the emission of any new pollutant. 42 U.S.C. §7411(a)(4). NSPS covers 50 major industry groups, including electric utility steam-generating units, fossil fuel-fired steam generators of more than 250 million Btu heat input, glass manufacturing plants, incinerators of more than 50 tons per day charging rate, iron and steel plants, municipal solid waste landfills, petroleum refineries, copper smelters, lead smelters, rubber tire manufacturing plants, and sewage treatment plants.

NSPS is the fifth key concept we must remember. These industry-specific standards require installation of the "best system of emission reduction" for any new source of pollution within a designated industry. A source of pollution may be a new process or merely an emission smokestack. The EPA may also prescribe NSPS for existing sources not already subject to NAAQS regulation, which has been used infrequently, although has been proposed by the EPA for CO_2 regulation which is not an explicitly identified criteria pollutant. 42 U.S.C. §7411(d).

These standards create a role for the EPA to analyze all technology in use to determine which methods are most effective, thus constituting the "best system of emission reduction." The EPA is required to consider what is maximally achievable in regard to potential percentage reductions of emissions and ultimate emission rates through implementation of a particular technology. Finally, the EPA must assess the financial implications for industry if a particular technology is mandated, and it must avoid a mandate that would cause "serious economic disruption in the industry." The Act implies that not all industries will be treated equally.

There is a federally dictated NSPS technology for most criteria pollutants for each major polluting industry. With the creation of uniform federal standards, it was assumed that no state would enjoy an advantage over another state in attracting business through lax pollution rules. Section 111 of the Clean Air Act requires the EPA to revise NSPS every eight years, although the EPA does not always meet this time line.

Where do you find the NSPS? For regulated industries, the Code of Federal Regulations describes the technology applicable to each criteria pollutant and often illustrates the technology with engineering diagrams. For example, in electric power plants, for particulate matter, a criteria pollutant, it might be application of a filter baghouse; for NO_x it might be non-catalytic reduction technology; for SO_2 it might be limestone scrubbers. The NSPS standard varies for each industry or process and for each criteria pollutant. Existing facilities are grandfathered.

National Emission Standards for Hazardous Air Pollutants (NESHAPs)

In addition to the six criteria pollutants, there are scores of hazardous (toxic) air pollutants potentially addressed by the National Emission Standards for Hazardous Air Pollutants (NESHAPs). Our sixth key concept is NESHAPs. These are additional federal emission limitations established for less widely emitted but dangerous, hazardous, or toxic air pollutants that are not covered by the NAAQS. These hazardous substances include carcinogens and mutagens. The "categorical" emission limitations are intended, by an "ample margin of safety," to regulate pollutants that "may cause, or contribute to, an increase in mortality, or an increase in serious, irreversible, or incapacitating reversible illness." This statutory language, as upheld by the court in NRDC v. EPA, 824 F.2d 1146 (D.C. Cir. 1987), emphasizes that these standards are intended to protect the public health and welfare with no consideration for the practicalities involved in their implementation through law. "This could mean effectively, that a plant could be required to close because of the absence of control techniques. It could include emission standards which allow for no measurable emissions." *NRDC* at 1154.

The EPA considers only health factors; the EPA is not allowed to consider cost and technological feasibility in determining what emission standards are "safe." "Safe" was not deemed to mean "risk-free." This "ample" margin of safety exceeds the "adequate" margin of safety for criteria pollutant NAAQS. The only safe level of certain toxics is zero exposure.

Between 1970 and 1990, the EPA regulated less than ten toxic air pollutants: asbestos, benzene, beryllium, mercury, vinyl chloride, coke oven emissions, inorganic arsenic, and certain radionuclides. We will consider the expanded current scope of NESHAPs later when we discuss the 1990 Clean Air Act Amendments.

New Federal Motor Vehicle Emission Limitations Under Title II of the 1970 Act, the EPA announced new motor vehicle emission controls pertaining to vehicle tailpipe emissions and fuel composition. These called for automakers to severely curtail new-vehicle emissions of hydrocarbons (HC) and carbon monoxide (CO) by 90 percent within five years, and to curtail nitrogen oxide (NO_x) within six years. Congress gave the EPA limited authority to extend the compliance deadline for one year provided specified conditions were met. EPA Administrator Ruckelshaus set off a firestorm of protest when he refused to grant the extension, stating that the conditions Congress established for granting the extension had not been met. In *International Harvester v. Ruckelshaus*, 478 F.2d 615 (D.C. Cir. 1973), the court reversed the EPA's decision not to grant the extension, reasoning that the risks associated with an erroneous denial of the extension outweighed the risks of an erroneous grant. The court shifted to the EPA the burden of rebutting the automakers' interpretation of the Act.

Perhaps unsurprisingly, the standards were not met in a timely fashion. A long succession of EPA waivers and congressional amendments relaxed the standards and deadlines. The HC and CO standards eventually were met. Major decreases in vehicle emissions resulted.

THE CLEAN AIR ACT AMENDMENTS OF 1977

As we have seen, the 1970 goals were not met. "Fast forward" to 1977. The basic structure of the Clean Air Act did not change as a result of the 1977 amendments. However, the failure of important existing provisions, especially the nonattainment of NAAQS for many regions of the country, led to substantive 1977 changes in some of the Act's key provisions.

First, the amendments addressed *existing* as well as *new* pollution sources. The application of "reasonably available control technology" (RACT) was required for *existing* major stationary sources of pollution in nonattainment areas that previously were grandfathered. RACT — "reasonable" — is less stringent than BACT — "best."

Second, additional *geographic*-specific standards were overlaid on the NSPS *technology* standards. In dirty air regions, a construction-permitting program was mandated that requires a "New Source Review" process for construction of *new* or *modified major* pollution sources to utilize pollution control technology that would ensure achievement of the "lowest available emission rate" (LAER). This standard is more stringent than BACT. These "new" sources were also required to meet offset requirements to prevent them from adding to the aggregate amount of criteria pollutant emissions already in a particular AQCR.

In clean air regions, the amendments require plans and permits for major new sources for *Prevention of Significant Deterioration (PSD)* of their healthful air. *New Source Review* and *Prevention of Significant Deterioration* are key concepts we need to remember.

The Concept of Nonattainment: Geographic Standards

The 1977 amendments combined the 1967 concept of AQCR with a new approach: Each AQCR was designated as having the status of *"attainment"* or *"nonattainment"* for the primary and secondary NAAQS. States are required to submit lists indicating which areas within their borders are or are not in timely compliance with the NAAQS. States are also required to list additional areas that were unclassifiable due to an absence of reliable air quality data. The Act imposed an obligation on the EPA to approve these designations or modify them accordingly within a short period of time. For cases that over-turned EPA designations, see *United States Steel Corp. v. EPA*, 649 F.2d 572 (8th Cir. 1981); *Western Oil & Gas Ass'n v. EPA*, 633 F.2d 803 (9th Cir. 1980). For cases that upheld EPA designations, see *Cincinnati Gas & Electric Co. v. Costle*, 632 F.2d 14 (6th Cir. 1980); *General Motors Corp. v. Costle*, 631 F.2d 466 (6th Cir. 1980). Changes in the borders of AQCR and nonattainment areas were allowed where necessary "for efficient program administration."

So what is *attainment*? Simply stated, it is a level of a specific criteria pollutant in ambient air in a region that is below the uniform federal NAAQS requirement. Similarly, *nonattainment* is a concentration of a pollutant that is above the federal standard. Therefore, for each of the more than 200 AQCRs, each of the six criteria pollutants could be in attainment or in nonattainment. As counsel you may want to think of the legal concept of

5.3   Criteria Pollutants by Region

AQCR	NO$_x$	SO$_2$	PM-10	Lead	Ozone VOCs (HC)	CO
1						
2						
3						
4						
etc.						

attainment or nonattainment as a matrix of geography (AQCR) and pollutant levels, as illustrated in Exhibit 5.3.

Any given region can be in attainment for some criteria pollutants and in nonattainment for others at the same time. A mosaic is created. As legal counsel, you must determine how this mosaic applies to a particular potential or existing polluting source. This mosaic will affect the type of permitting required and may suggest advantages in physically relocating a proposed new or expanded stationary source of pollution. It also will determine whether BACT, or LAER with offsets, is required. The lawyer's input is essential in making these kinds of business decisions.

Existing Sources: RACT

The 1977 amendments significantly extended the attainment deadlines for NAAQS until 1982, and as late as 1987 for the ozone and carbon monoxide criteria pollutants, in areas that could demonstrate that the 1982 deadlines were not feasible despite application of "reasonably available control technology" (RACT) to existing pollution sources. "RACT" is not federally defined and can therefore be defined by states in their SIPs. The extended deadlines of course necessitated state SIP revisions, and they placed tremendous pressure on the states to comply or face the loss of critical federal funding. Nevertheless, many states missed compliance in 1982 and again in 1987. Nonsignificant penalties attached to these failures.

Affected states were required to provide for all reasonably available control measures for "major sources" located in *nonattainment* areas. To achieve this goal, states had to adopt RACT as expeditiously as practicable for *existing* sources. 42 U.S.C. §7426, §7511. RACT is defined as "the lowest emission limitation that a particular source is capable of meeting by the application of control technology that is reasonably available considering technological and economic feasibility." *State of Michigan v. Thomas*, 805 F.2d 176, 180 (6th Cir. 1986). A demonstration of reasonable further progress (RFP) toward attainment of the NAAQS was required through stepwise reductions in emissions of criteria pollutants in nonattainment areas, until RACT implementation was complete. RACT is distinguishable from other control technology standards, as it applies to *already existing* sources. Affected states also were required to include in their SIP submittal packages a "comprehensive, accurate, current inventory" of actual emissions from all sources.

In *Air Pollution Control District of Jefferson County, Ky. v. EPA*, 739 F.2d 1071 (6th Cir. 1984), Jefferson County claimed that SO_2 emissions from the Gallagher power plant in Indiana were violating its SIP obligations by drawing from the same air resource as Jefferson County and degrading the county's air quality. Under the Kentucky scheme to control SO_2 emissions set forth in the 1977 amendments, Jefferson County's primary source polluter, Louisville Gas and Electric, was obligated to install scrubbers for smoke gas at a cost of $138 million. The Gallagher plant encountered no such requirements under the Indiana SIP.

The EPA refused to make a determination that would have triggered implementation of interstate pollution abatement measures against Gallagher. Jefferson County challenged the EPA's decision not to implement specific measures against Gallagher that would prohibit the emissions from a source in one area from "significantly contributing" to the failure of another state's effort to attain the NAAQS for a criteria pollutant. The court upheld the EPA, stating that Gallagher's emissions were "de minimis" and thus not serious enough to compel additional control measures. This case is a key RACT precedent.

In 1998, the EPA implemented its SIP Call to cut NO_x emissions throughout the eastern half of the country. The primary goal of the SIP Call is to reduce the transport of ozone precursors from plants in the Midwest and Southeastern states to downwind states in the Northeast. The authority for this was the §126 program under the Clean Air Act and general requirements for ambient air compliance. The EPA issued a separate §126 rule in 2000, which requires almost 400 electric power plants in 12 states east of the Mississippi River plus the District of Columbia to commence reducing NO_x emissions by May 1, 2003.

The U.S. Court of Appeals for the D.C. Circuit upheld the §126 rule as to its basic authority, but found that the EPA's system for allocating emission allowances among the states was not based on adequate data, and thus was arbitrary and capricious. *Appalachian Power Co. v. E.P.A.*, 249 F.3d 1032 (D.C. Cir. 2001). In a subsequent decision, the court held that the EPA had underestimated the projected growth in electric power generation in those states required to reduce NO_x emissions pursuant to the SIP Call, and that the EPA must reconsider the emission limitations. *Appalachian Power Co. v. EPA*, 251 F.3d 1026 (D.C. Cir. 2001).

Nonattainment Areas: New Source Review (NSR)

The 1977 amendments got tougher with new sources in dirty air areas. New Source Review (NSR) is authorized by 42 U.S.C. §7475(a). The seventh key concept is New Source Review. It is a *preconstruction* permitting *process* for major stationary new or modified sources of pollution. It applies geographically in addition to the NSPS standard. The NSR program is set forth at 42 U.S.C. §§7501-7515. A "modified" source is one that has any physical change or process change that increases the emission of a criteria pollutant by more than a de minimis amount. See §111(a)(4) of the Clean Air Act. It applies to any of the criteria pollutants that are in nonattainment in a given AQCR.

A primary goal of the NSR permitting program is to reduce the aggregate level of criteria pollutants in dirty air areas by preventing the addition of new sources, unless their potential emissions could be *offset* by the closing of, or the pollution source reductions from, an *existing* source or through other reductions. This is called an *offset*. Essentially, it requires a 1:1, or in some cases greater, reduction of the relevant existing criteria pollutant as a condition for adding new pollution sources that emit that criteria pollutant. Offsets must come from the same AQCR or an AQCR with an equal or higher nonattainment classification (discussed more later).

The offset must be real, permanent, quantifiable, surplus, and legally enforceable. This means it must be reflected in a permit or other legally binding document. *Citizens Against the Refinery's Effects, Inc. v. EPA*, 643 F.2d 183 (4th Cir. 1981) (finding offset where state SIP included a plan to discontinue using hydrocarbon-emitting asphalt in highway districts). In many cases, existing facilities will not be emitting criteria pollutants at their legally authorized potential to emit. For example, a facility under its permit may be allowed to emit 300 tons per year (tpy) of NO_x, but it actually emits only 200 tpy. The facility might want to sell the excess 100 tpy without changing its operations. Requirements, however, would not allow this 100 tpy differential between the *actual* emissions and the *potential* emissions to be sold as an offset. Only the *lower* of actual or potential emissions can be the base from which to create and sell offsets. The law thus attempts to hold the line in dirty air areas.

In addition to offsets, the NSR program allows new construction or modification of a major pollution source that would exacerbate an existing NAAQS criteria pollutant violation only if (1) the project utilizes the stringent control technology referred to as "lowest achievable emission rate" (LAER), (2) the state has an approved SIP, (3) any existing pollution sources owned or controlled by the owner of the proposed project are in compliance with the SIP, (4) and in some cases a cost-benefit analysis is performed. This is a tough set of standards. LAER is associated only with new or proposed major stationary sources in nonattainment areas. LAER normally is more stringent than BACT. LAER is defined as the emissions that reflect "the most

5.4 The NSR Process

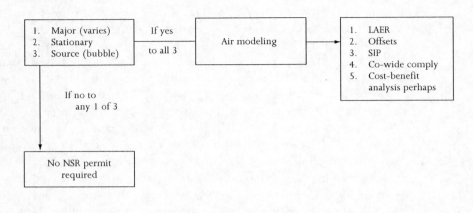

stringent emission limitation which is contained in the [SIP] for such class or category of source, unless the owner or operator of the proposed source demonstrates that such limitations are not achievable." 42 U.S.C. §7501(3)(A). In the C.F.R., LAER is specified in legal and engineering terms.

NSR is the most demanding of the air permitting processes. Legal counsel often try to avoid it. How do you think it could be avoided? First, it can be avoided by relocation: moving the specific criteria pollutant(s) emitted by the source outside the nonattainment area. Second, it can be avoided by reducing the scale of the new facility so that it is no longer "major." What is "major" is discussed later. Third, it can be avoided by not categorizing the new facility as a "source." This also is discussed later, as part of the "bubble" concept. Since there are multiple legal triggers, avoidance is possible. Exhibit 5.4 illustrates the process. Now let's look at the other side of geographically imposed standards.

Attainment Areas: Prevention of Significant Deterioration (PSD)

Prevention of Significant Deterioration (PSD) represents the other side of geographically determined air quality standards. PSD potentially applies wherever NSR does not apply. And vice versa. They are mutually exclusive permitting processes for individual pollution sources. They both overlie and are in addition to NSPS requirements. So, for every major new or modified pollution source, NSPS and NSR could apply, or NSPS and PSD could apply. PSD is our eighth key concept. The PSD program is set forth at 42 U.S.C. §§7470-7492.

PSD was formally codified by the 1977 amendments, but it was born in the decision in *Sierra Club v. Ruckelshaus*, 344 F. Supp. 253 (D.D.C. 1972). The Sierra Club desired to protect the unique vistas offered by national parks in the West. The federal district court in Washington, D.C., in a decision affirmed ultimately by the Supreme Court, held that the "EPA had a nondiscretionary duty to adopt measures that would improve air quality and prevent all but nonsignificant deterioration of existing high air quality levels." Once a state has made a showing factually that it is in attainment for ambient levels of a particular criteria pollutant, no further attainment progress is required to be made by that state for that pollutant, even if the state is not formally redesignated by the EPA as in attainment. See *Sierra Club v. EPA*, 999 F.3d 1551 (10th Cir. 1996).

PSD applies only in *attainment* areas. The PSD program attempts to maintain attainment status for each given criteria pollutant in "clean" air regions. This program is designed to prevent air quality in clean areas from deteriorating substantially from current acceptable levels. How does PSD work? It features three key elements.

First, there is a permitting process for *major new or modified stationary sources* that will emit pollutants for which the region is in attainment. PSD applies to criteria pollutants where the potential to emit is either 100 tpy or 250 tpy depending on the industry source category. The first PSD regulatory inclusion applies to 19 major sources that emit, or have the potential to emit, 100 tons per year or more of any pollutant. In an additional broader inclusion, PSD applies to all other sources having the potential to emit 250 tons per year or more of any criteria pollutant. 42 U.S.C. §§7471, 7479. Thus, PSD regulates some specific listed sources if they have the potential to emit more than 100 tpy and all sources, regardless of type, if they have the potential to emit more than 250 tpy. Compare this with NSPS, which only regulates certain listed high-pollution sources if over the ton threshold, and does not regulate unlisted sources regardless of emissions. The pollution-control technology is BACT, which with its consideration of control cost is a standard similar-to-best system of emission reduction that is required by the also-applicable NSPS requirements. BACT is defined as "an emissions limitation based on the maximum degree of reduction of each pollutant . . . which the permitting authority, on a case-by-case basis, taking into account energy, environmental, and economic impacts and other costs, determines is achievable for such facility." 42 U.S.C. §7479(3). Thus far, PSD may or may not add to what is already imposed by NSPS, depending on how stringently a state defines BACT.

However, here is a key distinction: BACT for PSD is determined on a case-by-case basis by the state; it is not detailed in the C.F.R. for only certain sources, as is NSPS. The requirement in establishing BACT for PSD review involves a top-down analysis of technical pollution control alternatives. Listed sources subject to PSD are provided at 40 C.F.R. §52.21(b)(1). The types of facilities that require PSD permits are listed in Exhibit 5.5.

5.5 Listed Categories of PSD Facilities

Fossil fuel steam electric plants (>250 mm Btu/hour capacity)	Phosphate rock processing plants
Coal cleaning plants	Coke oven batteries
Kraft pulp mills	Sulfur recovery plants
Portland cement plants	Carbon black plants
Primary zinc smelters	Primary lead smelters
Iron and steel mill plants	Fuel conversion plants
Primary aluminum ore reduction plants	Sintering plants
Primary copper smelters	Secondary metal production plants
Municipal incinerators (>250 tpd capacity)	Chemical process plants
Hydrofluoric, sulfuric, and nitric acid plants	Fossil fuel boilers (>250 mm Btu/hour capacity), petroleum storage and transfer facilities (>300,000 barrels capacity), and taconite ore processing facilities
Petroleum refineries	Glass fiber processing plants
Lime plants	Charcoal production facilities

Alaska's environmental permitting authority allowed Cominco (in an attainment area for NO_x) to discontinue its use of SCR NO_x control because it was deemed not economically feasible for in-state major stationary sources to install. The EPA deployed its power under 42 U.S.C. §7477 to order Alaska to stop construction at Cominco's facility. A state claim of economic infeasibility at the permitting stage must be supported from either the state or the source itself. *Alaska Dep't of Environmental Conservation v. EPA*, 540 U.S. 461, 468 (2004); 42 U.S.C. §7475(a)(4); *Navistar Int'l Transp. v. EPA*, 941 F.2d 1339, 1341 (6th Cir. 1991); *Citizens for Clean Air v. EPA*, 959 F.2d 839, 848 (9th Cir. 1992); *cf. Michigan v. EPA*, 213 F.3d 663 (D.C. Cir. 2000).

The second element of the PSD program is that each area is designated as Class I, II, or III. Class I is national parks and national scenic areas, where little additional air degradation is permitted. 42 U.S.C. §7472(a). In 1979, the EPA identified 156 such areas. Many are well-known national parks and wilderness areas. The EPA periodically requires SIP revisions for states with these areas to reach the goal of no visibility impairment in these highest-priority Class I classes. This is done by requiring the installation and operation of best available retrofit technology (BART) for controlling emissions. Class II is most other areas. Class III is certain development areas as designated by the states. States are allowed to re-designate areas originally designated as Class II to Class III areas for specific industrial development and emissions growth. The reclassification may not cause or contribute to the violation of any state or national ambient air quality standard or to a violation of the maximum allowable increases in any other areas. There is a different amount of degradation of existing air quality allowed in different class regions. Class I allows the least amount of additional cumulative air emissions, because there is an interest in not allowing pollution up to the maximum limit.

Under a separate Section 169A visibility program, in 1999, new rules were announced to combat migrating pollution known as "regional haze" in national parks. The goal is to return air quality at national parks to pre-industrial conditions by the year 2064. The main burden is placed on utilities that operate coal-burning power plants that contribute to regional haze at national parks.

Third, any new individual source of pollution is allowed to "consume" only a certain amount of the available remaining regional increment of clean air. This element of the law prevents any individual new polluter from fouling all of the available air. The allowed emission increment increases take into account both stationary and mobile sources. Sections 166(c)-(d) of the Clean Air Act provide specific numerical increments for particulate matter and sulfur dioxide and leave EPA discretion as to increments for other criteria pollutants. The increments allowed in the PSD area are uniform across all AQCRs, unless the full increment cannot be provided without violating the NAAQS. However, the amount allowed in each increment to a given new or major modified source varies, with Class III being the most generous available increment.

In 2005, the EPA proposed three options to allow states to meet PSD requirements for NO_x: (1) retaining the existing increment analysis, (2) implementing an interstate cap-and-trade program for sources of NO_x as embodied in the Clean Air Interstate Rule (CAIR) for the Eastern United States effective by 2010, or (3) demonstrating that the PSD standard for NO_x is satisfied through some combination of state and federal emissions controls. The CAIR rule affects 28 eastern states and the District of Columbia. States must adopt reasonably achievable control measures (RACM) to achieve attainment as soon as practicable and cause large pollution sources in their jurisdictions to adopt RACT measures unless they are in states that participate in CAIR. The CAIR rule was overturned by the D.C. Circuit in 2008 in *North Carolina v. EPA et al.*, 550 F.3d 1176 (D.C. Cir. 2008).

Summary of Permitting

Let's now recap the basics of the Clean Air Act, as illustrated in Exhibit 5.6. The federal government sets uniform NAAQS for six criteria pollutants. NAAQS are maximum permissible pollutant concentrations. They are enforced region-by-region in the many AQCRs that comprise airsheds within the states.

As counsel, you consult the Code of Federal Regulations to determine the boundaries of the AQCRs and the NAAQS for each criteria pollutant. You also determine from the C.F.R. whether each AQCR is "in" or "out" of attainment for each of the criteria pollutants. You will find that many urban areas are out of attainment for ozone precursors (NO_x, HC, volatile organic compounds). This attainment/nonattainment matrix determines the type of permit requirements imposed on new or modified major stationary sources.

NSPS is a technology-based standard that applies to major new or modified sources regardless of geographic location. Its standard, best system of emission reduction is a statutory legal standard of pollution control technology that is translated by the EPA in the C.F.R. into a specific level of emissions or pollution control device, process, or equipment on an industry-by-industry basis for each criteria pollutant. For example, BSER for NO_x, a criteria pollutant, may specify a different NO_x pollution control technology for steel plants than for copper smelters. And for steel plants, BSER will specify a different type of pollution control device for NO_x than for SO_2 or CO emissions.

5.6 Major New or Modified Source Regulatory Scheme

	Federal Level		**State Level**		
Ambient control	NAAQS		AQCR		
Mechanism	ppm standards		SIPs		
Air quality	*Criteria pollutants:*		*Attainment or nonattainment*		
Permit standard	NSPS	and	PSD	or	NSR
			Class I-III increments		
Requirement	Best system of emission reduction		BACT		LAER
Offsets	No		No		Yes

5. Air Quality Regulation

In *addition* to NSPS, there are *geographically* based pollution control standards applied to *individual* major new or modified sources, depending on whether the emitted pollutant is or is not already in attainment in ambient air in the particular AQCR. Where the pollutant is in attainment, PSD applies. PSD imposes BACT pollution control standards that are similar to those imposed by NSPS. The permit standard does not change because of the location or compliance of a region.

The states conduct the PSD and NSR permitting processes. PSD areas are categorized as Class I, II, or III, and the category determines the cumulative degree of additional air degradation permitted by new or expanded sources. Calculations are made to determine the amount of the available increment that can be consumed by any individual new source.

If the AQCR is not in attainment for a particular criteria pollutant, NSR applies. The NSR permitting standard is LAER *plus* at least 1:1 offsets of the pollutant, plus other requirements. LAER is more stringent than BACT. Offsets must be purchased or created, and obtaining them can pose a major obstacle. NSR thus imposes a significant additional challenge, transactional burden, and cost on the new or modified major source, as compared to NSPS or PSD. There are approximately 15,000 permits for major stationary sources filed with the EPA.

Examples

1. Can "Rolls-R-Us," an individual client in the bakery industry, obtain a variance from Governor Parrot's mandate for VOC reduction on this bakery because the mandate cannot feasibly be applied technologically or economically to Rolls-R-Us?

2. Because of your rising (no pun intended) reputation in the bakery industry, your new client, Rolls-R-Us, would like to locate more bakeries in the state. Describe in detail how you would inform this new client about its obligations under Clean Air Act regulations.
   a. What permitting process or standards potentially might apply?
   b. What process would you use to gain information for the new client concerning regulatory requirements imposed on business attempting to locate in the state?

3. As counsel, review briefly the techniques you have available to attempt to prevent a client that is proposing a new facility from being classified as subject to stringent NSR.

4. If one of your existing bakery clients, rather than build a new facility, elects to modernize and expand its existing facility, resulting in only a 1 percent increase in VOCs, is it subject to NSR?

5. Your new bakery client, Rolls-R-Us, is locating one new bakery in an AQCR where VOC emissions are in attainment. The client notes that PSD

review and NSPS standards both utilize BACT standards. If the client complies with NSPS, does this mean that PSD compliance is not required?

6. Your new bakery client, Rolls-R-Us, has an existing facility in a state located near the border. Does your client have to worry if its emissions of VOCs blow into the neighboring state such that it could be regulated by that state?

7. Your client, Rolls-R-Us, cannot find any available VOC offsets in the AQCR region in which it is located. There is an existing source of VOC emissions that is willing to make reductions for a price; however, this existing facility is located 50 miles away in a different AQCR. This other AQCR is in attainment for VOCs but not for carbon monoxide. Would you advise your client to purchase the VOC offset from this facility 50 miles away? Why or why not?

8. Your client wishes to purchase an offset of VOC from an existing facility that would emit 3,000 tpy of VOC if it operated around the clock. Its permit allows this operation. However, the facility operates on only two shifts daily and is closed between 11:00 p.m. and 7:00 a.m. Thus it emits only 2,000 tpy of VOC. Can this existing facility sell some of its unused 1,000 tpy to your client?

9. When, in the evolving process of designing a facility that will emit air pollutants — for example, obtaining the site, constructing the facility, or operating it — is one required to obtain a PSD or NSR permit?

Explanations

1. No. As the court held in *Union Electric Co. v. EPA*, 427 U.S. 246 (1976), there is no such thing as technological or economic infeasibility. A pollution source can always completely shut down, thereby ensuring compliance with even the most stringent environmental standards: zero emissions. Economic and technological feasibility are not proper considerations by the EPA in granting SIP approval.

2a. Bakeries emit volatile organic compounds (VOCs) as discussed in the earlier examples. These are criteria pollutants, since they are precursors to ozone. Bakeries may also emit certain *hazardous* pollutants to the ambient air. Therefore, you would want to consider (1) NSPS, which apply to all new major stationary sources, (2) NESHAPs, which apply now to 189 hazardous air pollutants, (3) and either PSD or NSR for each criteria pollutant that would be emitted, depending on whether the region is in compliance or noncompliance. Therefore, a range of considerations must be made.

2b. It is time to go check the Code of Federal Regulations. You need an inventory of all pollutants that will be emitted by the facility, as well as the quantities of these emissions *after* the application of pollution control equipment designed into the facility. Second, you want to determine whether additional pollution control equipment could minimize the emissions of certain pollutants below regulated levels. This is an important aspect of your legal advice.

In the C.F.R. you can determine the relevant AQCR for the facility location. This will determine whether the area is in attainment or nonattainment, and whether PSD or NSR applies. Determine next whether, under the applicable regulatory standards, the emissions of any criteria pollutants or hazardous air pollutants qualify the facility as a *major source* so as to subject it to regulation. If it is subject to regulation, determine the relevant standards for NSPS or PSD, determine the MACT standards for hazardous air pollutants, and determine the relevant LAER standards for NSR review. In addition, you will need to check with regulatory officials to learn the application of these standards to facilities in the state. PSD BACT standards are determined on a case-by-case basis by the relevant state authorities.

You will end up with a matrix of standards, pollutants, AQCRs, and definitional triggers. It is your job to understand and advise the client how these legal requirements apply to a particular facility. Always check the Federal Register to make sure you are using the most current version of the applicable regulatory standards.

RACT technology will not apply to your client for a new source, but it could be retroactively applied over time after the source is constructed. Typically, RACT is not as strict as BACT, MACT, or LAER standards that new facilities must satisfy at the time of construction prior to their first operation.

3. As counsel, you can advise several techniques. First, technical changes can be made in the process to drop its emission below the levels designated as *major* that trigger NSR. Second, as will be discussed in greater detail later in this chapter, one may be able to *bubble* the source determination so that the entity is not determined to be a *major source*. Third, one may be able to choose the location of the facility within an AQCR that is in attainment rather than nonattainment. Doing this will make the same criteria pollutant emissions less likely to be considered a *major* source and will impose less stringent BACT, rather than LAER, permitting standards if a source is major.

4. To answer this question, we recall the definition of a modified stationary source. A modified stationary source is one that has any physical process change that increases the emission of a criteria pollutant by more than a de minimis amount. In this case, a 1 percent increase

would not trigger NSR as a modified source. It is important to note that merely modifying or expanding a facility does not necessarily trigger NSR. The key issue is whether the actual or potential emissions from the modified facility are significant. If they are, NSR is triggered.

5. The fact that a similar standard is applied to criteria pollutants under both NSPS and PSD does not mean that you have to comply with only one and not the other. Compliance is required for both. As a practical matter, the technological pollution control standards applied may be identical. Recall, however, that best system of emission reduction is set federally and uniformly by the EPA for NSPS; BACT is determined on a case-by-case basis for PSD, often by the state agency. Compliance with both is required.

6. Although interstate pollution is a major concern, it will not be regulated by the neighboring state unless the bakery VOC criteria pollutants are a de maximis source of pollution in their AQCR. See *Air Pollution Control District of Jefferson, Ky. v. EPA*, 739 F.2d 1071 (6th Cir. 1984).

7. Be careful with this. The basic rule is that offsets can be obtained from other AQCRs, but only if the selling AQCR is of an equal or higher nonattainment classification. In other words, offsets must be obtained from relatively dirty air areas. This requirement ensures some progress for general cleanup. There is less value in obtaining an offset from an area that is already in compliance. Also, the pollutant must be a relevant pollutant. Generally, VOC and NO_x can be traded off, since they are both ozone precursors. Since the selling AQCR in the example is in attainment for VOC, it cannot provide the offset for your client. One must determine the attainment and nonattainment status of each criteria pollutant in an AQCR to see whether trades are possible.

8. Marketable offsets are calculated from a baseline that is the lesser of the *potential* to emit or *actual* emissions. Here, the potential to emit is 3,000 tpy and actual emissions are 2,000 tpy. Assuming that the 2,000 tpy figure is long-standing enough to constitute the baseline, this facility has no offsets of VOC to sell that are usable. You could acquire these "offsets" for your client, but since they may not exist, you would acquire nothing of value. The counsel for the purchasing entity must do his or her own due diligence to make sure that any offset credit purchase has legal significance and is certified by the state so as to be federally enforceable. Here, it is not promising.

9. The PSD and NSR permit processes are *preconstruction permits*. Therefore, prior to any significant groundbreaking at the site of a new or modified major stationary source, the permit must be in hand. In some cases, a state agency will issue these permits on a provisional basis, subject to later revision. Doing this allows construction to begin, at the risk of the project owner.

THE CLEAN AIR ACT AMENDMENTS OF 1990

An EPA report concluded that between 1970 and 1990 the Clean Air Act yielded benefits ten times greater than the cost of implementing the statute. A substantial part of these benefits came from reducing lead and particulate matter emissions, resulting in the reduction of premature deaths.

Major amendments to the Clean Air Act were made in 1990. While leaving the basic processes of the Act intact, the 1990 amendments added significant additional controls on key pollutants. Marketable allowance trading was a key innovation. NSR permitting became more rigorous. The EPA is authorized to treat tribes as states ("TAS"). 42 U.S.C. §7601(d)(1)(A). To qualify for TAS status under the Act, a Native American tribe must have a functioning governing body, the regulations must pertain to air resources within the tribe's jurisdiction, and the tribe must be capable of administering the federal programs. The 1990 amendments are organized into eight titles as set out below.

    I.   Attainment and Maintenance of National Ambient Air Quality Standards
    II.   Mobile Sources
    III.   Hazardous Air Pollutants
    IV.   Acid Deposition Control
    V.   Permits
    VI.   Stratospheric Ozone Protection
    VII.   Enforcement
    VIII.   Miscellaneous

We will focus on titles I-IV, VI, and VII.

Attainment and Maintenance of NAAQS: Title I

Failure to Achieve Compliance

Many of the new 1990 programs focus on ozone, particulate matter, and carbon monoxide (CO), the three most pervasive criteria pollutants violating NAAQS and contributing to persistent smog in many urban areas. Ozone is the most out-of-compliance of the criteria pollutants, with approximately 100 urban areas that failed to meet the primary NAAQS as of 1990. Seventy areas were in nonattainment for small particulate matter, PM-10, and approximately 40 areas failed the standard for CO. In 1988 the EPA estimated that the number of people in the United States living in areas that failed to meet the NAAQS for ozone, PM-10, and CO were 112 million, 25 million, and 30 million, respectively. With a few lingering exceptions, the NAAQS for the other criteria pollutants have been attained.

States are required to modify their SIPs to accommodate revised regulatory schemes for (1) CO, (2) PM-10, and (3) ozone precursors, which are commonly identified as NO_x and volatile organic compounds (VOCs) or nonmethane organic gases (NMOG). If a state fails in its obligation to provide an adequate and timely SIP, the Act instructs the EPA to impose sanctions. These sanctions deny a state access to federal highway funds and impose strict offset requirements from *existing* emission sources before any *new* major stationary source can be constructed.

The SIP process allows states to maintain primary responsibility for the air quality within their borders by establishing source-specific requirements to meet or maintain the NAAQS. Preconstruction review and notification measures also are required in relation to the "prevention of significant deterioration" program (PSD). The 1990 amendments require that SIPs contain provisions regarding pollution migration:

> prohibiting any source or other type of emissions activity within the State from emitting any air pollutant in amounts which will contribute significantly to non-attainment in, or interfere with maintenance by, any other State with respect to any such national primary or secondary ambient air quality standard.

A major component of these new schemes is a classification process used to assess the *severity* of the nonattainment problem for each pollutant in every nonattainment area. Based on an area's classification, intermediate emission reduction targets and ultimate attainment deadlines are established. These classifications are also used to determine the applicable pollution control technology to be adopted in each nonattainment area. The combination of control technology and ultimate attainment deadlines defines the scope of "reasonable further progress" toward attainment. Let's assess how this system works with ozone.

Pollutant-Specific Requirements for Nonattainment Areas

Ozone: Ambient Concentrations Ozone nonattainment areas are classified by statute into five categories of ozone pollution severity based on federal design values. The nonattainment classifications are "marginal," "moderate," "serious," "severe," and "extreme." A mathematical measure of the degree to which an area fails to meet the NAAQS for a criteria pollutant determines its design value. The state governor or legislature makes the classification.

Statutorily mandated NAAQS attainment deadlines are established for each of the five categories, with the more severe classifications given a longer period of time to achieve the NAAQS requirements. In return for the longer time, they inherit the mandatory application of stricter control measures to ensure compliance. Deadlines for attaining the primary NAAQS standard for ozone range from 3 years after enactment of the 1990 amendments for "marginal" areas up to 20 years after enactment for "extreme" areas.

By electing a "severe" or "extreme" classification, a state gets more time to reach NAAQS ozone compliance, but it must regulate new sources more strictly than less "extreme" areas. More time for the state to achieve *ambient* air compliance means more regulation of *individual* new sources. The deadlines and design values for each ozone category are presented in Exhibit 5.7.

Regulations by the EPA that would have provided certain areas of the country with an extra year to meet transportation requirements to reduce air pollution were deemed contrary to the plain meaning of the Clean Air Act. *Sierra Club v. EPA*, 129 F.3d 137 (D.C. Cir. 1997). Construing §176(c) of the Clean Air Act, the court found that "Congress intended a strict and broad ban on non-conforming activities in all nonattainment areas." By EPA

5.7 Deadlines and Design Values for Each Ozone Category

Ozone Nonattainment Classification	Number of Affected Urban Areas	Time to Reach Attainment (years after 1990) [date]	Definition of "Major New Source" (tpy)	Initial VOC Reduction (percent)	HC and NO$_x$ Reduction (percent)
Marginal	41	3 [1993]	100	15	—
Moderate	32	6 [1996]	100	15	—
Serious	18	9 [1999]	50	15	15 + 3/yr
Severe	8[*]	15 [2005]	25	15	15 + 3/yr
Extreme	1[†]	20 [2010]	10	15	15 + 3/yr

[*]Chicago, Baltimore, Houston, Milwaukee, Muskegon, New York City, Philadelphia, and San Diego. There were 12 AQCRs in the severe category in 2006, which included 111 counties with approximately 55 million people.

[†]Los Angeles. As of 2006, there were two AQCRs in the extreme category, which included 12 counties and approximately 17 million people.

regulation, nonattainment areas were deemed not to be afforded grace periods to achieve attainment.

In *Whitman v. American Trucking Assoc. Inc.*, 531 U.S. 457 (2001), Justice Scalia, writing for the majority, reversed the D.C. Circuit's nondelegation theory and reaffirmed the rule in *Lead Industries*; the EPA must remain oblivious to the cost of implementing a NAAQS when setting the initial standard. The Court held there was no textual commitment of authority allowing the EPA to consider cost considerations. However, the Court left unanswered the question of whether the particulate and ozone standards of the NAAQS were arbitrary and capricious. The D.C. Circuit on remand answered in *American Trucking Assoc. v. EPA*, 283 F.3d 355 (D.C. Cir. 2002), holding the EPA does not need to understand every risk a pollutant poses before it regulates it, and as long as the agency engaged in reasoned decision making, a court should be deferential to the agency's decision.

Section 110(a)(2)(D)(i)(I) of the Clean Air Act requires states to prohibit emissions that "contribute[ ] significantly to nonattainment in, or interfere with maintenance by, any other State with respect to . . . [NAAQS]." The EPA issued the Cross-State Air Pollution Rule (CSAPR) addressing interstate transport of SO_2 and NOx from fossil fuel-fired power plants in 27 Eastern states. CSAPR requires significant reductions in SO_2 and NOx; Hazardous Air Pollutants (HAP), including mercury from electric power; as well as certain $PM_{2.5}$ precursor emissions, with intrastate and limited interstate trading. SO_2 is a precursor to $PM_{2.5}$ formation, and NOx is a precursor to both ozone and $PM_{2.5}$ formation. Fifteen states sought review of CSAPR, while six states intervened to support the rule. In 2012, the D.C. Circuit struck the CSAPR cross-state rule, in part, because it did not defer to SIPS and state discretion in implementation.

CSAPR replaced and strengthened the 2005 Clean Air Interstate Rule (CAIR) whose revision was ordered. *North Carolina v. E.P.A.*, 531 F.3d 896, 929, 906 (D.C. Cir 2008) ("We must vacate CAIR because very little will 'survive[ ] remand in anything approaching recognizable form'"[; it is] "arbitrary and capricious" and "not otherwise in accordance with the law"). CAIR was intended to reduce or eliminate the impact of upwind sources on attainment of particulate and smog NAAQS in downwind states. Twenty-three states were required to reduce both annual SO_2 and NOx emissions, while twenty states were required to reduce NOx emissions during the ozone season (May through September). The EPA's state apportionment decisions were found to be "fundamentally flawed," unfair, and must be redone "from the ground up" because they allowed upwind sources to purchase tradable allowances rather than actually reduce their pollution and contribute to congressional requirements to have emission sources within the state measurably reduce pollution. The EPA's quantitative trading budgets were never rationalized. The cap-and-trade system thus could externalize responsibility by transferring actual reduction from the regulated state to other tradable sources, thus allowing upwind states to continue creating pollution that would contribute to downwind state nonattainment with Clean Air Act goals.

Also stricken was the EPA's mercury rule in characterizing EPA logic as "the logic of the Queen of Hearts, substituting EPA desires for the plain text [of the Clean Air Act]." *New Jersey v. EPA*, 517 F.3d 574, 582 (D.C. Cir 2008). Separately stricken was emission trading in ozone nonattainment areas. *NRDC v. EPA*, 571 F.3d 1245 (D.D.C. 2009). Also stricken was California's climate change regulatory program for improper approval of the options Scoping Plan prior to completing its environmental review, *Association of Irritated Residents, et al. v. California Air Resources Board*, and separately, California's low-carbon fuel program. *Rocky Mt. Farmers Union v. Goldstene*, 2011 U.S. Dist. LEXIS 149592 (E.D. Cal. Dec. 29, 2011).

Every state with a nonattainment AQCR for ozone must include in its SIP an emissions inventory that identifies and quantifies sources of ozone precursors — hydrocarbons (HC), and NO_x. HCs are synonymous with VOCs for our discussion purposes. Nonattainment AQCRs ranging from "moderate" to "extreme" classifications must achieve an initial 15 percent reduction in VOC emissions within six years to satisfy requirements. Additionally, "serious," "severe," and "extreme" areas must achieve 15 percent emission reductions for HC and NO_x during years one through six, followed by 3 percent reductions thereafter until attainment.

In *Conservation Law Foundation v. EPA*, No. 94-1692 (D.C. Cir. 1996), environmental organizations sought expedited review of a final EPA action that delayed implementation of the Clean Air Act. The EPA permitted downwind states to extend their own attainment deadlines on the basis of estimates of "overwhelming transport" of polluted air crossing their borders. In essence, states could extend their own deadlines by claiming that pollution migrates in from next door.

The case highlights the "Hobson's choice" faced by the EPA: Either insist that an upwind state adhere to the same earlier attainment deadline as any downwind state whose air it impacts, or impose stricter sanctions on a downwind state to achieve attainment regarding pollution crossing its borders from other states. Both the Fifth Circuit and Seventh Circuit courts of appeals struck the EPA's extension of ozone nonattainment deadlines for urban areas that claimed that upwind pollution was making it impossible for them to achieve local ozone standards. See *Sierra Club v. EPA*, 314 F.3d 735 (5th Cir. 2002).

Ozone: Stationary Sources   Under the NSR program, any entity proposing construction of a major new stationary source must devise a plan to reduce or offset emissions from existing facilities in the area by an amount slightly greater than that which the proposed new facility will emit. This offset ratio varies depending on an area's classification. Exhibit 5.9 later in this chapter illustrates the concept.

The definition of a *major* new or modified source of ozone precursor pollution subject to a permit now varies depending on an area's nonattainment classification. Under this "sliding scale" approach, a *major* source in a "marginal" or "moderate" area is defined as one that emits at least 100 tons per year (tpy) of a specified criteria pollutant. The major source classifications become more stringent: 50 tpy in a "serious" area, 25 tpy in a "severe" area, and 10 tpy in an "extreme" area qualify as *major* sources.

The EPA published control technique guidelines (CTGs) for various emission sources, setting the standard for existing sources achieving RACT. "Marginal" areas, treated more leniently, are only required to retrofit existing sources with RACT for CTGs that were issued prior to the 1990 amendments. "Moderate" to "extreme" nonattainment areas are required to implement RACT for all CTGs issued by the EPA either before or after implementation of the 1990 amendments.

Thus the ninth key concept we must remember is what constitutes a *major* source. It now varies for ozone by a sliding threshold depending on the ozone nonattainment classification. In attainment areas, for ozone it is constant. For other than ozone precursor criteria pollutants, the definition of *major* source is fixed. Any counsel dealing with air issues must understand these distinctions.

More sources avoid New Source Review (NSR) than obtain NSR offsets. Between 1976 and 1986, the California Southcoast Air Quality Management District issued permits to approximately 4,000 sources that were below the trigger level in this Southern California nonattainment area. These permits allowed the smaller sources to emit approximately 200,000 pounds per day of hydrocarbons. During the same period, offsets were procured for only 27,000 pounds per day of hydrocarbons. On balance, almost ten times as much additional hydrocarbons were allowed from smaller sources than were offset by new or major modified sources of hydrocarbons.

The three primary methods for avoiding New Source Review triggers are by designing, staging, or controlling existing equipment. "Designing equipment" is the selection and combination of pieces of equipment that utilize particular operating procedures to keep emissions of criteria pollutants just below the trigger thresholds of New Source Review. "Staging" equipment typically involves installing several small pieces of equipment that individually do not exceed emissions that would trigger New Source Review, whereas one larger piece of equipment would trigger this permitting requirement. "Controls" typically involve the addition of controlling equipment on existing sources to reduce their emissions after major modifications.

New entrants must purchase offsets, whereas existing facilities can employ netting at their existing facilities. Where emissions are netted, the reductions from other existing sources at the facility compensate for the increase from the new equipment. This can create inequities between new and existing facilities. Netting is possible only if an owner has other sources at the site, or within a certain distance of the site if a state allows netting among different locations of a commonly owned company. Netting is at the discretion of the states or regional districts that administer air programs. Typically, these rules encourage expansion at existing sites, which may be preferable from a land-use perspective but may or may not be preferable from an economic development perspective.

Emission reduction credits can be sold, leased, or temporarily transferred to other sources. It is becoming increasingly important to transfer mobile source emission credits to stationary sources. Unless this is done, growth of new industry can be severely restricted in nonattainment areas.

Mobile source emission reduction credits must meet the same criteria as stationary source credits. They must be real, quantifiable, enforceable, surplus, and permanent. For mobile credits, quantification is particularly difficult because commuter patterns, practices of vehicle fleet operators, and general variability of motor vehicle stock and its deployment varies over time. Key to quantification is determining the engine type and fuel of the large number of vehicles in a region.

Title I of the Clean Air Act delegates to states most of the implementation authority. As such, the federal government cannot compel states to participate in a regional emission trading program. The federal government can request states to achieve mandatory targets "voluntarily" through suggested means. It cannot mandate a particular means to achieve this, such as a cap-and-trade system for particular pollution credits. However, the EPA can disapprove a plan that does not meet its targets, or a particular means that does not viably achieve such targets.

Ozone: Mobile Sources Mobile sources are regulated to reduce production of smog-causing ozone. The 1990 amendments to the Clean Air Act require nonattainment states to improve existing Inspection and Maintenance (I/M) programs for automobiles. Some of you may have participated in these programs when you brought your vehicle to a registration inspection station and diagnostic equipment was used to analyze tailpipe emissions. All SIPs must mandate the use of vapor recovery controls by gasoline filling stations. These vapor recovery controls consist of plastic molding on the nozzle of the gas pump line that captures gasoline vapors before they can escape into the atmosphere.

Ozone *nonattainment* states additionally are required to mandate the use of "clean fuels" for any centrally fueled vehicle fleets in all areas except those classified as "marginal" or "moderate." Clean fuels are reformulated

213

gasoline, biodiesel fuel, natural gas, electricity, and other substitutes. "Severe" and "extreme" areas additionally are required to implement reformulated gasoline (RFG) programs. RFG contains high levels of chemical oxygenates, blended to produce fewer emissions when burned than customary grades of gasoline. Additional provisions in the Act require SIPs to consider transportation control measures (TCM) as another way to reduce emissions. Examples of TCMs are listed below.

- Ridesharing incentives
- Voluntary/mandatory no drive days
- Work schedule changes
- Prohibition of extended vehicle idling
- Improved public transit
- High occupancy vehicle (HOV) lanes
- Park and ride options
- Gas rationing/taxes
- Parking management
- Toll roads
- Improvement in traffic flow
- Trip reduction ordinances

Carbon Monoxide   Let's turn now to CO, which is in nonattainment in some urban areas. First, consider ambient air quality. Carbon monoxide nonattainment areas are classified as "moderate" or "serious."

Any "moderate" area that failed to meet the 1995 deadline was subject to additional controls and to reclassification as a "serious" nonattainment area. "Serious" nonattainment areas must adopt TCMs similar to those for ozone, so as to reduce the number of vehicle miles traveled. These "serious" areas also are required to adopt oxygenated fuel programs.

Second, consider individual permits. A *major* new or modified stationary source for purposes of the CO nonattainment restrictions is one that has the potential to emit 100 tpy or more of CO. The EPA may reduce this *major* source threshold from 100 tpy to 50 tpy, if it determines that stationary sources "contribute significantly" to the CO nonattainment problem. The EPA may waive requirements pertaining to TCMs, the I/M program, and the oxygenated fuels program if it determines that mobile sources do not contribute significantly to a nonattainment area's CO nonattainment levels. Major political tension surrounds both CO and NO_x, as to whether to regulate stationary or mobile sources more stringently.

New Source Review and PSD Revisited: [1]. Severity of Restrictions on New Sources   States continue to have the responsibility of administering New Source Review and Prevention of Significant Deterioration permitting programs under the 1990 amendments. But these requirements are never triggered if a new or modified source is not *major*. As you will recall, the 1990 amendments define "*major*" for ozone on a sliding scale depending on the severity of an area's nonattainment classification. Under this scheme, a new or modified "major source" in the "extreme" Los Angeles area would be any new or modified stationary facility with the potential to emit 10 tpy or more per year of an ozone precursor criteria pollutant in nonattainment. A source in a "marginal" nonattainment area (where the threshold is 100 tpy), with the potential to emit 95 tpy of the same precursor pollutant, would not be classified as a "major" source. *Potential to emit* is measured after taking account of the application of all pollution controls — it is the *final* value of the maximum operating pollution emission.

Thus the requirement to comply with any permitting process whatsoever is avoided by sliding *under* the relevant "major source" threshold for the AQCR. No LAER would be required. Similarly, no offsets would be required. If an NSR permit is required, a proposed "major" new or modified source must achieve the "lowest achievable emission rate" (LAER). LAER is based on the "most stringent emission limitation" contained in any SIP, or by the best available means demonstrated in practice by a like source. It is cutting-edge technology. What a difference the thresholds can make.

When NSR is triggered for ozone, the required offset ratios and netting ratios for a source vary by region. The offset and netting requirements, reducing emissions from existing sources to compensate for potential emissions from a proposed source, are more or less stringent depending on an area's nonattainment classification. The more extreme areas must offset a higher ratio of their proposed pollutants so as to achieve actual reduction in ambient pollutants, rather than merely maintain the status quo. These requirements are summarized in Exhibit 5.8.

Note that the trigger now varies for new versus modified sources, and the offset ratio varies between externally procured offsets and internal facility netting. Compare the legal complexity of these nonattainment area rules with the relative simplicity of attainment area requirements. The definition of a major new or modified source in an *attainment* area, subject to the PSD permitting program, is a source with the *potential to emit* greater than 250 tpy of a regulated criteria pollutant. For certain power plants, metal plants, and cement plants, the standard is 100 tpy. The potential to emit is measured with all pollution control technology in place. This requirement is much less stringent than the 10-100 tpy threshold in nonattainment areas.

Additionally, operators subject to PSD must commit only to the use of "best available control technology" (BACT) for any regulated pollutant emitted in "significant" amounts. BACT is defined as "the maximum degree of emission reduction . . . achievable," including consideration of economic, energy, and environmental factors. In other words, cost-effectiveness is a limiting factor in imposing BACT pollution control requirements. Thus the BACT standard is less severe than LAER. The permitting distinction

5.8 NSR Criteria

Classification	Major Source Size Emissions (tpy-VOC)	Modification Size Emissions (tpy-VOC)	Offsets Ratio (external source)	Internal Netting Ratio
Marginal	100	40	1.1 to 1	1 to 1
Moderate	100	40	1.15 to 1	1 to 1
Serious*	50	25	1.2 to 1	1.3 to 1
Severe*	25	25	1.3 to 1	1.3 to 1
Extreme*	10	Any	1.5 to 1	1.3 to 1
Ozone Transport Region	50	<Same>	<Same as classification>[†]	

*New sources and modifications are required to meet LAER, except for modifications to sources with existing potential to emit less than 100 tpy in serious, severe, and extreme areas, which are required to meet BACT.

[†]Marginal nonattainment areas and attainment areas are treated as if they were moderate nonattainment areas.

between the individual source restrictions in attainment and nonattainment areas has become more profound.

New Source Review and PSD Revisited: [2]. Bubbles   The tenth and final key concept to learn and remember is a stationary "source." *Source* is a key concept for NSPS, NSR, and PSD regulatory triggers. From 1970 to 1980, a source was defined by the EPA as any emitting structure, building, or smokestack. In the 1980s, the definition of what elements of a plant constituted a major source was changed by EPA regulation. The EPA adopted a facility-wide definition, contrary to the definition of the agency during the 1970s.

In essence, this change placed an imaginary "bubble" over an entire property or facility. Emission increases from any individual structure, building, or smokestack are ignored; only net emissions from this imaginary bubble over the entire facility or installation are evaluated. In other words, the legal bubble is the *aggregate* source. The bubble concept nets all structures as a parcel together for purposes of evaluating whether a source is "major."

Especially for purposes of NSR permitting, it is not in the interest of new or modified sources to be categorized as "*major stationary sources.*" A year of monitoring and modeling can be required prior to the permit, causing additional delay. Offsets can be expensive and, in many instances, unavailable.

Counsel for project owners often are asked to avoid "major stationary source" status wherever possible. If avoided, only the relatively tamer NSPS requirements may apply. To do this, counsel must cause the project not to fit the definition of "major stationary source." Let's look at each of these adjectives and nouns.

First, a facility cannot change its status as "stationary." End of discussion on this point. Second, a facility is not "major" unless it has the *potential to emit* more than the NSR trigger amount. Depending on the criteria pollutant and the regional degree of nonattainment in the AQCR, that threshold for new ozone precursor sources ranges between 10 and 100 tpy. Engineering changes in technology, fuel, and operating parameters might reduce emission of the particular criteria pollutant below the relevant quantitative threshold.

Third, if the second technique is not successful and the state has adopted a *bubble* policy, pursuant to EPA allowance, then the bubble policy may permit a redefinition of *source*. For example, a new or modified stack that exceeds the relevant "major" threshold may be reevaluated in the context of an entire "bubbled" facility. Reductions in emissions of the relevant criteria pollutant elsewhere in the facility are netted against the new or modified smokestack. This "netting" broadens the definition of *source* in ways that are of advantage to the project owner.

The environmental group NRDC calculated that 90 percent of individual new or modified sources that alone exceed the quantitative threshold for a major source evade NSR entirely when they are allowed to bubble their calculation of what constitutes a source. In 1984 the Supreme Court deferred to the EPA when the latter selected the bubble definition of a source for NSR purposes, in *Chevron v. NRDC*, 467 U.S. 837 (1984). In emphasizing that the role of the Court is not to interpret the wisdom of the agency's decision, the Supreme Court held that the EPA's construction of the "stationary source" term in allowing the bubble concept was a reasonable and acceptable policy decision. The *Chevron* case remains the primary Supreme Court opinion supporting deference to the environmental agency (see Chapter 2).

Previously, the courts had permitted a bubbled definition for sources subject to PSD review in attainment areas, in *Alabama Power Co. v. Costle*, 636 F.2d 323 (D.C. Cir. 1979). In *ASARCO, Inc. v. EPA*, 578 F.2d 319 (D.C. Cir. 1978), they had stricken a *bubbled* definition of sources subject to NSPS, applicable to all major new or modified stationary sources. Can you rationalize why bubbles should not be allowed for NSPS?

Since the 1985 *Chevron* decision, states are allowed to define sources as within a bubble for NSR and PSD purposes. The EPA policy allows each

5.9 Ten Key Concepts in Air Regulation

	Key Concept	Abbreviation
1.	Air Quality Control Regions	AQCR
2.	National Ambient Air Quality Standards	NAAQS
3.	State Implementation Plans	SIPs
4.	Criteria Pollutants	
5.	New Source Performance Standards	NSPS
6.	National Emission System for Hazardous Air Pollutants	NESHAPs
7.	New Source Review	NSR
8.	Prevention of Significant Deterioration	PSD
9.	Major	
10.	Stationary Source	

individual state discretion as to whether to adopt a bubble or individual definition of *source*. Supporters of the bubble concept argue that it encourages efficient pollution control in the most cost-effective aggregate manner. Critics argue that it allows evasion of the 1977 amendments, which were designed to tightly control additional pollution sources in nonattainment areas.

In *Environmental Defense v. Duke Energy Corp.*, 549 U.S. 561 (2007), the Court unanimously held that the EPA could apply inconsistent definitions of the statutory word "modification" at different places where it was placed within the Clean Air Act. The Court did not require that "modification" be consistently defined by the EPA in applying the term to the PSD program and the NSPS program. The EPA had interpreted the term "modification" more liberally under the NSR program involving net annual emissions, than it did under the NSPS program, and the issue was what should apply to the PSD program: whether in one instance an increase could apply to an amount, and in another instance to a rate of emissions. This case also is novel in that it is the first time since *Sierra Club v. Morton*, decided in 1972, that the court had granted *certiorari* in an environmental case at the request of an environmental organization over the objection of the federal government where no state supported the petition for review.

The ten *key concepts* are reprised in Exhibit 5.9.

Regulating Mobile Sources: Title II

Emissions generated by cars, trucks, and other mobile sources are addressed in Title II of the 1990 amendments. Collectively, mobile sources are our nation's single largest source of air pollution. Nationwide, vehicles are estimated to produce 70 percent of CO emissions, 50 percent of VOC emissions, 25 percent of CO_2 emissions, and 45 percent of NO_x emissions. Diesel exhaust is a complex mixture of particles and gases with hundreds of chemical compounds, including many organic compounds. Many of these are thought to be mutagenic and/or carcinogenic individually, let alone collectively. Total vehicle miles traveled yearly in the United States grew from 1 trillion miles in 1970 to 2.5 trillion miles in 1997. It is expected to continue increasing at the rate of 2 to 3 percent annually unless there are dramatic changes in the cost of vehicle travel.

Through a multifaceted approach, the 1990 amendments attempt to reduce the amount of emissions created by mobile sources. The Act mandates tighter emission controls and clean fuel requirements for existing mobile sources, and low emission vehicle (LEV) programs for new vehicles. Additionally, the amendments regulate the emissions generated by off-road vehicles.

Almost half of the passenger vehicles sold in the United States are higher polluting light-duty trucks and sport utility vehicles. These vehicles were not covered under former fuel efficiency requirements that regulated tailpipe emissions. Light-duty trucks and sport utility vehicles, including all passenger vehicles, are now subject to stricter tailpipe emissions. The EPA announced standards for lower sulfur content (by up to 90 percent) of motor fuels. The EPA projected that the lower emissions resulting from tightening these two standards would be equivalent, when fully implemented in 2007, to the removal of 164 million cars from the road. The EPA also estimated that the health benefits would be worth $25 billion, while the total cost to industry to implement these measures would be $5 billion. *Delaney v. EPA*, 898 F.2d 687 (9th Cir. 1990) (refusal of the EPA to require transportation control measures).

Emission Controls

The first component of the mobile-source emission reduction provisions creates a stricter standard for tailpipe emissions from passenger cars, light-duty trucks, and heavy-duty trucks. These standards are intended to cut hydrocarbon emissions by 35 percent and NO_x emissions by 60 percent from the 1990 levels.

The emission reduction approach also requires control of evaporative emissions of gasoline (discussed previously as part of the nonattainment SIP requirements in Title I). These evaporative emissions were largely ignored under previous amendments, despite the fact that, on a hot summer day, evaporative and refueling emissions of hydrocarbons are more substantial than hydrocarbon exhaust emissions. The amendments also require better "in-use" performance by motor vehicles. This is achieved through stricter warranty standards for emission control equipment, such as catalytic converters, and "onboard" vehicle diagnostics to indicate problematic emission control equipment.

All owners of urban buses in consolidated metropolitan statistical areas with a 1980 population of 750,000 or more must satisfy a standard for a 50 percent reduction of emission of particulate matter, PM-10. For new post-1993 urban bus engines, the EPA has specified tightened standards for NO_x and PM emissions. These standards can be satisfied directly by a fleet operator, but in lieu of, or in addition to, strict compliance, emission averaging, banking, or trading can be employed. There are three ways in which urban bus operators can comply with NO_x and PM emission standards for new engines. They can (1) purchase new, clean-technology urban buses, (2) deploy "retrofit/rebuild" technologies on existing buses, or (3) lower emissions of the total fleet through use of alternative fuels or other fleetwide technologies.

Fuel Programs

Congress also attempted to reduce mobile source emissions through fuel-related programs. The 1990 amendments seek to reduce fuel volatility (evaporation), desulfurize diesel fuel, and complete the phase-out of leaded gasoline successfully started in the 1970s. As lead was phased out of gasoline, greater fractions of aromatic organic compounds, such as benzene, toluene, and xylene were added as octane enhancements, increasing their share of gasoline from about 22 percent to about one-third of the volume. Benzene is considered a significant cancer risk when inhaled, and alone is responsible for 25 percent of the cancer risk associated with toxic air releases. Two-thirds of benzene releases come from motor vehicle emissions. Of note, these hazardous substances, as long as in gasoline in typical amounts, do not make gasoline a hazardous substance under CERCLA (see Chapter 9).

The RFG and oxygenated fuel programs designed for ozone and CO nonattainment areas were introduced. The amendments require the use of reformulated gasoline in the nine worst ozone nonattainment areas, with the intended result that the reformulated fuel be approximately 15 percent cleaner than conventional blends of gasoline. Other ozone nonattainment areas are given the option to "opt in" to the program. Additionally, the amendments require that all gasoline in CO nonattainment areas contain oxygenates during peak-level CO periods. This period is determined by the EPA and typically occurs during the winter months.

Renewable oxygenated fuels can contain a percentage of alcohols, like ethanol and methanol, which reduce the energy content of the fuel, and thus miles per gallon in use, and increase the emission of criteria pollutants. Ethanol is made from biomass, such as corn; natural gas is commonly used to produce methanol. Growing corn in U.S. agriculture is very energy-intensive and has environmental impacts from the use of petro-chemicals, nitrogen and phosphorous chemicals, and fertilizers (see Chapters 1, 6, and 14). With about one-third of the U.S. corn crop now used to produce ethanol, if ethanol were substituted for 10 percent of all U.S. petroleum, it would require about 40 percent of U.S. cropland be devoted to this purpose. Tariffs and duties limit the import of ethanol into the United States. The U.S. Department of Energy concluded that more energy was used to produce a gallon of ethanol than the energy value of that ethanol — a net energy loss.

The requirement that 30 percent of oxygen in reformulated fuels must come from ethanol or other reformulated fuels was stricken in *American Petroleum Institute v. EPA*, 52 F.3d 1113 (D.C. Cir. 1995). Provisions of the Energy Policy Act of 2005 amended §211 of the Clean Air Act to add a renewable fuel requirement for all gasoline sold in the United States. Some of this is satisfied by adding ethanol to gasoline formulations. Still, ethanol accounts for only about 2 percent of the total gasoline and diesel fuel consumption in the United States. The 1990 amendments limit VOCs through limiting gasoline Reid vapor pressure during summer months.

Vehicle Fleet Programs

The 1990 amendments mandate a clean-fuel vehicle program designed to govern the development of low-emission vehicles (LEVs) and zero-emission vehicles (ZEVs). This program will be implemented by requiring operators of centrally fueled fleets of ten or more vehicles in certain CO and ozone nonattainment areas to purchase and use clean-fuel vehicles beginning in 1998.

The EPA attempted to require 12 northeastern states and the District of Columbia to adopt California's tough vehicle emission program to help reduce ozone. This was challenged on the grounds that the evidence did not support the EPA's region-wide reduction requirements for NO_x and VOCs. In *Virginia v. EPA*, 108 F.3d 1397 (D.C. Cir. 1997), the court held that the statute did not grant the EPA the authority to require states to enact the California standards. Moreover, the EPA could not determine that the northeast states' SIPs were "substantially inadequate." Even where the EPA is justified in rejecting a SIP, the EPA does not have authority to mandate the specific measures necessary to have the state achieve SIP compliance: "EPA may not run roughshod over procedural prerogatives that the Act has reserved to the states."

5. Air Quality Regulation

The Clean Air Act Amendments of 1990 require the establishment of a Clean Fuel Fleet vehicle program. While often thought of as a procurement program, it is in fact a tailpipe emissions program that applies a stricter standard to new vehicle purchases. States must modify their SIPs to require certain central vehicle fleet operators to purchase a percentage of vehicles that exhibit cleaner exhaust emissions. States may opt out of this program if they achieve mobile source emission reductions or SIP reductions with alternative or complementary standards. The Fleet program does not apply nationwide, nor does it apply to all vehicles. Congress targeted only those operators that have, or potentially have, control over their sources of fuel for centralized fleets. Those areas covered are those with a 1980 population in the consolidated metropolitan area of 250,000 persons or more, and which exhibit "serious," "severe," or "extreme" ozone or CO nonattainment.

States with one of the 22 nonattainment areas covered by the Fleet program must revise their SIPs to include the program unless they opt out. The areas include the Northeast corridor, Atlanta, Baton Rouge, the urban areas of Texas, Denver, much of California, and Milwaukee. Most of these areas are in nonattainment because of ozone precursors. The only area that qualified for nonattainment because of carbon monoxide nonattainment was Denver. Complying vehicles that meet exhaust emission standards are low-emission vehicles (LEVs), or zero-emission vehicles (ZEVs).

This program applies only to fleets of ten or more vehicles that are capable of central fueling and are not otherwise exempted. The EPA altered its definition of "centrally fueled" fleets to limit it to vehicles that are centrally fueled 100 percent of the time; the definition of "capable of being centrally fueled" was limited by the EPA to vehicles that could be fueled centrally 100 percent of the time. To avoid coverage, a vehicle fleet operator need only show that occasionally it needs to fuel a vehicle somewhere outside the centrally controlled pumps.

If vehicles are taken home by employees at night, they are not deemed to be centrally fueled. In addition, any vehicles held for lease or rental to the general public, any used vehicles held for sale by dealers, any vehicles used for evaluations or tests, all law enforcement and other emergency vehicles, all nonroad vehicles including farm and construction vehicles, all Defense Department vehicles that the department deems to be exempt for national security reasons, and all heavy-duty vehicles above 26,000 pounds, are exempt from this program. This exempts many of the obvious central fleets. It also eliminates many of the obvious diesel fuel applications, by exempting heavy off-road vehicles, farm equipment, and construction equipment.

"Alternative" fuels for the Clean Fuel Fleet program include (1) biodiesel blends, (2) methanol, (3) ethanol or other alcohol fuels, including any mixture thereof containing 85 percent or more by volume of such alcohols with gasoline or other fuels, (4) reformulated gasoline, (5) diesel fuel, (6) natural gas, (7) liquefied petroleum gas, or (8) hydrogen.

Operators can comply with this program by purchasing LEV or ZEV vehicles, by purchasing credits from others who have exceeded their requirements under this Act and seek to trade surplus credits, or by converting existing conventional vehicles to clean fuels. Credits are earned for reduction of nonmethane organic gases and NO_x. Credits generated by doing more than required "may be used by the person holding such credits to demonstrate compliance with this section or may be traded or sold for use for any other persons to demonstrate compliance with any other requirements applicable under this section in the same nonattainment area." By purchasing credits, a vehicle operator need not purchase Clean Fuel Fleet vehicles.

Examples

1. If you are advising Governor Parrot on how he should designate his state for ozone nonattainment, review the trade-offs of selecting more or less extreme ozone classifications.

2. If your client, Rolls-R-Us, wants to locate a major new stationary source in a state that is labeled "severe" for ozone nonattainment, identify the relevant restrictions for ozone and NO_x that would accompany the permitting of air emissions for this facility. In formulating your answer, review the information and values in Exhibit 5.9. (Exhibit 5.7 may also be helpful.)

3. You are counsel in the Northeast United States to Nifty Car Rental Company. All of the Northeast is in ozone nonattainment. Nifty wants to know if it is subject to the Clean Fuel Fleet program, requiring use of clean fuels, for the following aspects of its conglomerate operations:
   a. Its 300 cars available for rental at the international airport.
   b. A pizza delivery company it owns that has 20 vehicles in the Metropolis urban area; its current policy is to refuel these vehicles at local filling stations rather than centrally.
   c. A fleet of 12 centrally dispatched minivans that are owned by the pizza delivery company to take fresh pizzas to the local international airport for shipment to other cities.

4. Your client is going to construct a new facility that has the potential to emit 300 tons per year (tpy) of VOC. If your client elects to use state-of-the-art pollution control technology, VOC emissions can be reduced to 45 tpy. If the facility is located in a "serious" ozone nonattainment area and uses the state-of-the-art pollution equipment, is it subject to NSR?

5. Your client, Spacely Space Sprockets, decides to manufacture a biodiesel fuel. Biodiesel is a combustible fuel substitute or additive made from

vegetable oil rather than petroleum. It is widely used in certain sensitive environmental regions in Europe, and it substantially lowers emissions compared to petroleum-based fuels. Spacely Space Sprockets purchases an existing soap factory to convert it into a biodiesel fuel facility. Advise the biodiesel company on the following questions:

a. The soap factory is in a region in nonattainment for ozone. The factory emits 500 tpy of VOC and 300 tpy of NO_x. After conversion to biodiesel production, the facility will emit 300 tpy of VOC and 500 tpy of NO_x. Is it subject to NSR?

b. If the facility closes for six months while it converts its soap manufacturing to biodiesel production, is it subject to NSR? Why or why not?

Explanations

1. By selecting a more extreme designation for ozone nonattainment, the state gains extra time to achieve attainment. Political fallout from not reaching attainment during the current gubernatorial administration is therefore unlikely. However, in return for the more extreme classification, smaller sources of ozone precursors are deemed *major* sources. This greater stringency means that the state will have to process more NSR permits for modernization and for new industry sites. It also means that there is more red tape associated with such smaller sources than might occur in other states. Annual percentage reductions of hydrocarbons and nitrogen oxides also are required for the more extreme classifications, and must be monitored.

2. In a "severe" area, while the state has until 2005 to achieve ozone compliance with the NAAQS, any source with the potential to emit 25 tpy or more of any ozone precursor is a major stationary source subject to full NSR review. In addition, NO_x offsets on a ratio of 1:1.3 are required for all new or modified major sources.

3a. The rental car company is not subject to the Clean Fuel Fleet vehicle program because rental car companies, taxicab companies, and other major fleets that would be prime targets can argue that they cannot always fuel centrally under the EPA definition. Moreover, they are legislatively exempt from this program. Many of the fleets that contribute the most emissions have effective regulatory exemption.

3b. Even though the pizza delivery cars are not centrally fueled as a matter of practice, the issue is whether they are *capable* of being centrally fueled. The answer to this seems to be "yes." Therefore, the program would apply to those cars unless it can be shown that they cannot be centrally fueled 100 percent of the time.

3c. The program covers minivans and light-duty trucks, so it would apply to the fleet.

4. The answer is no. The definition of a major source is determined *after* the application of all pollution control technology. The threshold for new sources is 50 tpy; 25 tpy for modified sources. The former standard applies. However, the facility will be legally required to keep in place such pollution control technology, once it avoids NSR permitting, because of the availability and application of this technology.

5a. The emission of NO_x actually is increasing. Technically, this is an increase of a major source; NSR would apply. However, NO_x and VOC both are ozone precursors. NO_x also is regulated separately. It is within the discretion of the administrative agency to *net* the increase and decrease of NO_x and VOC to conclude that ozone precursors as a whole are not increasing on balance. In such a situation, it might choose not to require a new NSR permit application process. It would behoove counsel to work with air officials to try to reach a compromise protocol for licensing the new facility. There might also be discretion as to whether existing soap factory permits would be transferable to the new owner, Spacely. Technically, the change in process (to create a different product) might cause the facility to be considered a *new* or *modified* stationary source. There is interpretive discretion here for state air officials in administrating a delegated Clean Air Act program. The change in ownership is not considered a "major modification."

5b. Closing the plant can also be a complication, especially since there is a change in ownership and manufacturing process. This closing of the facility could be regarded as an abandonment of the prior permit. Again here, it is important to negotiate with relevant air officials to obtain a determination that the facility operation is ongoing and not subject to characterization as a *new facility* or *modified facility* after the closure.

Hazardous Air Pollutants (NESHAPs): Title III

Two hundred seventy million Americans live in a census tract where the lifetime risk from exposure to one of 177 hazardous air pollutants is greater than ten additional cancer cases per million persons exposed. This includes about 90 percent of the American population. The EPA deems a lifetime cancer risk greater than one case per one million persons to be unacceptable. In most urban areas, the risk over a lifetime is 25 cancers per million persons exposed and in some urban corridors, the risk is greater than 50 cancers per million persons exposed.

Mitigating the impact of these statistics is the fact that the role of exposure to air pollution plays a relatively small role in all believed causes of cancer. One of every three Americans eventually contracts cancer, but less than 1 percent of these cancers is believed to be directly and primarily related to the inhalation of hazardous air pollutants. The hazardous constituent deemed to pose the greatest risk is benzene. Some advocacy organizations believe that diesel engine exhaust presents a risk of 365 cancers per one million persons exposed over a lifetime.

You will recall from our discussion of Title I that the NAAQS are aimed at controlling the emission of the six criteria pollutants. Title III of the 1990 amendments revamps the existing NESHAPs program for controlling air toxics. It focuses on air pollutants that are less pervasive than those in the criteria pollutant category, yet extremely harmful and dangerous to human health and air quality. Who emits toxics to the air? Chemical plants and other sources using chemical processes account for nearly 35 percent of hazardous air pollutant (HAP) emissions in the United States. Other industries that significantly contribute to HAP emissions include the auto, paper, plastics, rubber, and primary metals industries. The chemicals, compounds, and groups of compounds emitted from power plants subject to MACT include the acid gases hydrogen chloride (HC_1) and hydrogen fluoride (HF); HAP metals arsenic (As), cadmium (Cd), and lead (Pb); organic HAP dioxins benzene and methyl hydrazine; radionuclides; and mercury (Hg). 42 U.S.C. §7412(b)(1). Coal-fired power plants have been accused of producing in 2010 over 386,000 tons of 84 separate hazardous air pollutants from over 440 plants in 46 states.

In *NRDC v. EPA*, 824 F.2d 1146 (D.C. Cir. 1987), the Court of Appeals for the District of Columbia Circuit upheld the EPA's withdrawal of a proposal to amend the vinyl chloride NESHAPs standard. The court held that the NESHAPs must provide an *ample* margin of safety with regard to health risks created by the HAPs; however, the court did not equate safe levels to *risk-free* levels. The decision in this case required the EPA first to determine a "safe" level of emissions based on scientific health data, and then to determine what additional emission reduction requirements would be necessary to ensure an "*ample* margin of safety."

In commenting on the EPA's "safety" determination, the court stated, "The Administrator cannot under any circumstances consider cost and technological feasibility at this stage of the analysis." The EPA now approaches the "ample margin of safety" element of the program through a technology-based component that considers "additional factors relating to the appropriate level of control, including costs and economic impacts of controls, technological feasibility, uncertainties, and any other relevant factors." Exhibit 5.10 illustrates the difference in standards between HAPs and criteria pollutants.

The 1990 Clean Air Act amendments change the focus of regulating toxics to require the best demonstrated technology used by sources in an industrial category. In defining major sources subject to regulation under

5.10 Regulatory Provisions of the Clean Air Act

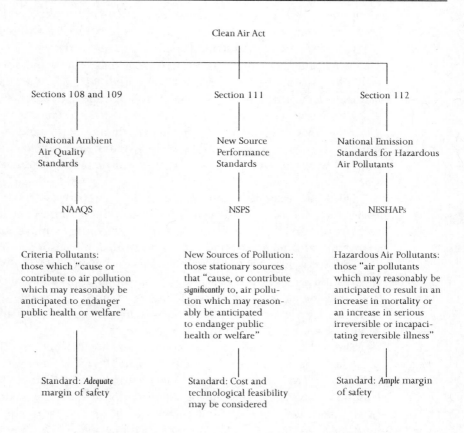

Clean Air Act

Sections 108 and 109	Section 111	Section 112
National Ambient Air Quality Standards	New Source Performance Standards	National Emission Standards for Hazardous Air Pollutants
NAAQS	NSPS	NESHAPs
Criteria Pollutants: those which "cause or contribute to air pollution which may reasonably be anticipated to endanger public health or welfare"	New Sources of Pollution: those stationary sources that "cause, or contribute *significantly* to, air pollution which may reasonably be anticipated to endanger public health or welfare"	Hazardous Air Pollutants: those "air pollutants which may reasonably be anticipated to result in an increase in mortality or an increase in serious irreversible or incapacitating reversible illness"
Standard: *Adequate* margin of safety	Standard: Cost and technological feasibility may be considered	Standard: *Ample* margin of safety

§112, the courts have held that the EPA is not bound to any single definition of a "major source." See *National Mining Ass'n v. EPA*, 59 F.3d 1351, 1359 (D.C. Cir. 1995).

One of the significant changes in the NESHAPs program under the 1990 amendments is that the number of *statutorily* listed HAPs has been increased to 189 substances, including hazardous organic chemicals and metals. The EPA is required to review this extensive list periodically, and the Act provides that a new substance may be added to the list if it can reasonably be expected to create adverse effects on human health or the environment. A substance may be delisted if it is not reasonable to anticipate adverse health or environmental effects. EPA rules will slash mercury and other toxic emissions by 2016.

violation, even without specific knowledge of the law. *U.S. v. Weintraub*, 273 F.3d 139, 147 (2nd Cir. 2001); Cf. *U.S. v. W.R. Grace*, 429 F.Supp.2d 1207 (D. Mont. 2006)("[t]he plain language of the Clean Air Act indicates that it is not a required element of §7413(c)(5) that the defendant know that his conduct is unlawful"), *W.R. Grace & Co. v. U.S.*, 554 U.S. 918 (2008). The statute states "circumstantial evidence may be used, including evidence that the defendant took affirmative steps to be shielded from relevant information," to demonstrate knowledge. 42 U.S.C. 7413(c)(5)(B). No federal agency may enter into any contract with any person who is convicted of any offense, if the good or service is produced by a violating facility. 42 U.S.C. §7606(a).

Privileged Legal Information

So, what is the duty of legal counsel with regard to information that demonstrates noncompliance or a violation of the Clean Air Act? Many companies audit or evaluate their operations as to environmental compliance. Environmental compliance audits and the information they produce create information that could have strong evidentiary value against a company's interest. The line between regulators' requirements for an abundance of detailed recordkeeping and the regulated community's claim to protection under certain privileges is thin.

The EPA policy on environmental audits is that the EPA will impose reduced civil penalties and will not seek criminal prosecution if violations detected by companies through environmental auditing and self-monitoring are voluntarily reported. This policy does not apply if the monitoring or sampling that reveals this violation is a result of monitoring required under a permit, order, or regulation. Reporting must occur within ten days or less of the discovery and additional measures must be undertaken to prevent recurrence. The policy does not apply if a recurring pollution situation is present.

This policy does not mean that one will escape fines, but merely that one will be eligible for lesser fines. This also falls short of establishing any statutory evidentiary privilege for environmental audits. Rather, this merely expresses an EPA policy for purposes of enforcement discretion. EPA policy rewards voluntary disclosure, but does not bar criminal penalties. Where there is doubt that a violation occurred, it is required by the policy that there be disclosure if a suspected violation "may have occurred." The EPA reserves the right to collect full civil penalties for criminal conduct, for repeat violations, and for imminent and substantial endangerment, while reserving the right to seek criminal actions. This policy does not create strong incentives for internal audit.

The information voluntarily disclosed to the EPA can still be used against a company, either in the form of a civil penalty prosecution, or prosecution by a state or local agency, or use in a citizen suit or toxic tort action against the company, or an individual action against corporate officers or employees. Therefore, these reports have to be viewed as potentially self-incriminating or detrimental when turned over to the agency.

A number of states have statutes exempting environmental audits from disclosure, as privileged communications. This means that such information is not accessible to the government or other third parties for purposes of use against the party that commissioned, and is the subject of, the environmental audit. Protected under these laws are raw data, opinions, photographs, maps, surveys, and other information.

Some of these statutes also prohibit those who participate in these activities from being compelled to testify or voluntarily testifying or disclosing the information of these audits. Some state statutes also provide immunity from criminal, civil, or administrative prosecution and any related penalties for environmental violations that are voluntarily reported by an entity (perhaps as a result of an environmental audit). The EPA does not recognize such state laws as binding for purposes of federal prosecution.

Several factors are necessary to establish the attorney-client privilege in the context of an internal environmental compliance audit. Initially, the privilege requires that the audit take place within the purview of an attorney-client relationship. Second, communications made to an attorney and information gathered by the attorney must be used for the *purpose* of providing legal advice. Presumably, this requirement would encompass the task of conducting an environmental audit for legal compliance purposes. The third element requires the communication to be relayed by the client to the attorney, outside of the presence of third parties not included in the attorney-client relationship. The fourth element requires that the party asserting the privilege has not intentionally or unintentionally waived his or her right to claim the privilege.

The privilege also accords information or materials assembled in *anticipation of litigation*, or in preparation for trial, a *qualified* privilege from disclosure to an opposing party. The EPA may well be the opposing party. The privilege is not allowed if the court determines that it will cause "undue hardship" for the nonmoving party, or if counsel asserts the privilege to protect materials that are not prepared in anticipation of litigation.

The attorney work-product rule provides a privilege from disclosure of facts contained in materials produced by attorneys or under their supervision, including environmental audits, if they are requested by an opponent during the discovery phase of litigation. This rule may not protect materials developed pursuant to an environmental auditing program that has been ongoing for a number of years; the court may consider the facts so gathered as regular business activity and, therefore, not developed in anticipation of litigation.

There is a recognized self-evaluative privilege regarding documents that contain constructive internal criticism, to encourage the free flow of self-critical information within companies. In contemplating application of the privilege, the Court in *Webb v. Westinghouse*, 81 F.R.D. 431 (1978), described three scenarios where the privilege has been applied: "(1) when the materials have been prepared pursuant to governmental requirements, (2) when the materials are subjective and evaluative, and (3) when the policy interests served by withholding the documents clearly outweigh the need of the party seeking the documents." In *United States v. Dexter Corp.*, 132 F.R.D. 8 (1990), the defendant corporation unsuccessfully asserted the privilege to protect certain self-evaluative documents by arguing that there was a "public interest" in encouraging candid and thorough internal self-criticism.

While the EPA recognizes the need for privacy in self-evaluations of environmental performance, corporations are forewarned that the EPA may successfully request disclosure of information from the audits. Additionally, some audit findings may by law have to be reported to government agencies.

The Clean Air Act authorizes the EPA to "demand such information as it may reasonably require to determine whether any person is in violation of any such standard or any requirement of such a plan or to carry out any provision of this chapter." *United States v. Excel Energy*, 759 F.Supp.2d 1106, 1111 (D.Minn. 2010). If the EPA's demand for information is not satisfactorily met, "EPA may seek an injunction or civil penalty for any source that refuses to comply with the foregoing demands for information." The civil penalty is up to $37,500 per day for each violation. 42 U.S.C. §7413(b). The Clean Water Act provides that, except for trade secrets, "[a]ny records, reports, or information obtained under this section . . . *shall* be available to the public." 33 U.S.C. §1318(b). Legislation allowing for the protection of a corporation's environmental audits has been passed in approximately 30 percent of the states.

All this makes audit data a double-edged sword: In the hands of the client, it may be helpful; in the hands of enforcement agencies, it may be evidence. The interposition of counsel in the design, collection, and evaluation of information on environmental performance may protect it.

Examples

1. If your client's facility is complying with its Clean Air Act permit, is it vulnerable to EPA enforcement actions?

2. If the EPA cites your client's facility for exceeding its permitted emissions of SO_2, NO_x, and particulate matter on ten days during the past month:
   a. Is your client subject to enforcement action?
   b. If your answer to the question above is "yes," what is the maximum aggregate civil penalty amount that could be collected on these facts?

3. A citizen group initiates litigation against your client's existing facility that admittedly emits air pollutants, subject to an existing Clean Air

Act permit. What is the impact on the citizen suit if the following occurs?

a. The citizen group immediately without warning sues your client for noncompliance with its permit.

b. Thirty days after litigation ensues, the EPA initiates prosecution against your client for the same violation alleged by the citizen group.

c. Can the citizen group collect attorney fees for its efforts, if the scenario in question (b) above occurs? Can it collect attorney fees if it prevails on the merits in the litigation?

4. Your client, the Spacely Space Sprockets biodiesel facility, desires to perform an environmental audit to gauge its environmental compliance. To attempt to protect this information from the EPA, it asks you as its counsel to hire the environmental consulting firm that will perform the audit. You hire the consultant team at EnviroSecrets, and it completes its audit work. EnviroSecrets produces a final report marked "Top Secret." Under each of the following scenarios, assess the strength of a claim of attorney-client privilege or attorney work-product protection of the information in the audit report, should the EPA attempt to discover it:

a. When the work is finished, you as counsel receive the sole copy of the final report, never read the results, and ship it on to the vice president for human relations of the biodiesel firm.

b. The client shows the results to its outside accountant, Libby Writeoff, for purposes of assessing cost and accounting implications.

c. Your client shows the results to another company that is a potentially responsible party at an unrelated Superfund site where the biodiesel company also is a potentially responsible party.

d. The client biodiesel company leaves the copy of the EnviroSecrets environmental audit report on a coffee table in the lobby of its corporate headquarters. It is unclear whether anyone outside the company reads this report.

Explanations

1. Compliance with a permit issued under the Clean Air Act operates as a "permit shield." Therefore, the facility is not subject to enforcement actions.

2a. A violation of any element of a standard or condition in a permit is an actionable violation for which the facility owner can be assessed a civil penalty. Here there are multiple violations in the fact pattern.

2b. On each of ten days there were violations of the emission standards for each of three criteria pollutants. This means that there are 30 separate violations. The maximum penalty is \$37,500 per day *per violation* (10 days × 3 violations). The maximum penalty would be 30 × \$37,500 = \$1,125,000.

3a. A citizen or citizen group is required to provide the EPA and the potential defendant with 60 days' notice prior to the initiation of litigation. This advance notice gives the EPA an opportunity to prosecute the violation itself. It also gives the target defendant a chance to remedy the violation. Litigation will be dismissed if it is initiated prior to the expiration of this 60-day notice requirement. Under these circumstances, the litigation is not ripe for prosecution. For discussion of the ripeness requirement, see Chapter 2.

3b. If the EPA initiates litigation, the litigation via the citizen suit is tolled and subsumed in the government action. The citizen suit is mooted mid-litigation.

3c. Attorney fees are available whenever the citizen group "prevails." See Chapter 2.

4a. To assert an attorney-client privilege, the information must be assembled for the purpose of providing legal advice to a client. If the attorney does not read the report, does not provide any legal advice based on the report, and does not even keep a copy of the report, a claim that the material is attorney-client privileged may well be defeated. The attorney should control, marshall, and access the information.

4b. Showing the report to a retained party consultant outside the firm, where the consultant has a reasonable need to see the information in order to furnish advice, is not a waiver of the attorney-client privilege. The accountant would likely satisfy this standard. It would be even more direct for the attorney to control access of the accountant to the report. However, showing the report indiscriminately to those who do not have to know its contents would constitute a waiver of the privilege.

4c. Showing the report to other potentially responsible parties who have environmental problems but are unrelated in any way to the internal auditing issues revealed in the report, would constitute a waiver of the privilege. It does not matter that these other parties would not be directly adverse to the corporation in litigation; the disclosure of the contents itself constitutes a waiver that destroys the privilege vis-à-vis other parties, such as the EPA.

4d. Public display of the report would constitute a waiver of the privilege, regardless of whether anyone *saw* the contents or read the report, unless there could be a showing that this was an inadvertent disclosure that was immediately rectified as soon as it became known. The mere treatment of the contents in a way that does not suggest respect of the privileged content could be deemed a waiver of the privilege.

CLIMATE CHANGE: GLOBAL WARMING AND CO_2 REGULATION

The Science of Warming

There is historical evidence that societal collapse has occurred from global climate change. Climate change is attributed to global warming, which is a result of the greenhouse effect from anthropogenic emissions of CO_2 and other greenhouse gases (GHGs). GHGs trap sunlight in earth's atmosphere, absorbing the longer infrared radiation, and turn the sunlight into heat, a phenomenon known as the "greenhouse effect." Every day, almost a hundred million tons of GHGs are released into the atmosphere. Every second, more than a thousand tons — two million pounds — of carbon dioxide is emitted from human technologies. The world emits more than 35 billion tons of carbon dioxide annually, or a half ton of CO_2 annually per world citizen. The average American is responsible for four times as much, or a hundred pounds of carbon dioxide emissions every day. While humans emit far less carbon dioxide than nature, the amount we emit exceeds the capacity of plants and oceans to absorb. Over the 50 years since 1960, the amount of carbon dioxide in the atmosphere has risen nearly 25 percent.

No environmental issue has emerged and risen in the public consciousness as rapidly as that of climate change from human-caused global warming. Prior to 2005, no nation had implemented any regulatory action to contain its contribution to warming; the international Kyoto Protocol began only in 2008, and the first U.S. states to regulate CO_2 commenced in 2009. Now there is a clear and present urgency to control climate change before the world passes a "tipping point" beyond climate restoration. Today, global warming has rapidly emerged at the center of the environmental regulatory focus. Carbon control has become the metavalue of the twenty-first-century environmental dialogue.

And there is good scientific reason: Some leading scientists warn that there are about five years left to dramatically reduce greenhouse gases (GHGs) before the world crosses a "tipping point." In 2009, the United Nations Environment Program also forecast upcoming "tipping points . . . that will alter regional and global environmental balances . . . irreversible within the time span of our current civilization." Prior to the Industrial Revolution, average earth temperature had been naturally maintained at 59°F. Since the Industrial Revolution, carbon emissions resulting from combusting fossil fuels to provide mechanical and electrical energy have poured into the atmosphere. Atmospheric temperature changes move in the same direction as atmospheric GHG concentrations.

For the past 10,000 years, the earth's temperature has varied by less than 2°F. Historically, there has been concern about cooling of up to 80°F during ice ages that lasted tens of thousands of years, sometimes dropping temperatures to −50°F. Glaciers used to cover 30 percent of the earth but have not been present to this extent for the last 12,000 years. These last ice ages created the Great Lakes and Hudson Bay in Canada.

Recently, global mean surface temperature rose 1.33°F over the last decade, and the rate of warming over the past 50 years has almost doubled. Atmospheric CO_2 levels now are approximately 33 percent higher than in preindustrial times, when they were about 382 parts per million (ppm). Limiting modern-era global warming to 4°F will require stabilizing CO_2 concentrations in earth's atmosphere at no more than 450 ppm. A top official with the United Nations Intergovernmental Panel on Climate Change (IPCC) has indicated that developed nations will need to slash CO_2 emissions by 80-95 percent — almost entirely — by 2050 to hold GHG concentrations to 450 ppm in the atmosphere. Burning a gallon of gasoline, which weighs 6.3 pounds, releases 5.5 pounds of carbon. In the atmosphere, the carbon combines into more than 20 pounds of CO_2.

Carbon is essential to living things and critical to the universe. The human body is slightly less than 10 percent carbon. Carbon dioxide was a critical part of the early atmosphere of the earth because the sun was originally much dimmer, and the presence of CO_2 and the resultant greenhouse effect kept the planet from freezing permanently when life was first being formed.

Some GHG emissions occur naturally, while others are anthropogenic. About 200 million tons of carbon are released into the atmosphere annually from decaying plants and volcanic activity. This is 30 times what humans expel from machines and cars. Water vapor, largely from ocean sources, is the major climate-forcing agent in the climate system. When there are CO_2 increases in the atmosphere through positive feedback, atmospheric water vapor increases correspondingly, amplifying climate change.

Heat-trapping greenhouse gases include water vapor, carbon dioxide (CO_2), methane (CH_4), nitrous oxides (NO_x), sulfur hexafluoride (SF_6), hydrofluorocarbons (HFCs), and perfluorocarbons (PFCs). The GHGs in Exhibit 5.12 are displayed in descending order of their impacts on the environment, which is a function of quantity released, heat radiation properties, and residence time in the atmosphere.

CO_2 concentrations in the atmosphere can persist for centuries. Within a century, if all nations of the world do not limit greenhouse gas emissions,

5.12 Greenhouse Gases

GHG	Global Warming Potential (CO_2 = 1)	Residency Time (years)	Amount of U.S. Total GHG Release (%)
Carbon dioxide (CO_2)	1	100	85
Methane (CH_4)	21	12	11
Nitrous oxides (NO_x)	310	120	2
Hydrochlorofluorocarbons (HCFCs)	140-11,700	Varies	<1
Chlorofluorocarbons (CFCs)	6,500	Varies	<1
Sulfur hexafluoride (SF_6)	23,900	Varies	<1

average global temperature will climb anywhere from 1.4-5.8°C (or 2.5-10°F). The IPCC reports that melting ice sheets could lead to a rapid rise in sea levels and the extinction of large numbers of species brought about by even moderate warming of 1-3°C. At the height of the last Ice Age, average temperatures were only approximately 5°C cooler than now, yet it resulted in much of the earth being covered by ice sheets. Therefore, an increase of an additional few degrees is a major shift. At recent average rates of warming, approximately 40 percent of the perennial ice cap will disappear by the year 2050. Melting of the entire Antarctic ice sheet could raise the level of the oceans by the height of a 20-story building.

According to NASA climatologist James Hansen, "The stakes, for all life on the planet, surpass those of any previous crisis. . . . If we stay our present course, using fossil fuels to feed a growing appetite for energy-intensive lifestyles, we will soon leave the climate of the Holocene, the world of prior human history." Global CO_2 emissions are rising at the rate of approximately 10 percent per year. The U.S. Department of Energy forecasts that a worldwide carbon *increase* of 54 percent over 1990 levels could occur by 2015. Ninety-eight percent of anthropogenic CO_2 emissions are from combustion of fossil fuels, and 83 percent of U.S. GHG emissions are attributed to CO_2. In 1949, only 11 percent of global warming gases in the United States came from the generation of electricity; today it is more than 40 percent.

Although they are emitting less than half of anthropogenic sources of CO_2 now, developing nations are expected to emit a majority of CO_2 emissions before 2035. The IPCC estimates that the present atmospheric concentration of CO_2 is at its highest level in the past 420,000 years, and the current rate of increase is unprecedented over the past 20,000 years. Because of this massive influx of carbon into the atmosphere, the global average surface temperature increased 0.6°C during the twentieth century and was likely the northern hemisphere's warmest in a thousand years.

As the Earth warms, polar ice sheets, ice caps, and glaciers melt, and ocean waters expand, all causing sea levels to rise. Over the last century, worldwide sea levels have risen approximately 4.8 to 8.8 inches. The IPCC estimates the average sea level will rise between 7.2 and 23.6 inches by 2100. A one meter rise in sea level would result in the loss of 10,000 square miles above coastal land in the United States.

Flooding and sea level rise resulting from climate change pose the most direct environmental risk to human settlement. They could threaten agriculture and water supply, displacing perhaps 200 million people in low-lying areas by 2080 and causing tens of billions of dollars of damage to coastal-area infrastructure. The economic loss from ordinary and extreme weather events has soared by a factor of 10.2 from $3.9 billion per year in the 1950s to $40 billion per year in the 1990s.

More than half of the naturally forested areas of the world have been destroyed or damaged during the past 8,000 years, with half of that occurring in the past 50 years. Thus the rate of deforestation has accelerated dramatically. One-third of the world's coral reefs have been severely damaged or destroyed. Under current rates of loss, half of the remaining reefs will be lost by 2030. A team of scientists concluded that human-induced carbon dioxide emissions will alter ocean chemistry to the point where it will violate EPA quality criteria by 2050.

About one-third of CO_2 from burning fossil fuels is absorbed into the world's oceans. This makes carbonic acid in the oceans, which can damage coral reefs and also hurt other calcifying organisms, such as phytoplankton and zooplankton. As carbonic acid concentrations intensify, they can corrode shellfish shells, disrupt coral formations, and interfere with oxygen supply. EPA Quality Criteria for Water state that ocean waters where the depth is substantially greater than the euphotic zone should not have a change of pH of more than 0.2 units outside the naturally occurring range. The euphotic zone goes from the surface to the depth of about 650 feet, the region where light can reach and photosynthesis can occur. To stay within this 0.2 limit, CO_2 concentrations need to remain at less than 500 ppm.

Energy is the biggest business in the world, with sales each year of about $2 trillion. Electricity generation and transportation account for 35 percent and 28 percent, respectively, of GHGs. Anthropogenic emission of greenhouse gases is driven by a fairly straightforward relationship, in which GHGs are a function of a three-part algorithm with inputs of:

- Population
- Degree of development and electrification
- Choice of technology

There is little doubt that world population will increase significantly during the next 50 years, especially in less industrialized, poorer developing nations, possibly reaching 8 billion people by 2020 and 9 to 10 billion by 2050. As previously mentioned, developing nations are expected to emit a majority of CO_2 emissions before 2035. China recently surpassed the United States as the largest CO_2 emitter in the world, currently meeting 70 percent of its electricity demand using coal-fired plants, the most prolific emitters of CO_2. Fifty-seven percent of India's electricity comes from coal.

Cap-and-trade is the legal regulatory mechanism through which world economies have decided to regulate carbon emissions. Cap-and-trade is the establishment of emissions limits on certain sources, and allocation or sale of the legal rights to emit, with the ability of entities to trade for more or fewer of such allowances. Before talking about U.S. regulation, let's set the international carbon context. Although the European Union (EU) since 2005, and most nations of the world through the Kyoto Protocol since 2008, have engaged in GHG control, there is no early evidence of success:

- The Kyoto Protocol has not been successful in achieving its reduced carbon emissions in either developed or developing countries.
- The 23 U.S. states presently regulating carbon emissions have become embroiled in legal problems involving constitutional issues.
- Nations are in dispute over which countries must shoulder burdens to implement reductions in GHGs, with coal generation a sticking point.

The Kyoto Protocol

The first global environmental conference was held in Stockholm, Sweden, in June 1972. The conference resulted in the Declaration of the United Nations Conference on the Human Environment, addressing population growth, sustainable development, and the preservation of natural resources, and created the United Nations Environment Programme (UNEP). The United Nations Framework Convention for Climate Change (UNFCCC) was adopted in June 1992 at the United Nations Conference on Environment and Development in Rio de Janeiro, Brazil. The Kyoto Protocol was adopted on December 11, 1997, in Kyoto, Japan, setting GHG emission reduction targets for 37 industrialized countries and the European Union. The Kyoto Protocol received sufficient national ratification and entered into force on February 16, 2005.

The Kyoto Protocol, prominently not ratified by the United States and, for a time, Australia, requires 37 developed nations by 2012 to reduce annual CO_2 emissions an average of 7 percent below 1990 baseline levels. The other GHGs must be reduced to 5-7 percent below either their 1990 or 1995 baseline levels between 2008 and 2012. The Kyoto Protocol in 1997 assigned to each Annex I country (developed nations) a maximum quantity of GHG emissions for the period 2008-2012. Developing nations successfully resisted efforts to include them in binding international obligations.

Emission allowance trading is allowed under the Kyoto Protocol. Any parties can purchase credits, even if they do not themselves require them for compliance, including traders who wish to speculate in these regulatory commodities. Kyoto includes the creation under its Clean Development Mechanism (CDM) of "offsets," called Certified Emission Reductions (CERs). Offsets are carbon reductions in unregulated projects that create additional allowance credits. The CDM apparatus is patterned on the U.S. SO_2 trading experience. Each CER generated in a developing country increases the GHG emissions allowed to be emitted in an Annex I country by the holder of the CER. Sixty-one percent of CDM projects were located in China, 12 percent in India, 7 percent in other Asian countries, 10 percent in Latin America, and 3 percent in Africa.

A second credit mechanism under the Kyoto Protocol is Joint Implementation (JI), which qualifies projects in signatory Annex I nations to remove GHGs by creating an Emission Reduction Unit (ERU). A JI ERU transfers a unit of allowed carbon emissions from a selling country's allowed cap to the purchasing country. Unlike a CDM CER, which creates an additional emission credit added to the cap, a JI project transfers an existing credit from one nation to another nation, as a zero-sum transaction.

Under the Kyoto Protocol, CDM, CERs, and JI ERUs are used to satisfy up to 2.5 percent of the holding party's annual allowed emissions. Those covered emitters of carbon needing additional allowances can either create or purchase additional allowances through the JI or CDM mechanisms. Emission credit creation and trading can serve as a means to transfer funds for carbon reduction to developing countries, as well as fostering least-cost emission mitigation projects internationally.

A significant problem with Kyoto, as with some other international mechanisms, is that it is a wholly voluntary agreement. There is no provision in the Kyoto Protocol to ensure compliance of any nation that fails to achieve its reductions or violates any provision. There is no effective international organization with any power over carbon-emitting nations. Achievement, at the end of the day, is voluntary and unenforceable.

The European Union Carbon System

The Kyoto Protocol has actually been on the ground for less time than the European Union's own carbon regulatory scheme. The European Union (EU) scheme is particularly important because:

- The EU system commenced three years before Kyoto commenced.
- 33 of the 38 Kyoto-regulated developed countries are in Europe; the others have no common borders with other regulated countries.

The EU system of regulation covers any combustion power source exceeding 20 MW, designed to exclude households, the agricultural sector, transportation, and aviation. The EU Emission Trading Scheme (EU ETS) covers approximately 5,000 European-based companies and 12,000 sources of industrial site emissions. EU ETS allowances, called EUAs, are issued by each country to their industries without charge within the EU carbon scheme. Trading of emission credits between members of the EU ETS and the Kyoto Protocol is allowed by the EU Linking Directive through the use of fully fungible CERs.

There are major serious policy disputes within the EU:

- Whether allowances to emit CO_2 will be auctioned to industry beginning in 2013, or freely allocated to industry
- Conflict between original and later-joining EU member states
- Future restrictions on coal-fired electric power production
- Whether states are willing to cede decision making to a central EU authority
- The speed and pace of program requirements

Poland and Bulgaria argue that more advanced Western EU countries should do more carbon reduction, while the poorer Eastern European countries should do less. Poland, the Czech Republic, Hungary, Bulgaria, Romania, and Slovakia launched legal actions against the EU Commission, asserting that even their relatively modest future carbon limits are too strict for the countries' economic growth. Poland generates 95 percent of its electric power from coal, which is locally produced but will require more auctioned CO_2 allowances than other fossil fuels, and could increase Poland's electric power prices by up to 90 percent. The alternatives of gas and oil supplied to Europe originate principally from Russia. Fresh in memory is Russia's quick strike into neighboring Georgia in August 2008, and its termination of gas supplies to the Ukraine in January 2006 and again in 2009, which then greatly diminished gas supplies throughout the EU. The U.S. Congress GAO noted regarding the EU ETS:

- The high cost of producing CDM offsets
- The failure of up to 40 percent of CDM offsets to meet "additionality" requirements
- Little positive impact to foster sustainable development

RGGI in the United States

To fill the vacuum left by the United States' refusal to participate in the Kyoto Protocol, many states have taken direct regulatory action. The Regional

Greenhouse Gas Initiative (RGGI), comprising ten East Coast states from Maine to Maryland, started in 2009 as the first program in the United States. The initiative calls for CO_2 emissions from larger power plants in the region to be capped at historic levels until 2015, with a phased-in 10 percent reduction between 2015 and 2018. By 2020, the program is expected to reach a power plant carbon emissions reduction of approximately 35 percent.

All RGGI states adopted virtually uniform state laws to implement the RGGI program, auctioning emission allowances to the highest bidders rather than freely allocating allowances. For even the relatively modest-sized state of Massachusetts, this auction at $5 per allowance would raise more than $100 million annually. It is unprecedented in U.S. environmental regulatory history that the allocations for emissions be auctioned; there also is no experience internationally with auctioning emission allowances.

The RGGI scheme also creates an offsets program, which excludes renewable energy generation as an eligible source. Offsets must be legally real, verifiable, permanent, enforceable, and "additional." There is no consensus on what the new legal concept of "additional" means, according to the Congressional GAO. RGGI initially allows offset projects to be sited anywhere in the United States if the average auction price of an emission allowance remains below $7 per ton. In each compliance period, each generator will be allowed to cover up to 3.3 percent of its emissions using offset allowances, which is roughly equal to half of that generator's emissions reduction obligation.

If allowance prices rise above $10 per ton, RGGI allows sources to cover up to 10 percent of their carbon emissions with offsets, allows offset projects from outside the United States, and recognizes international EU ETS-Kyoto allowances to be counted. Since EU ETS credits are given away without charge, this may work as an income and welfare shift, from U.S. power generation owners to EU industries selling allowances.

California GHG Regulation

California enacted a carbon regulatory scheme that requires reduction of GHG emissions to 1990 levels by 2020, counting all in-state and out-of-state generation used to serve California's electric load. This equates to an eventual estimated 25 percent reduction from current levels. Pursuant to AB 32, utilities are required to "account for greenhouse gas emissions from . . . electricity generated within the state or imported from outside the state." It does not distinguish the geographic source of power generation and covers the liberal import of power into California from other states.

Electric generators are required to meet a CO_2 emissions level no higher than that achievable by a combined-cycle gas-fired power generator. Any new contracts for a term of five years or more for the procurement of baseload generation must comply with a performance standard of emitting no more than 1,100 lbs. CO_2/MWh of power generation. "Baseload" generation is defined as generation that is designed and intended to operate at an annualized capacity factor of 60 percent or greater.

California environmental regulators shifted the point of control upstream to regulate power wholesalers at the first-seller transaction. This change makes it similar to the RGGI point of regulation. Many of these first-sellers own facilities outside the state, and engage in interstate wholesale power transactions, which are legally reserved exclusively to federal rather than state regulatory authority (see Chapter 12). RGGI regulates only CO_2 and regulates only the electric power sector. California regulates all GHGs, including CO_2. RGGI began in 2009; California's carbon program begins in 2012.

Regional U.S. Carbon Regulation

There are two regional carbon cap-and-trade initiatives in the United States, each involving multiple states and Canadian provinces. The Western Climate Initiative (WCI) comprised seven U.S. states and four provinces of Canada, with a regional, economy-wide goal to reduce GHG emissions to 15 percent below 2005 levels by 2020. The seven WCI states represented more than 20 percent of the U.S. economy, and the four associated Canadian provinces represented 70 percent of the Canadian economy. Six of the seven states withdrew in 2011, leaving California alone in this now-unitary consortium, along with the four observing Canadian provinces. Nothing was accomplished in its four years of existence.

Six participating Midwestern states and one Canadian province executed a regional greenhouse gas emission reduction strategy called the Midwestern Greenhouse Gas Reduction Accord. The group worked to develop a cap-and-trade carbon program originally scheduled for 2010. This accord will not set a specific target but will attempt to cut emissions by 2020. Recommendations would allow 10-50 percent of reductions to be achieved through use of offsets.

State Carbon Constitutional Issues

The constitutional issues confronting these state carbon regulations are that they may violate the Supremacy Clause or the Compact Clause of the U.S. Constitution (see Chapter 4). In addition, some carbon regulation auctions have been accused of constituting an unauthorized tax when they are adopted by executive branch regulation rather than by statute. Large (carbon auction) "fees" have been characterized by some courts as equivalent to taxes.

A major practical and policy problem is carbon "leakage." Leakage occurs when generators outside of the capped region export power to load-serving entities within the region without being covered by the regional carbon cap. The out-of-region sources of cheaper, unregulated power will then provide a larger portion of the power to the region, causing greater net emissions, or leakage, of CO_2. Because power can move at almost the speed of light almost anywhere in the continental United States, this leakage is a real phenomenon. The DC Court of Appeals, in August 2010, invalidated the third of three contested distinct cap-and-trade regulatory systems implemented by the EPA. *Arkema, Inc. v. EPA*, 618 F.3d 1 (D.C. Cir. 2010). This ruling invalidated cap-and-trade regulation for hydrochloro-fluorocarbons (HCFCs), which originally were regulated by the Montreal Protocol and are a global warming gas.

Some carbon-regulating states are considering surcharging or taxing wholesale power "leaking" in from outside the region. There are two legal issues. First, any state must be careful with such direct or indirect external carbon regulation, as the federal Constitution prohibits a state from regulating interstate commerce occurring in other states. Electric power has been identified by the U.S. Supreme Court as the quintessential article in interstate commerce. Regulatory impediments on the free flow of electricity from other states can run up against the dormant Commerce Clause of the U.S. Constitution (see Chapter 4). The Los Angeles Department of Water and Power (LADWP), the largest municipal utility in the United States, threatened legal suit over the California proposal to auction carbon emission allowances, alleging that it would result in a $1 billion-per-year transfer from coal-dependent utilities in the southern part of the state to northern utility ratepayers and companies.

Environmental officials in the various carbon-regulating states have declared that the rationale for the auction of 100 percent of the carbon allowances is to increase the cost of carbon-emitting power generation (via the requirement to purchase allowances). Electric-generating units in these states are allowed to operate in the order of the lowest operating price first, and then in ascending order of bid operating price. Thus, the RGGI auction policy is designed to alter, at the hand of state regulators, the "just" and "reasonable" rates previously established pursuant to federally approved wholesale market design. Higher-cost units are ordered not to run.

State regulations designed to change the wholesale price of certain power generation units could run afoul of the Federal Power Act's "bright line" of exclusive federal jurisdiction over such wholesale matters under the Constitution's Supremacy Clause and the filed rate doctrine. The Supreme

Court upheld the filed rate doctrine in 1986, 1988, 2003, and 2008 (see Chapter 12).

As set forth in Chapter 4, motive matters and was accepted at face value for preemption analysis, *Pacific Gas & Electric Co. v. California Energy Resources Conservation and Development Corporation, supra*, and subsequently in a later case was not accepted at face value, *Gade v. Nat'l Solid Wastes Mgt. Ass'n*, 505 U.S. 88, 107-08 (1992) (Court looked beyond "professed purpose" of challenged state statute because it "directly, substantially, and specifically regulate[d]" matters committed to federal regulators.). In 2009, the RGGI carbon regulatory program was challenged in New York by a Qualifying Facility cogeneration project under the Public Utilities Regulatory Policies Act (PURPA) (see Chapter 12). Separately, the Los Angeles Department of Water and Power filed comments with the California energy regulatory agencies challenging whether auction of allowances creates a tax in violation of Proposition 13 of the state constitution, violates home rule authority of the city, and unconstitutionally transfers funds from utility providers, by means of a forced regulatory gift.

Carbon Litigation

There has been a host of litigation regarding carbon. In *Massachusetts v. EPA*, 127 S. Ct. 1438 (April 2, 2007), the Supreme Court held that the EPA has authority under the Clean Air Act to regulate GHG emissions from new motor vehicles, and that even indirect harm from climate change can confer standing on these plaintiffs to sue the EPA for failure to comply with Act requirements. Note that the Court was not asked to hold that GHG emissions from stationary sources like power plants are regulated by the Act, that auto companies are liable for the harm caused by GHG emissions, or that the EPA is required to regulate GHG emissions from mobile sources. The EPA waited until the Obama Administration to decide to regulate CO_2.

The status of climate change litigation in the United States is such that no stakeholder was immune even *before* the 2007 Supreme Court decision, often raising claims under common law (see Chapter 1). Litigation on carbon issues divides along statutory claims and common law claims. Common law actions seek either monetary damages or injunctive relief. The statutory claims include attempting to pressure the government to act or refrain from acting.

These range from lawsuits involving NEPA applicability to attempts to stop states from regulating auto GHG emissions. There have been efforts to compel SEC disclosure of GHG emissions and public international law claims: *Korsinsky v. EPA*, 2006 U.S. App. LEXIS 21024 (2d Cir. 2006); *Coke Oven Envtl. Task Force v. EPA*, 2009 U.S. App. LEXIS 11003 (D.C. Cir. 2009) (petition for review challenging EPA's decision not to regulate CO_2

emissions); *Ctr. for Biological Diversity, the Sierra Club & San Bernardino Valley Audubon Soc'y v. San Bernardino Cnty.*, 188 Cal. App. 4th 603 (2010) — rehearing denial modified by *Ctr. for Biological Diversity v. County of San Bernardino*, 2010 Cal. App. LEXIS 1785 (Cal. App. 4th Dist. 2010); *California v. General Motors Corp.*, 2007 U.S. Dist. LEXIS 68547 (N.D. Cal. 2007) (against six automobile manufacturers requesting common law and nuisance compensation for damage inflicted by their vehicles' GHG emissions; the state withdrew its appeal after the bankruptcy filing of Chrysler); *Comer v. Murphy Oil USA, Inc.*, 839 F. Supp.2d 849 (S.D. Miss. 2012) (dismissing as nonjusticiable political question, lack of standing and lack of causal connection between global warming and hurricane damage claims related to oil, refining, and chemical manufacturing companies alleged to constitute a public nuisance resulting in monetary damages); *NW. Envtl. Def. Ctr. v. Owens Corning Corp.*, 434 F. Supp. 2d 957 (D. Or. 2006).

Even atypical defendants have been sued over carbon impacts. *Friends of the Earth v. Mosbacher*, 488 F. Supp. 2d at 892 (N.D. Cal.) (Overseas Private Investment Corporation and Export-Import Bank of the United States allegedly failed to comply with NEPA); *Petition to the Inter-American Commission on Human Rights* (claim by Native American citizens in Alaska that CO_2 emissions constituted a violation of fundamental human rights); *Kivalina v. ExxonMobil Corp.*, 663 F. Supp. 2d 863 (N.D. Cal. 2009) (suit against 14 electric utilities, 5 large oil companies, and Peabody Coal Company, alleging that defendants' emissions of GHGs collectively and individually constitute both a public and private nuisance and have contributed to climate change; subsequently dismissed by Ninth Circuit); *Brazos Electric Power Cooperative, Inc. v. U.S.*, 1997 U.S. Dist. LEXIS 23968 (W.D. Tex. 1997); *Ctr. for Biological Diversity v. Brennan*, 571 F. Supp. 2d 1105 (N.D. Cal. 2007) (suit to compel federal scientific bodies to prepare periodic scientific assessments of the effects of global climate change and to make research recommendations); *Montana Environmental Information Center v. Johanns*, Docket No. 07-01311 (D.D.C.) (NEPA challenge to the federal financing of coal-fired power plants); *Ctr. for Biological Diversity v. Kempthorne*, 607 F. Supp. 2d 1078 (D. Ariz. 2009) (failing to protect endangered species from effects of global warming); *Sunflower Electric Power Corp. v. Kansas Department of Health and Environment*, Docket No. 07-99567-A (Ks.) (final agency action of the Kansas Department of Health and Environment that prohibited power plant construction plans).

California's low carbon fuel program was enjoined as facially discriminatory under the dormant commerce clause against out-of-state fuel substitutes because it assigned a higher carbon index score to Midwest biofuels than it did to California-produced fuels due to the distances involved in delivery and use of coal in Midwest electricity production. *Rocky Mt. Farmers Union v. Goldstene*, 2011 U.S. Dist. LEXIS 149592 (E.D. Cal. Dec. 29, 2011).

While these weights were factually and environmentally accurate, no facially discriminatory regulation based on geography of the commerce can survive unless it embodies the least restrictive means of achieving a legitimate environmental objective. *Id.*

The Supreme Court unanimously held that the Clean Air Act, when coupled with the EPA's discretionary authority that the Court recognized in *Massachusetts v. EPA*, as well as the actions the EPA took to regulate GHGs, displaces federal common law causes of action addressing climate change. *Am. Elec. Power Co. v. Connecticut*, 131 S. Ct. 2527 (2011). The Court explained that its ruling does not affect *state* common law causes of action, which would be subject to a more exacting demonstration of congressional intent. Justice Ginsburg noted: "The Court, we caution, endorses no particular view of the complicated issues related to carbon dioxide emissions and climate change." The Court left open the question of whether common law suits seeking monetary damages (as opposed to claims seeking to enjoin emissions) remain viable. Such a nuisance case, *Native Village of Kivalina v. ExxonMobil Corp.*, seeking the costs associated with moving an Alaskan village to a new inland location due to climate change, was dismissed for lack of standing by the Ninth Circuit.

The D.C. Circuit dismissed the suit alleging that federal agencies had violated their fiduciary duties to preserve the public trust interest in the atmosphere. *Alec L. v. Jackson*, _____ F. Supp.2d _____, 2012 WL 1951969 (D.D.C. May 31, 2012). The Circuit relied on two recent Supreme Court opinions: *PPL Montana v. Montana* ("the public trust doctrine remains a matter of state law" and its "contours . . . do not depend upon the Constitution"), to find that the plaintiffs had not raised a federal question, and *American Elec. Power Co. v. Connecticut*, 131 S. Ct. 2527 (2011) ("the Clean Air Act and the EPA actions it authorizes displace any federal common law right to seek abatement of carbon-dioxide emissions from fossil-fuel fired power plants"), to find that common law was preempted by the Clean Air Act and nonjusticiable under the political question doctrine.

In late 2009, the EPA promulgated regulations under the Clean Air Act, following the Supreme Court decision in *Massachusetts v. EPA*, to require all emitters of more than 25,000 tpy of greenhouse gases to report those carbon emissions. The EPA did not include regulation of some greenhouse gases, such as water vapor, chlorofluorocarbons (CFCs), hydochlorofluorocarbons (HCFCs), halons, black carbon, and fluorinated ethers. If there was a new or major modified facility, it would trigger limitations on these emissions under PSD; the EPA also proposed to require amendments to existing Title V Clean Air Act operating permits to impose limits on carbon emissions. However, the Clean Air Act sets regulatory standards under PSD, NSR, and NSPS at any potential emission of more than 100 tpy or 250 tpy. The EPA by regulation unilaterally increased this threshold by 100,000 percent under its professed rationale of "administrative necessity" to avoid political backlash if small businesses or residents were regulated. The court upheld this EPA change by dismissing the claim for lack of standing, concluding that petitioners had failed to identify any "injury in fact" that they had suffered as a result of this relief of smaller emitters from coverage, or an redressable injury. *Coalition for Responsible Regulation, Inc. v. EPA*, 684 F.3d 102 (D.C. Cir. 2012) (states and regulated industries lack standing to challenge rules delaying and phasing in programs regulating greenhouse gas emissions).

Water Pollution

"Water water everywhere, not a drop to drink."

> Samuel Coleridge, Rhyme of the Ancient Mariner

"We are tied to the ocean. And then we go back to the sea. . . . [W]e are going back to whence we came."

> John F. Kennedy, 1962

"Having left the water planet, with all that water brings to the Earth in terms of color and abundant life, the absence of water and atmosphere on the desolate surface of the Moon gives rise to a stark contrast."

> Buzz Aldrin, Astronaut

"The use of the sea . . . is common to all. Neither can any title to the ocean belong to any people or private man for as much as neither nature nor regard of public use permits any possession thereof."

> Elizabeth I, Queen of England
> On the eve of the intended Spanish Armada invasion of England

THE IMPORTANCE OF WATER

It's everywhere — covering seven-eighths of the planet. Water — and its pollutants. Water is necessary for life itself. Without fresh water, an otherwise healthy person will be dead within a week. One can survive months without food.

Today, many people take for granted the availability of clean water. Yet an adequate supply of clean water cannot be guaranteed forever. The problem we face is not primarily the lack of an adequate *supply*, but rather the abuse of a limited resource and degradation of overall water quality. To understand the regulation of water pollution in the United States today, it is important to have a basic understanding of the properties and uses of water and of water pollution problems. The Clean Water Act, which is a colloquial designation for a series of federal acts and their amendments, tries to deal with these problems.

Water is in constant motion above, below, and on the earth's surface. The term used to describe the way in which water is circulated and transformed in nature is the *hydrologic cycle*. The principal actions in the hydrologic cycle are evaporation, precipitation, infiltration, storage, and runoff. To begin, water evaporates from the ocean, surface water bodies, and moist land surfaces and becomes part of the atmosphere. The moisture forms clouds, which return the water to the surface in the form of precipitation (rain, snow, sleet, hail, fog, and dew).

The precipitated water returns to the ocean, lakes, and rivers. A watershed is an area that is drained by a single water course. The area becomes a drainage basin leading to a stream or a river. Water also may be intercepted by plants, run over the ground surface to surface water bodies, or infiltrate into the ground. The water intercepted by plants is returned to the air by a process called transpiration. Surface runoff sooner or later returns to the air through evaporation. Infiltrated water may percolate to deep into the earth to be stored as groundwater, which will eventually discharge as surface water and evaporate into the atmosphere, completing the hydrologic cycle.

Groundwater and surface water are part of the hydrologic cycle. Groundwater is water beneath the earth's surface, and can exist in soil or in bedrock. Groundwater, like surface water, flows, though more slowly than surface water. The rate of flow depends on the characteristics of the geologic formation containing the water. These underground water-bearing formations are called aquifers.

The amount of water in the hydrologic cycle basically remains constant, although in the past century we have seen a tremendous increase in water usage in the United States and elsewhere. The factors responsible for increased usage include population growth, more indoor plumbing in homes, increased industrial demand, and greater agricultural use. Groundwater is the primary source of drinking water for about half the population of the United States. Groundwater is utilized in many areas because an adequate surface water supply does not exist or is too contaminated. Groundwater may also serve as a backup to surface water supplies in times of drought.

Water use in the United States has decreased in the past 15 years, apparently due to conservation efforts, rising water prices, and the introduction of water-saving technologies. Some of the most common industrial water pollution problems include oxygen depletion, increased suspended material, oil and grease, and release of toxic chemicals, including heavy metals. Some industrial processes may also cause significant thermal pollution or significantly change the pH (acidity or alkalinity) of the receiving water.

After agriculture, the United States uses more water for electricity production than for any other purpose. Two primary processes use water to produce power: In the first, *thermoelectric* power is generated primarily by converting water into steam by heating it with fossil or nuclear fuels. Water also is used for cooling purposes. Thermoelectric power provides nearly 90 percent of U.S. electric power. Second, *hydroelectric* power is generated by allowing water from dammed reservoirs to flow by gravity to drive turbines. In the United States, hydroelectric power generation on a major scale began with the creation of the Tennessee Valley Authority (TVA) in 1933. The environmental and regulatory aspects of energy production are addressed in more detail in Chapter 12. But note at this time that electricity production uses more water and consumes more clean air than any other single industry.

WATER QUALITY AND POLLUTION

Primary Sources of Water Pollution

The United States has more than 3.5 million miles of rivers and streams, and 40.8 million acres of lakes, ponds, and reservoirs. There are 58,421 miles of ocean shoreline. There are 34,388 square miles of estuaries, and 5,559 miles of shoreline along the Great Lakes. What relatively little monitoring there is for toxic pollution in these water bodies is of primarily biological, rather than chemical, pollutants. Water pollution remediation has had mixed results. Only 64 percent of surveyed rivers and stream miles supported the uses for which they had been designated (such as water supply, fishing, agriculture). Twenty-two percent partially supported their intended uses, while 5 percent failed to support their uses, and 9 percent were unknown in 1987. The similar assessments for lakes showed quality deterioration from 1984 to 1997.

To understand the regulatory framework governing water pollution, it is important first to understand the various sources of pollution. Sources of water pollution can be divided into two categories: (1) point sources and (2) nonpoint sources. This may seem straightforward, but it is more complex than it appears.

Point Sources

The federal Clean Water Act (§402) defines a "point source" to mean:

> any discernible, confined and discrete conveyance, including but not limited to any pipe, ditch, channel, tunnel, conduit, well, discrete fissure, container, rolling stock, concentrated animal feeding operation, or vessel or other floating craft, from which pollutants are or may be discharged.

It is litigation that has defined "point source." In *U.S. v. Plaza Health Laboratories*, 3 F.3d 643 (2d Cir. 1993), the Second Circuit found that the Act's criminal sanctions were not intended to punish human polluters; even a co-owner of a blood-testing laboratory convicted of dumping vials of hepatitis-B-infected blood into the Hudson River was not liable because there was no point source. However, human intervention does not rule out a finding of a point source. See *Sierra Club v. Abston's Constr. Co.*, 620 F.2d 41 (5th Cir. 1980) (finding point source where contaminated runoff spills out from holding area and funneled by mine operator to waterway). In the Clean Water Act itself, Congress has not been specific in its definition. Lower courts have deferred to the EPA's interpretation, applying total maximum daily loadings (TMDLs) to nonpoint sources as well as point sources. *Pronsolino v. Nastri*, 291 F.3d 1123 (9th Cir. 2002). The EPA has issued interpretive regulations to exempt certain categories of point sources from the permit requirements of §402. These exempted sources included all silva-cultural (forestry-related) point sources and all irrigation return flows from less than 3,000 acres.

The D.C. Circuit Court of Appeals held, in *NRDC v. Costle*, 568 F.2d 1369 (D.C. Cir. 1977), that the regulations exempting these discrete conveyances from the definition of point sources were invalid, but also that the EPA could build some flexibility into its program by issuing area-wide permits for specific classes of point source discharges. Therefore, while they must be regulated, they could be grouped into area blanket permits. In 1977, Congress categorically exempted from point source regulation return flows from irrigated agriculture.

Before discussing the regulatory significance of a point source, let's establish what, from a factual perspective, are the three major types of point sources: publicly owned treatment works, combined sewer systems, and industrial facilities.

Publicly Owned Treatment Works Publicly owned treatment works, commonly known as POTWs, are treatment plants for municipal sewage. Sewage is the used water supply of a community — including waterborne waste from residences, businesses, and industry. In some cases it may also contain stormwater runoff and surface water or groundwater. Domestic sewage from residential areas typically contains human and animal biological wastes and household wastes associated with bathing, clothes washing, and cooking.

"Sanitary sewage" is defined as domestic sewage plus industrial waste. The latter is associated with manufacturing processes. Some industries will discharge their process wastewater to the POTW to avoid the more stringent regulatory limits of discharging directly to a surface water body such as a river, lake, or harbor. We will address this aspect in greater detail later. Finally, "combined sewage" is a mixture of sanitary sewage and stormwater.

How does a POTW process operate? Sewage is treated at three different levels. The most basic level is *primary* treatment, which consists only of physical processes of treating the sewage. The function of primary treatment is to remove large suspended or floating organic solids (typically human waste), heavy inorganic solids called grit (plastics and so on), and excessive amounts of oil or grease. Primary treatment of municipal waste alone is of limited effectiveness.

Today most conventional sewage treatment systems also employ some type of secondary treatment. Unlike primary treatment, which is a *physical* process, secondary treatment is entirely *biological*. Through a process of microbial oxidation of organic matter as the water passes through a gravel bed, the treatment purifies the water, much like the self-purification action of a stream.

The most advanced, or tertiary, level of wastewater treatment is *chemical*. It allows treated municipal wastewater to be reused as part of the community's water supply. There are very few complete advanced treatment systems in the United States. The cost of this level of treatment is significant. However, as the demand for fresh water grows and the supply diminishes, we may see more communities that require advanced wastewater treatment technologies.

Combined Sewer Systems   In the mid-nineteenth century, cities in the Northeast and Midwest devised systems to get rid of animal waste associated with transportation. They combined the street storm sewers with the residential sewers, thereby eliminating the need for two separate systems. Many of these combined sewer systems (CSSs) are still in use today. The major problem with them is that "when it rains, it pours": They overflow with more wastewater than can be handled by the piping or treatment system. This overflow results in large quantities of untreated sewage being discharged into receiving surface waters. EPA reported that there were 828 federal NPDES permits authorizing discharges from 9,348 CSS outfalls in 32 states, discharging 850 billion gallons per year. Storm water can be considered a point source because it is often collected by storm drains, gutters, or ditches to go to treatment plants or to water bodies directly.

Industrial Facilities   Industrial facilities receive the most regulatory attention of all point sources. These facilities contribute to pollution of the water through direct discharges to surface water and through discharges to sewers that flow to municipal treatment facilities. Industrial facilities that discharge directly into surface waters are governed by the National Pollution Discharge Elimination System (covered later in this chapter). Industrial facilities that discharge into municipal sewer systems are subject to pretreatment requirements under the Clean Water Act, to prevent harm to the treatment facility and the ultimate receiving waters. Confined animal feedlots are defined as point sources even if they don't dispense manure via a human-made channel or conduit.

Nonpoint Sources

We will supply a universal definition of "nonpoint source": It includes everything that is not a "point source" or not associated with a discrete point of discharge.

Nonpoint sources are attributable to a variety of activities, principally farming, construction, and mining, as well as to urban runoff and spills of oil or hazardous materials. Rain and snow become contaminated with pollutants from various nonpoint sources and transport the contaminants to a point of discharge. As a generalization, nonpoint source pollution emanates from land use. Therefore, to control nonpoint pollution, land use activities must be controlled. The federal government historically has left this area of regulation to the states. We will cover it more in Chapter 10.

Nonpoint sources are blamed for 65-75 percent of the pollution in the nation's most polluted waters. In two-thirds of the states, nonpoint source pollution is the most significant form of pollution affecting streams, rivers, and lakes. Agriculture constitutes the largest source of nonpoint water pollution. We will return to it in greater detail after setting out briefly the science of water pollution.

Types and Measurements of Water Pollution

We have identified the basic sources of water pollution. The next step is to develop a basic understanding of the types of water pollution associated with these sources. Let's first introduce the common terminology of water pollution. In a nutshell, water quality is affected by (1) the amount of dissolved oxygen present, (2) the pH, (3) the water temperature, (4) the amount of light infiltration, (5) the rate and amount of water flow, (6) the amount of silt, (7) the nutrient load, (8) biological bacteria or parasites, and (9) the presence of oil or chemical contaminants. Definitions of these elements follow on the next page. Note the basic distinction between *biological* and *chemical* water pollution hazards.

Biological Hazards

When we release human and animal waste into water, we also release disease-causing organisms into the water. These pathogenic microorganisms may include bacteria, viruses, and parasites. Water quality is routinely tested for the presence of some of these organisms. If they are detected, the water is assumed to be contaminated with human or animal waste and, as such, is not suitable for human or animal consumption. We will revisit these pathogens later in this chapter when we discuss the Safe Drinking Water Act.

Biological hazards are illustrated by a 1993 water crisis in Milwaukee, when nearly 400,000 people were stricken with a waterborne disease caused by an intestinal protozoan parasite called *Cryptosporidium*. The organism is widespread in animal species and especially prevalent in cattle. *Cryptosporidium* cysts are able to survive for up to a year in low-turbidity water. They are susceptible to destruction by boiling but are resistant to chlorine treatment of the water. The effects of infection in most people are gastrointestinal and temporary in nature; however, the infection can be extremely debilitating and life-threatening in patients who are immuno-compromised.

Chemical Hazards

Large quantities of toxic compounds are added to water bodies through industrial activity, nonpoint source runoff, and atmospheric deposition. Chemical groups of particular importance include metals, pesticides, and polychlorinated biphenyls (PCBs). These chemicals can have direct effects on aquatic life, as well as indirect effects due to chemical changes in the water column.

In March 2008 the Associated Press revealed that in 24 of our nation's largest metropolitan areas, people were unknowingly drinking prescription drugs with their glass of tap water. There was cross-contamination from sewer and septic systems into drinking water supplies. Some of the pharmaceuticals were medicines for pain, infection, high cholesterol, asthma, epilepsy, mental illness, and heart problems, and included mood stabilizers, sex hormones, and antibiotics. The disposal of some pharmaceutical waste at health facilities is governed under RCRA (see Chapter 8) because the drugs are deemed hazardous waste, but most is not.

The EPA estimates that nearly 10 percent of the sediments underlying the nation's surface waters are sufficiently contaminated so as to pose potential risks to fish and to people and wildlife that ingest them. The persistent bio-accumulation of toxic chemicals, including DDT, dioxins, PCBs, and mercury, is the most predominant sediment contamination problem. These chemicals can last for years in sediment.

Before reading case law, it is important to be familiar with the definitions of key terms in the water pollution literature, which follow in the box below. BOD, total suspended solids (TSS), coliform, pH, and oil and grease are defined as *conventional pollutants*.

Algae: Microscopic photosynthetic plants of the simplest form, having no roots, stems, or leaves.

Bacteria/Coliforms: Bacteria are simple, one-celled plants that use soluble food and are capable of reproduction without sunlight. Many bacteria are harmless, but the presence of certain pathogenic bacteria in water can foster disease. Coliforms are bacteria found in the intestinal tract of humans and warm-blooded animals.

Biochemical oxygen demand (BOD): A measure of the waste material in a receiving body of water that will make a biological demand on the oxygen present. BOD is the most commonly used parameter to define the basic strength of a municipal wastewater or organic industrial waste treatment system.

Chemical oxygen demand (COD): A measure of the proportion of waste material that is susceptible to oxidation by a strong chemical oxidant.

Dissolved oxygen (DO): The amount of oxygen present in a surface water body. A certain concentration of oxygen is required to sustain fish, animal, and aquatic life. Insufficient levels of dissolved oxygen in the water column cause anaerobic (absence of air) conditions, formation of noxious gases, such as hydrogen sulfate, and production of malodorous conditions.

Fungi: Microscopic nonphotosynthetic plants, including molds and yeast.

Hardness: Generally, the sum of calcium and magnesium expressed as an equivalent amount of calcium carbonate minerals ($CaCO_3$). Hardness concentrations generally do not have public health impacts but can have economic impacts. It is difficult to create soapy lather in hard water. If water is very "hard" (>300 mb/L $CaCO_3$) it may be considered a nuisance condition and softening may be required.

Nutrients: Compounds including nitrogen, phosphorus, and carbon. They are classified as either macro nutrients (needed in large quantities) or micro nutrients (needed in small quantities). The amount of nutrients present in the water can have dramatic effects on biological processes in the water. In particular, nutrients directly encourage growth of algae, bacteria, fungi, and aquatic plants. Excessive presence of nutrients can also accelerate eutrophication, the natural aging process of lakes and reservoirs.

Parasitic protozoa: Any of a variety of microorganisms capable of surviving in water contaminated with human or animal waste. The ones most commonly associated with waterborne disease outbreaks in the United States are *Giardia lamblia* and *Cryptosporidium*.

pH: A value representing the negative log to the base ten of the hydrogen ion concentration. More generally, the pH value indicates how acidic or alkaline a solution is. The pH of the water is an important factor in the biological and chemical systems of natural waters. Water with a pH of 7.0 is neutral water. Acidic water has a pH less than 7.0. Some examples of acidic liquids are orange juice (pH = 4.2) and lemon juice (pH = 0.2). Alkaline or basic water has a pH greater than 7.0. Some examples of basic or alkaline liquids are bleach (pH = 12.7) and ammonia (pH = 11.3), and baking soda (pH = 8.3).

Total dissolved solids (TDS): Inorganic salts, small amounts of organic matter, and dissolved material. Excess amounts of dissolved solids may be objectionable in drinking water because of mineral taste and possible physiological effects. Sodium is frequently a principal component of dissolved solids.

Turbidity: A measure of the ability of suspended and colloidal materials to diminish the penetration of light through the water. Suspended matter in the water column may adversely affect chlorine disinfection. Turbid water interferes with recreational use and aesthetic enjoyment of water. Turbidity also may affect aquatic organisms.

Viruses: Biological agents, some of which, such as poliovirus and hepatitis A virus, are capable of causing waterborne disease.

Examples

1. The town of Eastwell passes an ordinance prohibiting cattle from grazing along the banks of the East River, which is the town's sole water supply. The groundwater aquifer is not suitable for drinking water purposes. The purpose of the ordinance is to protect the river from pollution. The local farmers are furious and allege that the town is trying to force them out because it wants to market the waterfront property. The farmers are threatening to sue. You are the town counsel. How does cattle grazing contribute to water pollution? Can you justify and defend the ordinance?

2. After one heated meeting with the farmers, the town Board of Health reports to the town a huge outbreak of gastroenteritis among Eastwell's residents. The culprit is believed to be *Cryptosporidium*. Do these events change your strategy? See Chapter 10 for more discussion of a health board's authority.

Explanations

1. The town is genuinely concerned about the quality of the water supply on several counts. First, livestock grazing is a problem because it increases erosion in the area, resulting in increased turbidity of the water. Turbidity affects chlorine disinfection. Second, the coliform counts in the surface water in that area will be high due to animal waste. Coliform affects potability. The grazing causes nonpoint pollution rather than point source pollution.

2. The presence of the parasite *Cryptosporidium* in the water supply requires more immediate action. The conditions associated with the livestock areas are extremely problematic for two reasons: (1) The cattle may be the source of the parasite. (2) The increased turbidity of the water makes identification of the organism more difficult. The cattle should be relocated immediately until remedial steps can be taken to control runoff from the grazing areas. The city, through its Board of Health authority or its general police powers, can take any reasonable emergency measures to protect the public drinking water.

EARLY WATER QUALITY AND EFFLUENT REGULATION

Though the technical aspects of water pollution are complex, its fundamentals are simple: Water moves, and waste materials deposited in water move as well. Water pollution results. But engineering assumptions and regulatory responses have not always proved successful.

In the nineteenth century, people widely believed that flowing water purified itself and that dilution would eliminate any hazard. In the 1850s in England, authorities decided to construct a system of underground brick sewers to transport both household waste and stormwater. The perceived benefits of this type of system were considered generally to outweigh its costs. As a result, a number of major U.S. cities built similar sewer systems in the late nineteenth and early twentieth centuries.

The anticipated public health benefit of the introduction of sewer systems was not realized. In cities that obtained their water supply downstream from the cities with sewer systems, the incidence of waterborne disease such as typhoid actually rose. Typhoid fever is caused by the enteric pathogen *Salmonella typhi*, which enters the water supply by the discharge of sewage. Sewage discharged upstream limited industrial and recreational uses of water downstream. The discharge of raw sewage by one community into another community's drinking water supply resulted in early common law nuisance actions.

The River and Harbors Act of 1899

The River and Harbors Act of 1899, also known as the Refuse Act, was enacted by the U.S. government to protect against potential interference with navigation in U.S. waters. This is the oldest environmental statute affecting any environmental medium. Section 13 of the Refuse Act specifically prohibits the discharge of *any* type of refuse, other than liquid discharge from streets and sewers, into navigable waterways without a permit from the Secretary of the Army. We will discuss the revival of this statute in the 1960s, when discussing the rationale for adopting the Federal Water Pollution Control Act in 1972.

Twentieth-Century Pre-1972 Water Pollution Control

As a result of frequent outbreaks of waterborne disease, the initial efforts to control water pollution focused on human waste, which was believed in the first half of the twentieth century to be the primary cause of such disease. Once the major cities began chlorinating their drinking water supplies in the 1930s, the incidence of these disease outbreaks decreased dramatically.

Prior to the end of World War II, any efforts to control water pollution were largely a state and local responsibility. The states developed water quality standards that focused on the water quality of the receiving water, not only on the effluent discharge to the water. Thus two ways to regulate water developed: from the perspective of the *individual* discharge and from the perspective of the destination or *receiving* water body. Depending on the designated use of the water, different water quality standards were established for temperature, pH, suspended solids, and dissolved oxygen.

The Water Pollution Control Act of 1948 was the first, if minor, involvement of the federal government in the regulation of water pollution in the twentieth century. During the latter half of the 1950s and throughout the 1960s, several more federal statutes addressing water pollution were enacted. The primary focus of these statutes was to direct federal assistance to municipal discharges and, to some extent, implement federal enforcement. By 1972 almost all the states had developed federally approved water-quality standards. These statutes focused on water-quality *standards* of the *receiving* waters. Ultimately, however, water-quality standards without any teeth were extremely difficult to enforce and had significant limitations:

- The enforcing authority relied on the dischargers to supply the data demonstrating their noncompliance.
- The enforcement agency had the burden of proof to demonstrate that a specific discharger was violating a standard or presenting a risk to public health.

- It was extremely difficult for the agencies to secure a meaningful judgment because the courts were required to consider the cost of cleanup in assessing the problem; the federal statute lacked civil or criminal penalties for violations.

The key to any statute limiting pollution is its enforcement. Prior to 1972, enforcement of water pollution violations was difficult because enforcement depended on a discharger's ability to reduce the *ambient* water quality of the *receiving* waters below a specific level. Think about this. Given multiple discharges to many water bodies, the agency's burden in proving which discharger was the sole cause of pollution was nearly impossible. The proof problems encountered were similar to those experienced in nuisance cases. Obviously, no discharger advised by counsel would admit that it was the sole cause of pollution.

The Supreme Court resurrected a statute that focused on individual discharges. In the Court's decisions in *United States v. Republic Steel Corp.*, 362 U.S. 482 (1960), and *United States v. Standard Oil Co.*, 384 U.S. 224 (1966), the River and Harbors Act of 1899 was deployed to prohibit harmful discharges into the navigable waters of the United States. Then the key question became, "What is 'navigable'?" The Court had an answer in a later case: almost all surface waters, regardless of whether they are *physically* navigable. *United States v. Riverside Bayview Homes*, 474 U.S. 121 (1985). "Navigability" thus is expanded to cover any tributary connected with a physically "navigable" waterway. Your backyard creek could qualify.

In October 1972 Congress overrode a presidential veto to enact the Federal Water Pollution Control Act of 1972.

Examples

1. You were recently appointed to a special advisory committee to the President. The Clean Water Act (circa 1966) is subject to reauthorization. The committee has been meeting for several months prior to your appointment. Most of the other members believe that the current legislation is largely ineffective at pollution prevention and cleanup. The committee's draft proposal recommends stricter water-quality standards. No other recommendations are made. Critique this position.

2. An alternative proposal, favored by a minority of the committee members, embraces a strategy modeled on the Clean Air Act's approach (see Chapter 5) of buying and selling pollution credits. How well do you think this strategy would work for water pollution and its various sources?

Explanations

1. It is very difficult to enforce water-quality standards against individual dischargers in the absence of *individual* discharge limits. Placing the burden of proof on the enforcing agency and lacking a definition of what conduct constitutes a violation, as well as lacking civil or criminal penalties, render meaningful enforcement akin to pushing a rock up a wet, slippery slope. What is required is individual limits on individual dischargers, *coupled with* the proposed water-quality standards for receiving water bodies.

2. An alternative based on the Clean Air Act strategy would create an economic incentive for preventing water pollution and could be viable. However, it might be too narrowly focused on point sources. Remember that nonpoint sources are a major source, and would not be addressed under the 1960s-era water statutes. To be able to trade emission credits, based on a maximum ceiling on receiving-water-quality degradation, there must also be *individual* limits on dischargers. This meets the shortcoming discussed in the prior explanation.

FEDERAL WATER POLLUTION CONTROL ACT

The Structure

Water pollution control entered the modern era in 1972 with the FWPCA. Since then the Act, like other key environmental statutes, has been transformed in subsequent iterations. The Federal Water Pollution Control Act Amendments of 1972 (FWPCA) was different from the previous federal water pollution laws: It set out the objectives of *restoring* the integrity of the nation's waters to fishable and swimmable quality by 1983, and total elimination of pollutant discharges into U.S. navigable waters by 1985. Further, the statute emphasized *individual* effluent discharge standards.

Section 101(b) identified the states as primarily responsible for meeting these goals. However, the federal government was not constrained, as it had been under previous federal water pollution statutes, from taking enforcement actions. Nonetheless, the nation did not achieve these deadline objectives.

In 1977 Congress adopted major amendments to the Clean Water Act. The amendments extended the deadlines for compliance with the technology-based effluent limits (see Exhibit 6.1 later in the chapter) and adjusted the specific requirements for certain dischargers. Congressional amendments continued. The Water Quality Act of 1987 made a number of significant changes but basically left the underlying structure of the Act untouched. The states are recognized as the primary enforcers of the federal regulations. The Act's 1987 amendments authorized the EPA to treat certain tribes as states for various purposes. 33 U.S.C. §1377(e). For a tribe to qualify as a state (TAS), it must have a functioning governing body, the water resource must be within reservation lands, and the tribe must be capable of carrying out the regulatory functions required. *Montana v. EPA*, 137 F.3d 1135 (9th Cir. 1998), *cert. denied*, 525 U.S. 921 (1998).

Permits for Point Source Discharges to U.S. Waters

Any discharge of a pollutant from a point source, or "vessel or other floating craft," requires a permit, whether or not it results in pollution of the receiving waters or has any other adverse environmental impact. Any point source discharge without a permit is illegal. The Supreme Court held that a discharge is not limited to situations in which a substance or contaminant is added to the water discharge. *Public Utility District No. 1 of Jefferson County v. Washington*, 511 U.S. 700 (1994). The FWPCA incorporates the River and Harbor Act's prohibition of discharge of any pollutant into a U.S. navigable water, unless such a discharge is permitted under the Act. "Navigable waters" are defined as those over which the federal government has constitutional authority. They need not be physically navigable in fact.

U.S. Army Corps of Engineers regulations define "waters of the United States," for purposes of the Clean Water Act, to include all waters "the use, degradation or destruction of which could affect interstate or foreign commerce." This definition does not require that the regulated activity have a substantial effect on interstate commerce, or even any nexus with navigable or interstate waters. "Waters of the United States" is broadly defined by federal regulation to include "all waters that could be used in interstate commerce and all intrastate lakes, rivers, streams, wetlands, sloughs, wet meadows, natural ponds, etc." 40 C.F.R. §122.2. Even small brooks, "intrastate lakes," and "prairie potholes" that are not physically navigable, unless municipally owned or privately owned, can qualify as "waters of the United States" by being tributaries of waters that are themselves navigable. *United States v. T.G.R. Corp.*, 171 F.3d 762, 1999 (2d Cir. 1999). Isolated wetlands are not within federal jurisdiction. *Solid Waste Agency of Northern Cook County v. Corps of Engineers*, 531 U.S. 159 (2001). See Chapter 11 for a detailed discussion of adjacent wetlands and the Supreme Court opinion in *Rapanos v. United States*, 547 U.S. 715 (2006), in which the Supreme Court closely divided 5-4 on what are federal waters of the United States subject to Clean Water Act jurisdiction.

Critics have argued that the purpose of the Clean Water Act was to protect all U.S. waters, instead of just federally jurisdictional "navigable" waters. In *United States v. Riverside Bayview Homes, Inc.*, 474 U.S. 121, 133 (1985), the Court stated that "navigable waters [are] the waters of the United States." In *Riverside Bayview*, the wetland actually abutted a navigable waterway, and the Court deferred to the agency interpretation. In the *Solid Waste Agency* (*SWANCC*) decision, it was determined that isolated wetlands were not navigable just because migratory birds might use them. *SWANCC* held that isolated intrastate waters and wetlands not connected by surface water to navigable waters lacked a "significant nexus" and were not waters of the United States.

In the *Rapanos* decision in 2006, a concurring opinion by Justice Kennedy held that it was important to give "navigable" waters meaning by finding a significant nexus between a contaminated water source and navigable U.S. waters. He wanted to remand for a determination of "significant nexus" by the trial court, which had not occurred under the standard applied. Justice Kennedy did not agree that navigable waters had to exhibit a permanence or surface water connection to standing water.

SWANCC and *Riverside Bayview* both held that each of the words "navigable waters" must be given meaning in defining the extent of federal jurisdiction; the use of the plural "waters" referred to "geographic . . . permanent, standing or flowing. . . . open water" features, which were less broadly defined than the intermittent or ephemeral channels, "storm sewers and culverts," definition that the Army Corps had used. *Rapanos* (plurality opinion). The Corps was found by the plurality of Justices to have stretched the Commerce power beyond limits and not employed a permissible construction of the statute. *Id* (citing *Chevron*). A more narrow federal definition was intended by Congress to leave in place "States' traditional and primary power over land and water use." *Id.* (quoting *SWANCC*).

At the same time, the Act requires compliance with water-quality standards, even by dischargers whose discharge is permitted under the Act. Water-quality standards, discussed in detail later, set pollution limits for navigable water bodies that receive pollutant discharges. Thus the initial discharge of pollution and the resultant public water body quality are both regulated.

What sources are regulated? As you will recall from the previous discussion, the regulated sources of water pollution are divided into *point* and *nonpoint* sources. The FWPCA of 1972 focuses primarily on point sources. The point sources are subdivided into (1) municipal sewage treatment plants (POTWs) and (2) industrial discharge sources. Effluent limits for all *industrial point sources* and POTWs are set pursuant to §301. Both of these point sources are required to apply for and obtain discharge permits. Under §208, the control of nonpoint sources is left primarily to the states, since nonpoint sources of pollution were considered to be primarily related to land use. Aquatic animal production facilities are deemed a point source by EPA.

What type of point source pollutants are regulated? There are three types of regulated point source pollutants: (1) toxic pollutants (§307),

(2) conventional pollutants including BOD, TSS, coliform, pH, and oil and grease (§304), and (3) nontoxic nonconventional pollutants. The administrator of the Environmental Protection Agency (the EPA) can add or remove substances from the list of 126 toxic priority chemical pollutants regulated by §307.

Title IV is the center of gravity of the Act, because it establishes the discharge permit program, the National Pollutant Discharge Elimination System (NPDES). This title permits and regulates the quantity and quality of a discharge. Section 401 requires certification by the potential discharger that it will comply with all the provisions of Title III. Under §301, the discharge of any pollutant is prohibited except for discharges made in accordance with the permit requirements of §402 (NPDES permits) and other sections of the Act. This results in the issuance of an NPDES permit allowing the discharge of certain pollutants from a point source. Compliance with the NPDES permit is deemed compliance with the Act (the so-called "permit shield" from prosecution).

There must be some addition of a substance to a navigable waterway to subject an industry or applicant to EPA regulation under the NPDES system. The EPA is not allowed to regulate substances which are not commonly understood to be pollutants: Under the NPDES system, the EPA may not regulate hydroelectric or dam facilities that do not add pollutants to a waterway. *National Wildlife Federation v. Gorsuch*, 693 F.2d 156 (D.C. Cir. 1982); *National Wildlife Federation v. Consumers Power Co.*, 862 F.2d 580 (6th Cir. 1988).

The NPDES program may be administered by the EPA or by states that have been delegated authority by the EPA to administer the program. There are still five states not delegated under the Clean Water Act to assume the federal authority to issue NPDES permits (Alaska, Idaho, Massachusetts, New Hampshire, and New Mexico). Section 402 authorizes the EPA administrator to issue permits for individual point sources and to review and approve the plan of any state desiring to administer its own permit program. The EPA lacks authority to issue state clean water permitting requirements beyond those that are enumerated in the statute. In *American Forest & Paper Ass'n v. EPA*, 137 F.3d 291 (5th Cir. 1998), the EPA was prohibited from requiring certain protections of endangered species as a condition of Louisiana's Clean Water Act permitting guidelines under §402 of the Act.

The First Circuit held that an EIS for a ski resort must consider the transportation and discharge of pollutants associated with snowmaking. In *Dubois v. U.S. Department of Agriculture*, 102 F.3d 1273 (1st Cir. 1996), *cert. denied, Loon Mountain Recreation Corp. v. Dubois*, 521 U.S. 1119 (1997), the court considered a proposal where a ski resort would extract water from a river for snowmaking, and when the snow melted it would be deposited in a pond. Although the water was hydrologically connected from the pond to the river, this was not its natural water course. Because the river contained different pollutants than the pond, this was a proper reason to reject an

EIS, or to condition an NPDES permit. The court noted that the deposition in the pond resulted indirectly through the conduit of the snowmaking pipes, therefore constituting a point source discharge subject to an NPDES permit.

It is of note that the Clean Water Act does not have jurisdiction over the 54 million acres of Native American lands. Five hundred fifty-seven recognized tribal governments make decisions in these lands held in fee and trust. Water quality is one of the primary environmental concerns of many Native American tribes. Native American tribes under the Clean Water Act can regulate discharges by tribal as well as nontribal members within their reservations. In *Montana v. EPA*, 137 F.3d 1135 (9th Cir. 1998), the court upheld the tribe's inherent power over environmental health and safety that could affect the tribe, even where nontribal members also are regulated. Even if not owned by tribal members, facilities on tribal land within the reservation can be potential pollution sources. These pollution sources can affect all residents. In *Albuquerque, New Mexico v. Browner*, 97 F.3d 414 (10th Cir. 1996), the court affirmed a tribe's authority to issue water-quality standards more stringent than the federal water-quality standards. Tribes may also set standards under the Clean Air Act.

Standard conditions are placed in all NPDES permits. One important condition requires discharge monitoring reports. 40 C.F.R. §122.41(j) and §122.41(l)(4). These reports provide the state and the EPA, as well as the public, with data on pollutant discharge. Citizen suits can be based on the contents of these documents. Provisions in the permit also deal with upsets and bypasses, types of exceedances that may be raised as an affirmative defense to an enforcement action for permit violations. These are discussed later in this chapter.

Effluent limitations in the permit are usually expressed numerically. The permit may also contain compliance schedules and other stipulations relating to enforcement. NPDES permits may be transferred to a new owner. The EPA and the state, however, can revoke the permit or reissue it with modifications if there is an alteration in the permitted activity and for various other reasons. 40 C.F.R. §122.41(b) and 40 C.F.R. §122.62(a).

Toxic Pollutants

Section 307(a) of the 1972 Act required the EPA to establish a list of toxic pollutants and to set within 90 days health-based standards for these chemicals. The Natural Resources Defense Council sued the EPA to require compliance. An agreement was reached and incorporated into a consent decree known as the Flannery Decree, named after the judge who approved it. The Flannery Decree required the EPA to establish technology-based standards for 65 toxic pollutants discharged by 21 primary industries. This list was later expanded to cover 126 toxic pollutants from 34 industries. These 126 pollutants came to be known as the priority pollutants. Discharges of toxic organics and toxic metals to U.S. waterways have declined markedly since the enactment of the Clean Water Act.

Health-Based and Technology-Based Standards

Health-Based Standards

Under the Clean Water Act, the EPA was to set standards to regulate the amount of pollutants in effluent by considering six factors: (1) the toxicity of the pollutant, (2) its persistence, (3) its degradability, (4) the usual or potential presence of affected organisms in waters, (5) the importance of the affected organisms, and (6) the nature and extent of the toxic substance's effect on the organisms. The agency was and is required to set the effluent standards at a level sufficient to ensure environmental protection with "an ample margin of safety." 33 U.S.C. §1317(a)(4). These are health-based standards, not predicated on existing technology.

The EPA does not have to consider costs when setting health-based standards for contaminants in wastewater discharges, as held in *Hercules, Inc. v. EPA*, 598 F.2d 91, 111, n.38 (D.C. Cir. 1978). Still, the task proved to be difficult. For one thing, scientists do not have enough information to evaluate the effect of all known toxins in the environment. For another, the nature and extent of pollutants discharged into waters cannot always be identified. Even when feasible, establishing effluent standards for one pollutant at a time is an extremely difficult and very slow endeavor.

Technology-Based Standards

Subsequently, the Clean Water Act was amended to move the EPA away from health-based standards and toward technology-based standards. Technology-based limitations rely on the ability of end-of-pipe equipment and process technology to reduce the amount of pollutants in industrial effluent. They are based on engineering criteria.

With the enactment of the FWPCA in 1972, Congress adopted a more aggressive approach to water pollution enforcement that includes best practicable control technology currently available (BPT), best available technology economically available (BAT), and best conventional pollutant control technology (BCT).

BPT Best practicable control technology currently available (BPT) is the first stage of effluent limitation. 33 U.S.C. §1311(b)(1). It is a minimum standard for each class of industry emitting pollution. Representing interim criteria, BPT is based on the average of the best existing performances by plants within each industrial category. See *National Ass'n of Metal Finishers v. EPA*, 719 F.2d 624, 657 (3d Cir. 1983).

The EPA determines the currently available BPT by assessing the total cost of applying the technology in relation to the effluent reduction benefits to be achieved. Other factors considered are the age of equipment and facilities involved, the process employed, the engineering aspects of various types of control techniques, process changes, nonwater-quality environmental impact (including energy requirements), and other criteria the EPA administrator deems appropriate.

The EPA has considerable freedom in choosing how to weigh costs and benefits when determining BPT standards, as upheld in *Metal Finishers*. The agency needs only to confirm that the effluent reduction required is not wholly out of proportion to the cost. This limited version of a cost-benefit analysis was sanctioned by legislators partly to avoid imposing a requirement on the EPA to determine the economic impact of controls on any individual plant in a single community. See *E. I. du Pont de Nemours & Co. v. Train*, 430 U.S. 112, 130 (1977) (quoting 118 Cong. Rec. 33696 (1972), Leg. Hist. 1700). If a discharger cannot raise performance up to BPT standards, it must go out of business, as dictated in *EPA v. National Crushed Stone Ass'n*, 449 U.S. 64, 75 (1980). Congress expected that some companies would close and jobs would be lost. BPT applies to all industry sources for all pollutants. It is the least restrictive of these three technology-based standards.

BCT Standards for best conventional pollution control technology (BCT) are determined for *conventional* or traditional pollutants such as suspended solids, biological oxygen demand (BOD), fecal coliform, and pH. See 33 U.S.C. §1314(a)(4)(1996). The assessment of BCT includes a two-step consideration. First, is there a reasonable relationship between the costs of attaining a reduction in effluents and the effluent reduction benefits to be derived? Second, how do the cost and level of reduction of the conventional pollutants at publicly owned treatment works compare with the cost and level of reduction of the same pollutants at industrial sources? See *American Paper Institute v. EPA*, 660 F.2d 954 (4th Cir. 1981). It essentially represents BAT standards tempered by economic reasonableness. BCT is more restrictive than BPT but less restrictive than BAT. It applies to conventional pollutants.

BAT Effluent limitations resulting from the application of the best available technology economically achievable (BAT) for a category or class of point sources is the most stringent phase of pollution control under the Clean Water Act. 33 U.S.C. §1317(a)(2). BAT limits are for dischargers of *toxic* and *nonconventional* pollutants. The EPA bases its BAT standards on the performance of optimally operating plants. See *Kennecott v. EPA*, 780 F.2d 445, 488 (4th Cir. 1986).

In the assessment of BAT, the EPA is mandated to take into account many of the same factors that apply to the determination of BPT — for instance, the age of the equipment — but not a cost-benefit analysis. Instead, the cost of achieving BAT effluent reduction is addressed together with all the other factors. 33 U.S.C. §1314(b)(2)(B). No balancing of costs and benefits is required, as upheld in *Reynolds Metal Co. v. EPA*, 760 F.2d 549 (4th Cir. 1985). In other words, cost considerations do not ratchet down the BAT standard. BAT for toxic pollutants is still health-based.

"Economically achievable" BAT does not refer to individual plant economics but to broad industry categories or classes of point sources. *Du Pont v. Train*, 430 U.S. at 126. There is no getting around the fact, however, that BAT does require that the standards be economically achievable. This means that dischargers need only to commit "the maximum resources economically possible," as articulated in *National Crushed Stone*, 449 U.S. at 74. Operators may qualify for modified BAT standards if they make use of technology within their "economic capability" and will demonstrate "reasonable further progress." 33 U.S.C. §1311(c); see *National Crushed Stone*.

In setting BPT and BAT, the EPA is permitted to draw on and borrow certain treatment technology from other industries, even if no one in the industry being regulated actually uses it. See *California & Hawaiian Sugar Co. v. EPA*, 533 F.2d 280, 285 (2d Cir. 1977). Although such transfer of technology can be treated as "available" and "achievable," the EPA must indicate for the record the reasons that such technology is feasible in a particular industry. See, e.g., *American Meat Institute v. EPA*, 526 F.2d 442, 463 (5th Cir. 1975).

In *Entergy Corp.v. Riverkeeper, Inc.*, 556 U.S. 208 (2009) (if Congress has directly spoken to an issue, then any agency interpretation contradicting Congress would be unreasonable), the Court issued Exhibit 6.1 which reviewed Clean Water Act technology-based standards and states that *Chevron* provides the appropriate standard of review.

6.1 Clean Water Act Standards and Regulated Entities

Statutory Standard	Statutorily Mandated Factors	Entities Subject to Regulation
BPT: "[E]ffluent limitations . . . which shall require the application of the *best practicable control technology currently available*." 33 U.S.C. §1311(b)(1)(A)(emphasis added).	"Factors relating to the assessment of best practicable control technology currently available . . . shall include consideration of the total cost of application of technology in relation to the effluent reduction benefits to be achieved." 33 U.S.C. §1314(b)(1)(B).	Existing point sources during the Clean Water Act's initial implementation phase.

6. Water Pollution

BCT: "[E]ffluent limitations . . . which shall require application of the *best conventional pollutant control technology.*" 33 U.S.C. §1311(b)(2)(E)(emphasis added).	"Factors relating to the assessment of best conventional pollutant control technology . . . shall include consideration of the reasonableness of the relationship between the costs of attaining a reduction in effluents and the effluent reduction benefits derived." 33 U.S.C. §1314(b)(4)(B).	Existing point sources that discharge "conventional pollutants" as defined by the EPA under 33 U.S.C. §1314(a)(4).
BATEA: "[E]ffluent limitations . . . which . . . shall require application of the *best available technology economically achievable* . . . which will result in reasonable further progress toward the national goal of eliminating the discharge of all pollutants." 33 U.S.C. §1311(b)(2)(A)(emphasis added).	"Factors relating to the assessment of best available technology shall take into account . . . the cost of achieving such affluent reduction." 33 U.S.C. §1314(b)(2)(B).	Existing point sources that discharge toxic pollutants and non-conventional pollutants.
BADT: "[A] standard for the control of the discharge of pollutants which reflects the greatest degree of effluent reduction which the Administrator determines to be achievable through application of the *best available demonstrated control technology.*" 33 U.S.C. §1316(a)(1)(emphasis added)	"[T]he Administrator shall take into consideration the cost of achieving such effluent reduction, and any non-water quality environmental impact and energy requirements." 33 U.S.C. §1316(b)(1)(B).	New point sources within the categories of sources identified by the EPA under 33 U.S.C. §1316(b)(1)(A).
BTA: "Any standard . . . applicable to a point source shall require that the location, design, construction, and capacity of cooling water intake structures reflect the best technology available for minimizing adverse environmental impact." 33 U.S.C. §1326(b).	N/A	Point sources that operate cooling water intake structures.

Amendments Regulating Specific Discharges

The statute was fine-tuned by subsequent amendments. Let's distinguish again between industrial dischargers and POTWs.

Existing Industrial Sources

The Standards The 1977 amendments to the Clean Water Act approached the previous 1983 deadline (established by the FWPCA in 1972) for industrial compliance with BAT effluent limits in a much more complex manner than in the original scheme. Different technology-based requirements and deadlines were developed for three categories of pollutants: (1) toxic (priority) pollutants, (2) conventional pollutants, and (3) nonconventional pollutants. The first category, toxic pollutants, initially included a list of 129 specific chemicals known as the priority pollutants. The second category, conventional pollutants, are designated by the EPA; they are nontoxic and include BOD, fecal coliform, suspended solids, and pH. The nonconventional pollutants are those not classified by the EPA as either toxic or conventional. The following standards were imposed by the 1977 amendments on discharges by industry, so as to be effective by 1984:

- *Toxics:* BAT was to be attained by dischargers of toxic pollutants.
- *Conventional pollutants:* For dischargers of conventional pollutants, a new standard, "best conventional pollutant control technology" (BCT), was established. The EPA was required to conduct a cost-benefit analysis and consider the reasonableness of the relationship between the costs of attaining a reduction in effluents and the benefits to be derived. BCT was required by 1984 if the incremental benefit of the pollution control upgrade exceeded the cost of the upgrade.
- *Nonconventional pollutants:* For dischargers of nontoxic nonconventional pollutants, BAT was to be achieved. If the limit was not yet established, compliance was required within three years of the promulgation of the nonconventional standard or by 1984, whichever was later.

The Water Quality Act of 1987 amends §301, giving industrial dischargers additional time to meet BAT and BCT effluent limitations. Compliance was to occur as soon as possible, not to exceed three years from the time of publication of the effluent limitations. Section 306 allows the EPA, with the state's approval, to set alternative BAT and pretreatment standards for an existing facility based on the existence of fundamentally different factors. These alternatives are known as FDF variances and are discussed later. The elements and deadlines of the 1972 FWPCA, the 1977 Clean Water Act Amendments, and the Water Quality Act of 1987 amendments are set out in Exhibit 6.2.

6.2 Existing Industrial Sources

Original Deadline in 1972 Act	Legal Requirement	Variance Available	Later Deadline by 1977 or 1987 Amendments
1977	Effluent limits on existing industrial dischargers must reflect "best practicable control technology currently available" (BPT) for all pollutants.	FDP	1979 on a case-by-case basis
1983	Effluent limits for conventional pollutants on existing industrial sources must reflect "best available technology economically available" (BAT); "BCT" later added.	FDP	1984, then 1992
1983	Toxic effluent limits are health-based BAT; nonconventional pollutant effluent limits are BAT.		1984, then 1989

Challenges to the Standard-Setting Process Section 402 of the Clean Water Act authorizes the EPA administrator to issue permits for individual point sources and also to review and approve the plan of any state wishing to conduct its own permit program. The permits serve to transform the effluent limitations developed according to §301 into legally binding effluent standards on individual dischargers, as articulated in *EPA v. California ex rel. State Water Resources Control Board*, 426 U.S. 200, 205 (1976). An EPA (as opposed to delegated state) decision regarding an NPDES permit is considered an adjudication subject to the provisions of the Administrative Procedure Act (APA). *Marathon Oil Co. v. EPA*, 564 F.2d 1253, 1262 (9th Cir. 1977); *United States Steel Corp. v. Train*, 556 F.2d 822 (7th Cir. 1977). As an adjudication, courts reviewing an NPDES permit determination apply the "substantial evidence" test. Id.; cf. *Weyerhaeuser Co. v. Costle*, 590 F.2d 1011 (D.C. Cir. 1978) (applying an "arbitrary and capricious" test and cautioning against de novo review). For more on the APA, see Chapter 2.

The EPA administrator must develop various kinds of technical data to provide guidance in carrying out responsibilities imposed on the agency and on the states by the Clean Water Act. 33 U.S.C. §1314. Effluent limitation guidelines described in detail under §304(b) of the Act are published by the EPA after consultation with interested parties. The guidelines survey and assess the effectiveness of an industry's options. They describe the methods the EPA intends to use to determine effluent limitations for new plants and existing point sources. However, the EPA does not have to publish effluent limitation guidelines before setting effluent limitations. See *Du Pont v. Train*, 430 U.S. 112 (1977).

Effluent limitations are achieved by the application of BPT, BCT, and BAT as described in §301(b) of the Act. Under §301, the EPA has the authority to limit the discharges of existing plants through the adoption of industry-wide regulations, upheld in *Du Pont v. Train*, 430 U.S. at 128. The EPA, though, must make some allowance for variations in individual plants.

Industry challenged in the courts almost every final technology-based standard developed by the EPA. The courts usually made favorable findings for the EPA. The courts deferred to the EPA regarding specific industry standards. In *American Meat Institution v. EPA*, 526 F.2d 442 (7th Cir. 1975), the Seventh Circuit Court of Appeals held that the BPT regulations set effluent limitations for the red meat processing industry that were appropriate and were already being achieved by some similar plants. Industry-wide effluent standards for the organic chemical industry were upheld in *Du Pont v. Train*, 430 U.S. 122 (EPA contended that §301 authorized the agency to promulgate regulations establishing effluent limits for general classes of plants without considering individual facility circumstances).

The Supreme Court held that it is permissible under a *Chevron* analysis and plain meaning interpretation for both utility companies and EPA to apply a cost-benefit analysis under the Clean Water Act to determine the specific technology required for cooling water intake structures, reversing a decision by then-appellate Judge Sotomayor. *Entergy Corp. v. Riverkeeper Inc.*, 556 U.S. 208 (2009). Cooling water intake structures expose aquatic species to impingement or entrainment by crushing or sucking species into the cooling structure. The Court held that just because the Clean Water Act "does not expressly authorize cost-benefit analysis," it does not show "an intent to forbid its use." Using a cost-benefit analysis weakens the technology thus required under Section 316(b) of the Act, 33 U.S.C. §1316(b).

Exactly where one physically discharges polluted wastewater is not a defense for industry. In 1978 the D.C. Circuit Court of Appeals upheld the EPA's refusal to consider the quality of a receiving water when determining the applicable BPT effluent limitations. Some pulp and paper makers challenged the validity of the BPT regulations set for their industry, arguing that their particular mills discharged into the Pacific Ocean and, as such, should not be forced to treat their waste stream as thoroughly as someone discharging into a smaller receiving surface water body. The D.C. Circuit noted in *Weyerhaeuser Co. v. Costle*, 590 F.2d 100 (D.C. Cir. 1979), that in the 1972 FWPCA, the Congress deliberately excluded any provision for treating waste based on the assimilation capacity of the receiving water.

The technological feasibility of individual company compliance with individual standards is not a factor in EPA standard setting. Nor is it a defense for industry. In *Crushed Stone*, the Supreme Court held that the EPA was authorized to adopt stringent technology-based effluent limitations, even if compliance with these levels would force some firms out of business.

There was one major industry victory. The 1977 amendments established the best conventional pollution control technology (BCT) effluent limits. The new BCT standards were challenged by industry groups. In a 1981 decision in *American Paper Institute v. EPA*, 660 F.2d 954 (4th Cir. 1981), the Fourth Circuit Court of Appeals held that the EPA's interpretation of the plain language of the statute was wrong, regarding the absence of cost factors in establishing standards. The EPA was required by the statute to use a cost-effectiveness test and a POTW cost comparison test: The court invalidated all of EPA's BCT regulations. Consequently, in 1986 the EPA adopted new BCT regulations considering cost.

Analysts, however, contend that BAT standards have proven to be compromises. One commentator concludes that BAT is driven by the most an industry will accept, not by the most it can do. See Oliver Houck, "The Regulation of Toxic Pollutants Under the Clean Water Act," 21 E.L.R. 10428, 10538.

POTWs

As we are already aware, POTWs are publicly owned wastewater treatment works, and their discharges after processing are classified as *point* sources. Title II of the Clean Water Act encouraged the construction of publicly owned waste-treatment works by providing federal grants-in-aid to states to construct facilities, including sewers and stormwater systems. States had to establish area-wide management agencies with planning and regulatory functions. In the 1987 amendments to the Act, Congress phased out Title II grants and replaced them with a loan program under Title VI, 33 U.S.C. §§1381-1387. Federal funds are disbursed through state revolving loan funds, which issue low- or no-interest loans to qualifying projects in communities.

About 40 percent of rivers, 44 percent of lakes, and 32 percent of estuaries are still not fit for fishing or swimming. A survey conducted by the EPA concluded that during the first two decades of the twenty-first century, wastewater handling systems in the United States will require approximately $140 billion in additional construction. These investments are necessary to construct wastewater treatment facilities, to upgrade existing facilities, to control sewer overflows when combined with stormwater systems, and to control agricultural and forest runoff. The EPA estimates that between the years 2000 and 2020, communities in the United States will need to spend $300 billion to replace existing water systems built in the first three decades following World War II. This equates to an annual figure of $21 billion, more than twice the capital budget actually being invested.

As of the 1977 Clean Water Act amendments, the EPA could permanently waive the POTW secondary treatment requirement for POTW discharges into marine waters, provided the sewage would not interfere with public water supplies, aquatic life, or recreational activities. In 1981 the Act was again amended, extending the secondary treatment deadline for POTWs to 1988. For political reasons, the definition of what constitutes secondary treatment also was relaxed. Biological treatment facilities such as oxidation ponds or lagoons were determined to be equivalent to secondary treatment, provided that the receiving water was not adversely affected. These amendments also eliminated the requirement for advanced or tertiary POTW treatment. Defenses to excess discharges from an "upset" POTW are possible.

Section 406 was amended to require the EPA to identify toxics in sewage sludge and establish numerical values for maximum allowable concentrations in the sludge. Sludge management requirements must be incorporated into the POTW's NPDES permit.

Industry avoids the need for a NPDES permit when it discharges to a POTW. The EPA demands pretreatment to avoid fouling POTWs. This program has been particularly difficult for the EPA to implement. Compliance of POTWs has been poor despite the relaxation of treatment requirements in the amendments to the Clean Water Act.

The EPA promulgated some pretreatment limitations that prohibit the industrial discharge of any pollutants that interfere with the POTWs or pollutants that may simply pass through the treatment facility. In *Arkansas Poultry Federation v. EPA*, 852 F.2d 324 (8th Cir. 1988), the court upheld the EPA's definitions of "interference" and "pass through," as a means of preventing excessive industrial discharges to POTWs. The POTW standards and deadlines imposed by the 1972 FWPCA, the 1977 Clean Water Act amendments, and the 1987 Water Quality Act amendments are set out in Exhibit 6.3.

New Industrial Sources

Section 306 requires the EPA to set performance standards for industrial *new sources* (that begin discharging after the statute was enacted) that reflect the best available control technology (BAT). They do not first meet BPT but go directly to the more restrictive BAT. The 1977 Clean Water Act amendments introduced new source performance standards (NSPS) for new sources. NSPS is defined as "the greatest degree of effluent reduction achievable through application of the best available demonstrated control technology." Effectively, EPA sets NSPS standards at BAT levels. These include water-quality-related standards when technology limits are insufficient to meet the applicable water-quality standards (§303(d)), and standards for toxic pollutants and pretreatment standards for industries that discharge pollutants into POTWs (§307(b)(1)). The elements and deadlines of the FWPCA and the 1977 amendments are set out in Exhibit 6.4.

6.3 POTWs

Original Deadline in 1972 Act	Legal Requirement	Variance Available	Later Deadline by 1977, 1981, or 1987 Amendments
1977	POTWs for BOD and TSS must meet effluent limits based on secondary treatment, or more stringent limits required by a state. Recall that secondary treatment is not a particularly stringent technology-based standard.	§304	1984, then 1988
1983	POTWs must meet effluent limits based on advanced treatment.		Requirement withdrawn

6.4 New Industrial Sources

Original Deadline in 1972 Act	Legal Requirement	Variance Available	Later Deadline by 1977, 1987, or 1987 Amendments
1983	New sources must meet "best available technology economically available" (BAT) per §306 for all pollutants. New Source Performance Standards: "greatest degree of effluent reduction . . . through . . . best available . . . technology."	None	Not changed

Nonpoint Sources

Nonpoint sources, the most significant source of water pollution, actually include a large universe of contaminants, including leakage from underground storage tanks, stormwater runoff, atmospheric deposition of contaminants, golf courses, and agricultural and forestry runoff. Nonpoint sources account for approximately half of all water pollution.

The 1987 Water Quality Act created a new section, §319, to address the problem of nonpoint sources. The states are first required to identify water bodies that cannot meet water-quality standards without control of nonpoint sources. The states then establish management programs for these water bodies. The plans are to include the "best management practices and measures," an implementation plan, and deadlines. The EPA must approve the plans.

Section 405 requires stormwater discharge permits. Stormwater is defined as "stormwater runoff, snow melt runoff and surface runoff and drainage." 40 C.F.R. §122.26(b)(13). Such stormwater discharges are defined to include a discharge from any conveyance from industrial yards, access roads, rail lines, handling sites, shipping and receiving areas, buildings, storage areas, and machinery exposed to stormwater. 40 C.F.R. §122.26(b)(14).

Since 1994, nonpoint discharges to waters of the United States require a permit for certain industrial discharges of stormwater and discharges from large and medium municipal separate storm sewer systems. Entities with discharges for which the state or federal environmental authorities determine there is a contribution to a violation of state water-quality standards or a significant contributor of pollutants to waters of the United States also can be required to obtain a permit for nonpoint discharges on an individual basis. Industrial facilities engaged in any kind of manufacturing or storage are subject to the stormwater permit requirements. This definition includes hazardous waste treatment, storage or disposal facilities, landfills, recycling facilities, scrap metal junkyards, salvage yards, automobile junkyards, battery reclaimers, steam electric power generating facilities, and sewage treatment works. Included as an industrial activity is any construction activity, including clearing, grading, and excavation, that results in the disturbance of more than five acres of total land area. Notification is now required prior to construction activity impacting one acre or more and must employ best management practices for erosion and sediment control during construction. 40 C.F.R. Part 450. States are allowed to enact more stringent requirements. There also can be a general permit for an area that authorizes certain types of industrial or stormwater discharges without the requirement of an individual notice of intent to discharge by the discharger.

The 1990 amendments required national guidance on nonpoint sources. These requirements apply only to states with Coastal Zone Management plans and apply only to the coastal portion of those 29 states with such approved plans. They do not apply to inland areas of those states or states without coastal zones. In addition, the national standards apply only to five sources of nonpoint contamination: marinas and recreational boating, hydro-modification, silviculture, agriculture, and urban runoff. Therefore, they are limited in the activities they target and the areas included. Beginning in 2003, EPA required NPDES permits for nonpoint waste discharged from several thousand large livestock operations to water bodies and application of animal waste as fertilizer. In 2008, EPA promulgated a new final rule requiring all concentrated animal feeding operations (CAFOs) to apply for NPDES permits if they proposed to discharge and to prepare a nutrient management plan for runoff, to contain nitrogen and phosphorus. A feedlot is only designated a CAFO and a point source if it contains over 1,000 animal feeding units, including hog, cattle, dairy, and poultry (which cumulatively produce 350 million tons of manure each year, three times what is generated by humans). A settlement requires a CAFO that "discharge" or "propose to discharge" to obtain NPDES permits, or self-certify that it does not need an NPDES permit. The federal court of appeals struck parts of EPA's CAFO rule as not limited to *actual* dischargers of pollutants. *Waterkeeper Alliance v. EPA*, 399 F.3d 486 (2d Cir. 2005).

FDF Variances

What about square polluters that do not fit in the EPA's round regulatory holes? When Congress decided to base the Clean Water Act on a technological approach employing *individual* discharger effluent limitations, the EPA developed these limitations for many broad categories of industries. The standards established for a particular *industrial category* may be inappropriate when applied to *individual* plants. The 1972 act did not specifically address this problem, except to allow the EPA to define subcategories for regulation within each industry.

The EPA has developed a "fundamentally different factor" (FDF) variance to ensure that its rough-hewn categories of point sources do not unfairly burden wastewater dischargers who are not typical among the group. See *Chemical Manufacturers Ass'n v. Natural Resources Defense Council*, 470 U.S. 116 (1985). The owner or operator subject to effluent limitation guidelines or pretreatment standards may demonstrate that the facility is fundamentally different with respect to the factors the EPA considered when the agency established effluent limitation guidelines or pretreatment standards for an industrial category. 33 U.S.C. §1311(n).

The Clean Water Act does not require the EPA to consider alleged FDFs of individual plants in promulgating national BPT limitations for an industry. *Chemical Manufacturers Ass'n v. EPA*, 870 F.2d 177, 185 (5th Cir. 1989). Both Congress and the Supreme Court expressed concern that the process of formulating nationally applicable water-quality standards would be unduly impeded if the EPA had to address the idiosyncrasies of individual plants in national rulemaking. So the FDF procedure serves as a safety valve to the categorical statutory scheme, allowing the EPA to address plant-specific variations through a separate and subsequent administrative process outside of national rulemaking.

The proposed alternative under the FDF variance has to be no less stringent than justified by the fundamental difference. It must not cause nonwater-quality impacts that are markedly worse than what the EPA considered in establishing the effluent limitation guideline in the first place. The EPA regulations list several factors that justify an FDF variance. They include the nature and quality of pollutants in the raw waste load, the volume of wastewater, nonwater-quality environmental impacts, energy requirements in complying with the standards, engineering and process differences, and cost of compliance with the required technology. A discharger's inability to afford the control technology is not a basis for requesting an FDF variance. *EPA v. National Crushed Stone Ass'n et al.*, 449 U.S. 64 (1980). But a facility could try to demonstrate to the EPA that, due to FDFs, the national effluent limitation would cost much more for it to achieve than other facilities in its category.

In any event, the EPA provides an exception for unavoidable exceedances. An "upset" is an affirmative *defense* in an action for noncompliance. 40 C.F.R. §122.41(n)(2); *Chemical Mfrs. Ass'n v. EPA*, 870 F.2d at 229. But the "upset" must be an exceptional incident caused by factors beyond the reasonable control of the permittee — not an operational error, a badly designed facility, lack of preventive maintenance, or carelessness.

The Supreme Court upheld the use of the fundamentally different factor (FDF) variance for BPT in *Du Pont v. Train*. However, in *National Crushed Stone*, the Court held that the EPA did not have to consider an individual company's ability to *afford* BPT requirements. Closure of a process or a plant is always an option for compliance. Therefore, while technical FDF factors can legitimize a variance, individual plant financial implications are not relevant.

In *Chemical Mfrs. Ass'n v. NRDC*, the Court upheld the EPA's decision to grant an FDF variance to discharges of toxic pollutants into sewage treatment systems, known as indirect discharges. Indirect discharges are governed by the pretreatment program in §307 of the Act. The Court held that the FDF variance was available despite the language of §301(l) prohibiting any modification of effluent standards for toxics.

Examples

1. You have a client who is a residential real estate developer. Several years ago he purchased some property along a major river. The river serves as a drinking water supply for three towns and is used extensively for recreational purposes. He wants to build individual septic systems for each home he constructs. The town does have a sewer system, but to connect to that system would be very expensive, because the nearest installed conduit is two miles away. The state does not yet have in place a Nonpoint Source Management Plan that has been approved by the EPA. The *proposed* plan, however, recommends drastic changes to septic system regulation to require sewer connection. What would you recommend to your client as the long-term solution?

2. To offset the costs of connecting the homes to the town sewer system, your client decides to lease a large piece of waterfront property to a commercial lawn and garden center. You are aware that this center has a long history of mismanagement and has frequently been cited for

releases of fertilizers and pesticides at its previous location. Your client wants your advice about environmental permitting before finalizing the lease and joining the business as a partner. What do you say?

3. Your client asks you if he needs an NPDES permit to discharge pollutants into a small nearby creek that is dry eight months of the year. What is your response?

4. Stan and Martha Murray are among thousands of entrepreneurs engaged in an outdoor profession that is spreading like wildfire. The Murrays mine for gold and other heavy minerals using a venerable gravity separation process known as sluicing. They run stream water over their pay-dirt in a box. The lighter sand, dirt, and clay are suspended in the wastewater and released. The ore collects behind dams built into the bottom of the box.

   a. The EPA decides to regulate sluice mining as an industrial subcategory under the Clean Water Act. The Murrays and the manufacturer of the sluicing equipment dispute the agency's authority, claiming they are not point sources, do not add pollutants to the water, and do not use navigable waters. Review the definition of "pollutant" at 33 U.S.C. §1362(6). Who prevails, and why?

   b. After a formal rulemaking procedure, the EPA decides that settling ponds are the best practicable control technology currently available for sluicing point sources and that settleable solids of 0.2 milligrams per liter (mg/L) of discharge is an achievable standard. The parties protest, saying that the EPA failed to use a cost-benefit analysis in determining BPT. Will they prevail?

   c. The EPA decides that zero discharge, that is, the recirculation of the process wastewater in the sluice boxes, is the best available technology (BAT). The petitioners do not deny that pumped recirculation rinsing technology is available, but they challenge its economic achievability. How should the court respond?

   d. The petitioners argue that any pollutants present in the sluice box discharges should not be subject to BAT limitations because the pollutants are in a naturally occurring solid form and are not toxic in that form. Does this argument change the judicial outcome?

   e. In desperation, the Murrays contend that the EPA may not regulate sluicing operations because the rules conflict with their water rights. They cite federal law at 30 U.S.C. §51: "Whenever, by priority of possession, rights to the use of water for mining, agricultural, manufacturing, or other purposes have vested and accrued, and the same are recognized and acknowledged by the local customs, laws, and the decisions of courts, the possessors and owners of such vested rights shall be maintained and protected in the same. . . ." If you need more information on water rights, read ahead to Chapter 7. Do these water rights defeat the EPA regulation?

Explanations

1. Because the plan is not yet effective, septic systems are still allowed and therefore are a viable option. The *long-term* solution, however, would be to connect the houses to the town's sewer system now. The additional cost incurred now could be offset in the sale price of each house. It will surely be more efficient than later having to replace the septic systems with sewer connections or to bring them into compliance with the future Nonpoint Source Plan. However, the client may wish to leave the long-term solution to subsequent purchasers of the houses.

2. Releases of fertilizers or pesticides along the river could have devastating effects on the marine environment. By entering into business with the garden center, the developer risks liability under the Clean Water Act as well as under other environmental statutes for any resultant nonpoint source pollution, even if he is a silent partner or lessor.

3. A *navigable* river need not be sailable or swimmable or even wet all year. "Navigable waters" are a constitutional rather than a physical concept. If a "navigable" tributary is connected to a navigable water of the United States, it is subject to an NPDES permit for any pollutant discharge. This means that a lot of merely wet areas are included. And similar state statutes may cover waters not federally navigable. As counsel, assume that a discharge permit is required until demonstrated otherwise. Call the EPA or the delegated state agency to determine jurisdiction.

4a. Congress views the words "navigable waters" in the Clean Water Act broadly and has defined them simply as "the waters of the United States." This includes nameless creeks and wetlands even if they are not connected to any river or lake. The Act can apply to the Murrays.

   The sluice is a physical structure, and the loadings emerge from a discrete point, thus the Murrays' operation is a "point source." We note that human beings are not envisioned by the law as point sources, as articulated in *United States v. Plaza Health Laboratories*, 3 F.3d 643 (2d Cir. 1993) (a man who puts vials of blood on a lake bank cannot be prosecuted as a point source under the Act).

   The Murrays excavate gravel and sand. The term "pollutant" encompasses these substances, as well as dredge spoil, solid waste, incinerator residue, sewage sludge, munitions, chemical wastes, biological materials, radioactive materials, wrecked or discarded equipment, cellar dirt, industrial, agricultural, and municipal waste discharged into water. 33 U.S.C. §1362(6).

Even when the material comes from the streambed itself, not from deposits nearby, the discharge is an addition of a pollutant to navigable waters because discharges regulated under the Act may include resuspension or redeposit of material drawn from the stream itself. The EPA wins this round if the stream is within U.S. jurisdiction.

4b. No, not if the EPA considered costs in determining what the BPT is for this industry and weighed the costs against the benefits. The petitioners would rightly expect to find in the record that the EPA had comprehensively analyzed model operations to estimate typical costs incurred by mining operations of various sizes, as well as to study the effect of compliance costs on the industry's profits. The BPT should represent the *average* of the best existing sluice mining operations. The effluent limitations on settleable solids will be upheld if they are supported by the record.

4c. The EPA must consider the cost of meeting BAT limitations but does not have to weigh the cost *against* the benefits of effluent reduction. See *Rybachek v. EPA*, 904 F.2d 1276, 1290 (9th Cir. 1990), citing *National Crushed Stone Ass'n*, 449 U.S. at 71-72; *Association of Pacific Fisheries v. EPA*, 615 F.2d at 818 (9th Cir. 1980). The agency measures costs on a "reasonableness standard"; it has considerable discretion in weighing the technology's costs, which are less important factors here than in setting BPT limitations. See *Natural Resources Defense Council v. EPA*, 863 F.2d 1420, 1426 (9th Cir. 1988); *American Iron & Steel Inst. v. EPA*, 526 F.2d 1027, 1052 n.51 (3d Cir. 1975), *modified in other part*, 560 F.2d 589 (3d Cir. 1977), *cert. denied*, 435 U.S. 914 (1978). The record must demonstrate that the EPA weighed the effect of recirculation costs on sluice mining. For example, the agency may have used various projections of gold pricing, assessed the cost for pumps, fuel, and maintenance, and calculated the number of operations that would be forced to close. On the basis of the data, the EPA must be able to conclude that recirculation is economically achievable and therefore BAT. If so, the EPA prevails.

4d. The petitioners will not be upheld if the agency has found on the record that naturally occurring metals in treated wastewater are toxic and cause environmental damage. Otherwise, the parties may prevail.

4e. If the Murrays do in fact have the water rights they claim, Congress has nevertheless spoken with sufficient clarity to affect the rights. The legislative history amply supports the argument that Congress foresaw and accepted the economic hardship, including the closing of some plants, that effluent limitations would cause. Cf. *National Crushed Stone Ass'n*, 449 U.S. at 79.

Water-Quality Standards

In addition to discharge limits, §302 imposes water-quality standards for *receiving water bodies* whenever the EPA administrator determines that meeting the §301 technology-based discharge limits fails to achieve the water quality designated for the particular water body or portion of a stream. In other words, if limits on individual pollutant dischargers fail to restore clean water, there is a general fail-safe standard for each water body measured against residual contamination levels. Section 304 requires the EPA to adopt water-quality criteria and guidelines for effluent limits, pretreatment programs, and administration of the NPDES permit program.

Pursuant to §303(d) of the Act, individual states must adopt water-quality standards, identify waters with insufficient controls, and limit pollutant discharge into those waters so as not to exceed the water-quality standards. Water-quality standards must include antidegradation provisions to protect against further deterioration. Section 301(b)(1)(C) requires that individual NPDES permits include these more stringent limits. State water-quality certification under §401 of the Clean Water Act is required only for point source discharges, and does not apply to nonpoint discharges. *Oregon Natural Desert Ass'n v. Dombeck*, 151 F.3d 945 (9th Cir. 1998) (U.S. Forest Service can issue grazing permit without obtaining state water quality certification regarding sediment created by cattle trampling stream banks; animals not included in the definition of point sources; "discharge" refers to a point source and does not include general runoff).

The states play a critical enforcement role. The state water-quality standards supplement national effluent limitations for individual point sources. The standards prevent water quality of water bodies from falling below acceptable levels as a result of numerous point sources discharging into waters even though, individually, the dischargers comply with effluent limitations. See *EPA v. California ex rel. State Water Resources Control Bd.*, 426 U.S. 200, 205, n.12 (1976).

A water-quality standard has two parts. The first is the designated use of a water body. For example, the state may declare water fit for agricultural use, for industrial purposes, for propagation of fish, for recreation, or as a public water supply. The second part of the water-quality standard is the water-quality criteria necessary to meet the designated use. Pursuant to §304 of the Act, the EPA publishes recommended nonbinding concentrations of pollutants, reflecting the latest scientific knowledge.

The use designated for a body of water is independently enforceable apart from any reference to corresponding water-quality criteria. *PUD No. 1 of Jefferson County and City of Tacoma v. Washington Department of Ecology*, 511 U.S. 700 (1994). In other words, the activities of a permitted facility cannot hamper the designated uses — discharges must be in keeping with the uses. It is not enough that the facility be in compliance with all water-quality criteria. Thus a hydroelectric power plant cannot diminish the flow of water below the minimum that a state agency regards as necessary for the propagation of fish or other values. Section 401 requires *states* to provide a water-quality certification before a federal license or permit can be issued. In §401, Congress has given the states authority to place any conditions on water-quality certification that are necessary to assure that the applicant will comply with effluent limitations, water-quality standards, and any other appropriate requirement of state law. See PUD *No. 1 of Jefferson County and City of Tacoma v. Washington Department of Ecology*, 511 U.S. 700 (1994).

Under the second part, for most pollutants, criteria are expressed as specific numerical concentrations, typically in milligrams per liter of water. *Mississippi Comm'n on Natural Resources v. Costle*, 625 F.2d 1269 (5th Cir. 1980). States may also establish narrative standards such as "no visible foam" or "no odor." States may consider economic factors when designating uses and, under limited circumstances, may remove an existing designation, a process called "downgrading."

The EPA requires states to adopt a controversial antidegradation policy embodied in 40 C.F.R. §131.12(a)(1). States cannot adopt water-quality standards that fail to protect existing uses. See *Mississippi Comm'n on Natl. Resources*. For high-quality waters, degradation to minimum levels for fishing and swimming is allowed only when necessary to accommodate important economic or social development. In addition, under §302 of the Act, the EPA can override state water-quality standards by changing the effluent limits for toxic pollutants in discharge permits whenever a source interferes with water quality on a targeted stream segment. 33 U.S.C. §1312. The EPA can substitute its judgment only if the state acts irresponsibly. The Court issued a unanimous opinion in *S.D. Warren v. Me. Bd. of Envtl. Prot.*, 547 U.S. 370 (2006), upholding states' broad authority under Section 401 to impose water-quality conditions on federal permits.

Lower courts have ruled flow control measures unconstitutional. See *Essex County Utilities Authority v. Board of Chosen Freeholders of Atlantic County*, 112 F.3d 652 (3d Cir. 1997). The court did not require the state of Michigan to elevate the water-quality protection level for Lake Superior to the highest level; the court deferred to the agency's interpretation of its own regulations as to such review. *National Wildlife Federation v. Browner*, 127 F.3d 1126 (1997). The EPA is not required by the Clean Water Act to approve or disapprove state decisions to leave unchanged their existing water-quality standards.

Approximately 40 percent of the rivers, 45 percent of the streams, and 50 percent of the lakes that have been assessed still do not support their designated uses. For water-quality standards to be useful, there must be a way to translate these limits into actual controls on individual dischargers. The Clean Water Act does this in §303(d) by requiring states to develop total maximum daily loadings (TMDLs). These values are subject to EPA review and approval. The TMDLs, once established in the aggregate, must be translated into permit limits for individual dischargers.

Unlike the Clean Air Act, the Clean Water Act does not set national ambient water-quality standards to be met in each water body nationwide. There are no uniform national standards as there are under the Clean Air Act. Instead, states classify the waters within their jurisdictions, varying state by state and region by region. The allowed pollutant discharges to water bodies are dependent upon the size of that water body, the number of others discharging to that water body, and the state administration.

States must then develop an implementation plan much like the SIP under the Clean Air Act. EPA provides itself the "hammer" to administratively discontinue individual water discharge permits if necessary to ensure that the TMDLs actually attain water-quality standards. This elevates the TMDLs for the first time to a major component of clean water implementation. TMDLs have been elevated from a quantitative calculation of the amount of pollution a water body could receive, to a tool for required implementation to achieve the water-quality standard. TMDLs apply to non-point sources, as well as point sources. This also focuses attention on ecological watershed management. While water quality is much more a local issue than air quality, this provides a mechanism to ensure local compliance. Once a TMDL is established, the total load amount is divided into units that can be bought, sold, or traded by individual resource users.

There is great disparity among the standards that states actually set for pollutants. Several states receive more than half of their water pollutants from upstream neighboring states, which may have much more lax restrictions on key pollutants.

The state of Oklahoma took legal action to prevent an NPDES permit from being issued to an upstream Arkansas wastewater treatment plant. Oklahoma argued that the Arkansas plant's discharges would lead to violations of Oklahoma's water-quality standards. The Supreme Court in *Arkansas v. Oklahoma*, 503 U.S. 91 (1992), held that Oklahoma was not able to impose its standards on Arkansas discharges. The court left the EPA discretion and ". . . authority to require a point source to comply with downstream water quality standards." *Id.* at 106. Therefore, the EPA may choose to protect the downstream state's water quality, but it is not compelled to do so and the downstream state may not force such a standard on the EPA.

Enforcement

Today, the EPA regulates more than 100 chemicals under the Clean Water Act, and more than 90 chemicals under the Safe Drinking Water Act (covered in the next section). Yet 40 percent of community water supplies in 2008 violated the act's pollution limits at least once. In the past five years, companies reported violating the Act on more than a half-million occasions. The number of exceedences of discharge limits has been increasing, rather than decreasing, and less than 3 percent of these violations resulted in penalties or prosecution, even though 60 percent were deemed significant noncompliance that could threaten public health.

The EPA has not set water-quality criteria for more than 1,000 chemicals routinely discharged into waterways in the United States, as well as pesticides and other sources of runoff contamination. An EPA report in 2003 concluded that 25 percent of major dischargers discharged in significant violation of their NPDES permits, seldom with any EPA penalties. Citizen suits, rather than the EPA, have often forced state compliance with the Clean Water Act. Section 505 permits any citizen to initiate a civil action on his or her behalf against someone who violates the Act. The term "citizen" is defined as a person who has an interest that is adversely affected, or that may be adversely affected. This broad definition comes from the test used in *Sierra Club v. Morton*, 405 U.S. 727 (1972), a standing case concerning forest service management practices and a Walt Disney resort (see Chapter 2). This section also allows a state to take action against the EPA administrator if the EPA fails to enforce the provisions of the Act and, as a result of the EPA's inaction, the state is harmed. Section 507 protects an employee or "whistleblower" who files an enforcement action under the statute.

Examples

1. For the last 50 years, the Famous Hat Factory has specialized in making hats. The factory is located on the banks of a large river. The factory has never discharged to the river or used river water for processing. The factory does use mercury to treat animal pelts prior to making them into hats. The technology is old, but the company follows all OSHA requirements in its workplace. The workers are very happy with the company and have a biannual physical. The company had been burning scrap waste, contaminated with mercury, in its furnace for years. This activity resulted in mercury-contaminated particulate matter being discharged into the air. For most of the years of its operation, the furnace was not required to have an air quality permit. Today the furnace no longer burns the waste scraps and operates in full compliance with existing air quality regulations. The company has an air discharge permit for its furnace. A study of the river conducted by the state environmental agency revealed that sediments and fish in the area of the Hat Factory are highly contaminated with mercury. The agency posted the area for "no fishing." Has the Hat Factory violated the Clean Water Act (FWPCA)?

2. About half a mile away from the Hat Factory, a medical waste incinerator has been operating for 20 years. The prevailing wind direction is toward the river. Studies reveal that medical incinerators are associated with discharges high in mercury (from thermometers, etc.). Has this incinerator violated the Clean Water Act?

3. The Hat Factory is located half a mile upstream from the state border. A fishing ban should extend into the next state as well, based on the elevated mercury levels in fish and sediments. May that second state take action to force cleanup?

4. A local group called "Friends of Fish" recently filed suit against the Hat Factory under the Clean Water Act. Is their action proper?

5. The EPA requires biological treatment under BCT. Biological treatment, however, works well only in warm climate conditions. If you represent a client subject to BCT in Maine, must you advise your client to implement this BCT standard?

Explanations

1. The Hat Factory has never been regulated as a point source under the Clean Water Act. This is correct as it never deliberately or directly discharged any liquid effluent into the river. It might be possible to allege that it is violating a river water-quality standard for mercury, but the mercury is not detected in the water column, only in sediment and fish. There are no current quality standards for sediment, which is where the mercury is found. The fish are migratory and not regulated per se. The Hat Factory has not violated the Clean Water Act.

2. The medical waste incinerator basically is in the same position as the Hat Factory: It makes no direct or deliberate discharge to navigable waters. It needs no NPDES permit. Pollution is incidental. It should, however, be checked for compliance of its discharge pursuant to the Clean Air Act.

3. The downstream state could sue for nuisance or possibly trespass, but not under the Clean Water Act unless the Hat Factory or the incinerator can be found to have violated the Act (see Chapter 1). To violate the Act, a facility must violate an NPDES permit or operate without a permit when one is required. The NPDES permit creates a "permit shield" against other statutory violations. If there is a violation of an NPDES permit, the down-river states' legitimate water-quality standards may be enforced through the NPDES process. Since no NPDES permit is required here, neither state has any immediate redress.

4. The citizens may bring suit under §505 of the Clean Water Act provided they meet the requirements set out. Most importantly, there must be an ongoing violation that is not being pursued by the EPA. Suit by the EPA negates a citizen suit. Since there appears to be no violation, the citizens may have no grounds for a substantive claim under the Act.

5. An FDF variance potentially is available when a fundamental factor does not apply. Maine has a cold climate that exhibits a fundamentally different technical factor for this BCT. You have an excellent case for an FDF variance. Apply for it. But it is important to comply fully until the variance is granted.

ADDITIONAL FEDERAL WATER POLLUTION STATUTES

Despite its complexity, the Clean Water Act does not do it all. Other important laws also deal with water quality. Section 404 of the Clean Water Act, concerning wetlands dredging, filling, or alteration, is discussed in Chapter 11.

The Safe Drinking Water Act

The Safe Drinking Water Act (SDWA) of 1974 established a federal regulatory system designed to protect and ensure the safety of public drinking water supplies. 42 U.S.C. §300(f)-(j). The Act operates primarily through assessment and demonstration programs designed to protect critical aquifer areas. Major amendments to the Act were added in 1986. The Safe Drinking Water Act was amended again in 1996 to require that the EPA regulate 25 new pollutants at least every three years, as it discovers new pollutants that actually occur in drinking water. Where the regulations are not cost-justified, the EPA may lessen the regulation. It prohibits "underground injection" that is not authorized by permit or rule under an approved Underground Injection Control Program. 42 U.S.C. §300h(b)(1)(A). Still today, almost 20 million Americans annually are thought to become ill each year from drinking water contaminated with bacteria, parasites, and viruses, not counting other chemicals (for more on the ecologic cycle and the role of bacteria, see Chapter 1).

Let's contrast this with the Clean Water Act. First, the SDWA standards apply to drinking water, regardless of its source. Drinking water resources include both surface water supplies and groundwater supplies. The law was designed to regulate the quality of water as it flows to and from the tap. This is a different goal and jurisdiction from that embodied in the Clean Water Act, which primarily seeks to eliminate ambient water pollution in rivers and lakes — surface water bodies. Note that prevention of water pollution is the first critical link in preserving high-quality drinking water.

The SDWA requires the EPA to set maximum levels for common contaminants in public water supply systems. A public water supply is a system that serves at least 25 persons, or has 15 service connections on a regular basis not less than 60 days of the year.

Private water supply wells or services are not regulated by the Safe Drinking Water Act or by any other federal statute. They may be regulated by state drinking water laws, though most states do not have such laws. In some states, local health boards have authority to make reasonable health-based regulations to ensure that drinking water is safe and of adequate supply (see Chapter 10 for more on boards of health). Some boards of health require testing of new wells prior to issuing occupancy permits for homes. Some towns may impose moratoriums on the drilling of new private wells. The contaminant levels established by the EPA under the SDWA are listed in Exhibit 6.5.

The Act restricts activities in geographic areas that have been designated as sole source aquifers. The primary enforcement of the Safe Drinking Water Act may be delegated to the states on their request. The individual states may adopt drinking water regulations no less stringent than the national standards. The states must also implement a monitoring and enforcement program. More than 90 percent of all public water systems are small. Due to an identified need for increased protection of the nation's drinking water supply after the September 11, 2001, events, the Public Health Security and Bioterrorism Preparedness and Response Act was enacted, which requires that EPA develop strategies for terrorist-related occurrences and increase drinking water security. Drinking water systems that serve more than 3,300 persons must conduct assessments of their susceptibility to terrorist attacks or other emergency-related acts and develop response measures.

The Safe Drinking Water Act authorizes the EPA to treat tribes as states ("TAS"). 42 U.S.C. §300j-11(a). This delegation provides qualified tribes with "primary enforcement responsibility for public water systems and for underground injection control."

Other Water Pollution Statutes

More than half of the U.S. population lives within 50 miles of the coast line or the Great Lakes, even though this comprises only 17 percent of the nation's total land area. Almost one million new homes are built every year within this coastal zone. The 95,000 miles of the nation's coasts are vitally important to the economy and well-being of the American population, and this region contributes half of the nation's gross domestic product.

The federal government, the adjacent states, and other nations all share jurisdiction over ocean waters to varying degrees. Federal authority over the coastline extends 200 nautical miles to sea, with the first 12 nautical miles considered U.S. territorial seas, the next 24 miles the contiguous zone, and the Exclusive Economic Zone out to 200 nautical miles, including sovereign rights to explore, exploit, conserve, and manage this zone, including the air space. The Fisheries Conservation and Management Act granted the federal government "the power to regulate all fishing within 200 miles of the United States." 16 U.S.C.A. §1811.

The Coastal Zone Management Act

In the Coastal Zone Management Act (CZMA) Congress declared a national policy "to preserve, protect, develop, and where possible, to restore or enhance, the resources of the nation's coastal zone for this and succeeding generations." 16 U.S.C. §301. Unlike many other statutes, CZMA focuses on an area rather than a pollutant. In this regard, it is similar to a land use statute. The secretary of commerce must approve state programs as consistent with the statute. Such approval makes states eligible for federal funding.

To be approved by the federal government, a plan must define the coastal zone's boundaries, identify activities permitted within the zone, and assign responsibility for administration of the program. The boundaries of the coastal zone are intentionally left vague by the federal Act to give the states flexibility in defining their management programs. Generally, the coastal zone includes waters *significantly affected* by land uses and extends inland to the extent necessary to control the shorelands. If there is a surface water discharge to a river, and that river flows to the sea, the original discharge could directly affect the coastal zone. If the discharge is inconsistent with environmental standards for the coastal zone, it could be impermissible. In order to continue to receive funds, the state must continue to meet federal standards.

6.5 Contaminant Levels Under SDWA

Standard	Definition
Maximum contaminant level goals (MCLGs)	The MCLGs are nonenforceable health values based on the risk of harm to health. Chemicals that have been classified as carcinogens (capable of causing cancer) have MCLGs of zero.
Maximum contaminant levels (MCLs)	The MCLs are enforceable primary standards applicable to public drinking water systems, set as close as possible to the MCLGs. The MCLs are based on consideration of the limits of analytical laboratory methodologies, the capability of water treatment technologies, and cost. The MCLs for drinking water include levels for microorganisms, turbidity, and organic and inorganic chemicals. Water supplies are required to come as close as possible to meeting the standards set by using the best available technology that is economically and technologically feasible.
Health advisories (HAs)	Health advisories are guidance values. These values are health-based and vary with the exposure duration.
Secondary maximum contaminant levels (SMCLs)	The secondary standards are concerned with color, odor, and appearance of water. The SMCLs are not enforced by the EPA but may be enforced by states. Individual states may also establish additional guidelines.

How far out to sea does the coastal zone extend? International law recognizes a 12-mile coastal area within the jurisdiction of each coastal nation under the 1982 United Nations Convention on the Law of the Sea (UNCLOSIII). The United States never formally ratified UNCLOSIII; however, American policy and legislation have recognized this 12-mile jurisdiction. The Coastal Zone Management Act, enacted in 1972, allows any state with an approved CZM program to "review activities that require a federal license or permit . . . for consistency with its enforceable program policies" and to issue a certificate of consistency as a prerequisite to any federal permitting. Thirty-five of those 38 states with a coastal zone have approved CZM programs. In 1990, amendments limited the state authority's seaward boundary to 3 miles, making it consistent with the limitations of the Submerged Lands Act, 43 U.S.C. §§1301 *et seq.* Almost all of the nation's shoreline is managed under states electing to implement federal coastal zone authority.

How far upland does the coastal zone extend? The coastal zone is "the coastal waters (including the lands therein and thereunder) and the adjacent shorelands (including the lands therein and thereunder) strongly influenced by each other and in proximity to the shorelines of the several coastal states . . . inland from the shorelines only to the extent necessary to control shorelands, the uses of which have a direct and significant impact on the coastal waters." 16 U.S.C. §304(1). States can include watersheds, areas of tidal influence that extend further inland than waters under saline influence, and Native American lands not held in trust by the federal government. CZMA covers activities directly affecting the coastal zone.

The legislative history indicates a broad construction of the term "affecting" the coastal zone. In 1990, the Act was reauthorized to require that states develop coastal nonpoint pollution control programs to protect coastal waters. States are authorized to "reflect the greatest degree of pollution reduction achievable through the application of the best available nonpoint pollution control practices, technologies, processes, siting criteria, operating methods or other alternatives." 16 U.S.C. §6217(g)(5). Implementation of these nonpoint source pollution programs is a prerequisite for funding under the Act as well as under the Clean Water Act §319.

"Directly affecting the coastal zone" was limited to activities occurring within the "coastal zone" in *Secretary of the Interior v. California*, 464 U.S. 312 (1984) (oil leasing outside the coastal zone pursuant to federal license was not inconsistent with the California coastal zone plan). In 1990, Congress amended and reauthorized the Act. These amendments specifically made oil and gas sale leases on the Outer Continental Shelf through the Outer Continental Shelf Lands Act expressly subject to consistency reviews with §307 of the Coastal Zone Management Act.

In *California Coastal Commission v. Granite Rock Co.*, 480 U.S. 572 (1987), the Supreme Court held that compliance with federal mining regulations on national forest land did not prevent Granite Rock from also having to comply with regulations imposed by the state coastal commission pursuant to the CZMA. The Court stated that the state could not apply *land use* regulations (those limiting how land can be used) to federal lands, but the state could apply environmental regulations (those dictating how the allowed activity is conducted).

States define the inland extent of the coastal zone differently. For example, the Massachusetts coastal zone extends 100 feet beyond the first major land transportation route encountered inland. California, by contrast, extends the coastal zone inland to the highest elevation of the nearest coastal mountain range, except in three large Southern California counties (Los Angeles, Orange, and San Diego Counties) where the coastal zone extends five miles inland from the mean high tide line.

The Oil Pollution Act

The Oil Pollution Act of 1990 (OPA) was Congress's response to the Exxon *Valdez* oil spill. For a variety of reasons, prior to OPA, the petroleum industry had escaped the brunt of most statutory environmental schemes, such as CERCLA. Generally, this resulted in the liability of the owners of oil tankers and offshore oil facilities being limited to after-spill value of the vessel, which could be very little. For example, in the *Torrey Canyon* oil spill, the $8 million cleanup costs could only be recovered by liquidating the value of the single lifeboat that survived the accident. The owners of the oil cargo that was spilled generally were not liable. Before OPA, only those who experienced actual physical harm to legal property interests were capable of recovering. There was no liability for damage to wildlife in which no one had a property interest. Loss of income was not compensated, such as lost profits or economic harm. While some inroads were made in this liability scheme by the Deepwater Port Act, 33 U.S.C. §§1501-1524 and the Trans-Alaska Pipeline Authorization Act, 43 U.S.C. §§1651-1656, comprehensive liability was not established prior to OPA.

OPA makes owners of vessels discharging oil liable for the costs of cleanup. A trust fund to pay for the costs of cleaning up oil spills also is established by the Act. To help prevent oil spills in the first place, the Act imposes minimum design standards for vessels operating in U.S. waters.

The Act imposed strict liability on any party that is responsible for an oil spill or the substantial threat of an oil spill. It carries with it liability for a Class D felony for violation, which can carry a prison term of up to five years and/or a $50,000 fine. The Act was designed to fill gaps in liability coverage of CERCLA and the Federal Water Pollution Control Act. Covered are costs and damages related to natural resources, real and personal property, loss of subsistence use, loss of revenues, and loss of profits and incapacity. 33 U.S.C. §272(a)(1)-(2). There is a three-year statute of limitations on claims, running from when the injury occurs or when reasonable discovery occurs.

299

6. Water Pollution

Under OPA, parties who suffer only economic losses from oil pollution, such as owners of waterfront stores and facilities, can recover from an oil spill in U.S. waters. Federal and state governments also may sue for damages for the loss of taxes, royalties, profits, or rents from injury to property or to natural resources. State government costs for additional fire, safety, or health hazard protection resulting from an oil spill also may be compensated. States are not preempted from imposing additional liability on parties responsible for discharged oil. 33 U.S.C. §2718(a)(1)(A). The number of oil spills in U.S. waters has decreased since the enactment of OPA in 1990.

OPA creates an Oil Spill Liability Trust Fund to pay for removal costs, claims, and damages not otherwise recoverable from responsible parties. The fund is created from a previous fund under the Federal Water Pollution Control Act, augmented by a nickel tax on each barrel of domestic and imported crude oil.

OPA regulates discharges of oil or hazardous substances affecting natural resources and occurring in "navigable waters, adjoining shorelines, or into or upon waters of the contiguous zone. . . ." 33 U.S.C. §1321(b). The EPA regulations under this Act require the preparation and implementation of a spill prevention control and countermeasure plan. 40 C.F.R. §112.3(b). This plan is only required from owners and operators of onshore and offshore facilities that could be expected to discharge harmful quantities of oil to the marine environment.

Contaminating a waterway, even though it is an inland facility, can be covered by the Act where the freshwater body eventually leads to a coastal environment. *Sun Pipeline Co. v. Comewago Contractors, Inc.*, 1994 U.S. Dist. Lexis 14070 (M.D. Pa. 1994). Therefore, a minimal nexus requirement is established between the locus of the spill and an eventual impact on coastal waters. All costs expended by the Coast Guard to prevent or minimize migration of oil pollution once spilled are recoverable costs. *United States v. Hyundai Merchant Marine Co., Ltd.*, 172 F.3d 1187, 1189 (9th Cir. 1999); *United States v. Murphy Exploration & Production Co.*, 939 F. Supp. 489, 491 (E.D. La. 1996); *United States v. Conoco, Inc.*, 916 F. Supp. 581, 589 (E.D. La. 1996).

There is a liability cap of $500,000 under §1,004(a)(2) of the Act, unless there is "willful misconduct or gross negligence" or the responsible party violated applicable federal regulations regarding safety or operating standards. *National Shipping Co. of Saudi Arabia v. Moran Trade Corp.*, 122 F.3d 1062 (4th Cir. 1997). Other limitations on liability, which act as a complete defense, are if the oil spill was caused solely by an act of God, an act of war, or an act or omission of a third party other than an employee or agent of the responsible party. There can be no contractual relationship in order to invoke the third-party defense. See *United States v. J. R. Nelson Vessel, Ltd.*, 1 F. Supp. 2d 172 (E.D.N.Y. 1998). These third-party defenses are quite analogous to the CERCLA third-party defense. Contribution provisions are provided. The UN Convention on the Law of the Sea also addresses marine ship pollution.

The Marine Protection Act

The Marine Protection Research and Sanctuaries Act was enacted in 1972. 33 U.S.C. §1400 *et seq.* The Act authorizes the secretary of commerce to designate areas of marine environment that exhibit significant ecological, aesthetic, historical, or recreational values as National Marine Sanctuaries. While oceans cover over 71 percent of the earth, only 1 percent is a Marine Protected Area.

There are 12 National Marine Sanctuaries in the United States. There also are United Nations Conventions on the Law of the Sea. One of these conventions pertains to protection of biodiversity in a marine environment, while another convention addresses conservation of marine resources. There is a 200-mile zone of exclusive economic control around coastal borders vesting the landed country with control over this sea zone. States in the United States have control over marine matters within a three-mile radius of their shores. The federal government has exclusive control over the zone from three miles to 200 miles from the shore.

The federal government regulates the dumping of all types of materials into ocean waters. It also funds comprehensive research on ocean dumping. All ocean dumping was designed to be stopped by the EPA by the end of 1981. Litigation by the City of New York extended this deadline for dumping that did not unreasonably degrade the marine environment. *City of New York v. EPA*, 543 F. Supp. 1084 (S.D.N.Y. 1981) (allowing continued ocean dumping in the New York Bight of sewage sludge from New York).

The Act was again amended in 1988, setting a deadline by the end of 1991 for the cessation of all dumping of sewage sludge and industrial waste into the ocean. New York counties again successfully challenged the ocean dumping ban. *United States v. County of Nassau*, 733 F. Supp. 563 (E.D.N.Y. 1990) (court extended congressional deadline for ocean dumping). Ocean disposal of some sewage sludge is still ongoing.

Petroleum can be "cracked" into plastics, which are organic synthetic or processed polymers of high molecular weight. Petroleum-based plastic leaches chemicals into the substances it encounters. Over the last 50 years, the consumption of plastic material has increased 20 times to about 100 million tons annually, consuming 8 percent of the world's oil production — 4 percent as feed stocks and 4 percent in the manufacturing process. Plastic is the dominant form of packaging material in the world and only 3-5 percent of plastics are recycled in any manner. Plastics are impervious to bacteria, water, acid, salt, rust, and most other agents except heat — they do not biodegrade.

Much of the plastic ends up in the world's oceans. Since most plastics are lighter than seawater, they float and slowly break down into smaller fragments, which can be consumed by the filter-feeding animals of the ocean. Even though the International Convention for the Prevention of Pollution from Ships (MARPOL) bans the dumping of plastics at sea, there is no enforcement of these provisions. There is now six times more plastic than plankton floating in the middle of the Pacific Ocean.

The Fish and Wildlife Coordination Act

The Fish and Wildlife Coordination Act provides that wildlife conservation shall be coordinated with "other features of water-resource development programs through the effectual and harmonious planning, development, maintenance, and coordination of wildlife conservation and rehabilitation. . . ." 16 U.S.C. §661. This Act applies primarily to the diversion or control of streams or impoundments by any arm of the U.S. government or by another entity acting pursuant to a federal license. In such instances, the agency is required to consult with the United States Fish and Wildlife Service, in order to conserve wildlife resources.

Examples

1. The price of water in Treetown has risen tenfold in the past five years. As a resident of the town, you are very concerned about these rising costs. The town has a long history of industrial use and, in the early 1980s, a number of the town wells were closed because of contamination with volatile organic compounds (VOCs) from local industry. You have been told that these compounds cause cancer, and there have been an unusual number of cancer cases in Treetown. The current water supply is piped from a reservoir several towns away. In casual conversation at a neighborhood party, you find out that five of your neighbors have installed private drinking water wells on their property because the town water is too expensive. Concerned for their safety, you contact the board of health, which tells you that the town has no authority to regulate these wells because the state and federal government do not regulate private wells under the Safe Drinking Water Act. Do you concur with this position?

2. You find out that the day care center where you send your children also has a private well. It has been in use for three months and has never been tested for possible contamination. What should you do if you are concerned?

Explanations

1. The town has broad-based public health powers under its police powers. The fact that the state and federal governments do not regulate private drinking water wells does not prevent the town from doing so. The town already regulates private residences to the extent that it issues occupancy permits. The health authority applies to any nuisances. The town may be compelled to act to require testing of drinking water wells in areas known to be contaminated with chemicals.

2. The additional facts do not really change the situation, except to make the desire to take action more compelling. If the well serves more than 25 persons, even if it is a private well system, it can be regulated as a *public* system under the Safe Drinking Water Act. Persons include "children and counts daytime only persons." However, this situation may also present you with an opportunity to address this problem at the state level if the state regulates day care centers for safety and compliance with public health. Every nexus is a potential additional lever to address a potential environmental problem.

Rights to Use Water

"When the well's dry, we know the worth of water."

Benjamin Franklin

"If there is magic on this planet, it is contained in water. . . . Its substance reaches everywhere; it touches the past and prepares the future; it moves under the poles and wanders thinly in the heights of air. It can assume forms of exquisite perfection in a snowflake, or strip the living to a single shining bone cast upon the sea."

Loren Eisley, The Immense Journey

"A man from the west will fight over three things: water, women and gold, and usually in that order."

Senator Barry Goldwater, Arizona

"Of all the elements, the Sage should take Water as his preceptor. Water is yielding but all-conquering. Water extinguishes fire, or finding itself likely to be defeated, escapes as steam and re-forms. Water washes away soft Earth, or, when confronted by rocks, seeks a way around."

Tso Cheng, Eleventh Century A.D.

Less than 1 percent of all the Earth's water is freshwater that is available for human use, and more than half of that 1 percent is within just 6 of the world's 200 nations, excluding the United States. One billion people lack access to safe drinking water, and half the world's population lacks adequate sanitation. Collectively these factors are responsible for 80 percent of all diseases and more than 5 million deaths annually. Groundwater is the source of drinking water for about half of the people in the United States and almost all people living in rural areas. Forty-seven states have wellhead protection programs. During the twenty-first century, water use is expected to increase dramatically in the southeastern and western parts of the United States, where population increases are expected to be greatest. More reclamation of wastewater will be required to help sustain water resources.

This chapter discusses the rights associated with use of water resources in the ground and surface portions of the hydrological cycle. Use of water resources fundamentally affects the environment. Misuse can alter interdependent ecological relationships. Use of water by individuals has led to its pollution. Constraints on the use of water may affect both water quantity and water quality. This chapter will analyze who has rights to use different sources of water. There are three types of water rights:

- English or natural flow: No water may be transferred away from the land for any reason, and all water may be taken on site.
- American or reasonable use: As long as the use of that water does not *unreasonably* interfere with other users, water may be transported off the land.
- Appropriation: A first-in-time doctrine.

The common law in the United States has spawned two alternative water rights systems: (1) riparianism and (2) prior appropriation.

SURFACE WATER RIGHTS

Who has water rights, and when do they arise? The answers depend on the allocation system. This section concerns the taking or use of surface water, such as lakes or streams. It does not concern groundwater, discussed in a later section.

American water law developed in the 1660s when King Charles II granted noblemen certain property rights to establish British colonies in the New World. Following English common law, land ownership included the rights to all resources present on the property, including the natural water sources abutting or transversing the land. That legal title did not necessarily include ownership of the water itself, but rather the right to use that water. The King retained the ultimate water control to appropriate water for the benefit of all citizens.

Following this English common law, the general ownership and property law principles did not attach to flowing water. With plentiful water and history of being colonies of England, the Northeast United States retained the English riparian system, which allowed adjacent owners unlimited use of the water supply, although not ownership. The need for more efficient use during the Industrial Age caused the evolution of a "reasonable use" standard applied to such water use. This causes shared rights among riparian owners, the government, and the general public.

The Western United States had more limited water resources and was not under English colonial rule. These states developed a system based on prior appropriation, which rewards the first user in time to put the water to a beneficial use. Early beneficial uses were, in order of priority, domestic potable use, agricultural, and industrial uses, with fish, wildlife, and recreational uses at the bottom of the hierarchy. The prior appropriator must actually divert the water and apply it to a beneficial use to protect his or her interest. Each western state distinctly defines what is a "beneficial use." Questions remain regarding traditionally protected out-of-stream use and in-stream water use, which is less clear. Priority attaches to the first in time. The most senior appropriators have superior rights to those more junior, or later in time, appropriators of water. This system tends to inhibit efficient and flexible use of water over time.

In the modern system, some elements of each of the prior appropriation and riparian systems have been retained and discarded. The "reasonable use" doctrine of the riparian system and a process recognizing permitted traditional or early uses have evolved in many states. First, we will explore the doctrine of riparian rights.

Riparian Water Rights: Geographic Determination

What Are Riparian Water Rights?

Water rights that spring from the ownership of property abutting a water source are called riparian rights. The owner of such land is called a riparian. Leaseholders on that land may also have riparian rights. Holders of easements have riparian rights only insofar as to use and enjoy the easement. Legally, holders of easements are not necessarily riparians. Geographic proximity dictates riparian rights.

The dictionary defines a "riparian" water right as

> the rights that accrue to owners of land on the banks of waterways, such as the use of such water, ownership of soil under the water, etc.; rights not originating in grants, but arising by operation of law, and are called natural rights because they arise by reason of the ownership of lands upon or along streams of water, which are furnished by nature.

Typical riparian rights include:

- Access to waterways
- Fishing
- Drinking
- Navigation and boating
- Household uses
- Industrial and commercial uses
- Production of hydroelectricity
- Turning of waterwheels

Notice that the listed riparian rights are all rights to *use* water for a purpose, and not the ownership of the water itself. Riparian rights are *usufructuary*, or rights to *use*. Because riparian rights are merely usufructuary and not possessory rights to the water, at law a riparian's *expectation* interests in those rights are less than his or her expectation in the rights normally associated with land.

Water Types Subject to Riparian Rights

Riparian rights attach to certain categories of *surface* waters, such as lakes and streams. Rights arising from proximity to lakes are called littoral rights. Because littoral rights are essentially the same as riparian rights, the terms littoral and riparian are both used in reference to lakes. Below, we briefly identify the types of *surface* waters and identify whether they are subject to riparian rights. As a basic rule, flowing water (watercourses) is subject to riparian rights. The rules determine whether a landowner with water on his or her land must share the water with other riparian owners.

Diffused Surface Waters — Not Subject to Riparian Rights Diffused surface waters are waters from precipitation or melting ice and snow that rest on the earth's surface but are not part of a watercourse or lake. The rule for diffused surface waters is that the owner of the land on which the water is located actually owns the water, and the water may be "captured" by the owner to use the water as he or she chooses. He or she need not share with others — it's a case of finders keepers. The only duty a landowner with diffused surface waters may have to neighbors is to allow drainage according to the natural drainage pattern.

Floodwaters — Not Subject to Riparian Rights Floodwater is water that flows over the banks of a waterway in times of high water and then returns to the stream. The laws pertaining to floodwaters vary by jurisdiction. Some states allow landowners to impound floodwaters for their own uses, while other states do not allow impoundment and require landowners to let the floodwater return to the original stream. There are no riparian rights to floodwater use. If impoundment is permitted, the owner need not share.

Springs — Sometimes Subject to Riparian Rights   The common law rule for a spring that is not the source of a running watercourse allows the landowner where the spring is located exclusive rights to the waters from the spring. The owner need not share. However, if the spring is a source of a running watercourse, the waters are subject to riparian rights, and the landowner will have a duty to share with other riparians.

Watercourses — Riparian Rights Attach   Riparian rights and duties attach to natural watercourses such as rivers and streams. For a body of water to be legally defined as watercourse, three elements must be present:

1. *Channel.* The channel of a watercourse must be well defined; waters must flow through a readily ascertainable impression in the land left by running waters.
2. *Bed and banks.* The stream bed and banks may be determined by an incline capable of retaining water, or by terrestrial organisms bordering aquatic organisms.
3. *Flow.* The water in a watercourse must flow or have a current in a certain direction. For seasonal streams, flow may be intermittent.

The nature of the specific riparian rights that attach to watercourses are defined according to *navigability*. Once a natural watercourse is determined to exist and riparian rights attach, a further delineation must be made as to whether that watercourse is *navigable*. Navigable waters are those waters over which commerce may be carried or that are used for transportation. Navigable waters usually provide a continuous course suitable for transportation. If a waterway is found to be navigable, then it is considered public and public rights attach. The general public has access rights to navigable waterways, and the private owners of property along the waterway have a duty to share the waters with the public. Public uses include commercial navigation, fishing, and recreation. If a conflict arises between private and public users, private rights may be suborned to advance public interests. If the waterway is nonnavigable, then no public uses exist and only private rights attach.

Riparian rights do not generally attach to artificial or human-made watercourses. Under changing circumstances over the passage of time, however, an artificial watercourse may evolve to become a natural watercourse, such as when a private mill run evolves to carry tributaries such as a natural stream. Conversely, substantial human-made changes to a natural watercourse may change the status of the watercourse to "artificial," and thus provide that its waters no longer need to be shared with other riparian owners.

Subsurface Streams — Riparian Rights Attach Wherever a subsurface stream is proven to exist, riparian rights will attach. However, proving that a water source is in fact a subsurface stream is a difficult proposition as the riparian proponent must demonstrate the boundaries and current of the stream before he or she may appropriate water. Exhibit 7.1 summarizes these five categories of surface water bodies and their relation to riparian rights.

Riparian Land

Riparian rights are tied to the ownership of riparian land. Riparian land is land that abuts or is adjacent to a watercourse during periods of normal flow. Since dry land naturally ends at the edge of the water body, the question arises: What is the legal boundary of the riparian land and its proximate water rights? The underwater boundaries of the riparian land are as shown in Exhibit 7.2.

The topography of an area may be altered through the natural forces of a stream's current. Drastic changes in a riverbed may occur within a very brief time span; gradual changes due to erosion or sediment may also take place. The rules for changes in riparian land area are set out in Exhibit 7.3.

Riparian land, as with any other type of real property, may be transferred in whole or in part or may have other tracts joined to it. Similarly, the right to water can be severed from the ownership of land: Riparian rights may be transferred separately from the land. Such transfers grant easements so that the transferee can exercise those rights. Riparian rights may be transferred in whole or in part by deed or other agreement. The transferor

7.1   Surface Water Bodies and Riparian Rights

	Water Body	Do Riparian Rights Attach?
1.	Diffused surface water	No
2.	Flood waters	No
3.	Springs	Sometimes
4.	Watercourses	Yes
5.	Subsurface streams	Yes

7.2   Underwater Boundaries of Riparian Land

	Water	Boundary
1.	Nonnavigable waters	The boundary line exists at the center of the stream.
2.	Lakes	The lake is split in a manner similar to a pie; in some states, however, the littoral owners may use and enjoy the whole, undivided lake.
3.	Tidal navigable waters	The state owns the streambed, and the private owner's boundary extends to either the ordinary high or low water mark, according to jurisdiction.
4.	Nontidal navigable waters	The state owns the streambed, and the private owners' lands extend to the vegetation line along the banks of the stream.
5.	Between states	State boundaries exist at the middle of the interstate waterway, unless defined otherwise.

7.3   Rules for Changes in Riparian Land Area

	Occurrence	Riparian Rule
1.	Gradual change from natural causes	Riparian takes possession and ownership of gradual augmenting changes (*accretion*) but bears the loss of gradual decreases (*erosion*). There are two types of accretion: (1) alluvion from sediment and (2) reliction from falling water levels.
2.	Sudden and perceptible loss (avulsion)	Boundary between properties remains where it previously existed in the old channel.
3.	Changes due to artificial causes	The same rules apply as in the case of naturally caused changes, except where artificial impediments are purposely erected to cause accretion, in which case the party who built the structure does not benefit from any gain to his or her land.

may convey a specific right to another, such as the right to fish, and retain his or her other riparian rights. The nature of the rights transferred is determined by the transfer instrument. The transferee may not convert any conveyed nonconsumptive uses into consumptive uses.

The Evolution of the Reasonable Use Rule

Originally, riparians had an *absolute* right to use the watercourse without any interference from other riparians. Riparians were permitted to make water withdrawals for their own noncommercial, domestic use to the detriment of others. At the beginning of the twentieth century, the absolute use rule was modified to allow for only *reasonable* withdrawals or diversions of water by a riparian for nondomestic, commercial purposes. The *reasonable use rule* that emerged grants rights that take into account the rights of other riparians along the same stream at any given time.

Because the nature of riparian rights is influenced by the rights of others, a *correlative* duty to share arises. Each riparian has a duty to exercise his or her rights only in relationship to the rights and duties of riparian neighbors. Whether a use is reasonable is a factual question. Additionally, rights to use may be established through covenants, prescriptive use for a period of time under a claim of right, government grants, or deeds.

The riparian interests of private landowners around a lake were subordinated by the Sixth Circuit to federal regulations to preserve the wilderness character and use of the entire lake, including areas that were outside the officially designated wilderness area in private hands. *Stupak-Thrall v. United States*, 70 F.3d 881 (6th Cir. 1995) (regulation was within federal power, even though federal statute expressly preserved private rights; which private rights were subordinated to those of adjoining sovereigns under state precedent; and in which local sovereign's shoes the federal government was allowed to stand for purposes of asserting these rights).

Riparian water rights are also subject to a sharing of those water rights with the public. A riparian has a right to use water, rather than own water. Riparian rights are severable from the land, and thus may be transferred to those who are not riparians. In some jurisdictions, such a transfer would only be valid against the transferring riparian, and not against other riparians.

Under the modern riparian system, the right to use water for either *consumptive* or *nonconsumptive* purposes must be reasonable. If the water is returned to the stream, the use is considered *nonconsumptive*. Nonconsumptive uses include fishing, boating, swimming, and turning turbines for hydroelectric power. However, if the water is consumed, incorporated into a product, or lost to evaporation, then the use is *consumptive*. Examples of consumptive uses are irrigation, the watering of livestock, and drinking.

Both consumptive and nonconsumptive uses are subject to the same legal test of *reasonableness*.

Water may be diverted and impounded for a period of time. Subsequently, the water may be either returned to the stream after undergoing some sort of nonconsumptive use or lost as a result of a consumptive use. The right to impound water also is limited by the reasonableness standard. The amount of water, period of impoundment, and the time and manner of discharge or return to the stream must be reasonable.

Some uses of riparian water are given preference over others. A preference is given to withdrawals for *domestic* purposes. Pollution and waste of water are considered unreasonable. Uses determined to be nuisances are also unreasonable. Use by a nonriparian may be enjoined as unreasonable. Through the balancing of these various factors, riparians may use waters reasonably, and they are protected against unreasonable uses by other riparians. We will see some examples of reasonableness (and its absence) in the Examples and Explanations.

During a water shortage, riparian owners would all suffer the loss of water more or less equally because each would be required to reduce water use in a reasonable manner. In the event of conflicts, the courts look at the reasonableness of each riparian's use and make a factual determination over which use is more reasonable. The use and suitability of that use is analyzed, as well as its social or economic value and the extent of harm caused to others by that use, in deciding how to ration riparian water uses.

This system is inherently flexible and allows judicial imposition of reasonableness standards. Conflicts between old and new uses are decided by the courts. In theory, new uses may replace less reasonable old ones. Ultimately, this system is designed to provide greater social, economic, and environmental protection by reallocating water rights to the most reasonable use over time. Although this flexibility exists, very few cases have reallocated water rights without requiring some form of monetary compensation.

The Effect of Non-Use and Prescription

The riparian need not actually use the water or exercise his or her rights in order to sustain those rights. Like other property rights, however, unexercised riparian rights may be lost under prescriptive theories if another party has made use of the water for a specific period of time in a manner inconsistent with the rights of a riparian. In effect, prescription creates an easement, or right to use the water, in the *user* to the exclusion of the riparian. The party asserting prescriptive rights may or may not be another riparian.

Example

1. Through the state of Anarchy runs the natural but tormented Angst River. The river is used by barges owned by Madonna in the course of carrying Ping-Pong balls in interstate commerce. The barges require a minimum depth of four feet of water for safe travel. Along the Angst River are located a number of properties. On the eastern bank of the river, George owns a tract to the north, and Paul to the south. On the western bank of the river, the property is owned by Ringo.

   George owns an old mill on his property that still has a waterwheel that had once powered its now defunct operations. George has since built a nightclub called the Liverpool Club on land next to the old mill, and he uses small amounts of water from the river to make ice for drinks.

   Paul wants to build a concrete pier so he can moor his boat, the S.S. *Yesterday*, on the river next to his private residence. The pier will extend some 100 feet into the river, which has a maximum width at this point of 250 feet. Paul also uses the river for his freshwater supply for his home. Only a small amount of water is used for drinking.

   Ringo is about to operate a huge kumquat farm on his property. His daily intake of water to irrigate his kumquat crop will reduce the level of the river from a normal depth of eight feet to a maximum depth of three feet at this point.

   Elvis turns up — why not, he's everywhere. He has entered into a lease agreement with George whereby he will convert the old mill into a power plant. In the lease agreement, George has conveyed to Elvis the right to use the river to turn the turbines in the proposed hydroelectric plant. Elvis plans either (1) to withdraw water at a rate of 500,000 gallons per day from the river to produce steam, or (2) to turn hydroelectric turbines by using the gravity of falling water before returning all water to the river. About one-third of this water would be consumed and not returned to the river under option (1) above.

   All parties wish to prevent Michael from sailing his yacht, the S.S. *Thriller*, in this part of the river and from swimming in "their" river. Their basis for opposing Michael's plans is "creative differences."

   The state of Anarchy employs the reasonable use rule of riparian common law to determine water rights and uses. How would this affect each of the parties below in the event of a dispute among them or a claim by downstream users? Advise:
   a. Paul
   b. Ringo
   c. Elvis

    d. Madonna
    e. Michael
    f. George

Explanations

1. Welcome to Angst! Let's set out the basic rights of the various parties. Exhibit 7.4 sketches the basic configuration. First, categorize the water body. The Angst River is a natural *surface* river and therefore subject to riparian law. Further, it is a *navigable* river and subject to the implied (1) navigation "servitude" and (2) public use. The riparian rights of the parties flow from their land ownership and river uses. George, Paul, and Ringo all are riparian owners with riparian rights. Elvis is not an owner, but he may have riparian rights as a tenant. Madonna is not a riparian (people have said worse!), but she has a right to use the river for commerce according to the implied *navigation servitude*. The same can be said for Michael, despite the creative differences. Let's look at each party's rights.

7.4   Parties Using the Angst River

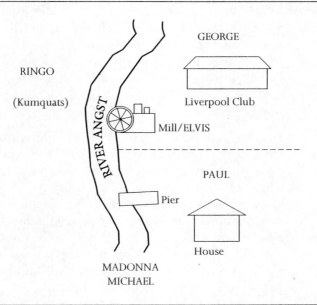

7. Rights to Use Water

1a. *Paul.* Paul's planned pier construction will be disallowed for several reasons. As part of the analysis, first categorize his use, and then look at riparian rights and implied public rights. Although boating and building accessory wharves are usually considered allowable recreational uses by a riparian, there is a rule of reasonableness. The proposed pier far exceeds the limits of reasonableness in terms of size. The pier would protrude into the river by 40 percent of the river's width and would potentially cause stream flow problems and water level problems to downstream riparian users. Furthermore, the planned pier would interfere with the navigation "servitude," or use, which takes precedence. The pier could be enjoined on that basis. As a final matter, the pier presumably would be constructed on piers sunk into the streambed owned by the state. To build on state property could constitute a trespass without permission, and the pier could be disallowed on that ground. Paul's pier may also be a nuisance and may be prevented as such. Result: A pier may be possible, but this pier is not reasonable and cannot be allowed as of riparian right. Paul's domestic uses of water are allowed, in reasonable quantities, as a riparian right.

1b. *Ringo.* Ringo's irrigation of his kumquat farm may be an allowable use of the Angst's waters. It is a traditional agricultural use and may be considered reasonable in concept. Note that it is a *consumptive* use. However, the *amount* of the daily consumption would render this use unreasonable. First, the amount of water withdrawn would affect downstream riparians' ability (including that of Elvis to construct his hydroelectric facility) to use the river current free from unreasonable interference. The amount of water consumed by Ringo's farm takes too much away from downstream users. Ringo's withdrawals would also substantially interfere with the navigation servitude, as barges could not use the river because it would be too shallow to permit passage. Irrigation would be disallowed as proposed, in these quantities. In theory, Ringo is entitled to *some* consumptive use.

1c. *Elvis.* The transfer of riparian rights from the riparian, George, to his tenant and licensee, Elvis, is allowed in the hydroelectric option. That transfer, in fact, is only for the *nonconsumptive* purpose of turning Elvis's water turbines. A hydroelectric facility diverts water from the river system, but then returns it. Elvis may not, however, use the conveyed nonconsumptive right in order to make *consumptive* withdrawals for a thermal steam turbine. (See Chapter 12 for a discussion of energy law and technologies.) The change in energy technology from hydroelectric to steam turbine changes the nature of the water use to one that is partially consumptive. Given that some discharge water would be returned and some lost to a steam turbine evaporation, the use must be reasonable on balance and the amount of the daily withdrawal must not interfere with the stream flow. Had *all* riparian rights been transferred to Elvis, the withdrawal of 500,000 gallons per day may have been reasonable for consumptive purposes for a steam turbine. If the transfer was for nonconsumptive purposes for hydroelectric power, there should be no problem if there is no reasonable interference with the river.

1d/e. *Madonna/Michael*. George, Paul, and Ringo may not prevent Michael from boating on the river. The implied navigation servitude applies. Because the river is navigable, public rights attach, and they are superior to riparian rights. Therefore, public boating and recreation are allowed, and private riparians may not enjoin or interfere with such use. Navigation rights for Madonna, although she is not a riparian, also are protected.

1f. *Domestic uses*. The only other stated uses allowed by the given facts seem to be George's icemaking and Paul's domestic consumption. Reasonable domestic uses are allowed. The other uses may be allowable if they are smaller in scale and not unreasonable under the circumstances.

The System of Prior Appropriation: First in Time

In the United States, the common law of prior appropriation was adopted and developed in the arid and semiarid western states. Evolved appropriation common law now forms the basis for administrative permitting systems employed by a large number of states across the country.

Under the prior appropriation doctrine, water rights do not stem from the ownership of land that abuts a waterway. Instead, prior appropriation law bases water use rights on *previous* withdrawals from a water supply. In essence, one is allowed to use presently what one used in the past, and one also has the future right to consume the same amount of water. The policy underlying the appropriation system is meant to ensure that limited water supplies are beneficially and efficiently used. But it also invests prior takers/exploiters with a right to use an increasingly valuable natural resource.

Development of Prior Appropriation

Miners and other water users in the public domain in the West were originally considered trespassers, unless they had obtained a federal patent. Naturally, water disputes arose even among trespassers. The rule that emerged was that the first trespasser had greater or priority rights against all subsequent trespassers. The rule of *first in time, first in right* formed the basis of the common law prior appropriation doctrine. The trespasser's rights, however, were still subordinate to federal authority.

7. Rights to Use Water

In 1935 the Supreme Court decided, in *California Oregon Power Co. v. Portland Beaver Cement Co.*, 295 U.S. 142 (1985), that the acts of 1866 and 1870, together with the Desert Land Act of 1877, severed water from the public domain. As a result, the federal government had relinquished all sovereignty over waters in the West, except in limited cases. After *California Oregon Power*, states were completely free to choose their water rights system, and many chose prior appropriation.

Because prior appropriation rights do not follow the ownership of property located along a waterway, like riparian rights, they may be acquired by anyone, and at any location. Parties may acquire the right to take and use a specific quantity from a water supply that they put to beneficial use. Some appropriators, like riparians, may transfer their rights to others. Once a party has established his or her right to extract a certain amount of water, he or she has rights *senior* to subsequent appropriators. This system of seniority rights is referred to as a priority system.

In an appropriation system, there exists no duty to share water with other potential users, unless they have priority. Because an appropriative right is an exclusive right, a senior appropriator can enjoin use by a junior user if the latter's appropriation infringes on the senior's ability to obtain his or her full amount of allotted water. In some circumstances exceptions to this rule are made, such as during periods of water shortage or by state-mandated action.

Obtaining Priority Rights: Appropriation

Parties wishing to appropriate from a water source must meet three criteria. First, a potential user must give *notice* of intent to appropriate water. Second, the party must make an actual *diversion* of the water. Third, the party must apply the water to *beneficial use*. When these conditions are met, an appropriator has "perfected" his or her right to extract water and has rights and liabilities according to the priority system of senior and junior rights. Where water is unavailable for further extraction, a senior appropriator may prevent a junior appropriator from diverting and using water. Let's examine the three necessary criteria.

Notice of Intent to Appropriate   Today, with the exception of Colorado, all states enforce priority rights through state administrative agencies. In states with administrative permitting agencies, notice of intent to appropriate is given when an application to withdraw is filed with the agency. Permit systems or Colorado's common law system require that the potential appropriator must indicate the location of the water supply. After an appropriator gives notice of intent to appropriate, he or she must next divert the water within a reasonable amount of time or lose the appropriative right.

7. Rights to Use Water

Diversion   Water is diverted when it is physically removed from its source. Diversion may occur when water is controlled in its natural course by artificial means, also known as an in-stream diversion. *Instream diversions* may be represented legally by simple stream flow or water level requirements. Exercising exclusive right to water where access to it is over public lands may involve statutes that allow a right-of-way for water ditches to transport the water to the place where it will be used. When access to a water supply requires a trespass onto privately owned land, a necessary easement must be granted.

Interestingly, the amount claimed *on paper* by senior appropriators may fully appropriate or even exceed the actual volume of water in a watershed. However, the amount *actually* diverted and put to beneficial use may be much less than the amount claimed by seniors. Because an appropriator's rights extend only to the amount put to *actual* use, a new appropriator may in some states be allowed to withdraw water if he or she can show that water is physically available. This dichotomy between claimed and actually diverted water is critical. Other states, however, rely strictly on the amounts claimed on paper by senior appropriators and will not allow further appropriations if a water body appears on paper to be fully appropriated.

Beneficial Use   In an effort to curb speculation and waste, the law requires an appropriator to put the diverted water to a specific beneficial use in order to perfect the right. Beneficial uses include domestic or municipal use, irrigation, stock watering, mining, power generation, recreation, fish and wildlife maintenance, and instream flow or water level protection. Wasting water is not a beneficial use. Either a *community custom* standard or an *efficient use* standard is used to determine whether a use is wasteful. When a use is determined to be wasteful or for a nonbeneficial purpose, the appropriation may be enjoined.

Instead of diverting water for immediate use, an appropriator may appropriate water and impound it. Water may be stored in off-stream ponds or reservoirs, or it may be kept behind in-stream dams. The storage of water is not a *per se* beneficial use unless the stored water is to be applied later to a beneficial use. Among other purposes, water may be stored for future irrigation or flood control. The appropriation still must meet the requirements of notice, diversion, and beneficial use.

The right to store water is a valuable asset in times of water shortages. Storage may provide an abundant water supply to an appropriator when other water sources are low. To capitalize on stored water in the hands of appropriators during shortage, some states have implemented *water banking* systems. A water banking system requires an appropriator to release a quantity of stored water or to forgo further appropriations in exchange for remuneration. The freed water is then distributed to users where water resources are scarce.

An appropriator who stores water may be strictly liable for damage caused by flooding as a result of inadequate impoundment. If an appropriator releases water from a reservoir into a stream, the amount released must not exceed the capacity of the stream. If a stream flow fluctuates, an appropriator releasing water into that stream has a duty to monitor the stream flow and adjust discharge amounts accordingly to prevent downstream flooding.

Water That May Be Appropriated

Surface Waters Surface waters, including streams and lakes, are subject to appropriation. Diffused surface waters are *not* subject to appropriation. Water may be appropriated when a new appropriator is capable of showing that water unappropriated by senior takers is physically available. Water availability in a stream or lake is a measure of the amount of water in a normal water year less the amount already claimed by senior appropriators. If a surplus exists, then water may be extracted by new (junior) appropriators.

Saved Water The amount of water unused by an appropriator because of the appropriator's use of conservation practices is *saved water*. Put another way, if an appropriator employs more efficient ways to put the water to beneficial use than he or she previously did, then the decrease in the amount of water used is *saved water*. In some jurisdictions, the saved water is not subject to appropriation by others, and the appropriator who "saved" the water has a right to the whole or partial amount of saved water. Other jurisdictions do not allow the water conservator to retain use of the saved water.

Reusable Water Water previously appropriated, put to use, and released as runoff may be recaptured and appropriated by others, so long as the runoff is in the tributary of a natural rather than human-made stream. Runoff that forms a tributary of a natural stream is called *return flow*; otherwise it is considered *seepage*. Return flow may be appropriated. The doctrine of return flow appropriation allows parties to appropriate the runoff from another party's land. If the water is considered *seepage*, the original user may reclaim the water and use it again. Once runoff has reached a natural stream, it is subject to appropriation by others.

Springs and Developed Water Springwater that originates and remains on the land where it originated is *not* subject to appropriation by others. Springs that are tributaries to natural streams *are* subject to appropriation. Water added to a natural stream that would not normally have become part of the stream is *developed* water. Developed water, such as water pumped from a mine, is not subject to appropriation by others. Modern law prohibits transfer of water out of a watershed area for use elsewhere. However, many transfers predating this modern doctrine continue currently. Moreover, government-sponsored water projections, subject to legislative directive, that divert public waters for irrigation or development projects are not subject to the common law doctrines.

The Transfer or Conveyance of Water Rights

Though appropriative rights do not arise from land ownership, they may be transferred incident to the sale of land. Appropriative water rights may also be transferred separately from the land. The only rights to appropriate water that may be transferred are for the amount of water put to actual *beneficial* use. This is a critical requirement.

Another limitation on the transfer of appropriative water rights involves the protection of junior return flow rights. Recall that runoff into a natural watercourse in the form of return flow may be appropriated by others. Proposed transfers of appropriative rights are not allowed to disrupt return flows. Similar to the way in which courts prevent a greater burden as a result of any assignment and delegation, they may prevent or condition water right transfers to protect a junior's right to that water.

An appropriator may lose rights to appropriate water as a result of abandonment. *Abandonment* is the intentional surrender of an appropriative right, while *forfeiture* is the loss of a right caused by failure to meet statutory requirements. Non-use alone is not abandonment. Proof must be presented showing an *intent* to abandon and an *act* of abandonment.

For forfeiture, by contrast, intent to abandon or forfeit need not be shown. Instead, noncompliance with statutes or regulations may be proven. Noncompliance generally involves non-use for a period of time — in many states, for five years. Non-use of water because of unavailability, as during a drought, does not rise to the level of abandonment or forfeiture. As appropriative rights may not be gained through prescription, those same rights may not be lost as a result of prescription.

Dual System States

Although the western states adopted the prior appropriation doctrine as a basis of water use law, in several of those states some riparian rights coexist with appropriative rights. How can this work? Conflicts between a riparian and an appropriator are resolved by converting riparian rights into appropriative ones. Similarly in many states, in both the East and West, administrative permitting schemes replace riparian common law systems. These transform riparian rights into appropriation rights, with appropriative priority relating back to the time of transformation. Only riparian rights that have been *exercised* are transformed into appropriative rights; recall that strictly traditional riparian rights usually do not need to be exercised to be retained. The idea of converting riparian rights into appropriative rights and the idea that those riparian rights must have been *exercised* are both important concepts.

Administrative Permit Systems

Administrative permit systems for water withdrawals and use are merely a codification and modification of the common law of prior appropriation. With the exception of Colorado, all western states have adopted administrative permitting systems. Many humid states also have adopted these systems. Administrative permit systems place the management of water resources in the hands of regulatory agencies. Often the administrative systems regulate both surface and groundwater uses under a system that follows a comprehensive state water resource management plan.

Under these administrative systems, an applicant must file an application for a water withdrawal permit with the regulating state agency. During the review process, the applicant must give notice of the proposed diversion to other rightsholders who may be affected by the new withdrawal, and a public comment period ensues. The application and comments are then reviewed by the permitting agency, and a permit may issue. The right to appropriate is *perfected* upon the permittee actually putting the *diverted* water to *beneficial* use. Note again these key concepts.

The agency may impose certain conditions based on environmental concerns, such as fish and wildlife protection, maintenance of stream flows and water levels, and pollution control. The public trust concept may also be used to limit the issuance of permits that would conflict with public trust purposes. If conflicting water uses arise, the state agency decides which use has precedence.

An examination of the Massachusetts Water Management Act is illustrative. M.G.L. c. 21G; 310 CMR 36. This 1985 statute enacts a comprehensive system for water management and withdrawals of water from groundwater or surface water to protect safe yields. The Act regulates water withdrawals in excess of 100,000 gallons per day (gpd). The Department of Environmental Protection also protects special watershed areas. The state DEP is given the authority to raise or lower this threshold upon a finding that such change is necessary to protect the public health, safety, and welfare.

There are two ways to withdraw water in excess of this threshold. One is to register a preexisting withdrawal; the second is to obtain a permit for any new withdrawal. Existing withdrawals of greater than 100,000 gpd prior to enactment of the statute can be registered with the agency. A baseline is determined looking at actual withdrawals during the five years prior to 1986.

Registrants are required to install flow meters to measure future withdrawals, maintain information on usage, verify any estimated withdrawals for the period 1981-1985, and submit additional historical water use data. All withdrawals of quantities in excess of 100,000 gpd had to be registered prior to 1988. Registrations gave a registrant the right to that water for a period of ten years. Renewals could be effected after ten years. Failure to register in a timely manner resulted in one not being able to grandfather an existing withdrawal. After this time, an existing use would have to register for a new permit as a new use. The department may attach to any permit conditions it deems necessary to further the purposes of this statute or to assure compliance with its regulations.

A new permit is valid for a period of 20 years from the effective date for a particular river basin. Therefore, the actual permit may be for a period of less than 20 years, depending upon the effective date for the region. In evaluating a permit application, the agency considers a variety of factors, including safe yield from the water source, long-term effect, land values, the use to be made of the water, reasonable conservation practices and measures, protection of public drinking water supplies, groundwater recharge, wastewater treatment, and hydropower resources.

"Preexisting users" are grandfathered: Instead of applying for a permit, they only file an annual registration statement to continue existing withdrawals for 10 years. The system tries to encourage communities to hold residential water use to 65 gallons per capita per day. State water regulation was unsuccessfully challenged as a "taking." *Molla et al. v. The Town of Franklin*, 7 Mass L.Rptr. 480 (Ma. 1997)(depriving a property owner of profit is not an unconstitutional taking; quoting *MacGibbon v. Board of Appeals of Duxbury*, 369 Mass. 512, 340 N.E.2d at 487).

There is an exemption for nonconsumptive uses. Where water is returned at or near the withdrawal point, in essentially unimpaired quality and quantity, it is determined to be a nonconsumptive use. These would typically include saltwater withdrawals, noncontact cooling water requirements, and use of hydropower resources. Generally, riparian systems did not allow the alienation of water rights from the riparian land. The Massachusetts system allows for the transfer of water rights.

In Massachusetts, approximately 1,200 individual entities have withdrawal permits. A large number of these are municipalities serving as water supply entities and agricultural uses (primarily cranberry bogs). Types of violations fall into the categories of willful failure to comply, violation of specific conditions on withdrawal permits, or failure to file required annual reports.

Constitutional Issues

The loss of property rights caused by state action raises constitutional questions of police powers, property takings, and due process.

Police Powers and Public Trust Doctrine   Courts allow a state to change from riparian rights to an appropriation system because of the state's right to exercise *police powers* — so long as the state action is rationally related to the protection or enhancement of the public's environmental health, safety, and welfare. States also have used the public trust doctrine to justify the change to an appropriative system of water management. The *public trust doctrine* does not create a legal trust, but it is a way to justify state action. The public trust theory declares that the water resources in a state are held in trust by the state for the use and enjoyment of the public. Because the state acts as trustee, it has the power to manage the trust *res* in a manner consistent with the public trust purposes of navigation, commerce, fishing, recreation, and so on.

Property Takings and Due Process   When a state converts exercised riparian rights to appropriative rights, the resulting loss of future, unexercised riparian rights raises issues of property taking by the government. Because the riparian rights are merely usufructuary and not possessory, courts have held that the riparian owner had a *diminished expectation* in those property rights. State interference in the exercise of those rights can be more readily justified than if the rights were possessory. The state appropriative schemes provide for the protection of *exercised* rights, so only an indeterminate amount of unexercised future rights are lost. In sum, courts reason that the owner of riparian rights suffers only a de minimis loss of rights. Since the rightholder's loss did not rise to the level of a substantial interference with his or her property rights, no taking occurred. For more discussion of "takings," see Chapters 10, 11, and 13.

Due process requirements are satisfied when a state gives (a) *adequate notice of the conversion of rights* to riparians, and (b) a sufficient or reasonable time period after that notice to exercise rights before vesting. Courts have held that five years is sufficient time to allow a riparian to exercise rights so as to determine the extent of his or her new appropriative rights.

Accretion occurs when sand builds up gradually on the beach over time, causing the adjacent property owner to gain land. The opposite of accretion is *reliction*, where sand is gradually removed from the beach, causing the adjacent property owner to lose land. *Avulsion* is the sudden loss or gain of sand which will not affect the adjacent property owner's rights. When sudden events or avulsions add land, the boundary between private and public land remains the high-water line, and any future accretions on the water side of that line belong to the state, not the beachfront owner. Maine is the only state that unconditionally guarantees littoral property owners common law rights of accretion and reliction.

The definition of the beachfront, or *littoral*, property line differs from state to state. Most states use the historic mean high-tide line. However, a few East Coast states use the historic mean low-tide line. Massachusetts is one of only five states (Delaware, Maine, Massachusetts, New Hampshire, and Virginia) that give private land title to the mean low-water mark. All other states give littoral owners title to the mean high-water mark. The states' boundaries extend from the line of the littoral owner (either high or low water line) to three miles offshore. 43 U.S.C.A. §1301.

There is no littoral right to contact with the water independent of the littoral right of access. The Supreme Court unanimously held that a state's decision to restore an eroded beach by filling in submerged land did not engage in an unconstitutional taking of beachfront property owners' property rights. *Stop the Beach Renourishment, Inc. v. Fla. Dep't of Envtl. Prot., et al.*, 130 S. Ct. 2592, (2010).

Example

1. Here's a challenging water rights problem that applies what we've just covered. As you work through the narrative, sketch the key dates, permitted withdrawals, and actual withdrawals in order to answer the questions.

   Melville owns a tract of property along the River of Discontent; the property historically had riparian rights. Melville has consumed an average of 1 million gallons of water per year from the river for more than 20 years for his small but profitable dandelion farm. He also conducts whale watching tours. In January 1989 the state passed well-publicized legislation converting all riparian rights into appropriative rights, administered by the state Water Agency. The state had already adopted an administrative permitting program a century before and was now just integrating riparian rights into the administrative scheme.

   The statute converting riparian rights into appropriative rights set forth a prospective six-year period during which consumptive water withdrawals by riparians were to be measured. At the end of the six-year period, the riparians were to be issued consumptive withdrawal permits in an amount equal to the average yearly withdrawal of each riparian over the six-year period. On July 1, 1996, Melville applied for and was issued a permit to withdraw 1 million gallons of water per year from the river. To this day, Melville still consumes 1 million gallons of water per year from the river.

However, Melville wants to expand his farming and consume 2 million gallons of water per year from the River of Discontent. Melville is unhappy that he has a permit to withdraw only 1 million gallons per year. He believes that he was shortchanged in the permitting process because in 1994 he told state officials of his expansion plans.

Dickens had received the right to appropriate 500,000 gallons of water per year from the same river for his chinchilla ranching activities, according to the deed and permit that he had received from Chaucer, the prior owner of the property. Dickens's ranch is known as Bleak House. Chaucer had used only 350,000 gallons of water per year before he conveyed the rights to Dickens. The date on Chaucer's water withdrawal permit for 500,000 gallons per year was August 2, 1934. The date that Dickens received the deed and permit from Chaucer was September 12, 1978. Since then, Dickens has used 350,000 gallons of water per year for his chinchilla ranch, but now wants to use 475,000 gallons of water per year for the ranch.

De Beauvoir produces Onion Patch Dolls. She filed an application with the Water Agency on July 2, 1996, and the next day received a permit to withdraw 500,000 gallons per year from the river. On July 12, 1996, she diverted water from the river and put 400,000 gallons of water to beneficial use in her onion patch in the year following.

Jong filed an application for a withdrawal permit with the Water Agency on July 3, 1996, and on July 9 received a permit to withdraw 600,000 gallons of water per year from the river. Jong operates a virtual airport for those with a fear of flying. Jong began diverting water from the river on July 11, 1996, to put to beneficial use at a rate of 100,000 gallons per year.

Finally, Capone never filed an application but began withdrawing water at a rate of 50,000 gallons per year from the river. Permits never were his thing.

After sketching out the key dates, amounts of water (both permitted and actual), and types of use, apply your knowledge to the following Examples:

a. Was the conversion of Melville's riparian rights legally allowable? Why or why not? What about his concerns of being shortchanged on quantity?

b. What is the priority of appropriations (senior to most junior and amount of water) among the five parties? In what volumes are they entitled to appropriate?

c. Assuming that a normal water year for the river is a total of 2.8 million gallons, how much water is available for appropriation based on paper rights? How much is available in physical actuality based on perfected rights?

d. Assuming that the total stream volume next year is only 2 million gallons, whose senior appropriations will be met, in what order or priority, and to what extent?

Explanations

1a. To answer this, you need to organize the dates and volumes. You must also recognize that we are now in the province of appropriative systems. The issue involves conversion of rights, police power, and "takings." Yes, the conversion to appropriative rights was legal and allowable. Look first at the state's interest. A permitting system had long existed in the state. The transition was well publicized. Due process is followed. The statute protects *exercised* riparian rights. The notice requirement has been met, and the measuring period is longer than five years and will be deemed adequate. The state validly exercised its police powers when it implemented the conversion law. There was no "taking."

Next, look at the individual rights. Melville had limited expectations in his riparian rights because they were usufructuary only. They were not possessory. The state action therefore did not constitute a "taking," because the intrusion was not substantial under the circumstances; it merely conditioned Melville's property rights and did not extinguish them. Unfortunately for Melville, his expansion plans were not realized, and he never *exercised* his riparian right to withdraw 2 million gallons of water before the conversion. He was not, under the law, shortchanged. He received the 1-million-gallon withdrawal right as a result of *his actual exercised* rights. Melville was entitled to no more than the 1 million gallons because, at the time of conversion, he had not given notice, diverted, or beneficially used any more. These three criteria must be satisfied.

1b. Here we need to distinguish *paper* versus *perfected* rights. The priority of *paper* appropriations plays out by earliest date of entitlement, as follows:

1. Dickens, August 2, 1934, for the amount of 500,000 gallons per year. Dickens assumes Chaucer's original legacy to priority and amount as of the date of Chaucer's vested entitlement (1934), not the date of the transfer (1978). The original vesting controls; the transfer does not extinguish the original right.

2. Melville, July 1, 1996, for the amount of 1 million gallons per year. The date of the permit application controls.

3. De Beauvoir, July 2, 1996, for the amount of 500,000 gallons per year. The permit application date controls.

327

     4. Jong, July 3, 1996, for the amount of 600,000 gallons per year.

     5. Capone has no enforceable rights as he cannot obtain appropriative rights through prescription. However, duck if you hear gunshots.

     Next, look at the *perfected* rights that control the shares. It is perfected rights that determine senior and junior rights. The priority of appropriations for *actual beneficial diversions* is:

1. Dickens, 350,000 gallons per year because he received the right to only that amount from Chaucer, who actually appropriated that much before conveying the rights to Dickens. The effective date is 1934. Chaucer could not convey a larger entitlement than he had perfected by actual use. This illustrates the "use it or lose it" nature of these rights. Dickens's expansion plans go to the end of the line as a new junior user in the order of his application.

2. Melville, as of July 1, 1996, perfects 1 million gallons per year. He also goes to the end of the line for additional appropriations as a junior user.

3. Jong, 100,000 gallons per year were perfected as of July 11.

4. De Beauvoir, 400,000 gallons per year were perfected as of July 12 when she diverted and beneficially used the water.

1c. During a normal water year, when the total stream flow is 2.8 million gallons, on *paper* there remain 200,000 gallons of water per year available for appropriation. In reality, based on perfected rights, 950,000 gallons of water are available for appropriation (because only 1,850,000 gallons were perfected). A first-in-time rule will apply to any additional filings for rights by Melville, Dickens, or other parties seeking additional beneficial uses as new junior appropriators.

1d. In a year when total stream flow is only 2 million gallons, on *paper* Dickens would receive 500,000 gallons, Melville would receive 1 million gallons, de Beauvoir would receive 500,000 gallons, and Jong would receive 0 gallons, there being none left. In reality, because not all interests are perfected, Dickens would get 350,000 gallons, as the senior interest, Melville would get 1 million gallons, Jong would get 100,000 gallons and de Beauvoir would get 400,000 gallons. In all events, Capone is entitled to none. In reality, he may be diverting or taking water — and once used, the water is gone.

GROUNDWATER ALLOCATION

In recent decades, the rate at which humans worldwide are pumping dry the vast underground stores of water, that billions depend on, has more than doubled. Groundwater represents about 30 percent of the available freshwater on the planet, with surface water accounting for only 1 percent. The rest of the potable supply is locked up in glaciers or the polar ice caps.

Groundwater, a primary source of drinking water, was discussed in detail in Chapter 6. Groundwater is also used for irrigation. One person's extensive use of groundwater can make it unavailable to others. The allocation of groundwater resources has not evolved in the same manner as surface water. Some prior appropriation jurisdictions have adopted variants of groundwater riparianism. The result has been a hodgepodge of laws controlling groundwater allocation that may or may not parallel that state's adoption of surface water allocation laws.

Riparian Rights

Where riparian rules have been applied to groundwater, two distinct doctrines have emerged. The first rule is the *English* or *absolute use* rule. Under the absolute use rule, a landowner may withdraw as much underground water as desired for any use, including uses that result in waste. The only duty on the landowner is that he or she may not extract groundwater with the *intent* of causing harm to others.

In contrast, the *American* or *reasonable use* rule permits groundwater pumping for reasonable uses. No duty to share with others exists so long as the use is reasonable. Only the reasonableness of the use is examined, and effects on others' uses are not considered. The water must be used on the land overlying the water source; that is, the groundwater may not be extracted and then transported elsewhere for use. This means that a tenant could use the water, but an off-site consignee could not. Use on overlying land is thus considered reasonable, but the use of groundwater on non-overlying ground is *per se* unreasonable.

Under both the *reasonable use* and *absolute use* rules, extractors of groundwater may withdraw water without much regard to other groundwater users. For example, under both rules, groundwater users may sink deep wells and withdraw large volumes of water, causing underground water levels to recede. This phenomenon is called drawdown. Because the water supply has been drawn down to a lower level as a result of deep wells, other users may not have access to the groundwater without digging or drilling deeper wells at great expense. Since no duty to share with others exists under the riparian rules, a groundwater extractor may draw down subterranean water levels without liability.

The Texas Supreme Court held that ownership of land includes a property interest in the underlying groundwater "in place" and that such a right cannot be taken through state action without adequate compensation. *Edwards Aquifer Auth. v. McDaniel*, 55 Tex. Sup. J. 343 (Tex. 2012). The Rule of Capture for groundwater resources allows landowners to withdraw groundwater from beneath their land regardless of any impact pumping may have on neighboring landowners or other hydraulically related waters. *Sipriano v. Great Spring Waters of Am., Inc.*, 1 S.W.3d 75, 76 (Tex. 1999). Few other states follow this absolute dominion rule which allows absolute right to subsurface rights from ownership of the surface land. Liability for this activity does not attach unless it intends to harm a neighboring landowner, results in the waste of water, or negligently causes subsidence of neighboring properties. *Id.* An overlying landowner owns the underlying groundwater "in place," even prior to capture through pumping, similar to the Texas law on oil and gas:

> To differentiate between groundwater and oil and gas in terms of importance to modern life would be difficult. Drinking water is essential for life, but fuel for heat and power, at least in this society, is also indispensable. Again, the issue is not whether there are important differences between groundwater and hydrocarbons; there certainly are. But we see no basis in these differences to conclude that the common law allows ownership of oil and gas in place but not groundwater.

This compromises both the states' and local governments' ability to manage groundwater resources. Courts elsewhere have held that certain governmental limitations restricting water rights can be a taking of private property without just compensation, rendering water rights property rights, rather than usufructuary rights to use. *Casitas Municipal Water District v. United States*, 543 F.3d 1276 (Fed. Cir. 2008), rehearing denied, 556 F.3d 1329 (2009).

Prior Appropriation Rights

The law of prior appropriation has also been applied to groundwater extractions. Appropriations of groundwater are permitted when a determination is made that underground water is available for use. Furthermore, prior appropriation law has been applied to curtail pumping and encourage conservation of water resources.

The priority concept has been followed to protect the rights of senior users. Unlike riparian groundwater law, prior appropriation systems protect a user's *right to lift*. As water is drawn down, it becomes more difficult to extract that water at deeper levels. The prior appropriation rule requires that junior appropriators limit their withdrawals so as to maintain the water table at a reasonable level — a level from which the water may be lifted by senior appropriators through reasonable means. The senior appropriator cannot demand that the water levels after use by juniors remain at a level where he can pump water in a manner most convenient, but only in a *reasonable* manner at reasonable cost.

For irrigation or processing industries, groundwater is mined as any other mineral may be mined, until depletion of the resource. Ironically, the prior appropriation system, which purports to conserve water, allows groundwater mining. The drawdown of water caused by water mining is not considered a violation of another's right to lift. Prior appropriation law has been modified so that other appropriators no longer have the right to certain volumes of water in the future.

FEDERAL AND TRIBAL RIGHTS

The discussion up to now has focused on *state* common law and administrative law. Federal jurisdiction also arises, under the commerce clause of the Constitution. Because navigable waterways facilitate interstate commerce, the federal government has jurisdiction to exercise control over those waterways. This is the basis for the Clean Water Act, analyzed in Chapter 6. The federal government may regulate uses of navigable waterways and make improvements to the same. This power gives rise to the navigation "servitude" that allows for public navigation of waterways without interference from private persons or states. Where the navigation servitude interferes with private parties, no "taking" occurs because private parties have no property rights in the streambeds of navigable waterways, and only limited usufructuary property rights, subject to the navigation servitude, in the water.

The supremacy clause of the Constitution also enables the federal government to exercise control over navigable waterways. Where state law is in direct conflict with federal law, federal law preempts state law. The federal government has shown deference to state laws, however, by incorporating some state policies into the federal permitting scheme. The Clean Water Act takes into consideration state standards regarding stream flows, water quality, and other state limitations, as well as the federal standards set forth by statute. The Federal Energy Regulatory Commission (FERC) hydroelectric licensing requirements also incorporate state standards (see Chapter 12).

The federal government also has jurisdiction over Native American water rights. Native American reservations have water rights in streams within their boundaries, running alongside the reservation, and in groundwater. Because Native American reservation water rights arise from treaties with the federal government, those rights are superior to state-granted riparian or appropriative rights. Native American water rights are limited to the amount of water needed to meet the needs of the reservation. That amount is measured in the amount potentially needed to meet the needs of the reservation, not the amount in actual use. Native American reservation water rights may be transferred to non-Native Americans only upon tribal and congressional approval.

When disputes arise between and among states regarding water rights, federal courts use the equitable apportionment method to resolve them. Courts examine reasonable and efficient uses as well as volumes of prior appropriations to determine allocation of water resources among states.

If a dispute arises between two states that have adopted prior appropriation law, the water supply is split according to the priority of appropriations of both states. Therefore, the seniority systems of both states are merged and water is appropriated to satisfy senior appropriators in both states. If the dispute is between two or more riparian states, courts will allocate water to effectuate a *reasonable* stream flow to all states involved.

States have attempted to manipulate water resource allocation by preventing the export of water to other states. Because water is an item in the stream of interstate commerce, the states may not prohibit the exportation of water because of the dormant commerce clause, discussed in Chapter 4. The Supreme Court in *Sporhase v. Nebraska*, 458 U.S. 941 (1982), held that states may not obstruct the exporting of water to other states.

Example

1. Diane and Sam own a tract of land on which they have a well. Traditionally, the water has been used solely for their domestic purposes. The well pumps a large amount of water out of an underground aquifer. Now they begin to pipe the water for commercial use to Norm's Airplane Repair Shop, which is located two miles away at Jong's airport. The Repair Shop is not located on the same parcel as the aquifer. Before they started pumping for Norm, the water table was 15 feet below ground level. Now that they have started pumping for Norm, the water table has fallen to a depth of 30 feet below. Sam and Diane's neighbor, Cliff, owns a tract of land located over the same aquifer; his well goes down to a depth of 20 feet. He uses this well for all his water requirements. It would cost Cliff $20,000 to drill a well through bedrock to reach water at the new 30+ foot depth.
   a. Under a riparian scheme, what relief would be available to Cliff? What are the key distinctions and rules in state law?
   b. Assuming that the parties are located in a state that has adopted a prior appropriation system for managing its groundwater, and that Cliff had senior priority over Sam and Diane, would Cliff have any remedy?

Explanations

1a. This example applies to groundwater rights. If the state employs the absolute use rule, Cliff would have no recourse. The absolute use rule allows an overlying riparian landowner to put the water to *any* use desired, and at *any* location. Under either riparian scheme, there is no right to lift, and Sam and Diane would not be liable to Cliff for the drawn-down water level. The facts also do not indicate that Sam and Diane pumped water from the aquifer with the *intent* of causing harm to Cliff. In an absolute use state, Sam and Diane's pumping would be permitted.

   The key distinction is reasonable versus absolute use rules. Had the state utilized the reasonable use rule, Cliff could enjoin their pumping. Non-overlying uses are *per se* unreasonable. Therefore Sam and Diane would have to stop sending water from their well to Norm's Airplane Repair Shop. Again there exists no right to lift in a riparian jurisdiction, so Cliff could not limit Sam and Diane's pumping for their own uses so long as they maintained the water table at a reasonable depth.

1b. Change gears now. In a prior appropriation jurisdiction, Cliff would have a remedy against Sam and Diane under the right to lift. Cliff is the senior appropriator, and the others are the junior appropriators as to their *increased* usage for export to Norm. The junior appropriators have a duty to maintain the water level at a reasonable level. If it can be determined that a water level at a depth of 15 feet or higher is reasonable, Cliff can limit Sam and Diane's pumping to maintain that reasonable level. This is a factual question. What a difference a change in common law jurisdiction makes.

The Management of Hazardous and Solid Wastes: RCRA

"A human being: an ingenious assembly of portable plumbing."

Christopher Morley, 1932

"Fair is foul, and foul is fair: hover through the fog and filthy air."

William Shakespeare, Macbeth

"Nature is trying very hard to make us succeed, but nature does not depend on us."

R. Buckminster Fuller, 1978

"Haste Maketh Waste."

John Heywood, Proverbs, 1546

We now turn to the statutes focused on hazardous wastes and substances. The United States generates 3 million tons of electronic waste annually, comprising 1-2 percent of the municipal waste stream. With only 13.6 percent of that electronic waste recycled, it is becoming the fastest growing municipal waste stream in the United States. The United States generates approximately 250 million tons of waste annually, of which 15 percent is hazardous waste. Municipal solid waste (MSW) is trash or garbage, between 55 and 65 percent of which is residential waste; the remainder is generated by commercial and institutional entities, such as schools, hospitals, and businesses. In 2007 alone, Americans generated over 254 million tons of MSW, with half sent to landfills. The EPA estimated that approximately 1 percent of

MSW contained hazardous substance. One-tenth of 1 percent of the hazardous wastes are exported and 99 percent of these exports go to either Canada or Mexico. RCRA regulates the import and export of hazardous wastes. 42 U.S.C. §6938.

Toxic or hazardous substances are of particular concern because of their potential to contaminate soil and groundwater, as well as the significant risk even small quantities pose to human health. Their regulation therefore needs to be fail-safe. For an operating business, there are at least five federal statutes (The Emergency Planning and Community Right-to-Know Act, RCRA, The Clean Water Act, The Clean Air Act, and OSHA), as well as state statutes, that regulate the emission of hazardous and toxic materials from these businesses. Each of these five federal statutes regulates a distinct and different list of regulated toxic substances. Although the Clean Air Act, the Toxic Substances Control Act, and the Clean Water Act, as part of their charge, regulate specific acts of manufacture or deliberate discharge of toxics, there are two statutes — RCRA and CERCLA — that comprehensively control all aspects of handling hazardous wastes from their origination to their final disposal and cleanup. The Resource Conservation and Recovery Act (RCRA), the topic of this chapter, regulates the handling, transportation, storage, and disposal of hazardous waste materials. CERCLA (discussed in Chapter 9) addresses the cleanup of, and liability for, released or spilled hazardous substances.

In this chapter, we address the following key questions:

- What is a "waste"?
- What wastes are hazardous?
- What escapes RCRA regulation?
- Who is regulated by RCRA?
- Where and how may hazardous waste be disposed of?

We will examine the EPA's powers to investigate, gather information and samples, and prosecute civilly and criminally those associated with wastes that threaten humans or the environment. We will also discuss efforts by individual citizens and citizen groups to commence civil actions under RCRA.

WHAT WASTE IS REGULATED?

RCRA's Purpose and Goals

In 1976, Congress enacted the Resource Conservation and Recovery Act (RCRA), 42 U.S.C. §6901 et seq., as a cradle-to-grave tracking and management system for hazardous waste. From the moment a source generates a hazardous waste, to its final disposal at a hazardous waste site, RCRA controls the movement and handling of this waste. More specifically, RCRA regulates the ongoing generation, transportation, storage, treatment, and disposal of hazardous wastes. Congress originally enacted RCRA to foster several goals:

- Increase the safety of land disposal
- Encourage alternatives to land disposal
- Increase safety requirements
- Promote the reduction of solid wastes ←————
- Maintain state responsibility for solid waste disposal by delegating to states the responsibility of permitting solid waste facilities
- Foster recycling

In 1984, Congress amended RCRA in an attempt to phase out land disposal of toxic chemicals and force the development of improved technology to detoxify hazardous wastes. Both the 1976 RCRA and its 1984 amendments (known as the Hazardous and Solid Waste Amendments) were amendments to the Solid Waste Disposal Act as originally enacted in 1965 and amended in 1970. The EPA codified its regulations implementing RCRA at 40 C.F.R. Subchapter I, Parts 240-271. RCRA is of primary concern to industrial facilities that create waste products and to parties that dispose of or transport wastes. Although RCRA covers nonhazardous solid wastes in its subtitle D and hazardous waste in subtitle C, the former is left largely to the states. New York City imposes a fine for persons who steal recyclable materials put out for curbside collection, with a civil penalty of $100 to $2,000 for the first offense and $5,000 for repeat violations. The law also sets criminal penalties consisting of fines from $1,000 to $2,000 and imprisonment for up to 90 days. *Solid waste regulation under the Commerce Clause was covered in Chapter 4 of this book. This chapter focuses on the hazardous waste regulations at 40 C.F.R. Parts 260-271.*

Trigger One: RCRA Regulates "Wastes"

We start with *what* is regulated. The primary trigger invoking RCRA is the definition of a material as a "solid waste." Section 1003(27) of RCRA defines "solid waste" as "any garbage, refuse, sludge from a waste treatment plant, water supply treatment plant, or air pollution control facility and other discarded material including solid, liquid, semisolid or contained gaseous material resulting from industrial, commercial, mining and agricultural operations and from community activity." Note that so-called "solid" waste may be in any form, including liquid or gaseous. In other respects, this definition seems straightforward.

In *United States v. CDMG Realty Co.*, 96 F.3d 706 (3d Cir. 1996), the court found that "disposal" for purposes of RCRA §1004(3) could not logically be interpreted to encompass passive action, but rather required affirmative human action. The court held that "the gradual spreading of contamination" cannot constitute "disposal," without rendering nugatory the RCRA definitions for current owner or operator liability. The court held that it would also nullify the innocent owner defense, as there would almost never be a point where an owner could own "after disposal," because contamination would always passively be leaking and spilling indefinitely in subsurface conditions.

Although the EPA does not regulate stored raw materials, it does claim jurisdiction if the material "exits the unit," or if the storage tanks remain on the site for more than 90 days after the unit ceases operation for manufacturing. It also regulates the material if the generator of the material does not immediately recover the waste for reuse as is or recycling to a new form.

The first trigger requires that the material constitute a "waste." Through its regulations, the EPA has defined RCRA's scope broadly. The EPA first defined "discarded" to include "abandoned" or "disposed of" materials. Further, it defined "disposed of" to include material "spilled or leaked," relying on RCRA's definition of "disposal," which includes "spilling" and "leaking." Both of these terms are passive gerunds, connoting activity that may occur passively in the *absence* of an actor's intent. This is indeed a broad scope.

Recycling

RCRA does not explicitly include "recycled materials" within the statutory definition of solid waste. "Sham" recycling operations may occur when persons attempt to evade RCRA regulation by claiming to recycle, or hold for recycling, wastes that are actually of no further use or value. RCRA regulations attempt to draw a line between legitimate recycling and "sham" recycling/disposal of wastes. The EPA has deemed that certain materials do not constitute solid wastes when recycled. These materials include industrial ingredients used or reused as effective substitutes for commercial products, or returned to the original process without reclamation (purification, treatment, or alteration). In sum, discarded wastes are covered by the Act; recycled materials are not.

What about recycling waste materials? EPA has the authority to regulate any process that constitutes "treatment." 40 C.F.R. §§270.1(c), 270.2. "Treatment" includes any method, technique, or process that changes the physical, chemical, or biological character or composition of any hazardous waste, including recycling. 40 C.F.R. §260.10. EPA considers recycling to include processes that recover energy and processes that recover material. Scrap tires that are managed by established tire collection programs and used as fuel for energy production are not considered "waste." Amid complex and often ambiguous-in-practice regulations, the courts struggled with what is legitimate recycling exempt from RCRA, and what is "sham" recycling that should be regulated by Subtitle C. In *American Mining Congress v. EPA*, 824 F.2d 1177 (D.C. Cir. 1987) (*AMC I*), the court concluded that the EPA need not regulate spent materials that facilities recycle or reuse in an ongoing manufacturing or industrial process, because these materials do not represent part of the waste disposal problem. Further, the court went on to articulate key active verbs that inform what is waste: Only materials *discarded* because facilities have *disposed* of, *abandoned*, or thrown them away constitute *solid waste*. See also *Connecticut Coastal Fisherman's Ass'n v. Remington Arms Co.*, 777 F. Supp. 173 (D. Conn. 1991) (lead shot and target debris had become part of the waste disposal problem); *Ass'n of Battery Recyclers v. EPA*, 208 F.3d 1047 (D.C. Cir. 2000) (improper interpretation of "discarded" under RCRA). Under RCRA, the EPA does not possess the authority to regulate in-process materials as wastes.

The court refined its definition of "discarded materials" in *American Mining Congress v. EPA*, 907 F.2d 1179 (D.C. Cir. 1990) (*AMC II*). The court limited *AMC I*'s holding to materials that are destined for *immediate* reuse in another phase of the industry's ongoing process and that have not become part of the waste disposal problem. The *potential* later reuse of a material does not prevent the EPA from classifying it as "discarded." Therefore, once a facility discards a waste, the EPA can subject it to RCRA regulation even if the facility intends to recycle it later. The EPA now defines a solid waste as any material abandoned by being disposed of or burned — or stored, treated, or accumulated *before* or *in lieu of* those activities. Such a material constitutes a solid waste unless industry (a) directly reuses it as either an ingredient in or effective substitute for some commercial product or (b) returns the waste, unregulated, as a raw material substitute to its original manufacturing process. *United States v. Self*, 2 F.3d 1071 (10th Cir. 1993) (materials burned for energy recovery are not subject to regulation because they are recyclable); *United States v. Marine Shale Processors*, 81 F.3d 1361 (5th Cir. 1996) (finding certain recycling of contaminated soil to avoid RCRA regulation to be sham recycling); *American Petroleum Institute v. EPA*, 216 F.3d 50 (D.C. Cir. 2000) (upholding EPA regulation of certain hazardous waste accumulation).

Trigger Two: RCRA Regulates Hazardous Wastes

Once the EPA establishes that a material falls under the definition of a *solid waste*, the second regulatory trigger under RCRA is whether the solid waste also is *hazardous*. If the EPA finds a solid waste hazardous, then it regulates the substance pursuant to subtitle C.

So what is a "hazardous waste"? Section 1004 of RCRA defines "hazardous waste" as a solid, liquid, or contained gaseous waste, or combination of wastes. Unless covered by one of the exemptions, RCRA regulates a waste as "hazardous" because its quantity, concentration, or physical, chemical, or infectious characteristics "may cause or contribute to an increase in mortality, or an increase in serious irreversible or incapacitating reversible illness," or may "pose a substantial present or potential hazard to human health or the environment when improperly treated, stored, transported or disposed of, or otherwise managed."

Criteria for Identifying Regulated Hazardous Wastes

Wastes can be regulated as hazardous because the EPA has determined either that they are hazardous — so-called listed hazardous wastes — or that they exhibit one or more key hazardous characteristics. For "listed" wastes, the EPA translates the general statutory definitions into a list of specific hazardous wastes that satisfy thresholds of hazardous properties. Where does one find the list? As a practitioner, you can find the current list in the Code of Federal Regulations — it must always be checked. The EPA has codified these lists at 40 C.F.R. §261, subpart D. RCRA waste can be F wastes from common manufacturing and industrial processes, K wastes from specific industries, and P and U wastes that are commercial chemical products. An Acute Hazardous Waste is normally designated by a "P" waste.

But the EPA list does not define or include *all* hazardous wastes. Other wastes qualify as hazardous because they exhibit one or more of the specific waste characteristics EPA applies in implementing §1004(5) of subpart C of RCRA. The EPA views these wastes as "characteristic" wastes subject to RCRA. Both *listed* and *characteristic* wastes are hazardous under RCRA.

EPA must consider a waste as characteristically "hazardous" if the waste meets any one or more of the characteristics in Exhibit 8.1. The "big four" of hazardous waste characteristics are illustrated in Exhibit 8.2.

8.1 Hazardous Wastes

Characteristic	Definition
1. Ignitable	Its flash point is below 140°F.
2. Corrosive	It has a pH less than or equal to 2.0, or greater than or equal to 12.5.*
3. Reactive chemically	It causes a chemical reaction when in the presence of other elements. Reactive wastes are unstable under "normal" conditions and can cause explosions, toxic fumes, gases, or vapors when heated, compressed, or mixed with water. Examples include lithium-sulfur batteries and explosives.

4. Exhibits "TC toxicity"	When tested according to the EPA's Toxicity Characteristic Leaching Procedure (TCLP), the extract or leachate contains one or more of 39 indicator toxins listed in 40 C.F.R. §261.24, Table 1, at concentrations at or above those set forth in the table. The TCLP test replaces the Extraction Procedure (EP) test. The EPA expects application of the new test to triple the amount of waste considered hazardous under RCRA.
5. Unstable	It is chemically unstable and can change violently without detonation, will detonate if heated, reacts violently with water, or produces toxic emissions when mixed with water or when exposed to noncorrosive-pH substances.
6. Fatal to humans in low doses or has an LD-50 or LC-50	It exceeds the lowest dose or concentration at which half the tested laboratory animals exhibit effects. If the LD or LC goes below levels set forth in 40 C.F.R. §261.11, it is deemed an *acutely hazardous waste*.
7. Contains toxic constituents	It contains one or more of the toxic constituents listed in Appendix VIII to Part 261 of the regulation, and after considering enumerated factors, the EPA concludes that the material can pose substantial harm if managed improperly. Appendix VIII lists substances shown in scientific studies to have a toxic, carcinogenic, mutagenic, or teratogenic effect on humans or other life forms. These wastes are called *toxic wastes*.
8. Listed	It is a waste that the EPA listed generically by industrial classification.

---

*For a discussion of pH, see Chapter 6.

8.2 Characteristics That Identify a Waste as Hazardous

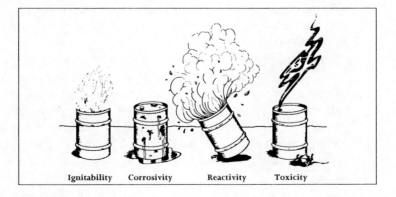

Ignitability   Corrosivity   Reactivity   Toxicity

Source: GAO, New Approach Needed to Manage the Resource Conservation and Recovery Act 18 (July 1988).

Thinking of mixing up a little waste cocktail? A listed waste does not evade RCRA's reach even if you dilute it. The EPA's mixture rule embraces mixtures of listed hazardous and nonhazardous waste. A mixture of a solid waste and a listed hazardous waste itself constitutes a hazardous waste if the hazardous component exhibits one of the RCRA subpart C *characteristics* above, unless the resulting mixture no longer exhibits any characteristic of hazardous waste identified in subpart C. Further, a mixture of solid waste and one or more hazardous wastes *listed* for reasons other than exhibiting the subpart C characteristics is *always* a hazardous waste. Therefore, dilution or mixture of hazardous and nonhazardous wastes may expand the amount of hazardous waste without taking care of any problem. Waste derived from a listed waste also is hazardous. Exhibit 8.3 summarizes these classifications.

Hazardous Wastes Regulated Under Other Statutes Are Excluded from RCRA Regulation

As a student of the law, you know by now that every statute has its exceptions. Some wastes that should be included as hazardous by virtue of their characteristics are nonetheless excluded.

Sewage   Section 1004(27) of RCRA excludes from the definition of solid waste any dissolved or solid material in domestic sewage; it also excludes industrial discharges subject to NPDES permits under §402 of the Federal Water Pollution Control (Clean Water) Act. The EPA has defined "domestic sewage" to mean untreated sanitary wastes that pass through a sewer system to a publicly owned treatment works (POTW) for treatment. The EPA's language limits the exclusion to wastes introduced into sewers intended for treatment at a POTW. See *Comite pro Rescate de la Salud v. Puerto Rico Aqueduct and Sewer Authority*, 888 F.2d 180 (1st Cir. 1989). The EPA has retained the domestic sewage exclusion because it favors regulating discharges by POTWs under the Clean Water Act. Regulation of POTWs was analyzed in Chapter 6.

As with the above sewage exclusion, the EPA intended its industrial point source discharge exclusion to prevent overlapping regulation under the Clean Water Act. Thus RCRA exempts the discharge of wastewater subject to regulation under the CWA. RCRA, however, still regulates on-site wastewater treatment or storage facilities and sludge produced by such facilities. Section 1004(27) of RCRA also excludes from the definition of solid waste any solid or dissolved materials in irrigation return flows.

8.3 RCRA Hazardous Waste Classifications

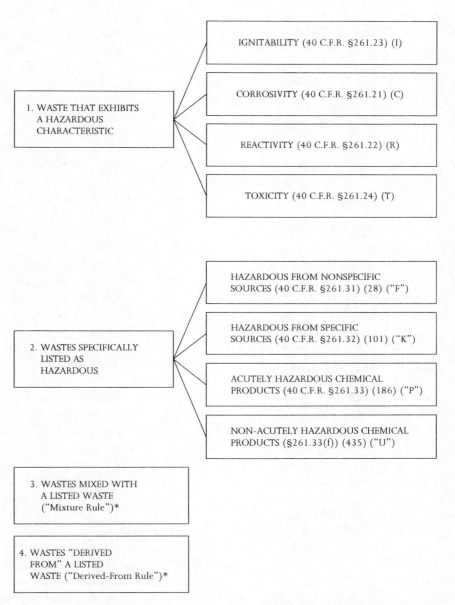

* Regulations temporarily reinstated, 57 Fed. Reg. 7628 (1992), after being invalidated on procedural grounds in *Shell Oil Co. v. EPA*, 950 F.2d 741 (D.C. Cir. 1991). Source: Robert V. Percival, *Environmental Regulation: Law, Science, and Policy* 199 (5th ed. 2003).

Nuclear Materials   RCRA excludes from its definition of solid waste any special nuclear or by-product material regulated by the Nuclear Regulatory Commission (NRC) under the Atomic Energy Act.

Energy Development   Although §1004(27) specifically includes waste from mining within the definition of solid waste, §§1006(c) and 3005(f) of RCRA require the EPA to defer to the Department of the Interior regarding coal mining wastes or so-called "overburden," because the Department of the Interior regulates such wastes under the Surface Mining Control and Reclamation Act of 1977. The EPA also excludes numerous other wastes from RCRA regulation by defining them as nonhazardous. Such materials include waste products of coal and other fossil fuel combustion including fly ash waste; bottom ash waste; flue gas emission control waste; wastes associated with the exploration, development, or production of crude oil, natural gas, or geothermal energy; and cement kiln dust waste.

Agricultural Waste   Also excluded from RCRA Subtitle C regulation are agricultural wastes returned to the soil as fertilizers and irrigation return flows. This exclusion permits the stockpiling of large amounts of waste material prior to field spreading, even though these wastes may be contaminated with pesticides. The EPA merely requires farmers to triple-rinse pesticide containers prior to disposal and to dispose of pesticide residues on their own land according to the pesticide package label's directions. Agricultural pesticides are toxic to humans at certain concentrations and can contribute to groundwater contamination (see Chapter 1).

Household Waste   The EPA has excluded other wastes despite their hazardous nature, including sludges, which are a by-product of wastewater treatment plants and some industrial processes; household wastes; and resource recovery/incinerator residues, which include household waste, hotel and motel waste, and household septic tank pumpings. Many of these exclusions are politically rather than technically motivated.

The Supreme Court in *City of Chicago v. Environmental Defense Fund*, 511 U.S. 328 (1994), expanded the scope of the EPA's regulatory control of hazardous waste under RCRA. EDF brought suit claiming that the City of Chicago's disposal of ash yielded 29 of 32 samples showing lead or cadmium levels that exceeded the minimum threshold for hazardous waste. Although RCRA §3001(i)'s exclusion for the household waste states, "A resource recovery facility recovering energy from the mass burning of municipal solid waste shall not be deemed to be treating, storing, disposing of, or otherwise managing hazardous wastes . . . ," this provision does not contain any exclusion for ash generated during incineration. Consequently, the Supreme Court concluded that while a resource recovery facility's management activities are excluded from subtitle C regulation, its generation of toxic ash is not excluded from subtitle C regulation. Therefore, the EPA regulates incinerator ash as hazardous whenever it shows the characteristics of a hazardous waste. Congress also statutorily exempted:

- Industrial wastewater discharges subject to the Clean Water Act (FWPCA)
- Mining wastes not removed from the ground
- Certain high-volume wastes that Congress directed EPA to study

Other Unregulated or Minimally Regulated Wastes

Small-Quantity Generators As with many environmental statutes, the meek and small may not inherit the earth, but they do receive different regulatory treatment.

Except for acutely hazardous waste and accumulated hazardous waste, the EPA does not include in its subtitle C regulatory program hazardous wastes that are generated by conditionally exempted small-quantity generators, which the EPA defines as a generator or less than 100 kg/mo, and that never accumulates more than 1,000 kg. Small-quantity generators can accumulate hazardous waste within the allowed limits for up to 90 or 180 days, or up to 270 days if ultimate disposal is more than 200 miles away, before actually disposing of the waste properly off-site. 40 C.F.R. §262.34(a)-(f). The EPA exempts from regulation only 1 kg/mo of *acutely* hazardous wastes, or 1,000 kg/mo of residue, soil water, or debris contaminated with *acutely* hazardous waste. It does, however, require small-quantity generators of hazardous wastes to meet certain minimal handling and disposal criteria. To the generator, the primary benefit of small-quantity generator status is exemption from the manifest system established under §3002 of RCRA (discussed later).

Energy Resources Instead of exemption because of size, certain materials just are not covered by RCRA. Exempt materials include used batteries held for regeneration, scrap metal, hazardous waste burned for energy recovery in boilers and industrial furnaces, and certain re-refined petroleum products. The EPA minimally regulates used oil by directly regulating oil recycling, without listing used oil as a hazardous waste. The court upheld the EPA's 1985 used oil regulations in *Hazardous Waste Treatment Council (II) v. EPA*, 861 F.2d 277 (D.C. Cir. 1988), *cert. denied*, 490 U.S. 1106 (1989).

Delisting Additionally, an individual can petition the EPA to exclude a waste at a particular generating facility from RCRA regulation. Such an applicant has to demonstrate that the waste produced by the facility does

345

not have any of the characteristics that ordinarily identify the waste as hazardous. The applicant also must provide an opportunity for notice and comment on its delisting petition. Similarly, an applicant may seek by petition a delisting of a waste regulated under the mixture rule. Applicants must follow the procedures set forth in 40 C.F.R. §260.22(i). Such exclusions apply *only to the specific facility* subject to the petition.

Summary   Now we know that there is a double trigger, subject to exceptions, as to what materials RCRA covers. A material must be a "solid" *waste* and it must be *hazardous*. For these covered materials, the RCRA obligations, however, are different for the different people who handle hazardous waste. These are explored after some Examples and Explanations.

Examples

1. Han Solo is the pilot of the *Millennium Falcon*, one of the fastest spaceships in the galaxy. He also operates an airport and maintenance and refueling station in the United States, on planet Earth. The Imperial EPA accuses Solo of RCRA violations for the following operations at his galactic airport. Evaluate which of the following categories of waste are and are not subject to RCRA jurisdiction and enforcement.
   a. Barrels of commercially purchased poisons for future use in pest control.
   b. Barrels of used waste oil from changing the oil in spaceships' and airplanes' internal combustion engines.
   c. Unauthorized storage of nuclear fuel for the "energizers" of space vehicles, which use the fuel to reactivate their depleted reactor propulsion systems.
   d. Overflows of sewage from the cesspool at the airport.
   e. Discharge of dirty water, created from washing airplanes that dock at the airport. This dirty water, which contains oil and grease, is discharged through an outflow pipe into a nearby river; the pipe enjoys an NPDES permit issued by the state on behalf of the EPA, pursuant to the Clean Water Act. (See Chapter 6 for a discussion of the NPDES permit process, if you need more information on this.)
   f. RCRA-listed hazardous chemicals, including solvents, used in spacecraft parts degreasing and cleaning vats until the chemicals evaporate, as well as old oily rags that are thrown in the shop trash barrels after being used to wipe airplane parts in the degreasing process.

2. At the facility, Han Solo stores antimatter from the moons of the planet Endor; the antimatter is used in airport operations and becomes a byproduct containing several hazardous wastes. Solo plans to incinerate the antimatter as fuel in his boilers to heat his airport facility. If he chose, he

could also sell this material to a recycler who would recycle this material into paperweights. What advice would you provide regarding RCRA compliance?

3. Han Solo maintains a large oil tank for backup fuel supply for his heating boilers. This tank has leaked oil through a ruptured seam onto the ground. A large oil stain is evident where the oil has soaked through cracks in the asphalt and entered the ground. Is this an RCRA subtitle C problem for Solo?

4. After Solo burns the antimatter from the moons of the planet Endor, he is left with waste ash in the incinerator. Solo needs to dispose of this waste ash. Is its transportation and disposal subject to RCRA as a hazardous waste?

5. Han Solo comes to you for advice. He would like to dilute some of his RCRA listed hazardous waste with his dirty wastewater from washing airplanes and spacecraft. By mixing 99 percent washing wastewater, which is not an RCRA hazardous waste, with 1 percent other listed hazardous wastes, Solo would produce a dilute mixture that he believes is not deemed hazardous waste under RCRA.
   a. What legal advice would you give Han Solo?
   b. Do you have any legal advice for Han Solo if he reveals to you that he generates as much as 130 pounds each month of hazardous waste from his airport operations?

Explanations

1. To answer this question, we must go back to the original "trigger" for RCRA regulation and its exceptions. Recall that the material must be a "waste" that is not within one of the exceptions in RCRA. Let's evaluate each example.

1a. RCRA materials, even if they would be a listed RCRA waste, are not a "waste" if they are not *currently* a waste material but still a useful product. Therefore, even the most toxic poison, if still useful as a product, is not a "waste," and therefore does not trigger RCRA. Even if the material were a recognized pesticide, the pesticide is categorically exempt from RCRA regulation. The pesticide user need only triple-rinse the pesticide container before disposal, and dispose of residues on its own property, pursuant to the pesticide formulator's instructions.

1b. Waste oil is not covered as a RCRA waste. However, if it is spilled, §7003 of RCRA (discussed later) would apply. Stored oil is not subject to RCRA subpart C.

1c. Nuclear fuel, regulated under the Atomic Energy Act, is exempt from RCRA regulation. Therefore, storage of nuclear materials would be exempt from RCRA regulation. The basic principle is that there is no dual-statute regulation of materials covered by a specific statute. Here, the more specific statute concerning the nuclear fuel takes precedence over the more general RCRA statute.

1d. So-called "sanitary" waste from a septic or cesspool system, as discussed in Chapter 6, has the potential to cause major environmental problems. However, domestic sewage is exempt from RCRA regulation. The reason for this is both technical and political. Solid waste normally is the province of local regulation, not federal law. Indeed, RCRA leaves regulation of solid waste largely to the state and local governments. (Technically, solid waste is regulated separately in RCRA subtitle D.) Finally, because every household in the nation generates sanitary waste, for political purposes it is exempted as a RCRA waste.

1e. Discharges of industrial wastewater are regulated by the Clean Water Act, whether or not the regulation is particularly effective. Here, the Clean Water Act NPDES permit acts as a "permit shield" and exempts this waste from RCRA regulation.

1f. The question of whether this qualifies as RCRA waste is a two-part inquiry. First, is this material a waste? Look at each material. The solvents held for future use or recycling are not "wastes." The oily rags, once thrown out, are wastes and are RCRA regulated. Second, there is a question of whether this shop waste is exempt as "household" waste. The waste stream here is a commercial/industrial waste stream and not likely to be categorically exempt as "household" waste, even though its constituents may be similar to waste created at the household level. For more discussion of this topic, see Steven Ferrey, "The Toxic Time Bomb: Municipal Liability for the Cleanup of Hazardous Waste," 57 *Geo. Wash. L. Rev.* 197 (1988).

2. We need to go back to the definition of a "waste" to answer this question. A "waste" must be "discarded." "Discarding" under EPA regulations includes burning or incineration. It also includes storage of the material for purposes of burning or incineration. Therefore, if this material is stored for purposes of burning or incineration, rather than for recycling, it is a "waste." It is RCRA regulated. Solo must comply with all RCRA requirements. However, there are two possible escape hatches. First, the example indicates that rather than merely burning or incinerating these materials, Solo is burning them specifically as a fuel source for his boilers. There is an RCRA exception for that

quantity of antimatter used as an energy source, rather than merely burned to destroy it with no energy recovery. This material therefore appears to be exempt from RCRA's "waste" definition. Second, if Solo were to legitimately claim that he was storing the material for purposes of recycling, it would not be a "waste" and would not be subject to RCRA subtitle C regulation.

3. Now we go back to our RCRA verbs. Here's the sequence for analysis: Trigger One requires that the material be a "waste." The EPA by regulation (and case law) defined a waste as a material that is "discarded." "Discarded" is further defined as a material "abandoned" or "disposed of." There's one more connection to make: "Disposed of" includes "spilling" or "leaking." Here, the material is "leaking." RCRA would apply to this material as a leaking, disposed-of waste. It is irrelevant whether Han Solo is a passive perpetrator of this leaking. Solo is subject to RCRA regulation once the material becomes a "waste" by entering the environment. The oil still in the tank is not subject to RCRA subtitle C regulation, although RCRA does implement standards for tanks. There also is no CERCLA regulation of leaking oil, as discussed in the next chapter.

4. Waste ash from burning of *fossil fuels* is exempt from RCRA regulation as a hazardous waste. However, antimatter is not any type of fossil fuel recognized in this galaxy. Therefore, it would not qualify for the exception and would be subject to hazardous waste regulation under RCRA if it exhibited any of the *characteristics* of a hazardous waste.

5a. This question asks you to interpret the RCRA "mixture rule." First, the wastewater, even though in liquid form and not "hazardous," is still considered a *solid* waste. The "mixture rule" assumes that a mixture of solid and a listed hazardous waste does not result in the more benign characteristic dominating the mixture, but rather in the more hazardous characteristic dominating. This mixture, even if it results in a dilute mixture that does not test as "hazardous," still is defined as hazardous for RCRA purposes if it contains a listed hazardous waste. The only way out is to specifically delist the mixture, an option you might pursue.

5b. Here again, think of exceptions from RCRA regulation. An exception can occur because of either the quality or quantity of hazardous waste. As a qualitative matter, the waste is hazardous. However, quantitatively, 130 pounds each month is less than the 100 kg/mo threshold for status as a small-quantity generator. A small-quantity generator is not subject to RCRA subtitle C plenary regulation. Set up Solo as a small-quantity generator, and exempt his operation from plenary regulation.

REGULATION OF HAZARDOUS WASTE GENERATORS

We now know *what* is regulated by RCRA. But *who* is regulated by RCRA? It is logical that the person creating a waste should be responsible for its disposal. This person who creates the waste is a "generator," which the EPA defines as any person, by site, whose act or process produces hazardous waste identified or listed in 40 C.F.R. Part 261, or whose act first causes the EPA to subject a hazardous waste to regulation. Under §3002 of RCRA, the EPA regulates generators' recordkeeping and labeling practices. Further, it requires generators to (a) specify the nature of containers used for hazardous waste containment, (b) inform transporters and waste treatment, storage, and disposal (TSD) facilities of the nature of the wastes they receive, and (c) submit reports to the EPA and the states as to the quantities of hazardous waste generated and disposed of.

Every site that generates hazardous waste must have an EPA identification number. The most important requirement, however, mandates that generators employ the *manifest system* and other reasonable means necessary to ensure that the generated wastes arrive at the permitted TSD facility. A manifest is the shipping document prepared by generators for waste (identified by a narrative description and waste identifier number) leaving their sites. The manifest system enables the tracking of hazardous waste "from cradle to grave." Every hazardous waste generator must comply with the manifest system's requirements. First, there is a uniform, one-page form or equivalent state version that all generators must use. This manifest has space for limited state-required information from the generator state and the TSD (recipient) state. Intermediate states cannot require additional information on the form. The information of each transporter is entered on the manifest. One benefit of the uniform manifest system is that generators and transporters have to produce only one piece of paper for RCRA compliance. The EPA, however, permits states to require the filing of additional *copies* of that piece of paper. Typically, generators will employ the manifest of the recipient state, to ensure that the waste shipment ultimately will be accepted by the disposal facility. Moreover, the generator normally is required to produce two copies of the manifest for himself, one for the initial transporter, a copy for each transporter in the chain of transportation, and a copy for the TSD owner-operator.

RCRA places on generators the responsibility for packaging their wastes, labeling the packages, marking them with the required warning, and offering to provide the transporter with Department of Transportation-required placards. Generators are the primary custodians of the paper produced by the manifest system. RCRA requires the TSD facility that receives the waste to send a copy of the completed, signed manifest to the generator, who must retain the record for three years from the date of passing the waste on to the initial transporter.

What happens if the waste disappears or is transformed? RCRA establishes two additional reporting procedures. A generator must file an exception report with the EPA or the authorized state if it does not receive confirmation of delivery of its wastes to the designated site. Conversely, a TSD facility must file a discrepancy report with the EPA or the authorized state if it receives wastes unaccompanied by a manifest, accompanied by an incorrect manifest, or in nonconformity with the manifest. Filing of either an exception or a discrepancy report triggers an investigation by the responsible agency. As stated above, manifests constitute public documents that the regulated entities must retain for three years.

Generators can be exposed to a double risk: Not only must they comply with the foregoing requirements, but they also run the risk of being considered an *operator* of a storage facility if they accumulate hazardous waste on-site for more than 90 days. The EPA can grant a generator a 30-day extension of the accumulation period, but only upon the occurrence of unforeseen, temporary, and uncontrollable circumstances.

What does it mean, once a generator becomes an operator? Each container of hazardous waste must bear on its label the date accumulation began and the date (if later) that the operator placed it into the container. The site operator must comply with the emergency preparedness and contingency planning requirements (40 C.F.R. Part 265 subparts C and D). Personnel must be trained to handle emergencies (40 C.F.R. §265.16). The EPA and courts hold these generators strictly liable, without proof of fault, for cleanup costs and natural resource damage at TSD sites at which treatment, storage, or disposal of a generator's waste has occurred. Attorneys must advise generators on how to comply with RCRA without also becoming an operator.

Examples

1. Han Solo takes some of his used aircraft hazardous material and sells it to young Luke Skywalker. Skywalker pays $4 per 52-gallon barrel for the used material. He puts it to productive use as a weed retardant on his Uncle Owen's farm in the United States (rather than in a galaxy far, far away). Skywalker could purchase other weed retardants for $10 per barrel. These other weed retardants are not considered RCRA-regulated substances. Advise Skywalker and Solo as to whether RCRA regulates either of their activities with regard to this used material.

2. Han Solo's airport is in California. Skywalker's farm is in Washington state. When shipping the used waste material, Solo asks you, his counsel, to fill out and sign the required manifest. He also indicates that the state of Oregon, through which the waste material will travel on its way to

Skywalker's farm, wants some additional, limited, Oregon state tracking information included on the manifest. What is your response?

3. If Solo has accumulated significant quantities of the hazardous waste material on-site prior to contacting you, what additional concerns are raised?

Explanations

1. May the Force be with you! Let's start with Skywalker. He is handling a hazardous material, hence is subject to RCRA. That's easy enough. How about Han Solo? Solo is selling his waste as a useful product to another party in an arm's-length transaction. Therefore, is the waste material an RCRA "waste" or not? It depends on one's perspective. From Skywalker's perspective, the material is of value as a product. From Solo's point of view, the material is "disposed of." When "disposed of" it is an RCRA waste. Solo does not escape RCRA regulation. Both parties are regulated, Solo as a waste generator and Skywalker as one who accepts the waste and disposes of it on the ground without an RCRA permit.

2. Limited state information may be included on the manifest — but only if required by the *generator* state (California) and the *recipient* state (Washington). States through which the shipment merely passes are not allowed to require information on the manifest. Therefore, Oregon may not require new information on the manifest.

   As counsel for Solo, it is permissible for you to execute the manifest. But be careful how you do this: As counsel, always designate your capacity as legal representative when signing. Otherwise, you might be mistaken for the generator if problems occur.

3. By accumulating more than a small quantity of hazardous waste on-site, Solo risks becoming subject to the operator requirements of RCRA, in addition to regulation as a generator. The operator requirements include additional recordkeeping, utilizing trained personnel, and contingency planning (discussed later).

REGULATION OF HAZARDOUS WASTE TRANSPORTERS

Who else is regulated by RCRA? Transporters handle and move waste that is shipped off-site. RCRA §3003 requires the EPA to regulate transporters' recordkeeping and compliance with the manifest system, and to require transporters to ensure that the wastes transported are properly labeled. Note that the EPA regulates only *off-site* hazardous waste transportation.

RCRA subjects hazardous waste transporters to minimal regulation, because the Department of Transportation (DOT) regulates them more extensively under the Hazardous Materials Transportation Act (HMTA). Although §3003(b) subordinates EPA's regulations to DOT's under HMTA, the EPA claims authority to enforce DOT's regulations.

Transporters play a crucial role in the manifest system because a transporter cannot accept hazardous waste from a generator unless the waste is accompanied by a properly executed uniform manifest and, for waste exports out of the country, an EPA Acknowledgment of Consent. Further, the transporter must sign the manifest and date it prior to commencing transportation of the waste, leaving one signed copy with the generator. Therefore, transporters have a continuing obligation to ensure that the manifest stays with the shipment to its destination.

In short, the manifest must accompany the waste throughout its journey, and each new transporter must sign and date the manifest, leaving a copy with the previous transporter, who must retain the record for at least three years from the date the generator turned the waste over to the initial transporter. The final transporter must secure the signature of the TSD facility owner or operator and retain his or her copy for three years.

If the transporter cannot make delivery in accordance with the manifest, the transporter must contact the generator for instructions on how to proceed, and then revise the manifest to reflect those instructions. A transporter must deliver all the waste accepted from the generator to the designated TSD facility, or to the alternate designated TSD facility if an emergency prevents delivery to the primary facility, or to the next designated transporter or extraterritorial delivery point designated by the generator.

RCRA's Part 263 regulations impose obligations on transporters who experience an accident or other release of hazardous waste. The transporters must clean up any hazardous waste that escapes into the environment. Also, a transporter who mixes hazardous wastes of different DOT shipping descriptions by placing them in a single container becomes a generator.

Similarly, RCRA treats transporters as treatment, storage, and disposal (TSD) facilities on certain occasions. A transporter can store manifested shipments of hazardous waste in complying containers at a transfer facility for a period of up to ten days without becoming a TSD facility requiring a permit. The EPA defines the term "transfer station" in Part 260 as any transportation-related facility including loading docks, parking areas, storage areas, and other similar areas where shipments of hazardous waste are held during the normal course of transportation. The EPA intended to exempt waste held for short periods as part of the routine transportation process. Because the EPA allows up to ten days' storage at each transfer facility along the transportation route, a transporter or a series of transporters could arguably hold on to the waste for a long time by tiering transfer facility storage periods.

Examples

1. In disposing of some old, unused oil that was stored at the airport, Han Solo employs Chewbacca the Wookiee to transport the waste. When Chewbacca, a licensed RCRA transporter, picks up some of the oil, he pumps it in bulk liquid form into one of his licensed disposal trucks. Then he goes down the road to pick up some tetrachloroethane (TCE), a nasty hazardous waste, from the establishment of the nefarious Jabba the Hutt. What are the legal repercussions for:

   a. Chewbacca?
   b. Han Solo?
   c. Jabba the Hutt?

Explanations

1a. Chewbacca has mixed hazardous and nonhazardous wastes. He inherits RCRA *generator* status, as well as *transporter* status, as a result of this commingling. He will now be doubly regulated. Your legal advice is that he should comply with both types of regulation in dealing with this one load of waste.

1b. As a consequence of Chewbacca's commingling, Han Solo can no longer segregate the waste he has shipped. Therefore, his waste can no longer go to an oil recycling or asphalt batching facility, where it could have been disposed of or recycled at modest cost. Instead, the entire mixture must be disposed of as a hazardous waste. Who should pay for this mixture's higher disposal costs? That's an issue for negotiation, which you as counsel may undertake.

1c. Jabba's waste is no longer segregated. But the consequences are not as severe for Jabba the Hutt, who contributed the more toxic substance and must dispose of his waste as hazardous in any case, as it is for Han Solo, whose oil waste is now an ingredient in a toxic waste cocktail.

TSD FACILITY REGULATION

One final category of persons is regulated under RCRA subtitle C. Sections 3004 and 3005 of RCRA erect a permit program under which all *owners* and *operators* of treatment, storage, or disposal (TSD) facilities must ultimately possess a permit as a prerequisite for doing business. These sections require the EPA to establish standards and other regulatory restrictions for TSD facilities. The EPA utilizes the RCRA permit as its device for enforcing

RCRA standards at TSD facilities. Under EPA regulations, a facility is given a lifetime permit unless the EPA has issued the permit specifically for a land disposal facility, storage facility, incinerator, or other treatment facility. The permits for these latter facilities run for a fixed term, not to exceed ten years. The EPA reviews land disposal facility permits every five years. The EPA may, for cause, modify, revoke, or reissue a permit prior to its expiration date.

RCRA prohibits the transporting, treating, or disposing of waste prior to submission of notification to the EPA. All generators, transporters, and TSD facilities, pursuant to §3010, must notify the EPA whenever they generate, transport, treat, store, or dispose of any hazardous waste — whether a listed or characteristic waste. Section 1004 defines the terms "storage," "treatment," and "disposal," but does not define "facility," "owner," and "operator." Further, the EPA requires these facilities to specify the location and describe the activity associated with the waste.

An important distinction, however, exists between the regulation of generators and transporters, on the one hand, and owners and operators, on the other hand. Unlike generators and transporters, whose activities must comply with certain RCRA requirements, but may be carried out as a matter of right, TSD facilities must operate pursuant either to the limited rights afforded by "interim status" or to a permanent permit issued by the EPA or an authorized state. These permits act as the principal enforcement mechanism for the substantive standards governing TSD facilities. There are two kinds of permit status, interim and permanent.

Interim Status Facilities

Interim status describes provisional accreditation for TSD facilities in existence when RCRA was enacted. Interim status lasts from November 19, 1980, until either (1) the EPA or an authorized state acts on the TSD facility's Part B permit application and issues a permit, or until (2) the EPA terminates interim status for failure to file a Part B application, or failure to certify compliance with applicable groundwater protection and financial responsibility requirements. The EPA, by regulation, limits and freezes an interim status facility to the specific wastes, processes, and design capacities set out in its application. Such a facility cannot accept different wastes or employ different processes without advance approval by the EPA or the state RCRA authority. *EPA v. Environmental Waste Control, Inc.*, 917 F.2d 327 (7th Cir. 1990).

Section 3008 of RCRA, as amended, allows the EPA to issue administrative orders requiring *corrective action* for releases of hazardous waste into the environment from interim status facilities, and to provide for judicial enforcement of the orders. In general, corrective actions include excavation of contaminated soil from which hazardous materials are leaching; collection of leachate or runoff; pumping out, treatment, and return of polluted groundwater; and measures to retard off-site groundwater migration. Interim status corrective action orders represent Congress's desire to give the EPA the authority to begin cleanup operations at existing facilities prior to TSD permitting, but outside CERCLA's purview (see Chapter 9). Practically, the impact is similar to that of CERCLA orders.

The EPA also requires all interim status facilities to have written closure and postclosure plans describing how the facility will close when it terminates its use, and how it contemplates decontamination procedures. The EPA's closure and postclosure approach to land disposers leaves essentially only two options: (1) capping the site and controlling any polluted leachate, or (2) removal and decontamination of all remaining wastes or constituents. Further, unless the EPA or the state regulatory authority grants an extension, the facility must complete closure activities within 180 days of receipt of the last waste shipment or approval of the closure plan, whichever occurs later.

The EPA mandates a 30-year postclosure monitoring, surveillance, and security requirement, and a qualified permanent prohibition against site disturbance for facilities where waste remains. Further, the qualified permanent prohibition against site disturbance also requires the recording of the prohibition with the deed or other instrument of title, and the preparation and filing in the local land offices of a record of the plat showing the restricted area and bearing a recitation of the restrictions. Further, subpart H requires owner/operators of TSD facilities to provide a means of assurance that they can meet the cost of closure in accordance with the closure plan. Similarly, they also must provide financial assurances for postclosure costs.

Unless terminated prematurely, interim status for a TSD facility continues until the EPA or an authorized state agency makes a final administrative disposition of the facility's permit application.

Permanent Permitted Status Facilities

As with the interim status standards, the EPA designed the permanent standards to be minimum national standards that define the acceptable management of hazardous waste. States, however, as with air and water, can elect to regulate more strictly. Consequently, RCRA imposes certain minimum standards on all TSDs.

Seven primary standards merit itemization. First, all TSDs must have an EPA identification number. Second, if a TSD receives waste from an off-site nonforeign source, the TSD owner/operator must notify the generator in writing that he possesses permits for, and will accept, the waste. Third, each time an owner/operator accepts a new kind of waste from a new generator, or if the TSD facility has reason to believe that an existing generator's process or operation has changed, the TSD facility must perform a detailed chemical and physical analysis of a representative waste sample. In addition, a TSD facility must sample each shipment of hazardous waste it receives accompanied by a manifest, to determine if the waste received equals the waste described on the manifest. Fourth, RCRA mandates that the design of TSD facilities must either (a) prevent potential injurious contact with the waste, structures, or equipment at the facility by people or livestock, or (b) have entry controls or barriers sufficient to prevent entry into the active area. Facilities must report releases, fires, explosions, and closures. Fifth, a protocol for inspections of operations and equipment, monitoring, and possession of emergency equipment is required. Sixth, RCRA orders personnel training involving various operating, safety, and emergency responsibilities. Finally, an owner/operator, upon receipt of a waste shipment, must sign and date the manifest, note any significant discrepancies from the manifest, and give the transporter one copy of the signed manifest. The TSD facilities must retain their copies for a minimum of three years from the date of delivery.

In summary, the seven primary requirements for TSD facilities are:

1. EPA identification number
2. Written notice of waste acceptance from TSD
3. Analysis of waste samples
4. Prevention of contact with wastes
5. Inspections, monitoring, emergency equipment
6. Operator personnel training
7. Completion and retention of waste manifest

What happens when the waste leaks or migrates — as it does at many TSD facilities? Cleanup requirements are similar to those for interim status. Section 3004(u) imposes an obligation on RCRA permit applicants to undertake *corrective action* to address environmental contamination caused by releases from solid waste management units at treatment, storage, or disposal facilities, regardless of when the waste was placed in a unit. The EPA's RCRA regulation, 40 C.F.R. §264.101, broadly interprets the word "facility" in §3004(u) of the statute to require permit applicants to address not only contamination existing on the portion of the property containing the leaking unit, but also on contiguous property under the owner's or operator's control.

What is the interface between RCRA corrective action and Superfund remediation? Both can leverage similar remedies against responsible parties. The EPA often defers placing sites on the CERCLA National Priorities List (NPL) when it can address such hazardous waste problems through corrective action under RCRA subtitle C. The EPA's official policy nevertheless includes placing RCRA units on the NPL when the owner/operator will not perform RCRA corrective action. This policy has strategic implications for generators and transporters, in particular, who get pulled into CERCLA actions. There is more discussion of these CERCLA issues in the next chapter.

Relation to Other Regulation

How does RCRA relate to NEPA? The RCRA permit process does not invoke NEPA's EIS requirement — ever. Because §3005 says nothing about a hearing, the EPA does not provide a hearing prior to issuing an RCRA permit. A party may, however, appeal the permit issuer's decision to the EPA administrator. The EPA gives the permit holder an opportunity for a full evidentiary hearing prior to terminating an RCRA permit, and prior to terminating interim status for failure to furnish information needed to make a final decision. As stated in Chapter 2, no right to judicial review exists until the contesting party has first exhausted an appeal to the EPA administrator.

Possession of an RCRA permit constitutes prima facie evidence of compliance with RCRA regulations and a delegee state's regulations. The permit, however, does not convey a property right or exclusive privilege. Further, the permit does not preempt the application of state or local nuisance, zoning, or environmental laws and regulations. For more discussion of local regulation, see Chapter 4. A summary of RCRA regulations applying to hazardous waste generators, transporters, and owner/operators of TSD facilities appears in Exhibit 8.4. For a discussion of environmental equity in the siting of waste facilities, see Chapter 1.

The Land Ban

A substantial body of political and scientific opinion holds that facilities should not, under any circumstances, dispose of hazardous waste in landfills. Landfill leachate is estimated to be approximately 20-100 times the strength of raw sewage. RCRA enacted a prohibition against land disposal of hazardous waste. RCRA requires the EPA to promulgate prohibitory regulations, unless the agency makes a positive determination that a particular method of land disposal is safe. See NRDC v. EPA, 907 F.2d 1146 (D.C. Cir. 1990). The EPA codified its regulatory implementation of the land disposal ban at 40 C.F.R. Part 268. In general, if the EPA decides to ban a given waste, then facilities may continue to utilize land disposal only if (1) the EPA grants an extension from the effective date, on a case-by-case basis, (2) an exemption exists covering the waste at a specific facility, (3) a small-quantity generator generated the waste, or (4) the waste constitutes contaminated soil or debris resulting from a response action taken under CERCLA §104 or §106, or a corrective action required under RCRA.

The RCRA land disposal restrictions require that concentrations of hazardous constituents not exceed those levels achievable by the best demonstrated available treatment technology (BDAT). A variance from these standards can be issued where a specific waste cannot be treated to these levels or where the treatment technology is not appropriate for the particular

8.4 Summary of RCRA Subtitle C Regulations

RCRA Requirements	Waste Generators	Transporters	Treatment, Storage, Disposal Facilities[*]
Determine if wastes are hazardous	X		X
Notify EPA if RCRA hazardous waste handler and obtain identification number	X	X	X
Train personnel in waste management procedures and emergency response	X	X	X
Implement preparedness and prevention measures and notification of releases	X	X	X
Facilitate contingency planning and emergency procedures	X		X
Inspect facility operations periodically	X		X
Track waste with manifest system	X	X	X
Keep records, make reports	X		X
Post signs: package marking, labeling, and transport vehicle placarding	X	X	
Ensure physical security	X	X	X
Use and manage containers, landfills, and other operating areas properly			X
Design and operate waste handling areas adequately[†]			X
Monitor groundwater			X
Ensure closure and postclosure care			X
Ensure financial responsibility for closure and postclosure care			X

*Treatment, storage, or disposal facilities in operation on or before November 19, 1980, could continue operating under "interim status" until a hazardous waste permit was issued, at which time the facility had to be in compliance with the final permit regulations.

†This includes the design and operation of tanks, surface impoundments, waste piles, land treatment facilities, landfills, incinerators, and injection wells.

Source: GAO, New Approach Needed to Manage the Resource Conservation and Recovery Act, July 1988, at 24.

waste. A variance can only be granted where the treatment will sufficiently minimize threats to human health and the environment that would result from the disposal. This can be satisfied where the regulator determines that the threat that would exist if the wastes were left in place without the treatment is minimal.

Before the EPA grants a variance from the hazardous waste land ban, the applicant must either meet the §3004(d)-(f) "no migration" criterion, establish that fundamentally different factors exist at this specific site, or prove that the national variance for insufficient treatment capacity applies. The "no migration" criterion requires that the EPA cannot permit the continued disposal of untreated hazardous wastes on land unless the owner/operator receiving the waste demonstrates that there will be no migration of hazardous constituents from the disposal unit or injection zone so long as the waste remains hazardous.

Land treatment is a form of land disposal, which RCRA disfavored and banned. In *American Petroleum Institute v. EPA*, 906 F.2d 729 (D.C. Cir. 1990), the court concluded that hazardous waste may not be disposed of on land unless the waste complies with RCRA's pretreatment regulations. The K061 steel smelting slag wastes were deemed "undisputably discarded" since they were allowed to lie on land for a period of time, thus contributing to the waste disposal problem. The court held that RCRA precluded the EPA from considering land treatment in conjunction with pretreatment as a method of treating hazardous wastes. In other words, wastes must be pretreated so as to be no longer hazardous before they are further treated or disposed of on land.

In *Chemical Waste Management, Inc. v. EPA*, 976 F.2d 2 (D.C. Cir. 1992), *cert. denied*, 507 U.S. 1057 (1993), the court held that the EPA had the authority to require the overtreatment of wastes to levels beyond the threshold of toxicity — i.e., to even more dilute or de minimis levels of hazardous constituents. The court also stated that dilution of characteristic hazardous wastes constitutes treatment only if no hazardous constituents that would endanger human health or the environment exist following dilution. Further, the court found dilution of wastes in Clean Water Act facilities acceptable as long as the facility minimized or eliminated the toxicity of the waste discharged, consistent with RCRA.

The availability of treatment capacity has come to mean the availability of incineration capacity, because incineration has become the EPA's primary treatment for hazardous wastes. Many scientists and policy analysts view incineration of hazardous wastes as a disposal method far superior to land disposal. Congress's 1984 amendments indirectly urged incineration for wastes such as solvents, dioxins, and PCBs that the EPA had essentially banned from land disposal. The EPA's regulations require 99.99 percent destruction of each principal organic hazardous constituent for most wastes, and 99.9999 percent destruction of the principal organic hazardous constituent for six dioxins.

The EPA governs both incinerators and land treatment facilities by a special set of permit requirements. For incinerators these requirements include trial "burns" and other air-pollution-related preoperational testing and monitoring. For land treatment facilities, these requirements include field testing. Parties cannot collaterally attack the validity of an incinerator permit issued under RCRA through a citizen's suit claiming that the operation of the permitted incinerator poses an imminent and substantial danger to health or the environment. Rather, the EPA must review permitting decisions on direct appeal under RCRA §7006(b).

State and Local Government Regulation

Many states, acting separately, regulate TSD siting. Regulatory decisions on new TSD facility siting have resulted in fierce citizen opposition. As with many other government regulatory programs, EPA can delegate RCRA's permit and enforcement authority to qualifying states. Section 3006 establishes the delegation parameters. Delegation occurs in two steps: interim authorization and final authorization. Section 3009 clearly allows state programs that are more stringent than the federal program.

The statute gives the EPA latitude in determining the acceptability of a state program. EPA regulations retain a right to override state permit conditions by inserting federal conditions in the state plan. Once a state has received federal authorization, parties alleging violations of the state program by state officials must bring suit in state court based on a final state action, not federal court. Further, parties cannot premise such lawsuits on the citizen suit provision of the federal statute. The EPA may withdraw authorization of a state program if it determines that the state is not administering and enforcing its program in accordance with the §3006 requirements, but the EPA must first give the state an opportunity to correct deficiencies.

RCRA does not allow states to enact a citizen suit provision that would be more stringent than the federal standards. See *Ashoff v. Ukiah, California,* 130 F.3d 409 (9th Cir. 1997). While it is permissible for states to enact stricter-than-federal standards implicitly under their non-preempted regulatory authority, the absence of express authorization in RCRA prohibits citizen suits based on such stricter standards.

What about the local role? Increasing numbers of municipalities have addressed the problems of hazardous waste disposal. Except for the general savings clause in §3009, however, the statute does not address municipal programs. Most municipalities are considered subagencies of the states. Therefore, if allowed by state statute and case law, municipalities should be able to regulate waste more stringently. Of note, as discussed in Chapter

4, the Supreme Court has held that state laws discriminating against out-of-state waste violate the U.S. Constitution's commerce clause. See *Chemical Waste Management, Inc. v. Hunt*, 504 U.S. 334 (1992); *Fort Gratiot Sanitary Landfill, Inc. v. Michigan Dep't of Natural Resources*, 504 U.S. 353 (1992); *C. & A. Carbone, Inc. v. Town of Clarkstown*, 511 U.S. 383 (1994); *Gilliam County v. Dep't of Environmental Quality*, 849 P.2d 500 (Or. 1993).

Overfiling

The states conduct 90 percent of all enforcement actions, as well as 97 percent of the inspections at regulated facilities, compared to the remainder, which are performed by the federal EPA. Some courts have ruled that principles of *res judicata* bar the EPA from pursuing an enforcement case against a company that is settling the same charges with the state regarding the same violation. See *Harmon Industries, Inc. v. Browner*, 191 F.3d 894 (8th Cir. 1999). The principle of *res judicata* comes from the Full Faith and Credit Act, 28 U.S.C. §1738. Intriguingly, the EPA had filed first in the *Harmon* matter, with the state filing second. The EPA administrative action was pending when the state court judge approved a consent decree between the company and the state.

Most federal courts, however, have not found a bar to overfiling. The Ninth Circuit rejected the *Harmon* overfiling decision. *United States v. Elias*, 269 F.3d 1003 (9th Cir. 2001) (RCRA supplants only the permitting and not the enforcement authority of RCRA via an authorized state RCRA program). See *United States v. Flanagan*, 126 F. Supp. 2d 1284 (C.D. Ca. 2001); *United States v. Murphy Oil U.S.A., Inc.*, 143 F. Supp. 2d 1054 (W.D. Wisc. 2001) (despite prior and ongoing state actions alleging identical issues, EPA allowed to proceed on Clean Air, Clean Water, and RCRA violations because lack of *res judicata*); *United States v. Power Engineering Co.*, 191 F.3d 1224 (10th Cir. 1999) (*res judicata* can only bar EPA overfiling where the federal government has employed legal counsel or aided the state in litigating the prior case); *United States v. LTV Steel Co., Inc.*, 118 F. Supp. 2d 827 (N.D. Ohio 2000) (Congress had anticipated overfiling and did not bar its enforcement in enacting the Clean Air Act); *United States v. Smithfield Foods, Inc.*, 191 F.3d 516 (4th Cir. 1999) allowing EPA Clean Water Act enforcement action despite state enforcement action.

The EPA has taken the position that if a state agency has merely notified a company of violation without prosecuting it to a final enforceable judgment, a prohibition on overfiling will not be respected by EPA. As a practical matter, EPA overfiles in less than one-tenth of 1 percent of state environmental enforcement cases.

Amendments to CERCLA in 2001 attempt to prevent federal overfiling, where both the state and federal government pursue simultaneous, and perhaps duplicative, enforcement actions. Except in limited circumstances, under the 2001 amendments, the EPA may not bring an administrative or judicial enforcement action to recover response costs at sites that have been addressed under a state program.

Examples

1. Princess Leia, "Her Royal Highness" as Han Solo affectionately calls her, now operates the Princess Wastatorium Bar & Grill, a licensed TSD facility featuring memorabilia from the planet Tattooine. She wants to know the RCRA requirements governing her operation of the landfill portion of the site, which is an RCRA permanent status disposal facility in the United States. Please advise her.

2. Princess Leia wants to expand the area of her landfill, which has proved a popular and successful destination for waste shipments from many star systems. The popularity is due in part to the fact that one can get a cold brew and a space burger while getting rid of toxic material. She would like you to see if you can modify her RCRA TSD permit to expand the landfill area. She also has read Chapter 3 of this book. Leia knows that community activists known as the Sand People could attempt to use a NEPA challenge to delay or frustrate her expansion efforts. How would you, as the princess's counsel, respond to a possible NEPA challenge by the Sand People?

3. Princess Leia wants to know how long a permit for her facility will run before needing to be renewed. What does the material you have just read suggest?

4. Darth Vader, a representative of the dark side of the Force, wants to dispose of his extremely toxic waste at Princess Leia's facility. He proposes two plans to the princess, who seeks your advice as to the legal acceptability of either:

    a. Plan One: Darth would send his extremely hazardous waste to the princess's facility, where she would mix it with other secret ingredients to neutralize the toxicity of Darth's waste.

    b. Plan Two: Darth would mix his waste with large quantities of water left over from operation of his TIE fighter aircraft. Thereafter, the diluted but still extremely hazardous waste would be safe in contact with persons, but it would kill the root systems of living plants. At this stage, he would ship the mixture to Princess Leia, who would bury the liquid waste at her facility in an area where there are only disposal pits and no vegetation or human activity.

Explanations

1. There are seven major requirements for permanent status TSD facilities. They follow a pattern of common sense and prudent management. Advise the princess that she must have an EPA identification number. This she obtains upon request from the EPA. Second, she must provide to waste generators a written notice of her acceptance of waste. Third, she must analyze samples of the waste received to ensure that it is what it purports to be on the waste manifest description. She should accept it only if it conforms to the manifest. Fourth, she must implement measures to keep the public isolated from the waste she accepts. Fifth, she must monitor her facility and submit to inspections. Sixth, she must employ trained personnel. Seventh, she must retain records of the waste received and its generators and transporters. While exacting, all this is just prudent business practice. The waste facility owner/operator will want to keep records so that it can pull in other responsible parties who contributed to the handling of waste, should remediation be required. More about this in Chapter 9.

2. It is obvious why the princess would like to avoid a NEPA challenge. NEPA delays a substantive permit. Delay allows opposition to mount, and it can imperil financing of a project. However, counsel the princess that an RCRA permit is categorically excluded from NEPA. It can be issued without NEPA compliance, and even without a hearing. The NEPA challenge, for failure to issue an EIS, can be dismissed for failure to state a claim.

3. Because Princess Leia operates a land disposal facility, these permits are granted for a period of not more than ten years. The permit can be renewed thereafter. The permit also is subject to review every five years, and it can be revoked.

4a. The court in *American Petroleum Institute v. EPA* held that neutralization of waste may not occur *during or as a part of* land disposal. Neutralization must occur before land disposal. Therefore, Darth's first plan violates the land ban (because the waste is still dangerous when it arrives at the princess's landfill for land disposal). If Leia first neutralizes the waste in an operation separate from land disposal, the plan is permissible. Land disposal may not play a role in the neutralization.

4b. Darth Vader's second proposal is a completely impermissible assault on the galactic (or at least U.S.) environment. Dilution of waste is permissible as a strategy to render it inert. However, as a result of dilution, the destruction of the hazardous constituents in the waste must be total and complete. This means that it can no longer endanger human health or the environment. Darth's dilution takes place prior to land disposal. So far so good. However, if the waste still exhibits a deleterious impact on plant systems, it has not lost all hazardous constituents. It does not matter that the waste will not be disposed of in an area of the site where there is no plant life. The waste is still hazardous regardless of the geographic area where it is disposed. Therefore, it still violates the land ban. Princess Leia may not treat or dispose of Darth Vader's wastes under this treatment plan. Tell the princess to reject any of Darth's waste and to send it back in a droid pod through hyperspace.

WRESTLING THE TIGER: ENFORCEMENT BY AGENCIES AND CITIZENS

The enforcement provisions of RCRA include §§3007 and 3013, which the EPA uses to acquire information about regulated entities; §3008, setting forth the basic administrative and judicial remedies available to the government; §7002, establishing citizen suit provisions; and §7003, which authorizes the government to bring lawsuits and to abate imminent and substantial endangerments to health or the environment. Let's see what each of these provisions does.

Information Gathering by the EPA: §3007

Government regulatory agencies need information about their regulatory targets, both to establish standards and permit conditions, and to marshall sufficient factual information to determine whether permittees are violating established requirements or endangering the public. Under RCRA, the EPA acquires information through voluntary industry self-monitoring, through TSD facility permit provisions, and through the manifest system imposed on generators and transporters. In theory, if the regulated entities adhere faithfully to those reporting requirements and freely provide EPA with access to their records, the extraordinary enforcement-related information-gathering tools provided in §§3007 and 3013 become unnecessary.

When necessary, however, the EPA utilizes RCRA §3007(a) as its primary information enforcement tool. It gives the EPA authority to (1) make formal, written demands for information relating to a regulated entity's hazardous waste activity, (2) gain access to records and copy them, and (3) enter sites for inspection and sampling purposes.

Information

In addition to getting information from RCRA-regulated entities, the EPA can address §3007 demands to any person who has handled hazardous wastes. Consequently, the EPA can extract information from persons who, though not themselves subject to RCRA regulation, may have handled, and thus gained information relating to, a particular waste. These persons include individuals, such as laborers, whom the EPA neither licenses nor otherwise subjects to direct regulation; and they include testing laboratories that analyze waste but that, because of the definitional structure of RCRA, the EPA might not consider waste generators or TSD facilities.

The "handled" phrase is broad and retrospective enough to encompass *past* generators, transporters, and TSD owner/operators who ceased activities prior to the advent of RCRA's regulation. Section 3007 does not authorize EPA to extract information from the owner of an *inactive* TSD site who did not actively manage the wastes at the site. Nor can the EPA demand information from a past passive owner of a currently active site. As a *passive* former owner, the entity does not "handle" waste, within the usual and customary RCRA meaning of the term. Such a person, because he or she no longer owns the site, does not equal one who currently stores, treats, or disposes of hazardous waste.

The EPA confers §3007 authority on any officer, employee, or representative of the EPA and on any duly designated officer, employee, or representative of a state having an authorized hazardous waste program. EPA employees always make their information requests in letter form. An RCRA-regulated entity can ask for confidentiality of data submitted in response to a §3007 request, under §3007(b) and EPA's confidentiality provisions. The entity must specifically designate the data as confidential, or give it to the EPA separately from nonconfidential data. Meanwhile, 18 U.S.C. §1905 and RCRA §3007(b)(2) prohibit knowing and willful disclosure of confidential information by federal employees to persons other than the EPA, the Department of Justice, or a duly authorized committee of Congress.

Inspections

The language of §3007(a)(1) and (a)(2) appears to authorize site inspections without a warrant. However, the Supreme Court, in *Marshall v. Barlow's, Inc.*, 436 U.S. 307 (1978), said that a nonconsensual entry cannot be authorized unless a judicially issued search warrant has been issued on the basis of an affidavit demonstrating either (1) probable cause to believe that evidence of a statutory violation exists on the site, or (2) that the inspection represents part of a neutral enforcement scheme. U.S. magistrates issue such warrants *ex parte*. Site inspections may be made either at presently active sites or at sites where hazardous wastes were formerly generated, stored, treated, disposed of, or transported. An inspection of an unregulated site may take place whether or not the site was previously owned or operated by a regulated entity. Inspections must occur at reasonable times.

Section 3007 also contains separate authority for EPA or state personnel to inspect and obtain samples from any person for any RCRA listed or characteristic hazardous wastes, and samples of any containers or labeling for such wastes. This section arguably allows entry to unregulated sites. If the EPA takes a sample, the EPA must leave a receipt describing the sample, and, if requested, must provide split samples to the site owner/operator. The EPA also must provide copies of analytical results to the entity promptly, even if unrequested.

To redress §3007 noncompliance, the EPA has available §3008(a)-(g) remedies. Additionally, a number of general federal criminal statutes relate to the gathering of information by the government. Upon nonresponse to a §3007 request, the EPA typically responds by threatening an administratively levied penalty, and then by issuing an administrative complaint and penalty assessment under §3008(a)(1) and (c). In sum, RCRA §3007 is quite compelling.

Monitoring and Testing: §3013

With environmental contamination, prior *existing* information seldom is sufficient. Section 3013 gives the EPA authority to order the owner or operator of a facility or site — or, if the present owner of a nonoperational site was not involved during the operational period, then the most recent previous owner or operator who reasonably has relevant knowledge — to undertake such monitoring, testing, analysis, and reporting as the EPA deems reasonable to ascertain the nature and extent of the hazards posed at the site. These activities are costly. A §3013(a) EPA order immediately requires the recipient to spend large amounts of money. Before issuing a §3013(a) order, therefore, the EPA must determine that the presence of hazardous waste from a facility or site presents a substantial hazard to human health or the environment. In practice, this is not a difficult showing for the EPA to make.

The EPA may issue a §3013 monitoring and testing order only to ascertain the nature and extent of the hazard at the site — the identity and properties of the contaminants, their distribution within the site or in the groundwater, the proximity, direction of flow, and rate of flow of groundwater, and other environmental fate information. The EPA can use this compulsion only for RCRA, not CERCLA, purposes. Section 3013, moreover, does not permit monitoring and testing for the purpose of formulating a cleanup plan, apportioning liability among potentially responsible parties, or ascertaining whose waste lies at the site.

When compelled by the EPA, the private party is not a free actor. A recipient of a §3013 order who wishes to comply must submit a monitoring, testing, and analysis proposal to the EPA for approval within 30 days of the order's issuance. If a recipient fails or refuses to comply with a §3013(a) or §3008(a)(1) order, or does an inadequate job in response to the order, EPA may bring a civil action seeking enforcement of the order and a penalty, or arrange for the required monitoring itself. Alternatively, the EPA can have state or municipal authorities execute the order, and then have the site owner or operator reimburse them for the costs. Section 3008(a) allows the EPA to respond to a violation of subtitle C either by issuing a compliance order, which may include an administratively issued civil penalty and/or suspension or revocation of a TSD permit, or by seeking injunctive relief and/or a civil penalty in a U.S. district court.

Sections 3006 and 3009 require state enforcement remedies to be as stringent as those of the EPA. This requirement is consistent with the entire pattern of environmental federalism. State enforcement procedures, however, can differ significantly from the EPA's. Occasionally a state will seek to enforce federal requirements by means of a citizen suit commenced under §7002. Although it will rarely do so, the EPA possesses the authority to enforce state program requirements against regulated entities in authorized states.

Citizen Suits: §7002

Citizens, as well as government agencies, can enforce RCRA. Section 7002 is RCRA's citizen suit provision. It provides that any person may commence a civil action against any other person — including the United States or any other governmental entity — to the extent permitted by the Eleventh Amendment. The action may allege a violation of any requirement or prohibition under the Act. An individual also can bring suit against the EPA administrator for failure to perform nondiscretionary functions. The next question, therefore, is: What is a *discretionary* act? Courts have held that EPA initiation of an enforcement action against an alleged RCRA violator constitutes a *discretionary* act, so failure to pursue the enforcement does not give rise to an RCRA citizen suit against the EPA.

RCRA §7002 authorizes citizen suits against past or present owners or operators of a site who generate or "contribute" to solid or hazardous waste at a site that poses an imminent or substantial endangerment to health or the environment. There is no prohibition against including a foreclosing lender as an owner or operator of a site who "contributed" to this problem, as there is with CERCLA, which protect lenders acting in the normal course of foreclosure on a contaminated property.

But one must notify before one leaps! RCRA requires citizen plaintiffs to give 60 days' prior notice of intent to litigate to enforce subtitle C requirements, and 90 days' notice for citizen *imminent hazard* actions. The EPA, however, may and does waive the 90-day notice if the suit alleges subtitle C violations as well. Section 7002(e) provides that a court may award payment of litigation costs, including reasonable attorney fees and expert witness fees, to prevailing or substantially prevailing parties. RCRA provides for payment of civil penalties in citizen suits under §§3008(a) and (g). The public also may obtain injunctive relief. Section 7002(a) provides that a U.S. district court has jurisdiction to enforce regulations and EPA orders, or to order the EPA administrator to perform an act or duty.

But that's not all: There are hoops and barriers to citizen suits. Substantial limits exist on exercising citizen suit authority under subtitle C. First, citizens may not seek to enjoin the siting of a new TSD facility or the issuance of a permit under §3005. Second, RCRA bars citizen suits if the EPA has commenced and is diligently prosecuting an RCRA §7003 or a CERCLA §106 action, is engaging in a CERCLA removal action, has begun a Remedial Investigation/Feasibility Study (RI/FS) under §104 of CERCLA, has begun remedial action at the site, or has issued a CERCLA §106(a) administrative order, under which responsible parties are conducting an RI/FS or undertaking remedial action.

Third, as discussed earlier, in certain circuits RCRA bars "overfiled" citizen suits if these overlap diligent enforcement actions brought by state agencies.

Fourth, individuals cannot predicate claims based on RCRA §7002(a)(1)(A) wholly on *past* violations of RCRA, but rather must allege either continuous or intermittent violations. This rule, however, does not defeat all claims under §7002(a)(1)(A) for past dumping. The continued presence of dumped materials, which may represent leaking hazardous substances, may constitute a continuous or intermittent RCRA violation. On the other hand, it is easier to bring citizen suits under §7002(a)(1)(B) against any person who has contributed to the *past* handling, storage, treatment, transportation, or disposal of any solid or hazardous waste that may present an imminent and substantial endangerment to health or the environment.

In *Meghrig v. KFC Western, Inc.*, 516 U.S. 479 (1996), the Supreme Court held that RCRA §7002 does not authorize a private cause of action for recovery of remediation costs; it applies only to situations where an endangerment to public health continues at the time of suit. In other words, §7002 is strictly injunctive (abating or enjoining), without sanctioning other equitable remedies, such as restitution of private cleanup expenses. Also, if one remediates a problem, §7002 is no longer available. The Court found RCRA's primary purpose to be waste management, rather than toxic waste compensation or remediation. The Court distinguished between the injunctive remedies available under RCRA and the broader private cost recovery provisions of CERCLA.

When a plaintiff does not have a cause of action under RCRA §7002, he or she often may also not have an action under CERCLA, which contains an exclusion of petroleum-related claims as well as omitting any private damage action or remedy (as opposed to restitution of response costs). After *Meghrig*, an action cannot lie unless there is an imminent danger, which implies that the remediation of the problem has not yet transpired. Every federal circuit has followed the *Meghrig* precedent.

In *Avondale Federal Savings Bank v. AMOCO Oil Co.*, 170 F.3d 692 (7th Cir. 1999), the cleanup occurred after the RCRA citizen suit, but before the court imposed any injunctive remedy against the alleged polluter. The unsuccessful plaintiff's enthusiasm to undertake cleanup prior to prosecuting its injunctive action was so that it could sell an uncontaminated property. This decision extends *Meghrig* to limit RCRA to remedial actions enforced by injunctions, and not sanctioning the award of damages after the cleanup.

Examples

1. The EPA decides to investigate Princess Leia's facility. It suspects that she may have been cutting corners in her acceptance of noncomplying waste and in her waste management. Which of the following attempts by the EPA to gather information are permissible?

   a. The EPA phones Darth Vader to demand information about the nature of the waste that he sent to Princess Leia.

   b. The EPA arrives unannounced on Princess Leia's doorstep at the facility and makes demands to take away her original records of waste acceptance and disposal activities.

   c. The EPA writes to C3PO, the chief analytic chemist of Droid Chemtech, the company utilized by Princess Leia to assess the constituents of waste samples she takes from incoming wastes. The EPA demands copies of records and samples from C3PO relevant to waste sent to Princess Leia.

   d. The EPA also writes Millennium Falcon Transport Company, the transporter for Darth Vader's waste sent to the Princess Leia site, demanding copies of all invoices, bills of lading, and manifests of waste shipments.

   e. May the EPA ask the former owner of Princess Leia's site, the Ewoks, to undertake monitoring, testing, or reporting to the EPA regarding contamination at the Princess Leia site? The Ewoks used the site as a junkyard.

2. Darth Vader immediately sends in copies of the requested information to the EPA. Afterward, Darth becomes concerned that proprietary information regarding his secret ingredients and production processes could be gleaned from the data he submitted. Is there any way Darth can thereafter keep this information out of the public domain?

3a. If the EPA does not pursue any action against Princess Leia's site, can the Sand People, a local citizen group, sue to compel the EPA to take action against alleged violations by Princess Leia?

3b. If the Sand People, the local citizen group, are unhappy about the lack of speed and lack of impact of an EPA action pursuant to §106 of CERCLA (see Chapter 9) that has been taken against the Princess Leia facility, can they bring suit under RCRA to push the process along?

Explanations

1a. The EPA is allowed to demand information from Darth Vader, in his capacity as a generator of RCRA-regulated waste. However, under §3007, the demand should be written, not oral. The request needs to be in written format. Darth can legally resist responding until written demand is made.

1b. Princess Leia, if she resists an unannounced entry of her premises, may be able to force the EPA to obtain a warrant, according to *Marshall v. Barlow's*. If she does not respond to the warrant, she is subject to penalties. The EPA is entitled to copy records. It is not unusual for the EPA or state authorities to take original records, but the EPA may not hold these original records for longer than necessary to inspect them and make copies. The original versions are the property of Princess Leia and should be recoverable by her. However, if a criminal prosecution is threatened, the government agency may attempt to keep the original records for purposes of introduction into evidence.

1c. RCRA does not regulate testing laboratories or its personnel — not even droids. However, the information-gathering scope of RCRA §3007 applies to anyone who handles waste. C3PO has handled waste — albeit only a sample of waste in his capacity as a scientist — and thus can be required to produce documents or samples. The request is in the proper written format. C3PO must comply.

1d. Millennium Falcon Transport Company must comply with a proper written request. Even though RCRA requires preparation and retention only of the formal manifest, other records such as bills of lading or invoices are discoverable by the EPA, if they exist. In other words, one need not prepare or retain any such records under RCRA, but if they exist, they can be obtained by the EPA. Counsel for various potentially accountable parties may advise on whether or not these documents should be created and/or retained, as long as such advice is prior to any requests for production or reasonable likelihood of same. Of course, once one has reason to believe that a request for documents may be forthcoming, or litigation has commenced that may be relevant, a party may not thereafter destroy documents, even in the course of routine document destruction. Counsel for a party must be vigilant to ensure that, even passively, he or she does not permit a client to willfully or inadvertently destroy documents once they become relevant to litigation or government enforcement actions.

1e. The EPA cannot apply RCRA monitoring or reporting requirements to those who do not handle waste, nor to prior owners or operators who were not in the waste business. This request is not legitimate. CERCLA is less protective of former owners and operators.

2. Once data are submitted without a claim for confidentiality, they are in the public domain. Darth's counsel should have designated the information as confidential by marking it as such prior to submission and formally requesting that it be kept out of the public domain. Once released to the EPA without such a claim, there is waiver of any confidentiality of the data. As counsel, a failure to so advise is dangerous.

3a. The citizen suit provisions of RCRA §7002 permit citizens to contest only *nondiscretionary* actions. Enforcement decisions of the EPA are considered discretionary acts. The Sand People are out of luck.

3b. The citizen suit provisions of RCRA do not allow such suits if they overlap with either state or federal enforcement actions against a facility. This provision includes CERCLA enforcement actions. Therefore, citizen suits are preempted once a government agency acts, even if such actions are less than vigorous. Again, the Sand People are out of luck.

Imminent and Substantial Endangerment Actions: §7003

The Contribution

The element of RCRA that is most covered in environmental casebooks is the venerable §7003. This section provides the EPA with substantial enforcement power. In essence, §7003 authorizes the EPA to sue to enjoin any person who *has* contributed to, or *is* contributing to, any solid or hazardous waste management practices that may present an imminent and substantial endangerment to health or the environment. Specifically, §7003 provides:

> Notwithstanding any other provision of this chapter, upon receipt of evidence that the past or present handling, storage, treatment, transportation or disposal of any solid waste or hazardous waste may present an imminent and *substantial endangerment to health or the environment*, the Administrator may bring suit on behalf of the United States in the appropriate district court against any person (including any past or present generator, past or present transporter, or past or present

owner or operator of a treatment, storage, or disposal facility) who has contributed or who is contributing to such handling, storage, treatment, transportation or disposal to restrain such person from such handling, storage, treatment, transportation, or disposal, to order such person to take such other action as may be necessary, or both. [Emphasis added.]

Therefore, §7003 allows the EPA to command actions from a wide variety of parties who contribute to or handle waste:

1. in the past or present
2. that is hazardous or solid
3. that *may* present
4. an imminent and substantial endangerment
5. to human health or the environment

These provisions cast a very broad net. The crucial element of proof under §7003 is whether the damage is threatening and "real" enough to establish the required "imminent and substantial endangerment to health or the environment." In applying this standard, the courts require only a relatively low level of danger as a trigger. Court decisions under §7003 and related statutory provisions have made it clear that harm is "imminent" even though it may occur in the distant future, and "substantial" despite the fact that it has not happened. This interpretation has been upheld in *United States v. Ottati & Goss, Inc.,* 630 F. Supp. 1361, 1393-1394 (D.N.H. 1985); *United States v. Price,* 688 F.2d 204, 211 (3d Cir. 1982). Therefore, proof of *actual* harm is not necessary to constitute endangerment.

Consequently, the government must demonstrate not actual damage but *exposure.* Courts have found it sufficient for the government to show merely that a number of hazardous chemicals were found at the site and have escaped into environmental media, to invoke §7003, as in *City of Philadelphia v. Stepan Chemical Co.,* 544 F. Supp. 1135 (E.D. Pa. 1982). The government need only prove that an existing dangerous condition creates a *risk of harm* to the environment or human health. Thus §7003 authorizes action against suspected danger, as well as against demonstrated harm. See *United States v. Waste Industries, Inc.,* 734 F.2d 159 (4th Cir. 1984) (describing RCRA as having enhanced the courts' traditional equitable powers not only in emergency situations, but when there is merely a risk of harm). See also *United States v. Price,* 688 F.2d 204, 211 (3d Cir. 1982).

The Actors

The pursuit of legal responsibility under §7003 turns up a host of candidates for liability. Section 7003 provides that liability reaches past and present actors who have contributed, or are contributing, to forbidden practices under RCRA. Specifically, §7003 authorizes suits "against any person (including past or present generator, past or present transporter, or past or present owner or operator) who has contributed or who is" contributing to the hazard.

For the most part, all owners — past and present, active and passive, virtuous and corrupt — are caught in the liability net. Section 7003's legislative history explicitly states that "non-negligent generators whose wastes are no longer being deposited or dumped at a particular site may be ordered to abate the hazard to health or the environment posed by the leaking of wastes they once generated and which have been deposited on the site." This standard of liability reflects the long-standing view that generators and other persons involved in the handling, storage, treatment, transportation, or disposal of hazardous wastes must share in the responsibility for the abatement of hazards arising from their activities.

Consequently, this scope of liability covers numerous individuals generally sheltered from tort liability. In *United States v. Northeastern Pharmaceutical & Chemical Co., Inc.* (NEPACCO), 810 F.2d 726 (8th Cir. 1986), *cert. denied*, 484 U.S. 848 (1987), the court held that §7003 did not require a finding of fault or negligence in order to hold past off-site generators and transporters liable for EPA site response costs. *United States v. Aceto Agricultural Chemicals Corp.*, 872 F.2d 1373 (8th Cir. 1989) (polluters liable and could not contract away their RCRA responsibility). Such parties are *strictly liable* even for acts of disposal that occurred before RCRA became effective in 1976. Further, persons liable can include officers and employees of corporate generators and transporters.

Remedies

Although in applying the "imminent and substantial endangerment" standard, courts have required only a relatively low level of danger as a liability trigger, courts in imposing remedies have balanced the hardship to the defendant against the public interest. Consequently, defeats for the EPA at the remedy stage have swallowed numerous substantive §7003 victories. The remedy aspect of §7003 suits, therefore, merits close attention.

In *United States v. Vertac Chemical Corp.*, 489 F. Supp. 870 (E.D. Ark. 1980), the court initially decreed that the defendant must implement some cosmetic dioxin containment and engage in study measures. The court was content to accept the former owner's pledge to contribute a "fair share" of the cleanup costs, and it declined to order it to take affirmative action on property it did not own. This nondecision contributed to a stalemate on the content of an acceptable remedial plan. Subsequently, another trip to court produced a decision favoring Vertac's less costly containment plan over EPA's more expensive proposals for soil excavation. The *Vertac* decision suggests that the assertive liability imposed in §7003 is achieved partially at the expense of the ultimate remedy. It is as if the courts pay heed first to the victims of pollution, and then to victims of proposals to clean it up.

In *United States v. Price*, 688 F.2d 204 (3d Cir. 1982), the court denied a preliminary injunction that would have required past and present owners of an inactive landfill to fund a diagnostic study of the possible threat to Atlantic City's public water supply, and to provide an alternative water supply to homeowners whose private wells had been contaminated by the landfill. The court of appeals held that although it was within the power of the district court to grant the preliminary relief requested by the EPA, the procedural posture of the litigation militated against granting it on appeal. Thus even at the preliminary injunction stage, some courts have qualified, moderated, and shunned relief sought by the government.

Section 7003 makes RCRA important not only for dealing with *present* hazardous waste disposal activities but also as a complement to CERCLA in securing judicially mandated cleanups of abandoned disposal sites. Section 7003 offers substantive advantages over CERCLA, including recovery of undesignated costs, broader definition of hazardous and solid wastes, and more extensive liabilities.

Criminal Violations

The EPA can seek not only civil but *criminal* enforcement under RCRA. Criminal liability can mean jail sentences. Corporations, of course, cannot serve jail time — but their employees can. RCRA contains both a general criminal liability provision governing *knowing* violations of the Act or regulations, and provisions that impose severe sanctions for "*knowing* endangerment." Congress established a complex set of special definitions and presumptions relating to the scienter requirement of "*knowing* endangerment," primarily to allay the fears of the corporate business community. One commits a criminal violation of RCRA if one:

1. *knowingly* transports or causes transportation of RCRA regulated waste to a TSD facility not possessing interim status or a permit for that waste;
2. treats, stores, or disposes of an RCRA regulated waste without a permit or in knowing violation of a material condition of a permit or interim status regulation or standard;
3. dumps an RCRA regulated waste into the ocean without a permit issued under the Marine Protection Research and Sanctuaries Act;
4. makes a false material statement or representation, or omits material information in documents filed, maintained, or used for the purpose of complying with EPA or state RCRA regulations;

5. destroys, alters, conceals, or fails to file a document or record required under the EPA or state RCRA program; transports or causes the transportation of hazardous waste without a manifest;
6. exports hazardous waste to a foreign country without consent of the recipient government, or in the absence of a treaty allowing export.

Scienter

The courts have addressed the nature of the scienter requirement for regular RCRA violations imposed by the "knowing" term in §3008(d). In *United States v. Hoflin*, 880 F.2d 1033 (9th Cir. 1989), *cert. denied, Hoflin v. United States*, 493 U.S. 1083 (1990), the court held that the defendant, who had participated in the unauthorized burial of paint, was guilty of violating RCRA, regardless of whether he knew that a permit had not been obtained authorizing such disposal. Additionally, in *United States v. Dee*, 912 F.2d 741 (4th Cir. 1990), *cert. denied, Dee v. United States*, 499 U.S. 919 (1991), the court held that the defendants "knowingly" violated the criminal provisions of RCRA, even if they did not know that violating RCRA was a crime, or that regulations existed listing and identifying chemical wastes as hazardous wastes under RCRA. In this case evidence existed that the defendants were aware that they were dealing with hazardous chemicals and that the materials handled by them were considered "wastes" under RCRA.

Further, in *United States v. Johnson & Towers, Inc.*, 741 F.2d 662 (3d Cir. 1984), *cert. denied sub nom. Angel v. United States*, 469 U.S. 1208 (1985), the court held that RCRA's criminal penalty provision covered *employees* as well as owners and operators of a facility that knowingly treated, stored, or disposed of any hazardous waste. The court concluded that employees can be subject to criminal prosecution if they knew or *should have known* that there had been no compliance with the statutory permit requirements. The court also determined that the knowledge required under RCRA's criminal penalty provisions could be *inferred* by the jury as to those individuals who held requisite responsible positions with the offending corporation. This is powerful precedent.

Appellate courts have been willing to imply the *mens rea* and scienter requirements for criminal prosecution by inference, even where the defendants claim no knowledge of limitations in their operating permits — i.e., defendants are imputed with knowledge of the law and permits thereunder. See *United States v. Hopkins*, 53 F.3d 533 (2d Cir. 1995), *cert. denied*, 516 U.S. 1072 (1996); *United States v. Weitzenhoff*, 35 F.3d 1275 (9th Cir. 1994), *cert. denied*, 513 U.S. 1128 (1995). But see *United States v. Ahmad*, 101 F.3d 386 (5th Cir. 1996) (one who honestly believes he or she is discharging a substance other than a restricted hazardous substance is not imputed with knowledge of the actual substance, even though he or she is imputed with knowledge of the law).

The key issue is proving knowledge of the facts of hazardous constituents, not knowledge of the law. Knowledge of potential to harm, inferred from knowledge that waste is RCRA regulated, is sufficient. *United States v. Greer*, 850 F.2d 1447 (11th Cir. 1988). Knowledge of the status of a permit is generally not a required element of proof. *United States. v. Laughlin*, 10 F.3d 961 (2d Cir. 1993); *United States v. Wagner*, 29 F.3d 264 (7th Cir. 1994). Mistake of fact, other than permit status, is a potentially tenable defense.

A person in a responsible position in a corporation can be imbued with imputed scienter, even if he or she possesses no actual knowledge. *United States v. Iverson*, 162 F.3d 1015 (9th Cir. 1998) (responsible corporate officer is criminally liable if he has authority to exercise control over the corporation and the activity that is causing the discharge); *United States v. Ming Hong*, 242 F.3d 528 (4th Cir. 2001) (relationship to the corporation can be grounds for Clean Water Act criminal misdemeanor conviction); *United States v. Elias*, 269 F.3d 1003 (9th Cir. 2001) (17-year prison sentence imposed for RCRA violation for failure to protect employees from imminent danger and improper disposal of hazardous waste without a permit, as well as making material misstatements).

Where the violation involves a public welfare statute, statutes do not require specific knowledge or intent in order to assign liability for a violation of the statute. *United States v. Hanousek*, 176 F.3d 1116 (9th Cir. 1999) (ordinary negligence sufficient to impose criminal penalty under the Clean Water Act, which is a public welfare statute); *United States v. Unser*, 165 F.3d 755 (10th Cir. 1999) (misdemeanor criminal conviction for entering a National Forest Wilderness Area when defendant became lost in a blizzard, without establishing *mens rea*).

Courts generally have not imputed knowledge of acts by subordinates to corporate officers, in light of the requirement of *actual* knowledge contained in §3008(d). In *United States v. MacDonald & Watson Waste Oil Co.*, 933 F.2d 35 (1st Cir. 1991), the First Circuit reversed the conviction of the president of a TSD facility charged with receiving waste not authorized by its permit. The government failed to prove that the officer had *specific* knowledge of the waste shipments in question. Since §3008(d) includes liability for a number of *paper* violations (such as failure to file required forms), knowledge imputation affects potential white-collar defendants who oversee the creation and filing of reports. This class of potential RCRA defendants is also exposed to potential criminal liability for the same acts under one or more of the "white-collar" crime provisions of U.S.C. Title 18.

The knowing endangerment offense arises when a transporter or TSD facility owner commits a substantive §3008(d) offense and *knows at the time* he or she commits the offense that he or she thereby places another person in imminent danger of death or serious bodily injury. The complexity of the "*knowing* endangerment" provision, however, will deter all but the most zealous white-collar prosecutors from seeking indictments. Although courts can employ circumstantial evidence, including steps taken by defendants to shield themselves from relevant information, to prove the requisite knowledge, courts may *impute* this level of knowledge only to an organization, not to a natural person. Because prosecutors will have an easier time proving a simple §3008(d) offense and the penalties available under §3008(d) fall within the felony range, prosecutors are unlikely to undertake the additional burden of pursuing "*knowing* endangerment" violations.

Penalties

RCRA criminal violations carry severe maximum penalties. Federal sentencing guidelines do not apply to fines pursuant to RCRA, where the statute governs. *United States v. Southern Union Co.*, 630 F.3d 17, 39 (1st Cir. 2010); cf. *United States v. Mancuso*, 428 Fed. Appx. 73 (2d Cir. 2011). Section 3008(d)(1)-(2) violations carry a fine of not more than $50,000 per day per violation and imprisonment for not more than five years, or both, for the first offense. Actions violating §3008(d)(1)-(2) include knowingly transporting or causing hazardous waste to be transported; or knowingly treating, storing, or disposing of hazardous waste without a permit or in knowing violation of a permit's terms; or knowingly treating, storing, or disposing of hazardous waste in knowing violation of an interim status regulation. Other violations, such as impermissible actions by hazardous waste generators or hazardous waste exporters, carry the same fine, with a maximum of two years' incarceration, or both. See RCRA §3008(d)(3)-(7). In each case, RCRA provides for the doubling of the sanctions on the second offense.

In *United States v. Elias*, 269 F.3d 1009 (9th Cir. 2001), an employee entering a tank was permanently disabled by hydrogen cyanide gas in the tank. For knowing endangerment of an employee at a fertilizer plant, pursuant to RCRA, and one count of providing false statements to OSHA by backdating a safety plan, the plant owner was sentenced to 17 years in jail and $5.9 million restitution to the employee's family.

The Department of Justice (DOJ) prosecution for environmental crimes is increasingly targeting individual corporate defendants, rather than the companies in which they work. There is no RCRA "safe harbor" for government installations. Section 6001 requires federal facilities to comply with both the substantive and procedural requirements of RCRA, as well as state hazardous waste programs, in the same manner and to the same extent as any person subject to such requirements, including exposure to sanctions for violations. Moreover, the Federal Facilities Compliance Act of 1992 allows the EPA and the states to enforce hazardous waste laws at federal facilities. Thus the EPA and the states now have explicit authority to impose fines and other penalties against federal agencies for hazardous waste violations.

RCRA Remedies and Bankruptcy Powers

RCRA (or CERCLA) owners and operators often file a bankruptcy petition when confronted with remediation obligations. To what extent does the filing of a bankruptcy petition serve to relieve the debtor of ordinary regulatory obligations, remedial action obligations, or penalty payment obligations? The filing of a bankruptcy petition normally operates as an automatic stay of the commencement or continuation of actions or proceedings against the debtor that were, or could have been, commenced prior to the filing date.

There obviously exists a tension between a trustee's bankruptcy powers and a state's police powers to remediate environmental pollution. Courts have upheld penalties assessed against the trustees in bankruptcy for regulatory transgressions that postdate the filing of the bankruptcy petition, and proceed outside any automatic stay provision.

As one aspect of the tension between bankruptcy and a state's police powers, bankruptcy may halt injunctions commanding performance. In *Penn Terra Ltd. v. Department of Environmental Resources*, 733 F.2d 267 (3d Cir. 1984), the court upheld a state court injunction ordering a bankrupt mining company either to perform land reclamation work or to forfeit a surety bond that it had posted with the state to guarantee performance of backfilling operations. Further, the court found the environmental injunction was a permissible exercise of state police and regulatory powers under 11 U.S.C. §362, rather than a prohibited proceeding to enforce a money judgment. In this instance, bankruptcy jurisdiction does not block injunctions.

Consequently, the critical question remains: To what extent must the bankruptcy trustee bear the remedial environmental costs at the expense of the creditors? Prepetition claims are dischargeable, while postbankruptcy petitions are not dischargeable. When the environmental claim arose — at the environmental release, at the incurrence of expense — is a critical factual and legal determination. In re *Chateaugay Corp.*, 944 F.2d 997 (3d Cir. 1991) (claim at environmental release); In re *Frenville Co.*, 744 F.2d 332 (3d Cir. 1984) (claim at right to payment). In *Ohio v. Kovacs*, 469 U.S. 274 (1985), the Court concluded that the state injunction ordering Kovacs to clean up a hazardous waste site he operated constituted an obligation only to pay money once the bankruptcy receiver took control of the site. Further, the Court concluded that such a money obligation was dischargeable in bankruptcy.

A bankruptcy trustee may abandon unproductive assets under §554(a) of the Bankruptcy Code. The polluted site of a failing treatment, storage, or disposal business clearly constitutes an unproductive asset. Accordingly, a number of trustees have sought to avoid compliance with remedial orders issued under CERCLA and RCRA by abandoning a TSD site. In In re *Smith Douglass, Inc.*, 856 F.2d 12 (4th Cir. 1988), the court held that under §544 of the Bankruptcy Code a bankrupt company could abandon property where violations of environmental law existed because the state had not demonstrated that the violations presented serious public health and safety risks and the company lacked the assets to clean up the site. This ruling protects the bankrupt at the expense of the environment.

In *Midlantic National Bank v. New Jersey Dept. of Envtl. Prot.*, 474 U.S. 494 (1986), the Court concluded that Congress did not intend for the Bankruptcy Code to preempt state laws that otherwise constrain the exercise of a trustee's powers. Specifically, the Court held, "Neither the Court nor Congress has granted a trustee in bankruptcy powers that would lend support to a right to abandon [contaminated] property in contravention of state or local laws designed to protect public health or safety." Other cases concur. See *In re Chateaugay Corp.*, 944 F.2d 997 (3d Cir. 1991). Therefore, a trustee may not abandon property in contravention of a state statute or regulation that is reasonably designed to protect the public health or safety from identified hazards. State mini-CERCLA statutes can impose such obligations and restrain the bankruptcy powers of trustees.

The court in *In re T. P. Long Chem., Inc.*, 45 B.R. 278 (Bankr. N.D. Ohio, 1985), concluded that remedial expenses fall into the category of expenses of administering and preserving the debtor's estate. Consequently, the court granted the remedial expenses priority for payment as administrative expenses, to the extent that the court found the expenses reasonable and necessary. If insufficient unencumbered assets are available to satisfy the regulatory obligation, the trustee may use assets subject to the interests of secured creditors, pursuant to the constraints imposed by §506(c) of the Bankruptcy Code. Thus environmental claims enjoy privileged status in bankruptcy proceedings.

SUBSIDIARY RCRA REGULATORY PROGRAMS

Underground Storage Tanks (UST)

Underground oil tanks are everywhere — at gasoline stations, at businesses, under homes. And they leak as they get older and corrode. Pipes and fittings, especially where pressurized, can leak during normal operations. Fiberglass as well as steel tanks leak. These leaks threaten groundwater, upon which about 50 percent of the population relies for drinking water. (See Chapters 6 and 11.)

The EPA estimates that there are more than 1.4 million USTs in the United States, 96 percent of which contain petroleum and 4 percent of which contain hazardous substances. The EPA estimates that 18 to 35 percent of the tanks holding petroleum motor fuels are leaking, and more will leak in the future. At an average cost of $100,000 per tank site, this represents a $35 billion potential cleanup bill. Oil is not filtered out of groundwater as it migrates. For more information on groundwater risk, see Chapters 6 and 7. The constituents of oil and gasoline — benzene, toluene, xylenes, ethylbenzene, and so on — are hazardous and carcinogenic.

Subtitle I of RCRA (§§9001-9010) establishes a subsidiary regulatory program within the overall RCRA framework aimed at identifying and regulating underground storage tanks. Regulated tanks must contain either petroleum or a CERCLA hazardous substance not regulated by RCRA subtitle C. Exceptions are made for heating oil tanks, agricultural tanks, and others. Therefore RCRA, and as discussed in the next chapter CERCLA, do not address or regulate domestic fuel oil tanks or releases of oil from these tanks.

Aside from these exceptions, RCRA subjects all tanks that are more than 10 percent below ground level to UST regulation. The subtitle contains its own enforcement provisions and exemptions. The UST program requires notification of tank existence, leak detection, records maintenance, chemical release reporting, corrective action, proper tank closure, financial responsibility of owners, and new-tank standards. The UST regulations contain detailed specific new-tank construction standards and piping standards, as well as spill and overflow prevention requirements. The EPA requires UST operators to have new-tank systems cathodically protected, or constructed of or clad with noncorrodible material, or designed to prevent the release of the contents. The basic UST reporting requirements provide that owners and operators must report, within 24 hours, knowledge of (1) discovery of released regulated substances in the neighborhood's environment, (2) unusual operating conditions such as evidence of unusual product loss or the presence of water in the tank for which no benign explanation exists, or (3) monitoring results from a leak detection system that indicate, after confirming the reliability of the results, that a release may have occurred.

The response program relies on two mechanisms to provide financial resources for corrective actions necessitated by tank leaks, which usually require groundwater remediation. The first safeguard is the RCRA mandate that owners and operators of regulated tanks must maintain evidence of financial responsibility sufficient to take corrective action and compensate third parties for any resultant property damage or personal injury. A UST operator may demonstrate financial responsibility by insurance, risk retention group coverage, surety bond, guarantee, letter of credit, self-insurance, trust fund, or state assurance, or a combination of two or more of these. The second safeguard is that the EPA or states may utilize a $500 million Leaking Underground Storage Tank (LUST) Trust Fund to pay response costs at "orphan sites."

So what laws govern oil spills from fuel oil tanks? If it is a commercial or industrial tank, RCRA corrective action regulates the spill. If the oil is in any way contaminated or adulterated, CERCLA governs the release. If the state has a state statute patterned on CERCLA, in many cases oil releases are covered by the strict liability state law. Otherwise, common law remedies of negligence, trespass, and nuisance will apply. Some state common law involves strict liability for landowners who conduct abnormally dangerous activities. See Restatement (Second) of Torts §520.

Medical Waste Tracking Act of 1988

There still remain approximately 2,400 hospital and medical infectious waste incinerators in the United States that combust approximately 850,000 tons of medical waste annually. However, this medical waste accounts for less than 2 percent of all municipal solid waste produced annually in the United States. Most of the medical waste is infectious waste. Regulations on the incineration of medical waste are promulgated under Section 129 of the Clean Air Act.

RCRA also includes, in subtitle J, the Medical Waste Tracking Act (MWTA). The EPA created seven categories of regulated medical waste: (1) cultures and stocks, (2) pathological wastes, (3) human blood and blood products, (4) sharps, (5) animal wastes, (6) isolation wastes, and (7) unused sharps. "Sharps" include needles and blades. More than 40 states independently regulate infectious waste; most do not regulate home health care providers or home disposal of infectious waste.

Examples

1. Recapitulate the factors that the EPA must demonstrate to seek an injunction against parties pursuant to RCRA §7003.

2. If the EPA seeks action to remedy problems at the Princess Leia site discussed in the prior group of Examples and Explanations, which of the following are subject to an EPA injunctive order under §7003?
   a. Princess Leia
   b. Millennium Falcon Transport Company
   c. Darth Vader
   d. C3PO

3. Assess the following transgressions, as to whether or not they impose any RCRA criminal liability:
   a. Darth Vader did not correctly identify the wastes he sent to the Princess Leia site.
   b. Princess Leia did not independently test Darth Vader's wastes but rather relied on Darth's representations as to the chemical constituents of his waste. Because of inaccuracies in this information, she disposed of waste that was other than it purported to be, and which she was not licensed to receive.

    c. Recently, upon learning of the discrepancy between Darth Vader's waste and his assertion of what was in the waste, Princess Leia altered some of her records, including the manifest, regarding the wastes sent to her site, so as to reflect the actual chemicals received rather than the chemicals as stated by Darth Vader.

    d. The Millennium Falcon Transport Company did not know that it had to manifest Darth Vader's wastes and did not do so.

4. Princess Leia ponders declaring bankruptcy in response to EPA demands that she remediate problems at her landfill site. She believes that doing so would allow her to conserve her resources to aid the Rebel effort in the Daggoba System, with which she is associated against the Empire. Advise her of the possible repercussions of declaring bankruptcy.

Explanations

1. To invoke §7003, the EPA must show that:
    a. A party fits one of the categories of handling waste or contributing to its handling.
    b. Such status was either in the past or in the present.
    c. The waste handled was either solid or hazardous waste.
    d. The waste may present an imminent and substantial endangerment.

      The presence of hazardous waste alone is enough to make this showing. Exposure of hazardous waste to the environment is enough, without any actual damage. There need not be any actual harm — only a risk of future harm, as interpreted by the courts.

      Liability is strict. There is no requirement to prove fault or negligence, as held in the *NEPACCO* case. 810 F.2d 726 (8th Cir. 1986).

2a. Princess Leia is liable as the current owner of the facility.

2b. Millennium Falcon Transport Company is liable as a transporter of RCRA waste and a handler of waste.

2c. Darth Vader is a generator of waste and is subject to RCRA §7003.

2d. C3PO does not fit any of the categories of parties covered by §7003. While he could be asked for information or samples in his possession, he is not potentially liable to implement remediation.

3a. The issue here is whether or not Darth knew of the incorrect identification. It is only a criminal violation if the violation was *knowing*. Does Darth Vader know everything?

3b. Princess Leia commits a criminal violation only if she knowingly disposes of something that is not allowed in her permit. However, if she fails to test, she violates her RCRA TSD permit. This could imperil the permit but is not in itself a criminal violation.

3c. Altering required information, even after the fact to make a correction, is an RCRA criminal violation. Princess Leia can supply additional information, but she should not alter any existing documents — ever.

3d. Millennium Falcon is criminally liable for failing to manifest the waste if it knew that a manifest was required. Courts likely will infer that the company should have known that a manifest was required. This is a potentially criminal violation. Failure to determine requirements of law is not an excuse. Good counsel is needed.

4. Bankruptcy is a commonly attempted escape hatch for owners and operators faced with RCRA liability. While the case law is not fully resolved, several elements of advice can be offered. First, under the *Kovacs* precedent, if the environmental obligation can be reduced to nothing more than a dollar amount prior to filing for bankruptcy, it should be discharged in bankruptcy as a personal debt. Otherwise, to the extent that assets exist, environmental claims can be afforded priority for payment as administrative expenses.

   However, in most cases, the automatic stay available in bankruptcy will not be an absolute bar. As many contaminating acts continue until addressed, there are ongoing environmental violations. If an order or penalty is assessed after the appointment of a bankruptcy trustee, the automatic stay will not apply, as in the *T. P. Long Chem.* and *Midlantic National Bank* cases. The bankruptcy protections often yield to the injunctive cleanup orders of environmental agencies.

   Finally, abandonment of contaminated property by the trustee, where such property constitutes a threat to the public health, is often blocked by the courts. Many contaminated properties can satisfy the relatively lenient standards for demonstrating public health threats. However, if there are insufficient assets and no demonstrated public health threat, the abandonment power survives, as in *Smith-Douglas*.

The Superfund: Hazardous Substance Remediation

"Avoid the unmanageable, and manage the unavoidable."

Thomas Friedman, Hot, Flat and Crowded, 2008

"True is it that we have seen better days."

William Shakespeare, As You Like It

"A land ethic for tomorrow should be as honest as Thoreau's *Walden*, and as corresponsive as the sensitive science of Ecology. It should stress the oneness of our resources and the live-and-help-live logic of the great chain of life."

Stewart L. Udall, The Quiet Crisis, 1963

"Man ain't really evil, he just ain't got any sense."

William Faulkner

While RCRA deals with the management of hazardous wastes, CERCLA (the "Superfund") regulates the remediation of spills or releases of hazardous substances. CERCLA is a federal statutory substitute or addition to the common law (see Chapter 1) for assigning responsibility for hazardous substance remediation. It designates who is potentially liable for cleaning up existing areas of contamination. It has been one of the most actively used and litigated environmental statutes.

In this chapter, we will highlight how CERCLA differs from other statutes, what substances are covered, and who is covered. We will examine the powers and tools of the EPA and private parties, the regulatory scheme that expands the statute, and the process of cleanup itself. We will look at different legal schemes and techniques for allocating liability, defenses to liability, and special liability issues involving municipalities, acts of war, trustees, bankruptcy, and parent or successor corporations.

THE MECHANICS OF CERCLA

How Superfund Is Different from Other Environmental Laws

The Superfund, or CERCLA, is a pillar of environmental law — and the object of attack from its detractors. More environmental lawyers may be involved with Superfund — in enforcing its provisions, defending potentially responsible parties, or litigating over insurance reimbursement of Superfund expenses — than any other single environmental statute. Close to 40,000 identified hazardous substance sites are directly affected by the statute.

Typically, when Congress wishes to increase the level of regulation in an environmental area, it amends and buttresses an existing statute, rather than enacting separate legislation. The logical question is: With RCRA subtitle C (discussed in the prior chapter) enacted in 1976 to address hazardous waste, why was there any subsequent need for new CERCLA legislation? The answer to why there are separate statutes: a more comprehensive scheme to address different categories of covered substances.

Prospective or Retrospective

CERCLA is *retrospective* in its fundamental approach, while many of the other primary environmental statutes are *prospective*. *United States v. Olin Corp.*, 107 F.3d 1506 (11th Cir. 1997) (retroactive liability for environmental cleanup). RCRA is principally a statute for the *prospective* handling and management of both hazardous *and* solid waste streams. As explained in Chapter 8, hazardous wastes are a subset of solid wastes, which include all wastes. Although RCRA does contain isolated provisions, such as its §7003, to address injunctively the consequences of past waste management practices, that is not its principal thrust. While RCRA works prospectively to control the current handling of waste streams, CERCLA works retrospectively to address and remediate demonstrated problems from past practices. In the life of a regulated substance, RCRA's requirements attach at the point when a substance becomes a "waste." CERCLA requirements do not attach until a substance is released to the environment and becomes a problem. The timeline in Exhibit 9.1 shows the points in a substance's chain of use at which various federal statutes come into play.

9.1 Major Environmental Statutes' Points of Regulation in a Substance's Chain of Use

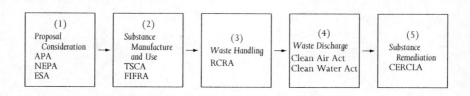

While other major environmental statutes regulate or provide permits to operators who want to emit pollution into the air or water or plan to handle toxic chemicals, CERCLA regulates toxic releases that have already occurred or are threatening to occur. CERCLA attaches late in a chemical's life and applies retrospectively. While counsel dealing with the Clean Air Act, the Clean Water Act, RCRA, and other primary environmental statutes typically engage in determining compliance requirements or obtaining permits pursuant to those statutes, counsel in CERCLA cases deal with sins already committed involving unpermitted releases of chemicals to the environment. Unlike many other primary environmental statutes, CERCLA often regulates unintentional emissions and releases of hazardous substances, rather than planned or permitted emissions.

Wastes and Other Substances

There are fundamental definitional distinctions between the focus of RCRA and that of CERCLA. Subtitle C of RCRA focuses on hazardous *wastes*. Wastes are defined specifically by RCRA with respect to four primary hazardous characteristics (discussed in Chapter 8). By comparison, CERCLA does not deal at all with wastes *per se*. CERCLA concerns hazardous *substances*, which need not be wastes as defined in RCRA. As shown in Exhibit 9.2, substances are a larger potential universe than wastes. The CERCLA universe includes the RCRA list of hazardous wastes, but it also includes hazardous chemicals that are regulated by the Clean Water Act, the minimum 189 hazardous air pollutants under the Clean Air Act, and substances regulated under the Toxic Substances Control Act.

While it is comprehensive, CERCLA is not all-inclusive. Excluded from its coverage for political reasons are petroleum and natural gas; also excluded, because they are covered elsewhere, are nuclear materials.

In 1999, CERCLA was amended by the Superfund Recycling Equity Act to exempt certain arrangers and transporters of "Recyclable Material" from liability under CERCLA. The Act exempts from liability under

9.2 Universe of All Chemical Substances

Hazardous	Hazardous	Nonhazardous
Hazardous wastes (RCRA)	Clean Water Act toxics	Benign nonwastes
TSCA hazardous chemical or mixture	Clean Air Act toxics	RCRA solid wastes

§107(a)(3)-(4), from liability as an arranger for disposal or transporter, those who arrange for disposal or transport recyclable material. "Recyclable Materials" include scrap paper, plastic, glass, textiles, rubber (other than whole tires), metal, used batteries; it does not include PCBs. Therefore, while not applying to whole tires, it might apply to chipped or shredded tires. To take advantage of this exemption, one must demonstrate that a market existed for the recyclable material, a substantial portion of the recyclable material was made available as feed stock for the manufacturer of a new saleable product, the recyclable material could have been a replacement or substitute for a virgin raw material or product, and the arranger or transporter exercised reasonable care to determine that the facility where the recyclable material was handled, processed, reclaimed, or otherwise managed by a third party was in compliance with all federal, state, or local environmental laws or regulations, including administrative or judicial decrees.

If one commences a contribution action under CERCLA against an arranger or transporter who is exempt by virtue of this exemption for recyclable materials, that person is allowed and authorized to recover all attorney fees, expert witness fees, and "all reasonable costs of defending" the action. The exemption applies not only to prosecutions undertaken by the government, but also to private cross-claims and third-party claims for contribution under CERCLA. *United States v. Atlas Lederer Co.*, 97 F. Supp. 2d 830 (S.D. Ohio 2000).

Let's look at the difference between CERCLA and RCRA in another way, as illustrated by the lifecycle of a chemical. Exhibit 9.3 depicts a chemical lifecycle from the creation of a material until its disposal. RCRA attaches only at stage (4) in the timeline of a substance's life. RCRA authority depends on the evolution of a substance to the status of a "waste." CERCLA, on the other hand, may apply at any point in a substance's lifecycle, depending on when the substance is released to the environment. Thus here is a critical

9.3 Stages in a Chemical's Lifecycle

distinction: RCRA is activated by *status* — the categorization of a substance as a "waste." CERCLA pivots on the *action* of a *release* of a hazardous substance. The action of releasing a hazardous substance is distinct from a hazardous substance becoming a waste material during its natural lifecycle.

Persons and Places

There are additional key distinctions between CERCLA and other environmental statutes. While the Clean Air Act, the Clean Water Act, and RCRA regulate persons (typically facility operators or material handlers), CERCLA regulates places. CERCLA applies when particular hazardous substances are or have been released to the environment at a particular place, called a "facility." So while CERCLA is a broad, overarching statute, encompassing and borrowing elements from other environmental statutes, it is fundamentally different in its approach. And these differences are important to keep in mind to fit CERCLA into the framework of environmental statutes.

CERCLA is multimedia in its scope. Any substance that would be hazardous, no matter what its environmental medium — as a land contaminant, water contaminant, or air contaminant — is governed by CERCLA regardless of the medium in which it is found at a particular facility. A substance is regulated by CERCLA even if it contaminates a medium other than the one in which it is regulated as toxic or hazardous by other statutes.

For example, asbestos is not recognized as an RCRA hazardous waste (see Chapter 8), but it is a toxic air pollutant (see Chapter 5). However, asbestos is actionable under CERCLA if it is released in any medium — air, water, or land. This is true even though asbestos disposed of on or in land is not an RCRA subtitle C hazardous waste. You must adjust to this lack of consistent integration of CERCLA with other statutes. CERCLA is *indiscriminately* and inclusively multimedia in its definition of hazardous substances.

CERCLA is also fundamentally different in that it creates private rights of action for individual persons to seek financial redress for their cleanup costs. (Personal injury is not covered.) The Clean Air Act, the Clean Water Act, and RCRA do not provide a similar private right of action. They permit citizen suits, whereby persons can sue as a private attorney general to enforce emission limits or practices; these private enforcement actions do not allow private recovery. In other words, no "damages" may be recovered privately; only equitable injunctions for enforcement and collection of penalties for violations of the statute are allowed (although under both the Clean Air Act and Clean Water Act, courts have allowed some penalty funds to be put aside in private trusts, to be managed in some cases by the plaintiff litigants, for environmental restoration, education, or benefit).

CERCLA allows both private rights of action and dollar recovery for cleanup costs, although claims technically are made in an equitable action for restitution, rather than at law for damages (the government but not private parties, under CERCLA, can recover for damage to natural resources). Thus CERCLA permits private rights of action, while other major environmental statutes do not.

Common Law Distinctions

Along with these key private liability provisions, the broad hazardous substance scope of CERCLA makes it one of the most powerful environmental statutes at the federal level. It is so compelling that it countermands, *impliedly* according to many courts, well-established principles of the common law:

- The common law tort principle of negligence finds no expression in CERCLA.
- Contracts that shift liability through indemnity provisions are ineffective as to third parties under CERCLA.
- Concepts of the corporate veil and insulation from personal liability for corporate acts *impliedly* are countermanded by CERCLA.
- The *mens rea* requirements of criminal law are stretched.
- Elements of the federal bankruptcy law *impliedly* are countermanded.

Significant elements of the first-year law-school curriculum, as well as certain statutory provisions, bend under the influence of CERCLA. Few environmental statutes are as comprehensive or compelling. However, ambiguities and gaps in its statutory scheme leave a wide range of issues for judicial interpretation. On many of these issues, the federal circuits have split authority and the Supreme Court has not yet spoken. Thus, in many ways, the Superfund is yet unsure of its full stride.

Basic Structure

In 1980, on the eve of President Reagan's assuming office, Congress enacted the Comprehensive Environmental Response, Compensation, and Liability Act (CERCLA) to provide a mechanism for response to releases of hazardous substances into the environment. It is important to understand the basic structure of this statute. CERCLA, as originally enacted, established four fundamental program elements:

1. A system for information gathering and analysis
2. Federal authority to respond to and clean up releases of hazardous substances
3. A Hazardous Substance Response Trust Fund (the "Superfund") to underwrite cleanup
4. A liability scheme for those responsible for releases of hazardous substances

These four elements form a logical sequence in which the EPA typically asserts its jurisdiction. The EPA (1) collects information, (2) responds to emergencies, (3) may tap a preestablished, segregated federal cleanup fund, and (4) pursues responsible parties. We examine each of these four elements in the following pages.

Information and Inspection: §§103 and 104

Notification   When there is a release of a pollutant or contaminant, reporting of that release may be required under CERCLA, the Emergency Planning and Community Right-to-Know Act, TSCA, FIFRA, RCRA, the Clean Water Act, the Clean Air Act, and/or OSHA. Notification of a release is set out in §103 of the statute. Section 103 is codified at 42 U.S.C. §9603 (the sections of CERCLA can be converted to their federal code sections by adding the numerical value 9500 to the CERCLA section). Basically, it is the responsibility of any person in charge of a "facility" who has knowledge of a "release" of a reportable quantity of any hazardous substance, to notify the EPA's National Response Center immediately of such release. The National Response Center, a federally administered information clearinghouse, then notifies the governor of any affected state, as well as the appropriate government agencies.

This system of notification enables the EPA, and other federal and state authorities, to compile a list of problem sites throughout the country, assess the relative potential danger of these sites to the public, and develop appropriate response plans. Penalties for failure to notify the National Response Center were increased to a fine as provided for in Title 18 of the United States Code, or a prison term of up to three years (and up to five years for a subsequent offense), or both. See 42 U.S.C. §9603(b)(3).

It is also the responsibility of an owner or operator of a facility, or one who arranges for storage, treatment, or disposal of hazardous substances, to notify the EPA administrator of the existence of such a facility and the nature of the substances stored, treated, or disposed of there. A temporary stoppage in transit of hazardous substances is not deemed to be storage. Penalties for knowing failure to so notify the EPA administrator include a fine of up to $10,000, a one-year prison term, or both. The EPA administrator is in turn authorized to notify the governor of any affected state, as well as the appropriate government agencies. 42 U.S.C. §9603(c).

There are exemptions from CERCLA reporting requirements (a) for hazardous substances that are reportable under other acts or sections, (b) for otherwise federally permitted releases, and (c) for the application of pesticides. While reporting the *release* of chemicals is required under §313 of the Emergency Planning and Community Right-to-Know Act (EPCRA), there is no federal requirement to report use of such chemicals. No court has required the reporting of a release that otherwise is consistent with a federally permitted release, and therefore exempt from CERCLA and EPCRA. EPCRA requires the facility where a hazardous chemical is produced, used, or stored to immediately report the release of reportable quantities of CERCLA hazardous substances, or any EPCRA extremely hazardous substances (listed at 40 C.F.R. Part 355, Appendices A and B), as well as to provide a written follow-up notice including information on the release, response options, risks, and medical advice.

Neither are accidents or malfunctions which result in unexpected releases deemed exempt by the EPA as federally permitted releases. Moreover, the EPA maintains that if an air permit does not provide for excess emissions during start-up or shutdown of a facility, any excesses during such times are federally reportable releases to the extent that they exceed the levels in the permit. Additional provisions regarding notification require recordkeeping and establishing penalties for failure to keep proper records.

Information   Pursuant to §104(e) of CERCLA, the EPA may request from any person information deemed relevant to a threat of release or release of hazardous substances. This information authority is very broad. It can compel persons to divulge information about financial ability and resources, as well as conduct with regard to hazardous substances. Refusal to comply with a §104(e) information request can subject the nonrespondent to treble damages in a later §107 cost recovery action or a later §112(c) subrogation action. (RCRA contains information-gathering provisions in §§3007 and 3013.)

Title III of the SARA amendments in 1990 created a free-standing statute known as the Emergency Planning and Community Right to Know Act (EPCRA). 42 U.S.C. §§11001-11050. This Act requires mandatory reporting of toxic substance releases annually to the EPA. The Toxic Release Inventory (TRI) includes releases of more than 320 chemicals, by statute. The annual reporting requirements apply to certain industries releasing more than 25,000 pounds per year.

EPCRA requires emergency release notification, hazardous chemical storage reporting, and toxic chemical release reporting. EPCRA also requires that states establish a state emergency response commission, which itself then creates local emergency planning committees, for purposes of notification and post-accident response to toxic releases from industry.

Each employer must have a material safety data sheet (MSDS) for each hazardous chemical that is produced or imported. These MSDSs must accompany chemicals that are shipped and also must be readily accessible to employees. The contents of the MSDS must show the OSHA permissible exposure limit (PEL) and threshold limit values. The MSDS must also be made available to the public under EPCRA.

Access   The EPA is authorized to enter property, conduct inspections, and take samples. It may demand access and entry to property from any private party for Superfund-related purposes. If a state has entered into a cooperative agreement with the EPA pursuant to CERCLA, state personnel also may enter or inspect private property to enforce the statute. It is undecided whether the EPA's access authority can be used to secure access on behalf of and for private parties who are undertaking various Superfund activities. The EPA also is authorized to exercise eminent domain authority for CERCLA-related purposes. The takings clause of the Fifth Amendment to the Constitution may require compensation of adjacent landowners whose property is used for implementation of a CERCLA remedy. (See Chapter 10.)

Key CERCLA Definitions

As with other environmental statutes, we must pay careful attention to statutory and regulatory definitions.

Facilities   First, the key noun, facility, statutorily includes "(A) any building, structure, installation, equipment, pipe or pipeline (including any pipe into a sewer or publicly owned treatment works), well, pit, pond, lagoon, impoundment, ditch, landfill, storage container, motor vehicle, rolling stock, or aircraft, or (B) any site or area where a hazardous substance has been deposited, stored, disposed of, or placed, or otherwise come to be located; but does not include any consumer product in consumer use or any vessel." 42 U.S.C. §9601(9). As Representative James Florio stated, the definition of "facility" is intentionally expansive: "[T]he definition of 'facility' is necessarily a broad one. It explicitly defines facility as, among other things, any site or area where a hazardous substance has been deposited, stored, disposed of, or otherwise come to be located."

The case precedent underscores this broad sweep. The term facility "includes every place where hazardous substances come to be located."

393

9. The Superfund: Hazardous Substance Remediation

United States v. Conservation Chemical Co., 619 F. Supp. 162, 185 (W.D. Mo. 1985). For example, the term includes roadside ditches where contaminated oil was spread. See *United States v. Ward*, 618 F. Supp. 884, 895 (E.D.N.C. 1985). A "facility" even transcends normal property boundaries: "Noncontiguous facilities may be treated as a single facility where they are reasonably related on the basis of geography or the actual or potential threat to the public health or welfare or the environment." See *United States v. Taylor*, 31 ERC (BNA) 1197, 1198-99 (M.D.N.C. 1989); *United States v. Bell Petroleum Serv., Inc.*, 31 ERC 1365, 1366 (W.D. Tex. 1989) (a site containing several contamination plumes constituted a single facility).

Release The key CERCLA verb, *release*, is defined in the statute as "any spilling, leaking, pumping, pouring, emitting, emptying, discharging, injecting, escaping, leaching, dumping, or disposing into the environment (including the abandonment or discarding of barrels, containers, and other closed receptacles containing any hazardous substance or pollutant or contaminant). . . ." 42 U.S.C. §9601(22). This definition includes words that describe the willful or inadvertent escape of pollutants into the environment. A little later in this chapter, we discuss whether or not these words refer to acts by totally *passive* nonpolluting owners.

Hazardous Substances The definition of "hazardous substances" is very broad. The hastily passed CERCLA simply incorporates by reference the lists of hazardous chemicals in other federal statutes regulating toxic substances. Thus it sweeps up all the toxic chemicals regulated by other divisions of EPA. "Hazardous substance" is defined as (1) any substance designated as a toxic pursuant to the Clean Water Act, §1321(b)(2)(A) or §1317 of Title 33, (2) any element, compound, mixture, solution, or substance designated pursuant to CERCLA, (3) any hazardous waste having the characteristics identified under or listed pursuant to RCRA, (4) any hazardous air pollutant listed under §112 of the Clean Air Act, and (5) any imminently hazardous chemical substance or mixture with respect to which the EPA administrator has taken action pursuant to the Toxic Substances Control Act (TSCA). Thus the release of almost any toxic or hazardous chemical or mixture to the environment can trigger CERCLA.

Exceptions However, there are statutory exemptions for certain kinds of releases, including workplace releases, emissions from transportation devices, emissions from pipeline pumping station engines, high-level radioactive substance releases regulated under other statutes, contamination from the application of federally permitted pesticides, and other federally permitted releases. 42 U.S.C. §101(22)(A)-(D). The term *hazardous substance* does not include petroleum or crude oil.

Federally permitted releases need not be reported to the EPA pursuant to the CERCLA reporting requirement contained at 42 U.S.C. §9603. This exception to CERCLA typically refers to releases to the water or air permitted under statutes primarily governing such discharges, such as the Clean Water Act or the Clean Air Act. The "federally permitted releases" exception does not apply to permits of the Bureau of Land Management, the U.S. Forest Service, or NEPA, because such land-use and environmental process permits do not qualify within the definition of federally sanctioned direct releases. Discharging a permitted hazardous constituent into the air or water in gross excess of the amount allowed under a permit violates that permit and does not qualify as a federally permitted release. Only releases in compliance with the express provisions of the permit count as federally permitted releases.

The pesticide exception applies only to the application of pesticides and does not affect the release of hazardous substances as part of the manufacture or disposal of pesticides. This pesticide exemption is from §107 of CERCLA, which provides for the recovery of response costs. No similar exemption is found in §104 or §111 of CERCLA. Therefore, it appears that the government, pursuant to §104, could expend Superfund monies on the remediation of hazardous substances resulting from pesticide application, but it could not recover Superfund monies from those parties responsible for the application.

It is noteworthy that the primary pesticide statute, FIFRA, contains no clear authority for the government to remedy groundwater contamination resulting from the release of registered pesticides. However, common law and state statutory remedies are expressly preserved by §107(i) of CERCLA. To the extent that such state or common law remedies exist, they may provide a cause of action regarding pesticide contamination where CERCLA does not. Certain "service station dealers" recycling used oil that contains hazardous substances, pursuant to RCRA recycling provisions, are exempt from CERCLA. 42 U.S.C. §§9601(37) and 9614(c)(1).

Cleanup Authority: §§104 and 105

Response   The second basic CERCLA element authorizes the federal government to clean up sites from which releases of hazardous substances occurred or are occurring. Two categories of federal response activities are authorized: (1) *short-term* removal or emergency response activities, and (2) *long-term* remedial activities. The President has the authority to act under §104 of CERCLA to

> remove or arrange for the removal of, and provide for remedial action relating to such hazardous substance, pollutant, or contaminant at any time (including its removal from any contaminated natural resource), or take any other

response measure consistent with the national contingency plan which the President deems necessary to protect the public health or welfare or the environment. . . .

42 U.S.C. §9604(a)(1).

Each of the key statutory terms is defined specifically in §§101 and 104 of CERCLA. Only $2 million of federal funds may be expended on a short-term removal or emergency response activity, prior to listing the site on the National Priorities List. The number of sites added to the NPL for 2003-2011 ranged between 8 and 35 annually, with 7-9 sites deleted annually, and final remediation accomplished at 11-25 sites annually. The EPA uses the money in the Superfund (discussed next) to fund and accomplish these actions. If the release or threat is perceived to constitute a public health or environmental emergency, and no one else is able to respond effectively, the President can take direct action. 42 U.S.C. §9604(a)(4).

The President takes remedial action contingent on a state's parallel assurances that the state will maintain and operate the cleanup activities initiated by the federal government for as long as necessary, ensure the availability of an adequate hazardous waste disposal facility in-state, and assume a portion of the government-funded response costs incurred. A state must agree to assume 10 percent of the response costs, or 50 percent if the facility is state-owned. If remedial action is deemed necessary on Native American-owned land, the state cost-sharing requirements of this section do not apply. When the EPA performs cleanup through its own contractors, according to GAO reports, inefficiency and unnecessary work continues to make these cleanups significantly more expensive than when PRPs perform cleanups themselves.

The National Contingency Plan Process   All federal actions must be consistent with the National Contingency Plan (NCP), a set of EPA regulations to order and guide cleanup activities. The content of the NCP is prescribed in general terms by 42 U.S.C. §9605. As part of the National Contingency Plan, the EPA established a National Hazardous Substance Response Plan, which sets forth guidelines for responding to releases of hazardous substances, pollutants, and contaminants. It is designed to ensure that only cost-effective measures are pursued. The NCP designates procedures to determine how much money should be spent at a site and to determine the appropriate extent of removal, remediation, or other actions. If remedial action is necessary, the EPA or the state lead agency develops a community relations plan.

If the EPA implements an outmoded remedy at a Superfund site, or ignores changed circumstances, some costs incurred may be "inconsistent with the National Contingency Plan" and PRPs will not be liable for such costs. See *United States v. Broderick Investment Co.,* 955 F. Supp. 1268 (D. Colo.

1997). To be consistent with the NCP, remedial actions must include (1) a site investigation and an analysis of remedial alternatives, (2) compliance with NCP regulations relating to development, screening, analysis, and selection of cleanup methods, (3) an opportunity for public comment on the selected remedy, and (4) a cost-effective response. 40 C.F.R. §300.700(c). Most private-party cost recovery litigation does not impose on private parties the same exacting NCP compliance that is required of the government, although private actions must be consistent with the NCP. A landowner loses any third-party defense if he or she knowingly transfers property containing hazardous substances without notifying the purchaser of such condition. Innocent purchasers who have been defrauded into purchasing contaminated property may seek rescission of the purchase contract pursuant to state common law.

As its basic approach, the EPA compiles lists of priority sites and potentially responsible parties to promote and maximize the number of privately funded cleanups, marshalling the Superfund to finance those priority cleanups for which private response activity is inadequate. To start, the EPA makes a preliminary assessment of each site to determine general health and environmental risks and priorities among various waste sites. Preliminary site assessment information is stored in the Comprehensive Environmental Response, Compensation and Liability Information System (CERCLIS), a compilation of hazardous substance release sites.

The EPA next quantifies the potential risks that characterize each site by conducting a "FITS" evaluation and translating this to a numerical score. The Hazard Ranking System (HRS) is found at 40 C.F.R. §300, Appendix A. The HRS evaluates toxicity, quantity, and concentration of wastes. The EPA evaluates the population at risk, the hazard potential of the hazardous substances involved, the potential for contamination of drinking water supplies, the potential for destruction of ecosystems, or direct public contact or damage to natural resources that may affect the human food chain. For each facility, the HRS produces a single risk value reflecting exposure potential and the degree of danger of the hazardous substances involved. This HRS score enables the EPA to determine which sites are most serious and belong on the National Priorities List (NPL). An HRS score greater than 28.5 makes the facility eligible for Congress to place it on the NPL. 42 U.S.C. §9605. The EPA continues to add sites to the NPL at an average rate of 20-30 per year. Sites are not listed on the NPL if corrective action pursuant to RCRA could address the contamination (see discussion in Chapter 8).

The NPL prioritizes facilities for remedial and removal actions. 42 U.S.C. §9605(a)(8)(A). These NPL sites are entitled to more than the $2 million limit of federal emergency funds to redress their problems. Until 2000, the EPA completed cleanup at about 85 NPL sites annually; since 2000, the completed number is about 40 sites annually.

After any emergencies are addressed, the EPA will conduct a Remedial Investigation (RI) to characterize the contamination at the site, and a Feasibility Study (FS) to evaluate different remediation options, prior to choosing the type of remediation as part of the EPA's Record of Decision (ROD). The ROD process involves public comment and a decision on the record, pursuant to administrative procedure (see Chapter 2). 42 U.S.C. §9605(a). Legal challenges to a cleanup remedy selected by the EPA are generally limited to review of the administrative record created by the agency and by public respondents (including liable parties). A summary of the NCP process is shown in Exhibit 9.4.

CERCLA provides that health-related authority is a joint responsibility of the EPA and the federal Agency for Toxic Substances and Disease Registry (ATSDR). Responsibilities of the ATSDR include (1) the establishment and maintenance of a national registry of serious diseases and illnesses of persons exposed to toxic substances, (2) the establishment and maintenance of literature, research, and studies on the health effects of toxic substances, and (3) the establishment and maintenance of a list of areas closed to the public or otherwise restricted because of toxic substance contamination.

States and Citizen Roles   States are responsible for all "future maintenance of all remedial and removal actions." That is, they must give full financial support to the operation and maintenance of cleanup actions. States must also provide at least one hazardous waste disposal facility, licensed pursuant to RCRA, to receive hazardous wastes removed from Superfund sites within their borders. States must cost-share 10 percent of remedial action costs at all sites within their borders, or 50 percent or more of such costs if the facility is state or municipally owned. A privately owned facility operated under contract to state or municipal entities is considered a state or municipal facility for purposes of cost sharing. States also can take over the EPA's lead remediation role, thus inheriting a §107 cost recovery action against potentially responsible parties (PRPs) for costs expended.

Citizens affected by a Superfund site may receive technical grants of up to $50,000 by participating in the Technical Assistance Grant (TAG) program. 42 U.S.C. §9617(e). These funds are used by the citizens to hire their own technical consultants to advise them about human health and

9.4   The EPA NCP Process in a Nutshell

(1) Preliminary assessment (CERCLIS)	(2) Emergency action (limit $2 million)	(3) FITS evaluation (HRS)	(4) NPL designation	(5) RI/FS	(6) ROD

environmental issues. These citizens and their consultants may take an intervenor or adversary position regarding agency decision making.

There are two citizen suit provisions in CERCLA. First, any person may bring suit in a federal district court against any other person, other than the EPA, alleged to be in violation of "any standard, regulation, condition, requirement, or order which has become effective" under CERCLA. Prior notice of sixty days must be given to both the alleged offender and the government. A copy of the complaint must be provided to the EPA and to the attorney general. The EPA or state may intervene in a citizen suit as of right. If the EPA prosecutes the alleged offense under CERCLA or RCRA, then the private litigation is barred. Attorney fees, costs, and expert witness fees are available for prevailing or substantially prevailing citizen parties, pursuant to CERCLA.

Second, a citizen may petition for a preliminary assessment at a site not otherwise scheduled for response actions. (In addition, states, but not municipalities or subdivisions of states, may bring suit in federal court to enforce CERCLA requirements.) These two provisions are in addition to the cost recovery provision of §107 and the contribution provisions of §113, described later in this chapter.

The private and citizen suit provisions of CERCLA are as follows:

- Citizen enforcement (60-day notice)
- Citizen preliminary assessment
- §107 Cost recovery
- §113 Contribution

Both injunctive relief and civil penalties are authorized by CERCLA. Civil penalties, which may be levied administratively or by the court, pertain to violations of the notification requirements, destruction of records, violation of §122(d)(3), or failure or refusal to carry out the terms of a settlement agreement. There is also a bounty provision in CERCLA: From the Superfund an "award" of up to $10,000 may be paid for information leading to the arrest and conviction of any person for a criminal CERCLA violation.

The Superfund: §§111 and 112

The third basic component of CERCLA is a Hazardous Substance Response Trust Fund, or "Superfund," to pay for federal government response to actual and threatened releases of hazardous substances, and for restoration of natural resource damages. 42 U.S.C. §9611. This fund pays the federal share of removal, response, or remediation activities. The trust fund originally was funded by sales taxes on chemical corporations and general U.S. government appropriations. As discussed below, this tax base subsequently ceased. The government acquires the right to seek reimbursement from potentially responsible parties (PRPs) for response costs incurred and paid from the Superfund in cleanup, administration, removal, oversight, and resource restoration. The money obtained through this reimbursement scheme replenishes the Superfund. 42 U.S.C. §9612(c)(3).

The Small Business Liability Relief and Brownfields Revitalization Act of 2001 provides federal grant money to encourage redevelopment of brownfields. Up to $200,000 per site for assessment, and up to $1 million per eligible recipient for remediation, can be funded by this program. Brownfields are defined as "real property, the expansion, redevelopment, or reuse of which may be complicated by the presence or potential presence of a hazardous substance, pollutant, or contaminant." Excluded from this definition are facilities that are the subject of a planned or ongoing removal action, sites listed on the NPL, certain RCRA sites, and sites that are the subject of unilateral administrative orders of the EPA, court orders, or consent decrees. The Act also requires that Davis-Bacon federal wages apply to workers at brownfield sites funded by the grant program.

Liability Allocation: §107

The fourth basic CERCLA element is a liability allocation scheme. CERCLA imposes strict, and often joint and several, liability for restitution of response costs incurred by the government or a private party as a result of actual or potential releases of hazardous substances. Four categories of responsible parties are liable: (1) owners and operators of a "facility" from which hazardous substances are threatened to be released or are actually released, (2) persons who owned or operated a facility at the time of hazardous substance disposal, (3) persons who arranged for disposal of hazardous substances, and (4) persons who transported hazardous substances and selected the disposal site. 42 U.S.C. §9607(a). As discussed later, these PRPs have only very limited defenses.

The term "owners and operators" does not include a unit of state or local government that acquired ownership or control involuntarily through bankruptcy, tax delinquency, abandonment, or other circumstances in which the government involuntarily acquired title by virtue of its function as the sovereign power. The exclusion does not apply, however, to any state or local government that has caused or contributed to the release or threatened release of a hazardous substance from the facility.

The D.C. Circuit held that the federal government has waived sovereign immunity as a defense to CERCLA liability whether it is acting in a proprietary or a regulatory mode. In *East Bay Municipal Utility District v. Department of Commerce*, 142 F.3d 479 (D.C. Cir. 1998), the court rejected the government's claim that the waiver of sovereign immunity does not apply to activities of the government as a regulator. Therefore, whether the government becomes an owner or operator by virtue of its role as a proprietor or a regulator, it has no sovereign immunity defense to liability.

If, in a rare situation, the state is guilty of negligent conduct in the selection, investigation, and design of a site remedy, in limited situations it has been held liable. See *U.S. Dep't of Commerce v. Stringfellow*, 20 ELR 20656 (C.D. Cal. 1990); *PFG Gas, Inc. v. Pennsylvania*, 740 A.2d 297 (Pa. 1999); *FMC Corp. v. U.S. Department of Commerce*, 29 F.3d 833 (3d Cir. 1994).

The 1986 SARA Amendments

Six years after Congress enacted CERCLA, significant amendments were enacted in the Superfund Amendments and Reauthorization Act of 1986 (SARA). Major SARA changes to CERCLA included revised cleanup standards, strengthened settlement and enforcement provisions, and a larger revenue base for financing and replenishing the Superfund:

1. Requirement that cleanups satisfy ARARs
2. Additional environmental taxes on corporations
3. Settlement incentives, codification of contribution rights, and mixed funding of cleanups
4. More expansive role for states
5. More public involvement
6. Participation by health authorities
7. Authority over contamination at federal facilities

First, the most significant change wrought by the 1986 SARA amendments was §121 of CERCLA, which imposes detailed remedial standards on CERCLA-funded or CERCLA-ordered remedial actions. The remediation now must be one that is "protective of human health and the environment, that is cost effective, and that utilizes permanent solutions and alternative treatment technologies to the maximum extent practicable." It is not necessary for the EPA to select a remedy that has already been achieved in practice; it may select and implement innovative technologies. This new provision in CERCLA is similar to the technology-forcing provisions of the Clean Water Act and Clean Air Act. Preenforcement judicial review of a remedial action chosen by the EPA is statutorily barred. 42 U.S.C. §9613(h).

The remedial option chosen must be "relevant and appropriate." Remediation must meet all ARARs. 40 CFR §300.430(b)(9). Thus remediation must be consistent with the Federal Water Pollution Control Act, 33 U.S.C. 1251-1376, the Safe Drinking Water Act, 42 U.S.C. §300(f)-(j), the Toxic Substances Control Act, 15 U.S.C. §§2601-2629, and the Clean Air Act, 42 U.S.C. §§7401-7642. Typically, Maximum Contaminant Levels (MCLs), which are drinking water standards, are adopted as ARARs for contaminants other than carcinogenic chemicals. States must be provided "substantial and meaningful involvement" in the "initiation, development and selection of remedial actions" within the state. Off-site transportation of materials for disposal is not favored.

Second, SARA created a broader source of Superfund revenues by levying a new "environmental" tax on corporations, which has since ceased. Third, in response to the onerous litigation ensuing from EPA enforcement attempts, SARA for the first time introduced extensive statutory settlement provisions. SARA encourages voluntary settlements between PRPs. It also introduces provisions for contribution rights among PRPs, mixed EPA and private PRP funding, and settlement provisions for de minimis parties. These provisions are each discussed in more detail in later subsections.

Fourth, SARA gave the states much greater status and responsibility for implementing responses to CERCLA violations. Originally, under CERCLA, the states assumed a partnership with the EPA in all stages of cleanup or settlement. Under SARA, the states take on even greater review and enforcement powers for compliance with cleanup standards, and participate to a greater extent in identifying priority sites and appropriate cleanup remedies.

Fifth, SARA introduced provisions for public participation in cleanup and response activities, including participation in enforcement settlements and consent decrees. SARA mandates community relations efforts to keep the public informed and to respond to EPA inquiries. Sixth, SARA provides for greater participation by health-related authorities and greater contribution of their health-risk expertise. Seventh, for cleanups at federal facilities, SARA introduced provisions which parallel those for nonfederal facilities suffering releases of hazardous substances. The amendments authorized the EPA to treat tribes substantially as states for notification of releases, access to information, and responsibilities related to the NPL; Native American nations are limited in their ability to access funds to remediate sites.

Examples

1. Your client, Curly, calls to inform you that he has discovered a number of potential environmental problems at his commercial property. He solicits your legal advice regarding his responsibilities under CERCLA. He first informs you that he has discovered asbestos-containing insulation flaking off heating pipes in his building. He wants to know if CERCLA applies.

   a. Walk through the analysis you would go through before advising Curly whether or not CERCLA covers his asbestos problem.

   b. Is there an obligation to notify the EPA of this release?

   c. Curly also has found flaking paint with high levels of lead on interior and exterior walls of his commercial building. Does this flaking have any significance pursuant to CERCLA, assuming that the lead in the paint is of such concentration as to be recognized as a hazardous substance?

   d. What if Curly discovers that oil has leaked from an underground storage tank at the facility into soil. Does CERCLA apply?

   e. If Curly indicates that he has discovered a pool of liquid near several drums of hazardous substances that he has on-site, what are his notification/reporting requirements, and how soon must he act? Would you advise him to report or to undertake additional activities?

2. Could Curly escape CERCLA liability because his property was never a treatment, storage, or disposal facility pursuant to RCRA and therefore not a "facility" for CERCLA purposes?

3. If the problems were significant, could the EPA take over and spend $5 million of emergency money to remove the threat at Curly's site so as to alleviate any future risks?

4. If Larry, from 1970 until the present, recycles and sends to the Curly property used oil taken from vehicles that have their oil changed at his service station, what are his liability, if any, and defenses for the contamination at the Curly property?

5. If the contamination at Curly's property was caused by the prior owner, Stooge Waste, Inc., who discharged wastewater containing various hazardous substances into a creek on the property pursuant to a then-valid federal NPDES permit, and some of those same contaminants are now present at the property:
   a. Is Stooge Waste liable?
   b. What additional information would you need to make this determination?
   c. If Stooge Waste is liable, is it liable only for the cleanup costs associated with the creek area?

6. If the city of Metropolis in which the Curly property is located has drinking water standards twice as stringent and restrictive as state or federal standards, will parties cleaning up the Curly property have to meet the stricter Metropolis standards or only the state and federal standards since CERCLA is a federal law? Would they have to meet Metropolis standards even if doing so would quadruple the price of remediation?

Explanations

1a. When you are contacted by Curly, your legal advice as counsel turns on whether there has been a "release" of a reportable quantity of "hazardous substances" at a "facility" that Curly, your client, owns or operates. Here, there is no doubt that Curly is an owner who is responsible for notification to the EPA's Hazardous Response Center. State laws in many states also require notification to state environmental authorities. It is always necessary for you, as counsel, to check parallel state and/or local reporting requirements. A failure to do so is a serious omission.

Although Curly clearly has an owner's responsibility, you need to determine next if, in fact, asbestos is a "hazardous substance." What do you advise? Your legal advice to Curly is that, while asbestos is not listed individually in CERCLA as a hazardous substance, CERCLA incorporates by reference hazardous substances or toxic chemicals addressed under several other federal statutes. Therefore, you must check those other statutes and their regulations to see if asbestos is covered.

Your first instinct, correctly, would likely be to check for asbestos on the RCRA list of hazardous wastes. After all, asbestos is a solid material that often is removed and, after removal, becomes a waste for disposal. RCRA lists hundreds of chemicals and compounds as wastes; consult the Code of Federal Regulations at 40 C.F.R. §261, as updated in the Federal Register. Wastes are listed alphabetically, which simplifies this task.

When you review these RCRA regulations, you see that asbestos is *not* listed as a hazardous substance. In fact, it does not seem to fit the RCRA criteria as either ignitable (asbestos is a flame *retardant*), corrosive, reactive with other chemicals (asbestos is a stable mineral), or a leachable toxic metal. In fact, RCRA treats asbestos as a "special" solid waste, requiring special handling and segregated disposal in a solid waste facility, but it does not require treatment as a *hazardous* waste.

However, if you check the list of toxic air pollutants pursuant to §112 of the Clean Air Act, you will find asbestos listed as an air toxin. And since CERCLA incorporates by reference §112 of the Clean Air Act, asbestos is a hazardous substance under CERCLA, even if the asbestos is not found in the air medium. You also recall that a "facility" is anyplace that hazardous substances may be located, so Curly's property is a "facility."

Your final inquiry, knowing that Curly as owner of a facility is responsible for notification and that a CERCLA "hazardous substance" is involved, is to determine whether a reportable quantity has been released to the environment. Since the definition of "release" is any " . . . emitting or escaping" into the environment, the flaking off of asbestos-containing materials certainly is a "release." But is this release "into the environment"? The release, as far as Curly has informed you, is still contained within a building.

Therefore, you need to define the term "environment" as used in CERCLA. Consulting the definitions section of CERCLA §101(8), you see that "environment" is "the navigable waters . . . under the exclusive management authority of the United States . . . and any other surface water, ground water, drinking water supply, land surface or subsurface strata, or ambient air within the United States or under the jurisdiction of the United States."

Has Curly described a release into the environment? The answer here involves two questions to determine if the release affects an environmental medium. First, is the asbestos on a land surface? The answer is no. Second, is it in the ambient air? While asbestos flakes may be airborne particles barely heavier than air that float (often for days) before reaching the ground, the *ambient* air does not include air inside a building or structure. Ambient air is outdoor air. Therefore, unless there is reason to believe that these asbestos fibers have escaped outside of Curly's building, there has not been a release into the environment.

While a building itself can be a part of a "facility," this does not equate automatically to a release to the environment. A building can be part of the contaminated area, which is generally described as a "facility." Indoor air is not a release to the environment, but a release inside a building could pose a *threat* of release to the (exterior) environment. Threats of release are actionable under CERCLA. If the EPA otherwise learned of a release inside a building, it could deem it to be a *threat* of a release to the exterior of the building and thus into the environment, requiring notification (see Exhibit 9.5). Your advice to Curly should include this element.

1b. At this point, Curly is not required to notify the EPA under CERCLA. Therefore no notification is required and he does not face CERCLA liability. However, you might wish to inform Curly that the removal and containment of asbestos materials typically is governed by federal and state regulations that do require a notification of both federal and state authorities prior to removal of asbestos fibers. Scraping or pulling down asbestos-containing materials could be deemed an unauthorized removal.

Moreover, since this building is occupied, Curly may be exposed to common law tort liability for not abating the public health threat posed by asbestos to occupants and visitors. In some states, the mere presence of asbestos would be deemed to make a building uninhabitable under health and safety precedent. Therefore, although Curly does not have CERCLA liability, other legal issues here suggest attention.

9.5 Actionable Threats of Release Under CERCLA

Hazardous substance → Release or threat → To the environment → At a facility → Owner Operator Generator Transporter

1c. The determination of whether lead-based paint poses a CERCLA problem proceeds in much the same way as the analysis discussed in 1(a) above for asbestos. While lead-based paints typically are regulated by state statutes that require covering up painted surfaces or removing the paint when children under age six or seven inhabit a dwelling, there potentially could be CERCLA liability. If the lead is leachable (capable of entering water or soil), it could pose a problem as an RCRA hazardous waste. Moreover, if the lead-based paint is sanded and dust is created, the lead could pose an airborne problem as an air toxin. Lead is a criteria pollutant under the Clean Air Act. Curly is liable as the owner of the facility, and the lead may constitute a hazardous substance.

However, to the degree that the lead is released inside the building, it does not constitute a release into "the environment" and does not implicate CERCLA liability, as discussed in 1(a) above.

However, peeling lead-based paint on the outside of a building is a different matter. To the degree that this falls to the ground and mixes with soil, it may be a release into "the environment." This would impose notification requirements on Curly as the owner if a reportable quantity is involved, and would potentially expose him to liability pursuant to CERCLA.

1d. Releases of oil are quite common. There are many underground oil storage tanks across the country. Most gasoline stations have underground tanks for gasoline and diesel fuels. These tanks historically have been of single-wall metal construction. Gasoline is corrosive, and over time many of these tanks have corroded and leaked. And even if the tank itself does not leak, the pipes and fittings used to fill and extract gasoline and oils from these tanks, often utilizing pressure, can leak oil to the environment.

In advising Curly, you must be careful. You recall that the Superfund does not cover oil. Therefore, Curly as an owner would have no liability pursuant to CERCLA for the release of pure oil. However, there is a notification requirement regarding oil releases. Curly has to notify the EPA about this release if it exceeds the reportable quantity identified in the Code of Federal Regulations, even if he does not face cleanup liability. You should check the CERCLA regulations to determine the reportable quantity of the chemical released. The reportable quantity for oil is ten gallons. Therefore, if it is likely that more than ten gallons has been released, or if the amount of the release is indeterminable, Curly has a notification requirement to the EPA.

There is a caveat, however, in dealing with oil. The definition section of CERCLA excludes from the definition of "hazardous substance" any "petroleum, including crude oil or any fraction thereof which is not otherwise specifically listed or designated as a hazardous substance. . . ." However, if petroleum or petroleum products are mixed with other hazardous substances, then that mixture is hazardous. For example, used motor oil drained from automobile engines at service stations contains high levels of toxic metals and other contaminants. It is no longer pure or so-called virgin petroleum but a combination of petroleum and contaminants. The entire mixture therefore is a hazardous substance. Similarly, PCB-laden transformer oils have been adulterated with PCBs and are not pure petroleum. They are hazardous substances. Therefore, one needs to determine whether it is so-called virgin petroleum or an adulterated petroleum product, mixture, or derivative that is released.

1e. The requirement to notify the EPA of a release of a hazardous substance is "immediate." The penalties are substantial for failure to so notify. Concomitantly, the potential liability from designating one's place of business as a hazardous substance disposal facility is palpable. It is Curly's obligation, not yours as Curly's counsel, to make the notification. An attorney acting in his or her advisory capacity does not have a responsibility to notify on behalf of the client, or to notify in the event that the client does not follow his or her advice and fails to make timely notification. As an aside, at least one state environmental official has expressed the opinion that attorneys should have a notification requirement separate from their client. However, an attorney-client privilege might be violated if the attorney made this notification over the client's silence or objections. Therefore, your only duty is to clearly advise the client of his or her obligation to make immediate notification.

However, you should not do this unless the client is sure that in fact a hazardous substance is involved. Mere suspicion, or even likelihood, that a leaking material is a hazardous substance does not require notification. As counsel, it would be prudent for you to advise Curly that he has every right, if he so desires, to have tests performed as soon as possible to determine, definitively, whether a hazardous substance is involved. Upon such confirmation, then you advise Curly that he must notify the EPA immediately to comply with federal law. In addition, you should check and advise Curly as to any notification requirements under state and local law, which may have their own time periods and their own penalties.

2. The definition of "facility" under CERCLA does not require that the facility have been a treatment, storage, or disposal facility as defined in RCRA, that it ever have handled hazardous waste pursuant to a RCRA permit, or that it ever have been intended for such purposes. Rather, a facility is any place, regardless of geographic boundaries or metes and bounds in property deeds, where hazardous substances have come to be located for any reason. Therefore, a facility is not so much a precise definition of type of land use as an inclusive description of a place where

the EPA may take action pursuant to CERCLA and with regard to which individual liability may be imposed. The fact that Curly never handled hazardous waste does not have any relevance as to whether his property can become a "facility" for CERCLA purposes.

3. The EPA can take immediate action if it determines that there is an imminent and substantial endangerment to public health or the environment. In practice, this is not a particularly difficult showing. Typically the EPA makes a determination, based on the opinion of one of its on-staff engineers or environmental specialists, that the site poses a risk. However, the EPA is limited to a gross expenditure of not more than $2 million at an individual site unless it obtains a waiver from the President. And of this amount, the state must contribute at least 10 percent. Therefore, if the state does not make this contribution, it can block effective EPA action. The EPA may not, then, spend $5 million to take emergency removal actions at Curly's property. Prior to expenditures of this amount, the EPA must characterize the site contamination pursuant to the NCP and if its problems are sufficiently serious have it placed on the National Priorities List.

4. You may recall that there is an exception to §101(37) of CERCLA that was added by SARA in 1986. This exception exempts from CERCLA liability the used-oil recycling activities of service stations if properly conducted. However, two questions still remain. First, did Larry, acting as a service station, properly recycle the used oil to an authorized recycling facility? If yes, the exception applies. If not, it does not apply.

   Second, there is an open question as to the effective application date of this exception. It was added in the SARA amendments in 1986. The service station exception takes effect as of the date of regulations promulgated under the Solid Waste Disposal Act (RCRA). 42 U.S.C. §9614(c)(4). This regulation was promulgated in final form in March 1993. There is a presumption against retroactivity in application of statutes, but an argument exists that the new regulation merely clarifies, rather than alters, the liability of service station oil recyclers. Therefore, it could apply pre-1986. In any event, oil recycling activities prior to there being proper RCRA recycling facilities would not qualify for the exception. Since Larry began recycling in 1970, some six years before the enactment of RCRA, some of those early years of oil recycling/disposal may not qualify factually for exception from liability.

5a. There is an exception from CERCLA liability for federally permitted releases. Releases of pollutants and contaminants pursuant to an NPDES permit under the Clean Water Act are recognized as federally permitted releases. Therefore, in concept, Stooge Waste is not liable for these releases.

5b. However, some additional factual information is required. Were the pollutants and contaminants that were released pursuant to the NPDES permit (1) limited to only those allowed in the permit and (2) not in excess of the amounts or concentrations allowed by the permit? This is a factual determination that can be determined by reviewing the self-monitoring data and any enforcement actions regarding Stooge Waste. If additional pollutants or contaminants not allowed in the permit, or allowed pollutants in excess of permitted amounts, were discharged, then those additional pollutants or amounts are not federally permitted releases. Since any minute quantity of a hazardous substance is sufficient to impose liability, additional contaminants or additional quantities of permitted contaminants trigger liability.

5c. If Stooge Waste is liable, it likely would be jointly and severally liable for all contamination at the facility. The "facility" will be the entire parcel of every area that is contaminated, which would include the creek as well as other upland areas of the property. The only way for Stooge Waste to limit its liability to the creek area would be to demonstrate that its contribution to the injury at the property is divisible, as discussed in the next section. Depending on the contaminants involved, their locations, and their pathways of migration, divisibility may or may not be possible at Curly's site. For PRPs at most waste disposal sites, demonstrating divisibility of the harm has proved difficult.

6. Drinking water standards are recognized as ARARs pursuant to CERCLA. Remediation must satisfy all ARARs, whether found in local, state, or federal statutes and regulations. The most stringent of these standards would apply. Therefore, the twice-as-strict Metropolis standards would apply to the remediation. The cost of compliance with ARARs is not a factor. As discussed in Chapter 4, states and localities, if allowed by state law, are allowed to promulgate standards more strict than federal requirements.

EPA TOOLS TO ACCOMPLISH POLLUTION ABATEMENT AND IMPOSE LIABILITY: §§106 AND 107

The Four Basic Tools

§106 Orders and Injunctive Remedies

CERCLA empowers the EPA with a toolbox of legal weapons. The EPA has four primary tools to cause a site to be remediated. Two of these four derive from §106. This section of CERCLA provides the EPA with the so-called "imminent hazard" authority to take such action "as may be necessary to protect public health and welfare and the environment," after the affected state is notified. The EPA may act if it determines that an "imminent and substantial endangerment to the public health or welfare or the environment" is posed by "an actual or threatened release of a hazardous substance from a facility." 42 U.S.C. §9606(a).

When the EPA acts, it may use either of two §106 tools: (1) civil judicial injunctive (similar to RCRA §7003) actions and (2) unilateral EPA administrative orders. A unilateral EPA order to a PRP may be issued without recourse to the judiciary. This is a very flexible and compelling tool.

CERCLA §106 directs the federal courts to use their equitable powers to cause responsible parties to abate the danger caused by the release or threatened release of hazardous substances. Courts have held that §106 administrative orders, although they appear to be sufficiently "final" to support review, are not reviewable except in defense of an enforcement suit. The majority view is that the EPA is not required to give a hearing to a PRP, to allow defendants to interpose good faith defenses, prior to issuing a §106 administrative order. Willful violation of a unilateral EPA §106 order can result in the imposition of a fine of up to $25,000 per day. 42 U.S.C. §9606(b). Responsible parties who, "without sufficient cause," fail to comply with a §104 or §106 order may be held liable for punitive damages of up to three times the amount of remedial response costs incurred by the government as a result of the noncompliance. 42 U.S.C. §9607(c)(3).

§107 Litigation

Section 107 is the third tool that the EPA can use to accomplish remediation. CERCLA §107 establishes liability for recovery of (1) costs incurred by state or federal governments that are not inconsistent with the NCP, (2) any other necessary response costs consistent with the NCP incurred by any other person, and (3) "damages for injury to, destruction of, or loss of natural resources, including the reasonable costs" for damage assessment. 42 U.S.C. §9607(a)(4). The regulations codified at 43 C.F.R. §11, separate from other CERCLA regulations, provide procedures to assess and determine compensation for natural resource damages.

CERCLA §107 enumerates four categories of persons who potentially may be liable for CERCLA response costs: (1) current owners and operators of facilities, (2) owners or operators of facilities at the time of hazardous substance disposal, (3) anyone arranging in any way for the disposal, treatment, or transport of hazardous substances, and (4) transporters of hazardous substances to a site they select "from which there is a release, or threatened release, which causes the incurrence of response costs."

Again, pay close attention to the statutory and regulatory definitions of the key terms. First, the entity must be a *person*. While "person" includes corporations, trusts, partnerships, and municipalities, the term "owner or operator" does not include a unit of state or local government that acquired ownership or control involuntarily through bankruptcy, tax delinquency, abandonment, or other circumstances in which the government involuntarily acquires title by virtue of its function as the sovereign power. When the disposal site owner or operator is a municipality, county, or state agency, CERCLA treats the entity as if it were a private person. 42 U.S.C. §9601(21). See *Artesian Water Co. v. Government of New Castle County*, 605 F. Supp. 1348, 1355 (D. Del. 1985) (finding that Congress did not intend to differentiate between governmental and nongovernmental entities for purposes of CERCLA liability); see also Steven Ferrey, "The Toxic Timebomb: Municipal Liability for the Cleanup of Hazardous Waste," 57 *Geo. Wash. L. Rev.* 197 (1988). Thus municipalities are in the group of PRPs as "persons" liable, but *out* if they succeed to property ownership by virtue of an involuntary acquisition.

Those who control hazardous substances must arrange for their disposal. "Disposal" is defined to mean the "discharge, deposit, injection, dumping, spilling, leaking, or placing of any solid waste or hazardous waste into or on any land or water so that such . . . waste or any constituent thereof may enter the environment or be emitted into the air or discharged into any waters, including ground waters." 42 U.S.C. §9601(29), §6903(3). A debate still exists as to whether this includes *passive*, unknown leaking or seeping. This issue is addressed later.

The EPA has been allowed to recover, as response costs in §107 litigation, costs expended for investigation, monitoring, and testing; response-related planning costs; EPA and Justice Department staff costs; and litigation and attorney fees. Prejudgment interest also has been held to be a consistently recoverable response cost under CERCLA. However, costs related to the investigation of a defendant, as opposed to investigation of the site, have been held not recoverable.

§104 Friendly Persuasion

A fourth enforcement tool available to the EPA is to convince the parties responsible for a release or threatened release of hazardous substances to take voluntary cleanup action. After gathering information from PRPs in response to CERCLA §104(e) requests, the EPA is in a powerful position statutorily to encourage voluntary cleanups through informal negotiations and settlement. The preferred EPA enforcement approach to hazardous substance releases under CERCLA is remediation by private parties, either voluntarily or pursuant to enforcement orders issued by the EPA. This cleanup is likely to occur under the threat of either a §106 order, or EPA expenditure of funds and a subsequent §107 action against PRPs. The former can involve fines, and the latter can involve multiple damages. Both can involve adverse publicity. Section 106 can result in a mandatory injunction; §107, by contrast, results in the reimbursement and restitution of monies spent by the government.

To recap, the government in litigation typically raises claims for relief under CERCLA §106(a) and RCRA §7003. It is clear that §106 applies to spill emergencies involving hazardous substances. Section 106 of CERCLA requires the government to demonstrate an imminent and substantial endangerment. It is not clear to what extent §106 applies to inactive or abandoned waste disposal sites. A majority of courts considering the issue have concluded that §106(a) does apply to inactive or abandoned sites. PRPs provide about 70 percent of the funds spent annually on Superfund cleanups.

Strict Liability

A key issue in the use of the EPA's CERCLA tools is whether the liability of individual PRPs is based strictly on a PRP's status or whether elements of negligence must be shown. Congress drafted and passed CERCLA hastily, omitting key provisions respecting liability, instead relying on the common law developed under other statutes. Because CERCLA incorporates by reference §311 of the Clean Water Act, which holds violators strictly liable for marine damages, courts overwhelmingly hold PRPs strictly liable in cost recovery actions under CERCLA §107, regardless of any negligence by owners, operators, transporters, or generators. Thus CERCLA liability is not negligence based. Neither is it based on common law tort. CERCLA liability is its own strict statutory species.

The strict liability has been consistently developed in cases including *United States v. Northeastern Pharmaceutical and Chemical Co.* (NEPACCO I), 579 F. Supp. 823 (W.D. Mo. 1984), *aff'd in relevant part, rev'd in part*, 810 F.2d 726 (8th Cir. 1986), *cert. denied*, 484 U.S. 848 (1987); *United States v. Price*, 577 F. Supp. 1103, 1113-1114 (D.N.J. 1983); *cf. United States v. Wade*, 546 F. Supp. 785, 793-794 (E.D. Pa. 1982) (finding a nonnegligent off-site generator not liable), *appeal dismissed*, 713 F.2d 49 (3d Cir. 1983). The concept of strict liability is mitigated somewhat by special treatment for small-quantity generators of hazardous waste and by the ability of PRPs to spread liability through contribution actions against other PRPs.

The Small Business Liability Relief and Brownfields Revitalization Act of 2001 provides specific exemptions for certain *de micromis* generators and transporters of waste, as well as exemptions for municipal and small businesses that sent municipal solid waste. The EPA had long used its discretion to exempt *de micromis* parties from liability by regulation and prosecutorial discretion. The 2001 amendments now statutorily exempt those generators or transporters of less than 110 gallons of liquid materials or 200 pounds of solid materials, where generation or transportation occurred before

April 1, 2001. To qualify for this *de micromis* exemption, the *de micromis* hazardous substances must not have contributed significantly to the cost of the response action or to natural resource damage restoration, the generator or transporter must not have failed to comply with a request for information or administration subpoena or otherwise impeded the response or restoration action of the EPA, and the generator or transporter must not have been convicted of a criminal violation regarding its particular CERCLA activities. The 2001 amendments also shift the burden of proof to any PRP initiating a contribution action against a *de micromis* party, to demonstrate that the *de micromis* party exemption does not apply.

Section 122(g) of CERCLA authorizes expedited settlement, with full releases from additional liability, for de minimis generators. The settlement requirement is that the amount and toxic characteristics of the waste sent by the de minimis party must be "minimal in comparison to other hazardous substances at the facility" and the settlement involved "only a minor portion of the response costs." 42 U.S.C. §9622(g)(1)(A). Section 113 contribution actions are treated in more detail later in this chapter as part of "allocation of liability."

Proximate Cause

A key issue in imposing conventional liability is some proximate cause of the defendant in causing damages. Proximate cause, including actual causation, is a nexus between conduct and injury. CERCLA imposes different proximate cause requirements on different PRPs. As a starting point, any quantity, level, or concentration of a hazardous substance, as defined by CERCLA, is sufficient to trigger liability for any PRP, as articulated by the courts in *United States v. Conservation Chemical Co.*, 619 F. Supp. 162, 238 (W.D. Mo. 1985); *Amoco Oil Co. v. Borden, Inc.*, 889 F.2d 664, 669-670 (5th Cir. 1989). At least one court has implied that if a PRP can prove that its waste was removed from a site, it may not be liable as a generator of waste at that site. *United States v. South Carolina Recycling & Disposal, Inc.*, 653 F. Supp. 984, 993 n.6 (D.S.C. 1984). Moreover, for purposes of CERCLA's cleanup requirements, the EPA can compel remediation on a showing of potential endangerment, even though no actual damage or harm is manifest.

CERCLA authorizes the imposition of liability on those having no ongoing relationship with a contaminated site. Courts hold that this "retroactive" application of current liability for past activities still requiring remediation does not violate the requirements of due process. See *SCRDI*, 653 F. Supp. at 997; *Conservation Chemical Co.*, 619 F. Supp. at 221-222; *NEPACCO I*, 579 F. Supp. at 839-843; *United States v. Monsanto Co.*, 858 F.2d 160, 173-174 (4th Cir. 1988).

Generators

The requirement of proximate cause for CERCLA liability varies, however, for different potentially responsible parties. Courts do not require a showing of proximate cause to impose liability on *generators* of hazardous substances that arranged for disposal at Superfund sites, despite some legislative history suggesting that proof of causation is required before liability may be imposed. See *SCRDI*, 653 F. Supp. at 992; *United States v. Wade*, 577 F. Supp. 1326, 1333-1334 (E.D. Pa. 1983); *Dedham Water Co. v. Cumberland Farms Dairy, Inc.*, 889 F.2d 1146, 1151-1154 (1st Cir. 1989); *Amoco Oil Co. v. Borden, Inc.*, 889 F.2d at 670-671. Sufficient causation exists if the PRP's hazardous substances or similar substances are on-site at a facility, and a threatened release of *any* hazardous substance requires or justifies some EPA response action. Thus once plaintiffs (typically the EPA) show a release or threatened release of a hazardous substance at a "facility," or that a substance sent by defendants is similar to the one released or posing a threat of release, and that plaintiffs incurred "response costs" to address a hazardous substance release or threatened release, plaintiffs establish the requisite causation. Divisibility of the harm is discussed later in the chapter.

The Supreme Court limited the definition of what sort of economic activity renders one a liable "arranger" of waste disposal pursuant to Section 107. *Burlington N. & Santa Fe Ry. Co. v. United States* ("BNSF"), 556 U.S. 599 (2009). Based on a "plain reading" of the CERCLA statute, the Court held that "an entity may qualify as an arranger when it takes intentional steps to dispose of a hazardous substance." Mere knowledge of future spills by others does not amount to an "intent" that they be spilled or otherwise disposed of so as to create "arranger" liability. *Id.*

Selling material to another plant is enough to find intent to dispose. *United States v. General Electric Co.*, 2010 DNH 203 (D.N.H. 2010); cf. *Celanese Corp. v. Martin K. Eby Construction Co., Inc.*, 620 F.3d 529 (5th Cir. 2010). However, the mere status of being the manufacturer of recycling products and preparing the instructions on their use were insufficient, absent actual individualized direction for their use at the facilities involved, to find the manufacturers liable under CERCLA. *Hinds Inv. v. Team Enter., Inc.*, 71 ERC (BNA) 2076 (E.D. Cal. 2010); *Team Enter., LLC v. W. Inv. Real Estate Trust*, 40 ELR 20227 (E.D. Cal. 2010); *see also, United States Virgin Islands v. Vulcan Materials Co.*, 2010 WL 2654631 (D.V.I. July 1, 2010) (chemical manufacture of PCE for dry-cleaning operations was "insufficient to qualify the Defendants as arrangers under" BNSF).

The United States was held liable as an "arranger" for historical contamination stemming from a private facility that refurbished and recycled rocket engines for the military during the Cold War. *Am. Int'l Specialty Lines Ins. Co. v. United States*, 72 ERC (BNA) 1687 (C.D. Cal. 2010).

Where a supplier provides chemicals in containers that it collects from the customer and disposes, it is still possible for the customer to be a liable PRP from evidence "inferred from the totality of the circumstances." See *United States v. Cello-Foil Products, Inc.*, 100 F.3d 1227 (6th Cir. 1996). A property owner's act of taking contaminated soils from one area of a site to another constitutes a new "disposal" for purposes of establishing generator CERCLA liability. See *Kaiser Aluminum & Chem. Corp. v. Catellus Dev. Corp.*, 976 F.2d 1338, 1342 (9th Cir. 1992); *Tanglewood East Homeowners v. Charles Thomas, Inc.*, 849 F.2d 1568 (5th Cir. 1988); *Redwing Carriers, Inc. v. Saraland Apartments*, 94 F.3d 1489, 1510 (11th Cir. 1996) (CERCLA's definition of disposal "should be read broadly to include the subsequent movement and dispersal of hazardous substances within a facility"); *Portsmouth Redevelopment & Hous. Auth. v. BMI Apartments Assocs.*, 827 F. Supp. 354 (1993) (moving contaminated dirt around the property in the course of construction constitutes "disposal").

Former generators of any disposed-of hazardous substance remain liable. Even if the wastes, once safely disposed of, are subsequently and perhaps illegally removed to a second site where contamination occurs, the original generator remains liable. See *Missouri v. Independent Petrochemical Corp.*, 610 F. Supp. 4, 5 (E.D. Mo. 1985); *Violet v. Picillo*, 648 F. Supp. 1283, 1285 (D.R.I. 1986) (finding generator liable for the ultimate disposal of waste diverted by the transporter from the site selected by the generator to a second site); *Conservation Chemical Co.*, 619 F. Supp. at 234 (stating that generators are liable for waste trans-shipped to unknown second sites); *Missouri v. Independent Petrochemical Corp.*, 610 F. Supp. 4 (E.D. Mo. 1985); *United States v. Cannons Engineering Corp.*, 720 F. Supp. 1027, 1046 (D. Mass. 1989) (stating that generators may be held liable under CERCLA for the ultimate destination of their wastes, regardless of intent to send the waste there); cf. *United States v. N. Landing Line Construction*, 3 F. Supp. 2d 694 (E.D. Va. 1998) ("arranger" liability requires knowledge of disposal at a particular site).

In *United States v. Distler*, 803 F. Supp. 46, 49 (W.D. Ky. 1992), the court held the generator liable for waste commingled or mismanaged as random unidentifiable waste and moved to other locations. In essence, the generator can be responsible for cleanup at remote sites, even though the government has not proved that the generator's specific waste was trans-shipped to that site, as long as waste similar to the generator's waste ended up there. Once a plaintiff has demonstrated the basic requisites of CERCLA §107 liability against a PRP, the burden shifts to that PRP to prove that its wastes, in fact, are not at a given site. Especially for a generator, this burden may be next to impossible to sustain.

Owners and Operators

Courts also hold that a showing of proximate cause is not required before liability may be imposed on current or former owners or operators of disposal sites. See *New York v. Shore Realty Corp.*, 759 F.2d 1032, 1043-1044 (2d Cir. 1985); *Pennsylvania v. Union Gas Co.*, 491 U.S. 1 (1989); see also *United States v. Price*, 523 F. Supp. 1055, 1073-1074 (D.N.J. 1981) (holding subsequent landowners liable merely by virtue of "studied indifference" to hazardous condition), *aff'd*, 688 F.2d 204 (3d Cir. 1982). The EPA has taken the position that lessees may be "owners" for purposes of CERCLA liability. A sole trustee and beneficiary of a real estate trust that owns a site is also deemed to be an owner pursuant to CERCLA. This is because persons who possess equivalent evidence of ownership can be deemed owners. A land purchase also can be deemed liable as an owner after a land-purchase contract is executed, but before the sale itself is executed. *NEPACCO I*, 579 F. Supp. at 847; *SCRDI*, 653 F. Supp. at 1003.

The federal circuits have split significantly regarding whether passive migration of contamination through soil constituted "disposal" that imposes liability on past owners. The Second Circuit has indicated that passive migration does not trigger CERCLA liability. *ABB Industrial Systems, Inc. v. Prime Technology, Inc.*, 120 F.3d 351 (2d Cir. 1997) ("prior owners and operators of a site are not liable under CERCLA for mere passive migration. . . . [N]one of the terms listed in the definition of 'disposal' is commonly used to refer to the gradual spreading of hazardous chemicals already in the ground"). The Third Circuit held that passive migration of contamination did not constitute disposal when the migration originated from direct placement of contaminants in or on the soil. *United States v. CDMG Realty Co.*, 96 F.3d 706 (3d Cir. 1996) ("the gradual spreading of contamination could not constitute (disposal), without rendering nugatory the RCRA definitions for current owner or operator liability or nullifying the innocent owner defense"). The Fourth Circuit held that passive migration does constitute disposal as it moves through the environment. *Nurad, Inc. v. William E. Hooper & Sons Co.*, 966 F.2d 837 (4th Cir. 1992) (§9607(a)(2) imposes liability for ownership of the facility at a time that hazardous waste was "spilling" or "leaking"). See also *Crofton Ventures L.P. v. G&H P'ship*, 258 F.3d 292, 297 (4th Cir. 2001) (any owner or operator at the time when hazardous waste leaked into the environment, whether or not such owner or operator was the cause of the disposal or had knowledge of it), *cert. denied*, 506 U.S. 940 (1992). The Sixth Circuit has held that disposal is confined to the movement of hazardous substances emanating from the involvement of human activity. *United States v. 150 Acres of Land*, 204 F.3d 698 (6th Cir. 2000) (distinction between "disposal" and "release" because "disposal" is defined primarily in terms of active words such as "injection," "deposit," and "placing," so potentially passive words "spilling" and "leaking" should be interpreted actively); *Bob's Bev., Inc. v. Acme, Inc.*, 264 F.3d 692, 697 (6th Cir. 2001) (the failure of the defendants to prevent passive migration of hazardous substances during their ownership does not constitute a disposal). The Ninth Circuit held that a former property owner can be held liable for passive migration only if the contaminants originated in a container or vessel. *Carson Harbor Village, Ltd. v. Unocal Corp.*, 270 F.3d 863 (9th Cir. 2001) (alleged passive migration of contaminants through soil during ownership was not a "disposal" under §9607(a)(2)). Some of these distinctions regarding whether hazardous substances were placed directly on the soil or whether they emanated from a container or vessel seem particularly curious.

These cases create a continuum across the circuits, with the Sixth Circuit taking an "active-only" approach in 150 *Acres of Land*; the Third Circuit, in *CDMG Realty*, and the Second Circuit, in *ABB Industrial Systems*, addressing only the spread of contamination, leaving unresolved whether migration must always be "active" to be a "disposal"; the Fourth Circuit, in *Nurad*, concluding that "disposal" includes passive migration, at least in the context of leaking underground storage tanks; and the Ninth Circuit, in *Carson Harbor*, concluding that there may be liability for passive migration where the contaminants originated in a container or vessel.

The sale of a site that later poses a threat leaves liable both the former owner who owned the site during the period of hazardous substance disposal and perhaps the current owner(s) purchasing with actual or constructive knowledge of likely contaminants, whether or not subsequent disposal occurs. Former owners who owned the site at any time when hazardous substances were disposed remain liable. See *Dedham Water Co.*, 889 F.2d at 1151.

The 1986 SARA Superfund amendments created an "innocent owner" defense to CERCLA liability for defendants who acquired the disposal site after the disposal or placement of the hazardous material, provided: (1) the defendant did not know or have reason to know of the hazardous material at the time the property was acquired, or (2) the defendant is a governmental entity and acquired the property by escheat, involuntary transfer, eminent domain, or the like, or (3) the defendant inherited the property. These provisions were added by SARA §101(f), codified at 42 U.S.C. §9601(35). See also *United States v. Monsanto Co.*, 858 F.2d at 168 n.14. The defense derives from the third party defense discussed in the next subpart. Technically, the innocent owner defense applies to owners, but not to tenants or lessees.

The 2001 Superfund amendments added a new §107(q) protecting contiguous landowners against liability for the spread of hazardous substances from their original loci. To enjoy this protection, the contiguous innocent landowner must not have contributed to the contamination, must not have known of the possible contamination at the time of his or her acquisition of the property, must have taken reasonable steps to limit the release once he or she became aware of it, and must not be too closely related to the liable PRPs.

The amendments also provide "bona fide prospective purchasers" of contaminated property a safe harbor from CERCLA liability if they can demonstrate by a preponderance of the evidence that they did not contribute to the contamination. The bona fide prospective purchaser exception requires constant vigilance and due diligence by the purchaser to meet ongoing EPA obligations, including to stop any continuing releases, prevent any threat of future releases, and prevent or limit human environmental or natural resource exposure to any previously released hazardous substance. The purchaser exemption does not expressly extend to tenants. 42 U.S.C. §9607(R).

However, if there are unrecovered EPA remediation costs, the government benefits from a "windfall lien" on the property up to the amount of its increase in fair market value due to the government's cleanup activities. Therefore, the government can recapture the enhanced value of the decontaminated property at the time of its prospective sale.

In late 2005, the EPA issued final rules for site assessments necessary to qualify one's status as an innocent owner or bona fide purchaser of contaminated property. "All appropriate inquiry" is satisfied by a site assessment conducted in accordance with the criteria drafted by ASTM International, and allows older assessments of properties to qualify as long as those assessments are updated. A prospective landowner must provide to its environmental professional who conducts the site assessment any information that the purchaser may have that has been embodied in other inquiries concerning the property. The site assessment must be performed by a person having a bachelor's degree, or a person with ten years of relevant full-time experience who undertakes the appropriate inquiry. CERCLA, RCRA, and EPCRA toxic release inventory programs have collectively resulted in a significant reduction in the generation of hazardous waste. A large industry has arisen to perform about a quarter-million site assessments annually, which is a prerequisite to obtaining innocent owner and bona fide prospective purchaser protections at the time of property transfer, as well as obtaining financing and property insurance for such transactions.

An on-site visit by the environmental professional is required, to assess the site and surrounding properties, including interview of current owners and occupants. In addition, a review of records and databases is required regarding the site and surrounding properties. The databases to be surveyed would include CERCLIS, the Emergency Response Notification System, the National Priorities List, RCRA lists, and registries of underground storage tanks. The review should go back as far as the property contained structures or was used for agricultural, commercial, industrial, governmental, or residential purposes. A prior investigative report has a "shelf life" of one year before the data is deemed not current. Grading or moving contamination at a site that worsens contamination can eviscerate the innocent owner defense and make one liable as a transporter of hazardous substances. *Franklin Cnty.*

Convention Ctr. Auth. v. Am. Premier Underwriters, 240 F. 3d 534 (6th Cir. 2001); *Tanglewood-East Homeowners Assoc. v. Charles-Thomas, Inc.*, 849 F.2d 1568 (5th Cir. 1988). If an owner leases to a tenant and ignores the known fact that the tenant is handling hazardous substances at the property, the owner can lose its innocence. *United States v. Monsanto Co.*, 858 F.2d 160, 165 (4th Cir. 1988).

The EPA is authorized to issue assurances that no enforcement action will be initiated under CERCLA and to provide protection against claims for contribution and cost recovery. However, these protections — whether a *bona fide* purchaser, an innocent purchaser, or a contiguous property owner — only protect against CERCLA liability. They do not protect against liability under RCRA. The "cooperation" standard imposed on *bona fide* purchasers may cause them to grant access without compensation to those undertaking cleanup efforts.

A majority of states have developed brownfields programs to encourage reuse of contaminated property. Typically, upon completion of a voluntary cleanup, owners receive liability protection in the form of letters of no further EPA action, certificates of remediation completion, and/or covenants not to sue. These releases typically apply to subsequent owners who did not contribute to the contamination. Under federal law, eligible sites may not be on the National Priorities List and must not have significant groundwater contamination.

Officer Liability

Under CERCLA, the corporate veil also can be pierced for "operator" liability where there is proximate cause and a reasonable nexus. Corporate officers of a company, if they personally arranged for disposal of waste or had direct supervision, can be held liable under §§106 and 107. This principle was first articulated in *United States v. Northeastern Pharmaceutical &. Chemical Co., Inc.* (*NEPACCO II*), 810 F.2d 726, 744 (8th Cir. 1986) (holding that an individual who participated in conduct that violated CERCLA may be held personally liable), *cert. denied*, 484 U.S. 848 (1987). See also *Conservation Chemical Co.*, 619 F. Supp. at 190 (holding that corporate officials who actively participate in the management of a disposal facility may be held personally liable); *Escude Cruz v. Ortho Pharmaceutical Corp.*, 619 F.2d 902, 907 (1st Cir. 1980) (stating that personal liability may be found when the corporate officer was the guiding spirit behind the wrongful conduct).

A corporate officer can be liable directly as an arranger for disposal if he or she had the authority and did exercise actual authority or control, directly or indirectly, over such activities. See *United States v. TIC Investment Corp.*, 68 F.3d 1082 (8th Cir. 1995). Active involvement in the day-to-day affairs of the company, absent a direct showing that the individual defendant "actually participated in the liability-creating conduct," is not sufficient to impose liability, even in a closely held corporation. See *United States v. USX Corp.*, 68 F.3d

811 (3d Cir. 1995). The formalities of a limited partnership corporate structure have been respected to prevent such limited partners, even where they hold a cumulative 99 percent interest in the partnership, from direct liability as owners or operators of a CERCLA site. See *Redwing Carriers, Inc. v. Saraland Apartments*, 94 F.3d 1489 (11th Cir. 1996). Shareholders also can be held liable under §107(a) if the corporation is closely held and the shareholder assumes an active management role. But remember that the reach of liability through to officers and shareholders requires a level of proximate cause or relationship not required for the strict generator, owner, or operator liability. These officer liability topics are reviewed in more detail later.

In *United States v. Iverson*, 162 F.3d 1015 (9th Cir. 1998), the Ninth Circuit adopted a very broad and inclusive standard for imposing criminal liability based upon positional status in the corporation. Even though not personally or directly involved with illegal environmental actions, a responsible corporate officer with some knowledge and authority with respect to the illegal activities can be found criminally liable. This decision erodes the *mens rea* requirement for criminal offenses. The court found that mere authority to exercise control over a corporation's activity that causes the illegal discharge is sufficient to impose criminal liability, notwithstanding that there was no authority exercised in fact, and the corporation did not expressly vest a duty in that employee to exercise control over an activity.

Transporters

A showing of proximate cause is required before imposing liability on transporters of hazardous substances. Both the statute and the case law link transporters to cleanup costs only if the transporters were responsible for selecting the disposal site. This liability is less extensive than RCRA's provision for transporter liability under §7003 (discussed in the prior chapter). Former transporters of hazardous substances who selected the disposal site also remain liable. See *Ottati & Goss*, 630 F. Supp. at 1402-1405; *SCRDI*, 653 F. Supp. at 1005; *NEPACCO I*, 579 F. Supp. at 846-847.

Basic Defenses

PRPs can avail themselves of one of the three extremely limited statutory defenses. 42 U.S.C. §9607(b). These defenses are available when releases of hazardous substances are caused exclusively by (1) acts of war, (2) acts of God, or (3) acts of unrelated third parties with whom a PRP has no direct or indirect contractual link, and where the PRP exercises due care with respect to any hazardous substances. The "Act of God" defense has only been argued a few times, and unsuccessfully due to other extraneous or mitigating circumstances.

9. The Superfund: Hazardous Substance Remediation

The third party defense has a variant known as the "innocent landowner" defense. In essence, to be an "innocent landowner," one must undertake at the time of acquisition "all appropriate inquiry . . . consistent with good commercial or customary practice in an effort to minimize liability . . . " and not know or have reason to know of any hazardous substance released or threatened to be released. The experience of the owner and the purchase price are relevant elements of this requirement. 42 U.S.C. §9601(35A). As discussed, the 2001 Superfund Amendments expend innocent owner defenses even where purchase of property is made with knowledge of contamination.

The Ninth Circuit held that Superfund applies to foreign corporations that undertake activities outside the United States that result in contaminating areas of the United States. In *Pakootas v. Teck Cominco Metals, Ltd.*, 432 F.3d 1066 (9th Cir. 2006), two tribal leaders brought suit against a lead and zinc smelter in British Columbia, whose slag was contaminating more than 100 miles of the Columbia River behind the Grand Coulee Dam in the United States. The defendant smelter argued that the heavy metals were discharged ten miles north of the U.S.-Canada border subject to a valid Canadian discharge permit, and movement was accomplished by acts of nature, such that Superfund could not apply. This was the first case against a foreign company brought under the citizen suit provision of Superfund.

Examples

Assume that Curly's property used to be, under prior ownership, a hazardous waste dump. After Curly bought the property, he erected a building on it. Now, hazardous substances are discovered at the site. Fortunately, the building, occupied by a tenant who operates a windsurfing equipment rental company, is not contaminated.

Here is the property history: Curly purchased the property two years ago from the town of Metropolis, which had taken the property from the prior owner, Stooge Waste, Inc., in lieu of property taxes owed and unpaid. During its period of ownership, Stooge Waste had operated the property as a waste disposal area. A guy named Shemp was the facility manager for Stooge Waste, Inc.

Larry operated a service under which he, as a broker, would make necessary arrangements to remove waste for various companies in the state. Although he never handled any of the waste himself, Larry, for a commission, would see that waste was handled and removed by various trucking companies with whom he contracted. Larry brokered waste that was sent to Stooge Waste for disposal. Moe ran one of those trucking companies delivering waste to Stooge during the time when the Stooge facility accepted hazardous wastes.

9. The Superfund: Hazardous Substance Remediation

1. Given the preceding information, assess the potential liability and potential defenses pursuant to CERCLA of each of the following:
   a. Curly
   b. Curly's current tenants who run a windsurfing equipment rental shop
   c. Larry
   d. Moe
   e. Shemp
   f. The town of Metropolis

2. Several years ago, when he was delivering waste to the Stooge/Curly site, Moe learned of contamination problems there. He ordered four hazardous substance trucks to halt and proceed no further. One truck full of hazardous chemicals stopped at the existing Metropolis city dump, where it awaited further instructions. Is Moe responsible for cleanup expenses at the city dump if the dump is then subject to EPA action?

3. During Stooge's period of ownership, its president decided she could make more money by taking in more waste than her facility could process. Unbeknownst to her waste-generator customers, she directed excess waste to a third-party remote location. Who would be responsible for waste at that third-party location should there be a threat or actual release of hazardous substances there?

4. If the EPA discovered contamination problems only after Curly bought the property, and if none of those problems resulted from Curly's activities, do any of the previous generators or transporters have defenses to liability based on late discovery?

5. A particular generator of hazardous substances sent asbestos-containing building materials in a solid physical state, encased in tight 55-gallon drums, to Curly's site when Stooge Waste owned the property. The waste release detected at the site is volatile organic compounds (not containing any asbestos) in a liquid state. Is that generator of asbestos potentially liable under CERCLA to remediate contaminated soil and groundwater? Is there a defense?

6. If Curly has not actively disposed of any hazardous substances during his period of ownership and has a willing buyer in an arm's-length transaction to purchase his site, can he make this sale? If he does so, is he relieved from his present or future liability?

7. To conclude this section, recapitulate the four primary tools that the EPA possesses in §§104, 106, and 107 of CERCLA, to cause or compel generators, transporters, owners, and operators to undertake cleanup action at CERCLA facilities.

Explanations

1a. Curly is a present owner of the facility. Hazardous substances have been discovered there only recently by the EPA. Curly owns the property, but he is not the operator. Even though the statute makes liable current "owners and operators," Curly need not be both an owner *and* an operator to be liable. Either status is sufficient under case precedent. As an owner, he is liable, even if he did not contribute to the disposal of hazardous substances at the site. This liability is strict, without regard to negligence or proximate causation.

However, there are possible defenses for so-called present innocent owners. One of the three enumerated CERCLA defenses in §107(b) may be invoked if a present owner establishes that the harm results solely from the act of omission of unrelated third parties with whom he or she has no indirect or direct contractual relationship. Review Curly's path to ownership: Curly has a direct contractual relationship, by virtue of his contract for purchase of the parcel from the town of Metropolis, the prior owner; he thereby has an indirect contractual relationship with all owners in the chain of title (at least one of whom would be responsible as the owner at the time of hazardous substance disposal). There is thus an indirect contractual relationship with the owner at the time of disposal.

However, there is possible hope for Curly. As provided in the SARA amendments, if Curly can establish that he did not know of the contamination, and had no reason to know of the contamination at the time of purchase, and used due care regarding the property, he may still be eligible for the so-called "innocent owner defense" (see Exhibit 9.6). 42 U.S.C. §9601(38); 42 U.S.C. §9607(b).

Curly will have to sustain the burden of proof of showing that he used commercially reasonable due diligence prior to property acquisition. The degree of due diligence depends on the nature of the property. A greater degree of due diligence and environmental evaluation is required for commercial and industrial properties than for residential properties, because of their higher potential for preexisting

9.6 Innocent Owner Third-Party Defense

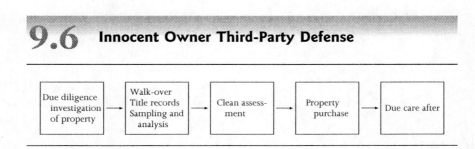

| Due diligence investigation of property | → | Walk-over Title records Sampling and analysis | → | Clean assessment | → | Property purchase | → | Due care after |

contamination. For former industrial property, this would involve, at a minimum, an on-site walk-over by a competent environmental engineer or specialist. It does not necessarily require the active sampling of soil or subsurface groundwater, depending upon the circumstances.

Here, however, since an investigation of the title records at the county registry of deeds, or discussion with town officials, would have revealed that the facility previously was a waste disposal facility, a much higher degree of due diligence is required. Moreover, this makes it almost impossible to establish the "innocence" necessary for the innocent owner defense. While the defense is potentially available to Curly, the circumstances in this case make it extremely difficult for Curly to invoke it successfully. Curly cannot successfully invoke the innocent-owner defense.

However, he may be able to establish by a preponderance of the evidence that he was a bona fide prospective purchaser, and thus evade liability. The government enjoys a windfall lien against the property in such event to secure any government investment in remediation.

1b. Tenants can be deemed operators of a facility. Note that the definition in 42 U.S.C. §9601(38) provides exceptions for innocent owners, not innocent operators. While a court might extend this exception to operators, the plain language of the statute would appear to limit it to owners. Owners certainly exercise not only ownership but typically greater control than lessees or operators. A tenant, for example, would be much less likely than an owner to undertake a due diligence investigation that would uncover and warn about prior waste practices at a site.

The scant case law that has interpreted the meaning of the term "operator" has tended, generally, to equate the status with some control over a facility or parcel. And it is hard to understand what would be more fundamental to such control than a lease for the property. There is not much precedent as to whether lessees are operators, and if so, how much control they must exercise to be liable operators pursuant to CERCLA. An argument can be made that if one leases a site but operates it for something other than waste disposal purposes, one should not be liable as a current operator of a prior waste disposal facility. A windsurfing business probably has no connection to waste disposal.

Even if not currently engaged in any waste operations, tenants could conceivably be liable as "operators" at a facility. Curly's tenants could be considered operators of a waste facility by virtue merely of their lessee status. However, the extent of their liability is still an open issue in the case law.

1c. Liability attaches for *arranging* for disposal of hazardous substances. This does not mean that one has to own, possess, handle, or touch the substances. Typically, those who *arrange* for disposal are the people who create the hazardous substances in their activities and directly dispose of such substances. A broker, such as Larry, could fit into the definition of an arranger for disposal. Larry is engaged in a commercial operation for which he receives a fee. If the decision as to where wastes are disposed or how they are assembled and packaged is Larry's decision, CERCLA scoops up Larry's conduct as potentially liable and makes him a PRP. If, on the other hand, Larry's activities are limited to providing a referral service, linking those wishing to discard waste materials with transporters or disposal sites, but not making the disposal decision, he does not "arrange for disposal." As described in this question, Larry appears to be selecting disposal sites. Therefore, he also is liable as a PRP. Liability is strict. No greater nexus is required.

1d. Potential CERCLA liability pursuant to §107, or potential RCRA liability pursuant to §7003 of RCRA, is distinctly different for Moe. As a transporter, Moe is liable under CERCLA only if he selects the disposal facility. Therefore, the relevant question becomes: Was Moe given waste to dispose of without any instruction or requirement as to where it was to be taken? If so, he is a PRP. If, on the other hand, he is a mere carrier of waste to a site selected by the company discarding the waste and arranging for its disposal, he should escape CERCLA liability.

As a practical matter this site selection determination can be difficult. Prior to 1980, there was no waste manifest system pursuant to RCRA regulations to record the handling and movement of waste. Even a hazardous waste manifest does not indicate who was responsible for site selection unless there is an accompanying waste contract that gives specifics. Of course, transporters typically claim that they had no role in site selection, while generators claim that it was the transporters who made site selections.

It is not unusual for the EPA or private PRP groups to attempt to hold both the generator and the transporter liable for a share of remediation expenses relevant to a particular waste shipment. If the transporter and generator of waste can work out a way to split this liability, that arrangement is usually accepted by the EPA or other PRPs. Typically, there should be no double-counting: The transporter and generator should not each have to pay in full for the same volume of waste shipments. However, if either the transporter or generator of the waste is unavailable, does not participate, is bankrupt or otherwise judgment-proof, the EPA or a private PRP group may look to the remaining solvent party to pay a full share of responsibility for that waste remediation.

The burden is on Moe, the PRP transporter, to demonstrate conclusively that he did not select the disposal site. This requirement can be a major impediment for transporters. As with other aspects of CERCLA, incurring the burden of proof often can be outcome-determinative and fatal. Here, Moe is potentially liable as a PRP unless he can make the exculpatory lack of site selection showings discussed here.

Pursuant to RCRA, unless transport was by common carriage by rail subject to a published tariff, Moe would be liable, whether or not he selected the disposal site. And the EPA can invoke RCRA simultaneously with CERCLA. Therefore, in pleading, if the EPA invokes §7003 of RCRA, Moe would be liable under any circumstances as one who contributed to the handling of waste that now poses a problem. Recall that there is no private right of action under RCRA, as there is under CERCLA. Therefore, whether or not the EPA pleads RCRA as a statute to establish Moe's liability, no private PRP can employ §7003 of RCRA for its own litigation.

1e. Shemp, in a position of management responsibility for the operating company at the time of disposal, can also be *personally* liable. CERCLA generally is interpreted to make "persons" liable without regard to corporate capacity. This is not a piercing of the corporate veil so much as a disregard of corporate formalities. Both Shemp and the Stooge Waste corporation, under the reasoning in *NEPACCO II* and in *Shore Realty*, are individually liable as operators. And there is no requirement that the company, if it is still viable, reimburse him for either defense or remediation expenses.

1f. Municipalities are liable as are any other "persons." However, here Metropolis became an owner by virtue of a foreclosure to satisfy tax delinquency. For public policy reasons embodied in the statute, municipalities in such circumstances are exempt from CERCLA liability imposed on present owners. However, if hazardous waste disposal activities, deliberately or inadvertently, continue during the time of town ownership, regardless of how that ownership was acquired, the town is liable. The defense that the town can assert is similar to the "innocent owner" defense discussed in 1a above. Therefore, it is important for towns, when they take properties for tax delinquency or by escheat, to use due diligence and take foreseeable steps to prevent hazardous waste or hazardous substance conditions to worsen during their ownership. Most towns have not taken such steps. Here, though, absent additional information, the town of Metropolis, as interim owner, is not liable.

2. Moe is not responsible for remediation expenses at the town dump by virtue of the temporary location of one of his trucks. Case precedent

offers an exception to transporters for the temporary location of vehicles. Even if the dump has become a "facility," Moe does not have transporter liability unless he selected the dump as a permanent disposal place for clients for whom he provided waste transportation. This reasoning assumes, of course, that his truck does not leak any hazardous substances while it is positioned at the city dump. In addition, should the truck be abandoned at the city dump, or left for a period of time such that it could be considered abandoned, then that act could be considered an act of disposal for which Moe would be liable.

3. The official of the former owner of Curly's parcel, Stooge Waste, Inc., made all the arrangements for transportation of the wastes to a third-party remote location. If it weren't for her unilateral and secret decision to redirect waste and cause it to be transported to that third-party location, the waste would not have ended up there. None of the original waste generators or transporters had any idea or intention that their waste would end up at that third-party location. Therefore, Stooge Waste, Inc., is clearly liable as an arranger for its disposal.

But is that all? Certainly the owner or operator of the third-party remote site would also be liable. What about Moe, the original transporter to Curly's site? Recall that transporters, to be liable, must select a disposal site. Assuming that the transporter did not have cause to question the waste redirection to the third-party site, the requisite proximate cause for Moe's transporter liability is not present. However, if Moe should have questioned the redirection, or if Moe rather than the generator was responsible for selecting Curly's site, Moe remains liable.

Can we say the same for the original generators? Certainly the generators never intended that their wastes should end up at the third-party site. They did not arrange for disposal at such sites. However, re-read the language of §107(a) of CERCLA. It does not require that one arrange for disposal at a particular site to incur liability as a generator. The requirement is only that one arrange for some disposal.

That evaluation is not made from the perspective of the specific plans of the party arranging for the disposal. The operative question is: Did the party generating the waste arrange for something to pass from the phase of being a usable substance to that of being a disposed substance? The evaluation of materials to waste status is made by the generator. Once material becomes a waste to the generator, even if some other party (including the next party to possess the waste) might use it productively, the material is considered ready for disposal. Whatever disposal the generator arranges for, and wherever the waste ends up, the generator remains strictly liable for any hazardous substances.

In other words, it is not critical that the generator intend for its substances to end up at a particular facility. It is only necessary that the generator intend disposal and arrange for transition to disposal status. Recall that liability is strict, with no need to show *proximate* causation by generators. As onerous as the burden may seem, the trend of the case law has been to hold generators strictly liable for transshipped waste, even when such transshipment contradicts the explicit instructions of the generator. Generators are liable as PRPs at the third-party site. See *Violet v. Picillo*, 648 F. Supp. 1283, 1285 (D.R.I. 1986); *United States v. Cannons Engineering Corp.*, 720 F. Supp. 1027, 1046 (D. Mass. 1989).

4. There is no estoppel doctrine that can be invoked against the government in its regulatory capacity. The fact that the government could have discovered the contamination at the facility at an earlier time, or even *should* have discovered the contamination at an earlier time, thus minimizing eventual cleanup costs, is bad luck and poor timing, but without legal consequence. Failure of the government to act does not create a viable defense for generators or transporters. The common law equitable defense of laches generally is not recognized in a §107 action by the government to recover its response costs. Originally some generators and transporters attempted unsuccessfully to argue that CERCLA liability was unconstitutionally retroactive. In other words, they argued that the government could not impose liability today for past actions which were legal at the time they occurred and which predated the enactment of CERCLA in 1980.

Some commentaries incorrectly stated that retroactive application of CERCLA had been deemed legal. This is not quite accurate. Rather, CERCLA imposes liability for current contamination conditions at a facility that were caused by past conduct of generators and transporters. Since the cost recovery and injunctive remedies of CERCLA are equitable, an order to restitute or redress a current ongoing threat is not retroactive application of the statute, regardless of when the conduct at issue occurred. An injunction or order for restitution mandates only *current* compliance with the order. CERCLA's equitable powers are not retroactive, and defenses based on such retroactivity will not succeed. The past generators and transporters remain liable.

5. To answer this question, we need to look once again at the operative verbs and nouns of CERCLA. Exactly what is required for generator liability? You will recall that there must be a release or threat of release of a hazardous substance at a facility which poses an imminent threat of substantial harm or endangerment to the environment or public health, and one must have arranged for disposal of a hazardous substance at the facility. Read closely, there is no requirement that one's precise

substances actually be released or even be threatened to be released. Moreover, there is no requirement that one's substances be those that pose the imminent and substantial endangerment or are the substances that require remediation. These requirements are sketched in Exhibit 9.7.

The requisite triggers to establish liability for broad classes of owners, operators, generators, and transporters are macro-level triggers: Is the site a facility? For any reason, is there a release or threat of release of *any* hazardous substance? Is there an imminent harm or endangerment? Did anyone arrange for disposal of any hazardous substance at the site? From these requirements there is no necessity to "fingerprint" the impact of any one generator's substances on the environment or the resultant specific risks posed. Liability is strictly imposed on broad classes of parties who have some macro-level relationship to the site, regardless of a micro-level impact of their particular conduct. In other words, the most careful, scrupulous, and commendable generator is swept into the same cauldron of liability as the careless, unconcerned, or unscrupulous generator of waste.

In addition, there is no requirement that one's specific waste *type* be causing the threat or release at a site. Courts articulate the requirement as wastes *like* the generator's wastes are released or threatened to be released at a facility. See *United States v. Monsanto, supra.* Courts have been very liberal in lumping together wastes of various kinds as *like* other wastes. There is the risk at any site that if one sends any hazardous substance, it may be deemed *like* all other hazardous substances, regardless of its physical state, or the condition of its containment or encapsulation at the time of delivery to the facility.

While there is still an argument for divisibility of one's liability, as discussed in the next section, there is no micro-level requirement to trace, fingerprint, or otherwise identify specific waste streams, let alone a particular generator's individual waste. And as a practical

9.7 Site and Party Requisites for CERCLA Liability

Site Requisites				Party Requisites	
Action	Element	Location	Risk	Liability Status	Event
Release or threat of release	Any hazardous substance	At a facility	For §106: Imminent harm or endangerment from any release or threat	Generators/arrangers Owners/operators Transporters	Wastes like those of PRP pose threat of release

matter, this tracing is often impossible at Superfund sites. By the time the EPA identifies a problem and takes action, there often is a complex chemical soup brewing below the site, with commingled waste streams making a wicked brew of contaminants. To impose an exacting fingerprinting requirement on the EPA or other plaintiffs would be to eviscerate the policy goals of swift and prompt action in a sea of endless discovery and factual disputes. To date, close identity of wastes has not been required under CERCLA, and mitigation of one's liability is thus not likely to be a successful defense.

6. Lucky Curly? Most contaminated facilities are not so lucky as to find a willing buyer. Contrary to common misperception, nothing in CERCLA prohibits or in any way restricts sale of contaminated property. If Curly can sell, he is not restricted by CERCLA. However, as counsel for Curly, you will want to check state laws. For example, New Jersey requires state approval prior to the sale of commercial and industrial properties where there may be contamination. State statutes and regulations can significantly affect the purchase and sale of contaminated property.

It is an intriguing issue as to whether Curly could escape liability once he completes the sale and becomes a *former* owner rather than a current owner. 'As a *current* owner, Curly is liable unless he can satisfy the so-called "innocent owner" defense or bona fide purchaser defense. As a former owner, Curly is liable only if he owned at the time of disposal. You will recall that "release" includes any "spilling, leaking, pumping, pouring, emitting, emptying, discharging, injecting, escaping, dumping, or disposing into the environment. . . ." As illustrated in Exhibit 9.8, "disposing" is one of the actions that constitutes a "release."

9.8 CERCLA Actions Constituting Initial and Possible Passive Continuing Releases

Initial Act of Discard	Possible Passive Act of Continuing Contamination
disposing	leaking
spilling	emitting
pumping	escaping
pouring	
discharging	
injecting	
dumping	

All of the verbs are in their gerund form (with "ing" on the end). The gerund typically connotes a more passive, less active form of activity. "Leaking" and "escaping" can continue after past disposal even without a distinct action by the current owner to start the release. However, in its normal usage, "disposing" connotes some action on the part of the disposing party.

Passive "leaking" and "escaping" of contaminants during Curly's period of ownership do not necessarily indicate that Curly owned at the time of disposal. The fact of a release during one's ownership is not the same as "disposing" during one's ownership. The requirement that an owner own at the time of "disposal" of hazardous substances would seem to exclude passive leaking and escaping. If so, Curly escapes liability by selling his property and becoming a former owner who did not own "at the time of disposal."

The courts are split on the requirement of active versus passive disposal. Some courts support the active requirement, holding that active disposal of former owners is required for liability. See *Ecodyne Corp. v. Shah*, 718 F. Supp. 1454 (N.D. Cal. 1989); *Cadillac Fairview/California v. Dow Chemical Corp.*, 14 Envtl. L. Rep. 20376 (C.D. Cal. 1984), *aff'd in part, rev'd in part*, 840 F.2d 691 (9th Cir. 1988); *United States v. Petersen Sand & Gravel, Inc.*, 806 F. Supp. 1346 (N.D. Ill. 1992). Other courts, however, expand CERCLA's reach by holding former passive nondisposing owners liable because preexisting contaminants continued to escape or leak during their period of ownership. This casts a very broad net indeed and diminishes the impact of the "innocent owner" defense. See *Nurad, Inc. v. William E. Hooper & Sons Corp.*, 966 F.2d 837, 844-845 (4th Cir. 1992), *cert. denied*, 506 U.S. 940 (1992); *New York v. Shore Realty Corp.*, 759 F.2d 1032, 1045 (2d Cir. 1985); *Emhart Indus. v. Duracell Intl.*, 665 F. Supp. 549, 574 (M.D. Tenn. 1987).

7. Let's review these in the order that the EPA tends to apply them: §104, then §106, and finally §107.

First, the EPA will use its extremely broad information-gathering powers under §104(e) to gather chemical, activity, and financial information relevant to PRPs. On the basis of this information, it will encourage PRPs collectively to organize themselves and volunteer to undertake necessary analysis and remediation, rather than face compulsory EPA action. In many cases, this approach is successful. The EPA prefers these "PRP-driven" site cleanups.

Second, the EPA can use its authority under §106 to issue unilateral administrative orders, compelling specific actions. These actions can include assessments, emergency removals, or long-term remediation activities. The EPA can target selectively just those PRPs that it wishes to compel with a §106 order. There is no necessity to send such an order to all PRPs. Failure to comply with a §106 order can result in penalties up to $25,000 per day for each violation. If several things are commanded in a §106 order, each might be construed by the EPA as a separate violation. Therefore, major publicly traded corporations or other entities concerned about public perception, or about having to declare liabilities in annual 10-K filings with the Securities and Exchange Commission, may be particularly sensitive to potential receipt of a §106 order.

Third, the EPA can seek an injunction from a federal district court pursuant to §106. This remedy mirrors that in §7003 of RCRA. While somewhat less flexible than a unilateral order pursuant to §106, there are times when an injunction makes sense as a tool for the EPA. For example, if the EPA is seeking court injunctive relief pursuant to §7003 of RCRA, it will often simultaneously plead §106 injunctive remedies pursuant to CERCLA.

Fourth, the EPA can expend trust funds from the Superfund to accomplish the remedy itself, pursuant to the NCP. The limit for EPA expenditures is $2 million, unless the EPA places the site on the National Priorities List or obtains a waiver of the dollar limit. Thereafter, it can expend whatever sums are necessary, consistent with its operating regulations in the NCP. As it incurs these response costs, the EPA can under §107 pursue equitable restitution of these response costs from PRPs. It need not sue all PRPs but can name those that it chooses. Moreover, if a PRP has failed to comply with EPA orders pursuant to §106, a court may treble damages in the response cost recovery action. These recovered funds replenish the Superfund. The §107 route is slightly disfavored by the EPA, because it requires prior expenditure of public funds and involves the risk of nonrecovery.

ASSIGNMENT AND ALLOCATION OF LIABILITY TO PRIVATE PARTIES

Approximately half of current CERCLA cost-recovery cases are brought by private parties rather than by a government agency. This section addresses instances in which the EPA prosecutes a §107 cost-recovery claim, as well as private-party §107 cost-recovery and §113 contribution actions. The legal posture and applicable theories for allocating liability vary in these disparate situations. Liability to the EPA under §107 is "joint and several." Liability to a private party can be either "joint and several," or "several." In this section we review three primary means that courts employ to allocate and assign liability among private PRPs:

- Divisibility of the harm by the nature of one's conduct or contribution to the harm
- Broad equitable factors
- Model allocation statutes

Each of these tools is used to divide the cost of remediating the injury/ cost of hazardous substance contamination among multiple liable parties. This is the exercise of dividing up the liability pie. The federal Superfund law forces a massive, and often invisible, reallocation of resources.

The statute clearly provides for complete reimbursement of costs incurred by the government. It does not, however, define allocation of liability among various potentially responsible private parties. First, CERCLA contains no express apportionment of liability among different categories of owners, operators, generators and disposers of waste, or transporters of waste. Second, §107 can create joint and several liability among this often unrelated group of responsible parties. Third, §§107 and 113 are two separate statutory mechanisms for allocating responsibility.

Joint and Several, or Several, Liability?

Although the final version of CERCLA deleted all reference to joint and several liability, courts typically hold that PRP liability is joint and several if there is no basis for dividing the responsibility for the injury. *NEPACCO I*, 579 F. Supp. at 845; *Conservation Chemical Co.*, 589 F. Supp. 59, 63 (W.D. Mo. 1984); *SCRDI*, 653 F. Supp. at 994; *Amoco Oil Co. v. Borden*, 889 F.2d 664, 673 (5th Cir. 1989).

Joint and several liability makes each responsible party liable for the *entire* liability, not just its proportionate share. Under joint and several liability, plaintiffs are not required to link their response costs with specific releases by particular defendants; to require such "fingerprinting" of wastes would eviscerate CERCLA's liability provisions and would be inconsistent with Congress's intent. To establish liability for the harm caused by the release at a particular site, "CERCLA only requires that the plaintiff prove . . . that the defendant deposited his hazardous waste at the site and that the hazard-ous substances contained in the defendant's waste are also found at the site." See *United States v. Monsanto Co.*, 858 F.2d at 169-170 (stating that it was sufficient for plaintiff to show that a waste *like* that sent by the defendants was found at the site); *Wade*, 577 F. Supp. at 1332-1333; see also *Shore Realty Corp.*, 759 F.2d at 1044-1045 (declining to find a causation requirement in

CERCLA §107(a)); *O'Neil v. Piccillo*, 883 F.2d 176 (1st Cir. 1989) (waste generators liable and have the burden of accounting for uncertainty).

Section 107 of CERCLA provides for recovery by the EPA or a private party of all costs of remediation *jointly and severally* against defined categories of responsible parties. No equitable factors are relevant. In contrast, §113 of CERCLA provides a statutorily authorized right of equitable contribution among jointly liable private parties. Section 113 liability is several only, so very different outcomes are likely. Section 113 also contains statutory contribution protection for any party that previously settles with the government in a judicially or administratively approved manner.

First let's look at §107, where liability can be joint and several. Courts have adopted two principal techniques for allocating liability among plaintiffs and defendants so as to mitigate the harshness of joint and several liability. The first technique involves divisibility of the injury. The second technique is the deployment of common law equitable principles.

Divisibility of the Harm

In a §107 cost recovery action, there are only the three statutory defenses, as mentioned earlier in the chapter — act of God, act of war, or liability of an unrelated third party. Divisibility is a judicially created additional technique that allocates liability based on a person's unique — not joint and several — contribution to the harm. This technique/defense offers the possibility of totally avoiding liability or, more likely, reducing liability to the divisible share of liability attributable to a particular party.

While many courts have articulated the theory of divisibility of the harm, very few have, in fact, actually divided the harm to reduce the liability of particular parties. See *United States v. Alcan Aluminum Corp.*, 97 F. Supp. 2d 248, 271 (N.D.N.Y. 2000); *United States v. Monsanto*, 858 F.2d at 165 (4th Cir. 1998). There are a variety of reasons why this is so. The burden is on the potentially responsible party (PRP) to demonstrate divisibility. *United States v. Saporito*, 684 F. Supp. 2d 1043, 1062 (N.D. Ill. 2010); *ITT Industries, Inc. v. Borgwarner, Inc.*, 700 F. Supp. 2d 848 (W.D. Mich. 2010). As a practical matter, this is a very difficult burden. It requires access to factual and technical information that usually is not within the control of the defendant. This is especially true when the problem occurs at a third-party waste site not owned by the PRP.

In a §107 cost recovery action, it is well established that liability for the mixed brew of pollutants in the ground below a site typically creates a common harm that is not divisible; liability is thus joint and several. It is actual harm, hazard, or injury that must be divided. Courts have both accepted and rejected the *volume* of waste sent to a site as a basis for divisibility. The harm, hazard, or injury, however, rarely is directly proportionate to the amount of substances or waste contributed to a site. Divisibility requires a much more sophisticated technical and factual determination of the pathways that cause such harm or injury and the segregated responsibility of a single person's contribution.

However, if a particular defendant PRP *can* demonstrate factually that the harm is divisible, it can limit the imposition of liability, on a "several" basis, to just the harm for which it alone is responsible. Several liability makes each party liable only for its individual share. *United States v. Monsanto Co.*, 858 F.2d at 172 ("While CERCLA does not mandate the imposition of joint and several liability, it permits it in cases of indivisible harm. In each case, the court must consider traditional and evolving principles of federal common law, which Congress has left to the courts to supply interstitially"); *Chem-Dyne*, 572 F. Supp. at 806; *Shore Realty Co.*, 759 F.2d at 1042 n.13; *United States v. Stringfellow*, 661 F. Supp. 1053, 1059-1060 (C.D. Cal. 1987).

The Supreme Court issued a clarification on §107 arranger liability under CERCLA and found 8-1 that the Ninth Circuit had wrongly held some PRPs liable. Shell Oil had arranged for delivery of a pesticide, which did not make it an arranger for CERCLA liability purposes; Shell did not plan the disposal of a "used and no longer useful" hazardous substance, and an accidental spill by another is not intended disposal of a useful product by the manufacturer. *Burlington N. & Santa Fe Ry. Co.v. United States*, 556 U.S. 599 (2009). Justice Ginsburg, in dissent, noted that "the control rein" on delivery should be liable. Joint and several liabilities was not upheld, instead finding apportionment of liability. The Supreme Court held that "divisibility may be established by volumetric, chronological, or other types of evidence," reversing the Ninth Circuit and adopting the divisible shares originally determined by the trial court. This will require a number of new case-by-case "fact-intensive inquiries" in the lower courts. Defendants may utilize principles of divisibility to achieve an apportionment among defendants for a §107 CERCLA liability that is otherwise joint and several.

Equitable Factors as Apportionment Tools

Despite the typically joint and several liability of §107, some courts reach into their inherent judicial powers to apportion liability equitably among plaintiff and defendant PRPs in a §107 action. This approach modifies a strict application of joint and several liability. It is different from divisibility in that it starts from the premise of equitable allocation of costs, rather than imposing the burden on a particular defendant. A few courts apply factors named in the congressionally rejected Gore Amendment to apportion liability among defendants. The Gore Amendment was proposed by then Senator Al Gore (more recently vice president) as an amendment to CERCLA legislation in 1980 to specify factors for allocation among PRPs. Although the amendment was not adopted, courts still have the responsibility to allocate liability and often find that the amendment's criteria are consistent with common law principles. The Gore Amendment would have apportioned damages according to these criteria:

1. The ability of the parties to demonstrate that their contribution to a discharge, release, or disposal of a hazardous waste can be distinguished.
2. The amount of the hazardous waste involved.
3. The degree of toxicity of the hazardous waste involved.
4. The degree of involvement by the parties in the generation, transportation, treatment, storage, or disposal of the hazardous waste.
5. The degree of care exercised by the parties with respect to the hazardous waste concerned, taking into account the characteristics of such hazardous waste.
6. The degree of cooperation by the parties with federal, state, or local officials to prevent any harm to the public health or the environment.

Where a PRP is not forthcoming with the EPA regarding its liability, under the Gore factors that party's liability can be doubled to reflect a lack of cooperation. *United States v. Consolidation Coal Co.*, 184 F. Supp. 2d 723 (S.D. Ohio 2002). It is of note that the Gore factors include weighing responsibility based on waste toxicity. As a matter of statutory interpretation, it would seem that apportionment using equitable factors is appropriate in a §107 action only if the contribution of two or more defendants is divisible; if the harm is indivisible, liability should be joint and several. Notwithstanding this fact, many courts equitably apportion liability even where the harm is not divisible. This practice mitigates some of the force of joint and several liability.

The next three sections, between here and the following Examples and Explanations, are quite detailed. This level of detail usually is reached only in advanced environmental law classes. You may want to skip these sections unless your course or interest proceeds to this level of detail.

Private PRP §107 Actions

CERCLA is written to permit private parties to employ §107 for cost recovery. But the federal circuit courts between 1993 and 2003 refused to allow private PRPs, as opposed to nonliable parties, to employ §107 to state a claim in private CERCLA cost recovery cases. The leading case showcasing the full potential of §107 is *United States v. Kramer*, 757 F. Supp. 397 (D.N.J. 1991).

Other primarily federal district courts originally endorsed the private party plaintiff's right to maintain only a §107 claim to recover response costs, without regard to contribution under §113. See *Key Tronic Corp. v. United States*, 511 U.S. 809 (1994) ("impliedly authoriz[ing] private parties to recover cleanup costs from other PRPs . . ."). However, between 1993 and 2003, 11 circuit courts found to the contrary: PRPs could not avail themselves of §107 to shift contamination response costs. In 2007, the Supreme Court reversed every federal circuit (discussed briefly below).

All but the D.C. Circuit took §107(a) claims brought by private PRPs against other PRPs and converted these to §113 claims without the consent of the plaintiffs. See United Technologies Corp. v. Browning-Ferris Industries, Inc., 33 F.3d 96 (1st Cir. 1994) (applying §107 only to actions initiated by innocent parties); Akzo Coatings, Inc. v. Aigner Corp., 30 F.3d 761 (7th Cir. 1994); United States v. Colorado & Eastern R. Co., 50 F.3d 1530 (10th Cir. 1995); In re Dant & Russell, Inc., 951 F.2d 246, 249 (9th Cir. 1991); Amoco Oil Co. v. Borden, Inc., 889 F.2d 664, 672 (5th Cir. 1989); Nurad, Inc. v. William E. Hooper & Sons Co., 966 F.2d 837 (4th Cir. 1992); Pneumo Abex Corp. v. High Point, Thomasville & Denton R.R., 142 F.3d 769 (4th Cir. 1998); Newcastle County v. Halliburton NUS Corp., 111 F.3d 1116 (3d Cir. 1997); Rumpke of Indiana, Inc. v. Cummins Engine Co., 107 F.3d 1235 (7th Cir. 1997); Redwing Carriers, Inc. v. Saraland Apartments, 94 F.3d 1489 (11th Cir. 1996).

Sequentially, next the Supreme Court in Cooper Industries, Inc. v. Aviall Services, Inc., 543 U.S. 157 (2004), abruptly restricted private cleanup of hazardous waste. The Supreme Court required that prerequisite to any §113(f) CERCLA contribution action is the necessity that the private party-plaintiff have either (1) suffered prosecution for liability from the federal government or (2) entered a judicially or administratively approved settlement of such dispute with the government. The Supreme Court seemed to disregard the language in the savings clause in Section 113: "Nothing in this subsection shall diminish the right of any person to bring an action for contribution in the absence of a civil action under Section 106 or Section 107." The Court maintained the distinction between §107 "cost recovery" and §113 "contribution actions." In the view of the Court majority, this was a plain meaning interpretation following the canons of statutory construction. See §113 discussion in the next subsection.

In more than half of recent EPA CERCLA actions, the EPA has elected to use a Section 106 order in lieu of a Section 107 suit. Therefore, when a Section 106 AOC is entered with the EPA, it can have significant implications regarding the inability of the recipient to subsequently bring a Section 113 contribution rights claim against other PRPs. Section 107 cost recovery does not require a prior settlement or litigation, as does Section 113.

While the Supreme Court decision was a 7-2 majority, the two dissenters did not seem to contest the core holding. Rather they sought to go farther to address the even more pressing issue of whether there was a private right to cost recovery under §107(a) of CERCLA, notwithstanding that ten circuit courts, over the prior decade, had walled off §107. However, the issue was not addressed in the circuit court opinion on review, and therefore was not before the Court on cert. Justice Ginsburg's dissent notes that in *Key Tronic*, the Supreme Court in *dicta* stated that §107 "unquestionably provides a cause of action for [PRPs]." Justices Scalia and Thomas, dissenting in *Key Tronic*, but in the majority in *Aviall*, in that dissent also favored a private right of action under §107.

The Supreme Court's opinion, and the previous still-valid opinions of ten federal circuits, created great legal uncertainty, affecting an estimated 450,000 contaminated waste sites. The problem was a decade in the making at the circuit court level — without any legislative history, contrary to the literal interpretive principles articulated in other Superfund jurisprudence, and contrary to the canons of statutory construction, 11 circuits closed off the alternative path embodied in CERCLA Section 107 to accomplish waste remediation and cost allocation.

In 2007, in *United States v. Atlantic Research Corp.*, 551 U.S. 128 (2007), the Supreme Court overruled the 11 circuit courts that held previously that §107 of CERCLA was not available to PRPs for private cost recovery. This reopened §107, which the circuit courts had closed, and §113 contribution to many PRPs, which had been closed after the *Aviall* decision in 2004. While in some instances the Supreme Court has applied "plain meaning" to interpret one statute and not another, in *Atlantic Research* it actually corrects the arbitrary and differential application of "plain meaning" employed by all circuit courts that had taken contrary positions on the applicability and availability of §107 of CERCLA. Cf. *National Ass'n of Home Builders v. Defenders of Wildlife*, 551 U.S. 644 (2007) (chose Clean Water Act over Endangered Species Act to apply "plain meaning").

With the Roberts Court, the Court appears often extremely divided in 5-4 splits in opinions. Recent environmental opinions are staking out new ground for "plain meaning" interpretation of environmental statutes. During the 2006-2007 term, the Court, twice in unanimous opinions and twice in split decisions, based its interpretation on "plain meaning." One such unanimous opinion was in *Atlantic Research*; the other was in *Duke Energy*, where the Court gave the EPA very wide latitude in its definition and interpretation of the statutory term "modification." "Plain meaning" also was the fulcrum for decision in *Massachusetts v. EPA*, 127 S. Ct. 1438 (2007) (EPA has authority to regulate greenhouse gas emissions from automobiles), and in *National Ass'n of Home Builders v. Defenders of Wildlife*, 551 U.S. 644 (2007) (Clean Water Act dominates Endangered Species Act in terms of potentially conflicting provisions regarding delegation of Clean Water Act authority from the EPA to the states).

Several federal circuits, post the *Atlantic Research* decision, held that a nonsettling PRP may intervene, by right given its contribution rights, in CERCLA settlement proceedings. The courts dismissed arguments that CERCLA's policies favoring early and efficient settlement outweigh a nonsettling PRP's right to intervene. See, *United States v. Aerojet General Corp.*, 606 F.3d 1142

(9th 2010); *United States v. Albert Inv. Co., Inc.*, 585 F.3d 1386 (10th Cir. 2009); *United States v. Union Elec. Co.*, 64 F.3d 1152 (8th Cir.1995); cf. *United States v. Alcan Aluminum, Inc.*, 25 F.3d 1174, 1184 (3d Cir. 1994).

Private Party Allocation: §113

A private party who incurs response costs, after settling litigation with the EPA, can shift costs to other responsible parties. The settling party can pursue nonsettlor PRPs via one of two alternative recovery and allocation avenues. The first avenue, pursuant to CERCLA §107, seeks restitution of response costs incurred by the settling party. Section 107 can follow theories of *joint and several* liability, subject to the equitable and divisible qualifications discussed immediately above.

The second avenue involves an action for contribution pursuant to §113 of CERCLA. Section 113 is equitable in nature. Added by the SARA amendments in 1986, it codifies a common law negligence principle to spread tort responsibility among multiple responsible parties. There are two model uniform tort acts adopted as state statute in many of the states. They have become the basis for principal CERCLA §113 decision rules as a matter of evolving federal common law. However, these model acts are potentially contradictory when applied as federal common law for allocation in the CERCLA private party context.

Uniform Contribution Among Tortfeasors Act (UCATA)

One state model statute employed to craft CERCLA precedent is the Uniform Contributions Among Tortfeasors Act (UCATA). 12 U.L.A. 57. It has been adopted in 19 states. UCATA stipulates that the settling party is totally discharged from all future liability, including liability for contribution to nonsettlors. In other words, the settlors are not liable for greater than the amount of their actual settlements with the EPA, even if a volumetric or other proportionate or "equitable" share would be greater than this settlement. This is known as the *pro tanto* rule.

A handful of jurisdictions construing §113 have adopted the UCATA rule. Section 113(f)(2) of CERCLA, as interpreted by the court in *In re Acushnet River & New Bedford Harbor Proceedings re Alleged PCB Pollution*, 712 F. Supp. 994, 1019 (D. Mass. 1989), *aff'd sub nom. United States v. AVX Corp.*, 962 F.2d 108 (1st Cir. 1992), allows a settlor of a CERCLA claim with the EPA to obtain contribution protection from the government, to extinguish its liability to the government, and to obtain contribution protection against claims by other private party nonsettlors. It also leaves nonsettlors liable for any remaining unpaid "orphan shares" attributable to other PRPs, including those that otherwise might be attributable to settlors. Where the government agrees not to sue

CERCLA settlors pursuant to a consent decree, even where it involves prior actions by other PRPs, if the consent decree does not extinguish the contribution rights of those other PRPs, they are free to bring private third-party actions against the settling PRP. Thus, both the scope and drafting of a consent decree with the government are important.

In *United States v. Cannons Engineering Corp.*, 720 F. Supp. 1027 (D. Mass. 1989), *approved*, 899 F.2d 79 (1st Cir. 1990), two dozen nonsettling defendant PRP parties ended up paying the government's unrecovered residual expenses which, on average, were nine times the defendants' proportionate (based on waste sent) volumetric shares of the total liability. Basically, this higher cost resulted from the nonsettlors' absorption of a discount accorded to 47 large settling PRPs, plus "orphan" and bankrupt parties' shares of liability. The defendant nonsettlors' liability is reduced by the *pro tanto* amount of the prior settlement—that is, the value of the settlement. Thus, when settling parties strike an advantageous deal with the EPA, nonsettlors are left to absorb the residual shortfall created by the beneficial settlement afforded the settling parties. The *Cannons* opinion gives voice to the concept that an allocation based on relative *toxicity* of waste contributed, as a determinant of proportionate liability, might be the most accurate yardstick. The EPA need not select the "best" or fairest means to allocate liability among PRPs, as long as the scheme is reasonable—a rough correlation with proportionate fault.

Pursuant to Section 113 and UCATA, some courts conclude that the amount paid in settlement by the settlers is *pro tanto*, locking that settlement amount in as all that the settlers must bear and making unsettled parties liable for remaining orphan shares and response costs, even if disproportionate. *Am. Cyanamid Co. v. Capuano*, 381 F.3d 6, 19-20 (1st Cir. 2004); *U.S. v. Davis*, 261 F.3d 1, 26 (3d Cir. 2001); *Akzo Nobel Coatings, Inc. v. Aigner Corp.*, 197 F.3d 302, 306-07 (7th Cir. 1999); *U.S. v. Charter Int'l Oil Co.*, 83 F.3d 510, 515 (1st Cir. 1996); *United Technologies Corp. v. Browning-Ferris Indus.*, 33 F.3d 96, 103 (1st Cir. 1994; *U.S. v. Cannons Engineering, supra*.

In *United States v. Rohm & Haas Co.*, 721 F. Supp. 666, 677 (D.N.J. 1989), the court held that if the settlement was basically fair, nonsettling PRP defendants should receive credit only for the amount actually paid in settlement by settlors to a plaintiff (typically the EPA). The court acknowledged that even in a subsequent §113 CERCLA private party contribution action, nonsettling private defendants would be barred from seeking any contribution against private settlor defendants who enjoy contribution protection.

Uniform Comparative Fault Act (UCFA)

The second relevant *state* uniform act adopted as federal common law to allocate CERCLA liability is the Uniform Comparative Fault Act (UCFA). 12 U.L.A. 41. It employs a *proportionate* credit rule regarding partial settlements. Applied to CERCLA, this Act would reduce PRP settlors' liability in a subsequent judicial action only by the causal or *proportionate* amount of their liability, regardless of the amount of the settlement. In other words, in a subsequent §113 contribution action, settlors would not receive the benefits of their settlement but only of their "equitable" share, however determined. "Orphan shares" and other uncollectible amounts typically would be reallocated proportionately among all the solvent PRP parties, not just among nonsettling PRPs.

As many courts have adopted the Uniform Contributory Fault Act, or the proportionate rule, in allocating responsibility between settlors and nonsettlors responsible for CERCLA cleanup, as have adopted UCATA. See, for example, *Agere Sys. v. Advanced Envtl. Tech. Corp.*, 602 F.3d 204, 229 (3d Cir. 2010); *U.S. v. Alcan Aluminum Corp.*, 990 F.2d 711, 723-24 (2d Cir 1993); *Lyncott Corp. v. Chemical Waste Management, Inc.*, 690 F. Supp. 1409, 1418 (E.D. Pa. 1988); *Allied Corp. v. ACME Solvent Reclaiming, Inc.*, 771 F. Supp. 219, 223 (N.D. Ill. 1990); *Hillsborough County v. A&E Road Oiling Service*, 853 F. Supp. 1402 (M.D. Fla. 1994).

Strategic CERCLA Litigation Choices and Outcomes

Substantive Distinctions

Settlement of private party liability under CERCLA can proceed either by the entry of a consent decree or by the EPA's issuing a unilateral administrative order under §106. Contribution protection is automatically granted only as part of a judicially or administratively approved settlement. 42 U.S.C. §9613(f)(2).

If the private party plaintiff has contribution protection due to its prior judicially or administratively approved settlement with a government entity, it is thereafter not subject to a §113 counterclaim in litigation. One court has held that claims under state environmental laws are not precluded contribution claims. This protection allows a PRP that has settled with the EPA to subsequently initiate a private party §107 claim to impose liability jointly and severally on nonsettling PRPs.

During the 1990s, as one federal circuit court after another cascaded into conformance prohibiting use of §107 by private PRPs, PRPs were forced to use the much less attractive §113 for cost recovery. After the Supreme Court issued the *Aviall* decision, the entire cost recovery mechanism was cast into uncertainty. The *Aviall* decision did not specifically overrule the 11 circuit courts regarding §107. So the Supreme Court in *Aviall* barred use of §113 where there is no prior settlement.

There are critical distinctions between these two litigation routes regarding the allocation and shifting of total response costs among the private PRP parties. Let's walk through these differences.

In a §113 private party claim, a PRP who previously settled with the EPA could theoretically recover from nonsettlor PRPs its equitably allocated remediation costs under §113 principles, but only *severally*. The plaintiff would have to prove the distinct several share of liability against each defendant it named. The court would employ either UCATA or UCFA principles to allocate shares equitably. If the settlement with the EPA were administratively or judicially approved, the settling PRP could defend absolutely against a counterclaim by nonsettlors asserting additional contribution against it. A state court has awarded attorney fees and costs in a contribution action to recover response costs where the recovering party has not contributed to or caused release of hazardous materials, and thus is "innocent." *Martignetti v. Haigh-Farr, Inc.*, 680 N.E.2d 1131 (Mass. 1997).

Contrast this process with what occurs under a §107 claim. If a PRP settled with the EPA and subsequently made a §107 response cost claim against nonsettling PRPs, a settlor could establish *joint and several* liability against nonsettlors potentially for all costs incurred by the settlor. It is much easier to prove joint and several liability of some member(s) of the PRP group than the several liability of each defendant. The plaintiff PRP can shift some or all of its costs to defendants named in the private cost recovery litigation and then assert its contribution protection to step away from the many counterclaims and cross-claims that are likely to follow as the defendants reapportion the shifted liability among themselves. This is a major advantage in private party litigation.

Coupled with the complete contribution protection afforded by a judicially or administratively approved settlement, a plaintiff PRP thus has a double advantage: It has a "shield" against incurring more liability and a §107 joint and several "sword" to recover its costs from the others. It is important to note that there are multiple advantages to a plaintiff employing §107: a much longer statute of limitations (six versus three years), a lesser burden of proof, joint and several versus several liability, less problematic requirements of proof, and fewer available defenses (limited §107 statutory defenses versus §113 equitable defenses).

How this allocation works depends on whether §107 or §113 is the basis of the claim. These two avenues of litigation can involve significantly different allocation of "orphan shares," the shares attributable to insolvent parties. Section 107 can shift all costs jointly and severally to defendants. In *Charter Township of Oshtemo v. American Cyanamid*, 910 F. Supp. 332 (W.D. Mich. 1995), the court applied this principle to allocate liability pursuant to a §107 claim among private parties. The court held that §107 plaintiffs and defendants would each be allocated a proportionate share of the orphan share of insolvent parties.

The government is allowed to settle with generators based on "mixed funding." In such situations, the government shares some of the costs of total cleanup using Superfund monies. 42 U.S.C. §9622(b). Mixed funding is left to EPA discretion. That discretion is insulated from judicial review. The EPA is more willing to utilize mixed funding when the nonsettling shares are neither orphan shares nor shares from municipal-waste origin. The reason is that the EPA can go after the private nonsettling PRPs in subsequent litigation to recoup the mixed funding share that it advances from the Superfund.

Statutes of Limitation and Review

A §107 cost recovery action must be commenced within three years after completion of a removal action, or within six years of the initiation of physical on-site construction of the remedial action at the facility. Subsequent §107 cost recovery actions must be filed within six years of completion of all response actions. A §113 contribution action must be commenced within three years after a judgment or administrative order related to settlements for given costs or damages. An action for subrogation must be commenced within three years of payment of any claim on which the subrogation is based. 42 U.S.C. §9613. For civil proceedings, the statute provides for nationwide service of process. A three-year statute of limitations is provided for natural resource damage claims, running from the date of discovery — or, for NPL sites, the date of completion of the remedial action(s) at the facility. Therefore, whether judicial action is brought pursuant to §107 or §113, the nature and staging of the cleanup activity, and the nature of the claim, are all affected by the statute of limitations, as set out in Exhibit 9.9.

Courts are statutorily prohibited from exercising any jurisdiction to review EPA-mandated cleanup standards or orders except at the §107 cost recovery stage or in an EPA action to enforce compliance with a §106 order. Judicial review is limited statutorily to the EPA-created administrative record, on an "arbitrary and capricious" standard; procedural errors by the EPA must be disregarded by the court unless they would have

9.9   CERCLA Statutes of Limitation

	Natural Resource Damages	Removal Action	Remedial Action	Subsequent Action	Subro-gation
Section 107	3 years	3 years	6 years	3 years	
Section 113		3 years	3 years		3 years

changed the outcome significantly. 42 U.S.C. §9613. These standards over-rule the normal requirements of the Administrative Procedure Act (see Chapter 2). EPA decisions on cleanup are not reviewable on an interlocutory basis. PRPs must decide whether or not to perform EPA-selected cleanup activities long before they have an opportunity to challenge the appropriateness of the cleanup. This presents a "catch-22" for many PRPs.

There can be a conflict between the Superfund statute of limitations to initiate a cost recovery claim pursuant to §107 and state statutes regarding dissolution of corporations. At certain times corporations are routinely (or in some cases because of potential liabilities, which might include Superfund liabilities) dissolved and the assets distributed to shareholders. The question remains whether those assets can be followed to satisfy Superfund liability. The Second Circuit held that once a corporation is no longer reachable after dissolution under relevant state law, that state law provision trumps the six-year statute of limitations for a Superfund cost recovery claim. *Marsh v. Rosenbloom*, 499 F.3d 165 (2d Cir. 2007); *Onan Corp. v. Indus. Steel Corp.*, 770 F. Supp. 490, 494 (D. Minn. 1989). The Second Circuit also held that there is no equitable trust fund doctrine that allows an equitable right to pursue corporate assets postdissolution.

If you have not read carefully the three prior sections, you may want to skip the Examples and Explanations that follow below.

Examples

1. Let's revisit Curly's facility from the prior Examples. Groucho sent 10,000 gallons of trichloroethylene (TCE) to the Curly site. In total 500 generators have been identified who sent a total of 10 million gallons of hazardous substances to the facility. A variety of organic and inorganic contaminants are discovered all mixed together in soil and groundwater at the facility. Included in this "duck soup" is TCE. This site promises to be a typical Superfund site, with expenses of approximately $40 million to remediate the facility.

    a. Groucho asks you, as his counsel, the conditions under which his liability would be divisible. Since Groucho sent only 0.1 percent of the volume of hazardous substances accounted for, he would like to pay only 0.1 percent of the $30 million expected cost, or $30,000. Advise Groucho.

    b. Given these facts, if a court uses equitable apportionment techniques to apportion liability, what is the likely outcome for Groucho? See the section on "Equitable Factors as Apportionment Tools," *supra*, if you need to refresh your recollection on this.

2. Harpo is a (very) silent partner in a small business that generated hazardous waste and arranged for disposal at the Curly site. Harpo sent

1 million gallons of hazardous substances to the site, representing 10 percent of the total waste volume. Harpo approached the EPA and negotiated a settlement of his liability for $1 million. Other generators, including Groucho, comprise the remaining 90 percent of waste volume sent to the site. Assume that 30 percent of that remaining 90 percent volume share is accounted for by parties that cannot be found, are no longer in business, or do not have the financial ability to pay (collectively called "orphan shares"). As in the fact pattern above, the cost of remediation will be $30 million.

a. If the EPA proposes to conclude negotiations by executing with Harpo an administrative consent decree for settlement, how does Harpo ensure that he gets the full litigation advantages of settlement? What do you advise, as counsel for Harpo?

b. If the allocation of liability were determined in a circuit that followed UCATA, such as the First Circuit in the *Cannons* decision, describe and trace how Harpo's and the remaining generators' liabilities would be allocated. Who would probably pay for the orphan share and why? See the section on UCATA, *supra*, to refresh your recollection.

c. If this matter were litigated after Harpo's settlement in a court that applied the UCFA allocation principle, as in the *Lyncott* matter, how would the liability of Harpo and the other generators be allocated? Who would be likely to absorb the orphan share under this allocation principle? See the section on UCFA, *supra*, to refresh your recollection.

3. Disregarding Question 2 above, assume that Zeppo, a major contributor (10 percent) of hazardous substances to the Curly site, elects to settle in full with the EPA for $30 million. Afterward, Zeppo attempts to spread to other PRPs the cost he incurred from the settlement. He will do this by means of private litigation. Assume that Zeppo chooses a jurisdiction that limits him to a §113 private contribution action to recover those costs. Review previous sections as necessary. In such circumstances, address the following questions.

a. To recover in full, how many of the other 99 identified PRPs at the site must Zeppo name as defendants?

b. What is likely to be the type of the liability (joint and several, or other), if any, that each liable defendant PRP will have?

c. To recover in full, Zeppo must prove liability against how many of the 500 defendants?

d. What must Zeppo, as plaintiff, demonstrate legally and factually against each PRP to be successful in recovering their shares of liability? Recall from earlier in this chapter the basic requisites of CERCLA liability and §113 contribution.

e. How is a 30 percent unrecoverable "orphan" share likely to be allocated in this litigation?

    f. Given the facts regarding this site, is this likely to be a low- or high-cost litigation scenario for Zeppo?

4. After agreeing to fund the entire remediation cost of $30 million in a consent decree with the government, Zeppo seeks to shift his response costs to some of the nonsettling PRPs by making claims under §107 of CERCLA. As in Example 3, above, answer the following:

    a. To recover in full, how many of the other 500 identified PRPs at the site must Zeppo name as defendants?

    b. What is likely to be the type of liability, if any, that each defendant PRP will have?

    c. To recover in full, Zeppo must prove liability against how many of the 500 defendants?

    d. What must Zeppo, as plaintiff, demonstrate legally and factually against each PRP to be successful in recovering their shares of liability? Recall the basic requisites of CERCLA liability and §107 cost recovery.

    e. How is a 30 percent unrecoverable orphan share likely to be allocated in this litigation?

    f. Given the facts regarding this site, is this likely to be a low- or high-cost litigation scenario for Zeppo?

Explanations

1a. Say the secret word and win $30,000: "divisibility." Divisibility is the so-called fourth defense. In addition to the three statutory defenses, divisibility typically is a way not to avoid one's liability *entirely*, but to limit liability. The burden, however, is on you as Groucho's counsel to demonstrate divisibility.

    Here the facts do not support a good case for divisibility. It is the harm or injury, not just the amount of hazardous substances delivered to the site, that must be divisible. Where wastes are commingled, the harm typically is not divisible. Here, where Groucho's TCE, or at least TCE from some source, is mixed in with the other liquid waste in a "duck soup," the technologies for addressing any of the liquid waste will likely address other liquid waste as well. There is thus little opportunity to segregate remediation costs for just *some* of the liquid wastes and not others. The wastes are physically and chemically mixed together. While Groucho's volumetric contribution to the site can be segregated, the harm that it may have caused at the site is not divisible. Therefore, Groucho's liability is not divisible and he cannot claim several liability based on divisibility of the harm. Instead he remains jointly and severally liable for the entire harm at the site, as do the other contributors of chemical wastes.

1b. If a court applies equitable apportionment techniques to divide liability among the parties, Groucho may be more successful than if he tries to claim divisibility. Typically, among generators of waste, volume of waste sent to the site is the starting point for apportionment. The six Gore factors, upon which equitable apportionment is often based, speak in terms of the "*contribution* to a discharge, release or disposal." Therefore, the *contribution* to, rather than the result of the accumulation of, hazardous substances is the starting point for equitable apportionment. As part of the total contribution, the Gore factors consider the amount of hazardous wastes involved (see Exhibit 9.10). Groucho's 0.1 percent contribution of waste (by volume) would create a presumption of his share of the remediation responsibility among generators.

The Gore factors also look at the toxicity of the waste, involvement of the party, degree of care exercised, and cooperation with government authorities. Typically, these four factors are difficult to translate to quantitative measure. While it is very appealing in theory to utilize toxicity as a determinant, actually doing so involves factual scientific and engineering determinations as complex as the chemicals and the contamination pathways that they traveled. Most judges find such determinations too complex; precedent has not given routine voice to these elements in any significant degree.

2a. Section 113(f) of CERCLA provides for contribution protection. But to ensure contribution protection, the settlement must be judicially or administratively approved, according to statute. As counsel for Harpo, *after* settlement is achieved you may request that the EPA initiate litigation against your client for the limited purpose of obtaining a judicially approved consent decree, if that seems more secure than administrative approval.

9.10

Gore Factors	Quantifiable?	Drives Allocation
1. Contribution to release	Quantifiable	Yes
2. Amount of hazardous waste		
3. Toxicity	Possibly quantifiable	Rarely
4. Involvement		
5. Degree of care	Usually not quantifiable	No
6. Cooperation with government		

This contribution protection is available as a bar against subsequent litigation by the government or by private parties only regarding the matters covered by the settlement. It does not bar subsequent litigation for new matters or matters not incorporated in the settlement. Therefore, it is up to counsel for Harpo to draft the settlement as inclusively as possible to provide the greatest possible bar against subsequent revisitation of these issues.

In settlements, the EPA may expressly specify "reopener" provisions in the event that new information regarding either the liability of the PRP or the nature of the site contamination is subsequently obtained. In other situations, the EPA may insert in settlement agreements specific "reopener" provisions triggered if remediation expenses exceed a certain threshold, or if other stated expectations regarding remediation are not satisfied.

2b. Under UCATA, Harpo's settlement reduces the liability of the nonsettling parties, who represent 90 percent of the waste volume, by the amount of Harpo's settlement. Harpo settled for 33 cents on the dollar of its volumetric share, or $1 million, on a proportionate volumetric share that would otherwise have been $3 million. Harpo has received a $2 million dollar benefit by this settlement, as opposed to his share under a strictly proportionate value.

And these figures do not consider the orphan share (see Exhibit 9.11). In effect, the remaining PRPs, representing 90 percent of the volumetric waste sent into the facility, must now assume 96.7 percent of the total liability. Recall, however, that only 60 percent of the remaining 90 percent of the volume of waste is represented by viable solvent parties. Therefore, this 60 percent share represented by viable parties will have to absorb the residual 96.6 percent of the waste volume. Thus the nonsettling parties have their volumetric liabilities increased, as a practical matter, by more than 50 percent.

9.11 UCATA Rule Applied to Harpo (in $ millions)

Share	Proportion	Volumetric	Pro Tanto	Savings	Percentage Borne
Harpo	10%	$ 3	$ 1	$ 2	3.3%
Other viable PRPs	60	18	29	(11)	96.7
Orphan share	30	9	0	9	0
Total	100%	$30	$30	$ 0	100%

The UCATA rule reduces the volume of the nonsettling parties only by the value of the settlement, regardless of the orphan shares. Therefore, the settlement by Harpo has a double benefit for Harpo: (1) he settled with the EPA for less than his proportionate share, and (2) he avoided any attribution of the orphan share to him. He has concomitantly increased the residual share for all nonsettlors. See *Acushnet River & New Bedford Harbor, Proceedings re: Alleged PCB Pollution, supra; United States v. Cannons Engineering Corp., supra; United States v. Rohm & Haas Co., supra.*

2c. The rights of the PRPs are quite different in a jurisdiction that applies the Uniform Contributory Fault Act. The liability of a settlor is reduced only by the equitable or causal amount of its liability, regardless of the settlement. Therefore, if there is no contribution protection (see Explanation 2a), in a subsequent action the court would ignore the value — good or bad — of a prior settlement in determining the ultimate liability of the settling party.

Since Harpo settled at a significant discount, that savings would not be recognized or preserved in a subsequent contribution action with nonsettling PRPs. Harpo's liability in such a proceeding would be his equitable share, typically determined on a proportionate basis with regard to waste sent to the site by each PRP. The amount of the original EPA settlement would not be a determinative value in the final allocation calculation. In addition, the 30 percent orphan share most likely would be divided proportionately among all parties, increasing each of their shares proportionately (see Exhibit 9.12).

If Harpo also obtained contribution protection by virtue of an administratively or judicially approved settlement, he would be immune from subsequent litigation or claims (see Exhibit 9.13). By this mechanism, he could preserve his negotiated share without any further attribution of liability, including liability for the orphan share

9.12 UCFA Rule Applied to Harpo with No Contribution Protection (in $ millions)

Share	Proportion	Volumetric	Proportionate	Savings	Percentage Borne
Harpo share	10%	$ 3	$ 4.3	$(1.3)	14.3%
Other viable					85.7
PRPs	60	18	25.7	(7.7)	
Orphan share	30	9	0	9	0
Total	100%	$30	$30	$0	100%

9.13   UCFA Rule Applied to Harpo with Contribution Protection (in $ millions)

Share	Proportion	Volumetric	Proportionate	Savings	Percentage Borne
Harpo	10%	$ 3	$ 3	$0	10%
Other viable PRPs	60	18	27	(9)	90
Orphan share	30	9	0	9	0
Total	100%	$30	$30	$0	100%

volume. See *Conservation Chemical Co.*, 619 F. Supp. 162 (W.D. Mo. 1985); *Lyncott Corp.*, *supra*. This would further enhance the value of an advantageous settlement with the EPA.

3a. In a contribution action, whether at common law or under the codified §113 of CERCLA, a liable party attempts to shift its common liability to other liable parties. In this scenario, Zeppo has already incurred 100 percent of the liability by virtue of his agreement with the government. Therefore, unless he successfully takes action, he must live with 100 percent of the liability, even though his proportionate share of the waste is much less. If there are 500 PRPs, Zeppo must successfully prosecute litigation against 500 PRPs if he is to move the shares of liability he has assumed over to each of the other PRPs. Therefore, all PRPs become potential defendants in a §113 contribution action.

3b. Recall that §113 is a codification of the common law concept of contribution. Section 113 is related to §107 — where courts have found joint and several liability — only by virtue of referencing §107 for its definition of potential defendants:

> any person may seek contribution from any other person who is liable or potentially liable under Section 9607(a) [Section 107] of this title, during or following any civil action under 9606 of this title or under Section 9607(a) of this title. Such claim shall be brought in accordance with this section and the Federal Rules of Civil Procedure, and shall be governed by Federal law. In resolving contribution claims, the court may allocate response costs among liable parties using such equitable factors as the court determines are appropriate. Nothing in this subsection shall diminish the right of any person to bring an action for contribution in absence of a civil action under Section 9606 of this title or Section 9607 of this title.

Therefore, the standard of joint and several liability of §107 is not grafted onto §113. In fact, §113 is a separate and distinct cause of action from §107. Section 113 uses §107 to define the four categories of PRPs by reference: owners, operators, generators, and transporters who select the site. The legislative history of §113, which was added by the SARA amendments of 1986, makes clear that the section is meant to codify only the common law right of contribution. The common law of contribution does *not* impose joint and several liability; it imposes *several* liability only. This line of reasoning reinforces the fact that Zeppo will have to sue all 500 parties because he must successfully impose several liability against each party to shift a share that he has incurred over to other liable parties.

3c. Zeppo will have to prove each of the 500 defendants *severally* liable to be successful in his litigation under §113. In other words, if a defendant PRP has a 1 percent share, Zeppo will be successful in shifting 1 percent of the liability he has incurred over to that particular PRP if he successfully proves the liability of that PRP defendant. Zeppo must proceed PRP-by-PRP to make his case. He cannot treat PRPs as a group or class; rather, Zeppo must litigate individually against each and every PRP, even if these suits are all consolidated in a single action.

3d. Recall the earlier discussion of what is necessary to demonstrate liability of a PRP. Zeppo must demonstrate these factors as to each PRP defendant named pursuant to a §113 contribution action. These factors are (1) that Curly's property is a facility, (2) at which there has been a release or threat of release, (3) of a hazardous substance(s) *similar to* but not necessarily the same as or identical to, (4) hazardous substances sent to the facility by the particular PRP defendant, (5) which has caused the plaintiff to incur costs consistent with the National Contingency Plan (NCP). Several of these elements can be proved a single time with regard to their application as to all 500 defendants. However, Zeppo must proceed defendant-by-defendant to demonstrate that each defendant sent a hazardous substance, or transported a hazardous substance and selected the site for disposal, and he must show that each PRP's hazardous substance is similar to hazardous substances released or threatened to be released at the site. This can be a painstaking undertaking that requires extensive discovery and the use of expert witnesses to testify as to the nature of particular hazardous substances.

3e. If there is a 30 percent orphan share because certain of the 500 PRPs are judgment-proof, have proceeded through bankruptcy, or don't respond to the litigation, then some PRPs will have to shoulder this orphan share.

There is a substantial risk to Zeppo that he will shoulder the entire 30 percent orphan share. This would raise his normal 10 percent share to 40 percent (see Exhibit 9.14). This allocation is discretionary with the court. Because liability is several rather than joint and several, and Zeppo as the plaintiff has the burden of proof, to the degree that he

9.14 Section 113 Contribution Action Applied to Zeppo as Plaintiff (in $ millions)

Share	Proportion	Original Settlement	Percentage Borne After Litigation
Zeppo	10%	100%	40%
Other viable PRPs	60	0	60
Orphan share	30	0	0
Total	100%	100%	100%

cannot locate viable defendants to shift their several shares, he risks retaining that orphan share. The litigation argument of financially viable defendants will be that they cannot be liable severally for more than their proportionate share.

The provisions of §113, quoted above in Explanation 2b, allow courts to allocate response costs among liable parties using such equitable factors as the court determines. Therefore, Zeppo has an opportunity to argue that it is only equitable that the orphan share be allocated proportionately among *all* viable PRPs. However, this would also include Zeppo, the plaintiff, as a viable PRP. The best that Zeppo can hope for in most circumstances would be that each party would incur 40.3 percent more liability than its proportionate share, to fully account for the orphan share. However, Zeppo will succeed in only incurring a 40.3 percent increase in his liability, from 10 percent to 14.3 percent, if he is successful in shifting liability under §113 to *all* viable PRPs. Unless courts make this equitable shift, Zeppo takes the very real risk of incurring the entire orphan share, thus increasing his share of total costs from 10 percent to 40 percent.

3f. As may be obvious from the Explanations immediately above, bringing a §113 contribution action pursuant to CERCLA is a substantial litigation undertaking. In addition to the extensive use of expert witnesses, Zeppo will have to conduct discovery individually against each of the 500 defendants he sues. Zeppo will want to conduct discovery to determine the quantity and type of substances sent to Curly's facility by each defendant. He will also want to determine their financial viability and financial resources. If the EPA has sent a §104(e) information request to some of these 500 parties, their responses may provide some of this necessary discovery information. Zeppo can eventually obtain access to this information through a Freedom of Information Act request to the EPA, or he can negotiate for such access as part of his settlement with the EPA. Although the EPA may attempt not to provide this information pursuant to the FOIA request because the information is necessary for its own litigation, it should eventually be accessible to Zeppo.

Moreover, in litigation Zeppo runs the very real risk that each of the 500 defendants will conduct separate and distinct discovery of Zeppo or that each will make separate motions for summary judgment, motions to dismiss or strike claims, and so on. These countermoves by the defendants can make litigation expenses exorbitant.

Can you think of any solution, drawing on your background in either civil procedure or courses in federal courts? The solution for Zeppo as plaintiff is to attempt to consolidate the defendants into groups and to control the pace of litigation through a case management order. If Zeppo can convince the court to force the PRPs to consolidate into classes (such as large generators, small generators, municipalities, owners, operators, transporters) each represented by a single liaison counsel, defendants will have to act in common in each of their liaison groups. This minimizes the number of individual discovery requests, depositions, and motions to which Zeppo must respond. Finally, the use of case management orders may control the pace of litigation.

4a. Zeppo, because of the nature of liability in a §107 action, as discussed immediately below, can if he chooses sue many fewer than the total 500 PRPs. No defendant PRP is an indispensable party. He can, for example, avoid suing those PRPs whom he knows to be judgment-proof or otherwise not easily reachable.

4b. In a §107 action, the courts interpret liability to be *joint and several*. In other words, any PRP shoulders the entire liability of all other PRPs. Each PRP is liable for the whole liability. This interpretation puts tremendous pressure to settle on any PRP named as a defendant either by the government or by a private party in §107 litigation.

4c. With joint and several liability, Zeppo need only prove his case against a single PRP. If he proves his case against a PRP that has, for example, a proportionate 2 percent liability share, that PRP jointly and severally can be forced to incur the entire liability for the site. Thus joint and several liability is a very powerful legal concept. By selecting only a few defendants and proving their liability, Zeppo may be able to shift the entire liability jointly and severally to the defendants.

4d. The elements that Zeppo must demonstrate for liability are the same as those for §113 above: (1) that Curly's property is a facility, (2) at which there has been a release or threat of release, (3) of a hazardous substance(s) *similar* to but not necessarily the same as or identical to, (4) hazardous substances sent to the facility by the particular PRP defendant, (5) which has caused the plaintiff to incur response costs consistent with the National Contingency Plan (NCP). While the elements of proof as to an individual defendant are identical, the consequences that flow from that proof — joint and several liability — are profoundly different in a §107 action.

4e. If Zeppo can prove his claim against any one single defendant PRP, that defendant PRP may inherit jointly and severally the liability for all orphan shares. Therefore, among its other advantages, §107 litigation can shift the orphan share away from Zeppo and onto the PRP(s) of his choosing (see Exhibit 9.15). Some sites have orphan shares that equal 60 percent or more of the total proportionate liability. Therefore, §107 is a very important mechanism by which plaintiffs can shift otherwise unrecoverable shares of liability. Section 107 does not contain the language of §113 allowing courts to invent and apply equitable common law concepts in allocating liability, although some courts take the liberty of doing so anyway. Equitable factors and equitable defenses are not mentioned in the statute. If a court applied the rule in *Charter Township of Oshtemo v. American Cynamid*, 910 F. Supp. 332 (W.D. Mich. 1995), it would allocate proportionately the "true" orphan share, but it would pass exclusively to defendants, on a proportionate basis, the share for viable PRPs not named or joined in the litigation. If there is an administratively or judicially approved settlement, the settling plaintiff PRP should be immune from counterclaims.

4f. Section 107 response cost actions can be a much lower cost litigation scenario than §113 contribution actions. First, fewer PRPs can be named

9.15 Section 107 Joint and Several Allocation of Liability (in $ millions)

Share	Proportion	Volumetric	Section 107	Savings	Percentage Borne
Zeppo	10%	$ 3	$ 0	$3	0%
Other viable PRPs	60	18	30	(12)	100
Orphan share	30	9	0	9	0
Total	100%	$30	$30	$0	100%

as defendants. No one is an indispensable party in a §107 action. Second, with fewer defendants, there is much less discovery and fewer motions to battle. Third, the factual burden of proof against a smaller number of defendants is obviously less cumbersome for the plaintiff. Less use of expert witnesses is needed to testify as to the many different types of hazardous substances. Case management orders can be requested from the court to attempt to bifurcate the proceeding to minimize plaintiff costs. In such a bifurcation, Zeppo would ask the court to adjudicate first his §107 claim, including the five elements discussed in Explanation 4d that he must demonstrate to successfully impose liability on the named defendants. In a second phase of the trial, liable PRP defendants could bring in any other PRPs as third-party defendants. If Zeppo had an administratively or judicially approved settlement with the EPA, he would not be subject to any counterclaims for contribution in the second phase of the trial, which would raise §113 claims.

Note, however, that Zeppo can partially or wholly avoid the litigation melee of the §113 action. Zeppo's liability will already have been determined in the §107 first phase. Moreover, if prior to litigation Zeppo has settled his liability with the government in a judicially approved settlement, §113(f) protects Zeppo against contribution claims. Any counterclaims from the named defendants, or cross-claims from the third-party defendants, would be in the nature of a §113 contribution claim. By virtue of his settlement, Zeppo is granted absolute protection from such claims. Therefore, he can partially or wholly remove himself from the second contribution phase of the litigation. Employed strategically, §107 can be a major element of leverage for a plaintiff party.

THE APPLICATION OF CERCLA LIABILITY IN SPECIAL SITUATIONS

Liability Status of Unconventional "Persons"

Municipal Liability

Municipalities may be liable just as any other "person," under CERCLA §107, as owners or operators of disposal sites or as persons who arranged for disposal of hazardous substances. For instance, in the seminal case of *B. F. Goodrich Co. v. Murtha*, 958 F.2d 1192 (2d Cir. 1992), potentially responsible parties brought an action against owners and operators of a landfill to recover past and future cleanup costs under CERCLA. In turn, the defendant landfill owner filed third-party claims for contribution and indemnification from various municipalities. Thereafter, the PRP complaints were amended to add the municipalities as defendants in the original action.

The court of appeals held that CERCLA does impose liability on a municipality that arranges for disposal or treatment of municipal solid waste that contains a hazardous substance, even though such solid waste contains primarily household solid waste: "CERCLA does not contain any exemption for municipal waste, and that the exclusion for household solid waste found in the Resource and Recovery Act (RCRA) is not incorporated into the CERCLA definition of hazardous substances. . . . [A] municipality disposing of hazardous substances at a site where there is a release or threatened release of such substances may be liable under [§107]." Municipal waste need not be "listed by name — instead of its constituent components — to fall within [CERCLA]." The court noted that CERCLA does not provide an exemption for municipalities arranging for disposal of municipal solid waste that contains hazardous substances simply because the municipality undertakes such action in the furtherance of its sovereign status.

Second, CERCLA's definition of hazardous substance makes no distinction based on whether the substance's source was industrial, commercial, municipal, or household. Whether the substance is a consumer product, a manufacturing by-product, or a component of a waste stream is irrelevant under the statute. Third, the court noted that quantity or concentration is not a factor in determining whether a substance is hazardous for purposes of CERCLA. All of these are important principles in the CERCLA case law.

The EPA released an Interim Municipal Settlement Policy in 1989. 54 Fed. Reg. 51,071 (1989). The EPA in 1997 implemented a new method to allocate responsibility at sites that contain both municipal waste and hazardous waste. 63 Fed. Reg. 8197 (1998). Such "codisposal" sites make up approximately one-quarter of those sites listed on the National Priorities List. The EPA now multiplies the known quantity of municipal solid waste contributed by a PRP, by an estimated unit cost for remediating municipal solid waste at a typical representative municipal solid waste-only landfill. This estimated cost is derived from data on clean, nonproblem municipal solid waste-only landfills that are not subject to CERCLA response actions or RCRA corrective action. Of course, CERCLA hazardous waste sites, in fact, are not model or typical clean municipal waste landfills. Where the municipality is the owner of the hazardous waste landfill, the EPA uses a 20 percent baseline share to reflect response cost liability.

In the face of litigation, the EPA stated in a written stipulation that the settlement policy is not a rule and has no binding force or effect. Subsequent litigation was filed contesting the policy. The EPA sought dismissal on the basis that should the EPA choose to apply this policy, appropriate court review would be of the settlement reached in such a specific instance. The court dismissed this challenge as not contesting "final agency action" of a policy ripe for judicial review and therefore not reviewable under the Administrative Procedure Act. *Chemical Manufacturers Ass'n v. EPA*, 26 F. Supp. 2d 180 (D.D.C. 1998).

The Small Business Liability Relief and Brownfields Revitalization Act of 2001 exempts certain arrangers for disposal of municipal solid waste (exclusive of "waste materials from manufacturing or processing operations"). Municipalities were already subject to a special municipal liability settlement policy. Those included in the 2001 CERCLA amendments are:

- owners, operators, or lessees of residential property generating MSW delivered to the facility,
- small businesses with an average of less than 100 full-time employees during the three tax years preceding notification of potential liability, and
- certain tax-exempt organizations employing less than 100 paid individuals at the location that generated the MSW.

In essence, this exempts consumers from individual liability for the approximately 1-2 percent of their average 4 pounds per day per capita disposed as MSW into landfills. It also exempts small businesses and tax-exempt organizations who may typically not be included in the MSW collection of a given town or municipality. Typically, a municipality, particularly with regard to any new businesses, will require that commercial and industrial entities provide separately for their own trash removal and waste disposal. The 2001 amendments also shift statutorily the burden of proof to a party challenging the exemption claimed by a residence or small business, to demonstrate why such entity is not entitled to this exemption. If a private third party seeks response costs from a residential or small business entity entitled to this exemption, all reasonable costs of defending this claim are imposed on the third-party plaintiff.

Municipalities already receive favored settlement treatment at mixed waste sites. Effectively, this exempts the great majority of contributors of hazardous substance MSW at a site, leaving a small minority of larger businesses to pay for remediating the waste legacy of the majority tonnage of waste. Moreover, should those responsible challenge the application or eligibility of these exemptions, they pay both their own and the defendants' reasonable costs of defending the action.

However, the EPA policy also states that it has no effect on the statutory right of PRPs to bring private contribution claims. Therefore, even if the government will not seek recovery of response costs from municipalities, the policy is not intended to foreclose other PRPs from doing so. Judicial decisions indicate that municipalities may be liable as "owners" or "operators" if they own or operate landfills at which hazardous substances are released; they may be liable as "arrangers" if they hire contractors to collect residential trash, and as "transporters" if municipalities own and operate trucks that collect and transport hazardous substances to chosen disposal sites. Municipalities are exempt from potential liability under §107 in two cases: first, if they acquired ownership or control of a facility involuntarily, such as through bankruptcy or foreclosure proceedings; or second, where the municipality responds to an emergency caused by the release of hazardous substances from a facility owned by another party and does not act with gross negligence or willful misconduct.

Liability of Trustees, Fiduciaries, and Lenders

Lenders   An "owner or operator" under CERCLA is one who has power or authority over the hazardous waste disposal facility. Although lenders and trustees generally are excluded from such a definition, they could be held liable as "owners or operators" under CERCLA if they exercise *actual* control of the hazardous waste contamination at the facility or if, as trustees, they merely possess such authority under the trust arrangement.

A "safe harbor" provision is provided in CERCLA for any person who, without participating in the management of the facility, holds indicia of ownership primarily to protect his or her security interest in the facility. The premier lender case is *United States v. Fleet Factors Corp.*, 901 F.2d 1550 (11th Cir. 1990), in which the court ruled Fleet Factors was not liable as a lender in the case, but it also stated that under the right facts, secured lenders may be deemed "owners" for purposes of establishing CERCLA liability even before they foreclose or own a facility. In dicta the court noted that a secured creditor would be liable if its involvement with the management of the facility was sufficiently broad to support the inference that the creditor *could* affect hazardous waste disposal decisions if it so chose.

Congress codified lender liability protection, when the lender does not participate in management, in the Asset Conservation, Lender Liability and Deposit Insurance Act of 1996. The 1996 Omnibus Budget Bill contained this CERCLA amendment meant to shield lenders from Superfund liability. A new definition in §101(20)(E) exempts from the definition of "owner or operator" those lenders that do not participate in the management or operational affairs of a facility. This provision allows lenders to foreclose or take property by deeds in lieu of foreclosure and participate in routine postforeclosure activities without being designated an owner or operator for purposes of CERCLA liability.

If one does not participate in management but only holds an "indicia of ownership" so as to protect the security interest, this is not deemed under federal law to expose one to "owner or operator" Superfund liability. A security interest is defined as a right under "a mortgage, deed of trust, assignment, judgment lien, pledge, security agreement, factoring agreement, or lease and any other right accruing to a person to secure the repayment of money, the performance of a duty, or any other obligation by non-affiliated person." 42 U.S.C. §9601(20)(G)(vi).

A deliberate foreclosure action is covered, even where the security interest holder purchases the property at a discount at a foreclosure or in the secondary market. See *In re Dufrayne*, 194 B.R. 354, 363 (Bankr. E.D. Pa. 1996). The lender has the burden of proof to demonstrate that it was within the secured creditor exception. *Organic Chemical Site PRP Group v. Total Petroleum, Inc.*, 6 F. Supp. 2d 660, 663 (W.D. Mich. 1998).

Under both federal and state so-called "Brownfields" initiatives — there are opportunities to obtain one of two negotiated legal protections. The first is an EPA comfort letter, an official statement by the EPA that it does not deem the current owner responsible for the contamination currently on the property, because of its source from off-property locations. But, it does not provide enforceable absolute liability protection under federal law. These comfort letters can fall into four categories: (1) a "no previous federal Superfund interest letter" where there is no historical evidence of federal involvement in the site; (2) a "no current federal Superfund interest letter" where the site is not federally listed as contaminated, or has been removed from the list, or is near but not within the boundaries of the contaminated site as listed federally; (3) a "federal interest letter" indicating that the EPA plans to respond in some manner or is already responding to the site; or (4) a "state action letter" where the state is taking the lead in dealing with remediation and control of the contaminated site.

Alternatively, the EPA has the power to enter a prospective purchaser agreement, with a prospective future purchaser who knowingly buys or procures an ownership interest in contaminated property subject to the federal Super-fund law. This does provide enforceable protection from EPA claims. However, it is time-consuming to obtain and requires negotiation with both the EPA and the Department of Justice.

As a third alternative, the EPA also has the power to enter *de minimis* settlements and *de micromis* settlements with potentially responsible parties, either of which can end the liability of anyone otherwise potentially responsible for a contaminated property. 42 U.S.C. §122(g). Such a settlement would provide protection from suit from both the EPA and from third parties with a claim. 42 U.S.C. §9607(f).

These amendments do not protect subsequent purchasers of the property from foreclosing lenders, which may, in turn, make the property harder to sell. The possible comfort of the Brownfields protections was previously discussed. These amendments do not affect any potential liability of foreclosing lenders pursuant to RCRA §7002.

Fiduciaries A trust is essentially a fiduciary relationship in which a trustee holds legal title to property subject to an equitable obligation to protect or use the property for the beneficiary of the trust, who holds equitable title.

Since a trustee holds legal title to the property, the trustee may be considered an "owner" for purposes of establishing CERCLA liability. Under §9607(a)(1), a trustee might be held liable as the *current* owner of contaminated property.

Courts initially found trustees personally liable, through a broad application of the term "owner." In 1990, in *Quadion Corp. v. Mache*, 738 F. Supp. 270 (N.D. Ill. 1990), the court determined that a trustee in a corporate context could not escape liability if a closely held corporation was involved. The *Quadion Corp.* court relied on the decision in *Kelley v. Thomas Solvent Co.*, 727 F. Supp. 1532 (W.D. Mich. 1989), which set forth the test for shareholder liability under CERCLA.

Section 107(n) of CERCLA was subsequently amended to provide: "The liability of a fiduciary under any provision of this chapter for the release or threatened release of a hazardous substance at, from, or in connection with a vessel or facility held in a fiduciary capacity shall not exceed the assets held in the fiduciary capacity." It does not absolutely shield fiduciaries who would otherwise be liable, to escape all liability by virtue of their fiduciary status. The statute provides a broad definition of "fiduciary," including trustees and guardians. If the fiduciary acts in other than a fiduciary capacity, is a beneficiary of the trust, or receives more than reasonable compensation, the fiduciary exemptions are vitiated. A key provision of the statute exempts the fiduciary from liability for administering property with preexisting contamination prior to the fiduciary relationship. This eliminates the necessity of asserting the "innocent landowner defense." Trustees may, however, still hold responsibility for releases or threatened releases occurring during their trustee tenure, unless other defenses included in the enumerated safe harbors or other defenses under CERCLA exist. The act's fiduciary safe harbor activities include:

(A) undertaking or directing another person to undertake a response action . . . ; (B) undertaking or directing another person to undertake any other lawful means of addressing a hazardous substance in connection with the vessel or facility; (C) terminating the fiduciary relationship; (D) including in the terms of the fiduciary agreement a covenant, warranty, or other term or condition that relates to compliance with an environmental law, or monitoring, modifying or enforcing the term or condition; (E) monitoring or undertaking one or more inspections of the vessel or facility; (F) providing financial or other advice or counseling to other parties to the fiduciary relationship, including the settlor or beneficiary; (G) restructuring, renegotiating, or otherwise altering the terms and conditions of the fiduciary relationship; (H) administering, as a fiduciary, a vessel or facility that was contaminated before the fiduciary relationship began. . . . 42 U.S.C. §9607(n)(4)(A)-(I).

Some states adopted statutes that provide immunity or limitations on liability for fiduciaries. Many of these statutes require some affirmative action, such as participating in day-to-day activities, or responsibility for either a willful or negligent release or threatened release of hazardous substances into the environment. These state protections are not absolute, and fiduciaries must evaluate their actions with respect to both state and federal requirements.

Liability of Parent Corporation for Acts of the Subsidiary

As may now be apparent, CERCLA creates law as much in its voids and silences as in its affirmative voice. The statute is silent on the issue of parent/subsidiary corporate liability. In *United States v. BestFoods*, 524 U.S. 51 (1998), the Supreme Court refused to extend liability to a parent company, if that parent company did not exercise actual control over the subsidiary's environmental practices.

BestFoods finally settled that direct actual control is the requirement under CERCLA for parent corporation liability. Because that control must be of the polluting facility itself, this narrows the prospect of parent corporate liability. In *BestFoods*, the court unanimously held that "a corporate parent could be held liable only as an 'owner' for CERCLA purposes when the corporate veil may be pierced" and this required active participation in exercising control over the operations of the polluting facility itself. Where the parent corporation pervasively controlled the facility, it could be liable as an "operator" even if neither the parent nor its subsidiary owned the releasing/polluting facility. The standard for "operator" liability is not quite as exacting as the traditional "veil piercing" corporate doctrine, but does require direct actual control. Near monitoring of the subsidiary's performance, supervision of its financing capital budgets, and general articulation of policies and procedures for the subsidiary is not enough to satisfy the standard of direct actual control. The Court held that an operator must "manage, direct, or conduct operations specifically related to pollution, that is, operations having to do with the leakage or disposal of hazardous waste, or decisions about compliance with environmental regulations."

The *BestFoods* court did not address whether the court should apply state or federal common law standards in adjudicating these matters. The exact degree of control over the subsidiary corporation's activities at the polluting facility are not articulated by the court. If the parent puts a director on the subsidiary's board of directors to serve the parent rather than the subsidiary, this may be enough control to impose parent liability. The veil piercing standard can apply to both owner liability and operator liability of the parent.

Parent corporation liability will not be the norm. Special importance, however, may be attached by courts to the actions of parent corporations that result in the exercise of control over particular hazardous waste management decisions.

Successor Corporation Liability

Corporate parties that sent waste to a particular Superfund site may no longer exist or they may have been succeeded by other companies. Are successor corporations liable under CERCLA for the acts of their predecessors? Well, at law it depends on how the succession occurs.

It is well-settled law that when one corporation purchases the stock of another corporation, or when two companies are merged or otherwise consolidated, the changes in ownership of the company stock do not affect the rights and obligations of the company itself. Assets and liabilities survive, even as ownership changes. As such, the liabilities of the former company are vested in the new shareholders or the surviving corporation. CERCLA liability is not abated.

However, when one corporation purchases or otherwise acquires all the *assets* of another corporation, without purchasing the company, the purchasing corporation typically does not become responsible for the liabilities of the selling corporation, which continues. Nonliability in such cases is based on the distinction that the purchasing corporation does not acquire the seller's liabilities by simply purchasing the seller's machinery or equipment. CERCLA liability here normally would not pass with the assets, but remain with the seller.

There are four well-recognized exceptions to the general rule that a successor corporation in an *asset purchase* will not be responsible for the liabilities of the seller corporation. The purchaser of assets assumes the seller corporation's liabilities only when (1) the purchaser expressly or impliedly agrees to assume the seller's obligations, (2) the transaction is entered into fraudulently to escape liability, (3) the transaction is effectively the same as a consolidation or merger of the corporations (the de facto merger exception), or (4) the purchasing entity is merely a continuation of the selling corporation. Also of note, the "product line analysis" or "continuity of enterprise" theory blends features of both the "de facto merger" and "mere continuity" theories into a more intuitive, "common sense" court analysis of whether the successor corporation is sufficiently tied to its predecessor to be held liable for the acts of the predecessor corporation under CERCLA. This theory is gaining force.

Liability of Persons During Acts of War

"War is hell." And so can be CERCLA liability. The term "act of war" is not defined in CERCLA. During wartime, the federal government exercises considerable regulatory control over private corporations, in order to mobilize the nation's industries to aid the war effort. These regulatory acts affect and control the nation's industrial output during war by allocating resources away from consumer production toward the manufacture of wartime materials. Like all other industrial activities, wartime production leads to the creation of hazardous waste that can be subject to CERCLA regulation.

The court in *FMC Corp. v. U.S. Department of Commerce*, 29 F.3d 833 (3d Cir. 1994), found the United States liable as an "owner," "operator," and "generator" of toxic waste under CERCLA for its regulatory acts during war related to rayon production. The court admitted this was quite a broad and expansive reading of CERCLA's liability provision but noted that to hold otherwise would violate the act's remedial goals.

Where the United States during wartime does not have firm control over a process leading to contamination, and does not have direct involvement in arrangements for disposal of hazardous waste and does not own any of the products (aviation fuel) that cause the harm, the government does not have arranger liability for waste by-products under CERCLA. See *United States v. Shell Oil Co.*, 294 F.3d 1045 (9th Cir. 2002). Where the government exercised direct control over a manufacturing site during wartime, even where it did not perform the (rubber) manufacturing, and agreed to indemnify the manufacturer, it is liable as an arranger for disposal. *Cadillac Fairview/California, Inc. v. Dow Chemical Co.*, 299 F.3d 1019 (9th Cir. 2002). No act of war defense applied to the private parties involved in either *Shell* or *Cadillac Fairview*, so government coliability was a critical issue in allocating expense. *FMC* and *Shell* waived sovereign immunity even where the government acts in a regulatory manner.

In *Boyle v. United Technologies Corp.*, 487 U.S. 500 (1988), the Supreme Court created a tort claim defense where a private contractor performed design for the U.S. military, effectively transferring government sovereign immunity to a private contractor. There must be a unique federal interest in significant conflict with state law, whereby the private company contracting with the federal government cannot comply with the state law obligation. Notice also the complication when warlike activities are carried out not as part of formal acts of war, but rather as less formal "police actions" or military activities.

Examples

1. The Stooges are famous for their cream pies, which they fling with reckless abandon in each other's faces. These "cream" pies do not contain real cream but rather a substance called CRM, made from petroleum. Suppose that cream pies become such a rage on college campuses that the Stooges sell the secret formula and the ingredients for making their Stooge "cream" pies to entrepreneurs on college campuses across the country. The Stooges get 10 percent of the sales revenues of all "Stooge Pies" sold by these licensed local vendors.

   The Stooge Pie Factory is owned in equal shares by Larry, Moe, and Curly through a trust, with Moe (the "smart" stooge) serving as trustee. During the early years of operation, CRM is disposed of along with other waste in the factory's garbage bins, which are removed weekly by the town of Metropolis and the waste placed in a landfill. During Operation Desert Storm in 1991, the Stooge Pie Factory was ordered by President Bush to divert its entire supply of pies for three months to the war effort, where the pies were dropped by B-2 Stealth bombers over enemy lines to demoralize the enemy. Recently, CRM was discovered in the soil and groundwater near the rubbish bin area at the factory. When told, Moe said, "Woop woop woop woop woop," and told employees to cover up the contaminated soil with empty pie crates, so that no one would notice.

On the advice of counsel, Moe takes two actions. First, in 2003 he spins the land ownership off into a subsidiary corporation called Fat Chance. The directors of Fat Chance are Larry, Moe, and Curly. To reduce potential losses, minimal assets are transferred to the subsidiary. Second, Moe, Larry, and Curly in 2004 decide to cash out all their assets. They sell the assets of Stooge Pies and Fat Chance to Pies-R-Us. In the sale contract, they carefully state that the sale is only an asset sale with no assumption by Pies-R-Us of any liability, particularly environmental liability. Pies-R-Us retains most of the former subordinate Stooge employees, and it continues in the CRM pie business, marketing pies under the Stooge and Fat Chance names.

Today, the EPA is on the scene. The CRM contamination is discovered. Try to answer the following questions.

a. Who is liable for CRM from the pie factory that ends up at the landfill utilized by the town of Metropolis to dispose of trash picked up at all residences and businesses? What must be established to prove liability?
b. What is Moe's liability as a trustee?
c. Is the U.S. government liable for CRM contamination because of its activities during Operation Desert Storm in 1991? Why? What factors are relevant?
d. What is the effect of the spin-off corporation, Fat Chance, with regard to CRM liability?
e. Does Pies-R-Us have any liability for the Stooge Pie CRM problem? Why?

Explanations

1a. Would you like to hold Stooge Pies liable? They appear to have arranged for disposal of CRM. An examination of §107 of CERCLA reveals no express requirement that the arranger designate the place of disposal. Arranging for *any* disposal is all that is required. But someone will need to prove that Stooge Pies disposed of CRM. Mere logic, inference, or circumstantial evidence is not sufficient.

However, the town may also be liable. Under B. F. *Goodrich* and other decisions, the town is liable just like any other person. Proof of the town's disposal or arranging for disposal of CRM still is required. As with Stooge Pies, the factual proof, not the legal issue, is the key to establishing liability. Towns typically dispose of trash in one of two ways: They (1) collect and haul the trash themselves or (2) contract with a private company for trash services. In the first case, the town actually takes title and executes the disposal. In the second case, the town does not take title but "arranges for disposal" of the waste. In either case, the town is liable as the trash disposer. There may be a claim by the town against Stooge Pies if disposal of CRM was not allowed in trash.

1b. Legally, Moe is a trustee. Nice work if you can get it. But he is *not* immune from CERCLA liability, under §107(n) as a fiduciary, because he is also a beneficiary of the trust. The trust itself is more a fictional shelter than an actual legal shelter. One can always "follow the cash" in the trust and reach those assets.

Moe may be personally liable as a trustee where he had the ability to control the property and then exacerbated the situation by not remedying the known release but rather allowing it to worsen by covering it up with boxes. He can be subject to *personal* liability. This means that the trustee's individual assets can be tapped to accomplish cleanup. Recall also that owners *and* operators can be liable for passive disposal, which can be interpreted as leaking and seeping. Moe has a problem here.

1c. The concept of government liability for its regulatory activities is established in the FMC case. However, the government essentially must operate the facility and its handling or disposal of hazardous substances. It can do so directly by operating a plant or indirectly through regulations controlling a plant. Key factors are whether or not the government so controls the manufacturing, storage, and disposal practices of a plant as to *require* conduct that results in the release of a hazardous substance. "Act of war," while a CERCLA defense, is not defined in the statute. In the modern era, "police actions" and "international peacekeeping" have replaced the constitutional prerogative of Congress to declare war. An issue remains as to whether the term "act of war" in CERCLA applies to Operation Desert Storm and similar military action.

Here, there is no evidence of such a commandeering role by the government. The government did redirect the supply of Stooge Pies during Operation Desert Storm. But it did not alter the ingredients, the manufacturing process, or the waste handling practices. Merely being a large and coercive customer neither imposes liability on the government nor exonerates Stooge Pies from liability.

1d. The spin-off is a subsidiary corporation. A variety of factors can make parent companies liable for the hazardous substance practices of their subsidiaries. In this situation, several factors argue in favor of parent liability:

- Thin capitalization of the subsidiary
- A lack of legitimate procedures, formalities, and records
- Possibility of a "sham" transaction in creating the subsidiary
- Parental control

These matters are decided on a case-by-case basis. But did you question the timing of the creation of the subsidiary? It was created *after* knowledge of possible problems. This bad timing does two things. First, it increases the possibility of a sham transaction and increases the possibility of parental liability. Second, it creates the likelihood of *dual* liability. Stooge Pies does not avoid *its* liability by this maneuver. Stooge Pies only changes its status from current owner to past owner at the time of disposal. Either status imposes liability. Check and checkmate. Moreover, Fat Chance is now liable as the *current* owner unless it can qualify as a bona fide purchaser, which is difficult here. Thus, dual liability is possible and the CERCLA problems may be compounded rather than redressed by creation of the subsidiary.

1e. This is an asset sale, which typically insulates the successor corporation from environmental liability. When you purchase assets, without taking over the entire company as a continuing entity, you can generally avoid the liabilities. There are four exceptions to this rule. In this case, counsel needs to analyze whether one of these exceptions, the *continuation of enterprise* exception, applies. Where, in fact, continuation of the enterprise is the result, the liabilities impliedly also continue with the successor company. The successor, Pies-R-Us, uses the former company's name, continues exactly the former product line, and retains the employees. In fundamental ways, the enterprise continues. There is a substantial likelihood that the continuation of enterprise exception would apply here to impose successor liability.

What about the statement in the sale documents that Pies-R-Us accepts no environmental liabilities? As a matter of contract law, this would be determinative. But the continuation of enterprise theory is not a contract law doctrine. It operates by imposing liability as a matter of equity, based on implied relationships. Therefore, the very acknowledgment by Pies-R-Us that it is trying to avoid known environmental liabilities strengthens the implied basis to apply the continuation of enterprise exception. Therefore, in certain circumstances such as these, the very attempt to avoid environmental liabilities may strengthen the case to impose those liabilities.

Interrelationship of CERCLA and Other Law

Effect of Indemnities and "Hold Harmless" Clauses

How does CERCLA affect contract law? CERCLA §107(e)(1) states that liability to the government may not be avoided by means of indemnification, hold harmless clauses, or other similar contractual devices. Such devices are commonly used to redistribute liability in the transfer of title to real property, or between parties such as generators, transporters, site owners, and operators.

However, indemnification language is effective between private parties. Therefore, while not effective against a government plaintiff in a §107 action, it is effective in a private party §107 or §113 action. See *Cadillac Fairview California, Inc. v. Dow Chemical Co.*, 299 F.3d 1019 (9th Cir. 2002). Therefore, the law of contract yields to government claims only. In applying private indemnity agreements in CERCLA actions, courts usually require clear indication that general indemnities are meant to apply to CERCLA liability and to release such liabilities.

Interplay with Bankruptcy Law

Although both the Bankruptcy Reform Act of 1978 (11 U.S.C. §§101-1330) and CERCLA were adopted by Congress to address certain indispensable needs of society, those needs can conflict. The Bankruptcy Code can be used by PRPs at Superfund sites to avoid paying their share of response costs. It is estimated that up to 30 percent of owners or operators of hazardous waste disposal facilities will petition for bankruptcy in the next fifty years.

In most CERCLA bankruptcy cases, courts consider the government an unsecured creditor for the amount of the environmental liability. The conflict between CERCLA and the Bankruptcy Act is palpable. The judicial resolution of the conflict between these conflicting federal statutes is discussed in Chapter 8 (RCRA).

The Petroleum Exclusion

Oil may be the most pervasive waste at Superfund sites. It naturally contains hazardous substances on the RCRA list. The definition of "hazardous substance" in CERCLA expressly excludes "petroleum, including crude oil or any fraction thereof not specifically listed or designated as a hazardous substance," 42 U.S.C. §9601(14). So the question becomes: "What is petroleum?" The legal answer is not easy to formulate.

Two key distinctions mark the jurisprudence. Courts distinguish between "waste" petroleum and reusable petroleum "product." In *United States v. Western Processing Co., Inc.*, 761 F. Supp. 713 (W.D. Wash. 1991), the court ruled that "tank bottom" (the "grunge" created from cleaning a petroleum tank), made up of petroleum residue contaminated with sand and rust from the tank, was not excluded from CERCLA. The fact that the tank bottom was "waste-like" supported the court's ruling. However, leaded gasoline tank bottoms have been excluded from CERCLA. *Cose v. Getty Oil Co.*, 4 F.3d 700 (9th Cir. 1993).

Second, the chemical components of the hazardous substance can be distinguished. In *Wilshire Westwood Assoc. v. Atlantic Richfield Co.*, 881 F.2d 801 (9th Cir. 1989), the court stated that refined gasoline containing a CERCLA hazardous substance is covered by the petroleum exclusion if the hazardous substance is "indigenous" to such products or additives. Under similar analysis, the court in *State of Washington v. Time Oil Co.*, 687 F. Supp. 529 (W.D. Wash. 1988), ruled that the petroleum exclusion is not applicable to hazardous substances that are found in oil products in *excess* of levels that are normally in a refined product. The exemption applies to gasoline additives. See *Southern Pacific Trans. Co. v. Calif.*, 790 F. Supp. 983 (C.D. Ca. 1991); diesel fuel, *Equitable Life Assur. Soc. of U.S. v. Greyhound Corp.*, 1990 WL 6143, 31 ERC 1079 (E.D. Pa. 1990); kerosene, *Andritz Spart-Bauer, Inc. v. Beazer East, Inc.*, 12 F. Supp. 2d 391 (M.D. Penn. 1998).

Therefore, every petroleum product manufactured within normal tolerances is exempt from CERCLA, even though it contains hazardous substances. The exclusion only covers CERCLA, but waste oil is still an RCRA solid waste. The petroleum exclusion is not countermanded by an actual detection of hazardous substances in the oil. But if oil is used or recycled so that it becomes a waste product, the evaluation changes. It then becomes critical *how* the hazardous substances got into the oil.

In *Mid Valley Bank v. N. Valley Bank*, 764 F. Supp. 1377 (E.D. Cal. 1991), the court held that "waste oil containing CERCLA hazardous substances does not fall within the petroleum exclusion." The court noted that if a hazardous substance, such as lead, is naturally present in the virgin petroleum as a result of the refining process, petroleum with the lead contamination would be excluded from CERCLA liability under the petroleum exclusion. However, if the lead contamination resulted from use of the oil in a vehicle engine, or is at abnormally high levels in the virgin state, it would not be excluded. On this distinction hinges "generator" liability at almost every Superfund site. *Accord, United States Western Processing Co. Inc.*, 761 F. Supp. 713 (W.D. Wa. 1991); *Acme Printing Ink Co. v. Menard Inc.*, 881 F. Supp. 1237 (E.D. Wisc. 1995). However, waste cutting oil has been excluded from CERCLA. *Marmon Group v. Rexnord, Inc.*, 822 F.2d. 31 (7th Cir. 1987). Used motor oil is not exempt, nor is oil mixed with another hazardous substance, *United States v. Amtreco, Inc.*, 846 F. Supp. 1578 (M.D. Ga. 1994), although petroleum is still exempt if mixed with a nonhazardous substance.

A state court in Indiana held that major oil companies were liable as "operators" under Indiana state law to correct underground storage tank

(UST) leaks and contamination at gasoline stations run by independent contractors carrying the trademark or logo of the major oil company. See *Shell Oil Co. v. Meyer*, 684 N.E.2d 504 (Ind. App. 1997). This liability was imposed even though the major oil companies whose brands were licensed to the independent operators had no control whatsoever over the operation of the tanks. The recovering plaintiffs were individual homeowners whose drinking water wells were contaminated by leaking petroleum from these gasoline stations. No effect was given the fact that Indiana had a separate UST fund created to cover such spills.

Liability of the major oil companies was predicated on (1) their understanding that steel USTs are subject to corrosion and leakage, (2) that slow leakage of gasoline tanks is difficult to detect without sophisticated technology, (3) that gasoline contamination of drinking water is carcinogenic, (4) that the major oil companies took steps to prevent such leakage and leak detection at gasoline stations that they directly owned, and (5) that the major companies transferred in the 1970s and 1980s tanks at independently owned stations to the independent owner to further remove themselves from liability. The court seemed to be particularly moved by the major oil companies forcing independent station operators to purchase the tanks that previously were owned by the major oil companies, as a means to avoid direct liability. Plaintiff's attorneys also recovered attorney fees under the statute.

Natural Resource Damages and Economic Loss

CERCLA §107(a)(4)(c) makes "damages for injury or destruction of, or loss of natural resources," including the reasonable costs of assessing such damage, recoverable by the government from responsible parties. "Natural resources" are defined as "land, fish, wildlife, biota, air, water, ground water, drinking water supplies, or other such resources belonging to . . . or otherwise controlled by the United States," 42 U.S.C. §9601(16). A claim for natural resource damages may be asserted only by the United States, a state, or a Native American tribe.

Assessment of natural resource damage is fraught with uncertainties. This is particularly the case when dealing with natural resources such as fish and wildlife, because such living resources are not ordinarily assigned monetary or market values. Trustees of natural resources must limit sums recovered from PRPs to those expenditures which "restore, replace, or acquire the equivalent of" lost or damaged resources. The Department of the Interior administers the federal trustee's responsibilities. The DOI's natural resource assessment regulations are complex; they are codified at 43 C.F.R. Part 11.

In *Ohio v. U.S. Department of the Interior*, 880 F.2d 432 (D.C. Cir. 1989), the court upheld the DOI's use of "contingent valuation" procedures, which are used when market value approaches to resource valuation are impractical or impossible. The natural resource damage regulations, as promulgated in

1994, were upheld in *Kennecott Utah Copper Corp. v. Department of Interior*, 88 F.3d 1191 (D.C. Cir. 1996).

There is a specific statutory provision against double recovery; §112(f) states that if funds have already been paid out for response costs or other authorized costs, then no other claim may be paid out of CERCLA funds for the same costs. Recovery is fully barred if both the release and the damages occurred prior to the effective date of CERCLA. The statute of limitations on pursuing natural resource damage claims against private parties is set, in §113(g)(1), at three years.

Natural resource damages are the only damages allowed under CERCLA. All other claims are equitable and restitutionary. Therefore, lost profits or other "damages" at law are not recoverable under CERCLA. But some *state* hazardous materials statutes include economic loss damages. In practice, counsel should check federal, state, and local provisions.

Some state statutes create a right to damages for private parties, and some of these damages can be so-called "stigma" damages to property value. Although some argue that stigma damages should not be awarded because they are based solely on public perception, the majority of state jurisdictions recognize that stigmatized property suffers from actual diminution of value and thus may be entitled to "stigma" compensation aside from any remediation costs. *Black v. Coastal Oil New England, Inc.*, 45 Mass. App. Ct. 461, 465 (Mass. 1998) (stigma from market fears associated with ongoing contamination); *Santa Fe Partnership v. ARCO Products Co.*, 46 Cal. App. 4th 967, 969 (1996)(recovery of damages for stigma in contamination cases based on the liability theory of continuing or permanent nuisance or trespass); *Walker Drug Co., Inc. v. La Sal Oil Co.*, 972 P.2d 1238, 1246 (Utah 1998) (repair of temporary injury will not return the value of the property to its prior level because of lingering negative public perception); *Adkins v. Thomas Solvent Co.*, 440 Mich. 293 (Mich. 1992) (recovery of stigma damages only for contamination that directly reaches the plaintiff's property). Licensed appraisers are usually retained to conduct market analyses of the property regarding damages associated with the nuisance of stigma.

Liens Against PRP Property

A 1986 SARA addition to CERCLA imposes a lien in favor of the United States on all real property that "belongs to" a §107 "responsible party" and is the subject of, or is "affected by," a removal or remedial action. Thus contaminated property is subject to the lien. The lien arises on the later of (1) the date costs are first incurred (with respect to a response action), or (2) the date on which notice of potential liability is given to the person. The lien takes normal priority. It is important to note that such a lien is narrower than some state "superliens," which spring into superior first position vis-à-vis prior lienholders.

The attachment of a §107 lien clouds title, often prevents sale or transfer of property, and can throw mortgages into default. *Reardon v. United States*, 947 F.2d 1509 (1st Cir. 1991), was the first successful constitutional challenge to any provision of CERCLA. In *Reardon*, the court struck down the attachment of a §107 lien on due process grounds. The court held that the CERCLA lien improperly deprived the Reardons of a substantial property interest without sufficient procedural safeguards. The court concluded that requiring the EPA to serve a notice of lien and allowing the property owner an opportunity for a hearing would not be unduly burdensome. As a result of the *Reardon* decision, parties claiming innocent landowner status, challenging a lien as overbroad, or otherwise asserting substantive challenges to the application of the lien, may be entitled to a hearing on the matters at an early stage of the enforcement proceedings.

In 1993 the EPA issued supplemental guidance on imposing federal Superfund liens. This guidance document requires the EPA to provide prior notice to property owners who are PRPs against whom the agency intends to perfect a lien. This notice must be given prior to filing the necessary papers to perfect the lien. Also, the agency must give the property owners the opportunity to be heard, either by submitting documents or by appearing before a neutral EPA official, or both. The guidance allows the EPA to perfect a lien prior to giving notice to the property owner only in exceptional circumstances.

Interlocutory Challenge: The "Take It or Leave It" Proposition

An important issue for PRPs is *when* and if to dispute liability for site clean-up expenditures and when to seek declaratory relief. The EPA's first step ordinarily is to send notification letters to the site owner or operator and other potentially responsible parties, informing them of the EPA's intention to recover any necessary expenditures under §107 and inviting them to confer with each other and the EPA regarding voluntary measures. At this point, the site owner and other PRPs may wish to assert defenses to liability before the EPA has expended significant monies on the cleanup effort.

When Congress added §113(h)-(j) to CERCLA in 1986, it essentially laid to rest the dispute over preenforcement review. Section 113(h) deprives the federal courts of jurisdiction over any action seeking to challenge a removal or remedial action decision made under §104 (response authorities), or embodied in a §106(a) order (abatement actions). Exceptions to this rule include (1) in the context of a cost recovery, natural resource damages, or contribution actions that have been instituted pursuant to §107(a) (liability provisions), (2) a §106-based action to enforce an order or collect a penalty for violation of an order, (3) a §106(b)(2) action against the government for reimbursement of voluntary cleanup expenditures, or (4) a citizen suit brought under §310 of CERCLA, or a §106 citizen action to compel remedial action. See *United States v. Princeton Gamma-Tech, Inc.*, 31 F.3d 138 (3d Cir. 1994).

CERCLA §106 provides authority for the EPA to act by administrative order instead of seeking judicial relief. Such orders appear to be sufficiently "final" actions to support an action brought by the recipient seeking judicial review. However, courts such as the one in *Wagner Seed Co. v. Daggett*, 800 F.2d 310 (2d Cir. 1986), have ruled that such orders are not reviewable except in defense of EPA enforcement suits. In contrast, in a wetlands permitting issue, a couple facing EPA sanctions for filling wetlands to build a home near a lake have the right to "immediately litigate their jurisdictional challenge in federal court. . . . The reach of the Clean Water Act is notoriously unclear." *Sackett v. EPA*, 132 S. Ct. 1367 (2012). While limited to wetlands statutes, this decision could foreshadow interpretation of a broader range of EPA statutes.

Whether the EPA must provide opportunity for a hearing prior to issuance of a §106 order is another significant, litigated issue. The argument for a prior hearing is bolstered by the fact that CERCLA imposes potentially enormous penalties (§106(b) calls for a $37,500 per day penalty for willful violation of an order) on PRPs who fail or refuse to comply with a §106 order. The current majority rule is that although a hearing is not required for due process to be satisfied, a defendant may assert a good faith defense and challenge any such order in a subsequent judicial enforcement action. The court in *United States v. Union Electric Co.*, 64 F.3d 1152 (8th Cir. 1995), held that nonsettling PRPs have the right to intervene, when the EPA settled with other PRPs, so as to protect their rights under the scope of such settlement and the contribution protection it automatically affords to the settlors, pursuant to §113(i) of CERCLA.

In 1995, the EPA established a National Remedy Review Board that functions as an appeal board for PRPs who are not satisfied that the appropriate remedy has been selected by an EPA region in the ROD process. This 20-member board of senior EPA officials can consider an appeal where the ROD is expected to cost (1) more than $30 million or (2) more than $10 million and cost at least 50 percent more than the least costly remedial action alternative scoped in the ROD that complies with ARARs. While remedies have seldom been overturned, there has been occasion where the National Remedy Review Board overturned a selected remedy. In at least one of these instances, PRPs complained that this reversal so embarrassed the overturned local regional EPA administrators, that they became vindictive in enforcing other elements of the settlement with the PRPs.

Criminal and Civil Penalties

CERCLA §109 was amended in 1986 to add criminal sanctions and a rather elaborate set of civil penalties. Civil penalties may be levied administratively, or by a federal judge, and are applicable to the situations in Exhibit 9.16.

9.16   Civil Violations Under CERCLA

CERCLA Section	Civil Violation
1. 103(a) & (b)	Violations of notification requirements
2. 103(d)(2)	Violation or destruction of records
3. 108	Violation of financial responsibility requirements
4. 122(d)(3) (enforcement of settlement agreements)	Violation of an order issued
5. 122 or 120	Failure or refusal to carry out the terms of a settlement agreement or interagency agreement

Two tiers of civil penalties, Class I and Class II, may be levied administratively in amounts up to $37,500. Substantively, Class I penalties apply to "per *violation*" offenses, while Class II penalties apply to "per *day*" violations. Procedurally, the two classes are quite different. Class I penalties are subject to a requirement of "notice and opportunity for a hearing." However, Class II penalties are subject to adjudicatory hearings under the APA, 5 U.S.C. §554 (see Chapter 2). Second and subsequent offenders subject to a Class II penalty are liable for up to three times the statutory amount, but no such multiplier is applicable to repeat offenders of a Class I penalty. The amended §109 also contains a bounty provision: §109(d) allows the government to pay out of the Superfund an award of up to $10,000 for information leading to the arrest and conviction of any person for a criminal CERCLA offense.

A short mention of corporate liability and its effect on the personal liability of individuals involved in corporations is in order. As we know, liability follows the status of an entity — as an owner, operator, transporter, or arranger for disposal.

Even if exact proof of chief executive or supervisory personnel involvement in arranging for disposal of hazardous substances is absent, it may be implied. The inherent authority and responsibility of corporate officials, as a class of individuals, can impose individual liability under §107(a) of CERCLA. *Control* is the critical variable in determining personal liability. But it is not necessary to have control over the polluting to be rendered liable; control over the corporation may be sufficient to render an individual personally liable. Under CERCLA, strict civil liability is imposed jointly, severally, and without the usual requirements of proximate cause.

Criminal corporate or individual liability requires a *mens rea* — knowledge and intent. The knowledge need only be that a particular released substance is hazardous. The intent can be implied from the circumstances.

CERCLA case law is moving beyond *actual* knowledge where a "knowing" violation is required. If a corporate officer "should have known" about a polluting activity, the officer can be found personally liable despite a lack of *actual* knowledge. Corporate officers can no longer avoid personal criminal or civil liability merely by closing their eyes and ears to corporate conduct. Criminal liability for hazardous waste is covered in more detail in Chapter 8.

Examples

1. Recall the situation from the most recent prior Examples and Explanations involving the Stooge Pie factory, and assume those facts here again. In that context, answer each of the following questions.

   a. If the Stooges received the following written warranty at sale from Pies-R-Us, how does it change their liability? "Pies-R-Us will assume and pay for any and all environmental liability associated with this property and its operations, from the beginning of time, and shall reimburse Stooge Pies for any such third-party liability."

   b. If it were revealed that the only ingredients of CRM were gasoline, water, sugar, egg whites, and air, would these facts change the liability of Stooge Pies?

   c. Soupy Sales, who owns property next door to Stooge Pies, and onto whose property CRM has migrated from Stooge Pies, sues Stooge Pies under CERCLA for damages representing the lost sale value of his property. Does he prevail? Why?

   d. Five years after the property is sold to Pies-R-Us, Soupy Sales sues Stooge Pies for damage to his plants caused by CRM. Does he have a claim?

   e. The EPA sues Stooge Pies for natural resource damages to Soupy Sales' property. Does the government have a claim? Why?

   f. The EPA sues Stooge Pies for CRM damage to the state forest adjacent to the pie factory. Does the government have a claim? Why?

   g. If the damage to the state forest from CRM occurred during the 1960s and 1970s, according to unrefuted scientific evidence, does this affect your answers to any of the four questions immediately above? Why?

   h. Should a bank with a first mortgage on the Pies-R-Us property be worried about a Superfund lien displacing its security? Why?

   i. If Pies-R-Us is the object of any of the following actions, can it immediately challenge the reasonableness of the action, prior to deciding whether or not to honor the EPA demand?

      (1) An EPA record of decision (ROD) under §104 choosing the most expensive and extreme cleanup measure

      (2) An EPA §106 cleanup order to Pies-R-Us specifying expensive remediation

(3) A §107 cost recovery action by the EPA against Pies-R-Us
(4) A natural resource damages action by the EPA against Pies-R-Us
(5) An EPA action against Pies-R-Us for failure to obey a §106 order and therefore seeking to collect penalties
(6) A citizen suit to compel the EPA to pursue Pies-R-Us

Explanations

1a. This is an indemnification clause. It is valid as a matter of contract law, but it has no effect as a matter of EPA CERCLA enforcement. Therefore, it is not a defense to a CERCLA §106 or §107 action by the government. It may be effective equitably in a private PRP action. It will be effective as a Stooge claim against Pies-R-Us, or to interplead Pies-R-Us in an action where there is a claim against Stooge Pies.

1b. Previously, we indicated that CRM was a listed hazardous substance. In fact, if the only hazardous substance it contains is motor gasoline, unadulterated by any other hazardous substances or compounds, then it should be delisted (see Chapter 8). Petroleum products, although actually hazardous, *legally* are excluded from CERCLA. This is true even if a refined petroleum product, such as gasoline, contains more hazardous substances than petroleum in its virgin state. See *Mid Valley Bank; Wilshire Westwood*.

1c. Sorry, Soupy! There is no private cause of action in CERCLA for *economic* loss or damages. This claim — diminution of value — is a claim for economic loss, not restitution, and so it fails at the summary judgment stage.

1d. Sorry again, Soupy! This is a claim for natural resource damages. There is no private right of action for any damages under CERCLA.

1e. Better, but sorry again, Soupy! Here, finally, a party — the government — has standing to bring a natural resource damages claim. However, it only has standing with respect to government damages regarding property over which it is trustee. Purely private property does not qualify. See *Ohio v. U.S. Department of the Interior*.

1f. Bingo! Standing: trustee responsibility over the land. Result: valid claim, Stooge Pies liability.

1g. Yes, natural resource damage claims must postdate CERCLA's 1980 enactment. On these facts, no such claims are valid. But the EPA could construe the damages as *ongoing* in an attempt to circumvent these limitations.

1h. No. A Superfund lien attaches in normal course of priority, unlike some springing state environmental liens. As long as the bank is properly secured, it retains priority of security. But the value of the property as security may decline if it is contaminated.

1i. Interlocutory challenges are difficult under §113(h)-(j), but not impossible. Here, in brief, are the answers:
  (1) No interlocutory challenge to §104 decisions.
  (2) Interlocutory challenge to §106 orders: unlikely but split authority.
  (3) Can challenge this §107 action.
  (4) Can challenge this §107 action.
  (5) Can challenge a §106 enforcement action.
  (6) Can challenge a §310 citizen suit.

Insurance Compensation for Contamination: Who Ultimately Pays?

Insurance coverage is a major asset of most corporations. For relatively modest premium payments, many corporations retain millions of dollars of untapped insurance coverage for accidents and damages. PRPs naturally seek to pass their environmental losses on to insurance carriers under one or more policies. If a PRP has few assets left, other PRPs may seek to get at the former's insurance assets, or at least to seek contribution from the insurance carrier.

Insurance litigation is a matter of state contract law. Unlike direct CERCLA litigation, which occurs in federal court, insurance litigation proceeds in a state forum unless there is diversity jurisdiction. Consequently, there is a checkerboard of case law and precedent from fifty states. The issues below are paramount.

The Duty to Defend

Ordinarily, one of the first determinations an insurer must make when notified of an insured party's involvement in an environmental dispute is whether or not the duty to defend the insured party has been triggered. This question of initial duty of the liability insurer to defend actions against the insured party is usually decided by matching the litigation complaint with the policy provisions. Moreover, in most jurisdictions, the "objectively reasonable expectation of the typical policy holder" will be considered by the court in construing the policy.

A comprehensive general liability policy (CGL) usually obligates the insurer to defend any "suit" against the insured that seeks damages. Since the term "suit" is generally not defined in the policy, the issue becomes at what point the insurer's "duty to defend" begins. Insurance companies typically argue that no duty arises until an actual lawsuit seeking damages is filed in a court. Conversely, insureds argue that the "duty to defend" is triggered by receipt of an EPA administrative notice that designates the insured as a PRP.

A majority of courts hold that an insurer's duty to defend is triggered by receipt of a PRP letter from the EPA or equivalent state agency. One reason for this position may be that these courts have concluded that if insurers were only obligated to defend insureds that were named in formal lawsuits, insureds might suffer unexpected hardship in light of governmental policy that favors nonjudicial remedies and quick cleanup of sites.

An insurer's duty to defend is analyzed separately from its duty to indemnify for losses. The duty to defend is distinct from, and broader in scope than, the duty to indemnify an insured party for damages that fall within the policy coverage. An insurer faced with an environmental coverage claim must examine the "complaint" (usually a PRP letter) and decide whether or not the allegations made are "reasonably susceptible to coverage" under the policy terms.

The insurer's initial duty to defend third-party actions against the insured is decided "if the allegations of the complaint are 'reasonably susceptible' of an interpretation that they state or adumbrate a claim covered by the policy terms." *Sterilite Corp. v. Continental Casualty Co.*, 17 Mass. App. Ct. 316, 318 (Ma. 1983). Whether a release occurred during the policy period is a material question of fact not appropriate for summary judgment. The duty to defend is triggered by the possibility that the property damage claim falls within the policy's coverage. *Id.*, at 319. An insurer's duty to defend or indemnify is not triggered by allegations of damages flowing from intentional actions that the plaintiffs claim resulted in climate change. *AES Corp. v. Steadfast Ins. Co.*, 283 Va. 609, 725 S.E.2d 532 (Va. 2012) (involving one of the defendants in the *Kivalina, supra.*, action seeking insurance coverage for third-party suit, which was deemed not an "occurrence" within the meaning of the general liability policies).

In the early stages of a CERCLA action, it is unlikely that the insurer will be able to make a definitive determination that no allegations are made in the complaint that may fall within the policy coverage. The purpose of the PRP letter is to notify a party of its potential liability for costs incurred by the government in responding to a release or threatened release of hazardous substances at a pollution site. Therefore, the PRP letter is rarely going to set out such specific allegations and descriptions of the way in which pollutants were released as to bar the contamination from being considered "reasonably susceptible to coverage" under a CGL policy.

An important trigger distinction was made in *Hazen Paper Co. v. United States Fidelity & Guaranty Co.*, 555 N.E.2d 576 (Mass. 1990). *Hazen* demonstrated that not all PRP letters will trigger the insurer's duty to defend the insured. The duty will arise only if the contents of the PRP letter assert a claim for damages resulting from covered property damage — i.e., an *actual* release of hazardous substances. Preventive measures taken as a result of a *threatened* release are not costs that would trigger the insurer's duty to defend, and they would not fall within the policy coverage.

The Requirement of an "Occurrence" Within the Policy Period

To be covered under the CGL policy, property damage or bodily injury must be caused by an "occurrence." CGL policies normally define occurrence as "an accident, including continuous or repeated exposure to conditions, which results in bodily injury or property damage neither expected nor intended from the standpoint of the insured." This definition has given rise to two major issues: (i) was the property damage "expected or intended" from the standpoint of the insured, and (ii) did the occurrence happen during the policy period (a trigger of coverage)? When analyzing an "occurrence," the inquiry focuses on the foreseeability of the damage caused by the discharge, not on the foreseeability of the discharge itself. *State Mut. Life Assurance Co. v. Lumbermens Mut. Casualty Co.*, 874 F. Supp. 451 (Ma. 1995).

To disclaim coverage on the basis that bodily injury or property damage was "expected or intended" from the standpoint of the insured, an insurer must ordinarily show that the insured either subjectively intended to cause injury or that the insured knew to a substantial certainty that such injuries would inevitably result. For an insurer to prevail in an environmental coverage dispute, it would have to convince the court that certain activities resulting in environmental harm impute to the insured's intent or expectation of such harm. A court ruling on this issue would need to move away from the traditional analysis of intent toward a more objective approach. In many jurisdictions that have employed such a standard, courts have found no occurrence in the following situations: where pollution occurred over a period of decades and the damage was predictable, or where an insured released hazardous substances into the environment as part of its regular business operations and damage was reasonably foreseeable. The cases that have been favorable to insurers on this issue have taken a commonsense approach by examining the polluter's pattern of conduct.

The "Trigger" of Coverage

Today, most CGL policies no longer offer coverage for pollution-related injury or damage. Therefore, it is often the older policies that are involved in current litigation. This is logical because of the long latency period for injury or damage caused by hazardous waste. When there is no exclusion in the CGL policy barring coverage for injury or damage caused by pollution, the courts have applied various theories in deciding when CGL liability is triggered.

The concept of "occurrence" ties into the concept of "trigger of coverage." A problem that frequently arises in interpreting the definition of occurrence is whether the alleged damage occurred during the policy period, thereby triggering the coverage. This problem creates not only disputes between insurers and insureds, but also among insurers that have written policies for the same risk in different policy periods. Keeping in mind that many waste sites involve pollution that has taken place over years or decades, and that many insurers may have written coverage for a particular PRP over the years, which policy will be triggered? Should it be the policy in effect when the pollutants arrived at the site, when the pollutants were released into the environment, when the released substances actually damaged the environment, or when damage was discovered?

Practically speaking, all the above points in time could possibly be the trigger because there are various theories for deciding when coverage is triggered, as set out in Exhibit 9.17. The use of one or more of these theories is jurisdiction-specific as well as fact-specific.

The "exposure" theory provides coverage under those policies in force at the time of exposure or introduction of the harmful agent. *Insurance Company of North America v. Forty-Eight Insulations, Inc.,* 633 F.2d 1212 (6th Cir. 1980). The manifestation theory provides coverage by those policies in force at the time the harm first manifests itself or is "reasonably detectable." *United States Fid. & Guar. Co. v. Johnson Shoes, Inc.,* 461 A.2d 85 (N.H. 1983). The continuous trigger theory provides coverage by all policies in force

9.17   Theories for Deciding When Coverage Is Triggered

Theory	Description
1. Wrongful act theory	Damage takes place when the waste is disposed of.
2. Release theory	Damage takes place when the waste leaches or releases into the environment.
3. Injury-in-fact theory	Damage takes place when the waste is released and the environment is actually injured.
4. Manifestation theory	Damage takes place when it is reasonably capable of diagnosis.
5. First-discovery theory	Damage takes place when the agency discovers the pollution.
6. Continuous trigger	Damage occurs at the time of exposure and manifestation.

during the period from the first exposure through the final manifestation. *Armstrong World Industries, Inc. v. Aetna Casualty & Surety Co.*, 45 Cal. App. 4th 1 (1st Dist. 1996). The injury-in-fact trigger theory affords coverage only under the policies in force at the time of the onset of the actual harm. *Northern States Power Co. v. Fidelity & Casualty Co.*, 523 N.W.2d 657 (Minn. 1994). This tends to most severely impact those insurance policies in the later years of a policyholder's history. Some courts have adopted a hybrid approach. *Stonewall Ins. Co. v. Asbestos Claims Management Corp.*, 73 F.3d 1178 (2d Cir. 1995).

The fewer single-year policies that are triggered, the sooner the primary-level insurance policies are exhausted, and thereafter excess layers of coverage for a particular year are invoked for supplemental coverage. Conversely, if a larger number of primary-level policies are triggered, the excess levels of supplemental insurance above them in a given year are less likely to be reached by a claim. The allocation among policies, which is in part a function of the trigger theory applied, determines how many deductibles or self-insurance contributions apply to the insured, and ultimately how much coverage over how many years is available. With multiple policies from multiple years, the courts have to derive decision theories to allocate risk among those policies, such as whether liability for coverage is joint and several, is a function of the proportionate size of the policy, or is a function of the time that each policy is exposed to a risk under the trigger theory of that state. Some courts have considered the aggregate policy limits in a hybrid approach to determine ultimate liability. *Carter-Wallace, Inc. v. Admiral Ins. Co.*, 712 A.2d 1116 (N.J. 1998).

The Pollution Exclusion Clause and Its Interpretation: "Sudden and Accidental" Polluting Events

Most CGL policies issued between 1970 and 1985 contain an exclusion designed to eliminate coverage for incidents involving damage or injury caused by the release of pollutants. The so-called "pollution exclusion" clause excludes coverage for such damage or injury unless the release of pollutants was "sudden and accidental." The analysis of this issue begins with well-settled principles of insurance law: (1) exclusionary language in insurance policies is to be strictly construed, and (2) ambiguities in insurance contracts are to be resolved against the insurer.

Because sudden and accidental occurrences are covered despite the pollution exclusion typical in insurance policies written during the 1970s and 1980s, the interpretation of what is meant by "sudden and accidental" is critical. Some courts have interpreted "sudden" to mean "abrupt." *Iowa Comprehensive Petroleum Underground Storage Tank Fund Board v. Farmland Mutual Insurance Co.*, 568 N.W.2d 815 (Iowa 1997). Other courts have held that the pollution exclusion clause language is ambiguous, and thus construed it against the drafting insurance carriers. *Hecla Mining Co. v. New Hampshire Insurance Co.*, 811

P.2d 1083 (Colo. 1990); *Claussen v. Aetna Casualty & Surety Co.*, 380 S.E.2d 686 (Ga. 1989). Yet other courts apply a regulatory estoppel against the mis-leading nature of the clause, which tends to mislead insureds. *Alabama Plating Co. v. U.S. Fidelity & Guar. Co.*, 690 So. 2d 331 (Ala. 1997); *Morton International, Inc. v. General Accident Insurance Co. of America*, 629 A.2d 831 (N.J. 1993), *cert. denied*, 512 U.S. 1245 (1994).

The difficulty involved in meeting an insurer's burden of proof on the "sudden and accidental" issue was demonstrated in *Goodman v. Aetna Casualty and Surety Co.*, 593 N.E.2d 233 (Mass. 1992). In *Goodman*, the plaintiff owned a gasoline station with leaking underground storage tanks, and it had been sued by an abutting property owner for damage resulting from leaking gasoline. Subsequently, the plaintiff brought an action against its liability insurer for indemnity in the underlying suit, along with a breach of contract claim for failure to defend. The trial judge, on the basis of stipulated facts that the storage tank had been leaking for eighteen months, decided that the release of gasoline had been going on too long to be considered "sudden." The highest state court reversed the trial court decision on the basis of the plaintiff expert's affidavit that the initial contamination was not gradual and had been caused by an abrupt discharge or release of gasoline. The court pointed out that although the discharge of pollutants occurred over a lengthy period of time, this fact alone does not automatically mean that the "suddenness" element has not been met. *Goodman* illustrates that when a case involves disputed facts, an insurer is not likely to get a determination on summary judgment of its obligation prior to trial. In the interim, the insurer is obligated to fund the defense of the underlying case, which could end up being more costly than the actual site cleanup.

The Absolute Pollution Exclusion

Most CGL policies issued after 1985 contain the so-called "absolute pollu-tion exclusion." The absolute pollution exclusion makes no distinction between sudden/accidental and gradual events, and clean-up costs are spe-cifically excluded. The "sudden and accidental" exception (previously dis-cussed) was removed from the exclusion, thereby excluding coverage for all pollution claims. In addition, a provision was added to the exclusion to address "cost or expense . . . arising out of any government direction or request . . . " and "litigation or administrative procedure in which the insured may be involved as a party." In both *Ascon Properties, Inc. v. Illinois Union Ins. Co.*, 908 F.2d 976 (9th Cir. 1990) and *Guilford Indus., Inc. v. Liberty Mutual Ins. Co.*, 688 F. Supp. 792 (D. Maine 1988), this absolute pollution exclusion has been interpreted by the courts to be an unambiguous bar to a PRP claim.

In *Jussim v. Massachusetts Bay Ins. Co.*, 610 N.E.2d 954 (Mass. 1993), the insureds were provided with a potential avenue for avoiding the application of the absolute pollution exclusion. In *Jussim*, a pollution exclusion in a homeowner's liability policy, which incorporated causation language, was found to not exclude coverage for an oil spill caused by the negligence of a third party. The court reasoned that "if the insurer desired to exclude contamination or pollution caused by a fortuitous negligent act, language accomplishing that purpose, and the means to do so are readily available." Although the *Jussim* holding was based on policy language different from the CGL absolute pollution exclusion, the principle of the case was argued by an insured in the case of *United States Liab. Ins. Co. v. Bourbeau*, 49 F.3d 786 (1st Cir. 1995), in which the CGL language was interpreted. In *Bourbeau*, the court interpreted the absolute pollution exclusion as it applied to lead paint contamination, holding that the lead paint contamination was a pollutant for purposes of the absolute pollution exclusion. The most difficult issue in cases involving this exclusion is determining whether a particular hazard can be considered a "pollutant." The validity of the absolute pollution exclusion has been confirmed by most jurisdictions despite numerous attempts by insureds to attack the validity of the exclusion.

Equitable Relief Versus Damages: Are Cleanup Costs Covered Under the CGL Policy?

The typical CGL policy provides, " . . . we will pay on behalf of the insured all sums which the insured shall become legally obligated to pay as damages because of bodily injury or property damage caused by an occurrence to which this insurance applies." Despite the seeming simplicity of this clause, its interpretation in the context of environmental liability has been the subject of extensive litigation. The dispute revolves around the scope of the word "damages" and whether the historical distinction between *legal* and *equitable* actions should be maintained for the purpose of interpreting an insurance policy. Recall that CERCLA redress is principally equitable. In determining whether or not costs properly fall within the coverage of the CGL policy, costs at issue ordinarily include (1) an insured person seeking coverage for cleanup costs sought by a governmental agency, (2) an insured seeking recovery of funds expended itself in the cleanup of a contaminated site at the request of the agency, or (3) costs incurred in complying with an injunctive decree.

A threshold question is whether or not there has been "property *damage*" as defined in the CGL policy. If *actual* harm to the environment has occurred, a majority of jurisdictions hold that the harm constitutes property damage. Insurers argue that remediation costs represent *equitable* relief and do not fall within the CGL coverage of "damages." Insureds argue that such a distinction is overly technical and is not a reasonable interpretation of the policy language by a typical insured party.

Courts are split on determining this issue. The majority of jurisdictions hold that environmental cleanup costs are damages and no distinction should be made between government action seeking equitable relief and that seeking legal damages. A minority of courts, as in *Continental Ins. Cos. v. Northeastern Pharmaceutical & Chem. Co.*, 842 F.2d 977 (8th Cir. 1988), have upheld the wordsmithing distinction, based on a finding that the term "damages" is unambiguous in the insurance context and that it refers only to legal damages, not equitable relief. See also *Maryland Casualty Co. v. Armco, Inc.*, 643 F. Supp. 430, 434 (D. Md. 1986).

Ultimately, the issue comes down to the perspective from which the court interprets the policy language. As easily as some courts have decided that the word "damages" has a particular legal meaning in the insurance context, other courts have held that the word, in its ordinary meaning from a layperson's perspective, encompasses environmental response costs. See *New Castle County v. Hartford Accident & Indem. Co.*, 933 F.2d 1162, 1188 (3d Cir. 1991). If such varying interpretations are possible, then the word is indeed ambiguous and the ambiguity, under rules of contract construction, is resolved against the parties who drafted the contract (the insurer).

Example

1. Reviewing the previous facts in the most recent Examples and Explanations regarding Stooge Pies, list any issues that would be raised should Stooge Pies make an insurance claim for defense and indemnification after the EPA issues a §106 cleanup order to Stooge Pies. Are any of the following issues likely to arise?
   a. Duty to defend
   b. A policy-period occurrence not expected or intended
   c. Trigger of coverage
   d. The pollution exclusion
   e. A claim for damages

Explanation

1a. Yes. The majority of courts require insurers to defend even against a letter claim or order of the EPA, rather than formal litigation. The §106 order is reasonably susceptible to coverage.

1b. Here there is a possible insurer defense. Assume that CRM was routinely discarded by Stooge Pies. When CRM pollution results from routine business practices and operations, the damage may not be considered accidental. No accident, no coverage.

1c. If only one insurer insured during all relevant times, the specific trigger is not an issue. But if there were two or more insurers, a dispute will ensue between Stooge Pies and its insurance carriers as to whose policy was "on the risk" when the damage, if any, occurred. Timing is everything. The answer depends on the "trigger" rule of the state whose law applies.

1d. This will be the most controversial clause. Was the polluting event "sudden and accidental" as required? Even expected pollution from an unknown accidental event can be "sudden and accidental." However, a result of deliberate discharges to the environment in many states is not covered. This issue will turn on how Stooge Pies' CRM handling activities are characterized.

1e. A §106 claim by the EPA is an equitable restitutionary claim or order. Nevertheless, a slight majority of states will recognize the EPA notice or order as a "damages" claim. Other states will not.

Local Environmental Controls

"I think that I shall never see
A billboard lovely as a tree.
Indeed, unless the billboards fall
I'll never see a tree at all."

Ogden Nash, Song of the Open Road, 1933

"Every man holds his property subject to the general right of the community to regulate its use to whatever degree the public welfare may require it."

Theodore Roosevelt, Speech at Osawatomie, August 31, 1910

"(N)othing so generally strikes the imagination and engages the affections of mankind, as the right of property; or that sole and despotic dominion which one man claims and exercises over the external things of the world in total exclusion of the right of any other individual in the universe."

William Blackstone, Commentaries on the Laws of England, 1782

LAND USE, PROPERTY RIGHTS, AND ENVIRONMENTAL LAW

The ability to own, control, and use land continues to hold a special place in our society because it is inextricably tied to the concepts of individual liberty and property rights. Land is the traditional basis of wealth, and it is closely tied to natural resource use. Water and energy from the land are key environmental resources, as well as the land itself. Two hundred years ago

485

Blackstone also articulated what has become the traditional view of the rights of landowners regarding use of their property: "So great is the regard of the law for private property, that it will not authorize the least violation of it; no, not even for the general good of the whole community."

In reality, property rights have never been as unlimited as Blackstone suggests. The public trust doctrine, which has its roots in Roman law, states that all navigable waterways belong to the public at large and cannot be privately owned (see Chapter 6). Activities on private land are also limited by the common law doctrines of waste and nuisance (see later in this chapter). These causes of action permit recovery when activities on private land cause damage to neighboring landowners or the public.

Today, a wide array of statutes regulate land use either directly or indirectly. Direct land use controls are those whose primary focus is the regulation of all activities on specific pieces of land. These controls include zoning laws and laws protecting critical environmental resource areas. Statutes that control land use indirectly include all of the major federal environmental statutes discussed in this book — the Clean Air Act, Clean Water Act, Endangered Species Act, NEPA, CERCLA, RCRA, and so on. These statutes are not generally thought of as "land use" laws because they primarily regulate specific actions wherever they might occur, rather than focusing on certain pieces of land.

This chapter focuses on four areas of environmental law most directly related to land use: (1) regulations targeted directly at land use control, such as zoning statutes and critical habitat regulations, (2) traditional common law land use controls, including the public trust, waste, and nuisance doctrines, (3) municipal environmental licensing powers, and (4) the limitations on land use regulation created by the Fifth Amendment requirement that private property may not be taken for public use without payment of "just compensation." Land use restrictions also differ from the jurisdictional confrontations posed in Chapter 4 of this book in that they are typically the province of state and local governments.

ZONING AND CRITICAL ENVIRONMENTAL HABITATS

Zoning and the Environment

History and Evolution of Zoning Techniques

We begin with a little historical context and a quick review of zoning techniques. The unlimited property rights that Blackstone describes did not exist even in his own time. England actually had a long history of regulating the use of private land in order to promote the public interest. As early as 1285, a law required that landowners keep the sides of highways clear of bushes and trees "whereby a man may lurk to do hurt," and all timber cutting was banned within 22 miles of London in the 1500s.[1] Not a bad idea even today.

Public interest in environmental values found broader expression following the Great Fire in London in the 1600s when that city enacted a building code which included restrictions on building materials, proportions, height, and the location of certain "noisome trades." In some of America's first environmental regulations, Massachusetts by 1692 restricted the placement of slaughterhouses, stills, and gunpowder storehouses. While these examples demonstrate that statutes did restrict private land use for the public good prior to Blackstone, they were limited in scope and targeted only the most dangerous and offensive uses.

These early regulations were based on the government's police power — the power to regulate in order to promote and protect public health, safety, and general welfare. Police power regulations are generally given a wide range of deferential latitude by courts because they have a limited range of options when a police power regulation is challenged. Courts can find that it does not advance a legitimate state interest, in which case it is deemed arbitrary and capricious and overturned. Or they can find that it is a valid exercise of the police power. If the regulation in question eliminates all economically viable use of the land, it amounts to a "taking." In this case, the regulation stands but the owner must be compensated. But, if using the land in the prohibited way creates only a nuisance, then the regulation does not amount to a taking.

As a general rule, courts before the modern era held that if there was no *physical* invasion of land, there was no taking. For example, in *Mugler v. Kansas*, 123 U.S. 623 (1887), a brewery in Kansas was made virtually worthless when the state enacted a prohibition statute. The Supreme Court held that the statute did promote a valid state interest and was therefore a valid exercise of the police power. They also concluded that there was no taking because operation of the brewery would have constituted a nuisance under state law. In addition, regulations aimed at controlling *specific* pieces of land *directly* were rare in nineteenth-century America.

Toward the end of the 1800s, the advent of factories and industrial production had a dramatic effect on land use in Western Europe and the United States. Drawn by the jobs that factories created, a large fraction of the rural population migrated to urban areas in the late nineteenth and early twentieth centuries. The crowded and unsanitary conditions that resulted prompted expanded efforts to control land use in urban areas. New York City created the United States' first comprehensive land use plan in 1916 by dividing the city into zones and restricting industrial, commercial, and residential uses each to specified areas. Other cities followed with similar plans, and the practice of regulating land use by dividing cities into

---

1. The state of Winchester, 13 Edw. 1, Stat. 2 (1285).

residential, commercial, and industrial sectors came to be referred to as zoning. The U.S. Department of Commerce heralded the modern era of land use control when it issued the Standard State Zoning Enabling Act in 1922.

Localities do not have inherent zoning powers; they originate from state police powers to protect the public health and welfare. Legally, the zoning power is legislative: The zoning enabling act passed at the state level spells out what a municipality must do prior to enacting a zoning plan and what the plan may include. The Standard State Zoning Enabling Act is the model by which most states have granted zoning power to their communities. This model, which has been updated several times since its original introduction, restricts the range of permitted zoning schemes in accordance with the limits of the state's police power and other constitutional requirements.

So what is modern zoning? Zoning is a more mature outgrowth of the fire and building codes of earlier times. The overarching goal of zoning is to segregate, as much as possible in an already built environment, residential areas from commercial and industrial uses and to isolate the most noxious industrial uses from other uses. As we have become more aware of the environmental impacts of human land development, planners have begun to push the envelope of the police power beyond direct human health and safety concerns. Zoning and other land use regulations have been used to preserve open space, protect watershed and wetland areas, save areas of aesthetic and historical value, and promote general environmental goals.

Can this be done legally in America? After 70 years of effort and litigation, the answer still is far from resolved. The basic answer is "yes," but with important qualifications. The U.S. Supreme Court approved of zoning as a valid exercise of the police power in 1926 in the case of *Village of Euclid v. Ambler Realty Co.*, 272 U.S. 365 (1926). Euclid had enacted a zoning ordinance creating residence-only zones, commercial zones, and unrestricted zones. The plaintiff owned land zoned for residential use that he believed was suitable for commercial or industrial use. He sued on the theory that the regulation had reduced the value of his land because it was more valuable if used for commercial and industrial purposes.

The *Euclid* court addressed the question of whether the zoning law was a valid exercise of the police power, given the absence of any evidence that the use proposed by the plaintiff would constitute a common law nuisance in a residential area. The court found that the zoning ordinance did promote general public health, safety, and welfare, and it thus refused to strike the ordinance as a whole. The majority indicated, however, that if the plaintiff had a specific use planned for the land and could show that the proposed use would not be detrimental to health and safety, they would be better able to determine that the law was arbitrary and unreasonable as *applied*, and thus unconstitutional. They refused, however, to overturn the law facially on such a broad and unspecific attack.

Challenging a zoning law *as applied* to a specific use can be more successful. Such an attack succeeded in overturning the Baltimore zoning code in 1925. A man named Goldman had a single sewing machine in his basement that he used to mend clothing. Because he took payment for his work and the home was in an area zoned solely for residential use, the city charged him with violation of the zoning law. In *Goldman v. Crowther*, 128 A. 50 (Md. 1925), the Maryland court of appeals found that this particular application of the zoning ordinance was arbitrary and capricious because the prohibited use did not present any threat to public health or safety and therefore was not properly regulated under the police power.

So how do you "bullet-proof" zoning? First, create a "master plan" designed to promote logical planned land uses. Courts have overturned zoning laws when they found that no master plan existed or that the zoning law did not follow the plan. Zoning schemes also have been rejected by the courts when they violate constitutional protections or fail to promote valid public interests. For example, minimum lot and building size requirements have been permitted up to a point to preserve family values, privacy, and peace of mind, but such minimums have been rejected when they are so large that they are perceived to be intended not to promote safety or health but to discriminate against persons of lesser income. Towns have an incentive to exclude all necessary but undesirable uses if they can get their neighbors to accept them. Of particular concern have been zoning law changes affecting small parcels of land to permit a specific "pet" project to proceed. Such "spot" or "contract" zoning occurs frequently to appease local employers or developers.

Since the court's decision in *Euclid*, zoning is now the leading form of direct urban land use regulation. Every major U.S. city has a zoning code with the exception of Houston, although some cities adopted their codes only after they had been ravaged by uncontrolled development. Zoning is almost universally accepted as a valid means of promoting community welfare and has been adopted through much of the country. Nevertheless, its effectiveness is still questioned, and it has caused a wide range of problems in its relatively short life.

Land use control, largely in the form of zoning, was dominated by local governments until the 1970s. As understanding of the environment and the complexity of biological interactions grew, the need to manage land use and development over a broader geographic area was recognized. Aquifers, lakes, rivers, wildlife, and other natural resources frequently cross municipal political boundaries and thus cannot be managed comprehensively at the local level. There is now direct *state* regulation of land use in critical areas.

The principles of the "smart growth" movement, which attempts to limit sprawl and encourage compact development, are:

- Mix land uses
- Employ compact building design
- Create a range of housing opportunities and choices
- Create walkable neighborhoods
- Preserve open space and farmland in critical environmental areas
- Provide a variety of transportation options

Examples

1. Taneyville is a typical American middle-class suburb about 15 miles outside of Kansas City. Taneyville commissioned the drafting of a master plan for the town and established a zoning code in accordance with this plan in 1934. At the time the town was only 50 percent developed and the areas around it were even less densely populated. The zoning ordinance created two types of residential zones, an industrial zone and two commercial zones. In 1962 Taneyville created a new type of zone, C3, which allowed only retail commercial enterprises of less than 800 square feet. The purpose of having this zone was to allow small businesses such as cleaners, small groceries, and purveyors of other common necessities to locate in residential neighborhoods and thus relieve congestion in the downtown business district. In the years between 1934 and 1962, the town and the areas around it had grown, as had the use of automobiles, and Taneyville was now a commercial center for several communities. The bylaw that created the new zone did not attach it to any particular areas in the town.

   Webster is the first citizen to file an application with the zoning commission to have a lot he owns rezoned from residential to C3 for use as a minimart. The commission, wanting to get their decentralization plan under way, granted the desired change despite heated public opposition, and several neighbors sued to overturn the decision. What do you think is the result in their suit?

2. Will the result above be any different if you are told that the lot is on a wide street which is a main thoroughfare through the residential neighborhood and that two gas stations, a drugstore, a coffee shop, and bar already exist on the street as nonconforming uses? A nonconforming use is a land use that predates the zoning restriction and was "grandfathered," or allowed to continue, even though it is not allowed as a new use. What if the zoning commission also undertook a thorough study of the proposed site prior to granting the exception in zoning to ensure that it was well suited to the proposed use and would not cause unreasonable hardship to neighboring landowners?

Explanations

1. The zone is not attached to a specific land area but applies anywhere to any applicant. The change will be overturned as an impermissible attempt at "spot zoning." A crucial element of zoning is that it must be done in accordance with a plan that has been developed to promote the general welfare. Zoning that is arbitrary and capricious or that is not in accordance with a reasonably designed master plan is not a reasonable exercise of the police power. Here, conditions in Taneyville have clearly changed since the master plan was developed and the zoning law enacted. Taneyville has recognized the need for amendments to their old zoning scheme, but they must make those amendments in accordance with a new plan which will ensure that the new zone is not applied in a haphazard and harmful manner.

2. Each of these conditions improves the commission's ability to defend its decision, but it is impossible to say whether they will be enough to prevail. There are no hard-and-fast rules in this area of law, and there are a number of competing considerations to be weighed by the court in deciding whether a zoning law is sufficiently supported to withstand judicial review. A zoning scheme must initially be consistent with the zoning master plan, and the plan must be grounded on a reasonably considered evaluation of the welfare of the community. The zoning board of a town has the power to deviate from the plan, but it must base its decision on a reasonable assessment of community welfare. Among the factors weighed by courts reviewing zoning board decisions are the sufficiency of the underlying master plan, whether there is a valid reason for deviating from the plan, the nature of the proposed change, how the change relates to existing and prospective uses in the area, the level of public protest, and the thoroughness of the administrative procedure followed in reaching the decision.

Legal Problems with Zoning

As noted by the plaintiff in *Euclid*, zoning laws can have a significant effect on property values. Zoning pushes real estate prices down when it forbids valuable uses and drives values up when it prevents noxious uses from being introduced nearby. As demand in an area changes over time, the original zoning scheme may be forced to give way to new realities. This has occurred in many areas of the United States as cities and suburbs have spread and "swallowed" towns that sought to maintain less dense development.

Another problem with zoning is that the traditional goal of segregating uses may have unassessed indirect costs in energy consumption and environmental pollution. The traditional segregated use model forces people into longer, inefficient commutes to get from their residential areas to the limited industrial and commercial areas where they work. Large-lot zoning for single-family houses forces development to spread and consume wilderness, wetlands, and farms rather than in-fill land with denser or multi-family housing. Centralization of commercial areas forces people to travel significant distances for everyday purchases. Zoning tends to create inefficiency and distorts development from the path it would follow if permitted to progress naturally.

The growth in environmental awareness since the 1960s has caused planners to create a number of new zoning techniques intended to promote environmental values and address shortcomings of traditional zoning schemes. State governments are more active in regulating local zoning activity and have even cooperated at a regional level where ecosystems and resources span political boundaries. The federal government has also entered the fray through statutes such as the Coastal Zone Management Act, the Clean Water Act, wetlands and floodplain regulation, and federal restrictions on industrial location via the Clean Air Act (see Chapters 5-7, 11).

Environmental Zoning Techniques

In theory, zoning's roots in the police power should allow it to be used as a tool generally beneficial to human welfare. However, focus on the quality of the *human* environment can promote development in ways harmful to the *natural* environment. Today, zoning is increasingly targeted to promote environmental goals. As more of the problems caused by traditional Euclidean zoning have come to light, new and more flexible techniques have been created that permit communities to control development but with greater flexibility. Primary zoning techniques are set out in Exhibit 10.1.

Each of these zoning concepts is explained below. Or, if you feel comfortable with the zoning concepts in Exhibit 10.1, skip ahead to the Examples and Explanations.

Euclidean Zoning

The zoning plan approved by the Supreme Court in *Euclid* (1926) became the model for the majority of zoning laws enacted for the next several decades. The primary concern of such traditional or "Euclidean" plans is the separation of residential, commercial, and industrial uses into logical zones. This is achieved by creating a master plan for the municipality designating zones for each type of use. Within residential areas of towns, a Euclidean plan attempts to maintain neighborhood character by imposing uniform lot sizes, building footprint maxima, height and setback requirements, and restrictions on multifamily use. Enforcement then focuses on ensuring

10.1 Primary Zoning Techniques

Zoning Techniques	Application
1. Euclidean zoning	Segregates commercial, residential, and industrial uses in distinct zones. Within each zone, focus is on individual lots to enforce setback, lot size, and other standards.
2. Cluster zoning	Concentrates development. Reduces infrastructure requirements, protects open space or critical areas. Runoff and other discharges from a point source are easier to control.
3. Planned unit development	Similar to cluster zoning; permits inclusion of nonresidential uses in regulated area to meet specific development objectives.
4. Transferable development rights	Used to protect critical areas from any development while avoiding takings problem through transference. Requires that community have suitable areas to receive transferred development rights from area to be protected. Complex system to administer.
5. Environmental overlay districts	Identifies critical areas that are then protected by other forms of environmental land use control.
6. Open space zoning	Specifies areas to be maintained as open space; may be classified as a taking.
7. Restrictions on growth	
A. Quotas	Limited number of units may be developed per year; difficult to justify.
B. Utility connection limitations	Effective only where connections are necessary; city must show plan to meet utility needs in the future.
C. Moratoria	Restricts all development, but must be for a limited, reasonable time as needed to study and implement permanent controls.
8. Exactions	Discourages inefficient development by making cost of development more accurately reflect demands placed on infrastructure and community resources.
9. Conservation easements, land acquisition, and taxation	Private groups have begun to play a significant role in conservation by acquiring land and development rights, often supported by tax incentives.
10. Performance standards	Development is allowed so long as it does not violate minimum standards set for critical areas.

that each individual lot within each zone meets the stated requirements. So long as the building plan for a given lot is in keeping with the requirements for that zone, the building must be approved by the city.

A project that is a minor part of the use of a lot may be permitted as an "accessory use." An accessory use is subordinate and customarily incidental to the principal use of the lot. See *Franchi v. Zoning Hearing Board*, 543 A.2d 239 (Pa. Cmwlth. Ct. 1988). The accessory use also must be associated with the main use. For example, a private air strip is not normally deemed an accessory use of a single-family residential lot. See *Town of Harvard v. Maxant*, 275 N.E.2d 347 (Mass. 1971).

Subdivision Control

Subdivision regulations provide the detailed lot-specific requirements of the zoning ordinance. Subdivision regulations apply only to the division of land in a subdivision, unless the state enabling statute adopts a broader purpose, such as in Hawaii. Subdivision control focuses on the division of land into multiple parcels and the provision of utilities and other infrastructure to the divided lots. It is a means to ensure that divided parcels are provided with necessary access and services at the expense of the developer, as a condition of the permit approval. Subdivision controls recently have begun to incorporate items that might be thought of as purely environmental. These include restrictions on septic systems to protect sensitive areas from phosphorus or nitrogen loading. In some cases, subdivision regulations have been used to require developers to dedicate land for public purposes, complete off-site improvements, or pay fees.

Cluster Zoning

In contrast to traditional zoning, which strives to create a uniform neighborhood character through regulation of individual lots, cluster zoning focuses on a larger area developed as a block. Under a cluster plan, the developer is excused from the rigid lot size, setback, and height requirements of the standard zoning plan. Instead, construction is concentrated or clustered on part of the land, and the remainder is devoted to open space or environmental uses. The exact plan is negotiated by the town and developer, permitting greater flexibility to locate construction in the most appropriate areas while leaving environmentally sensitive areas undisturbed. Clustering also has the advantage of reducing the length of roads and utility connections required and can lead to a more interesting and varied development pattern. Cluster zoning has been upheld by the courts. *Orinda Homeowners Committee v. Board of Supervisors, County of Contracosta*, 90 Cal. Rptr. 88 (Cal. App. 1970); *Cheney v. Village II at New Hope, Inc.*, 241 A.2d 81 (Pa. 1968).

Planned Unit Development (PUD)

A planned unit development is a single project planned as an entity based on a comprehensive plan. It is similar to cluster zoning in that it regulates not individually owned parcels, but a larger area where development is proposed. PUDs go beyond cluster development by regulating commercial use as well as residential. Permits are not granted on a lot-by-lot basis but via review and approval of a complete, integrated plan. The plan for a PUD will address a wide range of environmental issues including transportation, residential density, open space, utilities, and site design. Rather than apply traditional zoning requirements (lot size, footprint, setback, nature of use) to each lot in the area, PUD zoning allows flexibility so that development can be clustered in some areas and environmentally sensitive areas can be preserved. In addition the PUD can aggregate several small parcels into one large zoned parcel.

Doing this allows routine requirements such as setbacks and open space percentages to be assessed against the *whole* parcel, and not against each smaller parcel individually. When employed, local ordinances must specifically allow PUD zoning uses and limit the discretion of local authorities, or the plan may be susceptible to challenge as illegal "contract" or "spot" zoning.

Transferable Development Rights (TDR)

Transferable development rights are another tool similar to cluster zoning. To implement a TDR plan, a town must first designate one area as a preservation district and another as a development district. Landowners in the preservation district lose some rights to develop their land, but they are given development rights that they can sell to landowners in the development area. These latter owners are then able to develop their land more densely than they would have been able to without the new rights. Transferable development rights are particularly useful because they can allow cities to create restrictions in the preservation district that would otherwise constitute a "taking," without having to pay direct compensation to the affected landowner. In effect, the city pays the landowner indirectly by allowing him or her to sell the right of development which he or she can no longer exercise. Transferable development rights have been upheld against challenge. *Barancik v. County of Marin*, 872 F.2d 834 (9th Cir. 1989); cf. *West Montgomery County Citizens Ass'n v. Maryland-National Capital Park and Planning Commission*, 522 A.2d 1328 (Md. 1987).

In *Suitum v. Tahoe Regional Planning Agency*, 520 U.S. 725 (1997), the Court held that a landowner had a ripe challenge to regional environmental overlay restrictions even when TDRs were afforded the landowner as compensation. (These TDRs could be sold in the market or they could be used for the landowner to build elsewhere.) To be ripe, a person must obtain a "final decision" from the appropriate land use agency before bringing a takings claim. See *MacDonald, Sommer & Frates v. Yolo County*, 477 U.S. 340 (1986); *Williamson County Regional Planning Commission v. Hamilton Bank*, 473 U.S. 172 (1985). Therefore, whether some use of the parcel is still possible must be determined by the agency before judicial appeal on a takings claim. Where the local or state agency denies a permit to construct a particular usage, but leaves ambiguous whether some other usage is still possible, it frustrates the ripeness of the takings claim.

A related issue is whether the TDRs granted pursuant to a land use regulatory system are considered part of the property that generates them. The Tahoe Regional Planning Agency granted *Suitum* TDRs as an offset to the deprivation of a building permit. If these TDRs are considered part of the property that generated them, then there is not total deprivation of all property rights, since these TDRs allow construction at an alternative site in the same region. However, if TDRs are viewed as monetary compensation paid to the landowner for the restrictions on the use of the property, then the property itself has no further legitimate use and there is a total deprivation of all property rights, and a *per se* takings claim is ripe on the issue of whether there should be full, rather than partial (TDR), compensation. The court in *Suitum* did not reach this substantive decision, although three of the Justices in the majority clearly believed that TDRs are not part of the property, but merely detached compensation, making ripe a takings challenge.

As part of a cluster, PUD, or TDR zoning plan, a community must identify the environmentally critical areas to be earmarked for protection. Such areas may be designated by adding an overlay district to the standard zoning map. The standard zoning map includes designation of areas as residential, commercial, or industrial. The environmental overlay designates areas that are particularly environmentally sensitive (wetlands, wildlife habitat, water supply, flood zones, watershed drainage areas, and so on). These areas can then be subjected to additional controls beyond the residential/commercial designation. This technique is well accepted so long as the environmental areas are not created arbitrarily or managed retroactively. Courts have upheld the use of overlay zoning districts to protect wetlands and salt marshes (Maine), to protect flood plains (Massachusetts), to protect lake shore land (Wisconsin), and to protect scenic vistas (California).

Open Space Zoning

A government may take land via eminent domain and pay appropriate compensation to the owners. A number of cities have tried to avoid this cost by including open space requirements in their zoning regulations. In 1984 the city of Seattle enacted a Greenbelt Ordinance which required that landowners in the designated greenbelt area maintain as much as 70 percent of their land in an "undisturbed" state. The state supreme court held that while the law advanced many legitimate state interests, it forbade virtually all use of the affected land and thus constituted a taking: "Although [the landowner] still holds title to the property reserved as greenbelt land, he is denied the control over his property typically accorded landowners. We deem this to be a taking." *Allingham v. City of Seattle*, 749 P.2d 160 (Wash. 1988). Only when the requirements are less stringent and permit some reasonable use of the land are courts inclined to uphold such regulations.

Restrictions on Growth

In addition to restrictions placed on particular areas within a town via zoning, some communities facing high pressure from development have sought to restrict construction in general. Such restrictions are generally not specifically permitted by state zoning enabling acts and thus must be justified on other bases. Among the methods employed have been limitations on access to public services, quotas, and moratoria.

Where unlimited growth causes local environmental problems, restricted growth plans or moratoria have been upheld. See *Sturges v. Town of Chilmark*, 380 Mass. 246 (Mass. 1980); cf. *Building Industry Ass'n v. City of Oceanside*, 33 Cal. Rptr. 2d 137 (Cal. App. 1994); *Steel Hill Development, Inc. v. Town of Sanbornton*, 469 F.2d 956 (1st Cir. 1972). Limiting access to public services is the most accepted form of growth limitation because it most clearly derives from the application of the police power. Rapid development requires the city to provide roads, road maintenance, police and fire protection, schools, utilities (especially water and sewers), parks and recreational facilities, and environmental amenities. Thus a restriction on growth that is tied to the town's ability to provide these services is well supported by the police power.

In *Golden v. Planning Board of Ramapo*, 285 N.E.2d 291 (N.Y. 1972), the town adopted a plan that significantly restricted development for a period of 18 years. The plan called for the city to build the infrastructure needed to support planned development in an orderly fashion during this period. Only as services became available would building permits be issued. Builders could hasten the process themselves by building needed infrastructure facilities such as sewers and roads. In *Golden*, five essential facilities or services needed to be available before a special permit could be issued. The court noted that the plan would impose a severe restriction on landowners for a significant time, but it determined that the overall public purpose of the statute fell within the general planning powers envisioned by the zoning enabling statute.

At least one court has also permitted a city to restrict growth to a set number of new units per year. The city of Petaluma, California, was hit by a wave of development in the early 1970s that threatened to destroy its rural, small-town character. In response, the city adopted a complex plan intended to spread growth more evenly throughout the city and to promote more diverse housing options, while limiting the total units that could be built to 500 per year. The plan was challenged for being arbitrary and capricious as well as exclusionary. Following other zoning decisions that had adopted a broad definition of what "public welfare" could be promoted through zoning and land use regulation, the court upheld the Petaluma plan as a valid exercise of the police power. *Construction Ind. Ass'n v. Petaluma*, 522 F.2d 897 (9th Cir. 1975).

In certain circumstances, communities have been permitted to ban all new construction by imposing a moratorium. The most common use of this method is a moratorium on sewer or other utility connections, as in cases where treatment facilities are inadequate to handle added waste. Cities also have been allowed to not extend municipal water services, as long as the denial is rational and is not applied selectively or discriminatorily. *Moore v. City Council*, 105 S.W. 926 (Ky. Ct. App. 1907); *Dateline Builders, Inc. v. City of Santa Rosa*, 194 Cal. Rptr. 258 (Cal. Ct. App. 1983); *Swanson v. Marin*, 128 Cal. Rptr. 485 (Cal. Ct. App. 1976); *Wilson v. Hidden Valley Municipal Water Dist.*, 63 Cal. Rptr. 889 (Cal. Ct. App. 1968); *Mayor of Rockville v. Goldberg*, 264 A.2d 113 (Md. 1970). In *Dateline*, a developer tried to force the city to connect its existing sewer lines with the proposed "leap frog" development beyond the city's boundaries; the appeals court held that the city reasonably exercised its police power consistent with the city's land use and development policy, which ". . . envisioned that utilities will be extended when it is economically feasible. . . ." There was no taking, even if the water district does not seek to develop additional water sources, unless it prevents all practical use of property. *Lockary v. Kayfetz*, 917 F.2d 1150 (9th Cir. 1990). Municipalities have been permitted to enforce moratoria for a limited time when they can prove that construction poses a threat to public health or safety, or when they are required to prepare a new master plan or zoning law. These instances receive close scrutiny from courts because moratoria are viewed as extreme actions.

Exactions

Another solution to easing the cost to the community of new development is to exact more of the "public" infrastructure cost from the developer. This tends economically to slow growth and may provide environmental protection against urban sprawl. By the 1950s it had become "traditional" to ask developers to pay for roads, curbs, sidewalks, and water and sewer connections. Cities have begun to ask that developers pay for a variety of off-site infrastructure and environmental costs. Courts have been mixed in their response to such demands. In *Jordan v. Village of Menomonee Falls*, 137 N.W.2d 442 (Wis. 1965), the court upheld a town ordinance requiring developers to either dedicate land for schools and parks or pay a fee in lieu of dedication, assuming the fee is reasonably related and dedicated to the service provided. In contrast, other courts have rejected mandatory dedications and *particularly* fees in lieu of dedications.

Fees, or exactions, are distinctive from taxes because fees are in exchange for a governmental service that benefits the paying party in a way that others do not share. Fees are voluntary in that the paying party can choose not to use the governmental service and thereby skip the charge, and the charges are not collected to raise money, but rather to reimburse the governmental agency providing the services. *National Cable Television Assn. v. United States*, 415 U.S. 336, 341 (1974). A required payment is a tax, not a fee, where the user was not going to receive a special benefit or where the contribution did not compensate the town for services connected to expenses it had. *Id.*

The 1987 decision in *Nollan v. California Coastal Commission*, 483 U.S. 825 (1987), places some limits on the ability to demand exactions in return for a building permit. In this case, the state of California required that Nollan grant an easement across his property in return for a permit to expand his ocean-front home. The state had banned all new building in the area to prevent closely spaced houses from creating a visual and psychological (that is, environmental) barrier between the public and the beach. The court assumed that the state could ban construction under the police power in order to promote public welfare. But they noted that the easement required in return for the building permit gave the public *physical* access across Nollan's land and was thus clearly a taking, unless it was sufficiently related to the construction ban. The court ruled that the easement went too far. The ban on construction was meant to prevent visual and psychological barriers, but the easement granted *physical* access as well. Justice Scalia held that it lacked a sufficient nexus to the purpose of the construction ban and was unconstitutional.

Conservation Easements, Land Acquisition, and Taxation

A number of private organizations actively seek to preserve open space by acquiring land outright or by obtaining easements that limit development. Donation of a conservation easement also acts to separate development rights from land. The Internal Revenue Code promotes this technique by allowing a tax deduction for landowners who make a qualifying donation to a qualifying organization.

A number of states have moved to encourage the designation of land as open space or to preserve low-density uses, such as agriculture, through the property tax. The most common tax tool is the granting of a special reduced tax rate to property owners who agree, via contract, to maintain their land as farm or open space for a certain number of years. Vermont and Hawaii have gone even further. Vermont taxes gains on real estate transactions so that land held for a short period of time (less than six years) is taxed more highly, thus discouraging speculation and subdivision and encouraging agricultural use. Hawaii breaks down land use into a number of categories and grants preferential treatment to certain uses.

Performance Standards

Development can also be controlled indirectly by establishing standards for local resources that new development is forbidden to impair. The Clean Air and Clean Water Acts effectively do this at the federal level; states and localities also can establish similar performance standards for local resources.

The National Historic Preservation Act requires federal agencies licensing undertakings to "take into account the effect of the undertaking on any district, site, building, structure, or object" that is or may be eligible for inclusion in the National Register of Historic Places. 16 U.S.C. §470 *et seq.* If a project is located in an area of historic or archaeological importance, comments are taken regarding the project before licensing. This is primarily a consultation process to attempt to preserve historically significant places. Typically, state historic commissions provide a parallel function.

Examples

1. Trump owns a rare commodity — an empty, undeveloped piece of land in Manhattan. The parcel is the eastern half of a lot on which another developer built a large apartment complex several years ago. The empty portion was landscaped as an open park used primarily by the tenants of the adjoining building. Trump's lot is zoned to allow high-rise residential use. Trump proposes to build a conforming structure on the land for mixed commercial and residential use, and he seeks a building permit.

   Tenants of the building and other neighbors protest the plans and get the city to rezone the land. The city creates a new type of zone — Zone P — and applies it initially solely to the lot owned by Trump. Land in a P zone can be used only as park land open to the public. What is your legal advice to Trump as to this local action?

2. On the above facts, can you suggest any other zoning techniques the city could use to accomplish its objective of keeping the park open to the public, assuming it does so *before* Trump possibly vests his rights by applying for a building permit?

3. What if Trump's land comprises several small parcels that he has acquired "blindly" from various owners? How does he deal with the individual zoning setback and height restrictions that the New York zoning code imposes on *every* parcel?

4. On the above facts, the City of New York decides to prevent Trump's development by creating a watershed protection district that overlays his and other parcels. It manages to create this district *before* Trump applies for a building permit. The land covered is not allowed to be the place of any activities that

could cause any pollution, fouling, or turbidity of New York's potential drinking water supplies, because they are among the world's finest. What are your thoughts as to whether this impediment is legally permissible?

Explanations

1. This is not a legal rezoning for several reasons. By mandating that the land be made open to the public, the city stepped over the line from a regulation to a taking. The ability to exclude the public is one of the crucial rights of private land ownership. Permitting public access is, in essence, a *physical* invasion that must be compensated. This rezoning also smacks of "spot" zoning, which is highly suspect. Finally, it is *retroactive* zoning. Depending on local law, Trump's interests may vest as to the existing zoning as soon as he applies for a building permit to which he is otherwise entitled as of right. His rights vest prior to enactment of the zoning change. A city cannot legally entertain a permit application and thereafter change the zoning rules to defeat the application.

2. It is possible that a Transferable Development Rights (TDR) plan would work here. The city would name Trump's land as the transferor site and permit him to transfer his development rights for value to another site in the city, or to sell the TDRs to another developer. The transferee site/person would then be able to develop more densely than originally permitted. However, there are limitations to the availability of TDR as an option. If Trump can show that there is no market in the target area where he is permitted to use his development rights, then the city has not really given anything of value in return for the effective taking of his land. Without a viable market for the TDRs, Trump is likely to prevail. Exactions can extract a quid pro quo, but they cannot limit development. Restrictions on critical waste, sewage, or utility services — all of which are necessary for an occupancy permit — can frustrate development. However, they are only justified by technical requirements and must be applied evenhandedly to all similar parcels. New York City is not Petaluma. It would be harder to justify such limits in the Big Apple.

3. Satisfying individual restrictions on each parcel will prohibit any coherent development plan for the entire parcel, especially in a region such as Manhattan. Trump needs the city to deal with his parcel as a whole. Trump may need a PUD permit to site a mixed-use development that includes mixed residential and commercial use, or that combines several discrete parcels into one effective plot. In a PUD, zoning requirements as to setback, height, density, and so on are applied to the whole and not to each subparcel.

4. Environmental overlay districts are among the most direct zoning controls for environmental objectives. Watershed protection is very common, and

it is legal if based on objective criteria. Once enacted, an overlay district governs all uses not vested or "grandfathered" at that time. Even if the district is legal, it does not mean it would restrict Trump. If Trump handles no hazardous substances and does not engage in construction that threatens groundwater, the regulation may have no practical impact. New York, like almost all developed urban areas, does not rely on its own groundwater for drinking. It imports. Therefore, the connection between groundwater at the Trump parcel and public health may be quite attenuated. Trump probably can live with this overlay zone.

REGULATION OF CRITICAL ENVIRONMENTAL RESOURCES

During the late 1960s and early 1970s, a number of events led to a new focus on protection of particular types of land that are environmentally critical and especially threatened by human development. Among the resources that have been regulated as critical resources are the ocean coasts, wetlands, floodplains, and farmland.

The Coastal Zone

The coastal ecosystem is particularly fragile, while its proximity to the bulk of the U.S. population puts it under intense development pressure and exposes it to all kinds of pollutants. At the same time, it is a critical link in our natural environment, providing an important breeding and feeding ground for a wide variety of wildlife including some 70 percent of the nation's commercial fisheries catch (see Chapter 11). In 1972 when the combination of rapid coastal development and growing environmental awareness highlighted the need to protect the coastal zone as a unique national resource, Congress passed the Coastal Zone Management Act (CZMA).

The overriding goals of the CZMA are to preserve the unique value of coastal lands, preserve natural resources, prevent development in hazardous areas, protect water quality, and provide public recreation and an orderly process for siting new development. The Act seeks to achieve these ends by encouraging states to create and enforce land and water use plans for their coastal areas. The encouragement comes in the form of cash: Federal funds are granted to states that implement plans consistent with federally defined standards. The Secretary of Commerce must approve any state plan that meets the requirements of the Act and must award the state grants to pay for the administration of the state management program once approved.

Aside from funding, the other major incentive for states to create approved plans is that federal actions in the coastal zone of a state must comply with approved state plans. This consistency requirement applies to activities by federal agencies directly and to activities licensed or permitted by the federal government, including exploitation of oil and other resources on the continental shelf. The Act specifically excludes any land regulated solely by federal law.

The level of state regulation prompted by the CZMA varies from state to state. Twenty-four states now have approved coastal management plans. Of these, the majority employ a fairly simple regulatory scheme requiring a review and permit process before construction is allowed in coastal wetland areas and forbidding development in highly sensitive areas. A few states with acute coastal area problems, particularly North Carolina and the West Coast states, have created comprehensive management schemes with greater state involvement. These plans typically require state approval of local land use regulations and involve more extensive permit review procedures. Although federal funding and regulation have been decreasing in recent years, states continue to see the importance of coastal resources and have generally strengthened coastal regulations. See the end of Chapter 6 for a detailed treatment of CZMA.

Wetlands

Wetlands definition and regulation are akin to federal environmental overlay zoning in that they restrict land uses. Many states and municipalities also regulate wetlands. States' regulations must be more comprehensive than federal requirements, so as not to nullify the latter. The permitting process, jurisdiction, and process of §404 permits are set out in detail in Chapter 11. The federal government now regulates the filling of wetlands through §404 of the Clean Water Act, pursuant to its regulation of "navigable" waterways via the commerce clause. This jurisdiction extends not only to waterways that are themselves *navigable*, but also to their tributaries and to adjacent wetlands that *affect* the flow of water in the navigable waterway.

As described in Chapter 11, wetlands include swamps, marshes, bogs, and tundra that were once considered valuable only if drained and filled. Recently, it has become widely recognized that wetlands are extremely valuable environmental resources. They provide fertile breeding grounds for fish and birds and are natural controllers of erosion and flooding. They are also critical in the purification of water, effectively removing sediments, organic wastes, and other pollutants and producing oxygen and nutrients.

Wetlands are also fragile and particularly susceptible to development. They invariably are flat and easy to build on once the water has been eliminated, and they tend to be located near rivers, lakes, and coastlines — areas under high pressure from human development. Wetlands also are damaged by diversion of water for human use, changes in water table level, and agricultural runoff.

The environmental definition of a wetland has been the source of heated debate since the late 1980s. In 1989 the Army Corps of Engineers, which is charged with making an initial determination as to whether an area is a wetland, altered its definition in such a way that the area of the United States defined as wetlands nearly doubled, to over 100 million acres. The basis for a specific wetlands determination proceeds from a field study of the area's vegetation, soil, and hydrology.

Other Critical Areas

The federal government has singled out for special regulation several other natural land resources. These include floodplains, highly erodible land, and coastal barrier islands.

Dirt is important. Soil, as well as petroleum, water, or air, is a limited and fragile resource. Despite its seeming simplicity, soil is a complex system whose fertility arises from the interaction of many physical, biological, and chemical properties. Soil results from crumbled mineral matter. Creating six inches of topsoil requires tens of thousands of years of these interactions.

Traditionally, maintaining soil quality has been essential to maintaining the viability of a particular society. Poor management of soil resources led to the decline of numerous early dominant societies, including Classical Greece, Imperial Rome, several Pacific Island cultures, and the Mayan civilization. Today, the world is losing soil 10 to 20 times faster than it is replacing or replenishing it.

Tilling agricultural soil leaves it more susceptible to erosion, losing moisture, and being susceptible to wind and rain. When earth is cultivated, it releases carbon dioxide and nitrous oxide, losing plant nutrients and creating additional greenhouse gases. No-till farming has become more of a mainstream practice in recent times.

Soil erosion in the nation's agricultural heartland was first identified as a problem during the Dust Bowl of the 1930s. The 1977 National Resources inventory concluded that, despite almost fifty years of effort and the expenditure of some $30 billion, agricultural topsoil was eroding at a rate of 4 billion tons per year. This serious loss of topsoil led Congress to pass the Soil and Water Resources Conservation Act of 1977. This Act requires that the U.S. Department of Agriculture regularly assess the nation's soil resources and develop programs to conserve and enhance them. These programs require that farming on highly erodible land must be conducted in accordance with an approved conservation program and also establish a conservation reserve designed to take highly erodible land out of production.

By 1990 some 34 million acres had been protected under this program. This is a form of federal environmental land use overlay zoning.

Coastal barriers are long, narrow strips of land along a coast that are largely or completely surrounded by water. Their special value lies in their ability to protect coastal zones on the mainland from ocean storms. Important barrier lands include Fire Island in New York, Long Beach Island in New Jersey, and the Outer Banks in North Carolina. There are many smaller barriers along the East and Gulf Coasts. Human development in coastal areas weakens these barriers and makes them susceptible to erosion. Once a barrier land is eroded, ocean storms release their full fury on the mainland, causing damage to both human-made and natural resources there.

Although coastal barriers are within the area regulated by the CZMA, they have been singled out for special attention under the Coastal Barrier Resources Act of 1982 (CBRA). The CBRA does not create new regulation over the affected lands; it works simply by limiting federal funding for road and bridge construction. Such funding has effectively subsidized coastal development in the past. The CBRA effectively shifts the full costs and risks of coastal barrier development to the developer, making such development far less attractive and less profitable.

The largest federal regulation affecting *river* floodplains is the National Flood Insurance Program. Enacted in 1968, the NFIP was deemed necessary because private insurers were unwilling to insure properties subject to obvious floodplain risk. In return for running the NFIP, the federal government has been able to force states to enact stringent regulations in flood-prone areas. More recently the program has been criticized for subsidizing hazardous, uneconomical developments and has been curtailed to reduce this effect.

Examples

1. Cedar Stumps, Inc., conducts logging operations in national forests throughout the country. In 1994 it purchased a stand of timber on the western slope of the North Cascades, a mountain range in Washington state, some 100 miles from the nearest coastline. It plans to clear-cut the entire stand and has obtained all necessary permits from the U.S. Forest Service. A major river originates in the area that Cedar Stumps wants to log, and it flows directly into a large salt marsh which is critical habitat for a variety of wildlife including salmon, bald eagles, seabirds, otters, and small fish which in turn support whales and other ocean species. The state of Washington seeks to force Cedar Stumps to obtain a permit from the state Coastal Commission to ensure that the logging will not harm the marsh. Must Cedar Stumps get a permit from the state if it already has federal approval?

2. Wheaton Township has long been an agricultural area, but as suburban sprawl approached its borders, its downtown began to grow and single-family houses began to spring up on the edge of fields nearest the commercial area. In anticipation of continuing growth, the town installed sewer mains, improved its roads and water system, and generally upgraded its public services. Wheaton also created a master plan and a zoning scheme setting aside residential, commercial, industrial, and agricultural districts. McDonald then bought a small, 20-acre farm in an area zoned residential and continued to farm it. The township sued to enjoin her farming activities on the ground that they were not permitted in a residential district. McDonald's farm was particularly close to downtown and was served by new sewers and other services the town had installed. Can the town do this to Old McDonald? Why?

3. At the other end of town, J. R. Ewing owns a 50-acre farm he would like to subdivide into half-acre lots. His farm is in an area zoned agricultural with a minimum lot size of 10 acres. The master plan calls for much of the town to remain agricultural in order to maintain its traditional rustic character. The plan is supported by extensive studies which showed that the 10-acre minimum is necessary to support the type of farming traditionally practiced in the area.

Explanations

1. Yes. Cedar Stumps appears to have two good arguments for not complying with state coastal regulations, but the Supreme Court has rejected both of them. First, it appears that logging on dry land more than 100 miles from the ocean is an activity that would not affect the coastal zone. It is possible, however, that the logging will increase erosion of topsoil into the nearby river and thus add to silting and runoff in the critical coastal marsh. The coastal commission has the right to require that this possibility be reviewed before it grants a permit for the logging.

   Cedar Stumps may also argue that since its activities are confined to land owned by the federal government, it should be exempt from additional regulation by the state due to the preemption provisions of the CZMA. Recall the holding in *Granite Rock* regarding additional environmental requirements. Here, the state cannot create a statute stating that the national forest cannot be logged, but it can regulate how logging is conducted if it can show that the logging would directly affect the coastal zone. This interpretation is similar to one reached by the Supreme Court in *Commonwealth of Puerto Rico v. Muskie*, 507 F. Supp. 1035 (D.P.R. 1981), *vacated*, *Marquez-Colon v. Reagan*, 668 F.2d 611 (1st Cir. 1981), holding that the federal lands exclusion does not apply when activities on federal land affect areas outside federal ownership.

2. The city will probably fail in its attempt to bar Old McDonald from farming. It would give her only the choice of either letting her land lie unused or of building houses on it. This result has been held unconstitutional by at least one court. *Mindel v. Township Council of Franklin Tp.*, 400 A.2d 1244 (N.J. 1979). In that case the court ruled that the town must allow Mindel to continue to farm until the economic pressures of growth forced him to subdivide. The fact that a city has built sewers does not impose a burden on adjacent landowners to use them. Note that in *Mindel*, the farm owner was partly encouraged to continue farming by a state government program that gave landowners a tax incentive to farm. The state government was reacting to the rapid loss of farmland in the state due to the growth of New York and Philadelphia suburbs.

3. J. R. is unlikely to win at this point, but if the suburban growth continues he is likely to succeed some day. Agricultural and other large-lot zoning schemes have been upheld requiring minimum lots as large as 160 acres on the plains of the Midwest. The city will be able to enforce its zoning scheme so long as it can show that the regulations are based on a master plan that has been undertaken in good faith to promote the public welfare. Public welfare has been interpreted in zoning and other land-use-related cases to include general psychological well-being derived from peace and quiet, limited traffic, open space, and access to adequate parklands. But in heavily developed areas, courts have ruled one-acre lots to be an unjustifiable exercise of the police power, intended not to promote welfare but to exclude poor and moderate-income residents.

MUNICIPAL LICENSING FOR ENVIRONMENTAL GOALS

The Municipal Power to License

In addition to exercising its general zoning powers, municipalities issue a number of licenses and other approvals; they also assume principal responsibility for solid waste management, pursuant to RCRA (see Chapter 8). These other approvals are not directly environmental or zoning-oriented. But they can be used by municipalities and counties to accomplish environmental ends. Municipalities license certain types of businesses, pursuant to state law or local ordinance. Common licenses include annually renewable licenses for restaurants, victualers, vendors of alcoholic beverages, car dealers, used auto parts dealers, junkyards, pawnshops, dealers or collectors in second-hand articles, and so on.

Now what type of environmental authority could lurk within such municipal licensing? The potential is larger than it first appears. Any activities involving recycling may require a junk *collector's* license. If more than one corporation is involved, and recyclable materials change hands, a junk *dealer's* license might be invoked. Licenses to collect or store second-hand articles could be invoked. Does a facility that collects and converts used auto tires (which are comprised of petroleum and carbon black) into electrical energy require a license as a car dealer, a dealer in used auto parts, a junk dealer, a junk collector, or none of the above? It depends on the exact language and authority of the ordinance involved, as well as its interpretation and enforcement.

A municipality could employ its licensing authority to deny or restrict certain types of businesses from operating within city limits. By limiting the right to do business, one indirectly controls the environmental impacts of the potential business. The fundamental right to operate — and restrictions on that right — can provide indirect environmental controls.

Typically, local licenses are granted and renewed periodically — often annually. They are granted at the pleasure and convenience of the municipal body politic. The law varies in different jurisdictions as to the grounds on which such licenses may be withheld, suspended, or revoked. Some jurisdictions impose greater due process rights and presumptions in favor of the permittee, as well as a more favorable standard of review (see Chapter 2) on permit revocation as compared to permit issuance. A permit may only be able to be revoked on failure to satisfy the conditions originally placed in the permit. See *Derby Refining Co. v. Board of Aldermen*, 555 N.E.2d 584 (Mass. 1990).

The law also varies as to the due process rights of a license applicant or holder, the appeal process for an aggrieved license applicant or intervener, and whether or not the license is personal or runs with the property or business. Can a franchisee operate under the license of its franchisor? This determines whether the license could shelter the activities of tenants and licensees, or whether it pertains only to the holder of the license, who may be an owner of land or a business but not its operator.

Building and Occupancy Permits

A variety of local permits are routinely issued by local bodies to allow people to occupy buildings, park their vehicles, and hook into the utility infrastructure to consume water, dispose of waste, and store or obtain energy resources. A list of these typically required local permits is given in Exhibit 10.2.

Most of the permits on this list are routine and are granted as a matter of course. However, if an ordinance is broadly drafted or allows enforcement

10.2   Typical Local Permits

Medium	Permit
Waste	Sewer connection permit
	Waste handling certification
Use	Building permit
	Electric/wiring permit
	Plumbing permit
	Gasfitting permit
	Approval for boilers/furnaces
	Storage permit for fossil fuels
	Freshwater connection permit
	Occupancy permit
	Curb cut authorization

discretion, conditions can be imposed on the issuance of these permits. Some communities have successfully imposed limitations on utility service — for water or sewage hookups — to limit either residential or commercial growth within municipal boundaries (see the discussion of *Ramapo* earlier in this chapter). Vehicle traffic, as a modern environmental problem, can be controlled by curb cut authorizations, off-street parking requirements, or vehicular access restrictions.

Nonconforming Uses and Their Destruction

Grandfathering of existing established uses is generally required when a zoning law is enacted or modified. An existing, lawful land use cannot be eliminated by a zoning scheme or regulation unless it is determined to be an active threat to public health, safety, or welfare. Land uses that are less desirable but not actual nuisances are allowed to continue as "nonconforming uses." This treatment is necessary to prevent the zoning law from acting as a "taking" of property.

Nonconforming uses are *everywhere*. Every use that is not in the place required by the current version of the zoning code, and, moreover, is inconsistent with any environmental overlay zones, is nonconforming. But uses do change over time. Businesses expand, and they change the products or services that they sell, with consequent changes in land. Fire, flood, or earthquake can damage a building so that it needs to be rebuilt, use of the parcel for primary and ancillary uses can be reconfigured, the volume/success of the use can change, the personnel operating a business or its primary product or service can change.

Can these alterations occur legally under the umbrella of the earlier nonconforming use? Or do the alterations constitute a new use that goes beyond the protected area of nonconformance? The general rule is that nonconforming uses are acceptable only so long as they are not extended, enlarged, intensified, or abandoned.

What do these key legal terms mean? Since these are local concepts, they are governed by state law, and there is a patchwork of state interpretation. However, there are several general tenets of what is permissible. The key issue is whether there is a change in the *quality*, *character*, or *degree* of the nonconforming use. *Micro* changes within the basic character and form of the nonconforming use are generally allowed. *Macro* changes having a negative *qualitative* impact on the surrounding neighborhood are not allowed.

No use is completely static over time. When does reconstruction constitute enlargement or intensification of the nonconforming use? *Renovation* by itself is not an impermissible extension of a nonconforming use; *rebuilding* or reconstruction after destruction may be. See *Cullen v. Building Inspector*, 353 Mass. 671 (Mass. 1968). Some state enabling statutes or local zoning codes prohibit rebuilding a destroyed nonconforming use. Carry lots of insurance in such situations.

What about success? It is a double-edged sword for land-use purposes. A business's success on a particular site, which may occasion additional commerce, traffic, or pollution, generally is not sufficient to constitute an impermissible enlargement of the nonconforming use. *Jasper v. Michael A. Dolan, Inc.*, 355 Mass. 17 (Mass. 1968). Where there is a nonconforming use that is *incidental* to a *primary*, different nonconforming use, the expansion of that previously incidental or ancillary nonconforming use so that it dominates the uses can constitute an impermissible change in the character of the nonconforming use. *Town of Bridgewater v. Chuckran*, 217 N.E.2d 726 (Mass. 1966). Similarly, change from a retail operation to a larger wholesale operation may destroy the nonconforming use status. *Id.* However, merely finding a more efficient or modern means to conduct the same business on a parcel of land, without expanding the land area used, is not necessarily a destruction of the nonconforming character, even where it results in greater success and more commerce at the site. *Berliner v. Feldman*, 298 N.E. 2d 153 (Mass. 1973).

Ownership of land changes, as do the personnel who use or operate it. A change of *ownership* or *operation* of a land use, alone, typically does not destroy a nonconforming use, even if that new operator increases the amount of commerce on that particular land without changing the fundamental character of the use. *Sullivan v. Board of Appeals of Harwich*, 445 N.E.2d 174 (Mass. App. Ct. 1983).

How about enlargement of the land *area* occupied by the use? Dramatically increasing the amount of land used for the business can destroy a nonconforming use. *Cullen v. Building Inspector*, 353 Mass. 671 (Mass. 1968). However, one needs to distinguish a land use that basically dedicates an entire parcel to a particular purpose but does not consistently *use* the entire parcel. Interesting problems arise when the land use is cyclical and the land area actively used in the operation fluctuates over time. For example, a junkyard is the original recycler, accumulating scrap metal and materials for years, and then selling certain of those materials in bulk when the price for scrap materials rises. The amount of stored material at a junkyard therefore will ebb and flow in response to commodity prices. One year the lot will be full of used car hulks; another year it may be virtually empty and then slowly rebuild the inventory.

Expansion of active use of a larger area of the parcel, without changing the *quality* and *character* of the use, can in certain cases be considered a protected exercise of the nonconforming use. *Building Inspector v. Amaral*, 401 N.E.2d 158 (Mass. 1980). Nonconforming uses also can be abandoned, the legal consequence of which is to destroy the immunity from local restrictions vested in nonconforming uses. Abandonment occurs through nonuse of part of a parcel for an appreciable time. Case law in a given state will provide the period for what constitutes abandonment. However, mere failure to comply with any state or local licensing provision, where the defect is easily remedied, typically is not an abandonment. *Board of Selectmen v. Monson*, 247 N.E.2d 364 (Mass. 1969).

An *intensification*, or change in the *character* and *quality*, of a nonconforming use destroys the protection afforded by the nonconforming use. In other words, the nonconforming use shield is lost. The use need not constitute an environmental nuisance. Once the nonconforming use status is lost, the use is inconsistent with *current* zoning restrictions and can therefore be enjoined. A major battleground for environmental attorneys at the local level is thus the time when certain activities intensify, enlarge, change the character of, or abandon a nonconforming use. The legal significance of these determinations often is overlooked by counsel.

Board of Health Environmental Authority

Many municipalities invest authority in a board of health. A board of health, or a health agent, is an official municipal body empowered to enforce the general health rules of the state, county, and municipality. In certain cases, this can be a very dynamic job. Perhaps you saw the movie *Invasion of the Body Snatchers*. In that film, Donald Sutherland plays a health agent for the city and county of San Francisco. During the course of that 90-minute film, Sutherland goes from inspecting fancy French restaurants for mouse droppings in the French onion soup to battling intergalactic pod-people intent on ruining the city where Tony Bennett left his heart. Great work if you can get it.

Now, while we could wax poetic about the environmental repercussions of invasions of the pod-people, the point is that health agents have broad authority to protect the public health, however threatened by environmental disasters or space invaders. The enabling statutes for health authorities are very broad. Traditionally, health authorities concern themselves with restaurants and similar palpably health-related businesses. However, a municipality interested in enforcing environmental standards or impeding certain activities with environmental repercussions can use its health authority as a significant weapon.

The weapons in the arsenal of health authorities vary. The general common law power to arrest public nuisances can reside in health authorities. They can pick up at the local level the authority exercised at a broader scale by the county prosecutor or the state attorney general. They may be able to revoke licenses for an enterprise or issue "cease and desist" orders for certain activities. In other cases, they must report a matter as a complaint to state environmental enforcement authorities, and ask that agency to issue an order.

The application to potentially polluting activities should be apparent. Many activities involve emissions to the air, surface waters, groundwater, or discharge of effluent to septic systems. In addition, certain businesses entail substantial vehicle traffic or intensity of land use that poses a nuisance. Other businesses produce loud noise or unpleasant odors. Many of these environmental impacts may not be covered specifically by a particular statute or ordinance, but they can constitute a nuisance, or an impairment of health and welfare. The authority of boards of health can intervene in such situations. The very fact that board of health authority encompasses general nuisance authority to enjoin activities that constitute threats to public health and the environment makes them "wild cards" in the arsenal of environmental enforcement.

What limitations are there on board of health authority? First, boards of health or health agents can act only within their specific authority. State statutes and local ordinances will grant and prescribe the scope of authority. Second, preemption can limit board of health authority. As you will recall from Chapter 4, local environmental regulation can be preempted, either expressly or impliedly, by superior federal or state statutes. Similarly, local enforcement of state or federal laws may be limited by those statutes.

An analysis of the authority of boards of health begins with the presumption that their public nuisance authority is not expressly preempted. Few state or federal environmental laws specifically sanction the maintenance of nuisances. Boards of health or health agents are one of the most overlooked environmental authorities; they exercise both statutory and common law powers vis-à-vis the environment.

COMMON LAW LAND USE CONTROLS

The Public Trust Doctrine

The public trust doctrine also is treated in great detail at the end of Chapter 1. It traditionally has been applied only to navigable waterways. However, it has been expanded both by statute and by the courts to cover other public lands and to create more affirmative environmental duties. Several courts have taken the fairly small step of using the doctrine to protect fish and waterfowl in trust waters. In one case, an oil spill killed a number of birds on the Potomac River. When the federal government and state of Virginia sued the polluter, he moved for summary judgment on the basis that neither government owned the birds. The court held that, although neither government *owned* the birds in question, the public trust doctrine nevertheless gave them a duty to protect the public's interest in the nation's wildlife resources. Other courts have gone further and protected inland wild animals and nonsubmerged public land.

The public trust doctrine is generally limited as an environmental tool, however, because it is difficult to expand its traditional application only to navigable waterways. It is nonetheless worth noting because waterways, coasts, and wetlands are among the most fragile and important environmental land uses, and within these areas the public trust is extremely powerful. See Chapter 1.

Waste and Nuisance

Two other common law land-related doctrines are applied in efforts to conserve and protect environmental resources. Under the common law doctrine of *waste*, a current possessor of an interest in land is forbidden to do anything to diminish the value of the land if it is subject to a future interest. This doctrine prevents current possessors or users of land from extracting resources from the land or from polluting or altering it in any way that might harm the future interest. This doctrine was strictly applied in old English courts so that any change to the land was actionable, even if it was actually an improvement. This concept is of fairly limited application, however, since it only comes into play when there is a split in ownership between current and future interests.

Nuisance is a branch of tort law used to protect a landowner's right to quiet enjoyment of his or her land. A nuisance is any unreasonable use of land that interferes with another landowner's quiet enjoyment of his or her land but falls short of a physical trespass. Actions on one parcel that unreasonably interfere with the right of quiet enjoyment of the neighboring parcels are a nuisance. Traditional nuisance cases involve noises, vibrations, or gases passing from one property to a neighboring tract. A nuisance is created when an act by one party causes harm outside his or her property. As such, the nuisance doctrine is widely used to prevent air, water, and groundwater pollution, and in some cases erosion (through the duty to provide lateral support to neighboring lands).

If a party violates regulatory standards, however, a plaintiff has the option of pursuing the administrative remedy named by the regulation or suing under nuisance law. The violation of the regulation may be evidence that a nuisance exists. Conversely, the existence of a nuisance does not mean that a regulation has been violated. Therefore, nuisance may reach conduct that the statute does not. See Chapter 1 for much more detailed treatment on nuisance and common law doctrine.

Example

1. Leach bought a large oceanfront lot with the intent of building a large resort for the rich and famous to come enjoy the spectacular surf that pounded the soft, sandy beach much of the year. It was to be the fulfillment of their "champagne wishes and caviar dreams." He applied for a permit to construct a large seawall at the water's edge to keep the ocean from finding its way into his hotel once it was built, but his application was denied. Shortly thereafter a storm swept over his lot, reducing it to a saltwater marsh. He sued the state for taking his land by refusing the seawall permit. What would be the legal result?

Explanation

1. Leach should invest in some scuba gear, or at least waders, because that is the only way he can enjoy his land, or what used to be his land. The state may not accede to permit the seawall. Mother nature, not the state, took his land. According to the holding in *Carolina Beach Fishing Pier, Inc. v. Town of Carolina Beach*, 177 S.E.2d 513 (N.C. 1970), the land is now property of the state under the public trust because it is now below the high tide mark. C'est la vie à la mer.

Preservation of Natural Areas: Wetlands and Open Space

"Wilderness is the raw material out of which man has hammered the artifact called civilization."

Aldo Leopold

"The sea lies all about us. The commerce of all lands must cross it. . . . The continents themselves dissolve and pass to the sea, in grain after grain of eroded land. So the rains that rose from it return again to the rivers."

Rachel Carson, The Sea Around Us, 1951

"These trees shall be my books."

William Shakespeare, As You Like It

"The edge of the sea is a strange and beautiful place. All through the long history of earth it has been an area of unrest . . . for no two successive days is the shoreline precisely the same."

Rachel Carson, The Edge of the Sea

WETLANDS AND WATERWAYS

Consider this factor that distinguishes between wetlands and terrestrial open space: the natural topography of the earth. If the earth were symmetrically round and smooth, all areas would be under approximately 2.5 miles of

527

water. That would certainly alter the nature of life on this planet. However, the natural topography renders some areas above water and most under water.

Even more wetland areas have been lost than forests. One-third of the world's coral reefs have been severely damaged or destroyed. Rainforests harbor large numbers of animal species; coral reefs are home to large numbers of marine species. Under current rates of loss, half of the remaining reefs will be lost by 2030. The great majority of ocean fisheries have either collapsed or are in steep decline from overfishing. Farmland soil in areas growing food has been eroded away at 10 to 40 times the rate that it is replenished, and at 500 to 10,000 times the rate that naturally forested land loses topsoil.

The first section of this chapter assesses key water-related resources and the laws that protect them. Consideration of terrestrial open space follows later in this chapter. We begin by defining wetlands and wetland ecosystems. As part of this introduction, we consider the various human purposes that wetlands serve. U.S. regulation of wetlands began in 1899 with the Rivers and Harbors Act (see Chapter 6), augmented later by NEPA and §404 of the Federal Water Pollution (Clean Water) Act.

What Is a Wetland?

Wetlands, which include marshes, swamps, bogs, and fens, have been called "nature's kidneys" because of their ability to cleanse pollutants and sediments and regenerate freshwater supplies. There are approximately 110 million acres of wetlands in the continental United States, about half of what existed in the 1600s. The U.S. Fish and Wildlife Service has estimated that between the mid-1970s and the mid-1980s, the nation suffered a net loss of 2.6 million acres of wetlands. But according to the EPA, since 1980, the United States has experienced no net loss of wetlands. The importance of wetlands preservation was brought into the national spotlight in 1988 when then-vice president George Bush endorsed a "no net loss of wetlands" policy. Today the "no net loss of wetlands" concept remains national policy. However, the United States continues to lose wetlands at a rate of about 300,000 acres per year.

The average person would probably describe a wetland as a swamp or marsh, full of mosquitoes, snakes, and crawly critters. Wetlands can be very difficult to classify precisely because wetlands types tend to overlap and merge. It is not uncommon for an estuary to become a tidal marsh that then becomes a brackish marsh, and ultimately becomes a freshwater marsh, as one moves inland.

There is no single universal definition of a wetland. Part of the difficulty arises from the fact that wetlands can vary greatly in characteristics and functions. For many years there were no official guidelines for recognizing and delineating a wetland. In 1987 the U.S. Army Corps of Engineers developed the *Corps of Engineers Wetlands Delineation Manual* for identifying wetlands subject to regulation under the Clean Water Act. The manual does not attempt to identify every area that might be technically classified as a wetland; rather it seeks to define wetlands subject to the Clean Water Act by three parameters: (1) the presence of wetlands hydrology, (2) the presence of hydrophilic vegetation, and (3) the presence of hydric soil.

Today the wetlands definition used by both the Army Corps of Engineers (the Corps) and the U.S. Environmental Protection Agency (EPA) under §404 of the Clean Water Act is as follows:

> The term wetlands means those areas that are inundated or saturated by surface or groundwater at a frequency and duration sufficient to support, and that under normal circumstances do support, a prevalence of vegetation typically adapted for life in saturated soil conditions. Wetlands generally include swamps, marshes, bogs and similar areas.

Using the regulatory definition, there are three basic components to consider in evaluating whether an area is a wetland. First, consider the hydrology and determine if water is present at or near the surface for a period of time. If water is present for at least 5 percent of the growing season, an area meets the typical hydrology requirement for wetlands. Other factors may also be evaluated. These other factors include inundation, saturation within 12 inches of the surface, water marks, drift lines, water-stained leaves, the remains of aquatic vertebrates, and sediment deposit. Second, evaluate the type of vegetation present. Vegetation that grows in wetlands can be quite varied, but it must be capable of growth in very wet conditions. Finally, the type of soil present should be evaluated. Wetland soils are typically hydric soils, which are periodically saturated with water, creating anaerobic conditions.

Wetlands are often evaluated from the perspective of an ecological system or ecosystem. A biological community consists of living organisms that have relationships both among themselves and to the environment. The biological communities are in turn made up of populations. A population represents organisms of a particular species which occupy a specific area. "Species" is a term used to describe a population of organisms that are capable of interbreeding under natural conditions and producing healthy offspring. An organism is the smallest living unit of an ecosystem. Each organism within the community occupies a specific habitat, which includes all the necessary components for the organism's survival. In the case of wetlands, the human population is a major consideration.

529

In recent years the value of wetlands has become much more apparent. Wetlands serve five primary functions:

1. Reduction of the effects of flooding, soil erosion, and storm damage
2. Purification of both surface water and groundwater by filtering the water through wetlands soils
3. Prevention of pollution
4. Protection of critical habitat for a variety of wildlife species and fisheries
5. Protection of recreational, aesthetic, and property values

1. Flood Control

Wetlands provide temporary storage for floodwaters. The floodwaters can then slowly recede by means of evaporation, percolation into the soil, and downstream flow. (See Chapter 1 on the hydrologic cycle.) The wetlands act as a buffer during major storms, protecting the land nearby. They stabilize riverbanks and shorelines. When wetlands are functioning effectively, there is often no need for extensive engineering to prevent storm damage. When wetlands are destroyed, the water storage capacity is reduced and floodwaters can rise more quickly, creating the potential for erosion, downstream flooding, and property damage. The destruction of 90 percent of the Mississippi River's wetlands has resulted in torrential flooding that leads to loss of life and billions of dollars in property damage. The 2005 flooding and destruction of New Orleans by Hurricane Katrina is an extreme example.

2. Protection of Water Supplies

Although it is not always apparent, wetlands are often sources of water supplies. Water stored in wetlands may ultimately flow to surface water supplies or recharge groundwater supplies. By storing water during wet periods, wetlands make water available later when the weather is dry and water demand is high.

3. Prevention of Pollution

Wetlands can purify water that they receive by serving as natural settling ponds, where soils and vegetation can trap sediments. The sediments can bind pollutants such as heavy metals and hydrocarbons. Wetlands absorb and filter pollutants that would otherwise degrade rivers, lakes, and aquifers.

4. Protection of Habitat

Wetlands serve as breeding areas for many wildlife species. They can also serve as protective areas, providing food, shade, and cover. They provide habitat for one-third of the nation's resident bird species and for more than half of the migratory species. They also provide feeding, spawning, and nursery areas for over half the saltwater fin and shellfish harvested every year, and for freshwater game fish as well. Wetlands are the principal habitat for one out of three of the plants and animals currently listed on the federal registry of endangered and threatened species (see Chapter 13).

5. Protection of Recreational and Aesthetic Resources

Wetlands provide the human community with areas for fishing, boating, hiking, and other outdoor activities. The open space that wetlands provide can be extremely valuable, not only for the important functions identified above, but also for their beauty and solitude.

Example

1. You have recently been appointed to head an advisory committee. The committee is composed of scientists from both the private and public sectors, attorneys representing government and private interests, representatives of several environmental organizations, and representatives from the real estate development community. The main objective of the committee is to recommend to the EPA how the "no net loss" policy for wetlands can be advanced under the constraints of the existing laws. Reflect on the perspective that each of the interested groups is likely to bring to this policy.

Explanation

1. The biggest challenge facing a large group with such diversified, and even competing, interests would be the difficulty of reaching consensus. The environmentalists generally believe the best approach to "no net loss" is to curb all development in wetland areas. The real estate development interests are at the opposite end of the spectrum, recommending a narrowing of the way wetlands are defined under current practice; they do not believe it is necessary to count every puddle in order to achieve "no net loss." The representative from the U.S. Fish and Wildlife Service (FWS) may advocate mitigation banking, an approach by which saved wetlands are "banked" to allow offsetting destruction in other locations.

This approach was introduced by the FWS in the 1980s in an attempt to increase the effectiveness of wetlands destruction mitigation, while maintaining a reasonable cap on costs to the regulated community.

The concept of creating new wetlands where there were none is another controversial concept. Opposition generally comes from the scientific community. The creation of wetlands in an area that was not a wetland is difficult at best. Soil conditions play a major role in the success of the project. There is also a tendency to create those wetlands that are easiest and cheapest to create, specifically shrub wetlands and marshes. This type of wetland may not provide the type of habitat needed for area wildlife.

REGULATION OF WETLANDS

Early Regulation

The Rivers and Harbors Act of 1899

The Rivers and Harbors Act of 1899 (also discussed in Chapter 6) gave the Army Corps of Engineers authority to regulate construction activities involving dredging, filling, or obstructing navigable waters. The Act is still in effect today. Under §10, a developer needs to apply to the Army Corps of Engineers prior to building any structure in any water of the United States. Specifically, §10 prohibits the "creation of any obstruction not affirmatively authorized by Congress, to the navigable capacity of any of the waters of the United States. . . ." This regulation did not extend to most wetlands because most wetlands areas are outside the mean high water mark of navigable waters, the area over which the Corps has authority. In large part, the Corps does not regulate wetlands at all under this Act.

The National Environmental Policy Act (NEPA)

In 1969 the National Environmental Policy Act (NEPA) was enacted. As you recall from Chapter 3, NEPA requires all federal agencies to consider potential adverse environmental impacts in evaluating major federal actions, which include permit approvals. As a direct result of NEPA, the Corps could refuse to grant a permit to, say, fill in a tidal basin, not because doing so would impede navigation but because of anticipated adverse effects on marine life. The Fifth Circuit upheld the Corps's decision in *Zabel v. Tabb*, 430 F.2d 199 (5th Cir. 1970), *cert. denied*, 401 U.S. 910 (1971).

The Wild and Scenic Rivers Act

The Wild and Scenic Rivers Act creates a national regulatory system for protecting free-flowing rivers with recreational or scenic value. 16 U.S.C. §§1271-1287. Rivers are designated as either "wild," "scenic," or "recreational," with a greater degree of development allowed as one moves along this progression of designations. River status can be designated either by Congress or by state initiative upon approval of the secretary of the interior. As appropriate, activities such as logging, water diversions, and development projects are restricted after designation.

The Federal Water Pollution Control Act Amendments of 1972

§404 Overview

In 1972 Congress enacted the Federal Water Pollution Control Act (FWPCA), commonly referred to as the Clean Water Act (CWA). The Act is discussed extensively in Chapter 6. For the purposes of addressing wetlands, the most relevant section of the Act is §404, which regulates the discharge of dredged or fill material. It is important to note that the plain text of §404 only regulates the filling and dredging of a wetland, not the draining or altering of it (even though the Act does not use the term "wetlands"). The secretary of the army is responsible for issuing permits prior to discharging dredged or fill material into navigable waters. Issuance of the permit must be done in accordance with EPA guidelines and may be vetoed by the EPA if it determines that the discharge would have unacceptable adverse impacts on municipal water supplies, fishery areas, shellfish beds, wildlife, or recreational areas.

The Corps's regulations define "dredged" material as "material that is excavated or dredged from the waters of the United States." 33 C.F.R. §323.2(c). Dredged materials are primarily products of navigational maintenance. Dredged "spoils" are considered pollutants under the Clean Water Act. "Fill" material is defined as "material used for the primary purpose of replacing an aquatic area with dry land or of changing the bottom elevation of a waterbody." 33 C.F.R. §323.2(e).

Recall from Chapter 6 that, under the Clean Water Act, anyone proposing to discharge dredged or fill material to navigable water is required to obtain not only a §404 permit from the Corps but also a Water Quality Certification under §401. The §401 certification is a statement that there is reasonable assurance that the proposed activity will not violate the applicable state surface water-quality standards. The §401 certification may be issued with specific requirements for the project to ensure adequate environmental protection.

Under §404 the Corps may issue individual permits, or it may regulate entire categories of activities through the use of general permits issued on a state, regional, or nationwide basis. The underlying intent of general permits is to streamline the process. These general permits are allowed for activities that are similar in nature, that have minimal adverse environmental effects if performed separately, and that have minimal cumulative adverse effects on the environment.

The most important of the general permits are those that apply nationwide. These permits are issued from the Corps's headquarters in Washington, D.C. Nationwide permits incorporate a number of general conditions. There are about three dozen nationwide permits that cover a variety of activities. Approximately two-thirds of these permits do not even require the Corps to be notified prior to the property owner commencing the covered activity. The most controversial of the nationwide permits is Nationwide Permit 26, which exempts from individual permit requirements all activities that affect less than one acre in an *isolated* wetland or in areas above the headwaters of nontidal rivers and streams. Such one-acre activities still may result in significant cumulative loss of valuable wetlands.

In certain situations, applicants may apply to the Corps for "after-the-fact" permits. These effectively are retroactive permits that sanction any otherwise illegal activity. If an unpermitted activity is reported to or discovered by the Corps, the Corps may issue a "cease and desist" order, or upon consultation with other agencies it may request that the party apply for an "after-the-fact" permit. A 1989 memorandum of understanding between the Corps and the EPA states that applications for "after-the-fact" permits will not be considered by the Corps unless corrective actions have been taken and there is no enforcement action planned or pending.

Exemptions

The CWA completely exempts certain specific activities from §404 regulation. These exemptions can be found at §404(f)(1). No permit is required for discharges from normal farming, silviculture, and ranching activities. Other exempt activities include maintenance of serviceable structures such as dikes, dams, levees, riprap, causeways; construction or maintenance of farm or stock ponds and irrigation ditches; maintenance of drainage ditches; construction of temporary sediment basins at a construction site; and construction or maintenance of farm, forest, or mining roads.

The Army Corps of Engineers does not have authority under §404 of the Clean Water Act to regulate incidental "fallback" resulting from excavation, land clearing, channelization, and trenching operations in wetlands. *National Mining Ass'n v. U.S. Army Corps of Engineers*, 145 F.3d 1399 (D.C. Cir. 1998). The exemptions identified in §404(f)(1) are limited by §404(f)(2), which states that the exemptions are not available when the proposed activity will subject navigable water to a new use or impair the flow of navigable water. The courts have acted on several occasions to uphold the limiting language of the so-called "recapture clause" in §404(f)(2).

The Extent of Jurisdiction Under the Clean Water Act

Navigable Waters   In enacting the Clean Water Act, Congress's primary intent was to regulate the waters of the United States used in interstate commerce and the waters hydraulically connected to water of interstate commerce. Therefore, the Corps and the EPA have jurisdiction over a wetland only if destruction or degradation of that wetland could affect *interstate* commerce. How do we get from interstate commerce to wetlands and swamps? The term "wetland" is not used in §404, but the legislative history of the Act seems to indicate that wetlands should be protected. The CWA defines "navigable water" in §502(7) broadly to include "waters of the United States including the territorial seas. "Navigable" waters of the United States raises federalism issues, which are also raised in other areas of environmental and energy law (see Chapter 12)."

The Corps, however, originally interpreted the Act as extending federal jurisdiction only to waters that were *actually, potentially,* or *historically* navigable. This interpretation covered very few wetlands. Three-quarters of a century after the enactment of the Rivers and Harbors Act, environmental groups challenged this interpretation as being too narrow. In *Natural Resources Defense Council v. Calloway,* 392 F. Supp. 685 (D.D.C. 1975), the court held that Congress had not intended the term "navigable waters" to be limited to the traditional tests of navigability. On the contrary, Congress had intended to extend federal regulatory authority to the limits of its commerce clause powers. On the basis of *Calloway,* the Corps expanded its regulations to specifically include wetlands. How far can it go?

Adjacent Wetlands   Is it an overextension of EPA authority to attempt to regulate wetlands *adjacent* to navigable waterways? The Corps's regulations define "adjacent" as meaning bordering, contiguous, or neighboring. The issue of whether Congress intended the Clean Water Act to extend protection to wetlands was settled in 1985 in a unanimous decision of the Supreme Court in *United States v. Riverside Bayview Homes, Inc.,* 474 U.S. 121 (1985).

In this case the respondent, who owned 80 acres of marshy land near Lake St. Claire in Michigan, began filling the area in preparation for a housing development. The Corps considered this property to be an *adjacent* wetland, included in the definition of "waters of the United States." The Corps filed suit in a U.S. district court seeking to enjoin the respondent from filling without a §404 permit. The Supreme Court ultimately granted certiorari and reversed the appellate court's decision, holding that the correct interpretation of the Corps's regulations includes the respondent's property, and that a §404 dredge and fill permit was therefore necessary. The impacts of the filling affected navigable waters, extending the reach of the statute. The Corps is able to regulate adjacent wetlands that affect the quality of waters of the United States.

Isolated Wetlands The *Riverside* Court left open the issue of whether *isolated* wetlands were within the jurisdiction of §404. Isolated wetlands are those wetlands that are not hydraulically connected to "waters of the United States." The Corps's regulations, however, did extend jurisdiction over isolated wetlands if their use, degradation, or destruction could affect interstate or foreign commerce, where the wetlands in question are utilized by migratory birds.

In 1918, the United States and Great Britain entered into a treaty compelling Congress to pass the Migratory Bird Treaty Act, which regulated the hunting of birds that migrated between the United States and British-controlled Canada. Missouri appealed to the Supreme Court, arguing that Congress did not have the power to regulate under Article I, and that the Tenth Amendment reserved this issue for the states to regulate. Writing for a 5-2 majority, Justice Holmes rejected the states' arguments, and relying upon the language of the Supremacy clause of Article VI, concluded that Congress can advise the executive on treaties. *Missouri v. Holland*, 252 U.S. 416 (1920).

In *Solid Waste Agency of Northern Cook County v. United States*, 531 U.S. 159 (2001), an abandoned mining site that had become habitat for wildlife on seasonal ponds became the selected site for disposal of municipal non-hazardous waste. The Corps defended its Migratory Bird Rule on deference grounds under *Chevron v. NRDC* (see Chapter 2). A narrow majority of the Court found that the Corps had exceeded its authority by regulating isolated waters under the Migratory Bird Rule, and to uphold the Corps would be to ignore the requirement that waters be at least connected to "navigable" waters under the Clean Water Act. *Riverside Bayview* requires a "hydrological connection" to a navigable body of water, while *SWANCC* required a "significant nexus" between navigable waters and the water body regulated.

The federal government brought criminal charges against a property owner, John Rapanos, who, without a federal permit, filled in parts of his property, which was about 20 miles away from water that was navigable in the traditional sense, although it was within the drainage systems of Lake Huron and two navigable rivers. Rapanos brought suit alleging that the federal government did not have such far-reaching physical authority under the Commerce Clause of the Constitution to stretch the definition of his filling affecting waters of the United States.

In *Rapanos v. United States*, 547 U.S. 715 (2006), the Supreme Court closely divided 5-4, with three dissenting Justices joining an opinion by Justice Stevens supporting the broad definition of the Army Corps of Engineers to protect U.S. remote waters. Four other Justices in the majority opinion written by Justice Scalia applied a restrictive standard requiring a physical nexus between the alteration and navigable waters of the United States. This Justice Scalia opinion found that the federal government had stretched its authority under the Clean Water Act "beyond parody" by regulating land that contained nothing but storm sewers, drainage ditches, and "dry arroyos in the middle of the desert," and under the Commerce Clause had trampled on state authority by exercising a "scope of discretion that would befit a local zoning board." Justice Scalia found that the only wetlands subject to federal jurisdiction are those "with a continuous surface connection" to actual waterways, "so that there is no clear demarcation between 'waters' and wetlands," and "relatively permanent, standing or flowing" to be "the waters of the United States." Therefore, "adjacent" wetlands require a permanent hydrologic connection.

Justice Kennedy, the fifth vote in the majority, left the federal government authority over any alterations that had a "significant nexus" to actually navigable waters of the United States. Without precisely defining this significant nexus, this connection was a significant and technical case-by-case determination, on which the courts would need to give some discretion to the regulatory agencies. Under that test, regulators need not show that a wetland is adjacent to, or connected with, a navigable body of water. Rather, it is sufficient to show that it is adjacent to a small tributary that eventually itself flows into such federal waters.

Justice Kennedy stated that the federal government needed to identify those "categories of tributaries" that were "significant enough that wetlands adjacent to them are likely, in the majority of cases, to perform important functions for an aquatic system incorporating navigable waters." To affect "the integrity of an aquatic system," Justice Kennedy held that wetlands and tributaries that "either alone or in combination with similarly situated lands in the region, significantly affect the chemical, physical, and biological integrity of other covered waters more readily understood as 'navigable,'" are subject to federal jurisdiction. This nexus is not well defined, and there is confusion in the lower courts. Appellate courts have disagreed as to whether the opinion must be read in the narrowest of concurring opinions (Kennedy's) or can be applied by choosing between the plurality and Kennedy opinions.

As a result, the Army Corps subsequently either dropped or modified hundreds of enforcement actions involving wetlands alteration. Eventually, Rapanos agreed to pay fines for filling wetlands equal to $150,000, and to replicate 54 acres of wetlands that he had filled in to further his plans for residential and commercial development of his land. This settlement did not affect a parallel federal criminal prosecution against Rapanos. The federal government hailed settlement as vindicating its power over wetlands activities.

Types of Discharges The Clean Water Act at §404 clearly regulates physical discharges of dredge and fill materials into navigable waters. This process has been broadly interpreted in some cases. In a 1983 Fifth Circuit ruling, the court held that land-clearing activities with a bulldozer that resulted in redeposits of material from the wetland required a dredge and fill permit from the Corps. *Avoyelles Sportsmen's League, Inc. v. Marsh*, 715 F.2d 897 (5th Cir. 1983). A federal district court in Texas held that draining of a wetland was regulated under §404 even though there was no discharge, because the draining altered or destroyed the wetland. *Save Our Community v. EPA*, 741 F. Supp. 605 (N.D. Texas 1990). See also *Coeur Alaska, Inc. v. Southeast Alaska Conservation Council*, 557 U.S. 261 (2009) discussed infra.

Examples

John Wayne owns a piece of property that he has always used as a horse ranch. Wayne now wants to retire. He recently decided he would like to develop the area and build several homes for his immediate family members, Hopalong and Annie Oakley. One area of the property, one-half acre in size, collects rainwater. The area is slightly depressed, and the rainwater tends to remain there until it evaporates. The developer has told Wayne that this should not pose a practical problem for construction. As the first step in construction, Wayne has the entire parcel graded, including the wet area.

1. Shortly thereafter, Wayne receives a letter from the federal government informing him that his actions violated §404 of the Clean Water Act. What would be the basis of such a claim by the government? What is the basis of federal jurisdiction?

2. Convinced that surely there is some mistake, Wayne contacts the federal government and asks how this area could be within federal jurisdiction when it is hundreds of feet from any other water body? Moreover, how could his actions have possibly affected interstate commerce? Is there a government response?

3. You are a lawyer working in a small firm that does a bit of environmental work. Wayne contacts you seeking advice on what he should do. What is his best line of defense?

4. Suppose the government then issues an order requiring Wayne to remove the fill and provide mitigation. The estimated cost of complying with the

order is $150,000. If he does not comply, the government can assess penalties daily, up to $25,000 per violation. Wayne, with True Grit, wants to challenge this action. What can you as counsel do?

Explanations

1. The jurisdiction of the federal government under the Clean Water Act extends to *navigable* waters, as legally defined. Isolated wetlands can be within this definition if hydrologically connected to navigable waters. The definition includes three factors determined scientifically, described early in this chapter. Without this determination, there is no federal jurisdiction. But with this determination, grading the property could be deemed an unauthorized "filling" of wetlands.

2. The traditional government response has been that it does not matter that he is hundreds of feet from any other water body; migratory birds might use the area. Therefore it affects interstate commerce. The Court has found this too attenuated. Jurisdiction can also extend to isolated land subject to flooding, where such wetlands are hydrologically connected to waters of the United States. Thus Wayne's wet area could affect interstate commerce indirectly.

3. This situation presents both procedural and substantive elements. The first step should be to challenge the federal government's claim that it has jurisdiction over this piece of property. The government's claim would be based on the premise that the area in question is a navigable water, as defined. Wayne's claim would be brought in federal court. Procedurally, there is good likelihood that it will be dismissed by the court because courts generally will not grant administrative review of anything less than a *final* action by a government agency (see Chapter 2). Assuming, *arguendo*, that Wayne's complaint would be dismissed, the remaining options are (1) submit to jurisdiction and comply with the agency's requirements, (2) refuse to submit to jurisdiction and refuse to comply with the agency's requirements, or (3) begin the administrative proceedings required to get a final decision from the agency, which can then be challenged in court. If Wayne does not want to submit to jurisdiction and concede, the second alternative could subject him to substantial noncompliance penalties. Therefore, the final alternative of proceeding with the administrative process to get a final agency decision seems to be the safest, albeit most time-consuming, approach. Since Wayne's grading work is already completed, there is no urgency for a permit. A good-faith proceeding challenging the agency's determination also should

prevent the imposition of any additional penalties. But it would be wise for counsel to get a government stipulation to this effect.

4. In 1985 the Supreme Court ruled in *Riverside Bayview Homes* that the Corps had jurisdiction over wetlands that are adjacent to navigable waters. At a bare minimum, isolated wetlands must have some connection to or effect on interstate commerce to be considered "waters of the United States." If anything, Wayne's parcel exhibits only isolated wetlands characteristics. Once this is demonstrated, the wetland is not considered subject to interstate commerce and the federal government has no jurisdiction over the property. This is the best administrative or litigation line of defense.

JURISDICTIONAL OVERLAPS IN IMPLEMENTING §404

Jurisdiction under §404 is bifurcated between the Army Corps of Engineers and the EPA. The Corps and the EPA have concurrent jurisdictional authority under §404. The Corps has the authority to issue dredge and fill permits, as well as nationwide permits. The EPA thereafter exercises review authority. The Clean Water Act does not specifically state which of the agencies will make final determinations under §404, nor does it describe how to proceed in the event the two agencies do not agree. In 1980, as a result of a dispute between the EPA and the Corps, the agencies entered into a memorandum of understanding, "EPA/Department of Defense, Memorandum of Understanding on Geographic Jurisdiction of the §404 Program (MOU)," 45 Fed. Reg. 45,018 (July 2, 1980), providing that the Corps would continue to make most jurisdictional determinations, but the EPA would be involved in special cases involving specific technical or policy issues.

Initial Review of the Army Corps of Engineers

Who needs a permit? Almost everyone. Under §404(a) of the Clean Water Act, the secretary of the army (through district engineering offices) may issue permits for the discharge of dredged or fill material into navigable waters. All governmental and private parties must apply for permits. Over 90,000 projects each year require permits — either individual or general. Of this total, 80,000 are considered to need little or no individual review. The remaining 10,000 projects are subject to full regulatory review, and of those cases only 6 percent typically are denied permits — less than 1 percent of this subset of projects subject to jurisdiction. The Corps itself is excluded from the application process, but not from the substantive requirements of the law. Army Corps of Engineers regulations on §404 permits are at 33 C.F.R. §325.1.

What must a permit applicant show? Permits will not be issued unless four conditions are met: (1) there is no practical alternative that will have a less adverse impact, (2) no statutory violations will occur, (3) there will be no significant adverse impacts, and (4) all reasonable mitigation measures will be employed.

EPA guidelines also recommend against issuing §404 permits unless steps are taken to minimize the potential adverse effects of the activity. In the 1990 MOU, the EPA and the Corps agreed that in issuing a permit the primary objective should be to avoid potential impacts to the extent practicable. Compensation for restoration of resources should always be the last resort. Finally, both EPA and the Corps require cumulative impacts in a particular area to be considered. Although a number of individual permits considered alone may not have an adverse impact, the combination of all the permits may have a cumulative impact on the wetland that is not acceptable.

Prior to issuance of a final §404 permit, compliance with all applicable federal, state, and local laws is required. As previously noted, a §401 Water Quality Certification is required before the Corps issues a §404 permit. Other commonly encountered federal approvals or reviews involve the National Environmental Policy Act (NEPA), the Coastal Zone Management Act, the Endangered Species Act, and the Marine Mammal Protection Act. In addition, many states and cities have enacted wetlands protection laws. All of these must be complied with before the Corps will issue a final §404 permit.

Once the Corps has the complete application, a public hearing has been held, and all the public comment periods have closed, the Corps will issue a Statement of Findings, or in cases where NEPA is applicable a Record of Decision. If the Corps issues an individual permit at this time, it must state all conditions on the permit and the time frame for the permit. The Corps may also issue a nationwide permit if appropriate.

EPA Veto

Section 404(c) of the Clean Water Act authorizes the EPA to veto a §404 dredge and fill permit issued by the Corps. EPA guidelines govern the issuance of permits, and the EPA reserves a veto power over Corps permits. To do so the EPA (though its Office of Wetlands, Oceans, and Watersheds) must determine that "the discharge of dredged or fill materials will have an unacceptable adverse effect on municipal water supplies, shellfish beds and fishery areas (including spawning and breeding areas), wildlife, or recreational areas."

541

EPA guidelines for the issuance of §404 permits focus on two major criteria: the "practical alternatives" test and the "water dependency" test. Under the "practical alternatives" test, a permit should not be issued if a practical alternative to the proposed activity exists that would have a less adverse effect on the aquatic environment. The "water dependency" criterion asks whether water use is a critical component of the activity, as it would be when building a marina. When an activity is considered non-water-dependent, practical alternatives are assumed to be available unless specifically shown to be otherwise. The developer bears the burden of demonstrating that no such alternative location is available. The EPA guidelines describe "available" to mean another location that could serve the same basic purpose and could reasonably be obtained.

The federal district court in Florida upheld the Corps's decision to deny a permit in the case of *Deltona Corp. v. Alexander*, 504 F. Supp. 1280 (M.D. Fla. 1981), in which the Deltona Corporation wanted to build a resort on Marco Island. The corporation alleged that this was a water-dependent project and that there were no practical alternatives. The Corps had denied the permit, stating that the basic purpose of the project was housing, which is not a water-dependent use. The court agreed.

EPA guidelines regarding discharges to wetlands provide that permits shall not be issued if there is a practical alternative to the proposed discharge that would have a less adverse impact on the aquatic ecosystem or if there is significant degradation of an aquatic ecosystem. 33 C.F.R. §§230.1(c)-(d), 230.10(c). A permit from the Army Corps of Engineers cannot be issued until the state certifies that a discharge will not violate state water-quality standards. 33 U.S.C. §1341(a). An applicant for a permit must take all practical steps to minimize the adverse effects of the discharge and to mitigate any remaining damage.

The EPA has rarely exercised its veto power. The first veto occurred in 1980 and there has followed approximately one annually. The impact of the small number of final vetoes should not be underestimated, however. Many projects have been stopped or significantly modified under the threat of an EPA veto.

One of the most famous of the EPA veto cases is the Sweedens Swamp litigation, *Bersani v. U.S. EPA*, 850 F.2d 36 (2d Cir. 1988). In *Bersani*, the EPA vetoed the Corps's issuance of a §404 permit needed to construct a shopping mall because it determined that a non-wetland site had been available to the developer. The story begins in 1983, when Pyramid, the developer, decided to build a new shopping mall in North Attleboro, Massachusetts. A suitable site was available, but a competing developer bought an option on it in July 1983. Pyramid subsequently decided to build on some wetlands known as Sweedens Swamp. In August 1984 it applied to the Corps for a §404 permit, seeking to fill or alter 32 to 49.6 acres of swamp, excavate 9 acres of uplands to create artificial wetlands, and alter 13.3 acres of existing wetlands to improve its environmental quality. Under threat of an EPA veto if the Corps allowed the permit, Pyramid proposed to create additional artificial wetlands at a nearby gravel pit. The Corps approved the permit.

In May 1986 the EPA issued a final determination disallowing the use of Sweedens Swamp for Pyramid's development. The EPA found that (1) filling the swamp would adversely affect wildlife, (2) an alternative site had been available when Pyramid *began* to search the area for a site, (3) Pyramid failed to demonstrate that it had investigated other locations, (4) the alternative North Attleboro site had been feasible and would have had a less adverse impact on the wetland, and (5) the mitigation proposal did not make the project preferable to other alternatives because the likelihood of success was uncertain.

The major contention between the two agencies was the existence of practical alternatives. The Corps found that the North Attleboro site had *not* been available to Pyramid because another developer had an option to purchase it. The EPA, in vetoing the permit, found that the alternative North Attleboro site could have been available to Pyramid *at the time* they reviewed the area in search for a location. This is the "market entry" theory: The other developer did not buy the option for the alternative site until after Pyramid had entered the market. The Supreme Court rejected the developer's arguments and upheld the EPA veto. Timing of development alternatives is everything.

Review of EPA or Corps Decisions

Administrative Review

EPA can enforce its authority through compliance orders, administrative penalties, and initiation of civil actions. 33 U.S.C. §1319. The Corps may issue cease and desist orders. 33 U.S.C. §326.3. As illustrated by the *Bersani* case, if a §404 dredge and fill permit is denied, there is no administrative process for receiving an adjudicatory hearing from the Corps or EPA. If a party is denied a permit, he or she must go to court to appeal the decision. A final decision by the agency is subject to judicial review under the Administrative Procedure Act (5 U.S.C. §§701-706). See Chapter 2. The reviewing court will in most cases consider the agency's decision by reviewing the existing administrative record. A few wetlands cases have allowed for a de novo review of agency decisions, but that is rare. The court will admit new evidence only when the record is so scant that it makes review impossible based solely on the record. The court will reverse the agency's decision only if the agency is found to have acted in an arbitrary and capricious manner.

Citizen Suits Under §505

Citizens or environmental groups may bring suit under §505 of the Clean Water Act, the "citizen suit" provision. Citizen suits may seek compliance orders or civil penalties. They may not attempt to recover damages. Citizens may also sue federal agencies for failing to conduct nondiscretionary actions under §404.

A party wishing to challenge the issuance of a permit must file a lawsuit in federal district court under federal question jurisdiction because there are no direct agency appeal mechanisms for §404 permits. In addition, the issue must be ripe for review. Therefore the permit being challenged must be based on a final decision from the agency. This requirement is discussed in greater detail in Chapter 2.

Regulatory Takings

Applicants who have been denied a §404 permit may challenge the Corps's decision in federal court on constitutional grounds. These challenges are most commonly based on the theory of a regulatory "taking" of the applicant's property. The Fifth Amendment states: "No person shall be . . . deprived of . . . property, without due process of law; nor shall private property be taken for public use, without just compensation." Takings are discussed in greater detail in Chapter 10.

The government may be justified in denying issuance of a §404 permit on the basis of promoting environmental protection and conservation, which is a legitimate government interest. The court would need to balance that goal against the landowner being deprived of full use of his or her property. The issue of whether actions pursuant to a §404 application determination can result in a regulatory taking has arisen in a number of wetlands cases.

In *Florida Rock Industries, Inc. v. United States*, 21 Cl. Ct. 161 (1990), the court compared the value of the "taken" land based on its most profitable use *before* denial of the §404 permit with its fair market value *after* denial of the permit. The court found a taking in that case because the permit denial had essentially taken all the value of the property. *Accord, Lucas v. South Carolina Coastal Council*, 505 U.S. 1003 (1992) (involving a beachfront area, but not a §404 permit). See Chapter 10 for more detailed treatment of *Lucas* and other takings cases.

A couple facing EPA sanctions for filling wetlands to build a home near a lake have the right to "immediately litigate their jurisdictional challenge in federal court. . . . The reach of the Clean Water Act is notoriously unclear." *Sackett v. EPA*, 132 S. Ct. 1367 (2012). Otherwise, the Sacketts would have remained in limbo until the EPA decided to bring suit, all the while, accruing fees at a rate of $37,500 per day of noncompliance (EPA can assess an administrative penalty, initiate a civil enforcement action, issue a unilateral administrative compliance order). The Sacketts' APA challenge called the compliance order "arbitrary and capricious" and a denial of due process of law. In contrast, a lower court held that the issuance of a unilateral order by the EPA requiring cleanup of a parcel does not deny due process nor violate constitutional property rights. *General Electric Company, Co., v. Jackson*, 610 F.3d 110 (D.C. Cir. 2010)(powers of the EPA pursuant to Section 106 of CERCLA).

Examples

1. The Geo-Valley Company, a major developer, has proposed building a multifacility, integrated waterfront complex. It includes a marina, hotel, and waterfront arcade. You have been hired to prepare all the permitting applications. For the project to go forward as planned, many acres of existing wetlands will have to be filled. The developer has told you that she has worked on many projects very similar to this one, and they were all classified as water-dependent use projects. She expects you to proceed with the applications for a water-dependent use project.
   a. Analyze whether this is a water-dependent use or not.
   b. How does the "practical alternatives" test apply? What is the sequence of analysis?
   c. Can you think of any way to qualify any aspect of the project for water dependency?
   d. Who has the burden of proof?

2. Assume that you convince Geo-Valley, the developer, that the project will not qualify as a water-dependent use. You apply for a §404 permit as a non-water-dependent project and are denied. What legal recourse is available?

Explanations

1a. Under §404(b)(1) of the Clean Water Act the EPA established guidelines for the lawful discharge of dredged or fill material that identify a universe of two types of projects: water-dependent projects and non-water-dependent projects. A water-dependent project is one that *requires* access to water as part of its *basic and primary* purpose, such as a marina. A non-water-dependent project does not require water for its basic purpose, such as a motel. While a motel on the water might be nice, it does not *require* water. The guidelines treat these two types of projects

545

differently. Geo-Valley's proposed marina is water-dependent, but the other parts of the proposed development are not.

1b. The §404(b)(1) guidelines require a "practical alternatives" test to be conducted. This test prohibits discharging dredged or fill materials into waters of the United States, including wetlands, if there exists a practical alternative to the proposed discharge which would have a less adverse impact. An alternative is considered practicable when it is available and able to be utilized. Both water-dependent and non-water-dependent projects require a practical alternatives analysis. However, the water-dependent projects are *not* presumed to have an available alternative site that poses less of an adverse impact on the wetland.

To assist in identifying what these terms mean and how they should be applied to Geo-Valley, let's review the evolution of the case law on point. Given the court's ruling in *Deltona*, it seems unlikely that Geo-Valley could be considered a water-dependent use project. However, some of the Corps's decisions on similar projects subsequent to *Deltona* allowed the applicant to identify the use and alternatives available and then proceed with mitigation. Originally the Corps would conclude that if the mitigation proposed reduced the net impact of the project, the permit was allowed. However, the EPA veto in *Bersani* changed that.

The Corps and the EPA ultimately resolved the application of the practical alternatives test in their Memorandum of Understanding in 1990. The MOU established a sequence of steps to be considered in evaluating individual applications. The first step is to establish that no practicable alternative site is available. If there is no practicable alternative that would have less impact on aquatic resources, then impacts must be minimized. The last step in the sequence is to provide compensatory mitigation for destroyed wetlands resources.

It seems unlikely that the Geo-Valley project would be permitted as a water-dependent use project. Even if a §404 permit were issued by the Corps, the EPA could veto it under §404(c). Any application will require a detailed alternatives analysis. The EPA guidance does allow for consideration of cost and technology in light of the overall project purpose. It will also be necessary to develop a proposal for mitigation of the wetlands areas that must be filled for the portion of the project that inevitably will impact the wetlands.

1c. The only other option available would be to split the project and apply for two separate permits. The marina might qualify as water dependent.

However, the Corps's regulations require all reasonably related projects to be addressed by a single integrated permit. It could be difficult to present the water-dependent marina portion of the development as separate and not reasonably related to the rest of the project. However, as counsel to the developer, you should evaluate various ways to structure the terms on which you seek permission.

1d. The developer has the burden of proof. The agency has discretion.

2. The government's final action could be challenged as a regulatory taking. The government action may have placed such a heavy burden on Geo-Valley that the government for all intents and purposes has taken the property. The Supreme Court in *Lucas* held that if the government action deprives a property owner of all beneficial and productive use of its property, then the government action is a taking, and just compensation is due.

THE ROLE OF THE STATES IN WETLANDS PROTECTION

In addition to the federal programs designed to protect wetlands, over 20 states have enacted wetlands protection statutes of their own. State programs provide an additional statutory basis for restriction of private activities. In many cases the state's regulations are enforced by local boards. As counsel, you must always check federal, state, and local wetlands jurisdictions, processes, and definitions.

State Control of the §404 Program

The Clean Water Act under §404(g) authorizes individual states to assume responsibility for administering the §404 dredge and fill permit program. The state, if it wishes to assume this responsibility, must apply to the EPA for approval of its proposal to do so. If approved, the state assumes the duties of the Corps and issues §404 permits directly to applicants. The EPA still remains involved in the process in that it receives copies of all permit applications, retains its veto power, and may rescind the state's authority if regulatory requirements are not followed. Few states thus far have assumed responsibility for implementing the §404 program.

In *Coeur Alaska Inc. v. S.E. Alaska Conservation Council*, 557 U.S. 261 (2009), the Supreme Court reversed the Ninth Circuit to uphold the issuance of the original Clean Water Act §404 wetlands permit issued by the Army Corps of Engineers, treating gold mining waste slurry discharged into a lake and raising its bottom elevation, pursuant to its regulations, as "fill" rather than "pollutant discharges" subject to NSPS zero discharge. The circuit court previously had vacated Alaska's designation of a §404 "fill" permit, insisting that it be replaced by a Clean Water Act §402 NPDES permit for a point source discharge, given that the discharge would kill all animal and plant life in the lake. The Supreme Court applied *Mead*, 533 U.S. 218 (2001), analysis and deference and relied on and deferred to an internal EPA memo determining that waste dumped into a closed water body could be treated as "fill" of a wetlands rather than a point source of pollutants. The dissent lamented that this created a "loophole" for disallowance of this discharge under NSPS. Environmental groups immediately asked the Obama Administration to change the Clean Water Act.

State Wetlands Protection Jurisdiction

The Massachusetts wetlands protection program, which protects both inland and coastal wetlands, offers a vivid illustration of robust state regulation. The primary statute is the Wetland Protection Act (M.G.L. c.131 §40), which is a state law directing and empowering municipalities to protect and regulate development in inland and coastal wetlands resource areas. Enacted in the 1970s, the Act is designed to protect eight valuable public interests served by wetlands: flood control, storm damage prevention, protection of surface water supplies, protection of groundwater supplies, prevention of pollution, protection of fisheries, protection of land containing shellfish, and protection of wildlife habitats. Therefore it protects all environmental concerns of species, pollution, and even natural (flood) disaster.

The physical jurisdiction of the Wetlands Protection Act is broad and extends over any alteration of any bank, any freshwater wetland, any beach, any dune, any flat, any marsh, or any swamp bordering on the ocean, any estuary, any river, any stream, any pond, or any lake, without regard to navigability. Jurisdiction also includes land under any of the water bodies identified above, land subject to flooding, and tidal action or coastal storm flowage. Finally, jurisdiction includes any work within a minimum 100-foot "buffer" zone adjacent to any of the resource areas identified above. The rule is that if it's wet — or even within a 100-foot radius of something wet — it is subject to regulation. The actions regulated are *alterations*. An alteration is broadly defined to include removing, dredging, filling, or other changing of a wetland or the related physical areas described.

The wetlands protection program, even though created by the state, is administered at the local level by a conservation commission, a volunteer board that reviews each permit on a case-by-case basis. Assuming that the proposed project falls under the jurisdiction of the Wetlands Protection Act, the conservation commission accepts a permit application (known as a Notice of Intent) and holds a public hearing. The commission then will either issue an order of conditions permitting the project or deny the project.

The decision made by the conservation commission may be appealed to the Massachusetts Department of Environmental Protection (DEP), a state agency. The DEP, after review of the file and a site visit, issues a superseding order of conditions either upholding or overriding the conservation commission's decision. This order also may be appealed through an adjudicatory hearing at the DEP before an administrative law judge. The decision of the adjudicatory hearing may, in turn, be appealed to the Massachusetts superior court.

At the local level, many cities and towns in Massachusetts have local bylaws affording even greater protection to wetlands within their jurisdiction. These bylaws can go beyond the state requirements. If a property owner is denied an activity under a local bylaw, he or she must appeal that decision directly to the courts. Massachusetts has another law (M.G.L. c.91) regulating activities in tidelands, great ponds, and navigable rivers and streams. This Act, which embodies statutorily the public trust doctrine, is administered by the *state* environmental agency. The activities regulated here include dredging, filling, placement of structures, change in use, or structural alteration.

The Commission may impose fines under the state act only by going to court and getting a final judgment. Otherwise, the Commission may assess fines for violation of a local ordinance. M.G.L. c. 40, §21D (noncriminal "ticketing" procedure). Unlike other appeals, appeals of these enforcement orders go directly to court rather than the DEP. When a local commission bases its decision on a local wetlands bylaw that provides greater protection than the state statute, its decision cannot be preempted by a DEP Superseding Order. *DeGrace v. Conservation Commn. of Harwich*, 31 Mass.App.Ct. 132, 136 (Ma. 1991).

It is important to note that Massachusetts defines wetland resource areas differently from the Clean Water Act §404: Isolated lands subject to flooding are included irrespective of any connection to a navigable waterway. "Wetlands" are more broadly defined by the state, and protection extends at least 100 feet beyond the resource area. Therefore, the state's geographic jurisdiction may differ from that of the Corps. Moreover, a local bylaw may exert broader jurisdiction than that of the state or federal government.

These jurisdictions overlap. In Massachusetts, under the Massachusetts Wetlands Protection Act, when dredge and fill activities are proposed for a wetland, if the wetland is less than 5,000 square feet the property owner needs to apply for an Order of Conditions from the local conservation commission. If the wetland is larger than 5,000 square feet but smaller than an acre, the property owner must apply for an Order of Conditions, a water quality certification in accordance with the Clean Water Act §401, and — at the discretion of the Corps — an individual §404 permit. When the wetland is greater than one acre in size, an individual water quality certification (§401) and an individual dredge and fill permit (§404) are necessary, along with compliance with all state and local requirements. A Florida state court held that fisherman could pursue claims for economic loss due to pollution released in a public bay by a fertilizer company's waste storage facility even though they had no property interest in the bay or directly owned property affected. The Florida Supreme Court held that no property interest is required to have standing to sue under state water law that provides a private cause of action for negligent pollution releases under common law. *Curd v. Mosaic Fertilizer LLC*, 39 So. 3d 1216 (Fla. 2010).

Examples

1. You have recently inherited a piece of property from your grandfather. The property, which is located on Cape Cod in Massachusetts, was purchased years ago and has never been developed. You keep the property for several years and finally save enough money to build a house on it. You notice that some of the property is physically low-lying and decide to have the property surveyed to ensure that you will not violate any state or federal wetlands regulations. The survey indicates that you can build with no problem. You draw plans and prepare to begin building. You apply to the town for a routine building permit (see Chapter 10) and are notified that a recently enacted town bylaw disallows all building on property below an elevation of 88 feet. The bylaw was established to protect wetlands conservation land. Your plans require building at an elevation of 85 feet. You have hired an expert whose opinion is that there is no scientifically discernible difference in impacts to the wetland if the ordinance were based on 85 feet rather than 88. What actions, if any, are legally available to you?

2. What if, after your efforts, the law is amended to 85 feet? Could you file suit for a temporary regulatory "taking"?

Explanations

1. Work with the Massachusetts laws on this one. The first action should be an appeal to the town. Since the restriction is based on a town bylaw, no appeal is available through the Massachusetts Department of Environmental Protection. If the town does not have an appeal process, then the only available alternative is to file suit against the town. The basis of the suit would be that the ordinance is unconstitutional because it is a government taking of private property without compensation.

The cases to support this argument would be the Supreme Court's decision in *Lucas*, as well as a Massachusetts case, *Lopes v. City of Peabody*, 629 N.E.2d 1312 (Mass. 1994). The *Lopes* case was based on appeal of a town's wetlands ordinance. The fact pattern was similar to the case at hand. In *Lopes*, the case was remanded based on the ruling in *Lucas*. The Massachusetts court found that the basis for the ordinance was not related to any legitimate state interest. Therefore, the town was ordered to amend its ordinance in such a way as to allow the plaintiff landowner to build on the property. The original bylaw deprived the landowner of all economically beneficial use, but the court said this was not a taking because the statute eventually was amended. The case was later appealed to the U.S. Supreme Court. With this precedent, the taking should be easily established. The argument will be that the bylaw deprives you of all economically beneficial use of your property.

2. If the town amends the bylaw to reflect an elevation of 85 feet, you can now build the house. You can, however, sue for a temporary taking for the time that you were unable to build while you were in court. In *First Evangelical Lutheran Church v. County of Los Angeles*, 482 U.S. 304 (1987), a local ordinance prevented the church from rebuilding its campground because it was located in a flood area. The Court held that a taking had occurred and compensation was necessary. The Court tailored the holding to state that it was a *temporary* regulatory taking. When a private landowner is denied use of his or her property, the landowner must be compensated for the period of the taking.

PROTECTED NATURAL RESOURCE AREAS

Over the last three decades, one-third of the world's natural resources have been consumed, according to the World Wildlife Federation. The preservation of public natural resources is manifest in the legal rules that govern use, allotment, and preservation of lands owned by the federal government. Historically public land law was concerned with the distribution or land transfers of title from the federal government to the individual states or private citizens. Today, the law focuses more on the proper use and preservation of such precious resources rather than on their transfer.

There are almost 200 million acres of federal lands in the United States. Federally owned lands make up about one-third of the total national land surface area, which does not include the approximately 1 billion submerged acres offshore owned by the United States government. The United States owns land in all 50 states; most of these lands are concentrated in the West and Alaska. These parcels of lands are natural resources in and of themselves, but they also provide other economic benefits and opportunities ranging from mineral rights, oil, gas, coal, and timber. Most of these lands are predominantly unproductive for agriculture because of lack of water, which is why homesteaders never claimed these parcels.

The Antiquities Act of 1906 granted the President the power to declare historic landmarks, historic and prehistoric structures, and other objects of historic or scientific interest situated upon federal lands. 16 U.S.C. §431-433. Fourteen Presidents have used the Antiquities Act to establish 122 national monuments covering 70 million acres in 28 states, one territory, and the District of Columbia.

The most valuable public domain lands passed into private ownership many years ago. The major resources of public lands in approximate order of their values are water, minerals, timber, range, wildlife, recreation, preservation. These resources constitute a significant economic resource valued in the billions of dollars. But of importance also are the noneconomic benefits derived from public lands: Millions of people visit and explore these vast public resources every year.

The Agencies in Control

In the beginning there were parks. Originally, 2 million acres were set aside for Yellowstone National Park in 1872. By 1902, Congress had designated 6 national parks; there were 49 national parks in existence by 1986. The National Park Act of 1916 defines goals of preservation and recreation and gives the National Park Service (NPS) the mission of regulating park use to conserve the scenery and the natural and historic objects within these lands. The National Park System covers more than 84 million acres of land and is composed of 392 sites. Of those, 122 are historical parks and 58 are national parks.

Other important federal statutes invest various agencies with overlapping authority over natural resource areas. The statutory framework of natural resource law is a complex web of land management laws and resource-specific laws, both of which can overlap. There are land statutes that authorize the grant, sale, or acquisition of federal lands to or from state and private ownership. Resource regulations deal with hardrock minerals and fossil fuels.

The U.S. Fish and Wildlife Service (FWS) mission is divided between land management and regulation of wildlife protection. The Bureau of Land Management (BLM) is the agency in charge of all lands not reserved as parks or wildlife refuges. The Federal Land Policy and Management Act of 1976 (FLPMA) sets out some of the BLM's goals and missions though hundreds of federal statutes also apply to its operations. The Forest Service is responsible for the national forest management system with a charge to set strict

11.1 Main Administrative Authorities

	National Park Service	Fish & Wildlife Service	Bureau of Land Management	Forest Service
Location	Department of the Interior	Department of the Interior	Department of the Interior	Department of Agriculture
Headquarters	Washington, D.C.	Washington, D.C.	Washington, D.C.	Washington, D.C.
Offices	10 regional offices	7 regional offices	National office, 12 state offices, district offices	9 regional offices
General scope of authority	National parks, monuments, historic sites	Wildlife protection and refuges	All other land not classified as national parks	Management of timber resources

standards and limits on timber harvesting. These main administrative authorities are displayed in Exhibit 11.1 but there are also another half-dozen agencies that contribute to public natural resource law, such as the Army Corps of Engineers, the Bureau of Indian Affairs, and the Bureau of Reclamation. Which agency takes the lead? Timber sales: mainly regulated by the Forest Service; also by the BLM. Management of the nation's range: BLM; the Forest Service and FWS devote large portions of their lands to grazing, which is also allowed in some national park areas. Wildlife: FWS; each of the mentioned federal agencies has its own wildlife-related duties.

The four main federal land management agencies, NPS, FWS, BLM, and the Forest Service, are executive, as opposed to independent, agencies. This means that they are subservient to larger agency agendas. Three of these four agencies are housed within the Department of the Interior; the Forest Service falls under the purview of the Department of Agriculture. As long as an agency complies with proper procedures, it has the authority and discretion to decide whether to sell land, lease property, grant royalty interests, or not allow certain exploitation. BLM policies feature multiple-use management, striking a balance between recreational, mineral, timber, watershed, wildlife, scenic, and historical values and sustained yield, controlling the depletion resulting from uses over time so as to protect future uses. 43 U.S.C. §1702. Board of City Commissioners, 22 IBLA 182, 189 (1975). Actions must comply with NEPA and the Administrative Procedure Act (see Chapters 2 and 3 for more discussion of the NEPA and APA processes applicable to federal agencies). *Id*; *Walt's Racing Ass'n*, 18 IBLA 359, 365 (1975).

A general precondition to using or enjoying a public natural resource is having access. No one general rule applies to access to federal lands. Access issues are complex due to the actual physical fragmentation of federal lands and to the intermixing of private and state parcels among federal lands. There are untold numbers of alleged access rights by use or ancient statute rights. Many access questions are governed by the FLPMA, but many other statutes also exert authority. More users are demanding greater access to natural resources by requesting road access to harvest timber, coal, and minerals, and for access for recreational purposes.

The access problem is two-dimensional: rights and means. An individual may have a right to enter upon a federal land but the federal agencies aforementioned have a right to control and restrict the means for that access. Most persons who access federal lands do so under revocable licenses at the government's will. Many statutes authorize the federal land management agencies to close areas for resource protection purposes. In *American Timber Co. v. Bergland*, 473 F. Supp. 310 (D. Mont. 1979), the court upheld the Forest Service's decision to reduce timber cutting levels below those announced in its land plans because those numbers constituted maximum amounts only. In *Intermountain Forest Industry Ass'n v. Lyng*, 683 F. Supp. 1330 (D. Wyo. 1988), the court quickly dispensed the plaintiff's argument that a reduction in the amount of timber allowed to be cut violated its federal land plans. Lessees and contractors possess some contractual rights that may limit or impose conditions that alleviate the "at will" permissions and licenses.

Agencies in charge of federal land management have the power and authority to charge a fee for use of federal lands. 16 U.S.C. §4601-4604(f); *Rogue River Outfitters*, 63 IBLA 373, 381 (1982). These fees may be for use of the land, admission to the land, daily recreational use fees, and special recreation permit fees. Section 4 of the Land and Water Conservation Fund Act, 16 U.S.C. §4601 *et seq.*, permits such fees but does not define what kinds of recreational users are subject to fees. Fees are reasonable and permissible if they are fair and equitable considering the cost of the use to the government, benefit is received by the permit holder, and they comply with the public policy served by charging fees and comparable agency practice. *Rogue River Outfitters* at 384. Fees imposed on commercial users of federal lands are generally upheld as reasonable. *Upper Rogue River Outfitters*, 93 IBLA 103 (1986); *Noah's World of Water*, 141 IBLA 288 (1987).

The federal government is often sued for injuries. Individuals can sue the federal government, under the Federal Tort Claims Act, for injury or death caused by negligent or wrongful acts or omissions of an employee of the government within the scope of employment, to the extent that the federal government as a person would also be liable. 28 U.S.C.

§1346(b). Typically, the government is protected unless an employee has committed a willful, malicious, or intentional act. *Dehne v. United States*, 1991 U.S. Dist. LEXIS 14619 (N.D. Ill. 1991). To the extent that no fee is charged and warnings were posted to discourage the dangerous act, and such danger was not hidden by the government, recovery typically is denied. *Davidow v. United States*, 583 F. Supp. 1170 (W.D. Pa. 1984) (where federal employee failed to replace a buoy that directly led to a boat collision and injury, the federal government was liable); *Dehne* (when plaintiff ignored safety brochure, safety video, posted warnings, and signs before being injured rock climbing at a national monument in Utah, under Utah's comparative negligence law, the federal government was not liable).

Wilderness Areas

The Interior Department Board of Land Appeals defined a wilderness area as an area "where the earth and its community of life are untrammeled by man, where man himself is a visitor who does not remain . . . an area of undeveloped Federal land retaining its primeval character and influence, without permanent improvements or human habitation, which is protected and managed so as to preserve its natural conditions. . . ." *Animal Protection Institute of America*, 61 IBLA 222, 223 (1982). Deference is given to agency determinations of wilderness areas. *Conoco, Inc.*, 65 IBLA 84 (1982).

Once Congress declares an area a wilderness area, very few commercial or commodity uses are permissible. Wilderness lands are designated primarily for primitive, nonmotorized recreation. The Wilderness Act of 1964, 16 U.S.C. §1133(c), is silent on this point but the courts have held that logging in a wilderness area is prohibited unless specifically allowed by statute. However, the Forest Service is allowed to take such measures necessary in the control of fire, insects, and disease. There are a series of cases concerning tree cutting to deal with pine beetle infestation. In *Sierra Club v. Block*, 622 F. Supp. 842 (D. Colo. 1985), the court refused to preliminarily enjoin timber cutting because the balance of harms indicated that cutting would save more trees in the long run than not cutting. The court did order the Forest Service to cease cutting noninfested hardwoods and adhere to its strict policy of wilderness protection.

The Wilderness Act permits grazing to continue if it predates 1965, subject to reasonable necessary regulation. There is controversy: Does grazing by livestock actually contradict preservation of a wilderness area? The courts defer to the agencies in determining what are appropriate levels of grazing related to ecosystems. Judicial intervention is unlikely unless the levels allowed are so high as to cause obvious damage. See *Perkins v. Bergland*, 608 F.2d 803 (9th Cir. 1979) (courts will defer in substantial measure to management judgments on appropriate grazing levels).

As of January 1, 1984, wilderness areas became off-limits to new mineral location and leasing. Leases which were executed pre-1984 are still subject to reasonable regulation consistent with both the necessary mineral activity and restoration of the disturbed areas. Also not allowed in these protected areas is the use of motorized vehicles. In *O'Brien v. State*, 711 F.2d 1144 (Wyo. 1986), the court established that customary use of an area for landing airplanes was not a right and could be prohibited by the Forest Service.

Recreation is permissible, if not preferred, on all federal lands. Congress authorized recreation as one of the allowed uses in a wilderness area and one of the two dominant purposes for use on national park system lands. Hiking and camping raise few legal concerns; hunting, rafting, off-road vehicles, and skiing raise environmental concerns. Hunting and fishing have been held to be permissible forms of recreation for wilderness uses. Regulation of other permissible forms of recreation, such as hiking, camping, and rafting is within the agency's discretion.

The courts in numerous cases held that Congress may place restrictions on recreational access to federal lands. The courts generally afford recreation equal status with competing resource uses. In *United States v. Curtis-Nevada Mines, Inc.* 611 F.2d 1277 (9th Cir. 1980), the Ninth Circuit found an implied license to create free access to public lands. The court noted that Congress never required formal written permission and that agency regulations uniformly assumed free access, except to areas specifically closed or restricted. All Americans have a right to access public lands for recreation until Congress stipulates otherwise. Land management agencies have broad discretion to regulate the permissible types of recreation but they do not have absolute authority to revoke or place restrictive conditions upon basic access. By contrast, commodity uses such as grazing and lumbering require formal prior permission from an agency.

The increased use of off-road vehicles can seriously damage an ecosystem, interfere with or overwhelm other uses, and deprive others of recreational solitude. It is estimated that 42 million Americans participate in off-road travel annually. Almost 1 million all-terrain vehicles are sold in the United States each year. Where can they be used?

First, motorized vehicles are flatly prohibited in any wilderness area. A wilderness area, by definition, is roadless. But off-road vehicles are not necessarily barred from wilderness study areas not yet designated as wilderness if the agency retains enough control to prevent permanent damage. The National Park Service generally prohibits motorized off-road activity. The NPS allows the use of motor boats in some areas but it does have broad discretion to restrict such uses. Like the Park Service, the FWS has nearly complete control to regulate motor vehicle use in wildlife refuges. On the other hand, the Forest Service must allow recreation while avoiding permanent impairment of land productivity. The U.S. Forest Service rules on this topic are generally more relaxed.

Congress has not established legal guidelines for the use of motorized vehicles on BLM public lands. BLM has the power to close an area to off-road vehicles. In *Sierra Club v. Clark*, 774 F.2d 1406 (9th Cir. 1985), the court stated that the appropriate area for assessing damage by these vehicles was the entire 12 million acre California Desert Conservation Area (CDCA), not just the immediate area subjected to intensive use. Congress could alleviate this problem by changing the status of the CDCA to a wilderness area if it so chose and eliminate all such use.

The Supreme Court refused to force the BLM to take affirmative action promptly to restrict off-road vehicles that were using specific tracts of roadless lands in Utah. *Norton v. Southern Utah Wilderness Alliance*, 542 U.S. 55 (2004). This created de facto roads in roadless areas and thereby converted these areas (that were supposed to be kept as wilderness areas) into areas with roads, which effectively disqualified them from future wilderness status. The court refused to require that the agency keep these areas in a status consistent with their ultimate wilderness designation and refused to require the agency to act in a specific time frame or in a specific manner. *Id.* In this situation, the court refused to "compel agency action unlawfully withheld or unreasonably delayed," pursuant to 5 U.S.C. §706(1).

Timber Exploitation

The National Forest Management Act of 1976 (NFMA) contains many provisions that serve as limitations on the Forest Service's discretion to allow timber harvesting in certain areas or by certain means. First, the congressional budget appropriations determine how much timber may be harvested any fiscal year. Independent of the budget constraints, the secretary must limit annual timber sales to the amount that can be sustained in perpetuity. Timber harvesting must be limited to areas where no irreversible watershed damage will occur. Diversity of plant and animal species must remain. Several goals must be satisfied before clear-cutting is permitted:

- The Forest Service is generally prohibited from selecting a cutting method based solely on economic or gross production grounds.
- It must perform a review which finds that clear-cutting is the optimal method as judged by the land use plans.
- The harvest must be limited in size, shaped to blend with the existing terrain, and protect the current natural resources.

The courts have upheld the discretion of the President in setting aside areas for national monuments under the Antiquities Act, 16 U.S.C. §431.

Mountain States Legal Foundation v. Bush, 306 F.3d 1132 (D.C. Cir. 2002), *cert. denied*, 540 U.S. 812 (2003); *Tulare County v. Bush*, 306 F.3d 1138 (D.C. Cir. 2002), *cert. denied*, 540 U.S. 813 (2003). In both of these cases, the plaintiff counties were trying to limit, unsuccessfully, President Clinton's making a designation of national monuments involving a land area that they thought was greater than the minimum necessary to set aside to preserve the monument.

The NFMA does not require that the Forest Service reach any profit level from any of its timber sales or its annual sales. The Act requires the agency to prepare a cost benefit analysis in determining suitability of land for timber production. This allows challenge to such timber contracts. See *Thomas v. Peterson*, 743 F.2d 754 (9th Cir. 1985); *Big Hole Ranchers Ass'n v. U.S. Forest Service*, 686 F. Supp. 256 (D. Mont. 1988).

Before it can sell timber, the Forest Service must assess the value, determine conditions, advertise the sale, and comply with the provisions of NEPA. Several cases have held against the Forest Service for failure to comply with NEPA. See *Sierra Club v. Block*, 622 F. Supp. 842 (D. Colo. 1985) (no new EIS required); *NWF v. U.S. Forest Service*, 592 F. Supp. 931 (D. Or. 1984) (enjoined a timber harvesting plan for lack of an appropriate EIS on the adverse environmental consequences); *Sierra Club v. U.S. Forest Service*, 843 F.2d 1190 (9th Cir. 1988) (forestwide EIS required before timber sales).

The Endangered Species Act exerts a significant impact on the Forest Service timber program. *Sierra Club v. Lyng*, 694 F. Supp. 1260 (E.D. Tex. 1988) (enjoined the Forest Service permanently from clear-cutting within a three-quarter-mile radius of all known red-cockaded woodpecker colony sites, effectively ending a substantial number of timber sales); *Seattle Audubon Society v. Evans*, 771 F. Supp. 1081 (W.D. Wash. 1991) (enjoined the awarding of any timber contracts in areas suitable as spotted owl habitat until a protective plan was prepared).

Mineral Exploitation

Federal lands in the West contain immense quantities of coal. Historically, two paths were taken to delegate mineral rights. Where coal was known to exist, the Department of the Interior sold coal leases through a competitive bidding process. Alternatively, "preference right" leasing involved application for a permit to prospect for minerals in a certain area. If the applicant discovered coal, it would then apply for a preference lease. The Department of the Interior would grant the lease if the coal deposits were found by the prospector. The Federal Coal Leasing Amendment Act of 1976 (FCLAA) abolished preference leases, subject to maintenance of valid preexisting rights. This eliminated the noncompetitive process of preference leases and required competitive bidding on all new leases.

Generally now, federal coal leases are sold for a fixed royalty rate (a modest rental per acre) and a bonus bid. The bid will be awarded in competitive auction to the highest qualified bidder who meets or exceeds the sum predetermined to be the fair market value for the leasehold. No bid can be accepted below the fair market value. Leases issued under the FCLAA are for a term of 20 years and for such term thereafter as coal is produced in commercial quantities. But the lease will terminate if commercial quantities are not produced within 10 years after lease issuance. No individual or entity may hold or control at one time more than 46,080 acres in any one state or 100,000 acres in the United States.

In order to secure a mining claim, mining companies often put up fences around their mining areas. This can prevent the public from enjoying the benefits of the service area of what is otherwise public land. A mining claim on federal land is perfected by applying for a patent mining claim. 30 U.S.C. §612(b). Where a mining claim is granted, the government does not relinquish its ownership status.

Grazing

The federal government historically made little or no effort to protect the public lands from overgrazing or the resulting range wars that developed among cattlemen. In 1890, the Supreme Court ruled that the failure of the Congress to regulate such entry onto public lands for grazing purposes constituted an implied license, whereby anyone could graze livestock on unreserved lands for free. Although Congress has allowed some level of grazing in national parks, wildlife refuges, and wilderness areas, the majority of grazing is done on lands managed by the Forest Service. The Forest Service from its inception prohibited grazing without a permit and the Supreme Court upheld that policy in 1911. In an effort to protect wild horses on public lands, the Wild-Free Roaming Horses and Burros Act of 1971 was enacted.

The 1934 Taylor Grazing Act authorized the Department of the Interior to regulate and allocate grazing privileges by a preference permit system. The immediate result was that about 15 percent of permittees controlled over 80 percent of the BLM public lands. In 1974, the court in NRDC v. Morton, 388 F. Supp. 829 (D.D.C. 1974), ordered the BLM to prepare environmental impact statements on all its grazing programs.

Let's contrast grazing use and timber use. First, grazing differs from timber harvesting because grazing is an ongoing year-to-year activity, while timber exploitation is cyclical. Second, unlike exploitation of other federal land resources, federal grass is available only to adjacent landowners and permit use is limited to the number of cattle or sheep grazed in the baseline years 1929-1934. Third, the grazing permittee acquired his or her rights by virtue of use circumstances three-quarters of a century or more ago; the timber taking is a one-time license. Therefore, there are no preferential timber renewal rights as with grazing rights. Finally, if one wishes to harvest timber or drill for oil, one must seek case-by-case geographically specific permission. Grazing is sanctioned on nearly all BLM lands that contain enough grass.

The federal grazing permit or lease has surplus value because the fees ranchers pay for these privileges are far below the fair market value of the service. It thus represents a substantial federal subsidy, allowing users to graze for as little as one-tenth of private grazing fees. Setting of the fee at fair market value would reinvigorate the rangelands by eliminating economic incentives to graze marginal tracts of grasslands.

Energy and the Environment

"Energy is the only universal currency. One of its many forms must be transformed to another in order for stars to shine, planets to rotate, plants to grow, and civilizations to evolve. Recognition of this universality was one of the great achievements of nineteenth-century science, but, surprisingly, this recognition has not led to comprehensive, systematic studies that view our world through the powerful prism of energy."

Vaclav Smil

"The change in the scale of power opened the future. . . . Power is a new preoccupation, in a sense a new idea, in science. . . . Sources of energy were sought in nature: wind, sun, water, steam, coal. And a question suddenly became concrete: Why are they all one? What relation exists between them? That had never been asked before."

J. Bronowski, The Ascent of Man, 1973

"I sell here, sir, what all the world desires to have — power."

James Boulton (coinventor of steam engine), England, 1776

"I shall make electricity so cheap that only the rich can afford to burn candles."

Thomas Edison

"The basic tenet of high energy projections is that the more energy we use, the better off we are. But how much energy we use to accomplish our social goals could instead be considered a measure less of our success than of our failure — just as the amount of traffic we must endure to get to where we want to go is a measure not of well-being but rather of our failure to establish a rational settlement pattern."

Amory Lovins, Soft Energy Paths

ENERGY AND THE ENVIRONMENT

As Chapters 5 and 6 make clear, the production of electric power is a major source of environmental pollution. The burning of fossil fuels creates copious quantities of various criteria pollutants and other pollutants. Fossil fuels have been burned for only the last 300 years. Along with the automobile and industrial by-product pollution, conventional electric power production is a major source of environmental concern. In the view of some environmentalists, electric power is a *negative* — a major source of pollution. In a societal view, electric power is a resource that has shaped the modern era. While the United States uses approximately 25 percent of the world's energy resources annually, it produces approximately 30 percent of the world's gross domestic product. Just as the automobile has transformed land use and spatial patterns of human interaction — and has created a second major source of pollution — electric power is formative societally.

The Role of Electricity

Our sun is one of a family of stars known to astronomers as Yellow Dwarfs. It is powered by several kinds of fusion reactions that have consumed 11 billion pounds of hydrogen each second for the past 4 to 5 billion years, and are expected to continue for another 4 to 5 billion years. The earth's surface receives about 160 W/m^2 of the energy from this solar combustion. Energy used by humankind on the earth equals only about 0.01 percent of the total solar energy reaching the earth. In fact, no nation on earth uses more energy than the energy content contained in the sunlight that strikes its existing buildings every day. The solar energy that falls on roads in the United States each year contains roughly as much energy content as all the fossil fuel consumed in the world during that same year.

Unlike finite fossil fuels (which are comprised of decomposed organic matter, which is renewable but only over millennia), solar energy represents a constantly replenished flow, rather than an existing stock that is diminished by its use. Tomorrow, the earth will have exactly as much solar energy as it has today, regardless of how much solar energy is used and consumed each day. By contrast, burning a barrel of oil or a cubic meter of natural gas diminishes permanently that quantity of fossil fuels for the next day and for future generations. In 1997, all nations on earth consumed 26.4 billion barrels of oil, 81.7 trillion cubic feet of natural gas, and 5.2 billion tons of coal.

Approximately 20 large companies control and market about half of all the fossil fuel used in America. While many nations — particularly developing nations — have no significant reserves of oil, coal, or natural gas, every nation has renewable energy in some form — sunlight, wind, ocean wave power, and so on. This makes the interests involved in fossil fuel extremely concentrated, while solar energy interests are much more decentralized and diverse. Notwithstanding these elements, conventional fossil fuels, and not renewable fuels, are the primary energy sources deployed. Fossil fuels dominate electric energy production in the United States and worldwide. As of 2010, there were 150,000 MW of wind generation in the world. The bulk of this was installed in Europe.

The role of electric power is not always transparent. Without electric power, there would be no high-rise cities (electricity is essential for elevators and air conditioning, basic to the modern high-rise), no information superhighway, and no electric lights. There are perceived benefits from dense, high-rise urban environments: the proximity of many workers close together, the energy efficiency of dense urban development and the feasibility of mass transit to serve it, and the creation of vital, populated urban centers. There also are environmental disadvantages of high-rise development: There are significant wind vectors created by high-rise buildings, and unless mixed-use development is planned into the process, tall office blocks can be deserted and become lifeless communities in the evening. Note that while Paris is the most densely built city in the Western world, it has few high-rise structures and many parks and large people-friendly boulevards.

The first "skyscrapers" were invented in New York and Chicago around the turn of the twentieth century and became symbols of industrial might and power. In 1913, the Woolworth Building in New York soared 48 stories to 797 feet, and was considered one of the first modern skyscrapers. Yet, the desire to build tall structures did not originate only a century ago. Historically, those with the most resources have sought to build the tallest structures.

In the tiny town of San Gimignano in Tuscany, Italy, beginning about 1300, each wealthy family built an entirely useless tower to try to outdo its neighbors. At one point, this tiny town boasted 70 brick towers that soared as high as 175 feet taller than the height of Niagara Falls. During the Middle Ages, the church, at the height of its power, often constructed the tallest building on the most prominent piece of land.

During the twentieth century, the tallest buildings in the world were constructed by those with the most economic assets (the Chrysler Building in New York, 1931; the Empire State Building in New York, at 102 stories and 1,250 feet, in the 1930s; the World Trade Centers in New York at 110 stories and 1,368 feet, 1972; the Sears Tower in Chicago at 1,450 feet, 1974; the Petronas Towers in Kuala Lumpur, Malaysia, 88 stories rising 1,483 feet). With globalization, the skyscraper traveled abroad. Among the world's 20 tallest skyscrapers, not a single one was built in the United

States in the last 25 years of the twentieth century; 10 of the tallest 20 are in Southeast Asia, and 3 are in the Middle East.

Although an international phenomenon, the skyscraper would be impossible without four American inventions. First, using again an energy-intensive process, Americans invented the steel frame that allowed a thin steel skeleton on the interior to hold glass windows and metal panels on the skin of the building. This avoids the necessity otherwise to employ walls as much as nine or ten feet thick at the base, and allows much greater height.

Second, in 1857, the first passenger elevator was invented and installed in New York. Shortly thereafter, elevator technology soared to higher realms when powered by electricity, another new American "invention." This made the higher floors, with the best view, the most sought after. Electric high-speed elevators made height accessible and marketable (although elevators in very tall skyscrapers take up great amounts of interior space; at the World Trade Centers in New York, there were 104 passenger elevators in each tower).

The third American invention was Edison's invention of the electric light, which made possible illuminating the new larger interior spaces of massive skyscrapers, which can span as much as an acre of floor space per floor (the size of a football field). It is not possible to illuminate a large interior space only with natural illumination. Fourth, the invention of electric air-conditioning by Carrier Corporation in the United States made it possible to counteract the heat produced by electric lights, building occupants, and office equipment, and create a comfortable working environment.

Electricity is an absolutely essential resource in developing countries. For equatorial countries, which contain the bulk of the world's population, the ability to electrically air-condition space is a prerequisite to commercial growth. Lee Kuan Yew, founder and former prime minister of Singapore, identified the air conditioner as the most important invention of the twentieth century for Singapore, which may be a prototypic success story of recent commercial development.

While the industrial age increased physical mobility, expanding one person's range from a few hundred people in one's village to hundreds of thousands of people potentially within driving range, the electronic age increases virtual range of interaction by more than another thousandfold, to hundreds of millions of people within electronic reach. In fact, when you visit developing nations, one of the first things you notice is the relationship between electrification and the economic standard of living. The majority of the world's people do not have electricity, or the things that it brings, even today. There are almost 2 billion people in the world, primarily in South Asia and sub-Saharan Africa, with no access to electricity. Others in poor countries with access to electricity cannot afford to purchase it.

In this chapter, we will focus on energy as a *resource* — with polluting repercussions from its use. As a resource, while electricity does not always have

12.1 Electric Utility Net Generation, Total (All Sectors)

By Sector, 1989-2011

Trillion Kilowatthours

5 —
4 —
3 —
2 —
1 —

Electric Power

Commercial and Industrial

1989 1992 1995 1998 2001 2004 2007 2010

By Source Category, 2011

Trillion Kilowatthours

3 —
2 —
1 —
0

Fossil Fuels	Nuclear Electric Power	Renewable Energy
2.8	0.8	0.5

By Source, 2011

Coal 42%

Other[1] 6%

Natural Gas 25%

Hydroelectric Power[2] 8%

Nuclear Electric Power 19%

By Source, 1949-2011

Trillion Kilowatthours

2.5 —
2.0 —
1.5 —
1.0 —
0.5 —
0.0

Coal

Natural Gas

Nuclear Electric Power

Hydroelectric Power[2]

Other[1]

1950 1955 1960 1965 1970 1975 1980 1985 1990 1995 2000 2005 2010

[1] Wind, petroleum, wood, waste, geothermal, other gases, solar thermal and photovoltaic, batteries, chemicals, hydrogen, pitch, purchased steam, sulfur, miscellaneous technologies, and nonrenewable waste (municipal solid waste from nonbiogenic sources, and tire-derived fuels).

[2] Conventional hydroelectric power and pumped storage.

Note: Sum of components may not equal 100 percent due to independent rounding.

Sources: U.S. Department of Energy: Energy Information Administration (U.S. DoE EIA), *Annual Energy Review 2011*, tables 8.2a, 8.2b, and 8.2d.

substitutes, its efficiency and deployment involve critical decisions of which every environmental attorney and policymaker should be aware. Along with the automobile, electricity is the defining technology of modern America.

The History of Power

High Energy

Where does electricity fit in the energy mix? Energy is used in roughly equal shares by three sectors, the (1) transportation, (2) industrial, and (3) residential/commercial sectors.

The transportation sector uses energy principally in the form of refined petroleum for gasoline, aviation, and diesel fuels. The transportation sector utilizes more petroleum than the industrial, residential, commercial, and electric utility sectors combined. Increasingly, these petroleum imports come less from OPEC, and more from Mexico, non-Venezuelan Latin America, and other non-OPEC nations. In 1974, President Nixon pledged that the United States would not be dependent on any other country for energy by the end of the decade. By the end of that decade, oil imports into the United States had doubled. After the second oil disruption in the United States in 1979, President Carter promised that "beginning this moment, the nation will never again use more foreign oil than we did in 1977." Oil imports doubled yet again by 2006. There is minimal use of electricity by the transportation sector.

The industrial, commercial, and residential sectors burn fossil fuels directly. Oil, natural gas, and coal are burned in furnaces or boilers to produce heat to warm buildings or to produce heat for manufacturing processes such as glass, ceramics, pulp and paper, oil refining, and so on. Almost 20 percent of all energy in California is used to treat, transport, and deliver water in the state (see Chapter 7). Electricity is used to power machinery, operate lights, provide refrigeration, and sometimes to heat buildings.

The United States is a net importer of natural gas, principally from Canada, with some liquefied natural gas (LNG) from Algeria, the Caribbean, Indonesia, and elsewhere. The United States also is a net importer of electricity, again principally from Canada.

The principal fuel used for electric power generation in the United States is coal, followed in turn by nuclear power, hydroelectric power, natural gas, and oil. These energy sources are illustrated in Exhibit 12.1. Electricity is used in relatively equal amounts by the industrial, residential, and commercial/street lighting sectors. See Exhibit 12.2.

The industrial sector receives the lowest oil and natural gas prices, followed by the commercial and then the residential sectors. These relative prices are illustrated in Exhibit 12.3. As with gas and oil, the industrial sector also pays less for electricity than does the residential sector (Exhibit 12.4).

12.2 Electricity Overview

Overview, 2011

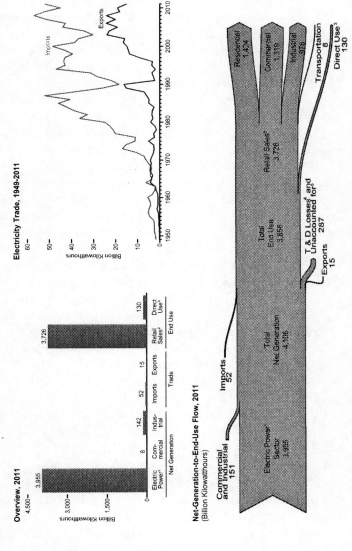

Electricity Trade, 1949-2011

Net-Generation-to-End-Use Flow, 2011
(Billion Kilowatthours)

[1] Electricity-only and combined-heat-and-power plants within the NAICS 22 category whose primary business is to sell electricity, or electricity and heat, to the public.
[2] Electricity retail sales to ultimate customers reported by electric utilities and other energy service providers.
[3] See table 8.1, footnote 8, in the source document.
[4] Transmission and distribution losses (electricity losses that occur between the point of generation and delivery to the customer). See Note, "Electrical System Energy Losses," at the end of Section 2 in the source document.
[5] Data collection frame differences and nonsampling error.
Sources: U.S. Department of Energy, Energy Information Administration (U.S. DoE EIA), *Annual Energy Review 2011*, tables 8.1 and 8.9.

Electricity as a Special Resource

In many ways, electricity is special. Electric energy cannot be stored, as can oil or natural gas. Electricity is an energy *carrier*, a way of transmitting energy rather than creating it. Carriers, such as electricity or hydrogen, provide mobility for energy sources. For example, if one were able to make direct use of lightning, then that would be a pure form of electric energy source, rather than a carrier.

If not utilized within a few nanoseconds of its creation, it is gone. There is no inherent "shelf life" for electricity as for energy sources in their chemical fossil fuel states. If not used immediately surplus electricity warms the transmission lines, is grounded, or overloads the circuits, but it does no work. So the challenge with electricity is to "use it or lose it." In certain circumstances, potential electric energy can be stored in the form of captured water — storing rainfall behind dams, to be released to turn water turbines when it is needed.

Electricity is a very high-quality energy source. Its production requires an additional step to convert the chemical energy in a fossil fuel into *electrical* energy. Many machines and devices can operate only with electricity — there is no substitute fuel. There are some tasks for which electricity has no peer, but there are other tasks for which it is a substitute — such as heating applications. One pays a premium price in lost efficiency and money for heating with electricity. Converting fossil fuels in their chemical states to electricity sacrifices as much as 60 to 75 percent of the potential energy inherent in the chemical fuel. To then reconvert this premium electric energy back to low-level heat sacrifices its premium energy status.

Most electricity is produced by burning fossil fuel to boil water.[1] The boiling water produces steam, which turns the blades of a turbine connected to an electric generating set, as it rapidly exits the turbine into which it is injected. Approximately two-thirds of the atoms burned in fossil fuels are hydrogen, with the rest being carbon.

The first commercial nuclear reactor for electric generation was completed in 1957 in Shippingport, Pennsylvania. In the 1960s, the AEC believed that by the year 2000 over 1,000 nuclear reactors would be operating in the United States. Nuclear power is generated in 104 commercial reactors in 65 nuclear power plants located in 31 states.

Commercial nuclear reactors operate by using radioactive fuel rods containing packets of enriched uranium to heat water into steam to turn turbines to produce electricity. Uranium oxide fuel assemblies for domestic power production reactors are produced in one of four facilities in South Carolina, Virginia, North Carolina, or Washington. Typically, a reactor needs

---

1. Some technologies for producing electric power do not boil water. These include hydroelectric power where running watercourses turn turbine blades connected to an electric generator; solar photovoltaic cells that use sunlight to create direct current electricity by causing a polarization of positively and negatively charged electrons; and fuel cells which create a chemical reaction that frees electrons to create electric energy without any combustion.

12.3 Natural Gas Consumption by Sector

By Sector, 1949-2011

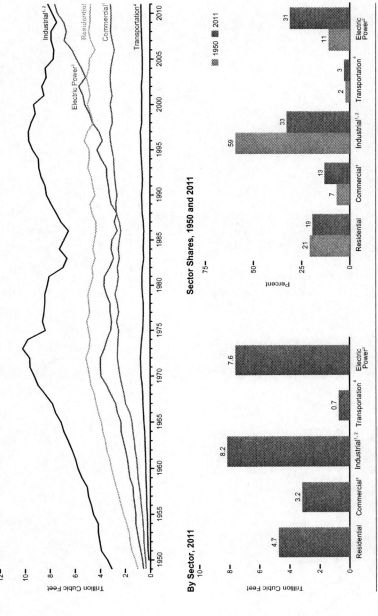

Trillion Cubic Feet

Industrial[1,2]

Residential[1]

Commercial[1]

Electric Power[3]

Transportation[4]

1950 1955 1960 1965 1970 1975 1980 1985 1990 1995 2000 2005 2010

Sector Shares, 1950 and 2011

▒ 1950 ▓ 2011

Percent

75 — 50 — 25 — 0

Residential[1] Commercial[1] Industrial[1,2] Transportation[4] Electric Power[3]

21 19   7 13   59 33   2 3   11 31

By Sector, 2011

Trillion Cubic Feet

10 — 8 — 6 — 4 — 2 — 0

Residential[1] Commercial[1] Industrial[1,2] Transportation[4] Electric Power[3]

4.7   3.2   8.2   0.7   7.6

[1] Includes combined-heat-and-power plants and a small number of electricity-only plants.
[2] Lease and plant fuel, and other industrial.
[3] Electricity-only and combined-heat-and-power plants whose primary business is to sell electricity, or electricity and heat, to the public.
[4] Natural gas consumed in the operation of pipelines (primarily in compressors), and as fuel in the delivery of natural gas to consumers; plus a small quantity used as vehicle fuel.
Source: U.S. Department of Energy, Energy Information Administration (U.S. DoE EIA), *Annual Energy Review 2011*, table 6.5.

Media	Permit	Purpose
	At the Local Level	
Noise	Local Ordinance	Limits ambient noise at site boundary
Waste	Sewer connection permit	
	Waste handling certification	
Use	Building permit	
	Electric/wiring permit	
	Plumbing permit	
	Gasfitting permit	
	Approval for boilers/ furnaces	
	Storage permit for fossil fuels	
	Freshwater connection permit	
	Occupancy permit	
	Curb cut authorization	
Land	Conformance with zoning	
	Site plan approval	
	Conformance with areas of critical environmental concern, such as wetlands, coastal zones, floodplains, aquifers	
Historic	Approval to avoid historic destruction/impact	

For three reasons the public entities typically have been able to produce power at lower cost. First, they do not need to produce a profit for stockholders — they have none. Second, as public entities, they can borrow money on a less costly tax-exempt basis. Third, they receive preference in utilizing the inexpensive public hydropower facilities across the country.

Since the 1930s, these 3,000-plus electric utilities have served customers in distinct monopolized geographic service territories. Retail customers there have no choice of supplier. In return for the monopoly, each private utility submits to plenary state, and in certain cases federal, regulation. All states except Nebraska regulate private utilities, 29 states regulate rural electric cooperatives, and 19 regulate public utility districts within their borders.

How Utility Rates Are Set

Entire books have been written on the process by which utility regulatory commissions, at the state and federal levels, set the wholesale and retail rates

581

for electric power. An unrestrained monopoly has the power to raise prices as high as it wishes, and if it provides a necessity of life to "captive" customers, it has no incentive to provide good service. To prevent a company from exploiting its monopoly over an essential commodity, public oversight on behalf of consumers is therefore necessary. Electric and natural gas utilities are one of the last of the regulated "cost-plus" industries. In other words, utilities are allowed to recover their costs (expenses) plus a return that provides for a profit. State regulatory commissions establish rates for a regulated utility at levels that allow the company an opportunity to earn a reasonable return on its assets; however, with this opportunity there is no guarantee of the outcome of utility profit. *Federal Power Commission v. Hope Natural Gas Co.*, 320 U.S. 591 (1944); *Bluefield Waterworks and Imp. Co. v. Public Service Commission*, 262 U.S. 679 (1923). Most commissions do not regulate the rates of public utility districts (cooperative utility districts operating on a nonprofit basis for their members) or municipal systems in the state.

The commission sets the *rates* that a utility can charge, but not actual utility revenues or the profits derived therefrom. The commission sets the rates that consumers will pay, and the utility's profit opportunity is provided for in the rates. The profit, or "return," may be more or less than anticipated, depending on how well the utility's expenses and sales match expectations.

The rate-setting exercise utilizes the concept of the "test year" as a proxy to model the hypothetical future operating period for the utility. The rate-setting process consists of two major phases: The first establishes the utility's allowed gross revenue, and the second disaggregates this amount into the sale of electricity at various rates to various classes of customers.

In the first phase, the objective is to determine the total revenue required for utility operations. The utility's legitimate expenses and allowed rate of return are calculated in an adjudicatory proceeding involving attorneys representing interested parties before the state utility regulatory commission. Disputes occur as to what expenses are legitimate and how much profit or return the utility needs. The simplified formula for revenue required is:

Expenses + (rate of return × rate base) = revenue requirement

The return is used to pay interest on the utility's loans and bonds, as well as to pay dividends to stockholders and to retain some earnings for expansion of facilities. The prudent amount of this return depends on the capital structure of the utility: How much of its capital is raised by borrowing, for example, rather than by issuing stock? Income tax impacts must be estimated and accounted for. The parties in the hearing present evidence from expert and factual witnesses, and they cross-examine the evidence of adversary parties. In most regards, the adjudicatory proceeding before the state commission resembles a trial.

Ultimately, the revenues the utility is allowed to earn depend on the "rate base" of the utility. The rate base typically is defined as the net book value of all the utility's plant and equipment investments "used and useful" for the provision of electricity. In other words, the cost of all the utility's assets — generating plants, poles, wires, and so on — less depreciation that has been taken on this equipment over the years and less any plant that is disallowed from the rate base because it is not operational or is deemed imprudently built, is counted in the rate base. These determinations, because they have major dollar consequences, are controversial. The more the utility spends on facilities, the larger the rate base and the larger the return earned when the allowed rate of return is multiplied by the rate base.

Assets of the utility company wholly unrelated to the provision of electric service are deemed to be "below the line." That is, their operating costs and revenues are not part of the rate base, and electricity customers do not pay for them.

The second phase of the ratemaking process, once the revenue requirement of the utility is determined, is to divide the gross amount of allowed revenue into per unit (KWh) rates for different groups of consumers. The first step in this process is to divide the total revenue requirement into different rate classes — typically different categories of residential, commercial, industrial, and municipal consumers. The per unit (KWh) rates for different classes of customers vary to reflect different costs to serve these different categories of consumers. Counsel for these different categories of consumers participate in the second phase of the adjudicatory proceeding to allocate these rates among different categories of consumers.

Horizontal and vertical equity among customers and customer classes should be reflected in rates that track the cost of serving different customers. This is true for electric utilities, gas utilities, and for utilities that provide water and sewer service. Horizontal equity among customer classes based on cost-of-service is particularly important to achieve and is much more objectively determined and achieved than vertical equity among different customers within the same rate category.

Even if a utility believes that its revenues do not cover its legitimate expenses, it may not retroactively recover any shortfall in expenses. Rather, it must petition the commission to increase its revenue requirement and rates to allow greater recovery in the future. Appeal of a state commission decision is to state courts, which apply a standard of "arbitrary and capricious" or "substantial evidence" in reviewing the commission's determination (see Chapter 2 regarding review of administrative decisions).

Examples

1. Onion Utility Company has higher than expected costs because Hurricane Bobby blew through town knocking down power lines and poles. The utility company purchased a new Lear Jet to facilitate cleanup activities after the storm. Since the cleanup, the company has used the jet for the past four months to take the company's CEO to and from her summer home in Aspen, Colorado. If the company now moves to recover the costs of the Lear Jet and other storm costs, what are the issues before the state regulatory commission?

2. The state of Anarchy elects a new governor who campaigns on a pro-consumer political platform. She appoints all new commissioners to the Anarchy Public Utility Commission to carry out her pledge to cut utility rates. The commission orders Orion Electric Company, which serves part of the state, to refund 10 percent of all revenues collected from consumers during the prior calendar year, because mild winter weather occasioned less than normal pole and line maintenance expenses for all utilities. For the future, the commission orders that Orion Electric may not pass through into consumer rates its costs to produce power from its Homer nuclear plant. This disallowance eventually will force Orion Electric into bankruptcy. If you were advising the commission as its legal counsel, what do you conclude about:
   a. The legitimacy of a new commission's taking steps in response to the new governor's agenda?
   b. The 10 percent refund?
   c. The prospective order restricting rate pass-through?

3. Here is a difficult question: To avoid bankruptcy, is there any reorganization of its corporate structure in which Orion Electric, a small, closely held power company, could engage to escape commission regulation? Think about which types of utilities are regulated by the states and how some types escape regulation.

Explanations

1. During the adjudicatory hearing, the first issue is whether the utility may recover for past expenses. The answer is "no." Such recovery would amount to retroactive ratemaking, which is not permissible. However, on the basis of this experience, the utility may argue that it should receive a higher future revenue requirement to account for hurricanes. So, the only way to recover is to achieve a higher base revenue requirement and rate to provide a legitimate contingency for

severe storm damage. This proposal will be controversial before the commission. Is hurricane damage normal or rare?

The second set of issues pertains to the Lear Jet. There are two issues here. One, was the Jet "used and useful" in electricity services even if devoted exclusively to these purposes? Two, was the jet appropriately devoted to these services? On both issues, the utility may lose. Jetting the CEO to her summer home will likely be adjudged imprudent and excessive. It would probably not be allowed as a legitimate rate expense. Even so, the utility would not be prohibited from providing this perk to the CEO. However, it must be paid for from utility profits and not out of or reflected in consumer retail rates.

2a. Political motive is not relevant as a defense to commission action. Commission positions change when the commissioners change. Motive is not objectionable if actual decisions are supported on the record.

2b. Retroactive ratemaking — even if factually supportable — is not permissible. To "undo" a validly approved rate retroactively is not allowed no matter how large the windfall. Similarly, in bad times, the utility may not collect more than authorized under a valid existing rate. The solution is a rate proceeding, initiated by any party or the commission, to alter rates *prospectively*.

2c. This proposed action does not involve a retroactive rate, but it still must have a defensible basis. A utility is allowed to have the opportunity to earn a reasonable return. A commission, no matter how motivated to slash rates, cannot act arbitrarily and capriciously. Whether this action is permissible depends on the factual record and on the legal basis of the commission action. A commission has authority to allow pass-through to retail rates only of those costs that are substantiated on the record. The commission has discretion as to how it views cost items. In addition, it has jurisdiction to disallow pass-through of costs that it deems imprudent. These discretionary powers give the commission some leeway. However, if the generating costs for the Homer power plant were prudently incurred, the utility is allowed to recover them as an element of its rate. A prudency determination is typically made when the costs of a new generating facility are first included in rates.

3. This is a very tough question. Don't worry if nothing springs to mind. Recall that most states regulate only investor-owned private utilities, like Orion Electric. Since the company is closely held, you might advise that a sale of the company should be arranged. The company assets could be sold and reconstituted as a public utility district. A public utility district in most states is not regulated as to the rates that it may charge its customers. Therefore, as a public utility district, the company could charge enough to recover all its costs in any given period, including

the costs of the Homer plant, without commission oversight. Although this would be a drastic step, most of the 3,000 public electric utilities in the nation do avoid direct rate regulation. One public utility, CP National Corporation in California and Oregon, did just this to circumvent a negative ruling from its state regulatory commission.

Federal Versus State Regulation

Federal regulation of electric utilities, as well as natural gas utilities, is invested in the Federal Energy Regulatory Commission (FERC). FERC has jurisdiction over four areas of electric power transactions:

- All wholesale power transactions
- Interstate power sales
- All power sales not regulated by the states
- Transmission of power in interstate commerce

Ask yourself what is missing from this list of federal FERC jurisdictions. Several things may occur to you. First, focus on the generation and sale of electric power. FERC does not regulate the sale of power intrastate, the retail sale of electric power, or self-generation and use of power.

However, these exceptions are not as broad as they might appear. For example, if Utility A sells power to Utility B, which then resells that power interstate to Utility C, the entire transaction, as well as all the utilities, can be regulated by FERC as interstate power sales. FERC can assert authority over a utility that places only a de minimis amount of power into interstate commerce. Once a small amount of interstate power is commingled with intrastate power, the entire amount becomes interstate power subject to FERC jurisdiction.

FERC regulates interstate power transmission, but intrastate distribution of power is state regulated. This division between interstate federal transmission and intrastate distribution of power is logically consistent with the jurisdictional line for sale of power.

While the inter/intrastate concept seems logical, its application is complex. Essentially all areas of the continental United States are physically interconnected by transmission lines. Therefore, in theory, an electron of electricity induced to move in a wire at any point in the United States could travel to and energize the wire at any other point in the United States. Of course, it is not possible to precisely track an electron wave along a certain path over the copper wire transmission network. Electrons flow toward areas on the transmission network where there is the greatest demand for electricity — in other words, power is "sucked" to the points of greatest demand for its use. We do not know and cannot control the actual physical flow of electricity. The unknown physical reality of the transmission path is an inaccurate barometer on which to establish a jurisdictional line.

If the physical test fails, how does one demarcate whether power transmission is in interstate or intrastate commerce? We are now on the cutting edge of an evolving legal issue. FERC in its 1996 Rule 888 attempted to make a distinction based on the legal *purpose* of power transmission. If the legal purpose is a *wholesale* transfer of power, it is deemed by FERC to be presumptively interstate. Therefore, the availability and pricing of this transaction is jurisdictionally and exclusively federal. Conversely, any transmission of power for a *retail* sale or purpose is more likely to be deemed intrastate and subject to state regulation. The crossing of state lines is replaced by the *purpose* of a transaction.

In 1983 about 8 percent of power was sold wholesale prior to being sold at retail to the ultimate consumer. The deregulation of power (discussed later) has changed that. Today more than half the power is traded or sold wholesale to someone other than its producer, prior to being sold at retail. Power is traded among utilities, from independent producers to utilities, and among independent entities.

The Filed Rate Doctrine

The division demarcating federal and state jurisdiction is less than a "bright line." One clear principle is the filed rate doctrine. This doctrine flows from the commerce and supremacy clauses of the Constitution (Chapter 4 surveys the commerce clause, the dormant commerce clause, and preemption). Essentially, the filed rate doctrine holds that if FERC issues an order or establishes a rate under its federal jurisdiction, any contrary state determination is federally preempted. A state must respect a legitimate decision of a superior authority.

Recall what rates FERC oversees — principally wholesale power rates. Therefore, if a utility moves power from one of its subsidiaries to another before selling it to consumers, those wholesale transactions are federally regulated by FERC. In such situations, the state regulatory authority would still regulate *retail* elements of the utility company's operations, such as the cost of poles, distribution lines, and administration costs. In the same state, there may also be a utility that generates its own power and does not engage in a wholesale transaction in that power. In such situations, there is no jurisdictional basis for federal regulation by FERC; all regulation is exclusively at the state level.

Once FERC renders a decision, it must be respected by the states. The state's only recourse is to get involved initially as a party before FERC when federal decisions are made. The Supreme Court has four times in the past 30 years upheld the filed rate doctrine in *Nantahala Power & Light Company v. Thornberg*, 476 U.S. 953 (1986), in *Mississippi Power & Light Co. v. Mississippi*, 487 U.S. 354 (1988), and in *Entergy La., Inc. v. Louisiana Pub. Serv. Comm'n*, 539 U.S. 39 (2003).

As one can imagine, there often is a substantial conflict between the regulatory positions of state and federal utility regulators. We know from Chapter 4 that while a state in a *proprietary* mode can seek to withhold from commerce its own resources, it may not accomplish the same result by regulation. *New England Power Co. v. New Hampshire*, 455 U.S. 331 (1982). In sum, whether a particular utility is a regulated private utility or one of the 3,000 public utilities that are largely unregulated by the states, and whether regulation is imposed at the federal or state level, or both, are important jurisdictional distinctions.

In *PPL Montana, LLC v. Montana*, 132 S. Ct. 1215 (2012), parents of students of the Montana public schools brought a diversity action in federal court against PPL Montana and two other hydroelectric power generators, seeking compensation for use of riverbeds that they alleged were state-owned school trust lands. PPL presented expert testimony that the dams were located on stretches of river where navigation was impossible due to the presence of falls or rapids. A district court and the Montana Supreme Court found for the state against PPL Montana, awarding damages of $41 million for river use from 2000 to 2007. In a unanimous opinion, the Supreme Court overturned the Montana Supreme Court's decision, holding that the river segments at issue had not been navigable at the time of statehood; therefore, those segments of the rivers were federal and not state, *See, e.g., United States v. Utah*, 283 U.S. 64, 77 (1931) (finding the Colorado River navigable for 4 miles, nonnavigable for the next 36, and navigable again for 149 miles). A state cannot rely on present-day river use as evidence of navigability at the time of statehood.

Examples

1. As counsel for a new utility company, you are asked how it should structure itself. It intends to generate all its own power and sell that power to consumers in the same state. The power will never cross a state line. FERC has been much more generous to utilities it regulates than has the state regulatory commission in the state where your utility will operate.
   a. What options take advantage of this distinction? How can the company structure itself and any subsidiaries it chooses to create so that it will be primarily regulated by FERC?
   b. If the company is regulated by FERC, what is the only way in which the state could influence power generation rates?

c. Even if the company is primarily regulated by FERC, what elements of its operations will still be regulated by the state?

2. The state of New Hampshire has many hydroelectric power facilities that are federally licensed by FERC to private multistate utility companies. The New Hampshire utility regulatory commission issues an order mandating that all inexpensive hydropower resources used to generate electricity in the state must be allocated by multistate utilities to New Hampshire customers. Is this order permissible? Why or why not?

Explanations

1a. Recall the four areas of FERC jurisdiction. FERC regulates power sales in interstate commerce, but, importantly, it also regulates every wholesale power sale transaction. So what is the definition of a wholesale transaction? A wholesale transaction is any power sale that is not made to the ultimate end-use consumer. This sale need not be to an unrelated party.

At this point, think how you might get creative with subsidiaries. Set up one subsidiary to own the power generating plants. Set up a second subsidiary to service the power generating plants. Set up a third subsidiary to handle retail service. All three are related and are wholly owned by the same parent company. Company One contracts with Company Two to operate the plants. Company Three contracts with Company One to purchase 100 percent of its long-term power requirements. These transactions are now wholesale transactions entirely regulated by FERC. The state has no direct regulatory influence. In fact, the filed rate doctrine requires that whatever wholesale power sale price FERC approves must be passed on by the state into retail rates, without alteration. Recall the holdings in the *Nantahala* case and the *Mississippi Power & Light* case. Because the transmission of power between the two subsidiaries is for wholesale purposes, the rates for such transmission also will be determined by FERC rather than by the state commission. As a practical matter, the operation of the consolidated company is not greatly changed under this subsidiary structure. But the regulatory oversight is shifted profoundly.

1b. The only opportunity for the state to influence power generation rates under this corporate organization is not regulatory but as a party intervener in rate determinations before FERC. The role of the state is changed from that of arbitrator to that of mere supplicant. The state must hire counsel to intervene before FERC, which sits only in Washington.

1c. All power generation and transmission costs and rates will be determined by FERC. These costs probably constitute two-thirds of the total operating costs of the utility. The remaining costs of Company Three are still subject to state jurisdiction. These include costs and rates for the local distribution of power, costs of billing and collecting from customers, salaries of Company Three personnel, and costs of equipment. But the two big-ticket items — the cost of power and its transmission — are federally preempted.

2. Sorry, Charlie. The problem here is the commerce clause. While the state could arguably elect to hold back from interstate commerce hydroelectric power from facilities that it owns, it cannot do so in a regulatory mode with regard to private power resources. See *New England Power Co. v. New Hampshire*, 455 U.S. 331 (1982). See also Chapter 4.

DEREGULATION OF POWER

Deregulation of Power Generation

In 1910, 59 percent of all electric power was self-generated by the power users. With the creation of large electric utilities over the next few decades, central supply of electric power became the norm. By 1950 only 17 percent of power was self-generated; by 1975 this value had shrunk to 3 percent. Since 1980 this percentage has increased; independent power is now more than one-third of total electric consumption and is still rising.

What spawned this renaissance in self-generation of electricity was the passage in 1978 of the Public Utility Regulatory Policies Act (PURPA). PURPA deregulated power generation for certain legal entities. These select entities were designated as Qualifying Facilities (QFs). A QF is a power generator that is one of two types of projects that Congress sought to encourage: a cogenerator or a small power producer. QF status is an exclusively federal matter determined by FERC. *Independent Energy Producers Ass'n v. California Public Utilities Commission*, 36 F.3d 848 (9th Cir. 1994). Essentially, this decision turns on the principle of implied federal preemption.

Benefits of QF Status There were tremendous economic and legal benefits accompanying QF status until some weakening in 2005 congressional amendments. If one is going to use all the power oneself, the benefits of QF status may be limited. The benefits of QF status principally apply to projects that sell their power to other utilities or persons. These numerous benefits of QF status are listed in Exhibit 12.8.

12.8 **Benefits of QF Status**

Benefit	Description
Federal exemption	The QF is exempt from regulation under the Federal Power Act and the Public Utility Holding Company Act administered by the Securities and Exchange Commission.
Local exemption	The QF is exempt from any state or local regulation of entities as utilities or energy producers — i.e., no "utility-type" regulation.
Power sale	The QF can sell any or all of its power output to the local electric utility or to any other utility it can reach with its electric power where (according to the 2005 changes) there are competitive nondiscriminatory wholesale markets.
Avoided cost	The price that the utility must pay for power purchased from a QF is equal to the utility's full avoided cost of generating or purchasing an equivalent amount of energy and capacity.
Interconnection	Utilities must interconnect their transmission grids with the QF to facilitate buy/sell transactions.
Backup power	The utility must supply necessary backup and supplemental power to the QF at nondiscriminatory rates, or it can be supplied by competitive suppliers.

These privileges allow a QF to self-generate power and to sell that power to a utility at the utility's full avoided cost. Full avoided cost is the utility's cost of generating power itself or purchasing it from others. The difference between the QF's cost of generation and the utility's full avoided cost payments is the profit kept by the QF. Some exceptions were made in 2005 to cause the QF to sell power into deregulated wholesale markets where those were available on a nondiscriminatory basis in certain areas of the country on a competitive basis.

A federal district court in Mississippi thought that the PURPA scheme was an impermissible transgression on states' rights and held it unconstitutional. On appeal, PURPA was narrowly upheld by the U.S. Supreme Court in *FERC v. Mississippi*, 456 U.S. 742 (1982). The requirement to pay full avoided cost for QF power and to interconnect with all QFs was unanimously upheld by the Supreme Court the next year in *American Paper Institute v. American Electric Power Service Corp.*, 461 U.S. 402 (1983).

Since the Supreme Court upheld the constitutionality of PURPA, there has been a proliferation of QFs nationwide. Every year since 1990, more new MW of power have come online from QFs and IPPs than from all new utility power facilities combined. QFs and other independent power facilities that states have allowed to compete are dominating the new power generation business, and their success spawned deregulation of wholesale and retail electric power. These benefits were changed a bit by the Energy Policy Act of 2005.

Cogenerators: "Useful" Thermal Energy Defined What is a cogenerator? A cogenerator sequentially produces at least two useful forms of energy — electric and thermal. Typically, the thermal energy, in the form of steam or hot water that the power generating equipment otherwise would exhaust as thermal or water pollution, is harnessed to heat a building or use in industrial processes. A cogenerator, as defined by federal law, can be of any size and can use any fuel to produce power, as long as it meets certain minimum efficiency criteria and as long as at least 5 percent of the total energy output of the facility is in the form of "useful" thermal energy.

When a QF files with FERC stating that it will achieve QF status, under the FERC rules from 1978 to 2006 there was a rebuttable presumption that the thermal output was "useful," as held in *Kamine/Besicorp Allegheny L.P.*, 63 FERC para. 61,320 (1993). "Usefulness" was determined by any common industrial or commercial application. If the use was not common, a more exacting test was applied. If the thermal energy user was related to the QF, a more careful examination without presumption of legitimacy was applied by FERC. If a challenger rebutted or raised questions about qualification, then FERC reviewed the actual contracts for thermal energy use to reach a decision. *EG&G, Inc.*, 16 FERC para. 61,060 (1981) (an aquaculture facility would not burn natural gas to heat pond water but for the desire to achieve QF status for the facility).

Thermal applications that would not be undertaken except for the by-product availability of inexpensive thermal energy may not necessarily be "useful" thermal applications. Use of by-product thermal energy for aquaculture purposes is particularly suspect, because conventional power plants routinely dump waste thermal energy into the water or the air. To be "useful," a thermal use should have an independent business justification, a determination that becomes problematic when the proposed application represents a new technology. See *Electrodyne Research Corp.*, 32 FERC para. 61,102, at 61,279 (1985).

However, where there is a close sizing of the facility to the *thermal* needs of the facility, rather than sizing to the maximum *electric* output available, an aquaculture use of the thermal output can pass muster as "useful" thermal output. In the matter of *John W. Savage*, 28 FERC para. 61,273 (1984), there were four factors that allowed an aquaculture thermal energy use to qualify as "useful." First, the facility was sized to deliver the appropriate amount of thermal energy — more than 50 percent of the useful energy output was thermal energy. Its primary purpose was not the production of electric power. Second, there was independent economic significance to the production of fast-maturing catfish. The production of catfish achieved a profit. Third, there was no ownership relationship between the electric and thermal projects. Each was independent of the other. Fourth, the heat was adequately controlled to best use the thermal output, rather than waste it.

New 2006 FERC regulations require that the thermal output be used in a "productive and beneficial manner," in a case-by-case analysis. This cracks down on potential new abuses.

If over 50 percent of the total energy output of the QF is used for "industrial, commercial, residential or institutional purposes," it is presumed used for an allowed, "safe harbor," purpose. 18 C.F.R. §292.205(d)(3); *Chugach Electric Ass'n, Matanuska Electric Ass'n*, 121 FERC 61,287, 2007 WL 4472021 (December 21, 2007) at ¶42 ("the Commission created a safe harbor"). "The Commission may waive any of the requirements. . . . upon a showing that the facility will produce significant energy savings." 18 C.F.R. §292.205(c) (2007). The Commission adjudges the usefulness of the output based on the facility's filing; it never inspects a plant and will refuse to view certain evidence or answers. *See Kamine/Besicorp Allegeny*, 63 FERC ¶61,320, 63,157-58 (June 24, 1993), 1993 WL 228191 at **2, **4 (rejecting petitioner's request that FERC review additional material); *Chugach Electric Ass'n, Matanuska Electric Ass'n, supra*, ¶18 (does not formally review self-certifications but relies on statements in submitted form); *Medical Area Total Energy Plant* 130 FERC ¶61,254, ¶8 (March 30, 2010).

Small Power Producers   The second type of QF is the small power producer. Typically, a small power producer is not a cogenerator; it produces only electricity (not useful thermal energy), and employs waste or a renewable resource as its fuel for power generation. A small power producer is limited in size, typically to a maximum of 80 MW, except for certain types of waste fuel projects that may be no more than 30 MW in size. A waste fuel is defined as any by-product fuel source that is "unessential and subordinate to the overall goal of an economic process and currently of little or no commercial value."

There is case law as to what constitutes a renewable or waste fuel. Small unproductive deposits of fossil fuels, as well as facilities that turn solid waste into energy, are eligible fuel sources for small power producers. See *American Lignite Prods. Co.*, 25 FERC para. 61,054 (1983); *Gabriel Mills Energy Co.*, 41 FERC para. 62,288 (1987). Likewise, producers that use renewable energy technologies, such as hydroelectric, solar, wind, and wood-based technologies, qualify as small power producer QFs. In any given year, not more than 25 percent of the fuel input into a small power producer can come from traditional fossil fuels.

Ownership Limitation   Only a limited number of projects qualified as QFs. The projects had to be either modest-sized units powered by renewable or waste resources, or units of any size employing any fuel that produced at least 5 percent of their total energy output as "useful" thermal energy. QFs did not include traditional utility-size or utility-type power plants.

In fact, QF status was lost if more than 50 percent of a project was owned by an electric utility or its subsidiary (not including gas or telephone utilities). What qualified as "ownership"? The close cases occur when a utility owns 50 percent of the equity in the company or takes more than 50 percent of the cash flow or tax benefits. The case law created exceptional flexibility that dwarfed the rule in defining how 50 percent ownership was calculated. The stream of benefits an owner received was the most determinative factor regarding calculation of the ownership share. *Ultrapower 3*, 27 FERC para. 61,094 (1984). The second most important factor was the control exercised by any particular owner. *Prodek/Hydro Resources Joint Venture*, 41 FERC para. 61,152 (1987). The time value of money had to be considered. The ownership limitation was eliminated by Bush Administration amendments in 2005.

Deregulation of Power and Wheeling

Wheeling is another term for the transmission of electric power. The transmission and distribution systems of the nation's electric power systems still are monopolized. But access to them is no longer restricted to utilities.

The Energy Policy Act of 1992 and FERC Rule 888 require all electric utilities to transmit, at a reasonable nondiscriminatory price, the *wholesale* power of any producer of power. In other words, an independent entity can move power in a wholesale transaction, to anyone not a retail user of power. Typically this transaction is a QF or other independent power producer transmitting power to a utility—a wholesale transaction.

Since 1998, 18 states have deregulated their retail electric markets. More would have done so but for the collapse of California's restructured market in 2001, which froze such changes.

Power Bidding and ISOs

Since the late 1980s, several state regulatory authorities have switched to bidding schemes as a way to administer power acquisition obligations. How does this change the equation? Recall that under the PURPA requirements, avoided cost is determined either by the price that the utility would pay to (1) generate power itself or (2) purchase that power from others. The standard state PURPA scheme administratively sets the avoided cost value and signs up as much power as is offered at that price.

A bidding system reverses that scheme: The *quantity* of power required is established administratively, and the power purchase *price* is established by the lowest winning bids in the solicitation process. As is demonstrated by Exhibit 12.9, bidding reverses the determination of the dependent and independent variables that must be administered under PURPA.

Eighteen of the states have deregulated retail power supply and utilize an independent system operator (ISO) to each day control regional wholesale power supply and transmission system operation, all eventually subject to FERC jurisdictional control. This bidding system causes the electric system to utilize competition to operate at the lowest wholesale cost of generation. Many of these states also have had their electric utilities sell their power generation units to independent companies.

Bidding is the official modus operandi for utility power acquisition in several states, including California and most of the northeastern states. These states allow large independent power projects (IPPs), which do not qualify as QFs, to participate in the bidding and supply. IPPs by definition are not limited to less than 50 percent utility ownership or by size or technology. They often resemble large utility-scale power plants.

In a bidding scheme, environmental pollution — called environmental "externalities" — can be factored into the scoring of different power project bids. For example, the Massachusetts state utility commission established an environmental externality pollution value for each kind of power generation. This scheme was stricken as beyond the regulatory authority of the state commission in *Massachusetts Electric Co. v. Department of Public Utilities*, 643 N.E.2d 1029 (Mass. 1994). In essence, the utility regulatory authority could not impose environmental standards that were stricter than the environmental regulatory authority, absent statutory grant of such power. This environmental regulation was ultra vires.

Retail Sales and Wheeling

The Energy Policy Act of 1992 requires utilities to wheel power for any wholesale produces. But the Act only pertains to *wholesale* power wheeling.

12.9 PURPA vs. Bidding Scheme

Scheme	Quantity of Power Sold	Price of Power Sale
Standard PURPA scheme	Variable	Administratively set
Bidding scheme	Administratively set	Varies by bids

And PURPA, which facilitates power sales by QFs, only applies to *wholesale* transactions among QFs and regulated electric utilities. The concept of wholesale transactions looms large in these federal laws. And for good reason: The Federal Power Act applies to interstate power sales. Although the commerce power would arguably allow Congress to assert jurisdiction over all power transactions, Congress has not done so.

However, there is ultimately a retail transaction at the conclusion of every power transmittal. Sale to the ultimate end user of power is, by definition, a *retail* transaction. Federal law says nothing about the retail transaction. Here the states have reserved exclusive jurisdiction pursuant to federal law. The states decide whether or not there is an exclusive retail utility supplier in an area, whether retail wheeling is allowed, and whether direct retail sale to end users by QFs, IPPs, or others is permitted.

Beginning in 1997 in Rhode Island, and then followed in 1998 by Massachusetts and California, 18 states have deregulated their retail electric power markets. This includes every large state except Florida, although California's restructuring has collapsed back into a black hole of state bailout and reregulation. Typically, this opens up retail electric sales to any party, including brokers, marketers, and independent power producers. While this includes Qualifying Facilities under PURPA, small QFs have difficulty competing against much larger and less regulatorily encumbered independent power producers.

In addition, many of these deregulating states have compelled or induced their traditional regulated electric utilities to divest themselves of all of their generating capacity. Thus, these divesting utilities thereafter retain only the poles, the distribution lines, and their brand name. FERC is encouraging these distribution utilities to form ISOs to coordinate their regional distribution activities. While these distribution functions remain regulated at the state level, generating capacity is held by unregulated independent companies who acquire power generating equipment from the utilities or build new independent power generation facilities.

This significant development in almost half of the states, including Texas and almost the entire northeast United States, changes the role and regulatory grip of regulators over the power system. In those traditionally regulated states, regulators could compel or induce utilities to build additional generating capacity, but the costs associated with overbuilding are incurred by consumers. In a deregulated retail environment, regulators have no direct means to control or require any independent generators to supply power or to build additional generating capacity. Moreover, the costs of any overbuilding are incurred by the owners of the generation, not utility ratepayers. The power supply operates by market forces. For more information on electric power regulation, deregulation, and environmental impacts, see S. Ferrey, *The Law of Independent Power*, West Publishing (republished in three volumes annually or available on Westlaw); S. Ferrey, *The New Rules: A Guide to Electric Market Regulation*, Pennwell Publishing, 2000.

In California, the dark side of the electricity market became visible in 2001. Power supply was inadequate, rolling blackouts occurred, businesses were closed, workers were dismissed without pay, and electricity prices skyrocketed. School budgets were shattered and Intel and other companies announced that they would not expand production in California because of the unreliability of the power supply there. Dramatically increasing demand for power in a high-tech economy, market manipulation by Enron and other IPPs, statutory and regulatory decisions of state regulators, and California's failure to facilitate the building of sufficient generating capacity to satisfy this demand created the market imbalance in California. California committed $43 billion of state dollars to save its system, creating the largest budget deficits in the nation. The nation's largest utility, PG&E, filed for bankruptcy protection, utility rates skyrocketed, and regulation was reimposed. These problems in the largest state have spurred new interest in cogeneration and renewable energy on site, in lieu of reliance on centralized production and distribution of electric power. For more on these technologies and the regulatory incentives involved, see S. Ferrey, "Exit Strategy," 26 *Harv. Envir. L.J.* 109 (2002).

Examples

1. Your client wants to construct and operate a Qualifying Facility for the generation and sale of electric power. The facility will use natural gas fuel and will send 5 percent of its total energy output to a greenhouse operation that the power plant owner plans to construct next door to the power plant. The client knows nothing about greenhouses or growing tomatoes, but she figures she can cart the produce out to the road and put up a sign: $10 a pound. She proposes to use low-quality glass in the greenhouse and leave all the windows open to utilize as much of the thermal output of the power plant as possible. Advise the client as to the legal issues associated with this plan. What are the legal tests that would be imposed?

2. Following the facts in Example 1, suppose the client abandons the greenhouse concept and shifts the fuel supply to a 60/40 blend of natural gas and wood. Has she solved her QF status? Why or why not?

3. The client in the above Example successfully develops a Qualifying Facility project. She provides steam and electricity from the facility to the paper company on whose property the Qualifying Facility is located. If she did not sell thermal output to the paper company, she would lose her QF status. Are there any problems with this arrangement?

4. The state adopted a bidding scheme whereby IPPs, QFs, and utilities would bid to supply designated quantities of power. Your client is a QF that loses the low bid to larger IPPs owned by electric utilities.

a. Is a bidding scheme legal as a means to determine the price that the purchasing utilities will pay?

b. What would be the basis of your best legal challenge to the bidding system?

5. In 1991 the California Public Utility Commission (PUC) adopted a QF monitoring and enforcement program. Under this program, the PUC authorized the utilities to monitor existing QFs from which they purchase electric energy to ensure that they are in compliance with federal PURPA operating standards. The program provides that if a utility determines that a QF is not in compliance with operating standards, the utility is authorized to suspend payment of the full avoided cost rate specified by PURPA and the standard contract for power sale, and to substitute an alternative rate equal to 80 percent of the utility's avoided cost for short-term economy power.

The utilities also are permitted to take back from the QFs payments already made that are above the 80 percent alternative rate for any period during which the QF has not been operating in compliance with federal efficiency standards, retroactively for a period up to three years from the last date on which efficiency data were submitted. Finally, the utilities are allowed to disconnect the electric interconnection under certain circumstances. Is the California program legal? Why or why not?

6. Utility A sells a very small amount of power each day from 5 p.m. to 5:15 p.m. to help with a peak need to Utility B, which then resells that power interstate to Utility C. Both Utility A and Utility B are in the state of Anarchy; Utility C is outside the state. Does the state of Anarchy or FERC have jurisdiction to regulate the sale by Utility A to Utility B?

Explanations

1. To qualify as a QF, this facility must be a cogeneration facility. Recall that a key requirement is that at least 5 percent of the total energy output of the facility must be "useful" thermal energy. This plan appears to be a close call, because it plans to use only 5 percent of the energy in this way. There are certain other problems with this plan, too. First, when a project is designed to waste thermal energy, it will not be deemed "useful." Exhausting heat through inefficient design or deliberate operation raises serious issues. The purpose of PURPA is to prevent the creation of "PURPA machines," large utility-type power plants that dump heat just to obtain QF status.

Here, because the business generating the power and the business using the thermal energy are related by common ownership, FERC will apply a more exacting test to determine QF status. Because the thermal use has an agricultural purpose, it is particularly suspect. The burden of proving QF status shifts to the applicant. It is also important to determine if the greenhouse business has an independent "stand alone" basis. If the greenhouse business is not capable of making a profit on its own and would not be undertaken but for the benefit of providing QF status for the power facility, it may not be deemed "useful." Nor is that the only problem.

Considering that this facility is sized for maximum electric rather than thermal output, that the heat produced is not efficiently used and controlled, that the heat-using facility is not independent, and that the product is not economic (i.e., the tomatoes will be dumped on the market to justify the QF status and electric production), the thermal application should not to be considered "useful." Here, QF status is likely to be denied.

2. Without a "useful" thermal application, the project cannot qualify as a cogenerator QF. However, it still may qualify as a small power producer. In any given year, the fuel used by small power producers can be no more than 25 percent traditional fossil fuels, such as natural gas. FERC has not been lenient in granting exceptions to this requirement. As proposed, this project will not achieve QF status. Your client's problem is not solved.

3. The sale of thermal output is fine. The potential problem lies with the sale of electricity to the paper company, which is the host for the facility. You were on track if you noted that the sale of electricity to the paper company is a *retail* sale. PURPA does not authorize retail sales — it only permits wholesale transactions. States control retail sales. Unless the state is one of the 20 that allow direct retail sales, this is an impermissible transaction. The problem is twofold. First, the QF has no certificate from the state regulatory authority to sell electric power. Second, a utility may still enjoy a monopoly to sell electric energy at retail, unless electric deregulation and competition are well advanced.

4a. Recall that the price at which a utility establishes its avoided cost rate can be set by reference to either the price at which the utility generates power or the price at which it purchases power. This is the second alternative; it is one of the means explicitly referenced by PURPA.

4b. Nonetheless, if your client is a losing QF in the bid process, it is disconcerting to lose to IPPs that don't have the same restrictions on their structure and operations as does a QF. There does appear to be a certain illogic to the way the system works. In a bid process, IPPs win the bids and establish prices not only for themselves but for nonwinner QFs as well, representing the avoided cost to the utility of purchasing power.

Therefore, the IPPs absorb the available blocks of bid-solicited power that otherwise would go automatically to QFs. Prices of power acquisition decrease for the utility system, but QFs do not realize their federal PURPA entitlements. That this state action de facto negates the realization of federal PURPA entitlements is the argument that you might make as counsel. No such challenge of a bid system has yet been made by a losing QF.

5.   California's regulation and interpretation of PURPA raises two issues. The first is the matter of preemption. In 1994 the Ninth Circuit found that authority over whether a QF in fact achieved the efficiency and output requirements of PURPA was preempted federally by the Federal Power Act. *Independent Energy Producers Ass'n, Inc. v. Calif. P.U.C.*, 36 F.3d 848 (9th Cir. 1994). The states are federally preempted, either by themselves or by delegation to utilities that they regulate, from exercising authority over enforcement of the QF requirements of PURPA.

The second matter of concern is a PURPA statutory issue. Recall that PURPA disallows any state applying "utility-type" regulation to a QF. By unilaterally imposing on any "noncomplying" QF an "alternative" rate equal to 80 percent of the utilities' avoided cost for short-term economy energy, the rate mandated by PURPA is negated by state action. The PUC program thus authorizes the utilities to deny to QFs one of the benefits to which they are statutorily entitled under PURPA: "What the state may not do, however, is to intrude into the Commission's exclusive jurisdiction to make QF status determinations by denying to certified QFs the full avoided cost rates to which they are entitled." *Independent Energy Producers, supra.*

6.   FERC has regulatory jurisdiction over all of these sales. When Utility A sells power to Utility B, which then resells that power interstate to Utility C, the entire transaction, as well as all utilities, can be regulated by FERC because the transaction involves interstate power sales. FERC can assert authority even over a utility that places only a de minimis amount of power into interstate commerce. Once a small amount of intrastate power is commingled with interstate power, the entire amount becomes interstate power subject to FERC jurisdiction.

OIL AND GAS RIGHTS

Oil and Gas in the American Economy

Petroleum dominates most accounts of twentieth-century energy history. The first oil well in the United States was drilled in 1859, in Titusville,

Pennsylvania. The industrialized nations since then have developed economies that depend on the use of petroleum and its derivatives, and electricity. As of 2010, the United States consumed approximately 24 percent of world petroleum, with only 8 to 9 percent of petroleum produced in America, which required the United States to import almost two-thirds of its oil. In 1974, President Nixon pledged that the United States would not be dependent on any other country for energy by the end of the decade. By the end of the decade, oil imports into the United States had doubled. Thereafter, President Carter pledged that the United States would never again import as much oil; oil imports doubled yet again by 2006.

Refined oil products (gasoline, aviation fuel, heating oil, diesel truck fuel, and so on) and natural gas are both products of petroleum. Petroleum is a complex chemical compound composed mostly of hydrogen and carbon, with minute amounts of sulfur, nitrogen, and oxygen. It occurs in liquid, gaseous, and even solid formations in sedimentary rocks. Sedimentary rocks include the layered remains of animals and plants deposited in shallow seas that later dried up and were subjected to great pressure over tens of millions of years. Thus fossil fuels are organic in origin. But within recorded human history, they are not renewable. They occur in pockets of the earth's crust, sometimes near the surface but often, in the case of petroleum, tens of thousands of feet below the surface. Oil and gas are extracted by drilling wells into these pockets.

Today about 40 percent of U.S. energy use is derived from petroleum, while 25 percent is derived from natural gas. In other parts of the world, the role of petroleum is even more profound. Petroleum and natural gas also comprise the dominant form of heating energy used by homes and industry. Fossil fuels are also the dominant fuel used to boil water to produce electric power in the United States.

But the greatest value of oil and natural gas may be in their uses as "feedstocks" for the production of synthetic materials that have become essential in the modern age: synthetic rubber, plastics, petrochemicals, nylon, synthetic coatings, and other materials. Petroleum drives the internal combustion engine, which powers most vehicles in the world. That mobility, especially since World War II, has shaped migration patterns, suburban sprawl, and the design of urban and suburban environments in this and other nations. Moreover, sprawled living and working patterns have made the daily commute, with its attendant transportation snaggles, loss of time, and pollution, a modern necessity.

Environmental Repercussions

The United States is the third-largest world oil producer. Petroleum consumption is a major cause of world pollution. The combustion of hydrocarbons creates a variety of pollutants, including organic compounds and nitrogen oxides. These pollutants are principally of concern as air pollutants.

The burning of fossil fuels also creates carbon dioxide, CO_2, which is not a criteria pollutant (see also Chapters 5 and 15). Put a gallon of gasoline in a gas tank, go for a drive, and that gallon of gasoline is transformed into about five and one-half pounds of carbon dioxide. Carbon dioxide emanates intractably from the very choice to burn fossil fuels — it is inherent in the fossil fuel base of industrial society.

Moreover, there are significant environmental repercussions from the drilling, extraction, processing, and transportation of oil and natural gas. The recent discovery of abundant natural gas resources under the Marcellus Shale has greatly increased projected U.S. natural gas resources, holding 827 trillion cubic feet. The amount of carbon dioxide produced by burning natural gas is less than oil and almost half as much as coal. Hydraulic fracturing fluids used to extract the gas can contain methanol, currently listed under the Safe Drinking Water Act (see Chapter 6), and benzene, toluene, ethylbenzene, and xylene, which have harmful effects on humans' nervous systems and must be properly handled, treated, or disposed.

Hydraulic fracturing, or "fracking," is a well-stimulation technique that employs high-pressure fluids consisting of water, sand, and a mixture of chemicals to create and prop open small fissures in shale rock to allow gas trapped in underground formations to move to perforated wellbore for extraction with new horizontal drilling techniques. Fracking requires 2 to 4 million gallons for each well. Injection water can become contaminated with traces of fracking chemicals. The potential for pollution of drinking water aquifers as well as surface waters exists. While the Safe Drinking Water Act (SDWA) is designed to protect underground drinking water sources from contamination caused by underground injection of fluids, hydraulic fracturing is specifically exempt from the Act. See, 42 U.S.C. §300h (d)(1)(B); Clean Water Act, 33 U.S.C. §1362(6)(B).

The oil spill from the Exxon *Valdez* oil tanker was an extremely visible environmental mishap. Nonetheless, as you may recall from Chapter 9, oil and refined petroleum products are exempt from coverage under CERCLA. The siting and construction of natural gas pipelines of less than several miles' length are categorically exempt from many of the state-version clones of NEPA, which otherwise would require examination of environmental impacts and alternative designs. (See Chapter 3 for more discussion of NEPA and equivalent state statutes.)

A large amount of wastewater is a by-product of oil well production. The majority of courts do not require an implied obligation to restore the premises of the production site, rather allowing reasonable use of the property. See *Warren Petroleum Corp. v. Monzingo*, 157 Tex. 479 (Tex. 1957); *Tenneco Oil Co. v. Allen*, 515 P.2d 1391 (Okla. 1973). The United States was found liable when federal oil leases which were about to lapse were not extended by the federal government after the state of California asserted Coastal Zone Management Act review authority over such extensions. *Amber Resources Co. v. United States*, Fed. Ct. Cl. (November 17, 2005); see also *California v. Norton*, 311 F.3d 1162 (9th Cir. 2002).

Ownership and Transfer of Oil, Coal, and Gas Rights

The coming age of relative scarcity of fossil fuels will increase the value of rights in control and allocation of these essential resources. Ownership of oil and gas rights did not originally fit within the common law tradition of the United States. At traditional common law, the owner of property owned it from the heavens to the core of the earth below. To develop fossil fuels, this concept had to change.

Coal resources and their exploitation were discussed at the end of Chapter 11 and are not repeated here.

When liquid or gaseous petroleum resources are extracted from beneath a tract of land, it is not possible to determine with legal certainty that those minerals physically emanate from directly below that parcel. Deposits of petroleum and natural gas do not coincide with land property boundaries; they migrate over time. Thus oil and gas resources may actually be drained from reserves physically located beneath a neighbor's parcel. Where the government breaches contracts for leases on federal land, even where the private rights were conditional on further government permits and not absolute, government repudiation results in restitution to the injured companies. *Mobil Oil Exploration and Producing Southeast, Inc. v. United States*, 530 U.S. 604 (2000).

Thus a common law precedent has developed during the past century: the "rule of capture." In short, the rule of capture allows the retention and ownership of all oil or gas resources that one can capture from drilling wells on land where one has the legal right to drill. This "finders keepers" type of rule is unusual at law for two reasons. First, it sanctions the expropriation of the associated land rights of another. Second, it is not an affirmative right as much as a shield from common law liability for appropriation of the associated land rights of another.

This rule allows, and even encourages, the owner of a tract of land to attempt to appropriate the minerals beneath not only his or her own land but also beneath neighbors' lands. This rule promotes energy development for an industrial economy, but it also promotes predatory practices and a "tragedy of the commons" syndrome.

This shield from liability for appropriating these mineral rights applies only if other common law principles are adhered to. One of these principles is that the appropriator may not trespass or otherwise interfere with the surface rights of another, and may not create a nuisance. The common law precedent has also developed to apportion and limit the otherwise unfettered rule of capture of fossil fuel appropriation in the following ways:

- The doctrine of correlative rights holds that each owner of a separate property has the right only to a fair and equitable share of the oil and gas underneath his or her property; the owner also enjoys protection from the negligence of neighboring appropriators. See *Elliff v. Texon Drilling Co.*, 210 S.W.2d 558 (Tex. 1948).
- To ameliorate incentives to create a "tragedy of the commons," states have enacted laws to limit owners' extraction of minerals to a fair share of the oil or gas formation below a particular property, as per state permissions or licenses. See *Wronski v. Sun Oil Co.*, 279 N.W.2d 564 (Mich. App. 1979). Typically, such statutes control the spacing of wells as a means to control fair appropriation, force the pooling of efforts as well as shared costs and royalties of different extractors, or regulate the amount of allowed production. See *Chevron Oil Co. v. Oil and Gas Conservation Commission*, 435 P.2d 781 (Mont. 1967).
- Hydrocarbons rights are personal, not possessory. Once extracted and captured, oil and gas resources become the personal property of the owner, and these are not forfeited just because possession subsequently is lost to another who drills into a reservoir or storage facility. They belong to the holder as personal property. See *Pacific Gas & Electric Co. v. Zuckerman*, 189 Cal. App. 3d 1113 (Cal. Ct. App. 1987).

So exactly what is the legal right that the owner of oil and gas rights possesses? Like so many other areas controlled by state rather than federal law, the answer depends on the jurisdiction in which one operates. In most jurisdictions, states follow and apply the "ownership in place" rule that vests these rights in fee simple absolute originally in the owner of the overlying land, until those rights are otherwise captured or divested. This rule creates in the owner corporeal (possessory) rights as to the oil and gas. The landowner owns the minerals beneath the land. They are not lost by failure to develop them or by abandonment.

A minority of jurisdictions follow the "nonownership theory," which vests title in whoever captures subsurface oil and gas. In such instances, the owner of the overlying land possesses only a *profit prendre*, an exclusive right to explore for and develop underlying mineral resources. This creates only incorporeal ("not of substance" *use* of land rather than possession) rights in the landowner. Possession of the mineral, not just the overlying land, controls the right to the mineral. Rights can be lost by abandonment.

Under either theory, the right is perfected only when the owner or his or her assignee captures the oil and gas. Incorporeal mineral rights—whether embodied in a leasehold, a royalty agreement, or other document — can be lost by abandonment at common law. See *Gerhard v. Stephens*, 68 Cal. 2d 864, 442 P.2d 692 (Cal. 1968). Corporeal rights cannot be lost by abandonment.

States also vary as to whether they characterize oil and gas interests as personal property or real property. The distinction has to do with the *duration* of the mineral interest, rather than whether or not it is possessory. Where the interest is of indefinite duration or for life, it is properly a real property interest. This is so even though the mineral itself in a given reservoir may be exhausted after a few years of exploitation.

Interests for a finite number of years are classified as personal property under the common law in most states. Where the right is to a royalty interest in certain profits of operation, rather than to the minerals themselves, this royalty interest is a right to a share of income and is not an interest in real property. Once severed from the land, the oil or gas resources become personal property, and eventually they become goods and articles in interstate commerce. In *BP America Prod. Co. v. Burton*, 549 U.S. 84 (2006), the Court affirmed that the federal six-year statute of limitations for government contract actions applies only to court actions and not to agencies' abilities to assess overdue administrative royalty payments on mineral leases.

There is no direct correlation between the ownership doctrines mentioned above, which relate to the *possessory* nature of interests in mineral rights, and the personal versus real property classification of various states. While this personal versus real property distinction does not affect the basic ability to transfer mineral interests, it does fundamentally affect second-order property rights, such as testamentary rights in the property, the application of lien statutes, and the taxation of mineral rights.

Interests in oil and gas rights can be transferred in fee, as an interest in the mineral, as a leasehold right, as a royalty interest, or as a right of profit in a corporation exploiting the minerals. These interests can be conveyed by contract, deed, lease, inheritance, judicial order, adverse possession, or other legal instruments. In short, all of the nuances of contract law and property law combine to create a common law of mineral interest rights and obligations. There is also a body of interpretive law on accounting for profits and royalty interest in mineral rights.

Example

1. The Muppet Corporation owned a tract of land with known mineral rights. In 1945 it announced that, as a gesture toward world peace, it would never develop oil and gas from the land. In 1985 the corporation went out of business. The rights as a successor to the corporation were later acquired by Kermit. In 1987, Kermit conveyed a leasehold for development of oil and gas rights on the property to the Miss Piggy Oil Company. Piggy profitably develops the mineral interests, without

objection from Kermit. Kermit then sells the property to Fozzie in 1996. Fozzie objects to the presence of oil drilling and production equipment on his property, which he wants to develop as a shopping center.

    a. Do you require more information to answer questions as to mineral rights of the parties?

    b. Fozzie brings suit to resolve title to the mineral rights in the property and to eject Piggy. Who has title to the mineral rights?

    c. Can Piggy grant its bank a secured interest in its real property rights in the mineral resources, to be recorded at the registry of deeds in the local county?

Explanation

1.   Let's walk through the issues raised. This is a difficult though not uncommon situation — where one owner in the chain of title sacrifices or potentially constrains the bundle of rights that can be transferred to subsequent owners. It often happens that subsequent owners of land have land-use plans inconsistent with uses in existence at the time of property acquisition.

1a. You do need more information to answer the question. In particular, you need to know the common law theory of a given jurisdiction to fully answer this question.

1b. In a state that applies the minority "nonownership theory," mineral rights are subject to abandonment. As a *profit prendre*, the owner's rights are incorporeal rights subject to loss by abandonment. There is no right to assert possession or ownership until the oil and gas is captured.

    See *Gerhard v. Stephens, supra*. Abandonment usually requires, as a matter of state common law, an intention to abandon and an extended period of nonuse. The conduct of Muppet as to the property may constitute the two requisites to determine that these mineral rights have been abandoned. Kermit cannot obtain, or transfer to Piggy, any more rights than those held by Muppet at the time of transfer. At law, Piggy as successor may not hold a valid lease from Kermit. Fozzie may be able to bring an action against Piggy Oil Company for ejectment or to quiet title as to the mineral rights. However, Piggy will have some equitable rights that will be weighed in any remedy in an action for ejectment.

    By contrast, in a state that applies the majority "ownership in place" doctrine, the rights are corporeal and are not lost by abandonment. There is a present possessory interest to the oil and gas in place. They are not lost by abandonment or by failure to develop the resources. Kermit would inherit the full possessory mineral rights that go with the land. He may transfer these to Piggy. Fozzie takes fee simple in the property subject to all disclosed or recorded leases or other conveyances of mineral easements or rights. The rule of law followed in the jurisdiction can determine whether or not abandonment is recognized, and therefore whether or not it can occur in the chain of title.

1c. In some states, Piggy would not receive a securable *real* property interest in whatever mineral rights it possesses. In these states, its interest would be considered personal property. To the degree that a state recognizes this right as a real property right, it could be secured by a security interest in the real property recorded in the registry of real property deeds.

The Endangered Species Act

In time of silver rain
The Earth
Puts forth new life again,
Green grasses grow
And flowers lift their heads.

Langston Hughes, "In time of Silver Rain"

"Every landscape in the world is full of these exact and beautiful adaptations, by which an animal fits into its environment like one cogwheel into another."

J. Bronowski, The Ascent of Man, 1973

"Descended from the apes. My dear, let us hope that it is not true, but if it is, let us pray that it will not become generally known."

Wife of the Bishop of Worcester

"The first prerequisite of intelligent tinkering is to save all the pieces."

Aldo Leopold

"We haven't the time to take our time."

Eugène Ionesco, Le Roi se Meurt, 1963

A HISTORY OF LIFE ON EARTH

Let's chart the 4.5 billion year history of the earth, one of billions of planets in the universe, as if it were a 24-hour day beginning at midnight. Life, in the form of single-celled microbes, appears first at 4 a.m. This is all there is for well more than half of earth's history, until 8:30 p.m., when plants first appear in the oceans, followed by simple jellyfish and marine animals. Around 10 p.m., plants (the final 10 percent of earth's history) make it to land, followed by insects, which eventually learn how to fly to avoid predation, and then larger animals. Forests containing carbon appear just before 10:30 p.m. and start the millions of years that it will take for the production of fossil fuels from their decay and compression.

Dinosaurs appear around 11 p.m. and rule the land until they vanish at 11:40 p.m., with mammals thereafter present. Human life starts one and one-quarter minutes before midnight, with recorded history just the last few seconds before midnight. Humans capable of speech have existed for only 0.0001 percent of the existence of the earth. During this compressed "day" of history, about three times every minute, a large meteor has crashed into the earth, destroying major parts of it. Such a major collision doesn't appear in the approximately one minute of human life on earth. (For more on the role of meteors in environmental damage, see Chapter 1.)

This places all living things in context. Most forms of life long predate us—not only plants, but also bacteria and viruses. Bacteria existed on earth billions of years before humans. Bacteria, often replicating in ten minutes and producing more than 100 billion offspring in a day, are an essential part of the environment: Their importance is linked to the creation and survival of humans. They create nucleotides and amino acids, make soil productive, purify water, and create oxygen. They make yogurt, cheese, and beer. Adding together all the living things on the planet, microbes constitute at least 80 percent of the volume of life by weight.

It is true that microbes are the number-three killer of humans, being responsible for malaria, yellow fever, encephalitis, and other diseases. Some of these can be spread through a simple mosquito bite. Bacteria in the environment are now being linked to ailments such as heart disease, arthritis, and some cancers. While we used to have antibiotics to successfully treat many of these bacteria, now more than 70 percent of antibiotics are mixed into animal feed to promote growth, and diseases have mutated around the antibiotics to develop immunity, rendering them ineffective (for discussion of the role of agriculture in environmental pollution, see Chapter 1). Although chemically simpler than bacteria, viruses are tiny and multiply prodigiously. They are responsible for influenza, which killed as many people in four months in 1918 as World War I did in four years between

1914 and 1917; smallpox, which killed 300 million people in the twentieth century; rabies; Ebola; polio; and HIV, which causes AIDS.

There has been massive extinction: Only approximately 1 living organism for every 10,000 that once existed is still alive today; 99.99 percent are now extinct. Hunters drove to extinction between 50 and 95 percent of the large animals on all continents. However, most of this global extinction is not from extinction by humans, but from the course of natural selection and evolution. There have been five major extinction events or periods, each wiping out between 75 and 95 percent of living species, according to fossil records. Three of these appear to be related to global cooling (see Chapter 5 for treatment of climate change). Meteor impacts also are blamed (see Chapter 1 regarding meteors and the environment); one that landed in Iowa had an explosive force equivalent to more than one Hiroshima-sized bomb for every person on earth today. Horses were reduced to only one species that survived — barely. At least 9,000 plants and animals are at risk of extinction in the United States alone, including 40 percent of U.S. fish species in U.S. lakes and rivers.

The distinction between animals and plants can be extremely subtle and often unappreciated. With apologies to SpongeBob Squarepants, the sponge spends its entire life not moving from a single place and has no heart, no brain, and no eye. Yet it is an animal. There are millions of protozoa in a drop of water.

The distinctions among people, as well as among various animals, are also chemically relatively minor. The DNA of all humans is 99.99 percent identical, with only a 0.1 percent variation. Humans have 96.4 percent identical DNA with chimpanzees, 90 percent identical DNA with mice, 60 percent identical DNA with fruit flies, about the same number of genes as a blade of grass; and half the chemical functions that occur in a banana also occur in human beings.

The cells of the human body are constantly being returned to the earth. The human body contains 10 thousand trillion cells; billions of them die daily, and skin cells are sloughed off into the environment. Each tiny human cell contains in its nucleus about six feet of DNA, the chemical code of life. Inside one human body, the length of DNA is more than 10 million miles, enough to stretch from the earth long past the moon. These dimensions are difficult to contemplate, but the connection of humans to other living things is evident in modern medicine: Nearly 40 percent of prescribed medicines are derived from plants, animals, or microbes.

Before looking at specific statutes, under common law, the government has the right to regulate access to wildlife, but does not have a property interest in the animals *per se* and is not liable for an animal's actions. Public ownership of wildlife is akin to a profit *a prendre*, allowing the government to impose limitations on the use of land as long as it does not constitute a "taking."

KEY STATUTES

Many species of plants and animals are essential for modern medicine. A fungus known as penicillin is an essential antibiotic. Certain tropical plants produce alkaloids used to treat heart disease, cancer, and other ailments.

Before the Endangered Species Act (ESA), only fragmentary legislation existed to protect wildlife. The states handled the earliest stages of wildlife management; intervention was limited. Established to regulate sport fishing and hunting, state laws operated on the premise that wildlife was a "public good." In 1900 the first federal legislation regulating wildlife focused on a few isolated species. The scope of federal protection was gradually extended, but only on a species-by-species basis. This first federal statute was the Lacey Act of 1900, which restricted interstate commerce of certain species taken in violation of state law. The Migratory Bird Treaty Act of 1918 was the first effective federal legislation to prohibit the taking of a species. Endangered species protection on a federal level was framed on a species-by-species basis until the 1960s (the Fish and Wildlife Coordination Act, 16 U.S.C. §661, is discussed at the end of Chapter 6).

The Lacey Act makes it unlawful to "import, export, transport, sell, receive, acquire, or purchase any wildlife already taken, possessed, transported, or sold in violation of State, Federal, American Indian Tribal, or foreign law." The Lacey Act has been interpreted not to include by implication violations of the Migratory Bird Treaty Act, and requires that something (a predicate offense) be done to wildlife that has already been "taken or possessed." *United States v. Carpenter*, 933 F.2d 748, 750 (9th Cir. 1991) (shooting a bird and having it fall on one's property is not a violation of the Act). A misdemeanor offense occurs when one with the exercise of due care should have known of the illegal nature of the act harming the animal. *United States v. Thomas*, 887 F.2d 1341 (9th Cir. 1989); *United States v. Hansen-Sturm*, 44 F.3d 793 (9th Cir. 1995). In 1969, Congress amended the Lacey Act to include amphibians, reptiles, mollusks, and crustaceans. More importantly, the Act's criminal sanctions increased to a fine of $10,000 for anyone who "knowingly and willfully" transported commoditized species across state lines for profit, and also allowed states to pursue offenders in civil courts for negligent violations. In 2008, plants and plant parts obtained in violation of foreign laws were included. By violating the underlying law or regulation, one necessarily violates the Lacey Act as well because it expressly incorporates foreign and international law, regardless of whether the underlying foreign law violation is criminal or civil in nature.

A felony offense requires *mens rea* as to the illegal status of the animal, even without knowledge of the illegality of the act or the provisions of the predicate law violated. *United States v. Todd*, 735 F.2d 146 (5th Cir. 1984); *United States v. Santillan*, 243 F.3d 1125 (9th Cir. 2001) (crossing the Tijuana border with parrots in a paper bag under one's car seat establishes *mens rea*); *United States v. McDougall*, 25 F. Supp. 2d 85 (D.N.Y. 1998) (defendant need not be a party that committed underlying offense to be liable). The foreign law that need be violated need only relate or refer to wildlife and need not be enacted necessarily for the protection of wildlife. *United States v. One Afghan Urial Ovis Orientalis Blanfordi Fully Mounted Sheep*, 964 F.2d 474 (5th Cir. 1992) (criminal penalties under the Act whenever predicate offenses involve foreign civil sanctions of any kind).

The Lacey Act also carries penalties for failure to mark or wrongfully mark any shipment of wildlife. 16 U.S.C. §§3372-3373. False labeling requires no predicate offense, as do other provisions of the Act. Filing false export declarations also is a violation of the Act. *McDougall, supra; United States v. Allemand*, 34 F.3d 923 (10th Cir. 1994).

A related statute is the Animal Welfare Act (7 U.S.C. §§2131-2159). Under this, the U.S. Department of Agriculture is required to promulgate regulations to provide standards to protect animals used in exhibitions. This includes providing a "physical environment adequate to promote the psychological well-being of primates." It was held that individual plaintiffs had standing to contest the failure of the agency to promulgate regulations to implement minimum standards for the protection of animals. *Animal League Defense Fund, Inc. v. Glickman*, 154 F.3d 426 (D.C. Cir. 1998) (plaintiff and the organization he represented had standing). The plaintiff alleged that he viewed animals mistreated at the zoo, which caused him to suffer a concrete, aesthetic injury, which would be redressed by properly promulgated regulations to protect not only the animal, but people like himself within the zone of interests the legislation was designed to protect. The injury was deemed to be distinct, aesthetic, and imminent.

This approach changed with the passage of the first Endangered Species Act in 1966, as subsequently amended by the 1973 Endangered Species Act, 16 U.S.C. §§1531 *et seq.* In this Act, Congress acknowledged the importance of biodiversity: "These species of fish, wildlife, and plants are of aesthetic, ecological, educational, historical, recreational and scientific value to the Nation and its people." 16 U.S.C. §1531(a)(3). The ESA set out to create the tools to conserve entire ecosystems necessary for the preservation of endangered species.

Congress used its earlier definition of species but extended it to embrace *any* member of any animal species or subspecies including entire populations. The 1973 Act extended protection to endangered species and also those threatened species that could foreseeably become extinct. The category of threatened species would also include species that have been "successfully restored" yet are still in need of protection.

Three major sections of the Act, §§4, 7, and 9, drive the machinery of the ESA. Section 4 lists the species. Section 7 requires interagency cooperation and consultation to prevent any federal action, including federal permits or funding, that places a species and or its "critical habitat" in jeopardy. Section 9 creates private party liability for prohibited acts against individual members of a species, specifically the "taking" of a species or destruction of habitat. The other operative sections of the Act are §10, which grants "incidental take" exemptions; §11, which delineates the enforcement provisions; and §6, which mandates state and federal cooperation. The Act's procedural requirements and guidelines are determined by the Administrative Procedure Act (see Chapter 2). Congress did not anticipate the potential powers of §§4, 7, and 9 of the Act. When Representative John Dingell itemized the nine principal changes that the Endangered Species Act would occasion, none of these included that §4 would cause many species to be listed without regard to economic considerations, or that §7 would halt federal programs that could jeopardize species, or that §9 would impose restrictions on private property land uses. 119 Cong. Rec. 30, 162-163 (Sept. 18, 1973) (statement of Representative John Dingell).

The ESA operates by listing endangered and threatened species of plants and animals, and their critical habitats. The Act applies to both federal and state actions. Any federal action requires consultation to prevent jeopardizing threatened species or their habitat. In addition, no private citizen can undertake any activity that will result in a taking of any species, even if the taking is unintentional. "Taking" can involve harming the habitat of an endangered species. Certain *incidental* takings are permitted, however. Let's look now at the specifics of the ESA.

Key Definitions

Key, broad-reaching definitions facilitate the purposes of the Act. The most important ESA nouns and adjectives are as follows.

Species is defined as a species, subspecies, or geographically separate population. In other words, very specialized, distinct branches of animals and plants are recognized for protection. Even though a species may have a healthy, viable population in one area, it could be threatened with extinction in another locale.

Endangered species is defined as any species threatened with extinction in all or a significant part of its range. *Fish or wildlife* is an unlimited term covering *any* creature dead or alive or its parts, products, offspring, or eggs. *Plant* takes in all seeds, roots, and other plant parts. Anything living or a part thereof is covered.

Threatened species refers to a species that is likely to become endangered within the foreseeable future throughout all or a large part of its range. By federal regulation, the same protection that shields *endangered* species applies to *threatened* ones. A little later, we'll discuss this distinction in more detail.

Places and activities also are key noun definitions in the ESA. *Critical habitat* is an area necessary for a species' survival. Unique food needs, shelter requirements, or breeding sites all delineate a critical habitat. Any physical or biological features essential to that species' survival or recovery can be designated for conservation based on a technical determination. A species does not have to *occupy* the habitat in question so long as the habitat satisfies fundamental behavioral needs. Critical habitat and the determination of an endangered or threatened species do not have to be established concurrently.

The scope of the habitat does not have to include the entire potential habitat. The *potential* geographical habitat for a species does not determine the *critical* habitat, except in cases where a limited area is the critical habitat. In *Palila v. Hawaii Dept. of Land and Natural Resources*, 852 F.2d 1106 (9th Cir. 1988), a state agency maintained a gaming program in which the game consumed the only possible food source for the palila, which is an endangered bird. The court scrapped the program, since it would render the endangered bird extinct. The destruction of the bird's habitat by sheep was deemed to threaten its ability to rebound from its endangered status. The result was that the sheep had to be removed from the forest to protect destruction of the endangered birds' habitat.

Conservation defines the purpose of the Act. As defined, conservation encompasses any and all measures of whatever kind necessary to remove a species from a threatened or endangered status. These measures range from scientific research to a regulated "taking." More about this below. Economic harm is not a factor in this analysis. In *Tennessee Valley Authority v. Hill*, 437 U.S. 153 (1978), the Court shut down a billion-dollar dam project so as to halt and reverse the trend toward species extinction, *"whatever the cost."*

One more noun and its modifier are important: *Commercial activity* extends to all activities of industry and trade and is not limited to mere buying and selling. However, exhibitions and the like by museums or similar cultural organizations are exempt from the "commerce" definition.

The Key Verb: "Take"

There is a single key verb to understand with respect to ESA. The Act operates to prevent the taking of any protected species. *Take* covers any possible conduct that could cause actual injury to an endangered or threatened species: to "harass, harm, pursue, hunt, shoot, wound, kill, trap, capture or collect or to attempt to engage in any such conduct." 16 U.S.C. §1532(3)(19). The verb *harm* is key in this string of definitions. *Harm* includes habitat modification as long as there is a showing of actual injury to wildlife. *Babbitt v. Sweet Home Chapter of Communities for a Great Oregon*, 515 U.S. 687 (1995). *Habitat modification* encompasses any activity that would significantly impair essential behavioral patterns such as breeding, feeding, or sheltering. 50 C.F.R. §17.3. So, *take* includes *harm*, which includes *habitat modification*, which includes impairment of breeding, feeding, or sheltering. Remember this key string.

Within the statute, the term "secretary" is a generic term that refers to the agency head who has authority for the implementation of respective sections of the ESA. The power vests according to the type of species. The secretary of the interior is responsible for land animals and freshwater fish, the secretary of commerce for marine mammals and saltwater fish, and the secretary of agriculture for the import and export of animals and plants. Command over the ESA is delegated to the U.S. Fish and Wildlife Service (FWS) and the National Marine Fisheries Service (NMFS), who then administer the ESA according to regulations promulgated by the respective "secretaries."

Examples

1. The piping plover, an endangered species, nests on the dunes of barrier beaches. The young birds are well camouflaged and remain on the ground for several weeks after hatching. Permits for off-road recreational vehicle travel on the beach generate considerable revenue for the state. Vehicle traffic crosses many nesting sites. Does the state have to close the beach to vehicle traffic? Why or why not?

2. The endangered palila's singular food source is threatened as a result of a state agency gaming program. If the gaming continues, the food supply will be eliminated.
   a. Can you enjoin the state from pursuing its gaming program?
   b. Evidence suggests the palila's population is increasing while the bird's singular food source is being threatened. Should the gaming program be halted under these circumstances? Why?

Explanations

1. Yes. Protection of a critical habitat is necessary whenever unique breeding, feeding, or sheltering patterns are interrupted. Thus in coastal New England, the piping plover's habitat is protected from beach traffic but only during nesting season while the fledglings are on the ground. Once the young birds are able to fly, the area is not restricted. The state does not do a balancing test weighing its economic interests against the plover's nesting requirements. The interest of the species is paramount.

2a. Since the gaming program directly interferes with the feeding habits of the palila, it meets the first prong of habitat modification: altering an essential *behavioral* pattern. The threat of injury is imminent to the species and that is enough to satisfy the *actual injury* requirement even without a corpus delicti.

2b. If the harm to the species merely affects the species' ability to recover from the endangered or threatened status, there is no proximate cause to suggest killing or actual injury. The status quo has not been altered.

However, if it is certain that the species will suffer injury as a result, protection should ensue since the purpose of conservation is to remove species from endangerment.

Listing of Species and Consultation

Listing Species and Habitat: §4

Listed species are protected. To protect species and enable them to recover before they become extinct, §4 of the ESA provides that species be identified and listed as either "endangered" or "threatened" species. Neither environmental impact statements (EIS) nor environmental assessments (EA) are necessary for listing of a species or its critical habitat, because the aims of the ESA are consistent with that of the National Environmental Policy Act (NEPA). You do not have to complete an EIS to satisfy the ESA, but you need to satisfy the ESA to complete an EA or a final EIS. Thus, while ESA is a factor in NEPA, an EIS is not necessary for ESA compliance.

No species receives full ESA protection until it is listed. The listing process is done "solely" in accordance with the "best scientific and commercial data available," because Congress intended for the secretary to use only *biological* criteria to determine which species are listed. 16 U.S.C. §1533(b). Economic factors are not considered when listing a species. Often species with similar characteristics are listed jointly or generically to increase protection for the truly endangered subspecies. Public notice is not necessary, but *actual* notice must be given to the affected state agencies.

To initiate the listing process, anyone may petition the secretary. Most actions to compel listing are brought by environmental groups under the citizen suit provision. Species proposed for listing must meet *any one* of five requirements in order for the petition to go forward:

1. The present or threatened destruction, modification, or curtailment of its habitat or range
2. Overutilization for commercial, recreational, scientific, or educational purposes
3. Disease or predation
4. The inadequacy of existing regulatory mechanisms
5. Other natural or manmade factors affecting its continued existence

16 U.S.C. §1533(a)(1).

In addition, §4 requires the secretary to list the species' critical habitat. The secretary uses the same listing criteria for both *species* and *habitat*. The critical habitat designation represents the geographic area necessary for the species' conservation and recovery from endangerment. Species *occupation* of a habitat is not a prerequisite for the classification.

A habitat may be excluded from protection if, after weighing the best scientific data available along with any other relevant impact, the secretary determines that the benefits of exclusion outweigh the benefits of inclusion. Unlike the listing of a species, the *economic* impact on a particular area may be considered in designating a habitat. This exclusion factor is widely used. Contrary to the mandate of the ESA, most species do *not* have a critical habitat listed for them.

In addition, the secretary must establish recovery plans for each listed species. He or she may allocate resources according to those species most likely to benefit from recovery efforts. Recovery is based on the secretary's reasonable belief as to what promotes conservation, and the plans are therefore discretionary. The Act allows the agency to acquire land to further the interest of conservation. However, due to limited appropriations, recovery plans do not receive first priority.

Because of limited funds, the biggest problem is the huge backlog of proposed or "candidate" species. In 1994 there were over 3,000 unlisted candidate species. These are often categorized by the secretary as "warranted but precluded" because of other species' more urgent listing demands. Since an unlisted or candidate species receives little protection, human activity is unaffected. There were more than 900 listed animal species and about 600 listed plant species as of 2010, with Hawaii being home to the largest number of these. Former Representative Richard Pombo (R. Ca.) charged that the Endangered Species Act has recovered only ten of the approximately 1,300 species on the list of threatened animals. He has equated the program with a "failed managed care program that checks species in but never checks them out."

Required Cooperation and Consultation for Listed Species and Habitat: §7

The federal government must consult proactively to protect species. Any person who requests federal action in the form of a federal permit, federal license, or federal funding for any project — federal, municipal, or private — must submit to a *consultation* between the appropriate wildlife agency and the concerned federal agency. Direct and indirect effects must be considered. *National Wildlife Federation v. Coleman*, 529 F.2d 359 (5th Cir. 1976). In every consultation, "each agency shall use the best scientific and commercial data available." 16 U.S.C. §1536(a)(2). Most consultations are informal, because most projects do not affect listed endangered species, candidate species, or their critical habitats. If questions arise as to the potential impact on a listed or candidate species or its critical habitat, formal consultation is necessary.

Once the formal process is initiated, the proposing agency may make no "irreversible or irretrievable commitment of resources." 16 U.S.C. §1536(d). Once again, we encounter a key term. The formal consultation process is designed to prevent any agency action that could "jeopardize the continued existence of any endangered species or threatened species or result in the destruction or adverse modification of habitat." 16 U.S.C. §1536(a)(2). The "jeopardy" analysis also extends to the continued existence of candidate species and the adverse modification of a proposed critical habitat.

The inquiry into jeopardy concerning the continued existence of a species centers on the potential effect on reproduction, population, or distribution, and that in turn generates a determination of the likelihood of the species' survival in the wild. The regulatory criteria for evaluating habitat modification include (1) space for individual and population growth, and for normal behavior; (2) food, water, air, light, minerals, or other nutritional or physiological requirements; (3) cover or shelter; and (4) sites for breeding, reproduction, rearing of offspring. 50 C.F.R. §424.12 (1992).

When a protected habitat or species is implicated, the same habitat modification criteria must be met to insure only an incidental taking. An incidental taking is a discrete event that does not jeopardize the species as a whole. The consultation process concludes once the proposal formally satisfies the jeopardy test.

In National Ass'n of Home Builders v. Defenders of Wildlife, 551 U.S. 644 (2007), the Court held that the EPA does not have to engage in consultation under the Endangered Species Act before delegating to a state permitting authority under the Clean Water Act. The Court also held that §7 of the Endangered Species Act only applies to agency actions that are "discretionary." In essence, the Act does not override independent authority that the EPA has under the Clean Water Act. The 5-4 majority of the Court accorded Chevron deference to the EPA to interpret a statute (the Endangered Species Act) that it does not administer.

State endangered species acts often parallel the federal Act, and add an extra layer of review and permitting which can restrict a project proposal. Typically, states will have similar administrative processes for identifying and listing the critical areas for endangered species. State endangered species can differ from the list maintained under the federal Act, and state wetlands protection acts may also protect wildlife habitat.

State action must comply with the purposes of the ESA, but it is not subject to the consultation process. Stricter state laws are not preempted by the Act as long as they do not contravene exceptions, exemptions, or permits granted under ESA §4, §7, or §10. The Supreme Court recognized "a conscious decision by Congress to give endangered species priority over the 'primary missions' of federal agencies." *TVA v. Hill*, 437 U.S. 153 (1978). If there is a conflict, "the firm opinion of the expert wildlife agency is entitled to a presumption of validity until overborne by contrary evidence." *Sierra Club v. Froehlke*, 534 F.2d 1289 (8th Cir. 1976). Judicial review of the secretary's actions is based on the APA's "arbitrary and capricious" standard. (See Chapter 2.)

Exemption from §7

Section 7 does create one narrow exemption whereby a project that will jeopardize a listed species or its critical habitat may proceed. If an application is denied in the consultation process, the applicant may pursue the matter with a cabinet-level group, the Endangered Species Committee (otherwise known as the "God squad"). This administrative route is rarely used because to succeed an applicant must first exhaust the consultation process and then demonstrate that the need for the proposed project meets a very demanding test. Only three petitions were considered over three decades, and only one of these, for the Grayrocs Dam, which jeopardized the whooping crane, was approved.

Five out of the seven members of the "God squad" must determine that:

1. no reasonable alternatives to the agency action exist,
2. the benefits of the action clearly outweigh the benefits of any alternative course of action consistent with the conservation of species or its critical habitat,
3. the action is in the public interest and of regional or national significance, *and*
4. neither the agency involved nor the exemption applicant has made an irreversible or irretrievable commitment of resources.

16 U.S.C. §1536(h).

In *Tennessee Valley Authority v. Hill*, the Tellico Dam was a billion-dollar project that did not meet this stringent test. If an exemption does issue, it is not subject to §9's prohibited acts (discussed after the Examples and Explanations). *Tennessee Valley Authority v. Hill* blocked the operation of the nearly completed Tellico Dam to save the snail darter, a small perch, because the Act makes the value of every endangered species "incalculable." Congress subsequently approved a rider to the Energy and Water Development

Appropriation Act of 1980 exempting the dam from §7 and allowing its completion and operation. Ironically, after operation, it was found that the snail darter was not present only on the affected river, but was present on other rivers in Tennessee; its status was down-listed from "endangered" to "threatened." See 50 C.F.R. §17.11.

Examples

1. A federally funded dam in Alaska is near completion, after being under construction for several years, when a previously unknown species of turtle, the arctic snow-turtle, is discovered in the riverbed. It is thought that the snow-turtle may only exist in this riverbed.
   a. Environmentalists want the project stopped, while Alaskan authorities urge that it should proceed. What should the result be? Why?
   b. The already "sunk" or expended cost of the dam is over a billion dollars. What impact should this have in the dispute? Is judicial review available?
   c. Suppose that the environmentalists' real agenda is to halt the project using the newly discovered rare species. What result?
   d. Assuming that the snow-turtle is an endangered species, must its critical habitat be designated at the same time? Why?

2. Do all federal permits and licenses require consideration of threatened species, endangered species, and candidate species as well as their critical habitats?

3. Do all state permits for private action require consideration of threatened, endangered, and candidate species as well as their critical habitats?

4. A proposed interstate highway will receive federal funding but will be constructed by the state Highway Department. It is to traverse the habitat of a rare species of crane. For the crane to survive, the habitat must retain its wilderness qualities. The Department of Transportation, in consultation with the U.S. Fish and Wildlife Service, has determined that the actual construction of the highway will have little or no direct effect on the crane's habitat. After it is built there will be indirect effects such as increased traffic, air pollution, and some development near the interchange exits. The Federal Highway Administration does not control development outside of the easements granted for construction of the highway.
   a. Does the state Highway Department have to consider both the direct effects and the indirect effects of its proposed action? Why?
   b. What is the effect if the secretary promulgates an emergency listing for the crane's critical habitat?

621

   c. If, under another statute, a Final Environmental Impact Statement has been issued, does the agency involved still have to initiate the consultation process?

   d. Can the U.S. Department of the Interior veto the action proposed by the Federal Highway Administration?

   e. Under what circumstances could a court find an abuse of discretion by an agency?

   f. If the FWS were to acquire a refuge for the crane in some other location, would that mitigate the Highway Department's obligation to protect the crane's habitat in the area of the proposed highway?

   g. If essential permits are denied to the Highway Department because it is not in compliance with the ESA, can the project still proceed?

5. Offshore oil drilling has many stages: exploration, development of wells, and production of oil. If stage one — exploration — is approved by the secretary, are additional subsequent consultations necessary for the later stages? Why?

Explanations

1a. No species receives ESA protection until it is listed. No protection for the snow-turtle is available until a petition for emergency listing is presented to the agency and adopted. Such adoption is a possibility, since there is a "significant risk to the well-being of a species." 16 U.S.C. §1533(B)(7). Two things must happen for the emergency regulation to have force and effect: It must be published in the Federal Register, and the secretary must give actual notice to the appropriate Alaskan state agency. A permanent listing must then be obtained within 240 days through the regular APA rulemaking channels (see Chapter 2).

1b. There is no judicial balancing test between the value of a species and the value of a project. Under the ESA, the obligation of the court is preservation of the status quo; thus all other options rest with executive or legislative branches. In *TVA v. Hill*, the Court held that it does not matter "whether a dam is 50% or 90% completed in calculating the social and scientific costs attributable to the disappearance of a unique form of life." The legislative mandate is for the preservation of biodiversity. Thus, the Court did not consider the economic effects of the ESA. Instead the judiciary pointed to the legislative branch to consider any adverse economic effects caused by implementation of the ESA.

1c. The snow-turtle would still be listed. Since listing decisions for species are based on science alone, personal agendas, emotional attachments, or economic impact do not factor in the listing process. Under the statute, scientific evaluation is intended to guarantee that all interested parties are treated equally.

1d. Yes. Whenever the designation of a species' critical habitat is determinable at the time of listing, the ESA dictates that the designation must be made at the time of listing. *Northern Spotted Owl v. Hodel*, 716 F. Supp. 479 (W.D. Wash. 1988). The goal is to prevent a *taking* of the listed species in the designated area.

2. Yes. Informal consultation is the first step to securing a permit or license. The secretary determines whether any listed or candidate species are affected by the plan. No further consultation is needed if there is no impact. A positive finding will trigger the need for a biological assessment and formal consultation. 16 U.S.C. §1536(c).

3. Yes. All state action must comply with the mandate of the ESA. However, if there is no need for federal funds, federal permits, federal licenses, or any other type of federal agency cooperation, §7 consultation does not operate.

4a. Yes. While the project in and of itself does not place the species in jeopardy, the inherent effects of highway construction will jeopardize the cranes' continued existence. Direct and indirect effects of proposed action must be considered in the consultation process.

4b. If the secretary determines that construction threatens part of the crane's critical habitat and that their significant well-being is in jeopardy, an emergency listing is warranted. Listing the crane brings its habitat under the express protection of §7. The rule restricts anything that would result in the destruction or adverse modification of a designated critical habitat.

4c. Yes. A satisfactory EIS does not waive the requirements of §7. An informal conference between the wildlife agency and the proposing agency must take place. If there are no implications for protected species or their habitat, the informal conference satisfies the consultation requirement.

4d. No. After the consultation process is finished, the requesting agency is not bound by the findings of the secretary. The action is then subject only to judicial review. Usually a citizens' group will attempt to enjoin the project until the ESA requirements are met. The court will determine if the requesting agency acted within the scope of its authority and then whether "the decision was based on a consideration of the relevant factors and whether there has been a clear error of judgment." *Citizens to Preserve Overton Park, Inc. v. Volpe*, 401 U.S. 402 (1971).

4e. Any contravention of the statute is viewed as an abuse of discretion. It is unlawful if an agency does not use the best scientific and commercial data available in the consultation process.

4f. No. Other protections afforded to a species in another locale do not alleviate the Highway Department's obligation to minimize disturbance to a habitat under its own proposal.

4g. No, not without an exemption. The last recourse is a petition to the Endangered Species Committee, the God squad, for an exemption. In order to get an exemption, all requirements of 16 U.S.C. §1536(h) must be satisfied.

5. At each level — exploration, development, production plan, and permission to drill — ESA reevaluation is necessary. It is implicit in the secretary's approval that every level of the project will comply with the ESA.

TAKINGS: §9

What Private Action Is Prohibited?

Individual acts that threaten species are prohibited. Section 9 enumerates all prohibited acts under the ESA. Any commercial activity (international, interstate, or in-state) involving a protected species is prohibited. Transport of a protected species is prohibited. Malicious destruction of a species or a habitat under federal jurisdiction is prohibited. The section does not apply to protected plants on private land if one is trespassing. Unlike §§6 and 7, §9 focuses on the activities of *any person*, not just on federal actions. The only exceptions are permits granted either by the God squad or incidental takings under §10 (discussed below).

The so-called "take" provision is the primary mechanism protecting listed species from the risks of development in the private sector. Most importantly, §9 declares that the "taking" of an *individual* member of a listed species is a prohibited act anywhere that federal jurisdiction applies. It does not matter that the taking was unintentional. One single taking is illegal. But, Section 9 does not apply to *plants on federal land* if a "taking" is *unintentional*. The scope of prohibited taking reaches the removal of any *part* or *stage* of a listed species (like eggs, body parts, or fur) or its habitat.

To further the national policy of protection and conservation, Congress defined "take" very broadly. From humble beginnings, this section has emerged as the subject of extensive and protracted litigation. Remember the string of terms defined earlier. The term *take* is defined by statute as "harass, harm, pursue, hunt, shoot, wound, kill, trap, capture, or collect or attempt to engage in any such conduct." 16 U.S.C. §1532(19). To construct a comprehensive understanding of the "take" definition, the secretary promulgated regulations to define *harass* as "an intentional or negligent act or omission which creates the likelihood of injury to wildlife by annoying it to such an extent as to significantly disrupt normal behavioral patterns which include, but are not limited to, breeding, feeding or sheltering." 16 U.S.C. §17.3.

Harm is defined in the same regulation as:

> . . . an act which actually kills or injures wildlife. Such act may include significant habitat modification or degradation where it actually kills or injures wildlife by significantly impairing essential behavioral patterns, including breeding, feeding or sheltering.

50 C.F.R. §17.3.

As a result of the "harm" definition, modification of a species' habitat can invoke a §9 "taking." This definition of harm is applied to protect and conserve listed species and critical habitat. To establish that a "taking" has occurred by habitat modification, one must show "significantly impairing essential behavioral patterns, including breeding, feeding, or sheltering." The regulation acknowledges behavioral patterns necessary to insure a species' survival. Harm to those patterns may be shown to be imminent, but it must not be too speculative.

It is possible to prevent an illegal *taking* by showing that no imminent actual injury to the species or habitat has occurred. One-time isolated disturbances are not enough to sustain a *taking* finding; however, a threat to the total population will constitute a taking. Without evidence substantiating a threat of injury, numerical probability or scientific data will not suffice. Actual injury to a species from habitat modification must be established for the court to find that a §9 taking has occurred.

In *United States v. Glenn-Colusa Irrigation Dist.*, 788 F. Supp. 1126 (E.D. Ca. 1992), an injunction was sought to prevent river water pumping that threatened to impinge upon and thus endanger Chinook salmon, a threatened species. The court restricted pumping rates during the salmon's high migration season in the river. In *Babbitt v. Sweet Home Chapter of Communities for a Great Oregon*, 515 U.S. 687 (1995), concerning the protection of the habitat of the red-cockaded woodpecker and spotted owl, the court interpreted the term "take" "to include significant habitat modification or degradation that actually kills or injures wild life." It held that resumption of logging activities would degrade the critical habitat causing loss of the species.

Circuit court opinions of "take" after *Sweet Home* are not consistent. Cf. *Marbled Murrelet v. Babbitt*, 83 F.3d 1060 (9th Cir. 1996) (no actual harm need to have happened if threat exists); *Strahan v. Coxe*, 127 F.3d 155 (1st Cir.

1997) (actual injury required for a "take"); *Loggerhead Turtle v. County Council*, 92 F. Supp. 2d 1296 (M.D. Fla. 2000) (past death sufficient to show "take"). Even where an endangered species is found only within a single state, there is a substantial enough interstate commerce issue for the ESA to regulate takes. *GDF Realty Investments, Ltd. v. Norton*, 326 F.3d 622 (5th Cir. 2003) (aggregating particular species with all other endangered species as part of larger regulatory scheme).

Incidental Takes Allowed: §10

Section 10 of the ESA grants the secretary authority to issue a permit for incidental "takes" pursuant to an otherwise lawful activity. The goal of the section is to balance development interests with conservation interests. Permits are available to private parties wishing to avoid §9 violations for incidental takes as long as the "taking is incidental to and not the purpose of, the carrying out of an otherwise lawful activity." 16 U.S.C. §1539(B).

The permit process requires a lengthy and potentially expensive notice and comment hearing. The permit will issue after adequate assurances are made to the secretary that the applicant will minimize and mitigate the effects of the taking and that the required habitat conservation plan will be implemented. A conservation plan must accompany the request for an incidental "take" permit.

The legislative goal behind the conservation plan is to retain enough of the habitat to encourage a listed species' recovery. The plan, which is mandatory, examines the impact to the species and ways to minimize and mitigate that impact. The conservation plan must meet the requirements for food, shelter, breeding sites, and the rearing of offspring, and it must specify how these steps will be funded. An applicant must document why alternatives are not feasible. The standard used to grant or deny the permit is the §7 regulatory criteria for evaluating habitat modification.

An incidental "take" permit, valid for one year, may issue for undue economic hardship, and allows development of private land. There is no limit for incidental takes. The applicant must have a contractual relationship that predates the notice of a *candidate* species' initial listing in the Federal Register. In addition, Alaskan natives are granted incidental "take" permits if such a taking is primarily for human subsistence.

Enforcement: §11

The enforcement provisions in §11 of the ESA create civil penalties and criminal penalties of up to $50,000 and a year in prison for a knowing criminal violation, and allow for citizen suits. A citizen may enjoin any person, including the United States, "who is alleged to be in violation of any provision of the ESA." 16 U.S.C. §1540(g). Intent is irrelevant as to whether or not a violation has occurred. Injunctions, warrants, forfeiture, condemnation, rewards, fines, and some expenses are all court remedy options under §11.

Standing was automatic under the language of the citizen suit provision. However, a Supreme Court decision altered the requirement for citizen suit standing. Now a citizen must show some direct injury. *Lujan v. Defenders of Wildlife*, 504 U.S. 555 (1992). However, the Ninth Circuit held that imminent past, present, or future injury to a species is enough to satisfy the distinct injury to plaintiff requirement. *Forest Conservation Council v. Roseboro Lumber Co.*, 50 F.3d 781 (9th Cir. 1995). The Ninth Circuit decision did not reach the issue of whether habitat modification that merely retards a species' recovery met the injury requirement to constitute a "taking."

In *Bennett v. Spear*, 520 U.S. 154 (1997), the Court held that any person, even one opposed to government protection of endangered species, is within the "zone of interests" to challenge the action. Justice Scalia, writing for the majority, found that "economic consequences are an explicit concern of the Act." This decision lets those opposed to species preservation challenge decisions under the Act. The petitioners also satisfied the zone-of-interest requirement under the Administrative Procedure Act to challenge the factual record assembled by the agency. (See Chapter 2.)

In the aftermath of the Supreme Court decisions construing the Endangered Species Act, the lower federal courts have generally deferred to broad restrictions enacted by responsible agencies (see Chapter 11 for discussion of federal agency responsibilities for public lands). See *Mausolf v. Babbitt*, 125 F.3d 661 (8th Cir. 1997) (upholding restriction of snowmobiles to minimize harm to the endangered gray wolf habitat); *Bensman v. U.S. Forest Service*, 984 F. Supp. 1242 (W.D. Mo. 1997) (preserving hibernation and breeding areas during the hibernation season of the Indiana bat); *United States v. Town of Plymouth*, 6 F. Supp. 2d 81 (D. Mass. 1998) (enjoining off-road vehicles on the beach that endangered the piping plover); *Loggerhead Turtle v. County Council*, 148 F.3d 1231 (11th Cir. 1998) (enjoining vehicles from driving on a beach and threatening baby turtles).

Examples

1. A train car derailed, spilling corn. The corn attracted grizzly bears, a listed species, to the spill site. The bears remained after the spill was removed. Subsequently, bears were killed by trains passing through the area.
   a. Has the railroad company committed a "taking"? Is the remedy foreshadowed in these facts? Why?
   b. Can the railroad company be held liable under §9? Why?

2. Sampson's Hill is being considered for a new housing development. Several species of endangered moths make this area their home.
   a. How can the developer proceed if it is certain some members of the species will be destroyed?
   b. What must the developer consider and do to go forward with his or her plans?
   c. Must the court balance the equities before issuing an injunction?

Explanations

1a. Yes, amazingly enough. Actual injury, necessary for a taking finding, was undisputed. The remedy, however, was effected by the routine removal of the corn. The unintentional disruption to the habitat was of a "localized nature" and [could] "not be characterized as significant." Therefore, no future restrictions will apply, once the corn removal is accomplished. There is no threat to the entire species.

1b. The corn spill modified the habitat on only a temporary basis. Once the disruption was removed, no further habitat modification resulted. A temporary modification of feeding habits where actual death did occur is not a "*significant* impact on the grizzly bear habitat." This is because not one of the habitat's essential elements — those needed for breeding, feeding, or sheltering — was modified. Therefore, there is no §9 liability for the railroad even though a taking occurred unintentionally. See *National Wildlife Fed'n v. Burlington N. R.R.*, 23 F.3d 1508, 1510 (9th Cir. 1994).

2a. If a taking is certain, the developer may consider applying for a special permit to proceed. A permit could allow for an *incidental* taking if all criteria are met and the species is not threatened with extinction because of this development.

2b. A habitat conservation plan must always be established to guarantee minimal interference with essential behavioral patterns. Thus the plan must address and meet the fundamental needs for the species' feeding, breeding, and sheltering. Perhaps an appropriate parcel of the site could be designated a permanent conservation area for the species. The species must be able to coexist with the development in spite of a few incidental losses in order for the development to be permitted to proceed.

2c. No. Allegations of irreparable harm to a species are enough for a plaintiff to obtain an injunction from the court. The balancing test is less rigorous for prohibited acts under §9 of the ESA. Injunctions will issue when substantial statutory violations exist that endanger the species' status quo.

TSCA and FIFRA: Regulating Chemical Manufacture and Distribution

"What is food to one, is to others bitter poison."

Titus Lucretius, De Rerum Natura (On the Nature of Things), 55 B.C.

"In time the sun will become mostly helium. . . . [C]arbon, for instance, is formed in a star whenever three helium nuclei collide at one spot within less than a millionth of a millionth of a second. Every carbon atom in every living creature has been formed by such a wildly improbable collision."

J. Bronowski, The Ascent of Man, 1973

"Double, double, toil and trouble; Fire burn and cauldron bubble. . . . Eye of newt and toe of frog, Wool of bat and tongue of dog. . . ."

William Shakespeare, Macbeth

Since World War II, tens of thousands of new, synthetic chemicals have been manufactured and released into the environment. Since then, more than 100,000 chemical substances have entered into the market, with most still in commercial use. Persistent organic pollutants, including polycyclic aromatic hydrocarbons and halogenated hydrocarbons, are toxic, persistent in the duration that they remain in the environment, and have a tendency to bioaccumulate in living organisms' fatty tissues. This can lead to cancer, damage to the central and peripheral nervous systems, diseases of the immune system, reproductive disorders, and behavioral abnormalities.

In Chapters 5, 6, 8, and 9, we examined how different federal environmental laws regulate chemical substances as *wastes* or when released to the environment (RCRA, CERCLA, the Clean Water Act, the Clean Air Act). Two key federal statutes, the Federal Insecticide, Fungicide, and Rodenticide Act (FIFRA) and the Toxic Substances Control Act (TSCA), control toxic chemical substances when they are produced and as they enter the market. These statutes focus on toxic *products*. TSCA also regulates unauthorized disposal.

Controlling market access can prevent irreparable injury because it potentially stops a product before it reaches the market. Because market access of a substance is integrally tied to interstate commerce, the constitutional basis for federal regulation is well established. First, an overview of TSCA.

THE TOXIC SUBSTANCES CONTROL ACT (TSCA)

The Toxic Substances Control Act (TSCA) was enacted in 1976 "to prevent unreasonable risks of injury to health or the environment associated with the manufacture, processing, distribution in commerce, use or disposal of chemical substances." It also covers importation of chemicals into the United States. It was intended to fill a regulatory gap by creating protection "upstream" of the final point when chemicals were discarded as wastes. TSCA regulates products, rather than wastes, becoming one of the first statutes to focus on pollution prevention rather than waste remediation. TSCA attempts to regulate the introduction of new chemical substances that could pose serious health and environmental risks. TSCA has become a major vehicle for advancing the EPA agenda of pollution prevention.

TSCA creates an inventory of all chemical substances in commerce; it requires submission of a premanufacture notice at least 90 days before the commencement of manufacture or import of a new chemical substance or an existing chemical substance is employed for a "significant new use." Ultimately, the EPA can ban or restrict the manufacture, processing, or distribution in commerce of new chemical substances or new uses of existing substances.

The basic structure of TSCA authorizes the EPA to promulgate chemical test rules (§4), regulate or ban chemical substances (§6), require reporting and recordkeeping regarding health studies and health impacts where a substance presents a substantial risk of injury to health or the environment (§8), and regulate the import and export of such chemicals (§13). Despite the relatively low profile of TSCA and the relatively specialized legal practice surrounding it, the EPA has elevated TSCA as a major enforcement mechanism in its arsenal. The fines and penalties generated under TSCA often exceed those fines and penalties imposed by the EPA under RCRA, CERCLA, the Clean Air Act, and the Clean Water Act regulatory provisions.

This Act was the first comprehensive statute to regulate the manufacture, distribution, and processing of chemical substances in order to protect public health and the environment. TSCA is a classic "catch-all" statute: If no other federal law regulates market access for a specific chemical substance, it is regulated under TSCA.

What Is a Chemical Substance?

The jurisdictional reach of TSCA is extremely broad, encompassing any "chemical substance" or "mixture." Section 3(2) of TSCA defines "chemical substance" as "any organic or inorganic substance of a particular molecular identity." It excludes substances already regulated under other federal statutes such as pesticides under FIFRA; foods, drugs, and cosmetics under the Federal Food Drug and Cosmetics Act; and nuclear material under the Atomic Energy Act, as well as "mixtures" from the definition. A "mixture" is "any combination of two or more chemical substances which does not occur in nature and is not the result of a chemical reaction." Section 3(8).

TSCA is potentially applicable to all chemical substances and mixtures that are manufactured, imported, processed, used, distributed, or disposed of in the United States. While mixtures are not themselves considered chemical *substances*, they are defined separately as unreacted *combinations* of chemical substances. TSCA is potentially applicable to almost every form of matter, be it natural or artificial, with exception to those specific substances already regulated by other federal statutes. We will employ the term "chemical substance" hereinafter to denote both "chemical substance" and "mixture."

TSCA divides all chemical substances into two categories: (1) existing chemical substances and (2) new chemical substances. When initially enacted, §8(b) of the Act directed the EPA to form and maintain a list of all chemical substances in the United States. The list was completed in 1980 and totaled approximately 60,000 existing substances. Any substance manufactured or processed after 1980, and not included on the TSCA inventory list, was labeled a "new" chemical substance. New chemical substances are subject to a stricter regulatory process than are existing chemical substances. Since 1980, more than 10,000 "new" chemical substances have been added to the inventory list.

Parties Regulated

TSCA regulates two principal parties: manufacturers and processors. A processor is one who prepares a chemical substance or mixture after its manufacture for distribution in commerce. Processing also includes the incorporation of a chemical substance into an "article" that is "distributed in commerce." If one purchases raw materials and manufactures products that contain a listed chemical substance, one can be regulated as a processor. The EPA will consider a company as a "processor" if it uses a TSCA-covered chemical substance and fabricates an article that is later distributed in commerce, and that article contains the substance or a mixture containing that substance, or a reaction product of that substance. It is important to note that even if one is a processor, TSCA will not regulate that entity unless there is "distribution in commerce" and ultimate end use of the product. Other sections of TSCA regulate parties who "distribute" chemical substances into the stream of commerce.

Testing Chemical Substances

Under TSCA, the EPA has the power to regulate the sale and distribution of chemical substances and mixtures. However, the EPA must prove the necessity of regulation in order to exercise this power. How does the EPA obtain the needed data to determine whether or not a chemical substance should be regulated? Unlike the FIFRA regulatory system, where the applicant has the burden of proving the safety of the product, the EPA can require testing only if it establishes the threshold standards embodied in §4 in the case of each individual chemical substance. If these standards are met, the EPA may require the manufacturer or processor to test the product in accordance with EPA standards, and to provide test results concerning health and environmental effects. The manufacturer or processor endures the time and expense of the testing.

The test results are used by the EPA to determine whether or not to regulate the product. Under TSCA, the EPA has the burden of proving the need for both the initial testing and the ultimate regulation. Section 4(a) of TSCA sets out three requirements for the EPA to require testing:

- Insufficient data exist on the chemical substance and its effects on health and the environment;
- Testing of the chemical substance is necessary to develop sufficient data; and
- Either (a) the manufacture, distribution, processing, use, or disposal of the chemical substance may present an unreasonable risk of injury to health or the environment, or (b) the chemical substance is, or will be, produced in substantial quantities and may enter the environment in substantial quantities or there may be significant exposure to it.

TSCA's requirement that the EPA formulate a rule to force testing has suffered severe criticism for several reasons. It has proven to be slow as well as costly: The required tests may cost as much as $2 million per substance. Due to its own budget constraints, the EPA may not be able to gather sufficient information to regulate a substance unless it can force testing by the industry.

The EPA rules on mandatory testing have been challenged by several chemical manufacturers. In *Chemical Manufacturers Ass'n v. EPA*, 859 F.2d 977 (D.C. Cir. 1988), an industry group attacked an EPA §(4) rule that required testing of 2-ethylhexanoic acid (EHA). The D.C. Circuit rejected the challenge, finding that EHA posed an unreasonable risk of injury to health, deferring to EPA interpretation on three central points:

- To establish an unreasonable risk, the EPA need only demonstrate "a more-than-theoretical basis for suspecting" that humans are exposed to the substance and that the substance is sufficiently toxic at that exposure level to present such unreasonable risk.
- The EPA is not required to produce direct evidence documenting human exposure; exposure may be inferred from the circumstances under which the substance is manufactured and used.
- Rare, brief human exposure may be enough to support a test rule; accordingly, a national survey that suggested that roughly 50 individuals might have occasional skin contact with EHA was sufficient to demonstrate exposure.

Notwithstanding the decision in *Chemical Manufacturers Ass'n*, the EPA rarely forces mandatory testing. During the first 18 years of TSCA's existence, the EPA issued only 30 test rules. It is more common that the EPA reaches a voluntary testing consent agreement with manufacturers and processors rather than implementing its mandatory power. In *Natural Resources Defense Council, Inc. v. EPA*, 595 F. Supp. 1255 (S.D.N.Y. 1984), the court declared that chemicals posing substantial health and environmental risks, upon which there are insufficient data, must be tested by the EPA pursuant to formal rulemaking proceedings.

Regulating Existing Chemical Substances

There are tens of thousands of existing chemical substances and mixtures. The EPA's authority over these existing substances depends on what the substances do and how they are used. These are highlighted below.

Existing Substances That Present an "Unreasonable Risk of Injury"

Once data are available, the EPA must conclude whether to allow the substance to be sold in commerce. TSCA §6(a) requires the EPA to establish a "reasonable basis" to conclude that the manufacture, processing, distributing, use, or disposal of a specific chemical substance presents an "unreasonable risk of injury to health or the environment" before disallowing a substance. The EPA under §6(c) considers (a) the effects of the substance on human health and the environment, (b) the magnitude of the exposure of humans and the environment to the substance, (c) the benefits of the substance, (d) the availability of substitutes for the substance, and (e) the reasonably ascertainable economic consequences of the rule. The EPA only allows a substance into commerce where the substance has benefits that outweigh its environmental costs.

The EPA can impose restrictions, but must choose the technique that will provide sufficient public and environmental protection against the risk "using the least burdensome requirements." Depending upon the circumstances, the EPA may do any of the following:

- Prohibit manufacture, distribution, or processing
- Limit the quantity that may be manufactured or distributed
- Prohibit the use of the substance for certain purposes
- Require warnings and instructions
- Prohibit or regulate the method of disposal
- Require that manufacturers give notice of unreasonable risk of injury to distributors, consumers, and the public

In *Corrosion Proof Fittings v. EPA*, 947 F.2d 1201 (5th Cir. 1991), the Fifth Circuit invalidated the EPA's asbestos ban, holding that EPA's lengthy and comprehensive study on asbestos was insufficient to justify the restriction imposed. This decision severely undercut the practical utility of §6, which led many to question the viability of the entire program. Under the *Corrosion Proof Fittings* decision, a complete products ban under §6 was unsustainable. The decision suggests that the §6 threshold may be so rigorous that it is unworkable in most instances, regardless of the EPA remedy sought.

PCBs are carcinogenic and mutagenic materials traditionally used as electrolytes in certain transformers, capacitors, and other electrical equipment. Section 6(e) provides a general prohibition for the manufacture, processing, distribution, or use of PCBs, "in a manner other than a totally enclosed manner." However, as toxic as PCBs are, at less than 50 ppm oils are not considered to be PCB containing. The EPA's PCB rule has not required the removal of PCB-containing equipment or of PCBs in soil. Therefore, PCBs remain in many electrical components and as potential contaminants. TSCA employs a PCB regulatory scheme that presumes that the presence of any PCB is an unauthorized release unless the property owner can prove otherwise by a preponderance of evidence — a difficult burden. It is unresolved whether such a burden satisfies basic due process requirements.

Asbestos was banned for most applications for new construction in 1989 by the EPA. EPA estimates that more than 100,000 schools and almost three-quarters of a million public and commercial buildings contain asbestos. The Asbestos Hazard Emergency Response Act (AHERA), enacted in 1986 as amendments to TSCA, requires schools to manage asbestos risk. Asbestos is also regulated pursuant to §112 of the Clean Air Act as a hazardous air pollutant.

On any removal project, EPA is required to be notified in advance if removing more than 260 linear feet of asbestos or more than 160 square feet of other components of asbestos-containing materials. Asbestos-containing material is that deemed to contain more than 1 percent asbestos. Supervision, training, and monitoring are required for asbestos removal. Residential buildings of four or fewer dwellings are exempt from asbestos regulations.

Workplace exposure to asbestos is governed by OSHA by the issuance of Personal Exposure Limits (PELs), which have been made more stringent over time. The courts have often stricken the EPA efforts to tighten the asbestos exposure standards. See *Asbestos Info. Ass'n of North America v. OSHA*, 727 F.2d 415 (5th Cir. 1984); *Building & Construction Trades Dept., AFL-CIO v. Brock*, 838 F.2d 1258 (D.C. Cir. 1988). Now workers exposed to asbestos levels of 0.1 fibers/cc or greater must be protected through the use of personal protection gear under OSHA and EPA regulations. 29 C.F.R. Part 1926, Subpart D.

"Imminently Hazardous" Existing Substances

Some substances may be discovered to pose substantial immediate risk. TSCA §7 authorizes the EPA to seek immediate judicial relief in emergency situations. This section authorizes the EPA to take action against "imminently hazardous" chemical substances when those substances present "an imminent and unreasonable risk of serious or widespread injury to health and the environment." Section 7(b) specifically empowers a court to grant "such temporary or permanent relief as may be necessary to protect public health and the environment." This section parallels §6(c)(1), which authorizes the suspension of a chemical registration when a pesticide poses an "imminent hazard." However, historically §7 has been overlooked and underutilized by the EPA.

"Significant New Uses" of Existing Substances

TSCA §5(a) provides the EPA authority to regulate a new use of an existing substance where the new use may endanger human health or the environment. This section requires that "a significant new use notice" (SNUN) be provided to the EPA by the applicant 90 days before the manufacturing or processing of certain combined chemical substances for new uses.

Supporting data must accompany the SNUN. However, this requirement is triggered only if the EPA issues a "significant new use rule" (SNUR) requiring notice for the category of the new use involved.

Section 8 imposes reporting and recordkeeping duties on manufacturers and processors. Section 8 directs manufacturers, processors, and distributors to maintain records with information about adverse reactions that the chemical substance may cause for human health or the environment, records of consumer complaints of personal injury or harm to health, worker reports of disease or injury, and reports of injury to the environment. The EPA is authorized to utilize this information in deciding whether or not to regulate a suspect chemical substance.

Regulating New Chemical Substances

New chemical substances are constantly created in commerce and as an unintentional by-product of chemical processes. Section 5(a) of TSCA empowers the EPA with the authority to regulate new chemical substances. Anyone who intends to produce a new chemical substance is required by TSCA to provide the EPA with a "premanufacture notice" (PMN) 90 days prior to manufacturing the substance or creating it as a by-product, with exceptions for R&D and low release or low exposure potential, among others. The 90-day period allows the EPA to decide whether or not to prohibit or restrict manufacturing, processing, distribution, use, or disposal of the substance. There are significant penalties for failure to file.

The PMN must include its chemical identity, trade name, anticipated maximum production volume, and intended types of uses. The PMN must also be accompanied by test data that demonstrate that the manufacture, processing, distribution, use, and disposal of new substances will not present an unreasonable risk of injury to health or the environment, if such data are already available to the applicant.

Filing the PMN can reveal the years of proprietary research and development. The PMN and accompanying test data often include trade secrets and other confidential information. Section 14(c) gives the applicant the possibility to protect the information from public disclosure by designating the information in the PMN as confidential and requesting protection. Such protection is at the discretion of the EPA.

Section 14 of TSCA requires that the EPA not disclose confidential business or financial information that is submitted under a claim of confidentiality. There is a confidential TSCA inventory that is not public, but which the EPA will search confidentially upon a bona fide request and submission of intent to manufacture. One risk is that those attempting to search the confidential inventory may not be truly intending to manufacture the substance, but just to obtain more information about the chemicals in a competitor's products. The EPA will disclose whether a particular chemical is in the confidential inventory to someone who submits a bona fide intent to manufacture the particular substance. In addition, a notice of commencement of manufacture is required within 30 days of first manufacture. At that time, the EPA adds the manufactured chemical(s) to the public or the confidential inventory, as appropriate.

Where a chemical substance is incorrectly listed, it may be corrected by the applicant. Inventory corrections take effect retroactively to the time of initial inventory submission; thus, the intervening production of the chemical substance would be considered to be consistent with the corrected inventory listing.

Where a chemical substance does not appear on any of the TSCA inventories, it is deemed to be a new chemical substance and may not be manufactured, processed, or distributed in commerce until a PMN has been filed. All test data in the possession of the applicant must also be submitted with the notice. The EPA can prohibit or restrict a substance's manufacture, distribution, processing, use, or disposal under §5 of TSCA, if necessary to protect the public health or the environment. Approximately 10 percent of registered substances are subject to some form of restriction as a result of the EPA review.

Evaluating the PMN, there are three bases upon which the EPA may regulate a new substance. First, §5(e) of TSCA allows regulation if:

- The information available to the EPA is insufficient to permit a reasoned evaluation of the health and environmental effects of the substance, *and*
- Either (1) absent such information, the manufacture, processing, distribution, use, or disposal of the substance may present an unreasonable risk of injury *or* (2) the substance will be produced in substantial quantities and either will enter the environment in such quantities or may cause "significant or substantial human exposure."

A second means of regulation occurs under §5(f), permitting the EPA to issue a "proposed rule" or "proposed order" that acts as a temporary ban or restriction on a substance. Third, the EPA may act under §6(a), discussed previously, when regulating a new substance, to impose a total ban on a substance. However, as previously discussed under judicial interpretation, there is a significant burden on the EPA to sustain such action.

There are a variety of exemptions from TSCA registration. These include intermediate chemicals which exist temporarily as a result of a chemical reaction where there is no human or environmental exposure and where no risk is presented, small research and development production of chemicals, exemption for certain polymers (which require a special polymer exemption notice), an exemption for production of a low volume of chemical (defined as less than 1,000 kilograms per year), and an exemption for substances having no separate commercial purpose.

ENFORCEMENT

TSCA and FIFRA vest the EPA with similar enforcement powers: They both authorize civil penalties. Section 16(a) of TSCA provides that the EPA may assess civil penalties in the maximum amount of $25,000 per day. The EPA operates a "gravity-based" penalty system, where the amount of fine is determined by the EPA pursuant to a complex penalty formula considering the nature, extent, and circumstances of the violation. The EPA considers whether or not to modify the penalty because of ability to pay, history of prior violations, cooperation, and degree of culpability. TSCA contains an affirmative requirement to report violations.

The EPA recovers penalties through administrative proceedings by filing an administrative complaint. The respondent is entitled to an adjudicatory hearing before an administrative law judge. This decision is first taken to the EPA Administrative Appeals Board, and thereafter to federal court. However, most cases are settled. The government also has additional powers to assess criminal penalties for knowing or willful violations, secure injunctions in district court to ensure compliance with TSCA, and sue in rem to seize illegally manufactured, processed, or distributed substances.

Section 20 of TSCA provides for private citizens' suits. This authorizes "any person" to sue anyone who violates any provision of TSCA or any rule under §4, 5, or 6, after adequate prefiling notice is given. However, TSCA does not allow for money damage awards to private claimants.

Examples

1. The Hare Club for Men, a company in Mexico, has a chemical substance that will increase hair growth for either men or rabbits suffering from male pattern baldness when applied correctly to the scalp. There are many companies, including Male Baldness America (MBA), that want to obtain the rights to sell this chemical to customers in the United States. A recent study, however, has shown that when the chemical substance is applied too liberally, or too often, it causes severe burning, skin rashes, and possible liver damage. Does TSCA apply? Why and how?

2. Homer Stimpson works with nuclear power and nuclear power plants. Mr. Stimpson created a new non-nuclear chemical combination of chemicals that would allow nuclear power plants to process their spent

nuclear fuel rods by dipping them in Mr. Stimpson's solution whereupon the rods disintegrate. This chemical is toxic to human beings and any dermal contact causes immediate and severe injury. What jurisdiction does TSCA have, if any, over Homer Stimpson's nuclear wonder chemical? What if the combination was not toxic but the chemicals are on the TSCA inventory?

3. If Stimpson in the above example produced the mixture in his laboratory but decided not to make the product available, would TSCA apply? Why?

4. If Stimpson is concerned that submitting his confidential data to the EPA will allow others to be able to pirate his formula, can he submit a PMN without the confidential data, or what should he do?

Explanations

1. The EPA would have grounds to require test data and possibly be able to regulate or restrict the product under §§5 and 6. TSCA covers imported products and their distribution. A PMN would have to be filed 90 days prior to manufacturing or importing and distributing the substance. Distribution would be the key trigger here. The 90-day period allows the EPA to decide whether or not to prohibit or restrict manufacturing, processing, distribution, use, or disposal of the substance.

2. While TSCA does not apply to nuclear materials, it applies to chemicals used in conjunction with nuclear materials. It also applies to mixtures, which this is. Under §4(a), three provisions allow the EPA to require testing. Provision number three states: "the manufacture, distribution, processing, use or disposal of the substance or mixture may present an unreasonable risk of injury to health or environment." This is subject to TSCA and to a PMN. Even if the mixture were not toxic, but the original chemicals are in the TSCA inventory, Stimpson still can be regulated as a "processor," but the chemical mixture may not be severely limited.

3. There is an exemption for R&D activities and a processor is not regulated unless the substance is distributed in commerce. Stimpson may not be regulated.

4. The PMN must be submitted with the confidential information, or it is not a complete application and the mixture cannot be manufactured or distributed until a proper application is filed. Stimpson may request confidential treatment and mark each page as submitted under a claim of confidentiality. The EPA ultimately makes the decision as to what is and is not protected. If the decision goes against Stimpson, the information is already out of Stimpson's control and subject to public disclosure at the EPA. A competitor could then access the information.

639

THE FEDERAL INSECTICIDE, FUNGICIDE, AND RODENTICIDE ACT (FIFRA)

FIFRA covers pesticides and herbicides. A pesticide is a substance produced and introduced into the environment purposely to kill or affect a particular plant or animal species. However, research has shown that some pesticides are toxic to both the "target pests" and a large quantity of nontarget species, sometimes including humans.

Like TSCA, FIFRA is a product licensing statute that uses a cost-benefit approach to decide whether or not to allow a product to be placed in commerce. FIFRA is unlike TSCA in that products regulated under TSCA can be processed, sold, and distributed without prior EPA approval. The EPA must affirmatively intervene to ban the product or otherwise restrict the product.

FIFRA, enacted in 1947 as a consumer protection measure with no deliberate concern for environmental protection, had two goals: (1) to ensure that the pesticide performed its intended function — to provide adequate toxic measures to kill the target pest, and (2) to protect the health of the consumer using the pesticide by placing proper use instructions on the label. FIFRA repealed the Insecticide Act of 1910, which prohibited the manufacture, sale, or distribution in interstate commerce of misbranded or adulterated pesticides. The statute assumed that the only parties likely to be affected by the pesticide were those applying the pesticide, such as farmers. The early ignorance about secondary impacts from pesticides was evident when, in 1957, a federal district court refused to stop the aerial spraying of DDT over suburbs of Long Island, New York, despite the active protests of affected residents.

In 1962, Rachel Carson's landmark book *Silent Spring* exposed the increasing hazards of pesticides and the inadequate laws surrounding pesticide use. In 1964, Congress bolstered FIFRA by empowering the Department of Agriculture to refuse or cancel pesticide registrations. Enforcement power was vested in the new Environmental Protection Agency in 1970. A series of later amendments, including the Federal Environmental Pesticide Act of 1972, restructured FIFRA into what it is today: the principal federal statute regulating pesticides to protect human health *and* the environment.

FIFRA operates primarily as a product licensing statute. Section 3(a) provides that a pesticide may not be sold or distributed in the United States without first being "registered" with the EPA. The EPA must protect the health of the public and the environment by denying or conditioning pesticide registration when the environmental costs of registration outweigh its benefits.

There are two other principal elements of FIFRA: Each pesticide is required to bear an EPA-approved label that sufficiently articulates the risks it presents, instructions on the proper way to use the pesticide, and other pertinent information. Second, FIFRA legally controls the use of pesticides in several ways. It makes it illegal to utilize a pesticide in any way except that which is expressly indicated on the label. Courts have adopted the FIFRA definition of "application of a pesticide" as the "placement for effect of a pesticide at or on the site where the pest control or other response is desired." *United States v. Hardage*, 733 F. Supp. 1424 (W.D. Okla. 1989) (adopting FIFRA regulations at 40 C.F.R. §162.3(j)). A particularly hazardous pesticide is registered for "restricted use" only, and only may be applied by "certified applicators." Moreover, FIFRA regulations mandate procedures to protect farm workers from pesticide exposure.

Pesticides Defined

FIFRA regulates pesticides. The sales and distribution of other chemical substances are managed by TSCA. Section 2 of FIFRA defines pesticides broadly as "any substance or mixture of substances" that is (1) "*intended* for preventing, destroying, repelling, or mitigating any *pest*," or (2) "*intended* for use as a plant regulator, defoliant, or desiccant." Note that this definition focuses specifically on the *intended* use of the substance, not its inherent toxicity.

Thus, more definitions become important: "pest" and "intended." "Pest" is defined in §2(t) to include any insect, rodent, or nematode (a type of worm, fungus, or weed). Beyond the statutory definition, FIFRA grants EPA the power to designate almost any living thing as a "pest."

The term "intended" is not defined in FIFRA. The EPA regulations focus on the intent of the manufacturer, seller, or distributor, not the intent of the user of the product. The EPA regulations define "intent" to include any one of the following: (1) the statement or implication (taken from labeling or otherwise) that the product can be used as a pesticide, (2) wherever the product has insignificant commercial value to be used as anything else except a pesticide, and (3) actual or constructive knowledge that the product will be used as a pesticide. Products such as household air purifiers and swimming pool additives are considered pesticides and subject to FIFRA regulation. There are approximately 20,000 "pesticides" registered under FIFRA.

Registration

Registration is the core of FIFRA. Through registration, the EPA is able to control whether or not a pesticide is distributed or sold, and ultimately utilized, in the United States. The registration process comprises three alternative procedures: (1) registering a product, (2) registering a product with a new active ingredient, and (3) reregistration.

To begin the process of pesticide registration, an application is submitted to the EPA. The application must provide the proposed labeling as well as enough scientific data to allow the EPA to decide whether or not the pesticide meets the legal standards for registration. Acceptable scientific data may consist of either the applicant's test results performed on the product, or citations to data of previous test results already available to the EPA. Where others have performed tests, these may be relied upon. The process of obtaining data and going through the registration procedure can take years for an applicant to complete.

FIFRA employs a cost-benefit analysis, rather than an assessment of risk, to determine whether a pesticide is capable of being registered. Its goal is to eliminate "unreasonable adverse effects" by weighing the costs and benefits. EPA conducts no independent testing regarding efficacy or safety of a pesticide.

The EPA is required by law to register a pesticide under §3(c)(5) if four requirements are met:

- Its composition warrants the proposed claims for it.
- Its labeling and other materials submitted in the registration procedure meet FIFRA standards.
- Its intended function will allow the pesticide to perform without causing "unreasonable adverse affects on the environment."
- When the pesticide is utilized in accordance with widespread and commonly recognized practice, it will generally not cause "unreasonable adverse effects on the environment."

Under §6(a)(2), the registrant must report to the EPA any later-obtained information concerning whether the pesticide causes unreasonable effects on the environment. This information may be used subsequently by the EPA to suspend or cancel the registration. If a registration is suspended or canceled, the pesticide may not be sold.

In *Environmental Defense Fund, Inc. v. EPA*, 465 F.2d 528 (D.C. Cir. 1972), the Environmental Defense Fund brought suit challenging the EPA's decision not to order an immediate suspension of the pesticide registrations for aldrin and dieldrin pending final EPA decision on cancellation. The D.C. Circuit held that under §4 of FIFRA, the EPA does have statutory power to suspend the registration of an environmental poison immediately if it finds that such action is necessary to prevent an "imminent hazard to the public." However, the EPA withheld an order of immediate suspension of the registration based on the conclusion that "present uses do not pose an imminent threat to the public such as to require immediate action." The use of DDT and DDE was banned by the EPA in 1972, and dieldrin was banned in 1974 because of concerns about impacts on human health and the environment.

In *Environmental Defense Fund, Inc. v. EPA*, 548 F.2d 998 (D.C. Cir. 1976), the D.C. Circuit reviewed suspension of pesticide registrations for heptachlor and chlordane. The manufacturers argued that mice studies showing carcinogenic effects after ingestion did not warrant an inference about the carcinogenic effects of inhalation or dermal contact. The court held that once the initial showing of hazard is made for one mode of exposure to a pesticide and that pesticide is shown to be present in human tissues, the burden shifts to the registrant to rebut the inference that other modes of exposure may also pose a hazard for humans.

Any pesticide that contains a *new active ingredient* is the most difficult to register. The EPA has practical difficulty testing the environmental effects of products containing a new active ingredient because of insufficient existing data. The applicant must bear the burden of the development of the test data, a process which is both expensive and time consuming. The EPA, as a general rule, will only register the product with a new active ingredient on a conditional basis, subject to additional review.

Prior to amendments to FIFRA, many pesticides were registered under relatively lax standards. The EPA mandated that any pesticide containing an active ingredient registered before November 1, 1984, must undergo the registration procedure again to evaluate and ensure that modern safety standards are met. The reregistration process is very slow. There are still thousands of chemicals on the market that were registered when the registration procedure was extremely lenient and largely ignored environmental concerns. State government has the principal responsibility to enforce FIFRA. The EPA, under §23(a), has delegated its enforcement authority to the states pursuant to cooperative agreements between the EPA and each state. In a few states the EPA has retained full authority because of inadequate state enforcement capability.

FIFRA allocates the burden of proof to the applicant. The problem with FIFRA implementation is slowness. The EPA has canceled or suspended only about 50 pesticides in the legislation's history. Most FIFRA provisions do not apply to pesticides that are manufactured for export. Exported pesticides may include those pesticides unregistered or banned for use in the United States.

Export of Pesticides

To export a pesticide manufactured in the United States, it does not need to be registered pursuant to FIFRA. It is estimated that approximately 30 percent of all pesticides that are exported from the United States are not registered. Such unregistered status may result from noncontroversial reasons, such as the manufacturer of the pesticide may have decided not to market the product in the United States and thus not to seek registration, or the registration application may be pending at the time of export. However, the reason for export may be precisely because the product cannot be registered, has failed registration, or had registration withdrawn in the United States, making the only possible commercial outlet export of the pesticide.

When an unregistered pesticide is exported, the foreign purchaser must acknowledge in writing that it recognizes that the pesticide is banned from all use in the United States, and such written confirmation must be provided by the manufacturer/exporter to the EPA. The EPA provides a copy of the statement to the United States Embassy in the importing country, which may then submit it to appropriate officials within those countries. This is the only method by which the importing country generally receives notification of the importation of a pesticide banned in the United States. FIFRA requires that the EPA advise the importing governments and the appropriate international agencies about those pesticides that have been suspended or canceled in the United States. The European Economic Community (EEC) in 1985 adopted directives for the laws regarding classification, packaging, and sale of various pesticides in the community. The directive also instructed member nations to ban the use and sale of certain pesticides, including DDT, aldrin, and dieldrin. However, it does not as stringently restrict pesticides exported from the EEC.

Pesticides not allowed to be used in the United States can be exported and applied to agricultural products in the receiving countries, and those agricultural products can then be exported to the United States with significant residual chemical levels. Chemical residues typically are not detected in imported agricultural products even though the hazards of these chemicals may have prevented their use in the United States. For example, teak trees harvested for lumber in Colombia became contaminated by the pesticide dieldrin. Wood shavings from the processing of such teak were used for cow litter in the United States, and were ingested by the cows, contaminating milk with dieldrin. Opinion in developing nations is split regarding the importation of pesticides banned in their country of origin: Some criticize this as the export of hazardous materials to the developing world, while others defend the right of developing nations to make their own determinations as to what pesticides are appropriate to utilize for the often more virulent strains of insects and insect-borne diseases in tropical climates.

Preemption

When the EPA approves a pesticide label, the approval is made on the basis of information and test results provided by the applicant. The EPA conducts no independent testing of the application of the data that is submitted. Therefore, an approval does not necessarily constitute an independent verification of the results.

FIFRA contains language of express preemption: States "shall not impose or continue in effect any requirements for labeling or packaging in addition to or different from those required" under FIFRA. 21 U.S.C. §136v(b).

In 2005, the Supreme Court decided that a state may regulate the sale and use of federally registered pesticides to the extent that such regulation does not permit any sales or uses prohibited by FIFRA. *Bates v. Dow Agrosciences LLC*, 544 U.S. 431 (U.S. 2005). The court interpreted federal preemption narrowly, as it had in *Medtronic, Inc. v. Lohr*, 518 U.S. 470. FIFRA preemption is now interpreted only to apply to state law requirements for labeling or packaging, and not to defective design, defective manufacture, negligent testing, or breach of express warranty claims that are common law causes of action. Therefore, a state may not impose or continue in effect any requirements for labeling or packaging in addition to or different from those required under Section 136(v)(b) of FIFRA. A claim of negligent failure to warn or fraud could more likely invoke the federally required labeling requirements, and could be preempted.

Many courts have found preemption of common law failure-to-warn cases against FIFRA-regulated parties. *Arkansas-Platte & Gulf Partnership v. Van Waters & Rogers, Inc.*, 959 F.2d 158 (10th Cir. 1992), *vacated and remanded*, 506 U.S. 910 (1992), *aff'd on remand*, 981 F.2d 1177 (10th Cir. 1993), *cert. denied*, 510 U.S. 813 (1993) (claim against manufacturer and distributor for failure to warn, as well as labeling, impliedly preempted because "Congress intended to occupy the field of labeling regulation"); *Papas v. Upjohn Co.*, 926 F.2d 1019 (11th Cir. 1991), *vacated and remanded*, 505 U.S. 1215 (1992), *aff'd on remand*, 985 F.2d 516 (11th Cir. 1993), *cert. denied*, 510 U.S. 913 (1993).

FIFRA also contains a savings clause providing that states "may regulate the sale or use of any federally registered pesticide or device in State, but only if and to the extent the regulation does not permit any sale or use prohibited by this subchapter." 7 U.S.C. §136v(a). See also Sen. Rep. No. 92-970, at 44 (1972) ("Generally, the intent of this provision is to leave to the States the authority to impose stricter regulation on pesticide uses than that required under the Act"). This provision allows states to regulate pesticides more stringently than FIFRA as long as no conflicting labeling material is required.

Several cases have preserved common law actions for failure to warn even where the federal government has imposed a strict product labeling requirement. See *Cipollone v. Liggett Group, Inc.*, 505 U.S. 504 (1992) (despite the Federal Cigarette Labeling Act of 1995 and the Public Health Cigarette Act of 1999, traditional state police powers were not clearly and manifestly preempted by federal statute; preemption under Supremacy Clause should be narrowly construed and federal acts should be governed expressly by their statutory language without engaging in any analysis of implied preemptive intent); *Ferebee v. Chevron Chemical Co.*, 736 F.2d 1529 (D.C. Cir. 1984) (injury from dermal exposure to Paraquat, a toxic herbicide causing pulmonary diseases, was not preempted under either an express or implied preemption analysis, noting that the purpose of federal labeling was to "insure from a cost-benefit point of view, that pesticides are not unreasonably unsafe, while state tort law encompasses broad compensatory goals beyond those of the FIFRA cost-benefit standard"); *New York State Pesticide Coalition, Inc. v. Jorling*, 874 F.2d 115 (2d Cir. 1989) ("Notification requirements such as cover sheets, signs and newspaper advertisements do not impair the integrity of the FIFRA label. . . . Labeling doesn't include materials designed to notify purchasers of services or the general public"). Some courts have found certain claims but not others to survive FIFRA preemption. See *Hawkins v. Leslie's Pool Mart, Inc.*, 184 F.3d 244 (3d Cir. 1999) (defective packaging claim not preempted by FIFRA); *Jeffers v. Wal-Mart Stores, Inc.*, 84 F. Supp. 2d 775 (D.W. Va. 2000) (defective packaging claim not preempted where container broken at Wal-Mart store permanently injuring a maintenance worker who cleaned it up).

The Court in *Wisconsin Public Intervenor v. Mortier*, 501 U.S. 597 (1991) (claim against manufacturer and distributor for failure to warn, as well as labeling, impliedly preempted because "Congress intended to occupy the field of labeling regulation") permitted a local regulation banning aerial application of pesticides, leaving to each state the allocation of regulatory authority between the state and its localities regarding those powers that are retained at the local level under FIFRA. Local regulation that conflicts with state law is preempted. See *Town of Wendell v. Attorney General*, 394 Mass. 518 (Mass. 1985). Some courts have held that since the FIFRA process is equivalent to NEPA, an EIS is not necessary regarding EPA FIFRA rulemakings and actions.

For more on environmental preemption, see Chapter 4.

Examples

1. Suppose a pesticide product was already permitted to be on the market and thereafter producers wanted to introduce a new active ingredient into the product. How would the registration process work? Would the producer register the new active ingredient or would the product be taken off the market until reregistration and registering the new active ingredient?

2. In the above fact pattern, suppose that the product also had an active ingredient that was registered before November 1, 1984. What then?

Explanations

1. The EPA, through registration, is able to control whether or not a pesticide is distributed or sold, and ultimately utilized in the United States. The product would be considered under the guidelines for *new active ingredient* registration. It would be licensed conditionally upon a showing by the applicant, unless the product could not be adequately labeled to protect the public during its use.

2. The product would have to meet the elements of *reregistration* under the more exacting current standards. If a product is a staple across the

United States with few substitutes, the EPA will take into consideration the product's use in the marketplace when reviewing it. If there are no substitutes, this increases the chance for maintaining registration because the benefits (no alternative product) outweigh the significant harm. Even though some pesticides can be harmful, they control pests that also can be harmful in spreading disease and crop damage.

International Environmental Law

"For you in my respect are all the world: then how can it be said I am alone, when all the world is here to look on me?"

William Shakespeare, A Midsummer-Night's Dream

"Let Rome in Tiber melt, and the wide arch of the ranged empire fall! Here in my space, kingdoms are clay."

William Shakespeare, Antony and Cleopatra

"Lost is our old simplicity of times,
The world abounds with laws, and teems with crimes."

Pennsylvania Gazette, *February 8, 1775*

International Environmental Law (IEL) is a body of law created by nation states to govern problems that arise *between* nation states. IEL is different from both international law and domestic environmental law in several ways. IEL differs from international law in that it owes much of its substantive laws and policies to domestic environmental laws. For example, nations often enter into treaties, or international agreements, that are driven primarily by their own internal environmental problems, and not necessarily because of the gravity of the international situation. However, despite the similarities, IEL is distinct because it is a compromise between nation states as to what environmental issues are most pressing to the world order.

The modern era of international environmental law began with the Stockholm Conference in 1972. This resulted in the Stockholm Declaration, a nonbinding statement featuring 26 general principles. Two of the principles dealt with transboundary environmental injuries and national sovereignty, which became the foundation of modern environmental law on an international scale. By the beginning of the twenty-first century, there were approximately 1,000 bilateral, multilateral, and regional documents containing provisions aimed at resource protection, prevention of pollution, and environmental principles.

Modern international environmental agreements increasingly embody sophisticated regulatory techniques, and often impose obligations on signatory nations beyond those embodied in national environmental laws. Environmental agreements increasingly recognize the sophisticated relationship between trade and development and international environmental harms. These are evidenced in the General Agreement on Tariffs and Trade (GATT) and the North American Free Trade Agreement (NAFTA).

There are significant problems with implementation of, and insuring compliance with, international environmental agreements. International environmental agreements are rarely self-executing. They constitute "soft law" that requires the good faith of nations to implement by adopting legislation or regulations at the national or regional level. For example, the Basel Convention on controlling international traffic in hazardous waste was never ratified in the United States because it would have required Congress to pass changes in RCRA. Compliance has been extremely spotty internationally with various environmental obligations imposed by international agreements. Environmental cases have been adjudicated in the European Court of Human Rights, the International Centre for the Settlement of Investment Disputes, and the Appellate Body of the World Trade Organization.

Since the seventeenth century, the guiding principle of international law is that international law is primarily by and for nation states. In the twentieth century, two crucial developments have compelled scholars and policymakers to question the adequacy of international laws, in particular IELs. The first is the rise and spread of the global market, including the transnational flow of people. The second is the steady emergence of the need to protect transnational environmental and human rights.

THE STRUCTURE AND LIMITATIONS OF INTERNATIONAL ENVIRONMENTAL LAW

The structure of IEL is very different from the familiar aspects of United States law. For example, there are no police officers in IEL, no immediate consequences or actions for violating IEL policy, and no organized systematic procedure for monitoring compliance with IEL. All IELs are nego-tiated and are the product of international compromise. No nation state is required to ratify or sign *any* treaty. There is no legislative body for IEL.

IEL allows nation states the exclusive authority to regulate conduct within their territories so long as those actions do not affect the international environment. If there are no policing bodies, then how do states react to the actual or alleged illegalities of another? Herman Kahn's "Escalation Ladder" describes four levels of response:

- *Retortions:* Acts by the government to seek redress for, or prevent recur-rence of, an undesired act by another government. These include the recalling of ambassadors, refusal to facilitate negotiations, denounc-ing of treaties, and pushing of resolutions against defying nation states in the United Nations.
- *Show of Force:* There are various ways of showing force: direct or indirect, silent or noisy. A direct show of force may include a massing of troops; an indirect show of force could include the test firing of missiles or a press campaign stressing the need to stop the defying nation's behavior.
- *Legal Harassment:* This type of enforcement may include an embargo on goods shipped to certain countries, an interference with shipping, confiscation of bank deposits, or the arrest or expulsion of the other state's nationals from within one's own boundaries.
- *Violent Harassment:* This form of enforcement is designed to harass, confuse, exhaust, violate, discredit, frighten and otherwise harm, weaken, or demoralize the opponent or his allies. Examples of this type of force include kidnapping, assassination, guerrilla warfare, piracy and border raids, probing operations, invasions, and other abusive and threatening activities.

How is IEL made, where can you find it, and how it is applied? You know there is no world legislature creating IEL, and that there is no global system of courts with jurisdiction to interpret the international laws and no international police force to implement and apply IELs. However, there are certain "sources" from which IEL may be extrapolated. This body of law includes the leading doctrines, principles, and rules that are applicable to global environmental protection. IEL comprises four general "sources" of law: (1) treaties, (2) custom, (3) general principles of law, and (4) supplemental information.

Treaties

Treaties are the preeminent method by which IEL is developed. A treaty is an international agreement made between states. Treaties are written documents that contain mutual promises by the signing states to follow the "rules" set forth in the document. The most important thing to remember about treaties are the principles that make treaties compelling. They represent compromises by nation states; by signing and ratifying a treaty, nations are consenting to be bound by the terms of the treaty; nations recognize that breaking the terms of the treaty may result in the other signatories "punishing" the defying nation through the methods explained in the Kahn Escalation Ladder.

There are two forms of treaties: (1) the bilateral treaty and (2) the multilateral treaty or convention. The bilateral treaty consists of two countries negotiating an agreement that establishes a relationship between them governed by international law intended to create a legal relationship. A multilateral treaty is the same as a bilateral treaty but is between more than two parties. A treaty may serve as an international contract between two or more states, or it may be a "lawmaking" treaty, or it may have a legislative effect. A contractual treaty simply states the mutual obligations that the parties have undertaken to perform. A "lawmaking" treaty is concerned with the norms of legal conduct that the parties to the treaty agree to act in accordance with in their relationship to the other signatories. A legislative treaty purports to determine law and obligations incumbent upon other states that are not parties to the treaty. The latter is the most highly controversial, hardest to enforce, and least used form of treaty.

Why do nations comply with treaties if there is no way to enforce them? There are primarily three reasons for compliance with treaties. First, nations do not usually enter into consensual treaty agreements unless they believe that these are in their own best interest. Second, there is a global common interest in complying with treaties in order to create a way to ensure a stable expectation of the outcome when one nation enters into a written agreement with another. Third, most nations believe obligations prove their trustworthiness and ability to keep their word. Most nations view treaties as a way to maintain their international "honor," "prestige," "influence," and "good reputation."

There are several steps to the conclusion and acceptance of negotiated treaties. When the final draft of a treaty is agreed upon, the text is made public for a certain period of time, and unless the nations agree to do away with the signature requirement, the treaty is signed by the representatives to authenticate its contents. Each state may sign the treaty at any time during the designated period, but after its expiration, no further signatories are allowed.

The effect of the signing of the treaty depends upon whether the treaty contains a clause within it that allows for ratification, acceptance, or approval. Where the treaty is subject to ratification, the nation representatives bring the treaty back to their governments for approval. In most nations the head of state will then decide whether or not to ratify the document. In the United States a two-thirds majority in the Senate is required to ratify a treaty.

Depending upon the treaty, some nations may also have the option of signing the treaty with reservations that they may agree to be bound by certain terms of the treaty but not to others. Furthermore, these same nations that have refused to be bound to certain terms of the treaty may still enforce those same terms against other signatories that did not express reservations against the terms.

Once the treaty is signed and ratified, it is "deposited" with a body or organization for its safekeeping. Most treaties are deposited with the United Nations.

What happens if a country is not present at the beginning of the treaty process but wants to become a later signatory? This depends on the terms of the treaty. Many treaties are left open so that other nations can come to the table and be a part of the treaty group throughout the process. After the treaty has closed, a nation may not be able to come into the treaty terms.

What if one party to the treaty breaches the agreement? If the treaty is bilateral, the other nation will have the option to either be bound or not be bound by the treaty. However, if the treaty is multilateral — for example, if five countries are bound by the treaty and one breaches — the other four are still bound; or, they may vote to suspend the treaty. Mutually, in the drafting of treaties, nations must provide clauses within the treaty to determine the choice of forum for disputes, rights and obligations of the nations, good-faith efforts by each nation to "police" its own citizens/corporations, definitions of pertinent terms, and the creation of an enforcement body for violations and sanctions.

The first treaty dealing primarily with the environment was the 1972 Stockholm Conference on the Human Environment. Prior to this convention, IEL had been addressed only sporadically and in an ad hoc fashion, and IEL decisions were based primarily on the thinking and ideology of individual nation states.

Custom

The second source of IEL is custom. Article 38 of the International Court of Justice statute describes "custom" as the behavior of nations in a general practice accepted as law. Custom is not a written law, but rather a belief by nations that an act or acts are against the law. This is known as *opinion juris*, or action based upon belief. For example, there is no written law regarding diplomatic immunity; however, every nation follows the "law" that you do not arrest or prosecute foreign diplomats under the law of your own nation.

How does one determine custom? There is no common law in the international arena; there is only agreed-upon law or consensual law. Therefore, all decisions in the World Court or the International Court of Justice (ICJ) are only binding on the parties before the court.

Similarly, there is no such thing as precedent on the international level. What we refer to as "precedent" in the United States can only be used as evidence of custom on the international level. Custom plays a major role in international decisions. For example, in *Cases Concerning Military and Paramilitary Activities In and Against Nicaragua (Nicaragua v. U.S.)*, 1986 I.C.J. 110 at 857, the United States allegedly was interfering with Nicaraguan affairs by funding "guerrilla freedom fighters" in their internal war against the Nicaraguan government. Nicaragua took the United States to court on the grounds that it is customary under international law for states not to interfere with another state's internal affairs. The ICJ held that the United States was, in fact, breaking international law by helping to fund the guerrillas and was therefore guilty of aiding and abetting. Although the United States did not accept the jurisdiction of the ICJ and the judgment was never enforced, it is still noteworthy that it was held to be against international law for one nation to interfere with the internal affairs of another nation because this violated international custom.

Additionally, the *North Sea Continental Shelf* cases (Federal Republic of Germany/Denmark; Federal Republic of Germany/Netherlands), 1969 I.C.J. 3, at 41-45, are examples of the ICJ's power to determine whether or not a scientific principle is considered a custom so as to rise to the level of international law. There, the Netherlands, Denmark, and Germany disputed how jurisdiction over the continental shelf was to be divided with regard to North Sea oil deposits. These cases presented the issue of whether the equidistance principle was a custom. This principle is that the area under the surface of the water out to a predetermined equal distance for all nations is considered a part of that nation's land mass. Here, it was held that the equidistance principle is not a globally accepted custom. In any analysis of IEL it is important to first determine if there are any binding treaties and then conduct a full analysis of customary law.

General Principles of Law

The third source of IEL is general principles of law. The basic notion behind general principles of law is that some propositions of law are so fundamental that they will be found in nearly every legal system. Some examples of general principles of law are (1) legal obligations must be fulfilled and rights must be exercised in good faith; (2) no person may be the judge in a case against him- or herself; and (3) breaches of legal duties entail the obligation of restitution.

The notion of general principles of law as binding IELs raises questions: Is a general principle of law binding on a state that has explicitly rejected or refused to recognize this principle? Are there situations where a general principle might take precedence over a treaty or a custom accepted as law? Generally, states will not be held to principles that they do not recognize. However, similar to the United States common law doctrine of estoppel, if a nation state has recognized the principle before and is merely denouncing it to avoid current liability, it will likely be estopped. As mentioned above, an analysis of IEL generally begins with treaties and customary law and progresses from there to include general principles of law.

Judicial Decisions and Scholarly Writing

Judicial decisions and scholarly opinions are also important sources of international law. However, this source, similar to all other sources of IEL, is not considered precedent, but might be used as evidence of custom in similar fact situations. For example, United Nations Resolutions are not necessarily unanimous but they are an attempt to codify custom or make a statement about the beliefs of many nations; they are thought to be indicative of the way in which the world community views and interprets an issue. Similarly, the writings of highly qualified publicists are also given obvious deference in IEL, but may only be used as evidence and not as precedent in any IEL case.

To what extent do scholarly writings actually contribute to the formation of international law? The answer is evidenced in several international opinions that cite scholarly writings in IEL. For example, in the famous decision of *The Paquete Habana*, decided in 1900, the court makes reference to the importance of the opinion of learned publicists:

> [W]here there is no treaty, and no controlling executive or legislative act or judicial decision, resort must be had to the customs and usage of civilized nations; and as evidence of these, to the works of jurists and commentators, who by years of labor, research and experience, have made themselves peculiarly well acquainted with the subjects of which they treat. Such works are resorted to by judicial tribunals, not for the speculations of their authors concerning what the law ought to be, but for trustworthy evidence of what the law really is. *The Paquete Habana*, 175 U.S. 677, 700 (1900).

Examples

1. The states of Abanda and Blotsphana enter into a treaty regarding the preservation of mountain lions and their natural habitat. Unfortunately, Blotsphana has decided that, due to increased consumption of livestock by mountain lions, its citizens may kill the lions if they believe them to be a threat to their livestock. In addition, the citizens are now selling the hides of the mountain lions on the global market, and the mountain lion

has been listed on the International List of Endangered Species. Abanda is obviously very upset with Blotsphana's decision to ignore treaty obligations by allowing their citizens to kill mountain lions. How might Abanda choose to react to the situation using the Kahn Escalation Ladder?

2. As counsel to Abanda, describe the most reasonable and effective means of dissuading Blotsphana from allowing its citizens to kill mountain lions.

3. The nations of Abanda, Blotsphana, and Colinga enter into a treaty that includes Article I, Article II, and Article III. Abanda and Blotsphana sign the treaty with no reservations, but Colinga signs the treaty pursuant to a reservation not to be bound by Article III. What rights are available if Blotsphana violates the treaty?

4. You are counsel to Colinga, primarily an agrarian nation with little industry. Abanda, a more industrial nation, is currently engaged in treaty negotiations with other states. The treaty is to lower the levels of sulfur emitted by industrial facilities in order to decrease the global acid rain level. What would you advise Colinga to do regarding joining this treaty?

5. Suppose the states of Abanda, Blotsphana, and Colinga all border the Purple Sea. Lately there have been numerous reports from fishermen that large pieces of a rare jewel, known as spade, have been dragged in with their fishing nets. Knowing the extreme value of spade, all three of the states have been making claims on areas of the Purple Sea surrounding their countries. The dispute will likely result in a lawsuit among the states. Under customary IEL do any of the states have a valid claim on the areas below the ocean surface within a certain distance from their country?

Explanations

1. If Abanda decides that the slaying of mountain lions is of global concern, it may:
   a. Under the retortions rung, recall its ambassadors to Blotsphana, or denounce its treaty obligations to Blotsphana.
   b. Under the force rung, Abanda may mass troops along its border or engage in a negative press campaign to compel Blotsphana to meet its treaty obligations. However, Abanda cannot send troops to Blotsphana to prevent the slaying of lions; this would be an invasion of Blotsphana's territorial sovereignty.
   c. Abanda may also choose to place an embargo on goods from Blotsphana, or if all else fails, engage in nefarious activities to prevent the execution of more mountain lions. It is important to note that this could be done by Abanda with or without a treaty.

2. If discussions with Blotsphana fail to prevent the killing of mountain lions, an embargo on Blotsphana's goods may be the most effective means of dissuading the killing. An embargo will likely directly affect the economy of Blotsphana, requiring it to make accommodations to Abanda on the issue. Similarly, another solution may be to provide monetary or technological assistance to Blotsphana to deter the mountain lions from eating the livestock without killing them (e.g., electric pens for the livestock, or moving the grazing areas outside of the mountain lions' habitat).

3. If Blotsphana defies Article III, Colinga and Abanda may still enforce the treaty and apply penalties against Blotsphana, even though Colinga is not bound by the terms of Article III.

4. Probably Colinga should try to approach the other states and request to become a signatory to the treaty. It is in the best interest of an agrarian nation to decrease the levels of acid rain in order to preserve its ability to grow healthy crops.

5. The court will allow the admittance of prior judicial decisions as evidence. Therefore, the court will likely look to the *North Sea Continental Shelf Cases* as a guide in determining if, under customary law, any of the states have made a valid claim to the area below the ocean surface. Under the *North Sea Cases*, the court held that it is not customary to apply the scientific principle that includes land under the sea in continental land mass. Therefore, the parcels of the ocean will probably not be considered as belonging to any particular nation, and will rather be considered part of the "global commons."

INTERNATIONAL FORUMS FOR JUSTICE

There are several international "courts." The most widely recognized is the International Court of Justice (ICJ), which is located in The Hague, but the ICJ is not the only permanent international tribunal. There is also the Court of Justice of the European Union in Luxembourg, the Benelux Court of Justice in Brussels, the European Court of Human Rights in Strasbourg, France, and the Inter-American Court of Human Rights in San Jose, Costa Rica. However, all of these courts except the ICJ have limited subject matter jurisdiction.

The ICJ and the International Law Commission (ILC) have become the two primary legal institutions of the globe. The ICJ is the principal judicial organ of the UN system and exercises jurisdiction by consent. The

International Law Commission (ILC) was created by the UN to work toward the codification and development of international law.

Judicial decisions have become a part of the substantive body of IEL. They include the *Corfu Channel* case (*U.K. v. Albania*), 1949 I.C.J. 4 (relating to the territorial jurisdiction of the international commission of the River Oder); the *Gavcikovo-Nagymaros Project* (*Hungary v. Slovakia*), 1997 I.C.J. 7 (concerning the use of water resources and their environmental implications); the *Fisheries Jurisdiction* case (*Spain v. Canada*), 1995 I.C.J. 87 (action to halt the destruction of fish stocks by prohibiting all fishing of straddling stocks off its coasts and in the adjacent high seas).

Equity in International Justice

The ICJ has appeared to interpret the concept of equity as implicit in the rules of international law. The court that is bound to administer justice must act equitably. For example, in the *North Sea Continental Shelf* cases, 1969 I.C.J. 3, the court indicated that just and equitable decisions find their "objective justification in considerations lying not outside but within the rules."

The concept of *ex aequo et bono*, which is found in Article 38(2) of the ICJ statute, gives the court the power to decide a case according to what is fair and appropriate, so long as the parties to the dispute agree. This is not the same as applying equity in national law. Rather, this implies deciding the case according to what suits the facts of the case, regardless of the law. In this way the court is able to create new law according to what is necessary. Generally, the equity concept finds most voice where the court must decide how to allocate environmental resources among several states. For example, the earth's system of boundaries is not formed around the earth's supply of natural resources, such as oil.

At least three approaches to equitable allocation of resources have emerged. The first, corrective equity, attempts to deal with unfairness that sometimes results from the application of strict law. The second, broadly conceived equity, is rule-based but tries to create a series of principles to be followed in equitable allocation. And the third, common heritage equity, determines the level of exploitation that is allowable without disturbing the conservation of humankind. Some scholars also propose a fourth type of equity, intergenerational equity, which would require that (1) each generation conserve the diversity of natural and cultural resources so as not to disturb the options available to future generations, (2) generations would maintain the quality of the planet so as not to pass it on to the next generation in any worse condition than when they received it, and (3) each generation should provide members with equitable rights of access to the legacy from the past generations.

Other sources of international law include the resolutions, declarations, plans, and agendas of the UN and other intergovernmental organizations, such as the Stockholm Conference. These types of law work by implementing the majority vote of nations that support both the practice and the opinion juris of the resolution or conference. It is suggested that when the UN passes a resolution by a unanimous vote, the content of that resolution is the unanimous consent of the nations present to be bound by the resolution.

THE APPLICATION OF INTERNATIONAL ENVIRONMENTAL LAW

In the United States, one is most familiar with legal decisions being determined by an impartial third party. This form of decision making is adjudicative. Conversely, international decisions are usually made through a process of unilateral determination and reciprocal response. There are four forms of unilateral response used in the international arena. First, when decisions are being made between foreign offices, a "diplomatic arena" is used—one where a series of fact-finding, negotiations, and reporting are used as instruments of policy. Second, formal conferences are used to make determinations between parliamentary bodies; this is known as the "parliamentary-diplomatic arena." Third, in discussions between legislative and quasi-legislative bodies regarding the global environment, decisions are made in the "parliamentary arena." Finally, secretariats of international governmental organizations, such as the UN, the European Council, and NATO, make decisions using the "executive arena."

The United Nations was founded in 1947 and has attempted to facilitate the protection of the environment. The UN charter does not create an environmental arena, nor does it specifically mandate the protection of the environment. Many of the UN-created agencies have assumed environmental responsibilities, including the Food and Agricultural Organization (FAO), the International Labour Organization (ILO), the World Health Organization (WHO), the World Meteorological Organization (WMO), the International Maritime Organization (IMO), the UN Educational, Scientific and Cultural Organization (UNESCO), and the International Atomic Energy Agency (IAEA).

Other funding organizations, such as the World Bank and regional development banks, exert tremendous international environmental influence. The World Bank environmental standards dictate emission limits for major new infrastructure funding. These become de facto international standards. In addition, several regional organizations play important roles in the development of IEL.

Major international environmental treaties entered since the creation of the United Nations two-thirds of a century ago are displayed in Exhibit 15.1. The United States has signed most of the treaties, but has not ratified many of those entered over the past decade, and so is not bound. The reason for failing to ratify is often because of conflict with preexisting U.S. law.

15.1 Multilateral Environmental Treaties

Name	U.S. Signed	U.S. Party	Entry into Force
Convention on the Intergovernmental Maritime Consultative Organization	X	X	March 17, 1958
International Convention for the Prevention of Pollution of the Sea by Oil	X	X	July 26, 1958 For U.S., Dec. 8, 1961
Convention on Fishing and Conservation of Living Resources of the High Seas	X	X	March 20, 1966
International Convention Relating to Intervention on the High Seas in Cases of Oil Pollution Causalities	X	X	May 6, 1975
The Convention on International Trade in Endangered Species of Wild Fauna and Flora (CITES)	X	X	July 1, 1975
Convention on the Prevention of Marine Pollution by Dumping of Wastes and Other Matter	X	X	Aug. 30, 1975
Ramsar Convention on Wetlands of International Importance	X	X	Dec. 21, 1975 For U.S., Dec. 18, 1986
UN Economic Commission for Europe Convention on Long-Range Transboundary Air Pollution (LRTAP)	X	X	March 16, 1983
Protocol of 1978 Relating to the International Convention for the Prevention of Pollution from Ships	X	X	Oct. 2, 1983
Convention for the Protection of the Ozone Layer	X	X	Sept. 22, 1988
Montreal Protocol on Substances that Deplete the Ozone Layer	X	X	Jan. 1, 1989
United Nations (UN) Basel Convention on the Control of Transboundary Movements of Hazardous Wastes and their Disposal	X		May 5, 1992
UN Convention on Biological Diversity	X		Dec. 29, 1993

Name	U.S. Signed	U.S. Party	Entry into Force
UN Framework Convention on Climate Change	X	X	March 21, 1994
UN Convention on the Law of the Sea	X		Nov. 16, 1994
International Convention on Oil Pollution Preparedness, Response and Cooperation	X	X	May 13, 1995
Law of the Sea Amendment, addressing deep-sea mining	X		July 28, 1996
UN Convention to Combat Desertification	X	X	Dec. 26, 1996 For U.S., Feb. 15, 2001
Cartagena Protocol on Biosafety to the Convention on Biological Diversity			Sept. 11, 2003
LRTAP Protocol on Persistent Organic Pollutants	X		Oct. 23, 2003
UN Rotterdam Convention on the Prior Informed Consent (PIC) Procedure for Certain Hazardous Chemicals and Pesticides in International Trade	X		Feb. 24, 2004
UN Stockholm Convention on Persistent Organic Pollutants	X		May 17, 2004
Kyoto Protocol to the UN Framework Convention on Climate Change	X		Feb. 16, 2005
Protocol of 1978, relating to the 1973 International Convention for the Prevention of Pollution from Ships (MARPOL) Annex VI dealing with air emissions	X		May 19, 2005

Judicial Decisions

The international courts are confronted with environmental laws that always represent a compromise between nations and, therefore, are quite vague. To develop a set of guiding principles based on vague statutes imposes political difficulty on most international tribunals. The courts are also reluctant to enunciate broad principles and context when a particular dispute before them is a narrow dispute between two nations. Therefore, the development of environmental jurisprudence has been extremely slow and insufficient on an international basis. Environmental disputes invariably also involve other substantive areas of law, such as trade agreements, human rights, the relationship between treaty and custom, or issues of state sovereignty. There is also a lack of unanimity internationally as to where environmental objectives stand in the general legal and political hierarchy. Priorities among nations differ.

Many treaties require parties to resort to diplomatic and other means of settling their differences before judicial remedies are allowed. However, judicial enforcement has successfully provided another avenue for securing compliance with IEL.

The United States has never ratified the Vienna Convention of the Law of Treaties, and is not bound by Article 63, which sets forth specific procedures to terminate a treaty. 1155 U.N.T.S. 331 (signed May 23, 1969, entered into force January 27, 1980, reprinted at 8 I.L.M. 679). This prevents any other country from bringing the United States before the International Court of Justice for a violation of the Law of Treaties. The United States included a "self-judging" clause as part of its reservation to jurisdiction of the International Court of Justice. The United States does not otherwise submit itself to compulsory jurisdiction of the International Court of Justice.

For example, in the 1984 *Nicaragua* case the United States issued a formal statement denying the court's jurisdiction and declaring withdrawal by the United States from further proceedings in the case. The United States then formally withdrew from the 1946 Declaration that applied compulsory jurisdiction by the ICJ. Similarly, in other cases, such as the *Nuclear Test* case (*Austria v. France*), 1974 I.C.J. 253, and the *Iranian Hostage Cases Concerning U.S. Diplomatic and Consular Staff in Tehran* (*United States v. Iran*), respondent states have chosen to boycott the court. These boycotts have forced the court to issue ex parte decisions that hold little force or effect.

Transboundary Harm

Environmental harm that is created in one state but affects the population in another is known as transboundary pollution. Several primary treaties dealing with air, water, and global pollution address transboundary harm. The Basel Convention Treaty regulates transboundary movement and disposal of hazardous wastes. The United States is a signatory but not a party to the Basel Convention because it would substantially interfere with RCRA. The Basel Convention includes "other wastes" such as household and electronic wastes.

Probably the most discussed IEL treaty is the Rio Declaration on Environment and Development (UNCED). The Rio Convention was held in 1992. Agenda 21 of the Rio Convention lays out the primary goals of the parties to the treaty, which include protection of wetlands and deserts, the reduction of air and water pollution, improved use of energy and technology, safer management of toxins, and the reduction of disease and malnutrition. Additionally, Rio created the United Nations Commission on Sustainable Development (CSD) to review the progress of national implementation of Agenda 21 and to help communications between the signatory nations.

Air Pollution

The migration of air pollutants has created major global problems, such as climate change, ozone depletion, and nuclear fallout. How do air pollutants migrate? When admitted into the atmosphere from industrial sources and automobile exhausts, they are suspended in small particles that dissolve in cloud vapors and rain. Depending upon the condition of the atmosphere and the weather, they may react with other chemicals to produce new, more harmful pollutants. The pollutants may be transported through water or air, or over hundreds or thousands of miles by the wind.

The Nuclear Test Ban treaty was enacted in 1963 to ban nuclear weapons testing in the atmosphere in outer space, and underwater. This treaty focused primarily on the prevention of any tests that would emit radioactive debris into the air of a country other than the one conducting the testing.

The first global environmental conference, the United Nations Conference on the Human Environment, was held in Stockholm in June 1972 and resulted in the Declaration of the United Nations Conference on the Human Environment and the United Nations Environment Programme. The first major international effort specifically intended to address climate change was orchestrated by UNEP and the World Meteorological Organization in 1988. Together, they established the Intragovernmental Panel on Climate Change (IPCC) for objective, scientific information about climate change. The United Nations Framework Convention for Climate Change (UNFCCC) was adopted in June 1992 at the United Nations Conference on Environment and Development (UNCED) held in Rio de Janeiro, Brazil. The 1982 UN Convention on the Law of the Sea codified customary international law. The United States has not ratified this, but its norms are considered to be customary international law and the United States has repeatedly acknowledged that it considers UNCLOS as a codification of customary international law.

In the mid-1980s two significant treaties were developed to protect the ozone layer. The Vienna Convention for the Protection of the Ozone Layer was held in Austria in 1985 to provide for a system of controlling human and nonhuman activities that produce adverse effects on the ozone layer. Similarly, the Protocol on Substances That Deplete the Ozone Layer was ratified in 1987 and required a 50 percent reduction in the production of chlorofluorocarbons (CFCs) by the year 1999, with some allowances for increases in developing countries. See Chapter 5 for more on U.S. regulation of these substances. Additionally, the 1990 Amendments to the Montreal Protocol created an accelerated phase-out of CFCs by increasing the reduction from 50 percent to 100 percent by the year 2000, and added several other toxins to the prohibited list of ozone-depleting chemicals.

The classic example of the effects of transboundary pollution is acid rain. In the landmark international case of *The Trail Smelter Arbitration (United States v. Canada)*, 3 R.I.A.A. 1938 (Mar. 11, 1941), a smelter located in Canada was found to have caused air pollution damage to a portion of Washington State. The Canadian plant was required to provide injunctive relief and a monetary award to the citizens of Washington.

This ruling has since become the basis for many more decisions regarding transboundary harm and various treaty provisions. Now Principle 2 of the 1992 Rio Declaration is the threshold for transboundary harm, codifying the *Trail Smelter Arbitration* decision into a well-settled rule of customary international law. It is now the principle of both treaties and customary law that one country may not cause significant transboundary environmental harm to another. See also Chapter 5 regarding air pollution.

Carbon regulation and climate change are covered domestically and internationally in Chapter 5.

Water Pollution

Approximately 70 percent of the earth's surface is covered in water. Large amounts of human waste are dumped into the oceans, rivers, and lakes every year. The water in these bodies is constantly recycled, resulting in the movement of pollution from one water body to another. Although water has the ability to change the composition of pollutants by dissolving and diluting them, this is dependent upon the location of the water body and concentration of the pollutant. Polluted water may cause not only biological damage, but also physical and economic damage.

Many states have agreed to a customary law that requires notification, consultation, and negotiation between states. In the *Lac Lanoux Arbitration* case *(Spain v. France)*, 12 R.I.A.A. 281 (Nov. 16, 1957), an arbitral tribunal held that France could not ignore Spain's interest in a planned hydraulic construction project on the Carol River. The tribunal further stated that no one state could use the hydraulic power of the watercourse to the detriment of another. Similarly, in the case of the *Diversion of Water from the River Meuse (Netherlands v. Belgium)*, 1937 P.C.I.J., it was determined that every state has the right to modify canals, and even the right to increase the volume of water in the canals, provided that such a change does not cause an interstate problem. This is similar to the later enactment of Principle 2 of the Rio

Declaration, whereby every state has the right to exploit its own resources, so long as it is not to the detriment of another state. The U.S. response to water pollution is discussed in Chapter 6.

The International Convention for the Prevention of Pollution from Ships (MARPOL) was implemented by the International Maritime Organization and is the primary international convention governing the prevention of marine pollution. The convention provides that the country where a ship is registered, known as its "flag state," is responsible for certifying the ship's compliance with MARPOL's regulations. It covers the prevention of pollution by both accidental discharges and from regular operations and states that "any discharge into the sea of oil or oily mixtures from ships to which this Annex applies shall be prohibited." 12 I.L.M. 1319, 1343.

Desertification

The term "desertification" refers to the process by which climatic changes, created by anthropogenic (human) impacts, create more desert regions on the globe. Human impacts include removal of natural vegetation, excessive cultivation, and exhaustion of water resources. The human impacts destroy the quality of the land and cause decreased ability of the soil to hold water. The decrease in water retention leads eventually to an advanced stage of land destruction known as desertification.

In areas of Africa, Asia, and South America, more than 70 percent of the agricultural land has suffered from desertification. The impacts appear to be worse in developing nations that have intensely used their land. Human activities have led to the overcultivation of land, and uncontrolled population increase has created a demand for increased food production.

The 1992 United Nations Conference on Environment and Development, also known as the "Earth Summit" or UNCED, created Agenda 21, a program for sustainable development that suggested preventative measures for decreasing the effects of desertification. These suggestions include rotation of crops and decreased use of the same farmland.

Environmental Warfare

Military tactics and weaponry can consume and destroy natural resources, waterways, forests, diverse species, and the atmosphere. The environment has been used as an instrument of war throughout history. During the Franco-Dutch War of 1672-1678, the Dutch destroyed a series of dikes, which stalled the French advance. During World War II and in the Korean War, thousands were killed when dams were deliberately destroyed. Power plants often are targeted during war. Now there are chemical weapons (such as nerve and blood agents that were used in World War I and the Iran-Iraq war) and biological agents (anthrax, smallpox) that spread disease as an element of war. The deliberate contamination of the hydrosphere by opening oil pipelines spilling millions of barrels of oil and the contamination of the atmosphere by setting oil wells on fire occurred during the Operation Desert Storm/Kuwait war against Iraq in 1991. The toxic plume rose four miles into the sky over an 800-mile area and took an international fire-fighting crew eight months to extinguish.

Rules of war established at the 1907 Hague Convention that limit environmental destruction did not specifically refer to the environment but limited the legal right to use excessive force on, derive profit from, benefit from, or damage property that belongs to another person. The Stockholm Conference of 1972 covered environmental preservation during times of war, and the United Nations General Assembly created the United Nations Environment Programme. The Geneva Convention of 1949 and the 1977 Geneva Protocol create customary international law prohibitions against environmental warfare acts that are not military necessities and require that distinctions be made between military and nonmilitary targets. The Environmental Modification Convention of 1977 (ENMOD), ratified by the United States, which grew out of concern for environmental modification tactics during the Vietnam War, prohibits environmental modifications that have "widespread, long-lasting, and severe" effects. It relies on good-faith compliance of signatory nations.

The United Nations Security Council passed Resolution 687 in 1991 and established the United Nations Compensation Commission (UNCC). The UNCC's specific mission was to address atrocities committed during the Gulf War with respect to the Iraqi occupation of Kuwait. Between 1993 and 1998, the UN Security Council established war-crime tribunals by statute for the former Yugoslavia, Sierra Leone, Lebanon, Cambodia, Iraq, and Rwanda.

The International Criminal Court (ICC) was established in 1998; the United States refused to consent to its authority. The ICC has global jurisdiction over environmental war crimes under the Rome Statute of July 1, 2002, which prohibits "[i]ntentionally launching an attack in the knowledge that such attack will cause . . . widespread, long-term and severe damage to the natural environment which would be clearly excessive in relation to the concrete and direct overall military advantage anticipated." In an effort to solidify immunity from the ICC, the United States began to sign independent treaties among and between nations. The treaties supersede the ICC's jurisdictional authority with legislative and executive branches of the government, rather than with the judicial branch. Since ICC inception, no state, party, or individual has been convicted of any environmental war crime by the ICC.

Nuclear Power and Weapons

Almost half the world's population has no electric power. It is one of the commodities most in demand in developing nations. Many nations have turned to nuclear power. The generation of power from nuclear energy creates approximately 17 percent of the electric power generated in the world. This form of power creates two forms of risk to humans. The first risk arises from nuclear accidents. Two primary examples are the Three Mile Island accident in the United States in 1979 and the Chernobyl accident in the former Soviet Union in 1986. Many people in Chernobyl died immediately from radiation and burns, and many more disastrous effects are predicted to occur long term. The Three Mile Island accident was not nearly as severe, but abnormal radiation levels were detected as far away as Europe. Since the Chernobyl disaster, international nuclear safety standards have been established by the International Atomic Energy Agency.

Second, many international laws have been formulated to deal with the disarmament of nuclear weapons. Some of these laws take the form of treaties, and others are customary in nature. The treaties include: the Strategic Arms Reduction Talks (START), the African Nuclear Weapon Free Zone Treaty, and various other regional negotiations. The customary law arises primarily from the threat of nuclear testing. It is well established that nuclear explosions pose a threat to the environment, atmosphere, hydrosphere, and outer space. However, many countries continue to test their nuclear weapons in areas that are potentially dangerous to other nation states.

The Nuclear Non-Proliferation Treaty, signed in 1968, provided nuclear technology for civilian power generation projects, in return for countries renouncing development of nuclear weapons. At the time, there were five nuclear weapons states — the United States, Russia, France, the United Kingdom, and China. However, outside the treaty, India (which never signed the treaty), Pakistan, South Africa (which has since dismantled its weapons under international inspection), Israel, North Korea, and perhaps Iran have developed nuclear weapons capabilities. Pakistan, through its nuclear chief, A.Q. Kahn, spread nuclear technology throughout the world.

During the period from 1967 to 1972, France conducted nuclear tests in the atmosphere that Australia claimed infringed upon the people of Australia's right to be free of radioactive fallout and violated Australia's sovereignty over its territory. Beginning in 1973 Australia and New Zealand brought separate actions against France in the World Court, in the *Nuclear Test Cases I (Australia v. France)*, 1973 I.C.J. 99; *(New Zealand v. France)*, 1973 I.C.J. 135. France rejected the jurisdiction of the ICJ. The ICJ found that France's cessation of testing constituted a binding commitment and therefore mooted the dispute. However, the court did provide the opportunity to reopen the case if France failed to adhere to the cessation.

The *Nuclear Test Cases II* arose when France declared that it would begin a round of underground testing in the South Pacific in 1995. Australia, which was primarily concerned with atmospheric testing, chose not to reopen its case. However, New Zealand made a claim that this new series of testing constituted a violation of rights under international law, and that it was unlawful for France to conduct such tests before undertaking an Environmental Impact Assessment in accord with international standards. The court, however, adopted a very narrow reading of the law and refused to reopen the case.

Species and Toxins

A variety of treaties try to protect species and their habitats and to prevent pollution of waters. The Wetlands Convention of 1971 established a list of internationally important wetlands and created programs under which nations would establish methods of wetland preservation. Similarly, the Convention on the Prevention of Marine Pollution by Dumping of Wastes and Other Matter of 1972 was an attempt to prevent the polluting of the ocean through regulation of dumping of certain materials at sea. MARPOL, or the Protocol of 1978 Relating to the International Convention for the Prevention of Pollution from Ships, was a treaty attempt at limiting the pollution emitted from seagoing ships. Additionally, the United Nations Convention on the Law of the Seas (UNCLOS), ratified in 1982, created a series of rules and laws for governing the ocean environment. This treaty went further than its predecessors by establishing a legislative enforcement body to control and prevent the pollution of the marine environment.

The Convention on International Trade in Endangered Species of Wild Fauna and Flora (CITES) was ratified in 1973 to protect endangered species from overexploitation. This treaty attempted to control the trading of living and dead animals through a system of highly monitored permits. The Convention on the Conservation of Migratory Species of Wild Animals was ratified in 1979 as an attempt to protect species of wild animals that migrate across international borders. The Biological Toxin Weapons Convention of 1972 prohibited the acquisition and retention of biological toxins not used strictly for peaceful purposes. This treaty was aimed not only at the prevention of pollution of air and water, but also at the preservation of human existence on the planet. The United Nations Conference on Environment and Development, held in Rio de Janeiro in 1992, adopted a blueprint called Agenda 21 to attempt to restrict the discharge to the environment of persistent organic pollutants.

Examples

1. Identify what type of international law is being followed when the countries of Abanda and Blotsphana affirmatively agree to make it illegal to build a nuclear reactor without consulting with other countries that may be affected by an accident.

2. The states of Abanda and Blotsphana enter into a treaty that neither state will hold a citizen of the other state in a prison without explanation of the charge. A municipal court in Abanda holds, erroneously, that the treaty between the two states does not give rights to Blotsphana citizens temporarily visiting in Abanda. As a result, a Blotsphana tourist is thrown into an Abanda jail without a hearing or any explanation as to why she is jailed. May the holding of Abanda's municipal court be upheld?

Explanations

1. Abanda and Blotsphana are demonstrating both practice and opinion juris. Opinion juris occurs where the vote for the resolution was premised on the assumption that there was no option but to so vote because it embodies established law, or because the state now accepts that it is the law. This may also show that the vote is an acknowledgment by the state that the content of the resolution accords with the requirements of international law and cannot legitimately be rejected. The resolution may enunciate principles or rules which later state practice adopted as customary law.

2. No, the decision of the Abanda court may not be decisive upon Blotsphana. Blotsphana likely will complain on a diplomatic level to Abanda.

Glossary

Abandonment. Nonuse of part or all of a parcel of land for an appreciable time. The intentional surrendering of an appropriative right.

Absolute pollution exclusion. Clause in Comprehensive General Liability insurance policies issued after 1985 that attempts to exclude coverage for all pollution claims.

Active ingredient. The ingredient in a pesticide or herbicide that is toxic to pests or plants.

Adjacent wetlands. Wetlands that border or are contiguous to navigable waterways.

After the fact permits. Retroactive permits that sanction otherwise illegal activity.

Agricultural waste. Waste returned to the soil as fertilizer. It is excluded from the definition of solid waste.

Air quality control regions (AQCRs). Regions or airsheds in which air quality is monitored and controlled.

Algae. Microscopic photosynthetic plants of the simplest form, having no roots, stems, or leaves.

Alteration. Removing, dredging, filling, or otherwise altering a wetland or the related physical areas described.

Ambient air. Outdoor air; does not include air inside a building or structure.

Annex I Countries. The 37 developed countries whose carbon emissions are governed by the Kyoto Protocol.

Apportionment. Method by which liability is divided among two or more parties.

Aquifer. A geologic formation, group of formations, or part of a formation that is capable of yielding a significant amount of water to a well or spring.

Asbestos. A mineral employed in many products as a fire retardant. The persistence of the asbestos mineral fiber, along with its physical structure and durability, cause the body's natural defense and cleaning mechanisms to destroy irreplaceable lung tissue. Asbestos fibers are extremely thin — typically less than 1 micron in diameter — with a length of 10-30 microns. Their length becomes aligned with airflow and penetrates deep into the lungs, where they are engulfed by a macrophage (large clusters of white blood cells that engulf and attempt to dissolve and degrade cellular invaders, including viruses and bacteria). Asbestos-related illness and death result because the macrophage cannot fully wrap around the entire length of an asbestos fiber, causing its tips to protrude from the engulfing cell. When the macrophage then injects enzymes and bleach-like chemicals into its interior to degrade the invading element, the perforated end of the macrophage allows reactive chemicals and digestive enzymes to leak through the cell along the shaft of the asbestos fiber and into the lung lining — destroying lung tissue and leading to lung disease.

Attainment. Level of a particular criteria pollutant in ambient air in a region, such level being below the uniform federal NAAQS requirement.

Avoided cost. The cost that a utility must pay for power that it generates itself or purchases from external sources. The power can include capacity costs or only energy costs, depending on whether the purchaser needs additional capacity in the future.

Bacteria. Simple, one-celled plants that use soluble food and are capable of reproduction without sunlight. Many bacteria are harmless. The presence of certain pathogenic bacteria in water can foster disease.

Glossary

Baseload generation.   Electric power generation that is designed and intended to operate around the clock, rather than cycling on and off as peaking power generation facilities do.

Best available control technology (BACT).   EPA standards based on the best of all technology in common use to control a pollutant.

Best system of emission reduction (BSER).   EPA technology standards for NSPS.

Biochemical oxygen demand (BOD).   A measure of the material in water that will make a biological demand on the oxygen present in a receiving water. BOD is the most commonly used parameter to define the basic strength of municipal wastewater or organic industrial waste.

Biological community.   Living organisms that have relationships both among themselves and to the environment. They are made up of populations.

Bottom ash waste.   An inorganic product of coal and other fossil fuel combustion; it is legally classified as nonhazardous.

Burden of proof.   The burden of proof lies upon the proponent of a position. The most common burden of proof for agency decisions is preponderance of the evidence.

Cap-and-trade.   The establishment of emissions limits on certain sources, allocation, or auction of the legal rights to emit, with the ability of regulated entities to trade for more or less quantity of such allowances.

Carbon dioxide (CO_2).   A "greenhouse" gas associated with global warming.

Carnot efficiency.   Ratio of the useful electric and heat output of an engine to its total energy input.

CDM.   The Clean Development Mechanism, an arrangement under the Kyoto Protocol allowing industrialized countries to invest in projects that reduce greenhouse gas emissions in developing countries in order to earn emissions credits.

Cement kiln dust waste.   Inorganic particulate waste matter produced by a cement kiln.

Certified Emission Reductions (CERs).   Climate credits (or carbon credits) issued by the Clean Development Mechanism (CDM) Executive Board for emission reductions achieved by CDM projects under the rules of the Kyoto Protocol.

Chemical oxygen demand (COD).   A measure of the proportion of the material that is susceptible to oxidation by a strong chemical oxidant.

Cluster zoning.   Development that concentrates structures on part of the land, leaving the remainder to open space or environmental uses.

Coastal barriers.   Long, narrow strips of land that are largely or completely surrounded by water. They protect coastal zones from ocean storms.

Coastal zone.   Waters and affected adjacent land subject to the public trust and interest, as defined by the Coastal Zone Management Act.

Cogeneration.   The simultaneous production of two forms of useful energy, typically electricity and heat.

Coliforms.   Bacteria found in the intestinal tract of warm-blooded animals, including humans.

Commercial activity.   Any activities of industry and trade, not limited simply to buying and selling.

Conservation (of species).   Measures of whatever kind necessary to remove a species from a threatened or endangered status. The measures range from scientific research to a regulated taking.

Conservation easements.   Easements that separate development rights from land ownership; used by private groups to restrict development.

Conservation plan.   A plan to guarantee minimal interference with a species' essential behavioral pattern. The plan must address and meet the fundamental needs for feeding, breeding, and sheltering under the ESA.

Continuous trigger.   The theory that environmental damage occurs continually at the multiple times of release of a substance to the environment, exposure, and manifestation of disease or injury.

Conventional pollutants.   BOD, total suspended solids (TSS), coliforms, pH, and oil and grease.

Glossary

Corrective action orders.   Administrative orders issued by the EPA, under RCRA, that require corrective action for releases of hazardous waste from interim status facilities. There is judicial enforcement of the orders. They give the EPA authority to begin cleanup operations at existing TSD (treatment, storage, or disposal) facilities.

Corrosive.   Tending to wear away a material gradually by chemical action. A waste is corrosive if it has a pH less than or equal to 2.0 or greater than or equal to 12.5.

Criteria pollutants.   Compounds that are not toxic in typical concentrations in ambient air but are undesirable in excess. There are six criteria pollutants: (1) particulate matter, (2) sulfur dioxide, (3) ozone, (4) nitrogen oxides, (5) carbon monoxide, and (6) lead.

Critical habitat.   An area necessary for a species' survival. Unique food needs, shelter requirements, or breeding sites all delineate a critical habitat.

Cryptosporidium.   A disease-causing intestinal protozoan parasite found in low-turbidity water.

De-listing.   The act whereby, upon petition by an individual, the EPA excludes a waste from RCRA regulation. The petitioner must demonstrate that the waste does not meet any of the characteristics that would identify it as hazardous.

Developed water.   Water added to a natural stream (but would not normally become part of the stream).

Dioxin.   A pollutant and a by-product of incineration, which is considered to be carcinogenic.

Discarded.   Burned, incinerated, or stored for such a purpose; abandoned or disposed of. A waste is a discarded material.

Disposal.   The discharge, deposit, injection, dumping, spilling, leaking, or placing of any solid or hazardous waste into or on any land or water so that the waste, or any constituent thereof, may enter the environment, be emitted into the air, or be discharged into any waters.

Dissolved oxygen (DO).   Oxygen present in a surface water body. A certain concentration of oxygen is required to sustain fish, animal, and aquatic life. Insufficient levels of dissolved oxygen in the water column cause anaerobic (absence of air) conditions, formation of noxious gases such as hydrogen sulfate, and production of malodorous conditions.

Diversion.   The physical removal of water from its source.

Divisibility.   A doctrine that allocates CERCLA (Superfund) liability according to a person's unique contribution to the harm.

Doctrine of correlative rights.   The doctrine that each owner of a separate property has the right only to a fair and equitable share of the oil and gas underneath the property. The owner is protected from the negligence of neighboring appropriators.

Domestic sewage.   Untreated sanitary wastes that pass through a sewer system to a publicly owned treatment works for treatment. Under RCRA, domestic sewage is excluded from the definition of solid waste.

Drawdown.   The receding of underground water levels as a result of groundwater users sinking deep wells and withdrawing large volumes of water. Consequently, other users may not have access to the groundwater without digging or drilling deeper wells at great expense.

Dredged material.   Material that is excavated or dredged from the waters of the United States. Dredged spoils are considered pollutants under the Clean Water Act.

Ecosystem.   The relationships between living things and their nonliving supporting environment.

Effluent.   A waste liquid discharge from a manufacturing or treatment process — whether in its natural state or partially or completely treated — that discharges into the environment.

Endangered species.   Any species threatened with extinction in all or a significant part of its range.

Environment.   As defined in CERCLA, the navigable waters under the exclusive authority of the United States and any other surface water, groundwater, drinking water supply, land surface or subsurface strata, or ambient air within or under the jurisdiction of the United States.

Environmental overlay districts.   Environmentally sensitive areas that are subject to additional local or state controls beyond typical zoning designations.

Euclidean zoning.   A zoning technique that separates commercial, residential, and industrial uses into distinct zones. The focus is on individual lots or parcels to enforce setback, lot size, and other standards.

Eutrophication.   A natural process by which aquatic systems are enriched with the nutrients, including nitrogen, that are presently limiting for primary production in that system. Agricultural runoff, urban runoff, leaking septic systems, sewage discharge, and other sources can accelerate this process.

Ex *parte* contact.   A contact with an administrative law judge or judge outside the formal protocol, which can lead to a disqualifying bias in an adjudication before an agency.

Exhaustion of administrative remedies.   This doctrine requires that the party seeking review demonstrate that it has exhausted all the possible avenues of redress within the agency, unless no adequate remedy would be available at the agency.

Facility.   Under CERCLA, any place where hazardous substances come to be located for any reason.

Federally permitted releases.   Releases to the water or air permitted under statutes primarily governing such discharges.

Filed rate doctrine.   A common law doctrine emanating from the supremacy clause of the Constitution. Under this doctrine, if FERC issues an order or establishes a rate, any contrary state determination is federally preempted.

Fill material.   Material used for the primary purpose of replacing an aquatic area with dry land or changing the bottom elevation of a water body.

First discovery theory.   The theory that environmental damage takes place only when an agency discovers the pollution.

Flow path.   The direction of movement of groundwater and any contaminants it may contain, as governed principally by the hydraulic gradient.

Flue gas emission control waste.   A waste product of coal and other fossil fuel combustion; it is excluded from RCRA regulation by the EPA.

Fly ash waste.   A waste product of coal and other fossil fuel combustion excluded from RCRA regulation by the EPA.

Forfeiture.   Loss of a right caused by the failure to meet statutory or other legal requirements.

Fossil fuel energy.   Energy produced by burning coal, natural gas, oil, and other carbon-based chemical energy sources produced by the slow degradation of organic matter. Fossil fuels are not considered renewable energy sources, even though they are continually produced slowly in the environment.

Fracking.   See Hydraulic fracturing.

Fuel cell.   Fuel cells convert fuel directly into electricity through a reaction between a fuel and oxidant that is triggered in the presence of an electrolyte.

Fuel fabrication.   Converting enriched uranium hexafluoride (UF_6) into fuel for nuclear power generation. The UF_6 is heated to a gaseous form and then chemically processed to form uranium dioxide (UO_2) powder. This powder is then processed into ceramic pellets and loaded into metal tubes that are subsequently bundled into fuel assemblies.

Fuel rod.   A long, slender, zirconium metal tube containing pellets of fissionable material that provide fuel for nuclear reactors. Fuel rods are assembled into bundles called fuel assemblies, which are loaded individually into the reactor core.

Fungi.   Microscopic nonphotosynthetic plants, including molds and yeast.

Generally available control technology (GACT).   Methods and procedures that are "commercially available and appropriate for application by area sources." GACT standards include consideration of the economic impact of regulation and the ability of the regulated industries to operate and maintain an effective emission reduction system.

Generator.   Defined by the EPA as any person, by site, whose act or process produces hazardous waste listed in 40 C.F.R. Part 261, or whose first act causes the EPA to subject a hazardous waste to regulation.

Geothermal energy.   Energy produced by bringing superheated subsurface waters to the land surface to produce steam to turn turbines and create electricity. Considered a renewable resource, it is very prevalent in California and the Pacific Rim.

Greenhouse gases (GHGs).   Six basic families of chemicals, which, when released to the ambient air, reflect and trap heat in the atmosphere, warming the planet. Heat-trapping greenhouse gases include water vapor, carbon dioxide (CO_2), methane (CH_4), nitrous oxides (NO_2), sulfur hexafluoride (SF_6), hydrofluorocarbons (HFCs), and perfluorocarbons (PFCs).

Grit.   Heavy inorganic solids (plastics, etc.) in sewage effluent.

Groundwater.   Water beneath the land surface in the saturated zone that is under atmospheric or artesian pressure. The water that enters wells and issues from springs.

Habitat modification.   Any activity that would significantly impair essential behavior patterns of species, such as breeding, feeding, or sheltering behavior patterns.

Hardness.   In water, generally the sum of the calcium and magnesium expressed as an equivalent amount of calcium carbonate minerals ($CaCO_3$). Hardness concentrations generally do not have public health impacts, but can have economic impacts. It is difficult to create soapy lather in hard water. If water is very "hard" (>300 mg/L $CaCO_3$) it may be considered to present a nuisance condition and softening may be required.

Harm.   Under the ESA definition of "take," harm is an act that actually kills or injures wildlife. It includes habitat modification as long as there is a showing of actual injury to wildlife.

Hazardous substance.   Under the CERCLA definition: (1) any substance designated as toxic under the Clean Water Act, (2) any element, compound, mixture, solution, or substance designated pursuant to CERCLA, (3) any hazardous waste having the characteristics identified under or listed pursuant to RCRA, (4) any hazardous pollutant listed under §112 of the Clean Air Act, and (5) any imminently hazardous chemical substance or mixture with respect to which the EPA administrator has taken action pursuant to the Toxic Substances Control Act.

Hazardous waste.   Any waste or combination of wastes that poses a substantial present or potential hazard to human health or living organisms. According to the EPA, a waste is hazardous if it exhibits any of the following characteristics: ignitable, corrosive, reactive chemically, toxic, unstable, fatal to humans in low doses, or has toxic constituents.

Heavy metals.   Metallic elements, including the transition series. Heavy metals include many elements that are required for plant and animal nutrition in trace concentrations but become toxic at higher concentrations. Examples are mercury, chromium, cadmium, and lead.

HEV.   A hybrid electric vehicle combines conventional power production and an electric motor.

Household waste.   Waste generated by single and multiple dwellings, hotels, motels, and other residential sources. The EPA has excluded these wastes from its definition of solid waste.

Hydraulic fracturing or "fracking."   Drilling that employs high-pressure fluids consisting of water, sand, and a mixture of chemicals to fissure shale rock to free underground gas for extraction with horizontal drilling techniques.

Hydric soil.   Soil that is periodically saturated with water, creating anaerobic conditions.

Hydroelectric power.   One of the two primary processes that use water to produce power. Hydroelectric power utilizes water from dammed reservoirs or in watercourses flowing by gravity to drive turbines. In the United States, hydroelectric power exploitation on a major scale began with the creation of the Tennessee Valley Authority (TVA) in 1933.

Hydrogen.   The most abundant element on earth. Hydrogen by volume weighs only 7 percent as much as air, is 4 times as diffusive as natural gas, and is 12 times as diffusive as gasoline.

Hydrologic cycle.   The way in which water is circulated and transformed in nature. The principal actions in the hydrologic cycle are evaporation, precipitation, infiltration, storage, and runoff.
Hydrophilic vegetation.   Vegetation capable of growth in very wet conditions.

Ignitable.   Flammable. A waste is ignitable if its flash point is below 140°F.
Incidental takes.   Section 9 of the ESA grants the secretary authority to issue a permit for incidental takes of endangered species pursuant to an otherwise lawful activity. The taking must be incidental to, and not the purpose of, the carrying out of an otherwise lawful activity.
Incorporeal rights.   A right to the use of the land, not to possession of the land.
Independent power projects.   Nonutility power generation projects that do not qualify as QFs. Pursuant to federal law, IPPs cannot demand that utilities purchase their power or interconnect.
Infiltration.   The flow of a liquid through pores or small openings.
Injury in fact theory.   The concept that environmental damage from a released waste takes place only when the environment is actually injured.
Innocent owner defense.   A defense created by the 1986 SARA (CERCLA) Amendments. It can be used by defendants who acquired a disposal site after the disposal or placement of a hazardous substance, provided the defendant (1) did not know or have reason to know of the hazardous substance at the time of acquisition, (2) is a government entity that acquired the property by escheat, involuntary transfer, eminent domain or the like, or (3) inherited the property.
Intensification.   A change in the character and quality of a nonconforming use. It can destroy the protection afforded by nonconforming-use status.
Interim status.   Provisional accreditation given to TSD facilities in existence when RCRA was enacted. An interim status facility is limited to the specific wastes, processes, and design capacities set out in its application.
International Court of Justice (ICJ).   An international tribunal located in The Hague.
International Law Commission (ILC).   The principal judicial organ of the United Nations; it exercises jurisdiction only by consent.
Inverter.   A device that converts direct current electricity to alternating current either for stand-alone systems or to supply power to an electricity grid.
Isolated wetlands.   Wetlands that are not hydraulically connected to waters of the United States.

Jeopardy test.   Under the ESA, a standard applied in formal consultations to prevent any agency action that could jeopardize the continued existence of any endangered species or threatened species or that could result in the destruction or adverse modification of habitat.
Joint Implementation.   A trading mechanism under the Kyoto Protocol for carbon credits.

Knowing endangerment offense.   A transporter or TSD facility owner commits a substantive §3008(d) RCRA offense and knows at the time he or she commits the offense that he or she thereby places another person in imminent danger of death or serious bodily injury.
Kyoto Protocol.   An international climate change protocol adopted in December 1997, entering into force after ratification in 2005.

Land treatment.   A form of land disposal banned by RCRA. Under RCRA, wastes must be pretreated so as to be no longer hazardous before they are further treated or disposed of on land.
Leachate.   A liquid that moves through or drains from a landfill.
LEV.   A low-emission vehicle emits less greenhouse gas than other vehicles.
Littoral rights.   Rights arising from proximity to lakes.

Manifest system.   RCRA requirement and system that tracks the movement, storage, and disposal of hazardous waste "from cradle to grave." It provides a paper trail for regulated hazardous wastes.
Manifestation theory.   The concept that environmental damage takes place only when it is reasonably capable of observation and diagnosis.

Maximum achievable control technology (MACT). EPA standards requiring the installation of control technology on "major sources" that will create the "maximum degree of reductions in emissions that is deemed achievable."

Maximum contaminant level goals (MCLGs). Nonenforceable health-based values based on the risk of harm to health. Chemicals classified as carcinogens (capable of causing cancer) have MCLGs of zero.

Maximum contaminant levels (MCLs). Enforceable primary standards applicable to public drinking water systems, set as close as possible to the MCLGs. MCLs are based on consideration of the limits of analytical laboratory methodologies, the capability of water treatment technologies, and cost. The MCLs for drinking water include levels for microorganisms, turbidity, and organic and inorganic chemicals. Water supplies are required to come as close as possible to meeting the standards by using the best available technology that is economically and technologically feasible.

Metal. A chemical element, usually characterized by lustrous appearance, malleability, and the ability to conduct electricity; tends to donate electrons and thereby become positively charged. Over three-quarters of all elements are metals.

Mixed funding. A process whereby the federal government shares some of the cost of total cleanup using Superfund monies. This is left to the discretion of the EPA.

Modified source. A source that has any physical or process change that increases the emission of a criteria pollutant by more than a de minimis amount.

Municipal licenses. Licenses granted by municipalities to businesses. By means of the licensing process, municipalities in so doing can indirectly control a business's environmental impacts.

National ambient air-quality standards (NAAQS). Geographically uniform standards for ambient air quality.

National emission standards for hazardous air pollutants (NESHAPs). Federal emission limitations established for less widely emitted but highly dangerous, hazardous, or toxic air pollutants that were not covered by any of the NAAQS.

National priorities list (NPL). A listing of the most contaminated hazardous substance facilities or sites eligible for long-term remedial action funding under CERCLA.

Natural resources. Land, fish, wildlife, biota, air, water, groundwater, drinking water supplies, or other such resources.

Navigable waters. Those waters over which commerce may be carried or that are used for transportation, including the territorial seas.

New source performance standards (NSPS). Industry-specific standards that require installation of the "best available control technology" (BACT) for any major new or modified source of pollution within a designated industry.

Nitrogen oxide. A primary air pollutant emitted by power plants and automobiles. It is formed by the conversion of chemically bound nitrogen in fossil fuels or by the thermal fixation of atmospheric nitrogen in combustion.

No migration criterion. EPA ban on the continued disposal of untreated hazardous wastes on land unless the owner/operator receiving the waste demonstrates that there will be no migration of hazardous constituents from the disposal unit or injection zone for as long as the waste remains hazardous.

Nonattainment. Concentration of a pollutant above the federal standard.

Nonconforming uses. Ongoing or continuing prior land uses that are inconsistent with the current zoning code, including all environmental overlay zones.

Nonhazardous wastes. Wastes not deemed hazardous by the EPA, including waste products of coal and other fossil fuel combustion including fly ash waste, bottom ash waste, flue gas emission control waste, and wastes associated with the exploration, development, or production of crude oil, natural gas, or geothermal energy, and cement kiln dust waste.

Nonownership theory.   The idea that title to the oil and gas found on land is given to whoever captures the subsurface oil and gas.

Nonpoint source.   A source of contaminants that is not a "point source" or associated with a discrete point of discharge. The contaminant enters the receiving water in an intermittent and/or diffuse manner.

Nuisance.   Any unreasonable use that interferes with another landowner's quiet enjoyment of the land but falls short of a physical trespass.

Nuisance exception.   In the law of land "takings" by the government, the concept that no taking exists when the law in question merely codifies what nuisance law would have prohibited anyway.

Nutrients.   Compounds needed for animal and plant life, including those with nitrogen, phosphorus, and carbon. They are classified as either macro nutrients (needed in large quantities) or micro nutrients (needed in small quantities). The amount of nutrients present in water can have dramatic effects on biological processes in the water. Nutrients directly affect the growth of algae, bacteria, fungi, and aquatic plants. Excessive amounts of nutrients can also accelerate eutrophication, the natural aging process of lakes and reservoirs.

Open space zoning.   Zoning law that requires specific areas to be maintained as open space. If too extreme, it may be classified as a taking.

Organism.   The smallest living unit of an ecosystem. Each unit occupies a specific habitat that includes all the components necessary for the organism's survival.

Orphan shares.   The shares of liability attributable to insolvent or nonresponsive parties at a CERCLA facility or site.

Ownership in place rule.   A rule giving the owner of the land where oil or gas is located a fee simple absolute right to the oil and gas.

Particulates.   A criteria air pollutant comprising small solid material. Particulate matter is defined as all finely divided solid or liquid material, other than uncombined water, which is emitted to the atmosphere. Particulates are produced as a by-product of the unburnable fraction of fuel, particularly coal, and they are also found in airborne dust and diesel truck exhaust, among other sources.

Petroleum.   A complex chemical compound composed of hydrogen and carbon, with minute amounts of sulfur, nitrogen, and oxygen. It occurs in liquid, gaseous, and solid forms in sedimentary rocks.

Planned unit development.   Similar to cluster zoning. It permits the inclusion of nonresidential uses in a residential area to meet specific development objectives.

Point source.   Any discernible, confined, and discrete conveyance, including but not limited to any pipe, ditch, channel, tunnel, conduit, well, discrete fissure, container, rolling stock, concentrated animal feeding operation, or vessel or other floating craft from which pollutants are or may be discharged.

Pollution exclusion clause.   A clause in Comprehensive General Liability insurance policies designed to exclude coverage for damage caused by the release of pollutants unless the release was "sudden and accidental."

Polychlorinated biphenyls (PCBs).   A group of organic compounds having two carbon rings, joined by a bridge, and two to ten chlorine atoms. Used in transformer fluid until recently when problems of persistence (they are not easily degraded by microorganisms) and toxicity became known. PCBs are relatively hydrophobic (strongly attracted to dry soils and sediments) and therefore move slowly in the groundwater system.

Populations.   Organisms of a particular species that occupy a specific area. They make up biological communities.

Potential to emit.   The maximum operating pollution emission to air of a pollution source.

Glossary

Practical alternatives test. A test under which a permit for the discharge of dredged or fill material into navigable waters will not be issued if a practical alternative to the proposed discharge exists that would have a less adverse effect on the aquatic environment.

Precursor chemical. A compound that reacts in the atmosphere with other chemicals to become or create a regulated compound.

Premanufacture Notice (PMN). The notification provided to the EPA at least 90 days beforehand, by a party who intends to create a new chemical substance or chemical by-product.

Prevention of significant deterioration (PSD). A permitting process for individual air pollution sources in attainment areas.

Primary treatment. The most basic level of wastewater treatment, consisting only of physical processes. The function of primary treatment is to remove large suspended or floating organic solids (typically human waste), heavy inorganic solids such as plastics grit, and excessive amounts of oil or grease.

Private nuisance. A nuisance that affects only one or a few specific neighboring properties.

Proportionate credit rule. Under the Uniform Comparative Fault Act, the rule that a potentially responsible party's liability can be reduced in a subsequent action by the proportionate amount of his or her liability regardless of the amount of settlement.

Public nuisance. A nuisance that affects a wide segment of the human population.

Public participation. In legislative rulemaking, the general public has a right to comment. In formal adjudication, the public may only have a discretionary intervention opportunity if it is not a party with participation rights. "Intervenors" are individuals who may participate as a party at the discretion of the agency.

Public trust doctrine. The concept that certain resources that are too unique and valuable to be privately owned without restriction should be regulated for the public benefit.

Qualifying facility. A cogenerator or small power producer that is entitled to special privileges and regulatory exemptions, including the right to sell electric power output to electric utilities.

Rate base. The value of depreciated capital, specified by the regulatory commission, on which a utility is permitted to earn a specified rate of return.

Rate setting. Process whereby unit prices for power are set. The objective is for the utility to achieve in future years a level of revenue sufficient to allow it to cover all reasonable costs and expenses plus a reasonable profit.

Reactive chemically. Said of a waste: likely to cause a hazardous chemical reaction when in the presence of other elements.

Release. Any spilling, leaking, pumping, pouring, emitting, emptying, discharging, injecting, escaping, leaching, dumping, or disposing into the environment.

Release theory. The theory that environmental damage takes place when a waste leaches or releases into the environment.

Renewable energy sources. Sources of energy quickly released by nature, such as biomass, water, wind, geothermal, solar thermal, and photovoltaic sources.

Renewable Portfolio Standard (RPS). State regulations that require an increasing portion in the gross electricity supply to be generated by defined renewable energy sources.

Return flow. Runoff that forms a tributary of a natural stream.

Riparian. Owner of land abutting a water source.

Riparian rights. Water rights that spring from the ownership of property abutting a water source.

Rule of capture. A rule allowing the retention and ownership of all oil or gas resources that one can capture from drilling wells on land on which one has the legal right to drill.

Salmonella typhi. An enteric pathogen that enters the water supply by the discharge of sewage and causes typhoid fever.

679

Sanitary sewage.   Domestic sewage plus industrial waste.

Saved water.   The amount of water unused by an appropriator because of the appropriator's use of conservation practices.

Secondary maximum contaminant levels (SMCLs).   Water standards designed to control color, odor, and appearance of water. The SMCLs are not enforced by the EPA but may be enforced by states. Individual states may also establish additional guidelines.

Secondary treatment.   An entirely biological process of treating sewage water that relies on biological oxidation. Through a process of microbial oxidation of organic matter as the water passes through a gravel bed, the treatment purifies the water, in much the same manner as the self-purification action of a stream.

Sedimentary rocks.   The petrified remains of animal and plant forms under great pressure in dried seas over tens of millions of years.

Several liability.   The concept that each party is liable for its own individual share.

Significant New Use Notice (SNUN).   The notification provided to the EPA at least 90 days before the new use of certain existing chemical combinations.

Silt.   A sedimentary material consisting of fine mineral particles intermediate in size between those of sand and clay.

Small power producer.   A power generator that produces only electricity, not useful thermal energy, and employs waste or a renewable source as fuel. Typically, it is limited in size to 80 MW.

Small quantity generator.   Defined by the EPA as those facilities generating less than 100 kg/ month of residue, soil water, or debris contaminated with hazardous waste or less than 1 kg/month contaminated with acutely hazardous waste.

Solar photovoltaic cells.   Electric cells that use sunlight to create direct current electricity by causing a polarization of positively and negatively charged electrons.

Solid waste.   A material abandoned by being disposed of, burned, or incinerated—or stored, treated, or accumulated before or in lieu of those activities.

Source.   Any structure, building, or stack that emits waste.

Special use permit.   Permits that apply to land uses that are technically in compliance with the zoning ordinance but cannot be carried out until city officials grant this kind of special permit.

Species.   A population of organisms capable of interbreeding healthy offspring under natural conditions.

Spent radioactive fuel.   Fuel left in a nuclear reactor during operation that is thereafter removed from the reactor and placed into an adjacent "spent fuel pool" while still highly radioactive.

Standing.   Standing of the plaintiff for judicial review of its claim has constitutional, statutory, and prudential elements. Plaintiffs must be positioned by their real interest to articulate the issues. Typically, this is an injury in fact to the plaintiff's personal or economic interest that is traceable to the agency action in question or having interest within the statutory zone of the interests protected by the statute. Prudentially for environmental group litigation, courts have added factors requiring that the injury be redressable if the relief is granted as well as some causation or proximity relationship between the defendant's action and the alleged resultant injury

Stationary source.   An unmovable facility, such as a power plant, that emits pollutants.

Sulfur dioxide (SO$_2$)   A compound that, when combined with nitrogen oxide (NO$_x$), is commonly recognized as a constituent in acid rain.

Surface water.   Water on the land surface—i.e., oceans, lakes, rivers.

Suspended organic solids.   Typically, human waste in sewage effluent.

Take.   Under the ESA, any possible conduct that could cause actual injury to an endangered or threatened species.

Tank bottom.   The residue created from cleaning a petroleum tank. It consists of petroleum residue contaminated with sand and rust from the tank.

Tertiary.   Third stage. An advanced form of treatment after primary and secondary treatment of effluent.

Thermal energy.   Typically steam or hot water that is harnessed to perform a heating function, such as heating a building or use in industrial processes.

Thermoelectric power.   One of the two primary processes that use water to produce electric power. It is generated primarily by converting water into steam by heating it with fossil or nuclear fuels. This process provides nearly 90 percent of U.S. electric power.

Threatened species.   A species that is likely to become endangered within the foreseeable future throughout all or a large part of its range.

Total dissolved solids (TDS).   Inorganic salts, small amounts of organic matter, and other dissolved material. Excess amounts of dissolved solids may be objectionable in drinking water because of mineral tastes and possible physiological effects. Sodium is frequently a principal component of dissolved solids.

Toxicity.   The ability of a material to produce injury or disease upon exposure, ingestion, inhalation, or assimilation by a living organism. A waste exhibits toxicity if it contains one or more of 39 indicator toxins listed in 40 C.F.R. §261.24, Table 1, at a concentration at or above that set in the table.

Toxic pollutant.   A substance that poses a significant or unreasonable risk of hazard to the public health or welfare.

Transferable development rights.   Rights, given to landowners in a preservation district, that can be sold to landowners in development areas, where previously towns had designated specific areas for preservation or development.

Transfer station.   Any transportation-related facility including loading docks, parking areas, storage areas, and other similar areas where shipments of waste are held or assembled during the normal course of transportation.

Transpiration.   A process by which water intercepted by plants is returned to the air.

Turbidity.   Measure of the ability of suspended and colloidal materials to diminish the penetration of light through the water. Suspended matter in the water column may adversely affect chlorine disinfection. Turbid water interferes with recreational use and aesthetic enjoyment of water. Turbidity may also affect aquatic organisms.

Uranium fuel rods.   The enriched uranium fuel assemblies used to produce heat and generate electric power in nuclear power plants.

Useful thermal applications.   Under PURPA, a thermal output that has an independent business justification. There is a rebuttable presumption that the thermal output of a Qualifying Facility is useful.

Usufructuary.   Having the right to use something.

Variance.   An individual exemption from the application of a zoning ordinance.

Viruses.   Biological agents, some of which are capable of causing water-borne disease, such as poliovirus and hepatitis A virus.

Waste.   An act by a possessor of land that decreases the value of the land.

Waste ash.   A by-product of power plant generation or other fossil fuel combustion.

Water dependency test.   A test determining whether a permit is issued for the discharge of dredge or fill material into navigable waters, depending on whether water use is a critical component of the activity.

Wetlands.   Land areas that are inundated or saturated by surface or groundwater at a frequency and duration sufficient to support, and that under normal circumstances do support, a prevalence of vegetation typically adapted for life in saturated soil conditions. Wetlands generally include swamps, marshes, bogs, and similar areas.

Wheeling.   The transmission of electric power.

Glossary

Wrongful act theory.   A theory holding that environmental damage takes place when the waste is disposed of, even if no damage to the physical environment has yet occurred.

Zoning.   Legislative action that separates or divides municipalities into districts for the purpose of regulating, controlling, or limiting the use of private property, as well as the construction and/or structural nature of buildings erected within the zones established.

Abbreviations

AEA Atomic Energy Act
APA Administrative Procedure Act
AQCR Air Quality Control Region
ARAR Applicable or Relevant and Appropriate Requirements
ATSDR Agency for Toxic Substances and Disease Registry

BACT Best Available Control Technology
BART Best Available Retrofit Technology
BAT Best Available Technology (Economically Achievable)
BCT Best Conventional Treatment
BLM Bureau of Land Management
BOD Biological Oxygen Demand
BPT Best Practicable Control Technology
BSER Best System of Emission Reduction

CAA Clean Air Act
CAFO Concentrated Animal Feeding Operations
CBRA Coastal Barrier Resources Act
CDCA California Desert Conservation Area
CDM The Clean Development Mechanism
CEM Continuous Emission Monitoring
CEQ Council on Environmental Quality
CERs Certified Emission Reductions under CDM.
CERCLA Comprehensive Environmental Response Compensation Liability Act
CERCLIS Comprehensive Environmental Response Compensation and Liability Information System
CFC Chlorofluorocarbon
CFR Code of Federal Regulations
CGL Comprehensive General Liability (policy)
CITES Convention on International Trade in Endangered Species of Wild Fauna and Flora
CO Carbon Monoxide
COD Chemical Oxygen Demand
CSAPR Cross-State Air Pollution Rule
CSD United Nations Commission on Sustainable Development

CSSs Combined Sewer Systems
CTGs Control Technique Guidelines
CWA Clean Water Act
CZMA Coastal Zone Management Act

DEP Department of Environmental Protection (MA)
DO Dissolved Oxygen
DOE Department of Energy
DOI Department of the Interior
DRE Destruction and Removal Efficiency

EA Environmental Assessment
EAJA Equal Access to Justice Act
EEZ Exclusive Economic Zone
EHA 2-Ethylhexanoic Acid
EIS Environmental Impact Statement
EP Extraction Procedures
EPA Environmental Protection Agency
EPCRA Environmental Protection Community Right to Know Act
ERU Emission Reduction Unit
ESA Endangered Species Act
EU European Union
EU ETS European Union Emission Trading System

FAA Federal Aviation Administration
FACA Federal Advisory Committee Act
FAO Food and Agricultural Organization
FCLAA Federal Coal Leasing Amendment Act
FDF Fundamentally Different Factors
FEIS Final Environmental Impact Statement
FERC Federal Energy Regulatory Commission
FIFRA Federal Insecticide, Fungicide, and Rodenticide Act
FIP Federal Implementation Plan
FLPMA Federal Lands Policy Management Act
FOIA Freedom of Information Act
FONSI Finding of No Significant (Environmental) Impact
FS Feasibility Study

Abbreviations

FTCA Federal Tort Claims Act
FWPCA Federal Water Pollution Control Act
FWS U.S. Fish and Wildlife Service

GACT Generally Available Control Technology

HA Health Advisory
HAP Hazardous Air Pollutant
HCFCs Hydrochlorofluorocarbon (chemicals)
HCs Hydrocarbons
HFCs Hydrofluorocarbons
HMTA Hazardous Material Transportation Act
HOV High Occupancy Vehicle
HRS Hazardous Ranking System
HUD Department of Housing and Urban Development

IAEA International Atomic Energy Agency
ICC Interstate Commerce Commission
ICJ International Court of Justice
IEL International Environmental Law
ILC International Law Commission
ILO International Labour Organization
I/M Inspection and Maintenance
IMO International Maritime Organization
IPCC UN Intergovernmental Panel on Climate Change
IPPs Independent Power Projects

LADPW Los Angeles Department of Water and Power
LAER Lowest Achievable Emission Rate
LEV Low-Emission Vehicle
LNG Liquefied Natural Gas
LRMP Land and Resource Management Plan
LUST Leaking Underground Storage Tank

MACT Maximum Achievable Control Technology
MARPOL International Convention for the Prevention of Pollution from Ships
MCLs Maximum Contaminant Levels
MCLGs Maximum Contaminant Level Goals
MOU Memorandum of Understanding
MPRSA Marine Protection, Research, and Sanctuaries Act
MWTA Medical Waste Tracking Act

NAAQS National Ambient Air Quality Standards
NCP National Contingency Plan
NEPA National Environmental Protection Act

NESHAPs National Emission Standards for Hazardous Air Pollutants
NFIP National Flood Insurance Program
NFMA National Forest Management Act
NFS National Forest Service
NMFS National Marine Fisheries Service
NMOG Non-Methane Organic Gas
NOAA National Oceanic and Atmospheric Administration
NOPR Notice Of Proposed Rulemaking
NPDES National Pollutant Discharge Elimination System
NPL National Priorities List
NPS National Park Service
NRC Nuclear Regulatory Commission
NSPS New Source Performance Standards
NSR New Source Review

OMB Office of Management and Budget
OSHA Occupational Safety and Health Administration

PCBs Polychlorinated Biphenyls
PEIS Program Environmental Impact Statement
PFCs Perfluorocarbons
PMN Pre-Manufacture Notice
POTW Publicly Owned Treatment Works
PRP Potentially Responsible Party
PSD Prevention of Significant Deterioration
PUC Public Utility Commission
PUD Planned Unit Development
PURPA Public Utility Regulatory Policies Act
PWSA Ports and Waterways Safety Act

QF Qualifying Facility

RACT Reasonably Available Control Technology
RCA Soil and Water Resources Conservation Act
RCRA Resource Conservation and Recovery Act
RFG Reformulated Gasoline
RFP Reasonable Further Progress
RGGI Regional Greenhouse Gas Initiative
RI Remedial Investigation
ROD Record of Decision

SARA Superfund Amendments and Reauthorization Act
SDWA Safe Drinking Water Act
SEIS Supplemental Environmental Impact Statement

Abbreviations

SF6 Hexafluoride
SIP State Implementation Plan
SMCLs Secondary Maximum Contaminant Levels
SNUN Significant New Use Notice
START Strategic Arms Reduction Talks

TAG Technical Assistance Grant
TCLP Toxicity Characteristic Leaching Procedure
TCM Transportation Control Measures
TDR Transferable Development Rights
TDS Total Dissolved Solids
TMDLs Total Maximum Daily Loadings
TSCA Toxic Substances Control Act
TSD Treatment, Storage, or Disposal (facility)
TSS Total Suspended Solids
TVA Tennessee Valley Authority

UCATA Uniform Contribution Among Tortfeasors Act

UCFA Uniform Comparative Fault Act
UNCED Rio Declaration on Environment and Development (United Nations Conference on Environment and Development)
UNCLOS United Nations Convention on the Law of the Seas
UNEP United Nations Environment Programme
UNESCO United Nations Educational, Scientific and Cultural Organization
UNFCCC UN Framework Convention for Climate Change
UST Underground Storage Tank

VOC Volatile Organic Compound

WHO World Health Organization
WMO World Meteorological Organization

ZEV Zero-Emission Vehicle

Table of Cases

Table of Cases

Table of Cases

Table of Cases

Table of Cases

Table of Cases

Table of Cases

Index

Index